Register Now for ~~~~
to Your I

MW00812940

Includes Student Resources

Your print purchase of *Social Work Practice* **includes online access to the contents of your book**—increasing accessibility, portability, and searchability!

Access today at:
http://connect.springerpub.com/content/book/978-0-8261-7853-4
or scan the QR code at the right with your smartphone and enter the access code below.

CH4889T9

Scan here for quick access.

If you are experiencing problems accessing the digital component of this product, please contact our customer service department at cs@springerpub.com

The online access with your print purchase is available at the publisher's discretion and may be removed at any time without notice.

Publisher's Note: New and used products purchased from third-party sellers are not guaranteed for quality, authenticity, or access to any included digital components.

SPRINGER PUBLISHING COMPANY

View all our products at springerpub.com

John Poulin, PhD, is a professor emeritus and adjunct professor at Widener University's Center for Social Work Education currently teaching the foundation field seminar in Widener's online MSW program. In 2016, he retired from Widener University where he had taught generalist practice, research, and policy courses for 32 years. Dr. Poulin received a BA from the University of Southern Maine, an MSW from the University of Michigan, and a PhD from the University of Chicago's School of Social Service Administration. The former director of Widener's BSW program, he founded its MSW program and served as the dean and director for 13 years. He also served for 10 years as the executive director of Social Work Consultation Services (SWCS), an innovative community-based field placement agency developed by the school of social work in collaboration with local community human service organizations. SWCS provides a wide range of free social work services to low-income community residents as well as free capacity building services to under-resourced, community-based human service organizations. Dr. Poulin has published numerous journal articles and book chapters and three editions of a generalist social work practice textbook and coauthored a new textbook designed for use in foundation field placement seminars and field placements. He has also delivered many national and international conference presentations.

Selina Matis, PhD, LCSW, is a proud social worker and lifelong resident of southwestern Pennsylvania. She earned her MSW from California University of Pennsylvania (Cal U). She received her doctoral degree in social work from Widener University. Additionally, she has a BS in elementary education and an MS in school psychology, both from Cal U. Clinically, she has worked primarily in the mental health arena supporting children and their families in a variety of settings. Her research interests include resilience, mental well-being, trauma, burnout, and self-care. Educationally, Dr. Matis has taught at both the BSW and MSW levels in a variety of subject areas including research, policy, human behavior in the social environment, and program evaluation. She has experience supporting students through the field process in a variety of ways, including as a field coordinator, field faculty liaison, and as MSW supervisor. Dr. Matis has published and presented on a variety of topics including resilience, trauma-informed social work, working with families, helping students succeed, and the social work competencies.

SOCIAL WORK PRACTICE
A COMPETENCY-BASED APPROACH

John Poulin, PhD
Selina Matis, PhD, LCSW

SPRINGER PUBLISHING COMPANY

Copyright © 2021 Springer Publishing Company, LLC

All rights reserved.

No part of this publication may be reproduced, stored in a retrieval system, or transmitted in any form or by any means, electronic, mechanical, photocopying, recording, or otherwise, without the prior permission of Springer Publishing Company, LLC, or authorization through payment of the appropriate fees to the Copyright Clearance Center, Inc., 222 Rosewood Drive, Danvers, MA 01923, 978-750-8400, fax 978-646-8600, info@copyright.com or on the Web at www.copyright.com.

Springer Publishing Company, LLC
11 West 42nd Street
New York, NY 10036
www.springerpub.com
http://connect.springerpub.com

Acquisitions Editor: Kate Dimock
Compositor: Exeter Premedia Services Private Ltd.

ISBN: 978-0-8261-7852-7
ebook ISBN: 978-0-8261-7853-4
DOI: 10.1891/9780826178534

Instructor's Materials: Qualified instructors may request supplements by emailing textbook@springerpub.com.

Instructor's Manual: 978-0-8261-7854-1
Instructor's PowerPoints: 978-0-8261-7856-5
Instructor's Sample Syllabi: 978-0-8261-7855-8

Student Ancillary can be accessed by visiting the following url: https://www.springerpub.com/swp

Student Ancillary: 978-0-8261-7857-2

19 20 21 22 / 5 4 3 2 1

The author and the publisher of this Work have made every effort to use sources believed to be reliable to provide information that is accurate and compatible with the standards generally accepted at the time of publication. The author and publisher shall not be liable for any special, consequential, or exemplary damages resulting, in whole or in part, from the readers' use of, or reliance on, the information contained in this book. The publisher has no responsibility for the persistence or accuracy of URLs for external or third-party Internet websites referred to in this publication and does not guarantee that any content on such websites is, or will remain, accurate or appropriate.

Library of Congress Cataloging-in-Publication Data

Names: Poulin, John E., author. | Matis, Selina, author.
Title: Social work practice : a competency-based approach / John Poulin,
    PhD, Selina Matis, PhD, LCSW.
Description: New York, NY : Springer Publishing Company, [2020] | Includes
    bibliographical references and index.
Identifiers: LCCN 2019027744 (print) | LCCN 2019027745 (ebook) | ISBN
    9780826178527 (paperback) | ISBN 9780826178534 (ebook)
Subjects: LCSH: Social service—Practice. | Social work education.
Classification: LCC HV10.5 .P684 2020 (print) | LCC HV10.5 (ebook) | DDC
    361.3/2—dc23
LC record available at https://lccn.loc.gov/2019027744
LC ebook record available at https://lccn.loc.gov/2019027745

Contact us to receive discount rates on bulk purchases.
We can also customize our books to meet your needs.
For more information please contact: sales@springerpub.com

John Poulin: https://orcid.org/0000-0003-2165-8242
Selina Matis: https://orcid.org/0000-0002-9492-4823

Publisher's Note: New and used products purchased from third-party sellers are not guaranteed for quality, authenticity, or access to any included digital components.

Printed in the United States of America.

To Oliver, Amelia, Lucy, Arlo, and Ezra—Love, Pepere
To my grandmother Mary Catherine Matis—Love, Selina

CONTENTS

Part II: Micro–Social Work Practice Competencies

ADDITIONAL CONTRIBUTORS

Marina Barnett, DSW

Marina Barnett, DSW, is currently an associate professor in Widener University's Center for Social Work Education. Dr. Barnett teaches social welfare policy, organizational practice and grant writing, and community organization at the BSW, MSW, and PhD levels. Dr. Barnett has served in the Philadelphia and Chester communities as a consultant to numerous community-based organizations and government offices. Her research interests include geographic information system (GIS) mapping of community assets and utilizing community empowerment approaches to train community residents to understand and conduct research in their own communities.

Stephen Kauffman, PhD

Stephen Kauffman, PhD, is a professor at Widener University's Center for Social Work Education, where he has taught community practice, program evaluation, research, and policy since 1991. Since receiving his PhD from Bryn Mawr College and his MSW from Washington University in St. Louis, his research and practice have focused on citizen participation and community and organizational responses to global problems, such as environmental decay, poverty (in all its dimensions), and education.

With this focus, major research projects have included program evaluations of U.S. Department of Justice (DOJ) violence prevention programs, U.S. Department of Health and Human Services (DHHS) housing programs, Century 21 school performance studies, lead abatement, and teenage pregnancy prevention. The programs (and evaluations) have received funding from the DOJ, the U.S. Department of Housing and Urban Development, the state of Pennsylvania, and several private foundations.

Most recently, his work has targeted the relationship between universities and their surrounding environments. He has published in *Social Work*, *Journal of Social Work Education*, *Journal of Community Practice*, *Journal of Baccalaureate Social Work*, and elsewhere.

PREFACE

This new social work practice textbook is designed and structured around the nine professional social work competencies as defined by the Council on Social Work Education's 2015 Educational Policy and Accreditation Standards (EPAS), with one or two chapters devoted to each professional competency. The chapter content covers all the components and topics described in the 2015 EPAS. The textbook's coverage of the professional social work competencies helps students develop the knowledge and skills needed to become effective social workers. Each chapter provides a comprehensive overview of the theories, concepts, and practice components of a competency.

In addition to providing detailed content related to the professional competencies, this new social work practice text has numerous case examples throughout each chapter as well as a detailed case summary that help students develop a deeper understanding of the application of the social work competencies from a practice perspective. The textbook focuses on mastering the professional competencies rather than just presenting content on social work practice. This approach helps students expand their competency knowledge, application, and integration by creating a purposeful approach to the development of their professional competencies that must be mastered by today's social work students.

This textbook is designed for use in undergraduate and graduate social work practice courses. It can be used in two-semester or one-semester practice courses that target upper-level BSW and foundation-level MSW students. It differs from other practice textbooks in that it is designed to fully cover the nine professional social work competencies. It is the only textbook currently available that approaches social work practice from the perspective of the 2015 EPAS social work competencies. The existing texts typically have charts that point to content related to the social work competencies. They apply the competencies to their existing textbooks. This new textbook uses the professional competencies as the structure of the book. The chapters cover all components of the professional competencies described in EPAS 2015. This approach ensures that the professional competencies are covered in the social practice course(s) and that students experience the relationships among the competencies and social work practice better, preparing them for their field education and future practice as social work professionals.

■ Key Features

Each chapter of this textbook begins with opening vignettes to help engage students in the chapter content, followed by chapter objectives that outline key concepts to be reviewed. In addition, each chapter has multiple case examples, critical thinking questions, and a detailed case summary with discussion questions. The critical thinking questions in each chapter help the student process and reflect upon the chapter content. The numerous case examples throughout the book bring to life the application of social work competencies in actual case situations. The same case summary is used in each chapter, providing students with an opportunity to reflect upon a case situation and describe how they would respond from the perspective of each competency. It is designed to engage students' critical thinking and decision-making skills in relation to the identified social work competency. Using the same case summary in each chapter illustrates the complexity of social work practice and the interconnections among the professional competencies.

Other key features of this book are the instructor and student supplementary resources. The Student Resources provides students with electronic access to all of the tools discussed in this book. The Instructor Resources include PowerPoint presentations for each chapter. The presentations cover the key points in each chapter and provide a structured guide for presenting the chapter content to students. The Instructor Resources also includes a competency class assignment with a grading rubric for each chapter and peer-to-peer or small group discussion assignments with grading rubrics. The two types of assignments (discussion and competency) are both applicable for use in site-based, hybrid, and online course formats. Sample MSW syllabi are provided for one-semester practice courses: one with a concurrent field placement and one without a concurrent field placement. There is also a sample syllabus for a 7-week online course.

Both authors are experienced social workers and social work educators. This book is designed as a companion to the authors' textbook *The Social Work Field Placement: A Competency-Based Approach* published by Springer Publishing Company in the fall of 2018.

In this book, we cover topics that students need for competency-based social work practice with individuals, families, groups, organizations, and community clients and constituents. The chapter topics and their associated competency topics shown in the following table illustrate the match between each chapter's content and the associated competency topics.

CHAPTER TITLE	CHAPTER TOPICS	EPAS COMPETENCY
Chapter 1. Theories, Paradigms, and Professional Competencies in Social Work Practice	Paradigms, Metatheories, Perspectives, Practice Models, Positivist Paradigm, Systems Theory, Ecosystems Perspective, Constructivism Paradigm, Social Constructivism, Strengths Perspective, Ecosystems and Strengths Perspectives, Social Work Competencies, Holistic Competency, Competency Model of Social Work Practice, Social Work Clients	This introductory chapter does not directly address a social work competency. It introduces students to EPAS 2015 and the professional competencies. It also introduces students to the major paradigms and theories that inform competency-based social work practice

(continued)

CHAPTER TITLE	CHAPTER TOPICS	EPAS COMPETENCY
Chapter 2. Ethical and Professional Behavior	Social Work Values and Ethics, Ethical Standards, Ethical Dilemmas, Value Conflicts, Interprofessional Collaboration, Supervision, Trust, Sharing and Vulnerability, Self-Reflection, Self-Awareness, Professional Development, Professional and Ethical Use of Technology, Online Professional Identity, Confidentiality, and Privacy	Competency 1: Demonstrate Ethical and Professional Behavior **Competency Components** Professional values, ethics, ethical dilemmas, personal and professional values, professional judgment, interprofessional collaboration, the use of technology, personal reflection, and supervision
Chapter 3. Diversity and Difference	NASW *Code of Ethics*, Conflict Theory, Intersectionality of Diversity, Oppression Theory, Oppression and Discrimination, Microaggressions, Diversity and Difference in Social Work Practice, Self-Awareness, Personal Values and Biases, Constituents as Experts, Cultural Competence Standards, Empowerment, Empathy, Humility	Competency 2: Engage Diversity and Difference in Practice **Competency Components** Impact of diversity and difference, identity formation, intersectionality diversity (age, class, color, culture, disability and ability, ethnicity, gender, gender identity and expression, immigration status, marital status, political ideology, race, religion/spirituality, sex, sexual orientation, and tribal sovereign status), forms and mechanisms of oppression and discrimination, micro-, mezzo-, and macropractice, self-awareness—personal values and biases
Chapter 4. Human Rights and Justice in a Social Work Practice Environment	NASW *Code of Ethics*, Maslow's Theory of Motivation, Theories of Social Justice, Distributive Justice, Oppression and Human Rights Violations, Global Interconnections, Forms of Oppression, Xenophobia and Ethnocentrism, Classism, Religious Oppression, Sexism, Homophobia, Biphobia, and Heterosexism, Transgender Oppression, Ableism, Types and Sources of Power, Social Processes, Conflict, Justice-Informed Practice, Anti-Oppressive Practice	Competency 3: Advance Human Rights and Social, Economic, and Environmental Justice **Competency Components** Fundamental human rights, global interconnection oppression and human rights violations, theories of human need and social justice, strategies to promote social and economic justice and human rights, elimination of oppressive structural barriers, advocacy at individual and systems levels, practice that advances social, economic, and environmental justice

(continued)

CHAPTER TITLE	CHAPTER TOPICS	EPAS COMPETENCY
Chapter 5. Engagement and Social Work Practice	NASW *Code of Ethics*, Object Relations Theory, Attachment Theory, Maslow's Theory of Motivation, Client-Centered Therapy, Feminist Standpoint Theory, Oppression Theory, Trauma Theory, Person-in-Environment Perspective in Engagement, Engagement With Different Client Systems, Affective Reactions, Self-Reflection and Biases, Trust Building, Collaboration, Helping Relationship Inventory, Helping Process, Engage, Elaboration Skills, Empathy Skills, Contracting Skills, Intervention Skills, Ending Skills, Evaluation Skills, Interprofessional Collaboration, and Building Professional Relationships	Competency 6: Engage With Individuals, Families, Groups, Organizations, and Communities **Competency Components** Ongoing dynamic interactive process, theories of human behavior, person-in-environment, self-reflection and affective reactions impact engagement, relationship building process (trust), interprofessional collaboration, empathy, reflections, and interpersonal skills
Chapter 6. Microsystems Assessment: Individuals, Families, and Groups	NASW *Code of Ethics*, Theory of Motivation, Psychosocial Development Theory, Stage Theory, Ego Psychology, Object Relations Theory, Self-Psychology, Systems Theory, Family Systems Theory, Person-in-Environment Perspective in Assessment, Assessment Process, Use of Self, Affective Reactions, Value Conflicts, Practice Context, Strengths-Based Assessment, Strengths Perspective Principles, Strengths and Obstacles Worksheet, Eco Maps, Genograms, Strengths-Based Assessment, Assessing Groups, Assessing Individual Group Members, Assessing the Group as a Whole, Strengths-Based Group Assessment	Competency 7: Assess Individuals, Families, Groups, Organizations, and Communities **Competency Components** Ongoing dynamic interactive process, theories of human behavior, person-in-environment, self-reflection and affective reactions' impact on assessment, apply knowledge to diverse clients, impact of practice context, interprofessional collaboration, impact of personal experiences and affective reactions on assessment and decision-making, develop collaborative goals and objectives, collect, organize, and apply critical thinking to interpret assessment data, apply theories, person-in-environment, and other multidisciplinary theoretical frameworks to client assessment

(continued)

CHAPTER TITLE	CHAPTER TOPICS	EPAS COMPETENCY
Chapter 7. Microsystems Intervention: Individuals, Families, and Groups	NASW *Code of Ethics*, Stages of Change, Generalist Practice Interventions, Case Management, Supportive Counseling, Group Interventions, Clinical Practice Models, Ecosystem Perspective, Life Model, Family Systems Therapy, Functional Family Therapy, Multisystemic Therapy, Brief Structural Family Therapy, Strengths Perspective, Narrative Therapy, Solution Focused Brief Therapy, Task- Centered Practice, Social Learning Theory, Cognitive Behavioral Therapy, Motivational Interviewing, Rational Emotive Behavioral Therapy, Conflict Theory, Empowerment Therapy, Feminist Therapy, Anti-Oppressive Practice, Transitions and Endings	Comptency 8: Intervene With Individuals, Families, Groups, Organizations, and Communities **Competency Components** Ongoing dynamic interactive process, evidence-informed interventions, theories of human behavior, identify, analyze, and implement evidence-informed interventions, interprofessional teamwork and collaboration, apply knowledge of human behavior, person-in-environment, and other multidisciplinary frameworks, negotiate, mediate, and advocate for diverse clients, facilitate effective transitions and endings
Chapter 8. Research-Informed Social Work Practice	NASW *Code of Ethics*, Positivism, Empiricism, Scientific Inquiry, Role of Research in Social Work Practice, Research-Informed Practice, Critiquing Existing Research, Evidence-Based Practice, Multiple Ways of Knowing, Translating Findings Into Practice, Evaluating Micropractice Effectiveness, Informal Supervision, Self-Reflection, Ongoing Client Feedback, Measurement Tools, Client Logs, Behavioral Observations, Rating Scales, Goal Attainment Scales, Measurement Guidelines, Standardized Measures, Designing the Evaluation, Analyzing Single-System Data	Competency 4: Research-Informed Practice and Practice-Informed Research **Competency Components** Qualitative methods, quantitative methods, evaluating practice, principles of logic, scientific inquiry, culturally informed research, ethical research, multiple ways of knowing, translating findings into practice, practice experience, using research to improve practice, policy and service delivery (research-informed practice, practice-informed research) Competency 9: Evaluate Practice With Individuals, Families, Groups, Organizations, and Communities

(continued)

CHAPTER TITLE	CHAPTER TOPICS	EPAS COMPETENCY
		Competency Components Ongoing dynamic interactive process, apply theories of human behavior to evaluating outcomes, use appropriate quantitative and qualitative methods, evaluate interventions, processes, and outcomes
Chapter 9. Mezzosystems Assessment: Organizations and Communities	NASW *Code of Ethics*, Scientific Management, Administrative Theory, Bureaucratic Theory, Rational Decision-Making Theory, Organizational Development Theory, Organizational Assessment, Internal Organizational Considerations, Organizational Environmental Considerations, Organizational Assessment Tools, Community Development Theory, Conflict Theory, Structural Functionalism, Community Needs Assessment, Community-Based Participatory Research, Asset Assessment, Asset Mapping	Competency 7: Assess Individuals, Families, Groups, Organizations, and Communities

Competency Components Ongoing dynamic interactive process, theories of human behavior, person-in-environment, self-reflection and affective reactions' impact on assessment, apply knowledge to diverse clients, impact of practice context, interprofessional collaboration, impact of personal experiences and affective reactions on assessment and decision-making, develop collaborative goals and objectives, collect, organize, and apply critical thinking to interpret assessment data, apply theories, person-in-environment, and other multidisciplinary theoretical frameworks to client assessment |
| **Chapter 10. Mezzointerventions in Social Work Practice: Organizations and Communities** | NASW *Code of Ethics*, Change Theory, Mezzointerventions, Setting Goals and Objectives, Developing the Intervention Plan, Education and Training, Planning and Program Development, Models of Community Practice, Coalition Building | Competency 8: Intervention With Individuals, Families, Groups, Organizations, and Communities

Competency Components Ongoing dynamic interactive process, evidence-informed interventions, theories of human behavior, identify, analyze, and implement evidence-informed interventions, interprofessional teamwork and collaboration, apply knowledge of human behavior, person-in-environment, and other multidisciplinary frameworks, negotiate, mediate, and advocate for diverse clients, facilitate effective transitions and endings |

(continued)

CHAPTER TITLE	CHAPTER TOPICS	EPAS COMPETENCY
Chapter 11. Policy Practice: How Policy Is Made	NASW *Code of Ethics*, Social Welfare Policies: What They are and Why We Care, Definition of Policies, Components of Social Welfare Policies, Social Work Role in Policy: Policy Practice, Policy Formation, Policy Foundational Concepts, Funding, Relationship Between the Federal Government and the States	Competency 5: Engage in Policy Practice **Competency Components** Social welfare policies at federal, state, and local levels, history of social welfare policies, factors that affect social policy (historical, social, cultural, economic, organizational, environmental, and global), policy formation, analysis, implementation, and evaluation, assess impact of policies on delivery and access to services
Chapter 12. Policy Practice: How to Conduct Policy Practice	NASW *Code of Ethics*, Policy Practice, Stages of the Policy Process and the Associated Primary Tasks, Problem Identification, Problem Characterization, Political Mobilization and Political Advocacy, Policy Implementation, Policy Evaluation	Competency 5: Engage in Policy Practice **Competency Components** Social welfare policies at federal, state, and local levels, history of social welfare policies, factors that affect social policy (historical, social, cultural, economic, organizational, environmental, and global), policy formation, analysis, implementation, and evaluation, assess impact of policies on delivery and access to services
Chapter 13. Practice-Informed Research	NASW *Code of Ethics*, Practice-Informed Research, Quantitative Research, Qualitative Research, Research to Improve Practice, Evaluating Outcomes, Logic Models, Process Evaluation, Outcome Evaluation, Dissemination, Conference Presentations, Journal Articles, Research Reports	Competency 4: Research-Informed Practice and Practice-Informed Research **Competency Components** Qualitative methods, quantitative methods, evaluating practice, principles of logic, scientific inquiry, culturally informed research, ethical research, multiple ways of knowing, translating findings into practice, practice experience, using research to improve practice, policy and service delivery (research-informed practice, practice-informed research)

(*continued*)

CHAPTER TITLE	CHAPTER TOPICS	EPAS COMPETENCY
		Competency 9 Evaluate Practice With Individuals, Families, Groups, Organizations, and Communities **Competency Components** Ongoing dynamic interactive process, apply theories of human behavior to evaluating outcomes, use appropriate quantitative and qualitative methods, evaluate interventions, processes, and outcomes

Qualified instructors may obtain access to supplementary material (Instructor's Manual, Sample Syllabi, and PowerPoints) by emailing textbook@springerpub.com

Student Resources can be accessed by visiting the following url: https://www.springerpub.com/swp

CHAPTER COVERAGE OF PROFESSIONAL COMPETENCIES

CHAPTER/ COMPETENCY	C1 ETHICS	C2 DIVERSITY	C3 JUSTICE	C4 RESEARCH	C5 POLICY	C6 ENGAGEMENT	C7 ASSESSMENT	C8 INTERVENTION	C9 EVALUATION
Chapter 1 (NC)	•	•	•						
Chapter 2 (C1 Ethics)	✓	•	•	•	•	•	•	•	•
Chapter 3 (C2 Diversity)	•	✓	•		•	•			
Chapter 4 (C3 Justice)	•		✓		•			•	
Chapter 5 (C5 Engagement)	•		•		•	✓		•	
Chapter 6 (C7 Micro-assessment)	•		•		•	•	✓		
Chapter 7 (C8 Micro-intervention)	•		•		•			✓	
Chapter 8 (C4 Research-Informed Practice and C9 Evaluation)	•	•	•	✓					✓
Chapter 9 (C7 Mezzo-assessment)	•		•				✓		
Chapter 10 (C8 Mezzo-intervention)	•		•					✓	
Chapter 11 (C5 Policy Practice)	•				✓				
Chapter 12 (C5 Policy Practice)	•		•		✓				
Chapter 13 (C4 Practice-Informed Research and C9 Evaluation)	•		•	✓			•	•	✓

✓, primary coverage; •, secondary coverage

I

SOCIAL WORK PRACTICE
METACOMPETENCIES

THEORIES, PARADIGMS, AND PROFESSIONAL COMPETENCIES IN SOCIAL WORK PRACTICE

Karen L is a first-year master's in social work student who had recently graduated from college with no prior social work experience. Her field placement was with a family service agency that provided individual and family counseling. During her first week, she observed her field instructor conduct three intake assessments. After each assessment, she and her field instructor debriefed and discussed the process and the case recommendations. During her second week, Karen's field instructor told her that she thought that Karen was ready to take the lead in conducting an intake assessment. Her field instructor would sit in, but Karen would conduct the interview. The intake was scheduled for that afternoon. Karen took a couple of hours in the morning to review the assessment form and prepare for the assessment. She was excited and felt comfortable about doing the assessment.

At the beginning of the interview, Karen was nervous and anxious about meeting with a client. The client was not very forthcoming with her responses and appeared angry about something. Karen found it challenging to ask all the questions and get the information recorded accurately. She became more comfortable as the interview proceeded. She was familiar with many of the terms on the assessment form, and getting her client to respond became easier. The assessment instrument had many open-ended questions and asked her to describe, among other things, the client's ecosystem, social supports, presenting problems that needed to be addressed, strengths and challenges, and potential factors that might influence the client's capacity to engage in a helping relationship and the treatment program. Karen met with her field instructor to debrief after she completed the assessment. Her field instructor gave her some constructive feedback on her documentation, but for the most part, she was very pleased with Karen's performance. Karen left her field placement that day feeling excited about her chosen career path and the learning opportunities she will have in her field placement. Although she was pleased with her first client assessment, she recognized that she had a long way to go in developing her professional social work competencies.

LEARNING OBJECTIVES

Conducting a client assessment is a complex process that involves some of the key concepts of social work practice. This chapter introduces some of the key social work practice concepts. It begins with a brief overview of the structure of the book and online student resources. This is followed by a discussion of the two major overarching theoretical foundations of social work practice: the ecosystems perspective and the strengths perspective. A review of the professional social work competencies is followed by a description of a competency model of social work practice. The chapter ends with a discussion of clients and a detailed case example with discussion questions. By the end of this chapter, you will be able to:

1. Describe the differences among paradigms, metatheories, perspectives, midlevel theories, and practice models

2. Describe the ecosystems perspective and its role in social work practice

3. Describe the strengths perspective and its role in social work practice

4. Identify the professional social work competencies

5. Describe the competency model of social work practice and the interrelationships of the competencies

6. Classify the different types of clients

7. Identify factors that might affect clients' willingness to develop helping relationships and engage in the helping process

■ Structure of the Book

This textbook is organized around the nine professional social work competencies developed by the Council on Social Work Education (CSWE) Commission on Educational Policy (COEP) and presented in the *Educational Policy and Accreditation Standards* (EPAS) (CSWE, 2015). The COEP develops curriculum policies for social work education. The EPAS are the guidelines social work programs must comply with to become and maintain their status as a CSWE accredited program. The 2015 EPAS define the core professional competencies for social workers. With the exception of this first introductory chapter, each chapter in this textbook is devoted to one of the nine professional competencies. Our goal is to provide social work students with a comprehensive understanding of each competency and the knowledge to begin developing their professional competence.

Each chapter reviews the knowledge base of a competency as well as the practice skills associated with the competency. To help put the chapter content into a social work practice context, there are a number of case vignettes with reflection questions as well as numerous critical thinking questions throughout each chapter. At the end of this chapter is a detailed case example that is used throughout the textbook. Each chapter has case example discussion questions that are related to the competency covered in the chapter. This provides you an opportunity to see how all the competencies come or can come into play with a single client. The case example and chapter discussion questions illustrate the interrelationships of the professional competencies and how they are integrated into social work practice.

The online student ancillary resources that come with this textbook provide you with electronic versions of many of the tools and forms discussed in the chapters. These resources can be accessed by visiting the following url https://www.springerpub.com/swp.

■ Paradigms, Theories, Perspectives, and Practice Models

There are a number of theories that influence the practice of social work with individual, families, groups, organizations, and communities. To most beginning social work students, the numerous theories and practice models are overwhelming and confusing. Adding to the confusion is a lack of standardization in terminology. Sometimes they are referred to as theories and other times as perspectives or paradigms. Sometimes an approach is called a theory and other times it is a model. In this text, we use the terms paradigms, metatheories, perspectives, midlevel theories, and practice models. Figures 1.1 and 1.2 show the relationships of the various theories and practice models covered in this book.

Paradigms are the broadest level of theory conceptualization. A paradigm is a distinct set of concepts, theories, and postulates that constitute a philosophical or theoretical framework. The two dominant paradigms in social work are positivism and constructivism. Within these two paradigms, there are a number of theories that help shape the practice of social work.

Metatheories in social work are broad general theories about concepts and propositions about what can or might happen in certain situations, given certain circumstances (Teater, 2014). As shown in Figure 1.1, there are seven metatheories reviewed in this book: systems theory, social constructivism, conflict theory, psychosocial theory, psychodynamic theory, social learning theory, and humanistic theory. These metatheories provide theoretical conceptualizations for social work practice with individuals, families, groups, organizations, and communities.

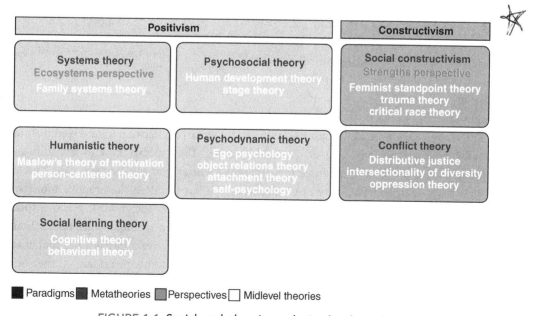

FIGURE 1.1 Social work theories and microlevel practice.

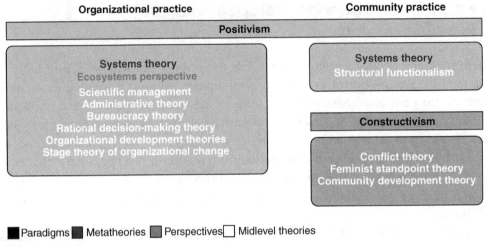

FIGURE 1.2 Social work theories and mezzolevel practice.

Perspectives are broad frameworks for practice. They provide a structure for approaching social work practice. A perspective is different from a theory as it does not necessarily predict but describes a way of viewing and understanding particular situations (Teater, 2014). Two major perspectives used in social work practice in the United States are the ecosystems perspective and the strengths perspective. A third perspective that is becoming more widely used in social work practice is the Afrocentric perspective.

Midlevel theories are theoretical propositions that fall under the broader metatheories. There are a number of midlevel theories that influence social work practice. As shown in Figures 1.1 and 1.2, there are numerous midlevel theories associated with the metatheories discussed in this book. All of the midlevel theories are reviewed in subsequent chapters.

▶ **Critical Thinking Questions**
1. In what ways do theories impact your social work practice?
2. What are the differences between metatheories and perspectives?

Practice models are specific approaches to social work practice that are derived from the metatheories, perspectives, and/or midlevel theories. They specify how to structure and approach social work practice from the different theories and perspectives. The practice models covered in this book are not exhaustive. We have limited the practice models to those that we believe are the major practice models used in social work practice today. The various practice models covered in this book are shown in Figures 1.1 and 1.2. and are grouped under their associated theories and/or perspectives. Please note that many practice models draw from multiple perspectives and/or metatheories. Many of the social work practice models shown in Figures 1.1 and 1.2 are based on concepts drawn from both the ecosystems perspective and the strengths perspective. For simplicity, we have listed the practice models under what we believe to be each practice model's primary metatheory and perspective.

This chapter reviews the positivist paradigm's systems theory and its associated ecosystems perspective. This chapter also reviews the constructivist paradigm's social constructivism theory and its associated strengths perspective. All of the other theories shown in Figures 1.1 and 1.2 are discussed in subsequent chapters of this book.

■ The Positivist Paradigm

Positivism has been one of the dominant paradigms in social work and the social sciences of this century (Peile & McCouat, 1997). Positivism is associated with a period of philosophical thought generally referred to as modernism. Positivists believe that knowledge grows out of careful observation and empirical verification. Positivists break down social phenomena into parts so that the causal connections can be empirically verified. The positivist paradigm assumes that there is an objective reality that can be scientifically tested and verified.

reliance on info

The social work profession is deeply rooted in positivism (Irving & Young, 2002). Until the mid-1990s, empiricism and the scientific approach dominated the social work profession (Dybicz, 2015). The early history of social work is characterized by a consistent adherence to the scientific model of knowledge (Montano, 2012). Social work's adherence to the scientific method began with the publication of Mary Richmond's *Social Diagnosis* in 1917. Richmond viewed "social diagnosis" as a scientific process of gathering facts and testing hypotheses about clients' social functioning. The psychoanalytic-oriented casework movement that began in the 1920s was also based on scientific principles of study, diagnosis, and treatment. In the 1960s, the empirical practice movement evolved (Reid, 1994). The empirical practice model stresses the application of scientific research methods to social work practice in assessing client situations, specifying goals, formulating solution-focused interventions, and evaluating their effectiveness. All of the practice models shown in Figures 1.1 and 1.2 under the positivism paradigm focus in part on the assessment of relevant facts, the specification of the problem in measurable terms, and the objective assessment of outcomes.

Systems Theory

Social work practice has a long tradition of helping individuals and promoting healthy environments (Gitterman & Germain, 2008). The focus on the person and the environment is a core defining feature of social work, and the person-in-environment approach has been a widely accepted principle of social work practice since its inception (Rothery, 2016). The theoretical perspective shaping the person-in-environment approach is the ecosystems perspective. This perspective is derived from the metatheory known as systems theory. Therefore, before we delve into the ecosystems perspective, a review of the origins and basic principles of systems theory is warranted.

Systems theory and its application to the social sciences is generally attributed to von Bertalanffy who proposed the idea of general systems theory (1968). Von Bertalanffy postulated that systems are holistic and that they contain properties that are not found within its separate parts. In other words, systems have their own characteristics that are separate and distinct from the individual components that make up the system. It is the interaction of the elements within the system that together form the entity (Bowers & Bowers, 2017). Systems theory provides a lens to view problems within a context and examine how the interactions of the various components create and/or maintain problems (Smith-Acuna, 2011). The elements in a system can be examined separately, but it is the interactions among and between the elements that create the system.

System components can also be composed of subsystems. For example, a family system could be composed of a parent subsystem, a child subsystem, a mother/daughter subsystem, and so on. Thus, in systems theory, there is the main system with multiple components and various subsystems within each of the main system components (Teater, 2014).

Systems theorists have developed language to describe the characteristics of a system. One characteristic is the degree openness. An open system allows information to flow in and out of the system. On the other hand, a closed system is one that is unresponsive or unaffected by outside stimuli (Teater, 2014). Closely associated with open and closed systems are system boundaries. A system boundary may be thought of as the point at which data flow from one system to another. The degree to which data are free to flow from one system to another is known as the permeability of the boundary. A permeable boundary allows data to flow freely, resulting in an open system. An impermeable boundary is one which strictly controls (or even restricts) the acceptance or dispensing of data, resulting in a closed system. System boundaries may be physical or psychological and they can vary in their degree of permeability.

Four other terms used to describe the characteristics of systems are homeostasis, equilibrium, disequilibrium, and steady state. Homeostasis is the tendency of a system to be resilient toward external factors and maintain its key characteristics. Equilibrium and disequilibrium are closely related to the concept of homeostasis. A system responding to conflicting messages from the environment and maintaining its internal sense of balance is considered to be in equilibrium. Disequilibrium is the opposite. The system is off balance, and the responses to and from the environment are negatively affecting the system. Systems are considered to be in a steady state when they are responding to the environment and experiencing positive growth and development.

Systems theory was conceptualized by von Bertalanffy as a way of understanding biology as an organized system of interrelated parts of a whole (Langer & Lietz, 2015). Ecological theory, an offshoot of systems theory, developed from the field of ecology. Ecological theory added the environment to systems theory. In addition to examining the relationships among organisms, ecological theory examines their interactions with the environment. The application of systems theory and ecological theory to social work gained popularity through the work of Gitterman and Germain (1976) with their publication of the life model of social work practice, which incorporates ecological theory as its framework. The combination of systems and ecological theory is now commonly referred to in social work as the ecosystems perspective.

Thus, systems theory and ecological theory together provide a lens to assess the individuals' behaviors and interactions within systems and betweensystems as well as the fit and effectiveness in achieving a steady state with positive growth and development. These two theories are consistent with social work's early focus on people and their environments. They also formed the basis for the development of the ecosystems perspective, which has been a widely adopted framework for the practice of social work in the United States (Payne, 2016).

Ecosystems Perspective

The ecosystems perspective has been the dominant framework of social work practice since the mid-1970s. The ecosystems perspective fits in well with social work's long-standing mission to address the situational and environmental factors that negatively affect disadvantaged persons.

The heart of the ecosystems perspective is the **person-in-environment concept,** which views individuals and their environments as an interrelated whole (Gitterman & Germain, 2008). Individuals are perceived as interacting with a variety of external systems, such as immediate family, extended family, peers, work or school, and community. The foci are on the interactions between the individual and the systems in his or her environment and on improving the interactions and transactions between individuals and the various systems in their environment (Teater, 2014). Figure 1.3 shows the potential systems in a typical person-in-environment system at the micro-, mezzo-, and macrolevels. It is important to remember that each system in the figure is potentially composed of a number of subsystems. Also keep in mind that each person's environmental system will be different for all three system levels and that those shown in Figure 1.3 are just examples that may or may not be part of a client's environmental system. It is also very likely that other micro-, mezzo-, and macrosystems could be part of a client's social environment.

The person-in-environment perspective recognizes the interdependence of these various systems. The relationship between individuals and their social environment is reciprocal, with

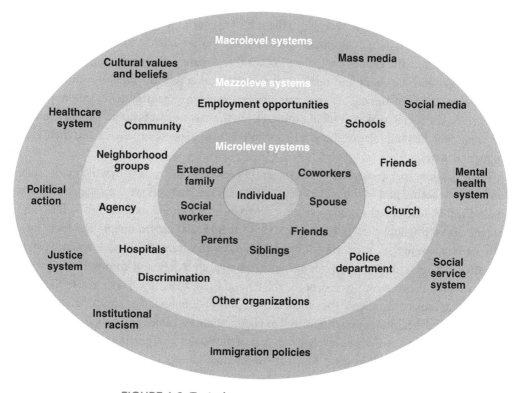

FIGURE 1.3 Typical person-in-environment systems.

each component in the client's system affecting and being affected by the others. The social environment influences individuals' perceptions of themselves and their interactions with others. Individuals, in turn, influence their environmental systems. Thus, the intervention might be focused on the individual, a system(s) within the person's environment, or both.

In the ecosystems perspective, understanding the person-in-environment fit is key. Assessing a person's needs, capacities, and aspirations and his or her environmental interactions is a core concept in the use of the ecosystems perspective in social work practice (Gitterman & Germain, 2008). The ecosystems perspective "helps the practitioner to see that all aspects of an individual's problem involve circular connections between the individual and environment, leading to a 'transactional focus' for practice that is consistent with social work's dual concern with person and environment" (Wakefield, 1996, p. 6).

A defining characteristic of the ecosystems perspective in social work practice is the importance given to improving clients' person-in-environment transactions to facilitate their growth, health, and social functioning. The focus is on the interactions and the fit for the individual. It is not an assessment of the individual and an assessment of the environ-ment. Rather, it is an assessment of the complex interactions between an individual and all the systems and subsystems in his or her social environment. The person-in-environment and the fit concepts are key to social work practice from the ecosystems perspective.

> ▶ **Critical Thinking Questions**
> 1. What do systems theory and the ecosystems perspective have in common?
> 2. What are the differences between systems theory and the ecosystems perspective?

The ecosystems perspective recognizes the role of the social worker in the client's environmental system (Gitterman & Germain, 2008). Social worker–client transactions are viewed as a component of the client's ecological system (see Figure 1.3). Interactions between the social worker and the client and between the social worker and the client's social environment become part of the client's dynamic person-in-environment system. This important system, you the social worker, is often omitted from the assessment process. Do not overlook the impact the helping relationship and your interactions have upon clients and their environmental systems.

The ecosystems perspective also recognizes different system levels with which individuals interact and that are part of the social environment. The microlevels are the systems closest to the individual. Microlevel systems are a client's friends and family members as well as other individuals with whom they have interactions in their social environment. The mezzolevel systems are those in the community or neighborhood with whom the client interacts. Possible mezzolevel systems are social service agencies, schools, churches, and community organizations as well as the community and/or neighborhood itself. Macrolevel systems are the larger systems that impact the client. They include state and national policies and programs, social service systems, healthcare systems as well as clients' cultural values and beliefs. Client interactions with systems at all three levels are all part of the ecosystems perspective in social work.

There are three possible ways in which individual clients can change the person-in-environment fit. The first is for the individual client to change and meet expectations or demands. The second is to change the environment to make it more responsive to client needs or demands, and the third is to change the person/environment transactions (Gitterman & Germain, 2008). The ecosystems perspective provides a lens to assess person-in-environment fit issues to identify the appropriate intervention targets and intervention strategies (see Case 1.1). It is not a practice model or an intervention. It does not address how to make the needed changes in the individual, the environment, or both but rather it helps identify where change is needed to promote positive growth and functioning. The various interventions and practice models that are compatible with systems theory and the ecosystems perspective shown in Figures 1.1 and 1.2 are discussed in subsequent chapters.

CASE 1.1   **NO TIME FOR ME: APPLYING THE ECOSYSTEMS PERSPECTIVE IN SOCIAL WORK PRACTICE**

John R is an 11-year-old boy with behavior management problems. He has attention deficit hyperactivity disorder and has a great deal of difficulty controlling his impulses. He is socially immature. His peers usually make fun of him and reject him. He usually plays with much younger children. In addition to his behavior problems, he has a very difficult family situation. His mother lives out of state. He lives with his father, stepmother, and 18-month-old stepsister. His stepmother resents his presence in the family and the difficulties he causes her.

John is a student at an alternative school, where he is in a special behavior modification program. Dawn W is John's social worker at the school and is also assigned to work with the family. The behavior management program is working well, but John's relationship with his stepmother is undermining his progress at home. The stepmother refuses to follow the treatment plan and is very rejecting. In fact, she openly tells John that he is bad and that she does not want him anywhere near his stepsister. When at home, John is generally either being punished or is alone in his room. John's father defers to his wife and pretty much lets her discipline John as she sees fit.

Dawn is approaching her work with John from an ecosystems perspective. One of the treatment goals is to improve the interactions between John and his stepmother. Dawn recognized that John is good with young children. He is thoughtful and caring and has a nice way of engaging them in play. Dawn suggested that John take care of his little sister for 1 hour a day. Her hope was that by having John demonstrate responsibility to his stepmother, the interactions between them would improve.

The intervention was successful. John took good care of his little sister, and his appreciation of being allowed to play with and care for her was evident. His stepmother's confidence in and patience with him improved. What other systems and/or subsystems in John's social environment could also be targeted to improve the person-in-environment fit?

■ The Constructivist Paradigm, Social Constructivism, and the Strengths Perspective

Postmodernism is a more recent period of philosophical thought that assumes that language is used to construct our perceptions of reality (Greene, Jensen, & Jones, 1996). Two of the dominant postmodern paradigms are constructionism and constructivism. Simply put, constructionism emphasizes the use of internal processes to understand the world and make meaning of one's reality. Constructivism also emphasizes internal processes as well as interactions with others and objects in the environment. The two terms are often used interchangeably. Constructivism is the term and concept used in this book.

While the modern period of thought stressed objective knowledge and verifiable facts, postmodern thought and constructivism stresses the creation of knowledge and the relativity of truth (Carpenter & Brownlee, 2017). Knowledge is constructed and not discovered. Within this paradigm, there are multiple realities based upon peoples' perceptions and constructions of their thought processes and experiences. There is less emphasis on the validity of knowledge and more on the variability of knowledge and subjective experiences.

A number of metatheories evolved out of the constructivist paradigm. They include relational, communal, radical, and social constructivism. Social constructivism is the metatheory that informed the development of the strengths perspective in social work and a number of midlevel theories and practice models. Social constructivism and the strengths perspective are discussed in the following. All of the practice models and theories shown in Figures 1.1 and 1.2 under the constructivist paradigm are discussed in subsequent chapters.

Social Constructivism

Social constructivism emphasizes the importance of culture and context in the construction of one's perceptions of knowledge and reality. Reality is constructed through human activity and interactions. Individuals create meaning through their interactions with each other and with the environment they live in (Teater, 2014). People construct their reality through their interactions with people, organizations, and institutions. These experiences are different from person to person (Greene & Lee, 2002). No two people experience an event or interaction the same. Each person's perception of reality is unique. Social constructivists value "each person's life experiences and acknowledge that each individual can experience situations very differently, particularly when one is influenced by social and/or cultural values" (Teater, 2014, pp. 76–77). Thus, "social constructivism takes the view that both individual and social processes are involved in the social construction of reality; it is not a matter of 'either/or' but rather 'both/and'" (Greene & Lee, 2002, p. 179).

Acknowledging that everyone has a different social construction of reality means that language must be used to begin to understand another's view of reality. In a world where individuals construct their own realities and the objective external world can only be viewed indirectly through perception, belief systems, and language, truth becomes what is agreed on. The agreement can be between two or more people or among larger social units. The agreed-on truth is usually determined by the dominant group within a culture. It is often not the truth for individuals and/or minority groups within the social environment. In summary, the basic premises of social constructivism are:

- Individuals have their own reality and their own way of viewing the world.
- People are active participants in developing their own knowledge of the world, rather than passive recipients of stimulus–response interaction with their environment.

- An individual's reality and knowledge are placed in a historical and cultural context; the reality is developed through social interactions within these historical and cultural contexts.

- Language is used to express an individual's reality.

- Reality is what we agree on; truth is agreement. (Teater, 2014, pp. 77–78)

Strengths Perspective

The strengths perspective draws heavily from social constructivism theory and its emphasis on individuals' subjective perceptions of reality based upon their social interactions within their social environment, the historical context, and their culture. The strengths perspective in social work provides a framework from which to approach practice with clients. It is a lens from which to view a client's perception of his or her reality and a set of guiding principles for interacting with clients. The strengths perspective is not a specific practice model. It is a framework or perspective that can be applied to a variety of practice models and/or interventions. The idea of building on clients' strengths has received a lot of attention in social work. Most social work agencies now claim adherence to "the strengths perspective." A strengths-based approach is very different from those that focus on client problems and history taking (Hepworth, Rooney, Rooney, & Strom-Gottfried, 2017). Social work has a long history of helping disadvantaged clients overcome individual problems and problem situations. Clients come to us with problems, and there is a natural tendency to attempt to resolve the problems and to view the clients from a deficit perspective. Often social workers' perceptions are different than their clients' self-perceptions. The clients view themselves as proactive, autonomous human beings who are using counseling services to enhance their functioning and competence. In contrast, social workers working from a medical model tend to focus on client problems and deficits that need to be addressed.

When social workers focus on problems, they tend to perceive clients in essentially negative terms, as a collection of problems and diagnostic labels. This negative perception may lower expectations for positive change. More likely than not, clients are seen as diagnostic categories or their presenting problems, or both. These labels may create distance between clients and helpers (Saleebey, 2013). They also create pessimism in both parties. Negative labels and expectations obscure the unique capabilities of clients. The social worker's ability to recognize and promote a client's potential for change is markedly reduced. The focus is on what is wrong and the client's inability to cope with his or her life situation. Saleebey (2013) suggests that instead of focusing on problems, we should focus on possibilities.

The pathologic problem approach searches the past for causes. How did the client get into this situation? Why is the client experiencing these difficulties? The search for causes and rational explanations assumes a direct link between cause, disease, and cure (Saleebey, 2013). Human experience is rarely that simple. More often than not, it is uncertain and tremendously complex. In addition, looking to the past diverts attention away from exploring the present. The shift from problems to strengths moves the focus from the past to the present and future. Strengths-oriented social workers seek to discover the resources clients currently have that can be used to change their futures. The past cannot be completely dismissed, because it provides a context for the present. However, in strengths-based practice, the focus is on the present and the future. Rather than focusing on why clients are having problems, social workers who have adopted a strengths perspective focus on what clients want, what they need, and how they have managed to survive (Saleebey, 2013). A strengths-based approach to social work practice emphasizes basic dignity and the resilience of people in overcoming challenging obstacles (Birkenmaier, Berg-Weger, & Dewees, 2014).

Adopting a strengths perspective does not mean that social problems such as domestic violence, child abuse and neglect, poverty, discrimination, and opioid addiction do not have devastating effects on many individuals, families, and communities. They do, and programs and policies to address these and other pressing social problems are needed. What the strengths perspective provides is a way of viewing and interacting with the individuals, families, and communities that balance the focus between the presenting problem and client strengths (Langer & Lietz, 2015).

The strengths perspective's fundamental belief is that all clients have strengths (Kondrat, 2014). Strengths can be internal and external. Internal strengths are internal qualities that help clients cope with the challenges they face and may include resilience, hope, determination, and motivation. External strengths are resources that can be used to support the client. External strengths may include extended family members, faith communities, community services, and informal support networks.

Saleebey conceptualized a "CPR" strengths triangle (2013). The C stands for competence, capacities, and courage. The P refers to promise, possibility, positive expectations, and courage. The R signifies resilience, reserves, and resources (Saleebey, 2013). The CPR triangle helps focus the identification of client strengths beyond the obvious personal strengths to the subtler internal capacities and external resources (Kondrat, 2014).

Strengths Perspective Principles

Saleebey (1992) identified six principles to guide strengths-based generalist practice. They also link the strengths perspective to the core values of the profession. Social work practice is not only about whether and how to intervene or about skills and techniques, but also about our profession's core values.

Principle 1: Every Individual, Group, Family, and Community Has Strengths

Regardless of the situation, every person, family, and community possesses assets, resources, wisdom, and knowledge that you need to discover (Saleebey, 2013). To become aware of these strengths, you need to be genuinely interested in your clients and respectful of their perceptions of their own experiences. The ultimate key to identifying client strengths is your belief in the clients and their possibilities. Adopting a strengths perspective requires you to view your clients as underused sources of knowledge and untapped resources.

Principle 2: Trauma, Abuse, Illness, and Struggle May Be Injurious, but They May Also Be Sources of Challenge and Opportunity

Dwelling on clients' pasts and hardships promotes an image of themselves as helpless. Focusing on past hurts and deficits leads to discouragement and pessimism. What is more extraordinary is that your clients have survived and that they are working with you to bring about changes in their lives. There is dignity and affirmation in having prevailed over trauma, abuse, illness, and other difficult situations. Posttraumatic growth illustrates the capacity for resilience and growth despite previous adversity. The strength of having survived and coped with numerous obstacles is often lost on clients who are struggling to meet life's daily challenges. A strengths approach recognizes clients' inherent competencies, resilience, and resourcefulness in having survived past difficulties as well as their current motivation for growth and development.

Principle 3: Assume That You Do Not Know the Upper Limits of the Capacity to Grow and Change, and Take Individual, Group, and Community Aspirations Seriously

Simply put, this means that you should set high expectations for your clients and help expand their hopes, visions, and aspirations. The strengths perspective is the perspective of hope and possibilities. Believe in clients' capacities for change, growth, and self-actualization. If you do not believe in their abilities and motivation, you really do not believe in the possibility of change. Creating hope where there is little to hope for, strengthening belief when there is little to believe in, and creating aspirations where there are none are the essence of social work practice from a strengths perspective.

Principle 4: We Best Serve Clients by Collaborating With Them

The strengths perspective calls for a partnership characterized by reciprocity and mutual respect between you and your client. There should be a sharing of knowledge and resources. You are not the sole expert or the only one with specialized information; your clients are experts who know more about coping with their situations than you do (Saleebey, 2013).

Take advantage of the wisdom, insights, and understanding your clients bring to the helping process by entering into a collaborative partnership with them. The strengths approach to social work practice requires it. Work with your clients in partnership. Do not presume to work on your clients or to do the work for them.

Principle 5: Every Environment Is Full of Resources

No matter how deprived a client's community, neighborhood, or family system, each has an abundance of untapped resources. "In every environment, there are individuals, associations, groups, and institutions who have something that can help" (Saleebey, 2013). Looking to these untapped resources does not negate our responsibility to work for social and economic justice, and it does not mean that we accept the notion that a disadvantaged person should assume sole responsibility for his or her situation and its amelioration. It does mean, however, that the possibilities for identifying and arranging needed resources for clients from within their own environment are more numerous than you would expect.

Principle 6: Caring, Caretaking, and Context Are Important

Caring for others and being cared for is a basic human right. Families can assist in caring for their members (Saleebey, 2013). Caring strengthens our social web, our interconnectedness. Social work is a caring profession, and the strengths perspective recognizes and embraces our dependence upon others for our well-being.

Strengths Perspective Practice Standards

Rapp, Saleebey, and Sullivan (2005) developed six standards that could be used to judge whether an intervention was strengths based or not (see also Case 1.2). The motivation for this was that the authors felt that while the original strengths perspective principles were being widely adopted in social work, much of the practice claiming to be strengths based was actually functioning from a deficit model (Simmons, Shapiro, Accomazzo, & Manthey, 2016). The six practice standards that define strengths-based social work practice are:

- *It is goal oriented.* Clients set the goals they would like to achieve. Social workers help clients define their goals. Clients are encouraged to consider the hopes and possibilities they have for the future (Saleebey, 2013).

- *There is a systematic assessment of strengths.* Strengths-based practice includes a systematic set of protocols for assessing and documenting strengths. The assessment focus is on understanding internal and external factors that help overcome barriers. The assessment searches for what is working well, instances when barriers are not present, and untapped coping strategies and skills.

- *The environment is seen as rich in resources.* The client's natural community is seen as a principal source for resources, supportive relationships, and opportunities (Rapp et al., 2005).

- *Explicit methods are used to leverage client and environment strengths for goal attainment.* Strengths-based practice entails matching a client's goals and strengths with resources. Assessing client strengths alone is insufficient. In strengths-based practice, the social worker helps the client mobilize his or her internal and environmental strengths (Simmons et al., 2016).

- *The relationship is hope inducing.* In strengths-based practice, the helping relationship is explicitly focused on increasing the client's sense of hopefulness. Building a positive helping relationship is a key component of the helping process that empowers the client to increase positive perceptions of his or her choices, abilities, and capacities (Saleebey, 2013).

> ▶ **Critical Thinking Questions**
> 1. What characteristics does the strengths perspective have in common with social constructivism?
> 2. How do the strengths perspective and the ecosystems perspective differ? In what ways are they similar?

■ *The provision of meaningful choices is central and individuals have the authority to choose.* In strengths-based practice, the social worker helps clients make choices and explore their options. Clients are seen as the experts in their own lives and are encouraged to assume the authority in directing the process.

CASE 1.2   ALWAYS ANGRY AND ISOLATED: APPLYING THE STRENGTHS PERSPECTIVE IN SOCIAL WORK PRACTICE

Jim L is a 15-year-old sophomore previously diagnosed as having a moderate learning disability. He takes regular college preparation courses and has managed to maintain a "B" average. He receives tutoring in math and science and uses the writing center at the school to help him write all of his papers. Although he struggles academically, he has been relatively successful in school.

Jim has no close friends and very few friendly acquaintances. His peers view him as odd and as a "loser." His attempts to fit in and make friends have met with rejection and ridicule, and he has withdrawn socially and makes no attempt to interact with classmates. He appears to have low self-esteem. Jim spends all of his free time at home watching television and playing computer games.

While at home, Jim appears to take out his frustration on his family. He is very demanding of his parents and causes many disturbances within the family. He gets angry quickly and lashes out at his parents over little things. He constantly picks on his younger sister, puts her down in front of her friends, criticizes her looks and abilities, and treats her with general disrespect.

Jim's parents are concerned about his lack of peer relationships and his behavior at home. They contacted the school social worker to inquire about help for their son.

You are the school social worker and you approach your cases from a strengths perspective. Based upon the aforementioned information, what are Jim's strengths? How would you go about applying the strengths perspective in your work with Jim?

■ Ecosystems and Strengths Perspectives Together

The ecosystems perspective and the strengths perspective are two frameworks that guide social work practice with individual, families, groups, organizations, and communities. Although each perspective derived from a different metatheory, they work well together in actual practice with a variety of different practice models. The ecosystems perspective focuses on the interactions between an individual and his or her social environment. The strengths perspective focuses on clients' internal and environmental strengths. The two perspectives can easily be utilized together in social work practice. For example, social workers often use ecomaps and the ecosystems perspective to assess a client's interaction and fit within his or her social environment. The same social worker can also employ a strengths perspective in helping the client identify internal and external strengths as well as use the helping relationship to inspire hope and encourage client autonomy in making goal and intervention decisions. Neither perspective is an actual practice model or intervention. They are frameworks from which a number of specific practice models or intervention can be used to help individuals, families, groups, organizations, and communities.

■ Professional Social Work Competencies

For social work education programs in the United States, the accrediting body is the CSWE Commission on Accreditation (COA). The CSWE COEP creates educational policy for social work education, and the COA creates accreditation standards. The educational policy and accreditation standards together form the EPAS, which guide the accreditation of baccalaureate and masters level social work educational programs (Poulin & Matis, 2015).

Accreditation and Social Work Competencies: EPAS 2015

Each of the nine professional competencies describes the knowledge, values, skills, and cognitive and affective processes that comprise the competency at the generalist level of practice, followed by a set of behaviors that integrate these components. These behaviors represent examples of observable components of the competencies, while the preceding statements represent the underlying content and processes that inform the behaviors (CSWE, 2015).

Competency 1: Demonstrate Ethical and Professional Behavior

Social workers understand the value base of the profession and its ethical standards, as well as relevant laws and regulations that may impact practice at the micro-, mezzo-, and macrolevels. Social workers understand frameworks of ethical decision-making and how to apply principles of critical thinking to those frameworks in practice, research, and policy arenas. Social workers recognize personal values and the distinction between personal and professional values. They also understand how their personal experiences and affective reactions influence their professional judgment and behavior. Social workers understand the profession's history, its mission, and the roles and responsibilities of the profession. Social workers also understand the role of other professions when engaged in interprofessional teams. Social workers recognize the importance of lifelong learning and are committed to continually updating their skills to ensure they are relevant and effective. Social workers also understand emerging forms of technology and the ethical use of technology in social work practice. Social workers:

- Make ethical decisions by applying the standards of the National Association of Social Workers (NASW) *Code of Ethics*, relevant laws and regulations, models for ethical decision-making, ethical conduct of research, and additional codes of ethics as appropriate to context
- Use refection and self-regulation to manage personal values and maintain professionalism in practice situations

- Demonstrate professional demeanor in behavior; appearance; and oral, written, and electronic communication

- Use technology ethically and appropriately to facilitate practice outcomes

- Use supervision and consultation to guide professional judgment and behavior

Competency 2: Engage Diversity and Difference in Practice

Social workers understand how diversity and difference characterize and shape the human experience and are critical to the formation of identity. The dimensions of diversity are understood as the intersectionality of multiple factors including but not limited to age, class, color, culture, disability and ability, ethnicity, gender, gender identity and expression, immigration status, marital status, political ideology, race, religion/spirituality, sex, sexual orientation, and tribal sovereign status. Social workers understand that, as a consequence of difference, a person's life experiences may include oppression, poverty, marginalization, and alienation as well as privilege, power, and acclaim. Social workers also understand the forms and mechanisms of oppression and discrimination and recognize the extent to which a culture's structures and values, including social, economic, political, and cultural exclusions, may oppress, marginalize, alienate, or create privilege and power. Social workers:

- Apply and communicate understanding of the importance of diversity and difference in shaping life experiences in practice at the micro-, mezzo-, and macrolevels

- Present themselves as learners and engage clients and constituencies as experts of their own experiences

- Apply self-awareness and self-regulation to manage the influence of personal biases and values in working with diverse clients and constituencies

Competency 3: Advance Human Rights and Social, Economic, and Environmental Justice

Social workers understand that every person regardless of position in society has fundamental human rights such as freedom, safety, privacy, an adequate standard of living, healthcare, and education. Social workers understand the global interconnections of oppression and human rights violations and are knowledgeable about theories of human need and social justice and strategies to promote social and economic justice and human rights. Social workers understand strategies designed to eliminate oppressive structural barriers to ensure that social goods, rights, and responsibilities are distributed equitably, and that civil, political, environmental, economic, social, and cultural human rights are protected. Social workers:

- Apply their understanding of social, economic, and environmental justice to advocate for human rights at the individual and system levels

- Engage in practices that advance social, economic, and environmental justice

Competency 4: Engage in Practice-Informed Research and Research-Informed Practice

Social workers understand quantitative and qualitative research methods and their respective roles in advancing a science of social work and in evaluating their practice. Social workers know the principles of logic, scientific inquiry, and culturally informed and ethical approaches to building knowledge. Social workers understand that evidence that informs practice derives from multidisciplinary sources and multiple ways of knowing. They also understand the processes for translating research findings into effective practice. Social workers:

- Use practice experience and theory to inform scientific inquiry and research
- Apply critical thinking to engage in analysis of quantitative and qualitative research methods and research findings
- Use and translate research evidence to inform and improve practice, policy, and service delivery

Competency 5: Engage in Policy Practice

Social workers understand that human rights and social justice, as well as social welfare and services, are mediated by policy and its implementation at the federal, state, and local levels. Social workers understand the history and current structures of social policies and services, the role of policy in service delivery, and the role of practice in policy development. Social workers understand their role in policy development and implementation within their practice settings at the micro-, mezzo-, and macrolevels and they actively engage in policy practice to effect change within those settings. Social workers recognize and understand the historical, social, cultural, economic, organizational, environmental, and global influences that affect social policy. They are also knowledgeable about policy formulation, analysis, implementation, and evaluation. Social workers:

- Identify social policy at the local, state, and federal levels that impacts well-being, service delivery, and access to social services
- Assess how social welfare and economic policies impact the delivery of and access to social services
- Apply critical thinking to analyze, formulate, and advocate for policies that advance human rights and social, economic, and environmental justice

Competency 6: Engage With Individuals, Families, Groups, Organizations, and Communities

Social workers understand that engagement is an ongoing component of the dynamic and interactive process of social work practice with, and on behalf of, diverse individuals, families, groups, organizations, and communities. Social workers value the importance of human relationships. They understand theories of human behavior and the social environment, and critically evaluate and apply this knowledge to facilitate engagement with clients and constituencies, including individuals, families, groups, organizations, and communities. Social workers understand strategies to engage diverse clients and constituencies to advance practice effectiveness. Social workers understand how their personal experiences and affective reactions may impact their ability to effectively engage with diverse clients and constituencies. Social workers value principles of relationship building and interprofessional collaboration to facilitate engagement with clients, constituencies, and other professionals as appropriate. Social workers:

- Apply knowledge of human behavior and the social environment, person-in-environment, and other multidisciplinary theoretical frameworks to engage with clients and constituencies

- Use empathy, reflection, and interpersonal skills to effectively engage diverse clients and constituencies

Competency 7: Assess Individuals, Families, Groups, Organizations, and Communities

Social workers understand that assessment is an ongoing component of the dynamic and interactive process of social work practice with, and on behalf of, diverse individuals, families, groups, organizations, and communities. Social workers understand theories of human behavior and the social environment, and critically evaluate and apply this knowledge in the assessment of diverse clients and constituencies, including individuals, families, groups, organizations, and communities. Social workers understand methods of assessment with diverse clients and constituencies to advance practice effectiveness. Social workers recognize the implications of the larger practice context in the assessment process and value the importance of interprofessional collaboration in this process. Social workers understand how their personal experiences and affective reactions may affect their assessment and decision-making. Social workers:

- Collect and organize data, and apply critical thinking to interpret information from clients and constituencies

- Apply knowledge of human behavior and the social environment, person-in-environment, and other multidisciplinary theoretical frameworks in the analysis of assessment data from clients and constituencies

- Develop mutually agreed-on intervention goals and objectives based on the critical assessment of strengths, needs, and challenges within clients and constituencies

- Select appropriate intervention strategies based on the assessment, research knowledge, and values and preferences of clients and constituencies

Competency 8: Intervene With Individuals, Families, Groups, Organizations, and Communities

Social workers understand that intervention is an ongoing component of the dynamic and interactive process of social work practice with, and on behalf of, diverse individuals, families, groups, organizations, and communities. Social workers are knowledgeable about evidence-informed interventions to achieve the goals of clients and constituencies, including individuals, families, groups, organizations, and communities. Social workers understand theories of human behavior and the social environment, and critically evaluate and apply this knowledge to effectively intervene with clients and constituencies. Social workers understand methods of identifying, analyzing, and implementing evidence-informed interventions to achieve client and constituency goals. Social workers value the importance of interprofessional teamwork and communication in interventions, recognizing that beneficial outcomes may require interdisciplinary, interprofessional, and interorganizational collaboration. Social workers:

- Critically choose and implement interventions to achieve practice goals and enhance capacities of clients and constituencies

- Apply knowledge of human behavior and the social environment, person-in-environment, and other multidisciplinary theoretical frameworks in interventions with clients and constituencies

- Use interprofessional collaboration as appropriate to achieve beneficial practice outcomes

- Negotiate, mediate, and advocate with and on behalf of diverse clients and constituencies

- Facilitate effective transitions and endings that advance mutually agreed-on goals

Competency 9: Evaluate Practice With Individuals, Families, Groups, Organizations, and Communities

Social workers understand that evaluation is an ongoing component of the dynamic and interactive process of social work practice with, and on behalf of, diverse individuals, families, groups, organizations, and communities. Social workers recognize the importance of evaluating processes and outcomes to advance practice, policy, and service delivery effectiveness. Social workers understand theories of human behavior and the social environment, and critically evaluate and apply this knowledge in evaluating outcomes. Social workers understand qualitative and quantitative methods for evaluating outcomes and practice effectiveness. Social workers:

- Select and use appropriate methods for evaluation of outcomes

- Apply knowledge of human behavior and the social environment, person-in-environment, and other multidisciplinary theoretical frameworks in the evaluation of outcomes

- Critically analyze, monitor, and evaluate intervention and program processes and outcomes

- Apply evaluation findings to improve practice effectiveness at the micro-, mezzo-, and macrolevels (CSWE, 2015)

■ Holistic Competency

McKnight (2013) proposes that competence is an "ongoing ability" to "integrate knowledge, skills, judgment, and professional attributes in order to practice safely and ethically" within one's professional scope (p. 460). The CSWE defines holistic competence as the "demonstration of knowledge, values, skills, and cognitive and affective processes that include the social worker's critical thinking, affective reactions, and exercise of judgment in regard to unique practice situations" (CSWE, 2015, p. 6).

Knowledge

The knowledge dimension is your mastery of the substantive content of the competency. Social work curricula are constructed to provide students with coursework that provides readings, assignments, and discussions that educate students on the current knowledge related to each competency. Students also increase their competency knowledge through their own research on the topics that comprise the underlying content and processes of each competency. A prerequisite of one's ability to demonstrate competence is a solid understanding and knowledge of the literature that comprises the competency.

Values

The value dimension is less clear than the knowledge dimension. Although Competency 1 is about values and professional behavior, the other eight competencies all have social work value dimensions as well. The value dimensions can have knowledge (social work values) as well as skill (ethical behavior and decision-making) components. Understanding the values and ethics associated with the application of the different social work competencies in unique practice situations is the fundamental aspect of ethical decision-making and professional social work competence.

Skills

The skill dimension refers to your ability to apply social work knowledge and values in your social work practice. There are numerous skills associated with each professional competency. Your field placement experience provides you with an opportunity to apply, refine, and learn social work skills in practice situations. Your skill is your ability to apply social work theories, concepts, and techniques in your practice with clients or client systems.

> ▶ **Critical Thinking Questions**
> 1. How do a social worker's cognitive processes and affective reactions impact his or her professional judgment?
> 2. What role do values play in a social worker's professional competence?

Cognitive Processes and Affective Reactions

This dimension has three associated subdimensions—critical thinking, affective reactions, and professional judgment. Critical thinking is the open-minded search for understanding. It is a process focused on explaining the why. The process includes "providing evidence, examining the implications of the evidence, recognizing any potential contradictions and examining alternative explanations" (Heron, 2006, p. 221). The CSWE (2015) defines critical thinking as an intellectual, disciplined process of conceptualizing, analyzing, evaluating, and synthesizing multiple sources of information generated by observation, reaction, and reasoning.

Critical thinking is a crucial component of professional competence because it ensures that your social work practice is reasoned and thoughtful and not the rote application of social work techniques. Affective reaction, on the other hand, generally refers to the affective component of social work practice with clients (Rubaltelli & Slovic, 2008). It is the worker's emotional response to the client's presentation and situation. It is tied to empathy and other affective processes. Affective reaction has relevance for social work competency in that effective social work practice requires cognitive and affective understanding of the client as well as one's own feelings, emotions, and reactions (Poulin & Matis, 2015).

Professional judgment is about decision-making in social work practice. A key issue debated in relation to decision-making in social work is the extent to which social workers use analytical versus intuitive reasoning styles (Collins & Daly, 2011). Thus, professional judgment is reasoned decision-making based upon evidence, knowledge, analytical reasoning, and practice wisdom. It is a process of examining all facets of the case and making a reasoned decision supported by both objective and subjective evidence. Exercising informed professional judgment is a critical component of professional social work competence (Poulin & Matis, 2015).

■ Competency Model of Social Work Practice

The nine social work competencies and the associated dimensions are the interrelated components of professional social work practice. The competencies are interconnected. They do not stand alone. Holistic competency is social work practice utilizing multiple professional competencies in each practice activity or client interaction. Figure 1.4 shows a conceptualization

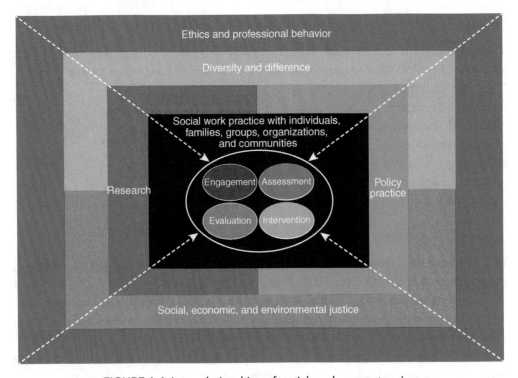

FIGURE 1.4 Interrelationships of social work competencies.

of the interrelationships among the nine professional social work competencies. The competencies in the two outer bands are those that apply broadly to all practice situations. The ethical and professional behavior, diversity and difference, and social, economic and environmental justice competencies are fundamental components of effective social work practice at all levels (Poulin, Matis, & Witt, 2019).

The competencies in the middle band of Figure 1.4 are the two areas of social work practice that are not client-based—policy practice and research. These competencies are informed by the ethical behavior, diversity, and justice competencies and in turn inform social work practice with clients and constituencies competencies. The center band represents the engagement, assessment, intervention, and evaluation competencies in social practice with individuals, families, groups, organizations, and communities. Thus, the ethical behavior, diversity, social justice, policy practice, and research competencies all inform the practice competencies of engagement, assessment, intervention, and evaluation with individuals, families, groups, organizations, and communities (Poulin & Matis, 2015).

▶ **Critical Thinking Questions**

1. How does the diversity and difference competency impact the social work practice with clients and constituencies competencies?

2. How does the research competency impact the social work practice with clients and constituencies competencies?

Thus, the nine professional competencies are interconnected in the delivery of social work practice with clients and constituencies. For example, a social worker's ability to engage with an individual client is influenced by his or her ethical and professional behavior competency; diversity and difference competency; social, economic, and environmental justice competency; and possibly his or her policy practice and research competencies. In short, most social work practice situations require the use of all or most of the nine professional competencies. Thus, to be a competent social work practitioner, you must develop knowledge, values, skill, cognitive process, and affective reaction competencies for each professional competency and be able to apply multiple competencies in a variety of practice situations.

Social Work Practice Competencies

The 2015 EPAS identify four social work practice competencies that are components of social work practice with clients and constituencies—engagement, assessment, intervention, and evaluation. These four components of social work practice are the framework from which all models of social work practice are employed. The four components of practice are used regardless of the theories or practice models used. For example, a social worker using the ecosystems perspective and an associated practice model would structure the work around engagement, assessment, intervention, and evaluation. Similarly, a social worker using the strengths perspective and an associated practice model would also structure the work around the four components of practice. The same would hold true for the other theories and practice models shown in Figures 1.1 and 1.2.

▶ **Critical Thinking Questions**

1. What role does the evaluation competency play in social work practice?

2. How does the engagement competency interact with the other three social work practice competencies?

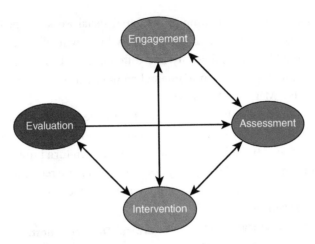

FIGURE 1.5 Social work practice components.

Figure 1.5 shows the interrelationships among the four components of social work practice with clients and constituencies. First of all, it is important to note that the four-component model is not linear and that the unidirectional arrows represent the dominant direction
of the relationships between the different practice components. While there is kind of a logical order, the process in actual practice is never linear, where one component is completed
and then you move onto the next. The components are often done together and there is
almost always a feedback loop (Birkenmaier et al., 2014). For example, one cannot build a
relationship with another person without some kind of interaction together. The engagement component is about building trust and a positive helping relationship. Engagement
almost always occurs as part of the assessment process. The worker/client relationship helps
with the assessment, and the assessment process helps build the relationship. Engagement
and intervention are also often bidirectional. Engagement affects the intervention process
and the intervention process affects engagement. The same is true for the assessment phase.
Assessment is usually an ongoing process that takes place throughout the helping process. In
fact, there is or should always be a continuous feedback loop between engagement, assessment, and intervention in the provision of social work practice to clients and constituencies.
Similarly, there is or should always be a continuous feedback loop between the assessment,
intervention, and evaluation components.

Engagement

Engagement is the process of building relationships among the social worker, the client, and
the client's environment. Social workers engage with their clients throughout the helping
process. It is ongoing and takes place during the assessment, intervention, and evaluation
phases of social work practice.

Engagement as defined by the 2015 EPAS involves applying knowledge of human behavior
and the social environment, person-in-environment, and other multidisciplinary theoretical
frameworks to engage with clients and constituencies; and use empathy, reflection, and interpersonal skills to effectively engage diverse clients and constituencies. Successful engagement

involves establishing trust and development of a bond between the social worker and the client (Birkenmaier et al., 2014). It requires effective communication and the ability to communicate empathy and understanding. Without trust and understanding, the relationship will not develop and hence the client will not truly engage in the helping process.

Assessment

Assessment is an ongoing interactive process. This component of social work practice entails an exploration of the client's internal and environmental challenges and strengths. Most social work agencies have some sort of client assessment that is conducted as part of the intake process. It is usually involves collecting data, analyzing the data, and developing goals and an intervention plan. The assessment process can vary depending upon the agency's theoretical orientation and practice model (Birkenmaier et al., 2014). For example, an agency employing the strengths perspective will structure a client assessment differently than one operating from an ecosystems perspective. The former will focus on the client's strengths and capacities to overcome barriers and obstacles. The latter will focus more on the interactions between the client and his or her environment looking for problems that need to be addressed.

Assessment is not limited to the intake process. It is ongoing throughout the helping relationship. The social worker is continuously gathering and analyzing information to better understand his or her clients and their needs and challenges. The initial assessment should be thought of as a starting point and that new insights and information are added to the assessment as the work progresses.

Intervention

This component refers to the implementation of the plan developed as part of the assessment. It is the actual work the client and social worker do to address the client's identified needs and challenges. Interventions vary widely depending upon the worker/agency's theoretical orientation and practice model, and whether the client is an individual, family, group, organization, or community. Although interventions vary, what they all have in common is that engagement and assessment are important aspects of the intervention. The social worker continues to engage and assess as the intervention is implemented with his or her clients.

Evaluation

Evaluation is also an ongoing component of the dynamic and interactive process of social work practice (CSWE, 2015). Evaluation methods and processes can take many forms and can vary depending upon the theoretical orientation of the social worker/agency. Generally, evaluation is the process used to assess a client's progress on the goals identified during the assessment component and development of the intervention plan. Evaluation can be qualitative, quantitative, or both. Its purpose is to obtain information on the effectiveness of the intervention in helping the client address the identified needs and challenges. Conducting ongoing evaluations is important in that doing so enables the social worker and client to adjust the interventions if progress is not taking place.

■ Social Work Clients

Social work practice involves work with client systems of all sizes. The client system could be an individual, a family, a small group, an organization, or a community. The primary client system is unlikely to be the only client system being helped or targeted for change. Typically, as shown in Case 1.3, social work practice involves working with more than one client system.

CASE 1.3   CAN'T TELL MY PARENTS: WORKING WITH MORE THAN ONE CLIENT SYSTEM IN SOCIAL WORK PRACTICE

Alice C is 17. She has been pregnant with her first child for 2 months. She is unmarried and very committed to her relationship with the teenage father of the child. They are both seniors in high school and plan to attend college in the fall. Alice's parents are devout Catholics who follow the teachings of the church. Although quite strict, they have always been loving, and have encouraged and supported their only adopted daughter.

Alice is afraid to talk to her parents about her situation. She is concerned about disappointing them and about the shame she will bring to the family. She has not told her boyfriend about the pregnancy either. She is unsure how he will react.

Alice does not know what to do. She is unwilling to confide in her family and friends, so she contacts the school social worker for help.

In the Case 1.3, if Alice agrees to work with the social worker, she will become the primary client. She needs help in assessing her options and deciding on a course of action. Depending on what she decides to do, her parents, her boyfriend, and the school are all possible client systems.

If Alice decides, for instance, that she wants to keep the baby and ask her parents to help her care for the child, Alice and her parents become the client. In this situation, the key to successfully assisting Alice is to help her parents respond supportively to her situation. The social worker would probably help Alice prepare for the meeting with her parents, might attend the meeting with her, and might offer to help the parents adjust to and cope with their daughter's pregnancy and the pending birth. In this case, Alice and her parents are both clients as well as the family as a whole.

Types of Clients

A potential client becomes a client only if and when there is an explicit agreement between the person and the social worker about the purpose of their work together. **Clients** are people who agree to work with you to achieve a specified outcome. There are three types of clients: voluntary, nonvoluntary, and involuntary (Seabury, Seabury, & Garvin, 2011).

Voluntary clients seek out the services of a social worker or social agency on their own because they want help with some aspect of their lives. A young mother who recognizes that she has a drinking problem and seeks help from a professional social worker is an example of a voluntary client. She has made the decision to get professional help and is voluntarily entering into a helping relationship with the social worker.

▶ **Critical Thinking Questions**

1. Engaging with involuntary clients is difficult. What would you do to engage an involuntary client in a helping relationship?
2. What theoretical framework would you use and why?

Nonvoluntary clients are being pressured to seek help by someone they know personally. They have not been given a mandate by a court of law or social agency to receive help. A friend, relative, or acquaintance believes they have problems; they themselves may or may not agree. Even if they acknowledge the existence of problems, they are not seeking help on their own volition. Someone in their life is forcing them to seek help (Seabury et al., 2011). A young mother who is being pressured by her husband to get help for her drinking problem is an example of a nonvoluntary client. She is meeting with a social worker only because her husband has threatened to leave her and seek custody of their child. She is essentially being forced by her husband to get professional help with her drinking problem and is complying with his wishes to prevent him from leaving her and possibly getting custody of their child.

Involuntary clients have a legal mandate to receive services. They have no choice in the matter. If the young mother with a drinking problem is arrested for drunk driving, part of her sentence might be a court order requiring her to participate in a 10-week counseling program. In this situation, she is an involuntary client.

Regardless of whether prospective clients are voluntary, nonvoluntary, or involuntary, they must make some sort of contract or agreement with the social worker in order to become clients. They must knowingly and willingly participate in the helping process. Clearly, it is easier to reach an agreement with voluntary clients than with nonvoluntary or involuntary clients. Voluntary clients are motivated to seek help. The others, at the point of initial contact, have probably not made the decision to seek help and engage in a collaborative helping process.

Client Change Process

Clients progress through five stages in self-initiated, professionally assisted change: precontemplation, contemplation, preparation, action, and maintenance. "**Precontemplation** is the stage at which there is no intention to change in the foreseeable future" (Prochaska, DiClemente, & Norcross, 1992, p. 1103). Clients at this stage are often unaware of their problems and are not seriously considering getting help. They are reluctant participants in the helping process. They have not chosen to seek help and probably are unhappy about the prospect of being helped. "**Contemplation** is the stage in which clients are aware that a problem exists and are seriously thinking about overcoming it but have not yet made a commitment to take action" (p. 1103). The key here is the lack of commitment to change. Many clients recognize the need to address concerns or problems but need help in making a genuine commitment to bring the change about. "**Preparation** is the stage that combines intention and behavioral criteria" (p. 1104). Clients at this stage have started to address the problem and are motivated to make the necessary changes. "**Action** is the stage in which individuals modify their behavior, experiences, or environment in order to overcome their problems" (p. 1104).

During the action stage, clients are engaged in the helping process and are taking necessary steps to achieve the desired changes. "**Maintenance** is the stage in which people work to prevent relapse and consolidate the gains attained during action" (p. 1104). In a way, maintenance is a continuation of the action phase. The client is actively trying to prevent a relapse.

The five stages of change highlight client differences in readiness to engage in the helping process. It is important to recognize these individual differences. Not all potential clients have reached the stage of contemplation or action. Many clients who are referred or have a mandate for service are in the precontemplation or contemplation stage. To become true clients, they must make a commitment to change. In the end, only those who willingly agree to work with the social worker to achieve a specified outcome can engage in a collaborative helping relationship. Nonvoluntary and involuntary clients might go through the motions because they are required to do so, but they will not truly become clients until they decide on their own to engage in a helping relationship.

The Reluctant Client

Social workers often work with clients who are in the precontemplation stage and are not interested in getting help. In the past, these clients were viewed as "resistant" and often blamed for not cooperating with their social workers (Anderson & Stewart, 1983). Many clients, at best, are going to be reluctant to engage in a helping relationship (Rooney & Mirick, 2018). The following discussion reviews some factors that affect clients' willingness and ability to move beyond the precontemplation stage in the helping process.

The Experience of Being a Client

A number of factors impact a person's willingness to become a client and engage in a professional helping relationship. Understanding these factors and the way a person feels about being a client can facilitate the helping process and the development of a collaborative helping relationship. Understanding the client's feelings about needing and asking for help as well as his or her perceptions of what it means to be a client can facilitate the process of reaching an explicit agreement about the purpose of working together. Whether the individual arrives on a voluntary, nonvoluntary, or involuntary basis, the worker's sensitivity to his or her feelings about being a client is critical to having that individual become a client.

Beliefs and feelings about receiving help from a professional are related to cultural mores. The dominant culture in American society has a strong tradition of individualism (Billups, 1992). Individuals who need psychological or social services are stigmatized and viewed negatively in American society because they are perceived as not living up to the cultural mandates of individual responsibility and self-reliance. This stigma keeps many who need the services provided by social workers from seeking them. Only after everything else has failed are they willing to get professional help.

Most clients have mixed feelings about getting help (Maluccio, 1979). People are uncomfortable about involving themselves in a helping relationship and admitting that they have failed or are unable to resolve their difficulties on their own. Clients may feel shame and embarrassment. They are concerned about what the social worker will think of them and what friends and family will think. Asking for help also raises negative feelings about themselves because they may view receiving professional help as a personal failure. Obviously, the intensity of these feelings varies greatly. However, it is probably safe to assume that every person is feeling some degree of discomfort when he or she asks for help and goes through the stages of becoming a client.

Clients are often afraid of the possibilities of change. Nevertheless, even the most reluctant nonvoluntary or involuntary client has the power to bounce back. The worker uses this resilience to infuse some degree of hopefulness and expectation about positive outcomes. At some level, all clients have what it takes to make changes. They may not know it, but we, as social workers, know it, and that is why we passionately look for a person's strengths when he or she is involved in difficult life situations. Clients may not be aware of their resilience because they are overwhelmed by feelings of failure and stigmatization.

It is only realistic to expect that clients have ambivalent feelings about working with the social worker and receiving professional help. The first interactions will probably determine whether clients decide to engage in the helping process or drop out. During initial meetings, it is critical for the worker to decrease the client's negative feelings and increase positive feelings about seeking help and engaging in the helping process. Empowerment starts during the first interview with the client.

Prior Experiences With Helping Professionals

Most clients who come to you will have received social services in the past and have had numerous prior contacts with helping professionals. Ignoring the possibility of prior negative experiences or assuming that all prior experiences were positive is a mistake. Clients' expectations about receiving help from a professional are influenced by their past experiences (Gambrill, 2013). Were they treated with respect? Were they given a voice in the decision-making process? Were the services helpful? Were their prior experiences with helping professionals satisfactory or unsatisfactory? Clients whose prior experiences were negative may expect more of the same and approach your work together with reservations, whereas those who enjoyed more positive experiences might be much more willing to engage in the helping process.

Early in the working relationship, preferably during the initial meeting, the social worker should explore the client's perceptions of prior experiences. The worker may not change these perceptions but recognizing them and learning what clients liked and did not like about earlier experiences is an important step in the helping process.

Clients' perceptions of the agency may also influence their approach to service (Seabury et al., 2011). Does the agency have a negative or positive reputation in the community? Does the agency communicate respect for clients and their cultures in its physical appearance and decor? Are clients greeted at the agency in a courteous and respectful manner? Is the waiting area pleasant and comfortable? Negative agency perceptions can impede the development of a helping relationship and the client's receptiveness to the helping process.

Understanding clients' perceptions of their prior experiences with helping professionals and their expectations for upcoming experiences with the agency is a critical step in the engagement process. Being sensitive to the possibilities of both positive and negative prior experiences enables you to directly address concerns. Communicating empathy about negative experiences and perceptions validates clients' experiences and perceptions. This validation begins the process of co-constructing a more positive mind-set regarding the helping process and a willingness to engage in a collaborative helping relationship.

Expectations About the Helping Experience

Social workers also need to be sensitive to clients' expectations about the helping process and their role as client. Ignoring or misunderstanding client expectations may result in the client dropping out prematurely (Gambrill, 2013). Client expectations about changes or outcomes should match those of their helpers. Different expectations will affect outcome and client retention (Gambrill, 2013).

Clients come to the helping process with various expectations. Some may have little or no hope of making any meaningful change in their lives, whereas others may expect a miracle. Some might be aware of the collaborative nature of the helping process, and others might expect the social worker to fix the problem. Early in your work together, although not necessarily during your first meeting, you need to discuss how you will work together and what your respective roles will be. Clients need to clearly understand the helping process as well as their roles and responsibilities in it. Inappropriate expectations and misunderstandings about how the work will proceed can lead to disillusionment and dissatisfaction. It is important to share your vision of the helping process. It is probably wise to assume that you and your clients have different visions and expectations. These differences need to be reconciled before meaningful work can begin.

Cultural and Ethnic Diversity

American society is characterized by cultural and racial diversity. Therefore, it is no surprise that social work clients have diverse cultural backgrounds and beliefs. Values and beliefs of different cultural groups might conflict with the values of the dominant culture or with the worker's values and beliefs. Even though social workers and clients often have a great deal in common, the expectation should be one of diversity and heterogeneity. Expect your clients to be unique individuals with different beliefs and values. Expect them to have a belief system that differs from yours in important ways.

The cultural or ethnic background of individuals may influence whether they become clients. Perceived similarities lead to understanding, empathy, and trust. Perceived differences may hinder the development of mutual understanding and trust (Miley, O'Melia, & DuBois, 2013). Perceived differences are barriers to clients' willingness to develop helping relationships. Most people seek out others with whom they feel a connection, a sameness, or a likeness. Individuals tend to trust those they perceive as similar and distrust those they perceive as different. The tendency to distrust those who are different makes the task of overcoming cultural and ethnic differences a challenge for all social workers.

The number of potential differences between you and your client is infinite. Differences in values, perspectives, and experiences create barriers to communication and trust. It is your responsibility, as the professional helper, to acknowledge differences directly and to communicate respect for your clients' values and beliefs. Rather than viewing cultural differences as threatening, view them as a resource that adds perspectives and options to your relationship with your client (Miley et al., 2013). Overcoming client–worker differences requires that you acknowledge the differences as well as communicate your understanding of the clients' values, perceptions, and beliefs. Value your clients' differences. Show respect and appreciation of diversity. The differences will remain; what will change is the perception that they are barriers to communication and trust. Directly acknowledging differences early in the helping process increases the likelihood that the individual will become a client. Ignoring cultural and ethnic differences tends to exacerbate the magnitude of differences and hinder the development of trust.

In working with people of color, women, gays and lesbians, and other oppressed populations, it is important to acknowledge that their perceptions and experiences have been subjugated by the dominant culture. To understand the experiences of clients, ask questions from a position of not knowing. Be curious and show a genuine interest in what the client has to say. The client, not the social worker, is the expert on his or her perceptions and experiences (Saleebey, 2013). Client expertise also encompasses cultural, ethnic, and racial experiences and perceptions.

Hartman points out that "in our attempt to become more skilled and more sensitive in our work with people of color, we have sought to gather information about cultures, to learn about difference, to become experts" (1994, p. 29). This approach leads to stereotyping and assumptions that all members of an oppressed group are alike. A better approach is to "abandon our expert role and really listen to our clients and believe and trust their experience" (Hartman, 1994, p. 29). If we listen to our clients, are open to their experiences, and take the position of learning with them and of not knowing, the chances of overcoming our differences are greatly improved.

Another important factor in cross-cultural practice is awareness of self and one's own cultural and ethnic heritage (Thomas, 2005). Being aware of your own ethnic and cultural identity will increase your comfort level in working with clients from different ethnic and cultural backgrounds (Poulin et al., 2019). A culturally self-aware person is capable of recognizing and acknowledging differences. Social workers who are not aware of their own cultural beliefs and values are more likely to impose their values and beliefs on their clients and to feel threatened by their clients' differences. The more you know about yourself, the more likely you are to want to learn about your clients.

Client Skills and Knowledge

Clients often seek professional help only after they attempt to resolve problems on their own, with assistance from friends, family, or informal community organizations, or with other helping professionals. First meetings with new clients usually occur after clients have made numerous attempts to cope with their situations. They have a wealth of experience in dealing with their problems. They know what has worked and what has not worked. They probably have ideas about what is making the issue difficult to resolve and what they need to do to successfully resolve it. Be open to and use this knowledge.

Clients bring unique skills to the relationship. Each client has interpersonal skills and competencies. Clients have developed coping strategies and have found ways to get by in spite of pressing life demands and circumstances. They have developed unique ways of adapting to their life experiences. They have been successful, at some level, in coping with their difficulties. They are struggling and need help, but they have managed to survive and cope with challenging situations. All clients bring strengths and skills to the helping relationship.

▶ **Critical Thinking Questions**
1. What are some of the feelings you would experience in asking for help from a social worker?
2. What can a social worker do to make becoming a client easier for you?

Clients are empowered when the social worker acknowledges their strengths, knowledge, and skills. They are also encouraged. Clients are given hope when they are viewed as capable and competent individuals. Regardless of their level of functioning, irrespective of the severity of their life circumstances, and in spite of the magnitude of the problems that need to be overcome, clients' knowledge and skills can contribute to the resolution of their problem situations. Look for strengths and abilities and expect to find them. It is your job to help clients identify and articulate the knowledge and skills that they bring to the helping process. Recognizing these strengths helps foster collaborative social worker–client relationships by increasing clients' willingness to engage in the helping process.

No matter whether a client is voluntary, nonvoluntary, or involuntary, and regardless of the circumstances that bring a client into contact with a generalist social worker, the client has to choose to participate in the helping process. For this to occur, the client has to have progressed at least to the preparation stage of change. The challenge for generalist social workers is to help clients move beyond the precontemplation and contemplation stages, so that clients do not drop out or go through the motions of changing without truly engaging in the helping process.

A number of factors influence clients' ability to engage in helping relationships. One factor is their feelings about getting help and the stigma they feel about asking for help from a stranger. Cultural values and beliefs as well as prior experiences with helping professionals influence these feelings. At best, most clients have mixed feelings about working with a social worker. The social worker must communicate understanding of these feelings and create an expectation that change is possible in order for clients to engage in the helping process. Being sensitive to clients' expectations and their role in the helping process and clarifying the collaborative nature of your work together also help promote client participation.

■ Summary

In this chapter, we have reviewed the differences among paradigms, metatheories, theories, perspectives, and practice models. Positivism, systems theory, and the ecosystems perspective were described and compared with constructivism theories and the strengths perspective.

In this chapter, we also presented the CSWE professional competencies, which provide the framework for the organization of this textbook. In addition, the concept of competency-based education and a discussion of how competency is conceptualized were reviewed. This was followed by a discussion of the four components that make up social work practice with individuals, families, groups, organizations, and communities. The relationships among the four components of engagement, assessment, intervention, and evaluation were discussed. The chapter ended with a discussion of social work clients, the client change process, and factors that affect client engagement and change.

CASE SUMMARY   "UNDOCUMENTED AND HOMELESS"

Practice Setting Description

Jackie is a first-year master's in social work student completing an internship at an inner-city family service agency in the Southwest. The agency is located in a section of the city that has a high crime rate, gang activity, and failing schools. The area has a diverse population with a large number of immigrants from Central and South America and a substantial African American population. The agency provides individual and family counseling services on a sliding fee scale. The agency also runs a number of educational and treatment groups as well as a temporary shelter for women and their children. Jackie has been assigned to work with the women and their children in the shelter. Her primary tasks are to provide concrete services and supportive counseling to the shelter residents.

Background Information

Elicia T and her daughter, Maria, are undocumented immigrants from Mexico. They have been in the United States for 5 years. Elicia and Maria fled to the area from another southwestern city to escape her abusive husband approximately 2 months ago. Elicia is 25 years old and Maria 8 years old. Elicia has a 2-year-old daughter, Sarah, who was placed in foster care because of suspected abuse in the home. Sarah is in a foster home in a small rural community in the state hundreds of miles from Elicia's current residence. Since moving to the area, Maria has not been attending school.

Elicia and Maria are currently residing in the agency's temporary shelter for families. They have been at the shelter for 2 weeks, and the agency has a 90-day limit. It is viewed as temporary housing, and the residents are only allowed to stay for 3 months. Prior to arriving at the shelter, Elicia and Maria were homeless and living on the streets.

Elicia is a high-school dropout and was a stay-at-home mother prior to leaving her husband and moving to a different part of the state. She chose to move there because she has two female cousins living in the area who are also undocumented immigrants. Elicia's native language is Spanish. She speaks some English but is not as comfortable speaking in English. Her English comprehension appears to be good. Maria speaks both English and Spanish well. When communicating with the staff, Maria acts as Elicia's interpreter since none of the staff at the shelter speak Spanish.

Maria appears to be behind academically. She struggles reading simple children's books written in English. It is unknown if her ability to read in Spanish is better than her English reading skills.

Other than her two cousins, Elicia has no other sources of support in the community. Her cousins have young families and limited resources but are well established and connected to a Latino community in the city and the local Catholic church. Her cousins refused to let Elicia and Maria live with them while she was trying to find her own place and a job. They stated that they did not have enough room and are concerned they would get in trouble with their landlord if it was found out that they were letting people stay with them. They sent her to the local church for help, and she was given the address for the agency's shelter by the priest.

Elicia has been looking for housing in the Latino community. The housing market is tight with limited options, and she has been unable to find anything that she could possibly afford. The only

(continued)

CASE SUMMARY

affordable housing she found was a room in a rundown motel that rents by the hour or by the month. It is in an area of town known for drug dealing and sex work.

On arrival in the community, Elicia found occasional work for a house cleaning company. The company hires undocumented workers, pays them very low cash wages, and threatens to turn them in to Immigration and Customs Enforcement (ICE) if they complain. The job bosses also exploit their female workers sexually, threatening to turn them in if they do not comply. Elicia was fearful about applying for other jobs because of her illegal status. She considered turning to sex work to be able to take care of her children, but her Catholic upbringing and thoughts of how doing so would shame her family have kept her from doing so. She is in constant fear of being detained, separated from her children, and having them placed in foster care. She is also afraid that she will end up homeless again and forced to live on the streets or return to her abusive husband.

Elicia is extremely reluctant to sign up for any federally funded services, even those that she and her children are entitled to receiving. On the suggestion that she enroll for supplemental food through SNAP, Elicia became nervous and refused as she has heard that participation in SNAP services, and others like them, would draw the attention of ICE, and she had heard stories on the news of individuals being deported after signing up for such programs.

Presenting Problems

Elicia and her children are facing multiple obstacles. They need to find permanent, affordable housing and a job that pays enough to cover her housing and living expenses. In addition, Maria needs to be enrolled in school. Elicia also wants to regain custody of her youngest daughter in foster care.

Additionally, Elicia is experiencing an immense amount of stress, anxiety, and possibly post-traumatic stress disorder (PTSD). She described an instance where she could not calm down her breathing, and she felt lightheaded. She is very fearful of men and tries to avoid all contact with men in the community. She reports difficulty sleeping at night and feeling exhausted most of the time.

She is concerned about Maria. She has started acting out at the shelter, getting into fights with the other children, disobeying her mother, and being disrespectful and defiant to the staff and other adults. Elicia and Maria fight frequently, and when Elicia tries to discipline Maria, she throws a temper tantrum until Elicia gives up.

Elicia has many strengths. She had the strength to leave her abusive husband and move to a different city. She loves her daughters. She wants desperately to keep Maria with her and hopes to have Sarah returned to her custody. She is resilient and has managed to survive and keep her daughter safe despite not having a place to stay, a job, and a limited support network. Additionally, Elicia is highly motivated to find her own accommodations and support her children.

■ Discussion Questions

1. What are the social justice issues affecting Elicia's case situation at the micro-, mezzo-, and macrolevels?

2. What are the micro-, mezzo-, and macrosystems that are in Elicia's person-in-environment? If you were her social worker, what systems or subsystems would you target for intervention and why?

3. Elicia has many strengths. How would you incorporate the strengths perspective in helping Elicia?

4. What client factors do you think will help you in developing a positive helping relationship with Elicia? What factors do you think will hinder the helping relationship? What would you do to try and build trust with Elicia?

■ References

Anderson, C. M., & Stewart, S. (1983). *Mastering resistance: A practical guide to family therapy.* New York, NY: Springer Publishing Company.

Billups, J. O. (1992). The moral basis for a radical reconstruction of social work. In P. N. Reid & P. R. Popple (Eds.), *The moral purposes of social work: The character and intentions of a profession* (pp. 100–119). Chicago, IL: Nelson-Hall.

Birkenmaier, J., Berg-Weger, M., & Dewees, M. P. (2014). *The practice of generalist social work* (3rd ed.). New York, NY: Routledge: Taylor & Francis Group.

Bowers, N. R., & Bowers, A. (2017). General systems theory. In F. Turner (Ed.), *Social work treatment: Interlocking theoretical approaches* (6th ed., pp. 240–247). New York, NY, Oxford University Press.

Carpenter, D., & Brownlee, K. (2017). Constructivism: A conceptual framework. In F. Turner (Ed.), *Social work treatment: Interlocking theoretical approaches* (6th ed., pp. 96–118). New York, NY: Oxford University Press.

Collins, E., & Daly, E. (2011). *Decision making and social work in Scotland: The role of evidence and practice wisdom.* Institute for Research and Innovation in Social Sciences. Retrieved from http://www .iriss.org.uk/sites/default/files/decision-making-wisdom-iriss-2011.pdf

Council on Social Work Education. (2015). *Educational policy and accreditation standards.* Alexandria, VA: Author.

Dybicz, P. (2015). From Person-in-Environment to Strengths: The Promise of Postmodern Practice. *Journal of Social Work Education, 51*(2), 237–249. doi:10.1080/10437797.2015.1012923

Gambrill, E. (2013). *Social Work Practice. A Critical Thinker's Guide* (3rd ed.). Oxford, UK: Oxford University Press.

Gitterman, A., & Germain, C.B. (1976). Social work practice: A life model. *Social Service Review, 50*(4), 601–610. doi:10.1086/643430

Gitterman, A., & Germain, C. B. (2008). *The life model of social work practice: Advances in theory and practice* (3rd ed.). New York, NY: Columbia University Press.

Greene, G. J., Jensen, C., & Jones, D. H. (1996). A Constructivist Perspective on Clinical Social Work Practice with Ethnically Diverse Clients. *Social Work, 41*(2), 172–180. doi:10.1093/sw/41.2.172

Greene, G. L., & Lee, M.Y. (2002). The social construction of empowerment. In M. W. O'Melia and K. K. Miley (Eds.), *Pathways to power: Readings in contextual social work practice* (pp. 175–201). Boston, MA: Allyn and Bacon.

Hartman, A. (1994). Social work practice. In F. G. Reamer (Ed.), *The foundations of social work knowledge* (pp. 13–50). New York, NY: Columbia University Press.

Hepworth, D. H., Rooney, R., Rooney, G. D., & Strom-Gottfried, K. (2017). *Direct social work practice: Theory and skills* (10th ed.). Boston, MA: Cengage.

Heron, G. (2006). Critical thinking in social care and social work: Searching student assignments for the evidence. *Social Work Education, 25*, 209–224. doi:10.1080/02615470600564965

Irving, A., & Young, T. (2002). Paradigm for pluralism: Mikhail Bakhtin and social work practice. *Social Work, 47*, 19–29. doi:10.1093/sw/47.1.19

Kondrat, D. C. (2014). The strengths perspective. In B. Teater (Ed.), *An introduction to applying social work theories and methods* (2nd ed., pp. 39–55). New York, NY: McGraw-Hill Education.

Langer, C. L., & Lietz, C. A. (2015). *Applying theory to generalist social work practice*. Hoboken, NJ: John Wiley & Sons, Inc.

Maluccio, A. (1979). Perspectives of social workers and clients on treatment outcome. *Social Casework, 60*, 394–401. doi:10.1177/104438947906000702

McKnight, S. E. (2013). Mental health learning needs assessment: Competency-based instrument for best practice. *Issues in Mental Health Nursing, 34*, 459–471. doi:10.3109/01612840.2012.758205

Miley, K., O'Melia, M., & DuBois, B. L. (2013). *Generalist social work practice: An empowering approach* (7th ed.). Boston, MA: Pearson.

Montano, C. (2012). Social work theory-practice relationship: Challenges to overcoming positivist and postmodern fragmentation. *International Social Work, 55*, 306–319. doi:10.1177/0020872812437226

Payne, M. (2016). *Modern social work theory* (4th ed.). New York, NY: Oxford University Press.

Peile, C., & McCouat, M. (1997). The rise of relativism: The future of theory and knowledge development in social work. *British Journal of Social Work, 27*, 343–360. doi:10.1093/oxfordjournals.bjsw.a011217

Poulin, J., & Matis, S. (2015). Social work competencies and multidimensional assessment. *Journal of Baccalaureate Social Work, 20*, 117–135. doi:10.18084/1084-7219.20.1.117

Poulin, J., Matis S., & Witt, H. (2019). *The social work field placement: A competency-based approach*. New York, NY: Springer Publishing Company.

Prochaska, J. O., DiClemente, C. C., & Norcross, J. C. (1992). In search of how people change: Applications to addictive behaviors. *American Psychologist, 47*, 1102–1114. doi:10.1037/0003-066X.47.9.1102

Rapp, C. A., Saleebey, D., & Sullivan, W. P. (2005). The future of strengths-based social work. *Advances in Social Work, 6*, 79–90.

Reid, W. (1994). The empirical practice movement. *Social Service Review, 68*, 165–184. doi:10.1086/604045

Richmond, M. (1917). *Social diagnosis*. New York, NY: Russell Sage.

Rooney, R. H., & Mirick, R. G. (2018). *Strategies for work with involuntary clients* (3rd ed.). New York, NY: Columbia University Press.

Rothery, M. (2016). Critical ecological systems theory. In N. Coady & P. Lehman (Eds.), *Theoretical perspectives of direct social work practice: A generalist-eclectic approach* (3rd ed.). New York, NY: Springer Publishing Company.

Rubaltelli, E., & Slovic, P. (2008). Affective reaction and context-dependent processing of negations. *Judgement and Decision Making, 3*, 607–618.

Saleebey, D. (Ed.). (1992). *The strengths perspective in social work practice*. New York, NY: Longman.

Saleebey, D. (2013). *The strengths perspective in social work practice* (6th ed.). London, UK: Pearson.

Seabury, B., Seabury, B., & Garvin, C. (2011). *Interpersonal practice in social work: Promoting competence and social justice* (3rd ed.). Thousand Oaks, CA: Sage Publications.

Simmons, C. A., Shapiro, V. B., Accomazzo, S., & Manthey, T. (2016). Strengths-based social work: A social work metatheory to guide the profession. In N. Coady & P. Lehmann (Eds.), *Theoretical perspectives for direct social work practice* (3rd ed., pp. 130–152). New York, NY: Springer Publishing Company.

Smith-Acuna, A. (2011). *Systems theory in action*. Hoboken, NJ: John Wiley and Sons.

Teater, B. (2014). *An introduction to applying social work theories and methods* (2nd ed.). New York, NY: McGraw-Hill Education.

Thomas, N. D. (2005). Generalist practice with people of color. In J. Poulin (Ed.), *Strengths-based generalist practice: A collaborative approach* (2nd ed., pp. 398–430). Belmont, CA: Brooks/Cole.

Von Bertalanffy, L. (1968). *General systems theory: Foundations, development, applications*. New York, NY: George Braziller.

Wakefield, J. C. (1996). Does social work need the ecosystems perspective? Part 1. Is the perspective clinically useful? *Social Service Review, 70*, 1–32. doi:10.1086/604163

ETHICAL AND PROFESSIONAL BEHAVIOR

Jill is a first-year master of social work student who has completed her field placement in a small homeless shelter that serves homeless families in a small Midwestern town. The shelter has a small full-time staff of five professionals plus Jill and another intern. The shelter serves four families at a time and collaborates with other service agencies in the county and surrounding counties.

Jill's client, Lisa, is a 25-year old Caucasian single mother of two toddlers; sheexperienced the death of her husband 12 months ago. She and her husband were attending a movie when a teenager opened fire with a semiautomatic rifle. Her husband was hit and died instantly. Lisa was not physically injured. Her mother is emotionally supportive but in poor health and unable to help care for her children. Lisa lost her part-time job in a supermarket due to missing work multiple times because she could not find the energy or motivation to go to work. Losing her husband, who was the primary breadwinner, and her part-time job caused Lisa to become homeless and move into the shelter with her two children.

Jill believes that Lisa's depression and lack of motivation to find employment are related to her grieving the loss of her husband and the trauma she experienced. Jill, as a first-year field placement student, does not feel qualified to provide the trauma-informed services Lisa needs. The other shelter staff members are also not qualified to provide trauma-informed care. Unfortunately, such services are also not available in the surrounding geographic area.

Jill is unsure how to proceed. She believes that providing case management services and supportive counseling to Lisa will not be effective until her trauma has been addressed. She knows how hard it is when one loses a loved one since her grandmother recently passed away. However limited her options, Jill feels strongly that she has an ethical responsibility to help Lisa.

LEARNING OBJECTIVES

This chapter focuses on ethical and professional behavior. The National Association of Social Workers (NASW) *Code of Ethics* (2017) is reviewed, which will enable you to identify the ethical issues facing Jill in the opening case example and identify the ethical principles that are most applicable to her case situation and decision-making process. This chapter also discusses policy, social justice, and diversity issues associated with the ethical and professional behavior competency. The chapter ends with a discussion of five practice issues associated with the ethical and professional behavior competency and a review of approaches to dealing with ethical dilemmas. By the end of this chapter, you will be able to:

1. Describe the various components of the ethical and professional behavior competency

2. Identify the NASW ethical principles and ethical standards for social work practice

3. Apply a framework for approaching and resolving ethical dilemmas

4. Describe the differences and relationships between personal and professional values

5. Apply guidelines for resolving value conflicts

6. Identify the challenges and strengths of interprofessional collaboration

7. Describe the role supervision and self-reflection play in upholding the NASW *Code of Ethics* and the Council on Social Work Education (CSWE) ethical and professional behavior competency

8. Discuss how professional development and the use of technology are related to ethical and professional behavior

9. Describe a policy and a social justice issue associated with the ethical and professional behavior competency

■ Competency 1: Demonstrate Ethical and Professional Behavior

Social workers understand the value base of the profession and its ethical standards as well as relevant laws and regulations that may impact practice at the micro-, mezzo-, and macrolevels. Social workers understand frameworks of ethical decision-making and how to apply principles of critical thinking to those frameworks in practice, research, and policy arenas. Social workers recognize personal values and the distinction between personal and professional values. They also understand how their personal experiences and affective reactions influence their professional judgment and behavior. Social workers understand the profession's history, its mission, and the roles and responsibilities of the profession. Social workers also understand the role of other professions when engaged in interprofessional teams. Social workers recognize the importance of lifelong learning and are committed to continually updating their skills to ensure they are relevant and effective. Social workers also understand emerging forms of technology and the ethical use of technology in social work practice. Social workers

- Make ethical decisions by applying the standards of the NASW *Code of Ethics,* relevant laws and regulations, models for ethical decision-making, ethical conduct of research, and additional codes of ethics as appropriate to context;

- Use reflection and self-regulation to manage personal values and maintain professionalism in practice situations;

- Demonstrate professional demeanor in behavior; appearance; and oral, written, and electronic communication;

- Use technology ethically and appropriately to facilitate practice outcomes; and

- Use supervision and consultation to guide professional judgment and behavior. (CSWE, 2015)

In summary, the ethical and professional behavior competency focuses on professional values and ethics, resolving ethical dilemmas, personal and professional values, professional judgment, interprofessional collaboration, the use of technology, personal reflection, and supervision. This competency, as shown in Figure 1.3 in Chapter 1, Theories, Paradigms, and Professional Competencies in Social Work, is the broadest of all the professional competencies. As such, the ethical and professional behavior competency influences one's competency in applying the other professional competencies in social work practice at the micro-, mezzo-, and macrolevels.

■ Social Work Values and Ethics

The practice of social work is based on a number of value positions and principles that guide the work with clients irrespective of the approach used, the presenting client problem, the client population, or the setting in which services are provided. These values and principles apply to all forms of social work practice (Poulin, Matis, & Witt, 2019).

Core Social Work Values

Social work is a value-based profession (Beckett & Maynard, 2005; Reamer, 2013). Values provide the basis for professional social work practice (Congress & McAuliffe, 2006; Gumpert & Black, 2006). They guide the actions we take and our evaluations of what is "good" (DuBois & Miley, 2014). Social work has a rich tradition of principles and beliefs. The heart of these is reflected in the NASW *Code of Ethics* (NASW, 2017), which identifies core social work values, which are referred to as ethical principles. The core professional values are: service to others, social justice, dignity and worth of the person, and importance of human relationships, integrity, and competence. These values and their associated ethical standards all play a critical role in social work practice. The NASW *Code of Ethics* is available online (www .socialworkers.org/About/Ethics/Code-of-Ethics/Code-of-Ethics-English).

Service Value

The ethical principle related to the service value is that social workers help people in need. This ethical principle emphasizes serving others and the fact that social work is a service profession dedicated to providing help to individuals, families, and groups in need and to improving community and social conditions (NASW, 2017).

Social Justice Value

The NASW's second ethical principle focuses on challenging social injustice (NASW, 2017). Social justice has long been valued in social work. Concern with social justice and inequality in the profession goes back to the advocacy efforts of Jane Addams and the settlement house movement of the early 1900s.

Social workers traditionally work with people who are victims of discrimination and prejudice. Many of our clients are unemployed or underemployed, have limited access to resources, received inadequate education and training, and are among the most disadvantaged members of society. They often face prejudicial attitudes and are identified as lesser persons (DuBois & Miley, 2014). Social injustice is manifested in discrimination on the basis of race, gender, social class, sexual orientation, age, and disability. Prejudicial attitudes provide justification for social structures that provide fewer prospects—fewer opportunities, fewer possibilities, and fewer resources—for those with lower status (DuBois & Miley, 2014).

Social workers' commitment to social justice is based on concern about the negative effect of discrimination and prejudice on disadvantaged populations. We often work with clients who have been denied basic rights and opportunities. We are called on to challenge social injustice and to increase the opportunities, possibilities, and resources of our clients. We have an ethical responsibility to address the social, physical, and economic needs of our clients as well as their psychological needs. The 2015 Educational Policy and Accreditation Standards (EPAS) expanded the concept of social justice to include economic and environmental justice (CSWE, 2015).

Dignity and Worth of the Person's Value

NASW's third ethical principle focuses on a person's individual worth and dignity (NASW, 2017). This entails treating our clients in a caring and respectful fashion, being mindful of individual differences and cultural and ethnic diversity. The underlying assumption of this value is that all human beings have intrinsic worth, irrespective of their past or present behavior, beliefs, lifestyle, race, or status in life (Hepworth, Rooney, Rooney, & Strom-Gottfried, 2017). As a social worker, you are expected to treat your clients with respect and dignity. They deserve respect by virtue of their humanness. This does not mean that you have to agree with your clients' life choices or decisions. It does mean that you should strive to affirm their dignity and self-worth. Not doing so can have profound negative effects on the helping process and doing nothing could potentially cause harm.

Before clients are willing to risk and trust, they need to feel accepted and valued. Doing so is even more important when clients' problematic behaviors involve moral, social, or legal infractions. A client whose behavior has violated social and cultural norms is not likely to engage in a collaborative helping relationship with a professional who communicates disapproval and condemnation.

Closely associated with respect for the individual is a nonjudgmental attitude. As a social worker, you must not blame the client in either your attitude or behavior. Focus on understanding your clients and their difficulties and on helping them find solutions or alternative ways of behaving. If you blame them for their difficulties and assign pejorative labels, most will become defensive and unwilling to trust you. The more you understand the life experience of your clients, no matter how personally distressing their behavior or beliefs may be, the more likely it is that you will be able to accept them as human beings (Hepworth et al., 2017).

Many of our clients' behaviors conflict with our personal values and beliefs. More often than not, there will be a clash of values between you and your clients. These differences should be viewed as a normal part of generalist social work practice. Expect them and accept them. There are going to be differences; in fact, there are going to be major differences. If you focus on your values and assign blame to clients for adopting behaviors or attitudes with which you disagree, you will not be able to help them.

Adopting nonjudgmental attitudes is a prerequisite for developing effective working relationships (Poulin, 2010). The challenge is to maintain your own values without imposing them on others and without judging those whose behavior and beliefs are in conflict with your belief system. To accomplish this, you need to be open to others and treat everyone with respect and dignity. This is difficult when you have negative feelings about your client. You are human, and you will have negative feelings about some clients. Pretending that you do not have these feelings will not work; clients will sense insincerity and negative reactions. The best approach is to try to understand your client and to communicate that understanding in a caring and nonjudgmental manner. Clients are not seeking your approval; they are seeking your help. They need to feel that they have been heard and that you understand them and their situations. They need to feel that you care and that you want to work with them. Communicating care and concern facilitates the helping process. If clients perceive you as judging and blaming them, they are not likely to accept help from you.

Importance of Human Relationships Value

NASW's fourth ethical principle focuses on relationships (NASW, 2017). Focusing on the relationship issues of clients is common in generalist social work. Many clients need help in improving their human relationships and interpersonal interactions.

Historically, the helping relationship has been given a central role in the helping process (Perlman, 1979). The *Code of Ethics* states that "social workers engage people as partners in the helping process" (NASW, 2017). Relationship implies that there is a reciprocal interactive process between two people. In social work, the helping relationship is a partnership. You and the client both have input and make decisions together. You are joint participants. Social workers do not solve problems for their clients; they work with clients and help them solve their own problems.

▶ **Critical Thinking Questions**

1. Which social work value do you identify with most strongly? Why?

2. Are there any social work values that you feel are less important than the others? Why?

Beginning social workers often feel that unless they are doing something specific and concrete for their clients, they are not being helpful. You will be tempted to do things for clients, using your skills and abilities to get the task done and hand over the results to clients. It will make you feel useful and productive. Avoid the temptation because it is a trap. More often than not, clients will not appreciate your generous efforts on their behalf. By doing work for them, you will put them in a dependent position, highlighting their inability to manage their lives. No one likes feeling incompetent and dependent. Rather than making your clients dependent on you, empower them. Help them help themselves. Help them do whatever they need to do to manage their own lives as best they can. Ultimately, your clients must become confident and learn to do tasks for themselves. The helping relationship in social work is a collaborative partnership. Social workers do not work for clients; rather, they work with clients.

Integrity Value

NASW's fifth ethical principle focuses on being trustworthy (NASW, 2017). You have probably heard the sentiment that honesty is the best policy; in the social work profession, we value honesty very much. Social workers should demonstrate integrity at all times through honesty, sincerity, and responsibility. This is the key to developing trust and a positive helping relationship. Be open and honest. It is ok to admit that you do not know or are unsure about something. If that happens, let your clients know that you will find out and then follow through and get back to your clients with the information.

Competence Value

NASW's sixth ethical principle focuses on competence and professional expertise (NASW, 2017). Social workers are to practice within their areas of trainings and seek ongoing supervision, education, and support on a regular basis. As social work interns, the primary learning objective of your field placement is to become a competent generalist social worker. This is done by demonstrating proficiency through your practice experiences as they relate to the nine professional competencies defined by the CSWE (2015). The development of competence is a lifelong undertaking that involves critical thinking, reflection, and ongoing professional development.

Ethical Standards

The core social work values and ethical principles embody the ideals to which all social workers should aspire. The *Code of Ethics* sets specific standards and explains how the core values and principles influence the actions of professional social workers. The standards spell out social workers' ethical responsibilities to clients, to colleagues, in practice settings, as professionals, to the social work profession, and to the broader society (NASW, 2017). They are detailed, comprehensive guidelines for professional behavior. The NASW *Code of Ethics* (NASW, 2017) identifies the six areas of professional behavior: responsibilities to clients, to colleagues, to practice settings, as professionals, to the profession, and to the broader society. Each area of responsibility includes a number of subareas. It is important that you carefully review the detailed descriptions of the standards found in the NASW *Code of Ethics* available online (www.socialworkers.org/About/Ethics/Code-of-Ethics/Code-of-Ethics-English).

As social work students, it is important that you become very familiar with the areas of professional responsibility in preparation for your field placements and social work practice with clients. A thorough knowledge of the NASW *Code of Ethics* early in your field placement experience will help ensure that you engage in ethical practice and will help you avoid unethical behavior. It is your responsibility as a professional social worker to be familiar with the *Code of Ethics* and follow it in your professional behavior in your social work practice.

> ▶ **Critical Thinking Questions**
> 1. How will your ethical responsibilities to the broader society affect your professional life?
> 2. Which of the six areas of ethical responsibilities do you think will be most difficult to implement? Why?

The NASW Ethical Standards cover a very broad range of behaviors from interactions with clients to participation in larger societal change. Thus, as a social worker, it is your ethical responsibility to have these standards of behavior guide your professional behavior in all aspects of your professional life. Without a doubt, doing so will create challenges when different ethical standards are in conflict in your practice with clients, experiences with colleagues, and at your agency or field placement. The ethical standards related to being a professional, the social work profession, and society are more under your own control and the choices you make. Nevertheless, conflicts are possible among and between the areas of professional responsibilities. These conflicts referred to as ethical dilemmas are discussed in the following.

Ethical Dilemmas

Social workers frequently have ethical obligations to several parties at the same time. For example, we have ethical obligations to both our clients and our employing organizations. This creates the possibility of conflict or ethical dilemmas. An ethical dilemma occurs when one or more social work values are in conflict. In these situations, you are forced to choose between two competing values or undesirable courses of action. Because we have ethical responsibilities to our clients, our colleagues, our practice settings, the profession, and the broader society, value conflicts and ethical dilemmas occur often within and among the six areas of professional responsibilities.

Resolving ethical dilemmas is never easy or straightforward. Rarely is there a clear-cut right or wrong choice. The choice is between two seeming "rights"; the task is to determine which "right" is more so given the circumstances.

The first step in addressing ethical dilemmas is to refer to the *Code of Ethics* for clarification of the standards of practice. The code, however, does not offer bases for choosing between two or more conflicting standards. A number of guidelines have been developed to help resolve ethical dilemmas. A hierarchy of value assumptions is the basis for decision-making. The hierarchy developed by Reamer (1990) is shown in the following.

 Ethical Guidelines

1. The rights to life, health, well-being, and necessities of life are superordinate and take precedence over rights to confidentiality and opportunities for additive "goods" such as wealth, education, and recreation.

2. An individual's basic right to well-being takes precedence over another person's right to privacy, freedom, or self-determination.

3. People's right to self-determination takes precedence over their right to basic well-being, provided they are competent to make informed and voluntary decisions with consideration of relevant knowledge and as long as the consequences of their decisions do not threaten the well-being of others.

4. People's rights to well-being may override laws, policies, and arrangements of organizations.

The first guideline proposes that a person's right to health and well-being takes precedence over the right of confidentiality. If you had to choose between protecting a person's health and well-being and violating a client's confidentiality, you would choose health and well-being. For example, the right of neglected and abused children to protection takes precedence over their parents' rights to confidentiality.

The second guideline proposes that a person's right to health and well-being takes precedence over another person's right to privacy, freedom, or self-determination. When you must choose between protecting a person's freedom and protecting another person from harm, the choice is to protect the person from harm. For example, if a client reveals plans to seek physical revenge on his or her former spouse, you should warn the former spouse.

The third guideline states that a person's right to self-determination takes precedence over his or her own right to well-being. That is, an individual's self-determination supersedes that person's well-being. The principle promotes freedom to choose and possibly fail or make mistakes. It protects the right of people to carry out actions that do not appear to be in their own best interests, as long as they are competent to make informed and voluntary decisions. However, the first guideline takes precedence if the individual's decision might result in death or serious harm. For example, you must act to protect a client who is at risk of committing suicide.

The final guideline proposes that the right to well-being may override agency policies and procedural rules. Social workers are obligated to follow the policies and procedures of social work agencies, voluntary associations, and organizations. When agency policy has a negative effect on a client's well-being, however, violating the policy or procedure may be justified.

Congress (1999) developed another model of ethical decision-making to help social workers make ethical decisions quickly. The model's acronym of ETHIC stands for the following:

E   Examine relevant personal, societal, agency, client, and professional values.
T   Think about what ethical standard of the NASW *Code of Ethics* applies as well as relevant laws and case decisions.
H   Hypothesize about possible consequences of different decisions.
I   Identify who will benefit and who will be harmed in view of social work's commitment to the most vulnerable.
C   Consult with supervisor and colleagues about the most ethical choice (Congress, 2000, p. 10).

The guidelines described previously—or any other guidelines—will not always provide clear-cut courses of action. They will, however, help you prioritize values to help clarify your thinking about an ethical issue. Resolving ethical dilemmas almost always entails making value judgments and subjective interpretations. For example, Reamer's third guideline states that a person's right to self-determination takes precedence over his or her right to basic well-being, provided he or she is competent to make an informed decision. A social worker may have to apply this guideline to a person who is mentally ill and homeless, who prefers to remain on the street, and who has little or no interest in participating in a treatment program. Does this person have the right to refuse treatment as well as the right to live wherever he or she wants? The complicating factor in this situation is determining the person's competence and the degree of physical or mental harm that is likely to ensue. Can a person who is mentally ill, delusional, and exhibiting psychotic behavior make informed decisions? At what point does refusing shelter or treatment create a serious risk of physical and mental harm? Clearly, the answers to these questions are subjective and open to value judgments.

In attempting to resolve ethical dilemmas, always invoke the concept of shared responsibility and decision-making (Reamer, 2013). Do not make the decision on your own; enlist others in the process. Get your supervisor's or administrator's advice and approval before you act on an ethical dilemma. Case 2.1 illustrates the difficult decisions involved in resolving ethical dilemmas.

CASE 2.1   AN ETHICAL DILEMMA IN SOCIAL WORK PRACTICE

Desiree is a first-year master of social work student who has been placed in an after-school program for emotionally disturbed children. The program is run by a comprehensive mental health agency that offers a wide range of services for children and adults. The agency is a subsidiary of a larger organization that owns and operates a number of inpatient and outpatient mental health facilities. The after-school program has two full-time social workers, a case aide, a half-time supervisor, and a quarter-time program administrator.

Approximately 20 children with emotional and behavioral problems are provided with on-site services 5 days a week and in-home services once a week. Because of a technicality, the program lost its primary source of funding and was slated to close. Desiree found out about the pending closing of the program from her supervisor. She was told not to tell the other staff or the children. The program administrator had decided that it was best for the children, their parents, and the staff not to know in advance about the closing.

Desiree was concerned about the children's need to have enough time to deal with their feelings about leaving the program and about the parents' needs to have time to make other arrangements for the treatment and after-school care of their children. She also wondered how the lack of process about closing the program would affect the staff and their morale. Desiree believed that the well-being of the children was being subjugated to the perceived needs of the agency. She suspected that the agency administrator felt that telling the children and their parents would upset them and that the children would act out more than usual during the time remaining in the program.

She also suspected that her supervisor wanted to avoid having the parents put pressure on the agency to continue the program. It appeared to her that the closing policy was designed to protect the agency from disruption at the expense of the children and their parents.

Desiree is faced with an ethical dilemma. She has been told by her supervisor to follow an agency policy that she believes is not in the best interests of her clients. Does she advocate for changing the agency's policy? What are the consequences for the children of following the agency's policies? For their parents? Using Reamer's guidelines or Congress's ETHIC model, assess Desiree's ethical dilemma, propose a case decision, and provide an explanation for your decision.

Value Conflicts

"Value conflicts occur when an individual's personal values clash with those of another person or system" (Birkenmaier, Berg-Weger, & Dewees, 2014, p. 54). Ethical dilemmas, on the other hand, occur when a social worker must choose between two contradictory ethical principles or standards. Value conflicts occur when your personal values are different from the values of the profession, clients, or colleagues. Value conflicts in social work practice occur when the actions taken by your agency, colleagues, or your clients go against your personal values (Reamer, 2013). See Case 2.2 for an example of a value conflict.

CASE 2.2   GET A JOB: EXAMPLE OF A VALUE CONFLICT IN SOCIAL WORK PRACTICE

Shureka is a first-year master of social work student completing her foundation field placement in a shelter for women and children in Georgia. The shelter's mission is to help homeless women find employment, permanent housing, and the resources they need to care for their children. Trish is a 20-year-old single mother with a 2-year-old child. She moved from South Carolina to the area with her boyfriend, Carl, when her daughter was born because of a work opportunity for her boyfriend. She has no family in the area. Four months ago, Carl lost his job and left for somewhere out West. Carl was the wage earner in the family, and after he left, Trish was not able to pay her rent and became homeless. She moved into the shelter shortly after Shureka started her internship.

Trish had completed high school and had become pregnant shortly after. She has never really worked at a full-time job. Her only work experience was some part-time employment at a supermarket when she was in high school. Shureka conducted Trish's intake assessment and had been meeting with her twice a week as her social worker. Trish liked meeting with Shureka and talking about her hopes and dreams. Together they established Trish's treatment goals, which were to find employment and then permanent housing. Each week they would set tasks for the week and weekly goals. Each week Trish, for one reason or another, would not complete her tasks or goals. Trish seemed happy in the shelter. She had childcare and did not have to look after her 2-year-old daughter all the time; she had food for her and her daughter as well as a place to live. She also liked the attention she got in talking with Shureka and the other staff members.

Shureka was frustrated in her work with Trish and found that she was losing her patience and willingness to try and help her. She was beginning to avoid Trish, which was difficult to do in the shelter, and she was finding excuses to cancel their scheduled meetings. Shureka's field instructor and supervisor noticed the change in her behavior and brought it up in supervision. As Shureka reflected upon her change in behavior toward Trish, she realized that she had been raised in a family with a strong work ethic that valued independence and hard work. She also realized that she is most comfortable in helping clients who want to help themselves and that she is less comfortable with clients who are content to rely on the services provided and not become self-sufficient. Shureka's supervisor pointed out that her personal values around work and independence were probably the cause of her behavior toward Trish. She was experiencing a value conflict with her client's behavior and actions or lack of actions. Shureka and her supervisor talked about ways she could address her value conflict. They both agreed that her awareness and understanding of how her personal values were affecting her work with Trish was an important first step. What are the next steps Shureka should take to resolve her value conflict? What ethical principles and standards are relevant in this situation?

There are five types of values: social, cultural, religious, professional, and personal. Social values are generally accepted norms, customs, and beliefs of a particular society. These types of values are regulated by social pressure rather than public policy (Edwards & Seek, 2018). For example, beliefs about individual responsibility, competition, and hard work are social values associated with the United States. Social values can vary from society to society. In contrast to the United States, common social values in Japanese society include harmony, obligation to the group, and collective responsibility.

Cultural values are similar to social values. The difference is that cultural values are beliefs that are integrated into public policy (Edwards, 2014). They are institutionalized as standards for the culture. An example of a cultural value is our laws regarding education. Our beliefs about education have codified into laws that require young children to attend school. Another American cultural value is the belief in self-government. The idea that Americans have a say in how and who runs their government is institutionalized through voting laws and regulations.

Religious values are those associated with specific faith communities. These values can vary from religion to religion. They tend to be doctrinal statements about behaviors, such as sexual behavior, interpersonal behavior, dietary restrictions, and religious practices. Professional values are those designed to regulate behavior of people within a profession. In social work, the NASW *Code of Ethics* spells out the expected professional behavior for social workers. The final type of values is personal values. These are the values individuals adopt from the previous four value categories as guiding principles for their lives. Individuals have a core set of principles or a core belief system. Thus, one's core beliefs can conflict with the values of the profession, one's organization or agency, peers and professional colleagues, and clients.

There are personal and professional value conflicts in social work practice (Osteen, 2011; Valutis & Rubin, 2016). Gough and Spencer (2014) found in a survey of 1,800 Canadian social workers that 53% had experienced a conflict between their personal values and the profession, 82% between their personal values and their organizational workplace, and 75% between their personal values and a client (p. 26). Clearly, even though a student's motivation for choosing a social work career has been found to be a desire to help others and make positive contributions to society (Osteen, 2011) and that their personal values are aligned with the professional values of social work, conflicts between personal values and the values of the profession, employers, colleagues, and clients will arise.

Resolving value conflicts is never easy. By definition, values are beliefs that we hold dearly. They help define who we are and how we behave. When a conflict arises, it is natural to feel that your belief and values are correct and that the conflict value or behavior in is not. Valutis and Rubin (2016) found that the vast majority of social workers in their study indicated that they use professional values as a decision-making guide when faced with a value conflict. Chechak (2015) suggested that social workers must conform personal values to the profession's values and that ethical codes and practice guidelines cannot be made to conform to individual belief systems. Social work's values and ethics have always been the cornerstone of social work practice (Reamer, 2013). Gough and Spencer (2014), however, found in their survey of Canadian social workers that the most common approach to dealing with value conflicts was to consult with colleagues and supervisors. We believe that both approaches should be used in addressing value conflicts in your social work practice. The following lists the steps for addressing value conflicts in your practice:

- Identify your own value that is causing the conflict. Determine if it is a social, cultural, religious, or a personal value. Assess the importance of the value to your sense of self-worth and identity.

> ▶ **Critical Thinking Questions**
> 1. What are three personal values that are very important to you? How do they fit with core social work values?
> 2. What are some potential value conflicts you might encounter in your social work practice?

- Identify the behavior, action, or decision that is in conflict with your value. Determine if it is a social, cultural, religious, professional, or a personal value. Assess the importance of the value to your agency, colleague, or client.

- Determine the consequences of choosing one value over the other. What are the benefits of each and for whom? What are the possible negative consequences and for whom?

- Review the values' positions from the perspective of the NASW *Code of Ethics* ethical principles and ethical standards. How does each value position correlate with social work values and principles? Are the values in conflict with the values and principles of the profession?

- Discuss your value conflict with colleagues and your supervisor. Get other professionals' opinions and thinking about your course of action. Is there a consensus about how to deal with your value conflict? How do others see the pros and cons of your options?

- Make the decision on how to resolve your value conflict a shared decision with your supervisor and/or agency administrators.

■ Interprofessional Collaboration

Both the CSWE competency on ethical and professional behavior and the NASW *Code of Ethics* identify interprofessional collaboration as a component of social work practice. The competency on ethical and professional behavior states that "social workers also understand the role of other professions when engaged in interprofessional teams" (CSWE, 2015, p. 7). The NASW *Code of Ethics* Ethical Standard 2.03 addresses interdisciplinary collaboration. The standard has two subsections. The first states that

social workers who are members of an interdisciplinary team should participate in and contribute to decisions that affect the well-being of clients by drawing on the perspectives, values, and experiences of the social work profession. Professional and ethical obligations of the interdisciplinary team as a whole and of its individual members should be clearly established. (NASW, 2017, Ethical Standards, Interdisciplinary Collaboration, para. 1)

The second states that "social workers for whom a team decision raises ethical concerns should attempt to resolve the disagreement through appropriate channels. If the disagreement cannot be resolved, social workers should pursue other avenues to address their concerns consistent with client well-being" (NASW, 2017, Ethical Standards, Interdisciplinary Collaboration, para. 2). CSWE and NASW recognize the importance of interprofessional collaboration in the provision of social work services.

There has been an increase in recent years in the use of interprofessional teams in the provision of healthcare services and in other areas of practice in the United States and globally (Bayne-Smith, Mizrahi, Korazim-Kőrösy, & Gracia, 2014; West, Miller, & Leitch, 2016). The World Health Organization (WHO, 2010) recognized the importance of interprofessional collaboration in addressing the global health crisis. Similarly, the Institute of Medicine (2003), the American Public Health Association (2008), and the CSWE (2016) all have issued statements in support of interprofessional collaboration in education and practice.

Interprofessional collaboration is the process of bringing together professionals from different disciplines, such as nursing, medicine, physical therapy, psychologists, and/or social workers, to provide team-based care. WHO defines interprofessional collaborative practice as "when multiple health workers from different professional backgrounds work together with patients, families, carers, and communities to deliver the highest quality of care" (2010, p. 7).

The movement toward interprofessional care is driven by the belief that solutions to complex health and social problems need the coordinated interventions of more than single disciplines (Perreault & Careau, 2012). There is growing evidence that interprofessional collaborations result in more positive patient outcome in healthcare and other service areas (WHO, 2010). WHO, summarizing existing research, reported that interprofessional collaborative practice increased patient access, made better use of specialists, improved patient outcomes, increased caregiver and patient satisfaction, had greater acceptance of treatment, reduced costs, and resulted in shorter treatments than noncollaborative approaches to the delivery of healthcare services (WHO, 2010, pp. 18–19). The Institute of Medicine (2003) also reported improved patient outcomes and more effective service delivery with interprofessional collaboration approaches. Similar results have been found in nursing, social work, and other allied health disciplines (Caven & Bland, 2013; Freshman, Rubino, & Chassiakos, 2010). Conversely, lack of collaboration and poor communication have been found to negatively affect outcomes and reduce patient satisfaction (Fewster-Thuente & Velsor-Friedrich, 2008).

▶ **Critical Thinking Questions**

1. How might interprofessional collaboration affect your identity as a social worker?
2. What do you see as a benefit of interprofessional collaboration to your development as a social worker?

Interprofessional Collaboration Competencies

The Interprofessional Education Collaborative (IPEC), in 2011, issued a report of an expert panel that outlines four core competencies for interprofessional collaborative practice. The four competencies are: (a) adopting values/ethics for interprofessional practice; (b) understanding interprofessional roles/responsibilities; (c) enhancing interprofessional communication; and (d) facilitating teams and teamwork (IPEC, 2011).

Values and Ethics for Interprofessional Practice

Each discipline brings to the team its own set of professional values and ethics. Competency is interprofessional collaborative practice required for the development of a professional identity that includes interprofessional ethics.

> Mutual respect and trust are foundational to effective interprofessional working relationships for collaborative care delivery across the health professions. At the same time, collaborative care honors the diversity that is reflected in the individual expertise each profession brings to care delivery. (IPEC, 2011, p. 17)

This philosophy is reflected in IPEC's general competency statement for values and ethics, which states that interprofessional collaborative team members "work with individuals of other professions to maintain a climate of mutual respect and shared values" (IPEC, 2011, p. 19).

Roles and Responsibilities

Interprofessional collaborative practice requires an understanding of the roles and responsibilities of each member/discipline on the team. Team members need to be able to clearly describe their own professional roles and responsibilities and understand others' roles and responsibilities in relation to their own roles. Understanding your role and how your role interfaces with the other team members' roles is a critical component of effective interprofessional collaboration. Doing so also requires you to have a clear understanding of the other team members' roles and responsibilities. All team members need to understand their roles and responsibilities, with a clear understanding of the roles and responsibilities of the other team members and a clear understanding of how the various roles and responsibilities interface among and between each other. This concept is reflected in IPEC's general competency statement for roles and responsibilities, which states that interprofessional collaborative team members "use the knowledge of one's own role and those of other professions to appropriately assess and address the healthcare needs of the patients and populations served" (IPEC, 2011, p. 21).

Interprofessional Communication

Developing effective communication skills is a core competence for all professional disciplines but communication skills across disciplines are often problematic. Professional jargon creates a barrier to effective interprofessional collaboration. Communicating readiness to work together and finding a common language for the collaborating team members are important steps in developing effective communication among and between interprofessional collaborative teams. This concept is reflected in IPEC's general competency statement for interprofessional communication, which states that interprofessional collaborative team members "communicate with patients, families, communities, and other health professionals in a responsive and responsible manner that supports a team approach to the maintenance of health and the treatment of disease" (IPEC, 2011, p. 23).

Teams and Teamwork

Being on an interprofessional collaborative team requires teamwork and being a good team player.

Teamwork behaviors involve cooperating in the patient-centered delivery of care; coordinating one's care with other health professionals so that gaps, redundancies, and errors are avoided; and collaborating with others through shared problem-solving and shared decision-making, especially in circumstances of uncertainty. (IPEC, 2011, p. 24)

Understanding group dynamics and team functioning are important skills to becoming an effective team member. Conflict resolution skills are also important. Conflicts will arise and being skilled in resolving misunderstandings and differences requires effective interprofessional communication and a shared commitment to improved client outcomes. "Staying focused on patient-centered goals and dealing with the conflict openly and constructively through effective interprofessional communication and shared problem-solving strengthen the ability to work together and create a more effective team" (IPEC, 2011, p. 24). The concept of teamwork is reflected in IPEC's general competency statement, which states that interprofessional collaborative team members "apply relationship-building values and the principles of team dynamics to perform effectively in different team roles to plan and deliver patient-/population-centered care that is safe, timely, efficient, effective, and equitable" (IPEC, 2011, p. 25).

Mechanisms That Support Interprofessional Collaborative Practice

WHO identified three practice-level mechanisms that influence the effectiveness of interprofessional collaborative practice. The three mechanisms are institutional supports, working culture, and the environment. These three factors support successful interprofessional team collaboration.

Institutional Supports

Institutional supports shape the way collaborative teams can function. "Staff participating in collaborative practice need clear governance models, structured protocols and shared operating procedures" (WHO, 2010, p. 28). They need administrative support and the organization's commitment to the collaborative model. Collaboration by definition means giving up some autonomy and sharing resources. The organization's leadership and the leadership of the participating partners all need to support the collaboration conceptually and through the development of supportive management practices and the sharing of operating resources. Adequate time and space need to be provided to support collaboration. Without strong institutional support, interprofessional collaborations are doomed to failure.

Working Culture

Interprofessional collaborative practice needs opportunities for shared decision-making and regular ongoing team meetings. Getting together to share perspectives, viewpoints, and ideas as a team is critical to effective collaboration. This process in itself helps build a collaborative culture of respect and helps keep the focus on client goals and outcomes. "Structured information systems and processes, effective communication strategies, strong conflict resolution policies and regular dialogue among team and community members play an important role in establishing a good working culture" (WHO, 2010, p. 29).

Environment

Another factor affecting collaboration is the physical environment. Having team members housed in different physical locations can hinder the effectiveness of the collaboration and the development of a working culture (West et al., 2016). The physical space can also enhance or detract from effective collaboration. "Most notably, physical space should not reflect a hierarchy of positions. Additional considerations could include developing a shared space to better facilitate communication or organizing spaces and rooms in ways that eliminate barriers to effective collaboration" (WHO, 2010, p. 29). Refer to Case 2.3 for an example of a successful interprofessional collaborative team.

> ▶ **Critical Thinking Questions**
> 1. In your experience, how does the physical environment affect communication patterns?
> 2. How has the use of digital forms of communication affected team building and collaboration?

In summary, WHO recommends the following action steps to advance interprofessional collaborations:

- Structure processes that promote shared decision-making, regular communication and community involvement;

- Design a built environment that promotes, fosters and extends interprofessional collaborative practice both within and across service agencies;

- Develop personnel policies that recognize and support collaborative practice and offer fair and equitable remuneration models;

- Develop a delivery model that allows adequate time and space for staff to focus on interprofessional collaboration and delivery of care; and

- Develop governance models that establish teamwork and shared responsibility for health-care service delivery between team members as the normative practice. (WHO, 2010, p. 30)

CASE 2.3   INTERPROFESSIONAL COLLABORATION OF THE HOSPICE TEAM

Gail is a social worker employed by a nonprofit agency providing hospice and bereavement services. The agency serves approximately 400 individual and families daily. The hospice services are all provided by interprofessional teams. The teams are composed of a physician, nurse, pharmacist, social worker, chaplain, and volunteer coordinator. The nurse on the team functions as the case manager for all the patients assigned to the teams. The team meets weekly to review the patients and to make case treatment decisions. All the team members provide input on the patient from their discipline perspectives, and the team collectively decides the respective tasks of each team member.

(continued)

CASE 2.3

The roles and responsibilities of each team member are clearly defined and understood by the other team members. Gail's responsibilities included conducting biopsychosocial assessments, helping the patient and/or family obtain needed resources, and making referrals to other community service providers. The chaplain provides spiritual counseling to the patient and family members and works closely with Gail in terms of assessing the patient's and family's social/emotional needs. The nurse, who functions as the case manager, oversees the patient's medical needs in consultation with the physician and pharmacist as well as input from the volunteer coordinator, who has patient information via volunteer visitor reports, Gail, and the chaplain. This structure ensures that patient information from all the different perspectives are taken into consideration on a weekly basis.

The team members' offices are all located in the same building and in close proximity to one another. The physical arrangement of the team members' offices helps facilitate informal and formal communication. Program policies and procedures all support the functioning of the collaborative teams, and the agency has a strong culture of mutual respect and collaboration. Gail loves her job and being part of a well-functioning interprofessional team.

■ Supervision

As with interprofessional practice, supervision is recognized as a component of the ethical and professional behavior competency defined by CSWE (2015) and also an ethical standard specified in the NASW *Code of Ethics*. The competency on ethical and professional behavior states that social workers use supervision and consultation to guide professional judgment and behavior (CSWE, 2015, p. 7). The NASW *Code of Ethics* Ethical Standard 3.01 addresses supervision and consultation. The standard has four subsections. The first states that social workers providing supervision should have the necessary knowledge and skills. The second indicates that social workers providing supervision set clear, appropriate, and culturally sensitive boundaries. The third subsection is about not engaging in any dual or multiple relationships with supervisees and the fourth is about providing fair and respectful evaluations of supervisees. Thus, the CSWE competency focuses on how to use supervision and the NASW ethical standard focuses on the provision of supervision. Both are important components of ethical and professional behavior in social work practice. In this context, we are referring to clinical supervision that focuses on your work with clients and your social work competencies.

Social work supervision can be traced back to the beginning of the profession in the early 20th century as it was described and used with charity workers in New York (Kadushin & Harkness, 2014). Supervision within social work has long been a means to pass along practice wisdom from the trained professional social worker to the learner. It is through social work supervision that you can hone your social work skills based on your work with clients and constituencies. Social work supervision is a collaborative process where both you and the supervisor work together in order to enhance your practice skills and develop your professional self (NASW & Association of Social Work Boards [ASWB], 2013). Through social work supervision, your professional social work identity can mature (Field, 2016). Social work supervision serves to ensure that you are developing the appropriate skills necessary to be an ethical and competent social work practice professional (Caras, 2013).

To supervise is to direct, watch over, or keep an eye on the work of another. In supervision, the supervisor monitors the actions of the supervisee. Social work supervision goes beyond this basic definition. Social work supervision involves a dynamic engagement between the supervisor and supervisee. Good quality supervision provides a foundation for the developing social worker. As a social work student, we encourage you to make the most of your weekly supervisions during your field placements in order to set a strong foundation for your future as a professional social worker (Poulin et al., 2019).

Developing a supervision agreement can be helpful cement (Field, 2016). A supervision agreement serves to ensure that both parties are clear on what to expect from each other throughout the supervision relationship. Caras and Sandu (2014) set forth that "supervision requires a learning alliance, which empowers the person to acquire relevant skills and knowledge for his profession. This alliance aims to develop interpersonal skills in supervision relationship" (p. 76). Since social work supervision is multidimensional and can have multiple functions or purposes, it is important to be clear on what to expect out of supervision. Social work supervision can serve many purposes, including:

- Developing and assessing your professional social work competencies
- Developing your professional self and increasing a sense of professional autonomy
- Personal development by exploring how personal values and beliefs align and merge with those of the profession
- Promoting professional values within all elements of practice
- Reflecting upon ethical considerations related to your social work practice

Social work supervision consists of three primary domains: support, administration, and education (Kadushin & Harkness, 2014; NASW & ASWB, 2013). Figure 2.1 illustrates the three domains and their interrelationships.

Social work supervision serves as a means to support your work as a social worker. Support is very important within the profession of social work. At times, practicing social work can be quite demanding and stressful. It is important to learn ways to diminish and manage stress whenever possible. Through supportive supervision, you, as the developing social worker, can address situations, experiences, or processes that are difficult for you. Together with the support of your supervisor, you can brainstorm and problem-solve potential solutions in order to ameliorate such conditions. There may be simple changes that you are able to make that your supervisor can help you see. In the event that it is something beyond your control, your supervisor may be able to provide you with suggestions for ways to cope or better manage the stressor.

Social work supervision covers administrative processes. Through supervision, you can review agency policies and procedures. You can review macrolevel policies that relate to your practice as well. Reviewing professional ethical values and standards is also a part

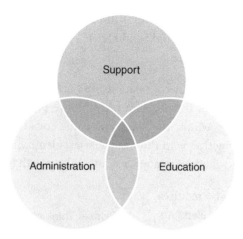

FIGURE 2.1 Three domains of social work supervision.

of administrative supervision. Administrative supervision is often a central component to employment supervision, which we discuss later in this chapter. Within administrative supervision, work tasks and assignments are often explored in order to ensure that agency mission, goals, and objectives are being met and clients are being served appropriately, both effectively and efficiently.

Last, social work supervision can serve as an educational process. Educational supervision seeks to increase your knowledge, skills, and training and help push you toward mastery of the social work competencies. Educational supervision is a pivotal aspect of clinical supervision and your development as a professional social worker. It is necessary to understand not just what to do in a situation with a client, but it is important to understand why you are doing it. The why is often connected to theories, perspectives, models, or evidence-based practices that have been found to be well-suited for the situation you are experiencing as a social worker. Good social work practice is grounded in the research and derived from the wealth of practice knowledge available to us.

Trust, Sharing, and Vulnerability

In order for social work supervision to be most beneficial, it is important that there is trust between the supervisor and supervisee. Trust involves many factors but ties closely to the social work value of integrity. Related to the value of integrity, we can increase trust by being honest and truthful. We can follow through with what we say we are going to do and be dependable and reliable (Poulin et al., 2019).

Open, honest sharing is important in social work supervision. It is important to use your time in supervision not as a time to try and impress your supervisor by saying what you think the "right thing" is, but rather as a time to sort through your thoughts and feelings in order to become a competent social work professional. At times, you may need to explore your own personal thoughts, feelings, and beliefs in supervision regarding how they are impacting your practice as a social worker. You may also need to discuss situations or experiences with clients or systems that you work with during your placement that are triggering to you.

Though social work supervision often involves discussing personal issues, it is not to be confused with personal therapy. Unguru and Sandu (2017) put forward the following distinction between counseling and supervision:

> While counseling involves the direct relationship between the social worker and the beneficiary, the reflection on the problem being the responsibility of the beneficiary guided by the counselor, within the supervision the social worker is the one who reflects upon his own practice, with the beneficiaries, identifying the best professional solutions he approached/is about to approach in working with his customers. (p. 18)

Social work supervision requires self-reflection not only on elements of social work practice but also on the practitioner's thoughts, feelings, and behaviors. Effective social work professionals must engage in continuous self-reflection. We must be mindful of how our thoughts, feelings, and behav-

▶ **Critical Thinking Questions**

1. How does clinical supervision differ from supervision in a nonsocial work setting?
2. In what ways would your behavior as a supervisee differ in a social work setting versus a nonsocial work setting?

iors influence our practice. Self-reflection is discussed in more detail in the following section. Brown (2017) puts forth the acronym BRAVING in order to better understand trust. In this acronym, the B stands for maintaining boundaries. As we know as social workers, boundaries are very important. We talk about having healthy boundaries with our clients quite often. Regarding social work supervision, it is important to also have boundaries. One way to have clear boundaries in your field supervision is to maintain a professional relationship and be clear on each other's roles and responsibilities in the supervisory process. The R stands for reliability. As you may recall from a research course you have taken, being reliable refers to consistency. We can develop trust by being consistent. As we have discussed, one way we can do this is to demonstrate the social work value of integrity. We can do what we say we are going to do. By following through on our words with actions, we are demonstrating integrity and demonstrating that we are reliable. Accountability is what the A stands for in the acronym. Being accountable requires that you are responsible for what you have done (or maybe did not do). The V represents the concept of vault. By its definition, a vault is a storage compartment. In Brown's analogy, the vault refers to holding information as secret or in confidence. In order to have a relationship of trust, we should not share things that are meant to be held in confidence. The I represents integrity. As social workers, through the NASW *Code of Ethics* (2017), we understand integrity as being "continually aware of the profession's mission, values, ethical principles, and ethical standards and practice in a manner consistent with them" while being honest and responsible (p. 6). The N stands for nonjudgment. Trust requires that we integrate a nonjudgmental stance and attitude. Last, the G stands for generosity. Brown suggests that generosity means that we give the benefit of the doubt to the person we are in a relationship with. By being generous, we assume goodwill toward the person and try not to take offense or become defensive.

Once you have a foundation of trust in your supervisory relationship, you can proceed with sharing and vulnerability. Sharing is a necessary aspect of supervision. Sometimes it can be difficult to determine what to share. Sometimes we may not want to share certain things because they make us feel vulnerable. Vulnerability refers to a state of being open or exposed in which we could possibly get attacked. Vulnerability can be scary. Despite that, vulnerability is necessary for many things in life including true connection and in order to feel emotions such as joy. Brown (2012) defines vulnerability as "uncertainty, risk, and emotional exposure" (p. 34). Vulnerability is connected to having the courage to speak our truth (Brown, 2012). As a social work student, you may at times feel vulnerable during your field placements. For example, if you are presented with a task to complete at the agency and you do not know how to do it, you may feel vulnerable to say you do not know and ask for help. We encourage you to remember that during your field placement (and throughout your social work career), it is okay to be vulnerable. It is okay not to have all of the answers. It is okay to ask for help. In fact, the NASW *Code of Ethics* lists competence as one of our values— it is our duty to ask for help when it is needed to ensure we are meeting the expectation of competence in our work.

■ Self-Reflection

The CSWE (2015) ethical and professional behavior competency states that social workers "use reflection and self-regulation to manage personal values and maintain professionalism in practice situations" (p. 7). Thus, in order to be a competent professional social worker, you will need to engage in self-reflection and self-regulation.

When we are thinking deeply or carefully about something, we are engaging in reflection. Self-regulation refers to our ability to maintain or control ourselves regarding our thoughts, feelings, and behaviors. Successful reflection and self-regulation require self-awareness. It is impossible to engage in reflection and self-regulation if you are unaware of your thoughts, feelings, and behaviors. Effective social workers are self-aware and continually examine their own selves so that they can be more effective helping professionals (Poulin et al., 2019).

Self-Awareness

Self-awareness is a term used to describe the recognition of personal thoughts, feelings, and behaviors. When your stomach growls and feels the sensation of hunger, that is self-awareness. Another example would be when you are texting with someone you are interested in and you feel butterflies in your stomach—that is self-awareness. Any time that you can recognize your thoughts, feelings, and behaviors, you are being aware of your *self*. Some people naturally seem to do a better job at self-awareness than others, but do not worry; self-awareness is something that you can practice and improve. Being present in the moment and practicing mindfulness are ways that you can improve your self-awareness.

Self-awareness is critical and necessary in social work practice. Social workers often use their *self* in helping clients. Just as accountants would use a calculator to do their job, social workers use their self to do their job. A big piece of social work is being present with the client. In order to be fully present with the client, we must be present with ourselves.

How do we get to know our *self* better? Hopefully, your education, especially your social work courses, has served as a catalyst for self-exploration and critical thinking. Throughout your social work education, you have learned about the use of self in your practice classes.

In addition to what you learn in the classroom, you may also gain insights into yourself from a variety of other sources. Maybe you have received feedback from people you are close to or maybe you have sought your own avenues to get to know yourself better through books, groups, or activities designed with such a purpose. Self-awareness, or personal knowledge about the social worker's self and needs, can be achieved in a variety of ways (Bogo, 2010). Throughout your field experiences, you can explore your self-awareness and use of self in the following ways: field supervision, process recordings, feedback from others (including field supervisors, faculty members, colleagues, peers, clients), and personal reflection.

Focusing on self-awareness as a component of field education is critical. In order to provide sound, ethical social work services, social workers need to be aware of their biases, beliefs, and values and how these are connected to their personal experiences, feelings, and reactions. Throughout your social work education, you have learned to pay attention to your verbal and nonverbal behaviors (making eye contact, nodding, etc.) to demonstrate to the client that you are concerned and listening. In a similar way, now that you are in the field, you must turn your attention inward and pay attention to your thoughts and feelings while working with others. Though it is important that you are aware of what is going on with you, you cannot allow that to be the focus of the session. It is a delicate balance and requires some practice in order to be able to be reflective while still focusing on the clients in front of you. As you develop this skill, you will become a more effective social work professional.

■ Professional Development

The CSWE (2015) ethical and professional behavior competency states that social workers "recognize the importance of life-long learning and are committed to continually updating their skills to ensure they are relevant and effective" (CSWE, 2015, p. 7). The NASW Ethical Standard 1.04 Competence also addresses the importance of ongoing professional development. Subsection (c) states that social workers take "responsible steps (including appropriate education, research, training, consultation, and supervision) to ensure the competence of their work and to protect clients from harm" (NASW, 2017, Ethical Standards, Competence, para. 3). Also, state licensing requirements for social workers all need a specified annual number of continuing education hours to maintain a social work license. The continuing education workshops, conferences, and trainings have to be approved for credit by the state authority in charge of licensure. Licensed social workers are required to engage in professional development activities by their state licensing boards and are encouraged by the NASW Code of Ethics and the CSWE competency on ethics and professional behavior.

Updating your social work skills and knowledge can take many forms. Attending professional conferences is an excellent way to stay current on a number of topics in a short period of time. The CSWE, the Association of Baccalaureate Social Work Program Directors, and the Society for Social Work and Research all hold annual conferences on a variety of social work topics. There are also a number of social work related national conferences on specialized topics, such as aging, health, addictions, trauma, and other topics. Additionally, NASW holds regional and state conferences.

In addition to conferences, social workers can attend local, state, national, and international training workshops in person or online. Training workshops can cover the whole range of social work relevant topics. Many social workers' places of employment also provide workshops and trainings related to the populations they serve.

Finally, many graduate social work programs hold symposia and lectures on current best practices in social work and other topics. Many schools of social work also offer certificate programs for advanced training on a range of specialized topics.

▶ **Critical Thinking Question**

1. As a social work student and future social worker, how will you have to change your use of social media and electronic communications? Why?

■ Professional and Ethical Use of Technology

The CSWE (2015) ethical and professional behavior competency states that social workers "understand emerging forms of technology and the ethical use of technology in social work practice" and they "use technology ethically and appropriately to facilitate practice outcomes" (CSWE, 2015, p. 7).

It is important that as professional social workers, we are caring and genuine with our clients. In demonstrating that connection, we may be friendly toward our clients, but we must be clear that though we are friendly, we are not our clients' friends. Establishing and maintaining appropriate boundaries is a critical component of competent social work practice. The responsibility for the development and maintenance of boundaries falls totally on the social worker. So, as the social worker, you need to establish and be clear about these professional boundaries with your clients. It is inappropriate to be friends with clients on social media. Social work professionals should not accept requests and invitations from clients on social media platforms in order "to prevent boundary confusion, inappropriate dual relationships, or harm to clients" (NASW, 2017, p. 11). Furthermore, social workers should not engage in personal communication with clients through any electronic forum.

According to Loue (2016), "social workers are increasingly relying on the Internet to provide information to clients/patients, to seek advice about patients, to provide mental health treatment, and as part of an ongoing supervisory or consultant relationship" (p. 1). With a growing focus on telehealth services and a rise in app-based video conferencing as a way to connect with helping professionals, social workers must be aware of the benefits and potential limitations of such advances. Furthermore, several social work professional organizations came together recently to release technology standards for social workers. The NASW, ASWB, CSWE, and Clinical Social Work Association (2017) clearly set forth that social workers must continue to practice within the guidelines of the NASW *Code of Ethics* as well as:

> [w]hen using technology to provide services, practitioner competence and the well-being of the client remain primary. Social workers who use technology to provide services should evaluate their ability to assess the relative benefits and risks of providing social work services using technology. . . reasonably ensure that electronic social work services can be kept confidential. . . reasonably ensure that they maintain clear professional

boundaries. . . confirm the identity of the client to whom services are provided electronically at the onset of each contact with the client. . . assess individuals' familiarity and comfort with technology, access to the Internet, language translation software, and the use of technology to meet the needs of diverse populations, such as people with differing physical abilities. (pp. 11–12)

Professional Online Identity

Developing a professional online identity is another important step to consider. For some social workers, developing this professional online identity is necessary (especially if they deliver services electronically). Curington and Hitchcock (2017) suggest that professional social workers who utilize social media for professional purposes should create a professional online identity, post for professional reasons, and create a social media policy. Your professional online identity is different than your personal online identity that we have previously discussed in this chapter. Your professional online identity may utilize social media platforms, blogs, business websites, or other online forums. Through these forums, you are clearly identifying yourself as a professional social worker. Since this is a professional presentation, your postings should be aligned with social work values and principles while following guidelines set forth by professional organizations. As this is a professional presentation, you should develop a social media policy regarding how you utilize technology and your response to various situations.

Confidentiality and Privacy

As professionals, we must always consider the intended and unintended consequences of behaviors. When utilizing electronic communication and the assistance of technology, we must be aware of our limitations to safeguard information. In this day and age, it is common to hear about hackings and data breaches, but we must never get accustomed to these terms to forget what that means for us as social workers and for the clients we serve. When serving vulnerable populations and dealing with sensitive and confidential information, we must take all of the steps possible to protect the information of our clients. We should follow all state and federal guidelines related to privacy and compliance. There are many considerations in ensuring confidentiality while using technology-driven social work practices (Groshong & Phillips, 2015). We should ensure that we are Health Insurance Portability and Accountability Act (HIPAA) compliant when using technology that often involves levels of encryption and agreements with servers. HIPAA was passed into law in 1996 in the United States and serves to safeguard protected health information (PHI). The Act also has provisions to ensure that any PHI that is transmitted electronically (ePHI) is safeguarded to ensure confidentiality and privacy.

■ Policy Issue

A policy issue associated with the ethical and professional behavior competency concerns licensing social workers. The primary reason for the licensure of social workers, as with other professions, is to protect people from mistakes and ethical misconduct that may occur in the provision of services (Donaldson, Hill, Ferguson, Fogel, & Erickson, 2014). Although all 50 states and the District of Columbia now license social workers, there are a number of reasons why licensure is a policy concern.

The licensing of social workers is state regulated. Each state has its own laws and regulatory bodies to govern the licensing of social workers. All 50 states and the District of Columbia use the ASWB licensing exams for licensure. There are four types of licensing exams: Bachelor's (BSW), Master's (MSW), Advanced Generalist, and Clinical (ASWB, 2018). The BSW and MSW licenses require degrees from CSWE accredited programs and no postdegree experience. The Advanced Generalist and Clinical licenses require 2 years postdegree supervised experience. Although the ASWB exams are used throughout the United States, the fact that the licensing of social workers is state regulated raises a number of policy concerns in terms of protecting people in a uniform way state by state.

The first concern is the eligibility requirements for licensure. While every state requires that the candidate's social work degree comes from a CSWE accredited program and that the candidate passes an ASWB licensing exam, eligibility requirements for each type of license as well as the licenses offered vary from state to state. For example, some states require completion of specific courses and/or types of field placements for the advanced licenses and others do not.

A second concern is that the continuing education requirements for maintaining a social work license vary from state to state. There are no uniform expectations for staying current in the social work knowledge and best practices. Some states have rigorous criteria regarding what qualifies as professional development as well as substantial continuing education hours and others much less so. This variation can lead to vast differences in the ability of licensed social workers to provide competent and ethical services state by state.

A third concern is that the requirements for postdegree supervised experience vary from state to state. The number of supervised practice experience hours is not standardized. Some states require a substantial number of supervised practice hours and others lesser amounts. Regardless, the important point is that there is a lack of standardization regarding the requirement of an advanced social work license.

A fourth policy concern is that the state licensing boards vary in their composition and definitions of social work (Donaldson et al., 2014). Many are composed of social workers, some are collaborative boards composed of representatives from related disciplines, and others are composed of state administrative personnel. Thus, in many states, there are one or two or no social workers determining the licensing requirement for social workers.

The final and perhaps most troubling concern is that the CSWE accreditation and competencies are not in sync with the ASWB identified competencies. CSWE, in the most recent version of its EPAS, defines the professional competencies for social work education at the BSW and MSW levels. The CSWE competencies, as presented earlier, are broadly defined and the accredited social work programs are given wide latitude to develop curricula to help social work students master the nine professional competencies. The ASWB competencies that are used to develop their licensing exams are very specific (Donaldson et al., 2014). The fit between the two approaches to defining social work practice and competency is of concern. Social work education is preparing social workers to operate and practice social work with an emphasis on critical thinking, self-reflection, and the development of holistic competence. ASWB's licensing exams, on the other hand, focus on very specific practice behaviors that may or may not be covered in a student's educational curriculum. This results in students completing their degrees under one set of expectations and then preparing for their licensing exams on another set of expectations. Perhaps this works to some extent, but the lack of a unified approach is of concern.

■ Social Justice Issue

At least two of the NASW Ethical Standards connect the professional behavior of social workers with social justice issues. The first concernsethical responsibilities to the profession and not engaging in or tolerating any form of discrimination (NASW, 2017). The other ethical standard related to social justice is under ethical responsibilities to society and advocating for changes in policy and legislation to promote social justice (NASW, 2017).

Clearly, the ethical standards on discrimination and social and political action call for social workers as professionals to engage in actions and activities that address social justice–type issues in organizations, institutions, communities, and society. Our professional values and ethics define professional behavior and the expectation that social workers be active participants in the promotion of social justice and in change efforts to address social injustice.

Unfortunately, today in the United States and in many other countries there are a number of social justice issues that are in the news on a weekly basis if not daily. It appears that tolerance of others is declining, and divisions are increasing. In our opinion, the need for social action to fight injustice is as great now as it was a century ago. In the United States alone, transgendered persons are being denied the right to use bathrooms of their choice, and school bullying is still an issue in many communities. According to the U.S. Department of Health and Human Services website on bullying, almost 30% of students aged 6 to 12 have been bullied, and over 55% of LGBT youth have experienced cyberbullying (Facts About Bullying, 2018). Human trafficking for the sex trade and some other industries is an ongoing problem. In a 2017 report from the International Labor Organization and the Walk Free Foundation, an estimated 24.9 million victims are trapped in modern-day slavery. Of these, 16 million (64%) were exploited for labor, 4.8 million (19%) were sexually exploited, and 4.1 million (17%) were exploited in state-imposed forced labor (Human Trafficking by the Numbers, 2017). Discrimination against people of color, LGBT persons, immigrants, persons with physical and mental challenges, Jews, Muslims, and women has not abated. Persons seeking asylum at our borders are being arrested and families are separated and children detained separately from their parents. Hate crimes have risen for three straight years with a 17% rise between 2016 and 2017 (Eligon, 2018). The majority of violent attacks on people were based on their race, ethnicity, religion, and sexual orientation (Eligon, 2018). These are but a few of the social injustices that occur all too frequently in the United States and globally.

The NASW *Code of Ethics* and the CSWE professional competencies make addressing these human rights issues part of what it means to be a social worker. There are many ways this could be accomplished. Social workers can engage in social and political action at the neighbor or community level. They can become active in addressing injustice at the organizational level and at all levels of government. Case 2.4 describes a social worker's involvement in social action to address potential discrimination against LGBT persons in the State of Massachusetts.

CASE 2.4   PROTECTING THE RIGHTS OF LGBT PERSONS IN SOCIAL WORK PRACTICE

Bill is a social worker employed at a service center for LGBT youth in Boston. In 2016, the State of Massachusetts passed a law protecting the rights of LGBT persons from discrimination to their sexual orientation or identity. A group of conservative Christians obtained the necessary signatures on a petition to have the law repealed as a referendum question in the 2018 midterm elections. The referendum question called for the repeal of the Massachusetts 2016 law banning discrimination against LGBT persons.

Bill joined a citizens group organized to turn out the vote against repealing the ban on LGBT discrimination. It was a statewide effort with committees operating in almost every municipality in the state. Bill took a leadership position in his community. It was a grassroots effort with almost no funding. They used a committee structure to organize their tasks. One committee raised funds for lawn signs urging votes against the repeal, another committee organized a door-to-door campaign to encourage residents to vote and to vote against the repeal, and a third committee solicited volunteers to staff polling places to encourage voters. Bill volunteered his time to help defeat the referendum question. He felt it was his ethical responsibility to fight to protect the rights of his clients and other LGBT persons in his community and state.

■ Summary

This chapter focused on the various components of the ethical and professional behavior competency. For reference, the competency defined by CSWE in the 2015 EPAS began the chapter. We then reviewed in detail the NASW *Code of Ethics* (2017). The *Code of Ethics* describes the core social work values, which are called ethical principles. The ethical principles are social justice, dignity and worth of the individual, importance of human relationships, integrity, and competence. These are the guiding principles for social work practice. The *Code of Ethics* Ethical Standards specifies ethical behaviors in six domains. The domains are ethical responsibilities to clients, ethical responsibilities to colleagues, ethical responsibilities in practice settings, ethical responsibilities as professionals, ethical responsibilities to the social work profession, and ethical responsibilities to the broader society. These ethical standards taken together define ethical behaviors and responsibilities for social workers in all practice settings and as a professional social worker. The discussion of ethical principles and standards was followed by a review of ethical dilemmas and frameworks for resolving ethical dilemmas and a review of personal and professional values and approaches to resolving value conflicts.

The chapter then reviewed interprofessional collaboration, interprofessional collaboration competencies, and mechanisms that support effective interprofessional collaboration. This was followed with discussions on supervision, self-reflection, professional development, and the ethical use of technology in social work practice. The chapter ended with a policy example and a social justice example related to ethical and professional behavior.

CASE SUMMARY   "UNDOCUMENTED AND HOMELESS"

Practice Setting Description

Jackie is a first-year master's in social work student completing an internship at an inner-city family service agency in the Southwest. The agency is located in a section of the city that has a high crime rate, gang activity, and failing schools. The area has a diverse population with a large number of immigrants from Central and South America and a substantial African American population. The agency provides individual and family counseling services on a sliding fee scale. The agency also runs a number of educational and treatment groups as well as a temporary shelter for women and their children. Jackie has been assigned to work with the women and their children in the shelter. Her primary tasks are to provide concrete services and supportive counseling to the shelter residents.

Background Information

Elicia T and her daughter, Maria, are undocumented immigrants from Mexico. They have been in the United States for 5 years. Elicia and Maria fled to the area from another southwestern city to escape her abusive husband approximately 2 months ago. Elicia is 25 years old and Maria 8 years old. Elicia has a 2-year-old daughter, Sarah, who was placed in foster care because of suspected abuse in the home. Sarah is in a foster home in a small rural community in the state hundreds of miles from Elicia's current residence. Since moving to the area, Maria has not been attending school.

Elicia and Maria are currently residing in the agency's temporary shelter for families. They have been at the shelter for 2 weeks, and the agency has a 90-day limit. It is viewed as temporary housing, and the residents are only allowed to stay for 3 months. Prior to arriving at the shelter, Elicia and Maria were homeless and living on the streets.

Elicia is a high-school dropout and was a stay-at-home mother prior to leaving her husband and moving to a different part of the state. She chose to move there because she has two female cousins living in the area who are also undocumented immigrants. Elicia's native language is Spanish. She speaks some English but is not as comfortable speaking in English. Her English comprehension appears to be good. Maria speaks both English and Spanish well. When communicating with the staff, Maria acts as Elicia's interpreter since none of the staff at the shelter speak Spanish.

Maria appears to be behind academically. She struggles reading simple children's books written in English. It is unknown if her ability to read in Spanish is better than her English reading skills.

Other than her two cousins, Elicia has no other sources of support in the community. Her cousins have young families and limited resources but are well established and connected to a Latino community in the city and the local Catholic church. Her cousins refused to let Elicia and Maria live with them while she was trying to find her own place and a job. They stated that they did not have

(continued)

CASE SUMMARY

enough room and are concerned they would get in trouble with their landlord if it was found out that they were letting people stay with them. They sent her to the local church for help, and she was given the address for the agency's shelter by the priest.

Elicia has been looking for housing in the Latino community. The housing market is tight with limited options, and she has been unable to find anything that she could possibly afford. The only affordable housing she found was a room in a rundown motel that rents by the hour or by the month. It is in an area of town known for drug dealing and sex work.

Upon arriving in the community, Elicia found occasional work for a house cleaning company. The company hires undocumented workers, pays them very low cash wages, and threatens to turn them in to Immigration and Customs Enforcement (ICE) if they complain. The job bosses also exploit their female workers sexually, threatening to turn them in if they do not comply. Elicia was fearful about applying for other jobs because of her illegal status. She considered turning to sex work to be able to take care of her children, but her Catholic upbringing and thoughts of how doing so would shame her family have kept her from doing so. She is in constant fear of being detained, separated from her children, and having them placed in foster care. She is also afraid that she will end up homeless again and forced to live on the streets or return to her abusive husband.

Elicia is extremely reluctant to sign up for any federally funded services, even those that she and her children are entitled to receiving. Upon the suggestion that she enroll for supplemental food through SNAP, Elicia became nervous and refused as she has heard that participation in SNAP services, and others like them, would draw the attention of ICE, and she had heard stories on the news of individuals being deported after signing up for such programs.

Presenting Problems

Elicia and her children are facing multiple obstacles. They need to find permanent, affordable housing and a job that pays enough to cover her housing and living expenses. In addition, Maria needs to be enrolled in school. Elicia also wants to regain custody of her youngest daughter in foster care.

Additionally, Elicia is experiencing an immense amount of stress, anxiety, and possibly post-traumatic stress disorder (PTSD). She described an instance where she could not calm down her breathing, and she felt lightheaded. She is very fearful of men and tries to avoid all contact with men in the community. She reports difficulty sleeping at night and feeling exhausted most of the time.

She is concerned about Maria. She has started acting out at the shelter, getting into fights with the other children, disobeying her mother, and being disrespectful and defiant to the staff and other adults. Elicia and Maria fight frequently, and when Elicia tries to discipline Maria, she throws a temper tantrum until Elicia gives up.

Elicia has many strengths. She had the strength to leave her abusive husband and move to a different city. She loves her daughters. She wants desperately to keep Maria with her and hopes to have Sarah returned to her custody. She is resilient and has managed to survive and keep her daughter safe, despite not having a place to stay, a job, and a limited support network. Additionally, Elicia is highly motivated to find her own accommodation and support her children.

■ Discussion Questions

1. What is a possible ethical issue facing Jackie that comes under ethical responsibilities to clients?

2. What is a possible ethical issue facing Jackie that comes under ethical responsibilities as a professional?

3. What is a possible ethical issue facing Jackie that comes under ethical responsibilities to the broader society?

4. What is a possible ethical dilemma facing Jackie and how would you resolve it?

■ References

American Public Health Association. (2008). *Policy statement on promoting interprofessional education*. Retrieved from https://www.apha.org/policies-and-advocacy/public-health-policy-statements/policy-database/2014/07/23/09/20/promoting-interprofessional-education

Association of Social Work Boards. (2018). *About licensing and regulation*. Retrieved from https://www.aswb.org/licensees/about-licensing-and-regulation

Bayne-Smith, M., Mizrahi, T., Korazim-Kőrösy, Y., & Garcia, M. (2014). Professional identity and participation in interprofessional community collaboration. *Issues in Interdisciplinary Studies, 32*, 103–133.

Beckett, C., & Maynard, A. (2005). *Values and ethics in social work*. London, UK: Sage.

Birkenmaier, J., Berg-Weger, M., & Dewees, M.P. (2014). *The practice of generalist social work* (3rd ed.). New York, NY: Routledge: Taylor & Francis Group.

Bogo, M. (2010). *Achieving competence in social work through field education*. Toronto, Canada: University of Toronto Press.

Brown, B. (2012). The power of vulnerability: Teaching on authenticity, connection, and courage. Boulder, CO: Sounds True, Inc.

Brown, B. (2017). *Braving the wilderness: A quest for true belonging and the courage to stand alone*. New York, NY: Random House.

Caras, A. (2013). Ethics and supervision process: Fundamentals of social work practice. *Procedia – Social and Behavioral Sciences, 92*(10), 133–141. doi:10.1016/j.sbspro.2013.08.649

Caras, A., & Sandu, A. (2014). The role of supervision in professional development of social work specialists. *Journal of Social Work Practice, 28*, 75–94. doi:10.1080/02650533.2012.763024

Caven, M., & Bland, R. (2013). Depression in primary care: Current and future challenges. *Canadian Journal of Psychiatry, 58*, 442–448. doi:10.1177/070674371305800802

Chechak, D. (2015). Social work as a value-based profession: Value conflicts and implications for practitioner's self-concepts. *Journal of Values and Ethics, 12*, 41–48.

Congress, E. (1999). *Social work values and ethics: Identifying and resolving professional dilemmas*. Chicago, IL: Nelson-Hall.

Congress, E. (2000). What social workers should know about ethics: Understanding and resolving practice dilemmas. *Advances in Social Work, 1*, 1–25.

Congress, E., & McAuliffe, D. (2006). Social work ethics: Professional codes in Australia and the United States. *International Social Work, 49*, 151–164. doi:10.1177/0020872806061211

Council on Social Work Education. (2015). *Educational policy and accreditation standards for baccalaureate and master's social work programs*. Retrieved from https://www.cswe.org/getattachment/Accreditation/Standards-and-Policies/2015-EPAS/2015EPASandGlossary.pdf.aspx

Council on Social Work Education. (2016). *Setting priorities, serving the nation: A shared agenda for social work education*. Retrieved from https://www.cswe.org/getattachment/764a1611-84dc-48e6-b667-be14ab602274/A-Shared-Agenda-for-Social-Work-Education-2016.aspx

Curington, A. M., & Hitchcock, L. I. (2017). *Social media toolkit for social work field educators*. Retrieved from http://www.laureliversonhitchcock.org/2017/07/28/social-media-toolkit-for-social-work-field-educators-get-your-free-copy

Donaldson, L. P., Hill, K., Ferguson, S., Fogel, S., & Erickson, C. (2014). Contemporary social work licensure: Implications for macro social work practice and education. *Social Work, 59*, 52–61. doi:10.1093/sw/swt045

DuBois, B., & Miley, K. K. (2014). *Social work: An empowering profession* (8th ed.). Boston, MA: Pearson.

Edwards, A. (2014). *Family stress and divorce: Implications for human behavior and social work practice.* Charlotte, NC: Kona Publishing and Media Group.

Edwards, A., & Seek, M. M. (2018). Ethnicity, values, and value conflicts of African American and White social service professionals. *Journal of Social Work Values and Ethics, 15*, 37–47.

Eligon, J. (2018, November 13). Hate crimes rise for the third straight year, FBI reports. *The New York Times*. Retrieved from https://www.nytimes.com/2018/11/13/us/hate-crimes-fbi-2017.html

Facts about Bullying. (2018). Retrieved from https://www.stopbullying.gov/media/facts/index.html

Fewster-Thuente, L., & Velsor-Friedrich, B. (2008). Interdisciplinary collaboration for healthcare professionals. *Nursing Administration Quarterly, 32*, 40–48. doi:10.1097/01.NAQ.0000305946.31193.61

Field, P. (2016). *Practice education in social work: Achieving professional standards.* St. Albans, Hertfordshire, UK: Critical Publishing.

Freshman, B., Rubino, L., & Chassiakos, Y. (2010). *Collaboration across the disciplines in health care.* Sudbury, MA: Jones & Bartlett.

Gough, J., & Spencer, E. (2014). Ethics in action: An exploratory survey of social worker's ethical decision making and value conflicts. *Journal of Social Work Values and Ethics, 11*, 23–40.

Groshong, L., & Phillips, D. (2015). The impact of electronic communication on confidentiality in clinical social work practice. *Clinical Social Work Journal, 43*, 142–150. doi:10.1007/s10615-015-0527-4

Gumpert, J., & Black, P. (2006). Ethical issues in group work: What are they? How are they managed? *Social Work with Groups, 29*(4), 61–74. doi:10.1300/J009v29n04_05

Hepworth, D., Rooney, R., Rooney, G. D., & Strom-Gottfried, K. (2017). *Direct social work practice: Theory and skills* (10th ed.). Belmont, CA: Cengage.

Human Trafficking by the Numbers. (2017, January). Retrieved from https://www.humanrightsfirst.org/resource/human-trafficking-numbers

Institute of Medicine. (2003). *Health professions education: A bridge to quality.* Washington, DC: National Academy Press.

Interprofessional Education Collaborative. (2011). *Core competencies for interprofessional collaborative practice: Report of an expert panel.* Retrieved from https://www.aacom.org/docs/default-source/insideome/ccrpt05-10-11.pdf?sfvrsn=77937f97_2

Kadushin, A., & Harkness, D. (2014). *Supervision in social work.* New York, NY: Columbia University Press.

Loue, S. (2016). Ethical use of electronic media in social work practice. *Romanian Journal for Multidimensional Education, 8*, 21–30. doi:10.18662/rrem/2016.0802.02

National Association of Social Workers. (2017). *Code of ethics.* Silver Spring, MD: Author. Retrieved from http://www.socialworkers.org

National Association of Social Workers & Association of Social Work Boards. (2013). *Best practice standards in social work supervision.* Retrieved from https://www.socialworkers.org/LinkClick.aspx?fileticket=GBrLbl4BuwI%3D&portalid=%200

National Association of Social Workers, Association of Social Work Boards, Council on Social Work Education, & Clinical Social Work Association. (2017). *NASW, ASWB, CSWE, & CSWA standards for technology in social work practice.* Retrieved from https://www.socialworkers.org/includes/newIncludes/homepage/PRA-BRO-33617.TechStandards_FINAL_POSTING.pdf

Osteen, P. J. (2011). Motivations, values, and conflict resolution: Student's integration of personal and professional identities. *Journal of Social Work Education, 47*, 423–444. doi:10.5175/JSWE.2011.200900131

Perlman, H. H. (1979). Relationship: The Heart of Helping People. Chicago: University of Chicago Press. doi:10.1093/sw/25.1.71-a

Perreault, K., & Careau, E. (2012). Interprofessional collaboration: One or multiple realities? *Journal of Interprofessional Care, 26*, 256–258. doi:10.3109/13561820.2011.652785

Poulin, J. (2010). *Strengths-based generalist practice: A collaborative approach* (3rd ed.). Belmont, CA: Cengage Learning.

Poulin, J., Matis S., & Witt, H. (2019). *The social work field placement: A competency-based approach.* New York, NY: Springer Publishing Company.

Reamer, F. G. (1990). *Ethical dilemmas in social service* (2nd ed.). New York, NY: Columbia University Press.

Reamer, F. G. (2013). *Social work values and ethics* (4th ed.). New York, NY: Columbia University Press.

Unguru, E., & Sandu, A. (2017). Supervision. From administrative control to continuous education and training of specialists in social work. *Romanian Journal for Multidimensional Education, 9,* 17–35. doi:10.18662/rrem/2017.0901.02

Valutis, S., & Rubin, D. (2016). Value conflicts in social work: Categories and correlates. *Journal of Social Work Values and Ethics, 13,* 11–24.

West, A., Miller, S., & Leitch, J. (2016). Professional socialization and attitudes towards interprofessional collaboration among graduate social work and health professionals. *Advances in Social Work, 17,* 134–150. doi:10.18060/19809

World Health Organization. (2010). *Framework for action on interprofessional education & collaborative practice.* Retrieved from https://www.who.int/hrh/resources/framework_action/en

DIVERSITY AND DIFFERENCE

Tara is a hospital social worker at a large urban children's hospital that is one of only two in the state. At the hospital, children and their families come from across the country for specialty care. As a result, Tara often works with people from a variety of cultural backgrounds. During her social work education, Tara studied human behavior in the social environment and diversity, so she felt that she had a good understanding of the importance of appreciating diversity and how culture influences an individual.

Tara is often interacting with individuals from diverse backgrounds. Thankfully, the hospital recognizes the diversity in the patients they serve, so they have set up a "lunch and learn" series on issues related to cultural competence. At these 30-minute sessions, hospital workers who are on their lunch break can meet together and learn about various diversity issues and topics. Tara appreciates the opportunity to learn more about the cultures of others so that she can better serve the patients and their families. Tara understands that she cannot know everything about every single culture, but rather operates from a position of cultural humility, honoring that the cultural experience of each person is unique to them. The individual is the expert of his or her own culture.

LEARNING OBJECTIVES

In this chapter, we address diversity and difference. Social workers value diversity and promote equality regardless of difference. Differences can include a variety of areas such as age, class, color, culture, disability and ability, ethnicity, gender identity and expression, immigration status, marital status, political ideology, race, religion/spirituality, sex, sexual orientation, and tribal sovereign status. Social workers value all people and appreciate differences. Social workers are cognizant of their own personal culture and are cautious to not allow their own experience of culture to supersede that of their clients. Self-awareness is necessary in order for social workers to be culturally competent professionals. By the end of this chapter, you will be able to:

1. Understand the role of intersectionality as it relates to diversity
2. Describe theories that inform practice with diversity and difference
3. Define and provide examples of microaggressions
4. Describe levels of oppression and discrimination
5. Recognize and identify how personal biases could interfere with the helping process

6. Define intersectionality and describe how it relates to understanding and appreciating individual experiences of diversity and difference

7. Identify the 10 standards of culturally competent social work practice

8. Describe and appreciate the value of constituent experts

9. Describe cultural empathy and humility

■ Competency 2: Engage Diversity and Difference in Practice

Social workers understand how diversity and difference characterize and shape the human experience and are critical to the formation of identity. The dimensions of diversity are understood as the intersectionality of multiple factors including, but not limited to, age, class, color, culture, disability and ability, ethnicity, gender, gender identity and expression, immigration status, marital status, political ideology, race, religion/spirituality, sex, sexual orientation, and tribal sovereign status. Social workers understand that, as a consequence of difference, a person's life experiences may include oppression, poverty, marginalization, and alienation as well as privilege, power, and acclaim. Social workers also understand the forms and mechanisms of oppression and discrimination and recognize the extent to which a culture's structures and values, including social, economic, political, and cultural exclusions, may oppress, marginalize, alienate, or create privilege and power. Social workers:

- Apply and communicate understanding of the importance of diversity and difference in shaping life experiences in practice at the micro-, mezzo-, and macrolevels

- Present themselves as learners and engage clients and constituencies as experts of their own experiences

- Apply self-awareness and self-regulation to manage the influence of personal biases and values in working with diverse clients and constituencies

■ National Association of Social Workers (NASW) *Code of Ethics*

Social workers are called upon to serve populations that are diverse while carrying out the professional mission to enhance human well-being. The ethical principles of social justice as well as dignity and worth of the person clearly illustrate the value social workers place on appreciating diversity and difference. Specific standards that social workers must adhere to that relate to diversity include cultural awareness and social diversity, discrimination, social welfare, as well as social and political action. The NASW *Code of Ethics* is available online (www.socialworkers.org/About/Ethics/Code-of-Ethics/Code-of-Ethics-English).

Social workers are mandated to challenge discrimination and other social injustices (NASW, 2017). Social justice requires equity of opportunity and resources for people to achieve their fullest potential. In order to promote social justice, social workers must be aware of social injustices that are occurring. Social workers must be aware of what is happening in their communities, country, and the world. Once a social worker recognizes an injustice, he or she then needs to seek out social change. Social workers should seek change at all levels of practice to ensure social justice for all.

At all times, social workers are also mandated to treat people with respect, regardless of their cultural and ethnic backgrounds (NASW, 2017). Social workers understand that diversity and cultural appreciation enhance the tapestry of society at all levels. Social workers are supportive of individual differences. Social workers see diversity and differences as something to be highlighted and celebrated.

Social workers are trained to be aware of culture. Through human behavior in the social environment and diversity courses, social workers learn about diversity and oppression based on a myriad of differences. Social workers are called to appreciate culture, identifying strengths existing in all cultures. Social workers are called to present with a level of cultural competence related to the clients they are serving. Beyond cultural competence, social workers should possess cultural humility in understanding that individuals present with a unique lived experience and their experience of their culture may be different.

Words have power. Social worker should not use language that is disrespectful to clients (NASW, 2017). Derogatory language can be explicit hate language but can also include a more covert bias or suggestive disrespect. Social workers should be considerate of words they choose to use and avoid using language that is disrespectful to any group of people.

Discrimination based on any type of difference is unethical (NASW, 2017). Social workers do not engage in discrimination. The great poet Maya Angelou is credited with saying "Once you know better, you can do better." Social workers should know better and in turn do better with regard to promoting social justice. Discrimination cripples social justice. Social workers do not accept the status quo of intentional or unintentional discrimination at any level. Social workers do not condone discrimination. Social workers speak up against any type of discrimination and do not collaborate with any form of discrimination either.

Caring for the welfare and well-being of all is a cornerstone for the social work profession. Social workers are called to advocate for all and promote cultural values that promote social justice (NASW, 2017). Social workers do not operate from an ethnocentric lens, rather they operate from a multicultural perspective that understands that culture influences all aspects of person's life. Social workers do not diminish the culture of others, but rather celebrate those values and ensure that regardless of difference, individuals are able to meet their own basic needs.

Social workers are also called upon to engage in social and political action whenever necessary in order to ensure that all people, regardless of difference, have equal access to their basic needs (NASW, 2017). Social workers are called to be a voice for those, who at times, may not have a voice at the table. We must speak for others, especially those who are discriminated against or oppressed in any way.

At all levels of practice, social workers should strive to promote respect for all regardless of difference. In fact, social workers should work to promote the honoring of differences. By engaging in social and political action, social workers can inform policies to ensure that they are supportive of differences and not biased against particular groups (regardless of whether that bias is intended or unintended).

Social workers are called to end discrimination and prejudice that any person or group may experience based on any type of difference. Discrimination and other forms of oppression are toxic, and social workers seek to reduce them. Social workers, personally and professionally, value diversity and difference and do not stand for discrimination in any form.

■ Conflict Theory

Conflict can be defined as a serious disagreement, dispute, or struggle. Some theorists suggest that conflicts are to obtain status, resources, or social change (Bartos & Wehr, 2002). Theories related to conflict set out with the goal to explain conflicts and provide an understanding of the conditions that create (or prolong) conflict. These theories also attempt to explain the process by which conflicts can be resolved or addressed by parties on both sides of the disagreement.

Karl Marx was an early conflict theorist who addressed conflict based on class struggle, and much of conflict theory is based on his initial works (Salem Press, 2014). Conflict theory is often used to describe social, economic, and political power struggles that occur within and between systems (Fogler, 2008). Some principles of conflict theory that Marx put forth were that conflict was inevitable, power differences exist in relationships, resources are scarce, and whoever is in power has control of the limited resources (Langer & Lietz, 2014).

Marx's work was based on works that suggested that conflicts can be understood considering the thesis, antithesis, and synthesis. The thesis can be understood as the current situation or status quo. The antithesis is the opposition or opposing perspective to the thesis. This is the alternative view. Conflict occurs between the thesis and antithesis. As a result of this conflict, a synthesis is created. The synthesis is a new way or situation. Eventually the synthesis evolves into the thesis, and the process can resume with the new thesis and the new antithesis. Figure 3.1 illustrates this relationship. Let us consider an example to understand this concept related to diversity and difference. For many years in the United States, only heterosexual couples had the opportunity to marry; this was the thesis. The antithesis to this position was that all people have the right to marry the person they love. Through years of conflict that included rallies, marches, and policy advocacy, a new synthesis of marriage equality was achieved nationally in 2015 in the United States.

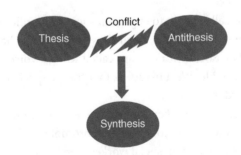

FIGURE 3.1 Conflict Theory: The conflict between thesis and antithesis results in synthesis.

The use of conflict theory to understand diversity can be useful because it wards against pathologizing oppressed groups; rather, it promotes "recognition of the historical, cultural, economic, and political context of their behavior" (Hutchinson, 2017, p. 37). Social workers strive to identify the influences on a person's experience in order to be better able to understand his or her current situation. When considering a person without paying attention to contextual influences, one risks misunderstanding the individual and his or her current state.

■ Critical Race Theory

Critical race theory has been adopted by various helping professions (Stovall, 2016). Critical race theory views race and racism to be multifaceted, complex social constructs. Critical race theory presents a counterposition to the dominant, or majority view, focusing on the experience of minority groups while demonstrating an inherent commitment to equality and social justice. This theory sets out the premise that racism is so engrained in culture that it can be difficult to recognize for those whom are a part of the dominant group and familiar with the culture (Stefancic & Delgado, 2013).

■ Intersectionality of Diversity

When you think of an intersection, you may think of an area where multiple roads meet and cross, or intersect, each other. Intersectionality is a crossroads of human identity, so to speak. Human beings are complex and multidimensional. It would be difficult and inaccurate to boil a person down to a single dimension. Figure 3.2 illustrates the intersectionality of four components of diversity: gender, race, class, and sexual orientation. When considering intersectionality, there can be a myriad of intersections related to any of the areas of difference we have previously noted. Through intersectionality, we are able to consider how the multiple levels of a person's cultural identity inform their experience. Intersectionality allows social workers to view the client in his or her entirety (Cox, Tice, & Long, 2016). If we only considered one level of this person's identity, we would lose the complexity that comes with being all of those things. Case 3.1 provides a brief introduction to three individuals. After reading their introductions, consider the various intersectionalities that are present for each.

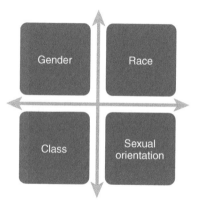

FIGURE 3.2 Intersectionality of gender, race, class, and sexual orientation.

CASE 3.1   UNDERSTANDING THE ENTIRE PERSON USING INTERSECTIONALITY IN SOCIAL WORK PRACTICE

Li

Li is a 36-year-old Asian American. Her parents were both born in Korea and immigrated to the United States when Li was 7 years old. Li's parents have worked quite hard to provide for her and her three younger siblings at the family restaurant. As Li's parents began aging, working 7 days a week in the restaurant was starting to take a toll on them. As the oldest child, Li felt obligated to step in at the restaurant to ease the burden on her parents. Li now works 7 days a week but still finds herself struggling to make ends meet financially. Since taking on more responsibility at the restaurant, Li's relationship with her partner, Amy, has been struggling.

Taylor

Taylor is a 20-year-old college student who is gender nonconforming. Taylor's parents are not supportive of what they call Taylor's "lifestyle" because they believe it will not be well received in their devout religious community. Taylor is disappointed by this because church has always been enjoyable. Taylor is African American.

Teresa

Teresa is a 79-year-old Mexican American. She lives in community housing with her oldest son, Riccardo, and his family. Teresa has a history of major depressive disorder that has been worsening as her physical health has declined in recent years and since the death of her husband 2 years ago.

The idea of intersectionality is based on the work of feminists of color. During the feminist movement in the mid-20th century, several authors put forth that the experience of women varied based on other areas of difference. They suggested that there were different experiences based on each level of difference, or intersectionality. For example, experiences based on gender identity were different. On the next level, among people who identified as the same gender, there would be differences based on race. For example, the experience of Caucasian females is different from that of African American females. Though both groups may experience oppression based on gender, African American females have the additional oppression based on race that Caucasian females do not. Furthermore, adding the additional intersectionality of sexual orientation could potentially add another layer of oppression.

Several theorists have contributed to the body of knowledge related to intersectionality. A contemporary theorist on this issue is Kimberlé Crenshaw. Crenshaw, a legal scholar, used the term "intersectionality" in an attempt to describe the cumulative experience based on difference. Intersectionality demonstrated how "single-axis thinking undermines legal thinking, disciplinary knowledge production, and struggles for social justice" (Cho, Crenshaw,

& McCall, 2013, p. 787). According to Bubar, Cespedes, and Bundy-Fazioli (2016), "intersectionality is now considered to be one of the most significant contributions to feminist scholarship in the late 20th century" (p. 284).

Intersectionality allows for the exploration of social discrimination processes in various social identities or categories of difference (Risberg & Pilhofer, 2018). Intersectionality can illustrate how some groups are more prone to social injustices due to the multiple dimensions of discrimination and oppression (Crenshaw, 2012). Using the concept of intersectionality provides a framework to deconstruct concepts of privilege and oppression based on differences (Bubar et al., 2016; Liu, 2018).

▶ **Critical Thinking Questions**

Reflect about your personal identity. How would you describe your personal intersectionality based on age, class, color, culture, disability and ability, ethnicity, gender identity and expression, immigration status, marital status, political ideology, race, religion/spirituality, sex, sexual orientation, and tribal sovereign status? How does your intersectionality inform your worldview? How might your worldview be different if the elements of your intersectionality were different (e.g., you identified as a different gender)?

Privilege is a term used to describe the "sum of earned advantages of special group membership" (Marsiglia & Kulis, 2016, p. 23). Just as being a member of a specific group can place an individual in a position of oppression, some group memberships provide privilege simply by being a part of that group. Groups that maintain privilege are often considered the dominant group, whereas the group that is oppressed is often considered the minority group. The terms dominant and minority are not solely based on number; rather, it is a much more complex dynamic of social and political capital and power that results in some groups having power and other groups being oppressed. For example, though rates of males and females in the United States are nearly mathematically equal, gender equality does not exist.

In the United States, as with most areas of the world, males are considered the dominant group and in turn possess privilege related to being assigned to that gender group.

▶ **Critical Thinking Question**

Describe how privilege and oppression can cross in regard to your personal intersectionality.

By viewing all of the dimensions of the person through the lens of intersectionality, we can see how at times individuals may experience oppression on multiple levels of their identity. Intersectionality provides a way to not only explore between-group differences but within-group differences as well. Systems of inequality are often interrelated (Marsiglia & Kulis, 2016). Intersectionality allows one to explore the multiple dimensions of inequality or oppression that a person may be experiencing based on his or her identity.

Social workers must be able to attend to the individualized needs that each client system presents. In addition to considering intersectionality, a culturagram may be a tool to assist workers helping diverse populations. A culturagram is much like an ecomap but focuses on cultural aspects of an individual or family system (Congress, 1994). Components of the culturagram include 10 content areas (Congress & González, 2013). Figure 3.3 illustrates the components of a culturagram.

FIGURE 3.3 Culturagram: A social work assessment tool that illustrates the cultural aspects of an individual or family system.

■ Oppression Theory

Theories of anti-oppression, multiculturalism, and culturally sensitive practice serve to provide social workers with a framework from which to view and better understand "ethnic barriers, conflicts and differences in societies so that they may practice in ways that respect people's individual and social identities and respond to oppression by dominant social groups" (Payne, 2016, p. 373). These theories underscore the importance of considering the whole person in light of his or her diversity and difference as that is a formative piece to his or her identity.

Understanding oppression "contribute(s) an understanding of how low social power and lack of societal validation for certain individuals illuminates ways that populations can be marginalized, invalidated, and deemed invisible" (Congress & Chang-Muy, 2015, p. 100). Bulhan (1987) suggested a theory regarding oppression that explored constraints including social limitations on rights and other inequalities, personal feelings and perceptions referred to as strains, as well as the presence of cultural norms. In order to understand the function of oppression in the lives of clients, Bulhan (1987) suggests exploring physical and economic space, roles and responsibilities, energy flow, access to information, as well as personal mobility.

■ Forms and Mechanisms of Oppression and Discrimination

Social workers must understand oppression and discrimination in order to be able to stand against it. Gil (2013) sets forth:

> Oppression" refers to a mode of human relations involving domination and exploitation—economic, social, and psychological—among individuals, among social groups and classes within and beyond societies, and, globally, among entire societies. Injustice refers to coercively established and maintained inequalities, discrimination, and dehumanizing, development-inhibiting conditions of living (e.g., slavery, serfdom, and exploitative wage labor; unemployment, poverty, starvation, and homelessness; and inadequate healthcare and education) imposed by dominant social groups, classes, and people upon dominated and exploited groups, classes, and people. (p. 12)

Components, or important aspects, related to oppression are power and privilege (David & Derthick, 2017). Oppression exists as both an act and as a process. Common examples of oppression include racism, sexism, ageism, classism, ableism, and xenophobia. There are various forms of oppression. The forms of oppression we will be exploring are interpersonal, institutional, and internal.

Interpersonal oppression occurs between people at an interactional level. This type of oppression exists as attitudes and beliefs. This form of oppression can occur between people and may be overt or covert, intended or unintended. Hate language or slurs, jokes about groups of difference, bullying, and intimidating are all examples of interpersonal oppression.

Institutional oppression occurs at the community or organization level and can pervade society. Some examples of institutional oppression would be oppressive laws, policies, and standards. At a macrolevel, societies can be oppressive or nonoppressive. Oppression of groups can at times be built into society's social structure (Beckett & Maynard, 2013). Nonoppressive societies are ones in which all people have equal rights and access to the resources that are necessary for them to meet their basic needs (Gil, 2013). Oppressive societies that have built-in mechanisms of oppression would represent institutional oppression.

Another form of oppression is internalized oppression. Internalized oppression is a type of oppression that is self-imposed within a group that has been oppressed by others. David (2014) suggests that "because of its pervasiveness, oppression can also become internalized—the hidden injury of oppression that is often ignored or minimized" (p. 3). Internalized oppression often presents with shame or embarrassment. It is important for social workers to not view the oppressed as lesser due to the oppression. It is crucial not to consider the oppressed as "passive victims who do not even understand their own situation" (Beckett & Maynard, 2013, p. 124).

Discrimination is a prejudicial or unjust treatment of a person or group based on difference. There are a variety of types of discrimination including direct, indirect, associative, and perspective that are based on the Equality Act of 2010 (Gast, Wonnacott, & Patmore, 2012). Direct discrimination refers to treating a person negatively due to a characteristic of difference. Indirect discrimination occurs via policies that can disadvantage members of a particular group. Associative discrimination is a type of discrimination in which a person is associated with a member of a diverse group and is treated negatively due to that association. Perspective discrimination occurs when an individual is believed to possess characteristics of difference and treated negatively as a result of that perception.

Microaggressions

For this text, we define microaggressions as "brief and commonplace daily verbal or/and environmental indignities whether intentional or unintentional that communicate hostile, derogatory, or negative racial slights and insults to the target person or group" (Sue et al., 2007, p. 273). Microaggressions can be blindly assuming characteristics of a culture and applying them to others; for example, believing that all Asian Americans have above-average intelligence or all African Americans are athletic. A lack of awareness does not excuse a microaggression.

> ▶ **Critical Thinking Questions**
>
> Describe a microaggression that you have witnessed. How could a social worker address the microaggression you described?

Microaggressions also include the denial of personal bias (Fisher, Moore, Simmons, & Allen, 2017). For example, when people posit that they hold no bias related to race and state that they are in fact "color-blind," this minimizes the role of race in a person's experience and the existence of cultural diversity (Fisher et al., 2017). Social workers must combat such microaggressions by not allowing the histories of groups to be diminished or forgotten.

Microaggressions can also occur environmentally (Sue, Jackson, Rasheed, & Rasheed, 2015). Environmental microaggressions target groups and have the consequence of making members of that group "feel unwelcome, isolated, unsafe, and alienated" (Sue et al., 2015, p. 121). Case 3.2 illustrates some environmental microaggressions.

■ Diversity and Difference in Social Work Practice

The mission of the social work profession calls upon social workers to provide services to all, with particular attention to individuals who are vulnerable and oppressed while being sensitive to all forms of social injustice. As a result, many social service agencies are filled with diversity in one form or another. Often, individuals mistakenly take for granted that all diversity and difference are visible. On the contrary, sometimes areas of difference are not outwardly visible (e.g., sexual orientation, class, ability).

CASE 3.2   (NOT-SO-)WELCOME TO THE COMMUNITY: EXAMPLES OF ENVIRONMENTAL MICROAGGRESSIONS IN SOCIAL WORK PRACTICE

Alice is a social worker at a community resource center in the heart of the Appalachian region. This area lacks much diversity; it is prudentially White and low- to middle-class. Much of the region lives in poverty. There is little racial or ethnic diversity. Many of the families in the region have been in the area for generations and do not often "venture out" to the nearby cities that are much more diverse.

Alice recently learned that a large Syrian refugee population is going to be settled in the community where her resource center is located. The contact at the refugee resettlement agency had reached out to Alice to ensure a smooth transition for the refugees. The resettlement agency was able to find several vacant properties in the area that they were able to secure for the refugees. While they would continue to assist the families, since their agency was based within the city (approximately 40 miles away), they were hopeful that Alice and her agency would be a local point of contact and support for the refugee families. Alice was excited to work with this population and assist them in their transition.

Move-in day finally came, and Alice and her team of social workers from her agency were there to support the refugees and welcome them to the community. Unfortunately, not everyone in the community was as welcoming. Nearby, neighbors sat on their porch and stared at the refugees as they were moving in. The neighbors stood with their arms crossed, staring and muttering about the group moving in, while shaking their heads with disapproval. Some people yelled slurs as they passed by. Alice was not expecting this reaction.

The first week was very difficult. When the refugees attempted to go to community establishments, they were treated poorly. For example, when a couple went to the local market, no staff would assist them even though it was obvious that they were having trouble navigating the store. At the local gas station, the normally chatty clerk would not make eye contact with the refugees and kept the conversation limited to the amount due. When walking in the community, long-term residents would switch sidewalks or hold their bags a little tighter when passing the new residents.

The community was not accepting of the new residents. Talk throughout the community continued about how they did not want "those kinds of people" in their town. At a town council meeting (which is normally near empty), dozens of community members packed the meeting room to express their concerns about the new residents. Alice, who often attends these meetings in order to be engaged in political action at the community level, was present. After hearing community member after community member spout off discriminatory, prejudiced comments, she decided she needed to speak up.

Alice waited in line for her chance to talk at the meeting. Though she was nervous, she knew that she needed to speak up for the refugees. Alice shared that she is a social worker and has been assisting the new residents. She urged the community to be more open to the refugees. She began describing her interactions with the refugees over the past week and how she has taken time to get to know them on a personal level. She encouraged other community members to do the same as well. She also encouraged the town council members to set up community dinners and other events

(continued)

CASE 3.2

to allow the long-term residents a chance to meet and interact with their new neighbors. The town council liked this idea and encouraged Alice to spearhead the event since she was both familiar with the local community and connected to the refugee population. Alice did not really expect to be in charge of this event, but she knew that it was important; so she took on the task.

The next day at work, Alice and her team of social workers began discussing ideas for the event. The team agreed on the goal of bringing people together and giving them a chance to experience each other's cultures in a way that would allow them to appreciate their diversity. One of the workers suggested a community street fair, filled with food and music that incorporates both cultures. Alice reached out to her contact at the urban refugee resettlement agency and asked if they wanted to be involved at the event as well. They were excited to join the event.

The day of the street fair arrived. Alice and her team had worked hard getting the word out about the event and offering giveaways and other attractions in order to entice people to attend. The refugee resettlement agency pulled upon several urban resources to bring a Middle-Eastern food truck to the event that was a big hit among the long-term residents. The event went well and had a great turnout. Alice knew that this was just the start and there was still much more work to be done in order to assist the community in fully welcoming their newest members; but for one night, the community was able to come together as one.

Social workers not only serve diverse populations but welcome diversity into the profession (Thyer, 2010). In addition to NASW, there are a variety of professional organizations that support diverse social workers. Here are two examples. The National Association of Black Social Workers (NABSW) promotes a mission that is "committed to enhancing the quality of life and empowering people of African ancestry through advocacy, human services delivery, and research" (NABSW, 2018, para. 1). The North American Christian Social Work Association (NACSW) promotes a mission to integrate their faith with professional practice.

Self-Awareness

Professional social workers must be reflective and possess self-awareness skills. Self-awareness refers to social workers' ability to reflect upon and consider their own thoughts, beliefs, and reactions. Social workers utilize self-awareness to monitor their use of *self* in practice. Effective use of self requires social workers to consider how and why they are experiencing what they are as a result of their current situation and circumstances. Social workers can utilize supervision to assist them in finding meanings and connections that assist in an increased level of self-awareness. Social workers must possess self-awareness in order to be fully able to attend to the needs of clients and ensure that their own issues are not interfering with treatment. Yet, we fully understand and appreciate that social workers are human and as a result have their own experiences. However, professional social workers must be diligent to not allow their own issues to interfere with the help-ing process and work for the client. If social workers cannot contain themselves or lack self-awareness, they should seek support immediately as the well-being of clients is of paramount concern.

As we have noted, self-awareness is necessary for professional practice. Whether work-ing with clients of dissimilar or same cultures, it is necessary for social workers to be aware of different experiences of culture and challenges that could potentially occur as a result (Akhtar, 2013). Self-awareness leads to a social worker's ability to understand and work from a multicultural perspective. Social workers must first be self-reflective regarding their own cultural experience as well as their personal values and any potential biases that may exist. Congress and Chang-Muy (2015) set forth the following questions that social workers can ask themselves regarding self-awareness related to diversity and difference:

1. What awareness does the [social] worker bring in relation to culturally based countertransference and societal projection?

2. What motivation and commitment does the [social] worker have to explore these issues (e.g., same-ethnicity workers of different class backgrounds and/or accul-turation levels)?

3. How will the [social] worker manage his or her comfort and discomfort levels in practice (i.e., explore the trig-gers), particularly in relation to differences in affect con-veyed in communication (i.e., differences in communication styles)? (p. 103)

▶ **Critical Thinking Questions**

Reflect upon your answers to the three questions posed here regarding diversity and self-aware-ness. How can you improve your self-awareness as it relates to diversity and difference?

In addition to considering these questions, social workers should think critically about their personal experiences with their own culture as well as the culture of others. Social workers should honestly reflect upon experiences and interactions that have been positive, negative, and indifferent. Then the social worker should consider mitigating circumstances to those situations and consider why and how they informed the experience on both sides of the interaction.

Self-reflection can also be very important in recognizing issues such as transference and countertransference. Transference refers to when the client takes feelings from his or her past and applies them onto the social worker. At times, social workers may encounter a transfer-ence experience on behalf of the client. The feelings transferred can be positive or negative. It is important for the social worker to recognize transference when it arises in order to ensure that it does not interfere with the helping process. On the other hand, countertransference is when a social worker applies feelings onto the client as a result of his or her interactions with others. Again, these feelings can be positive or negative. Regardless of the type of feelings, countertransference must be recognized, and the social worker should take immediate steps to address the issue including supportive supervision. Case 3.3 illustrates scenarios of trans-ference and countertransference.

Transference

Susan, a 24-year-old female, is seeking counseling services from a licensed clinical social worker, James, to address issues stemming from a conflicted romantic relationship. From their first meeting, James strives to build a rapport with Susan, engaging her in treatment and creating a safe place for her to explore her feelings. During the third session, Susan shared, "I am so comfortable with you, I can tell you anything. I have never felt this way with a man before. I feel so connected to you. Do you feel it too?" James recognized that Susan may be experiencing some transference. Since Susan was currently in a relationship where her communication needs were not being met, she transferred those needs and desires onto her relationship with her social worker, where she was being heard. James thought about how to respond for a second and then said, "I am glad that you feel comfortable as that is important in the counseling process. I enjoy meeting with you as well and I feel a connection through a social worker–client relationship." James understood that in transference responses, it was common for clients to treat the worker as an idealized figure. By responding the way he did, utilizing a self-involving disclosure, he was able to reflect Susan's sentiments, and allow her to feel heard while setting a boundary regarding the nature of their relationship being solely a professional one.

Countertransference

Katie is a social worker at a long-term nursing and rehabilitation facility. Katie is tasked with meeting with all patients upon admission and completing an assessment, monitoring their progress, and when ready, preparing for discharge ensuring the appropriate services, supplies, and supports are in place for transition to a lower level of care. One day, Katie walked into a patient room to meet with a new resident. She was taken aback at first when she saw the patient, an 88-year-old petite female who very much resembled Katie's own grandmother who had passed away a year ago. Katie smiled, introduced herself, and began the assessment with the new resident. Throughout the assessment, Katie noticed she was having a hard time staying on task and focused. She found herself just staring at the patient and reflecting upon memories with her grandmother, with whom she had always been quite close. After the interaction was complete, Katie went back to the social work office to complete her documentation of her visit. When another social worker returned to the office, Katie shared her experience. Katie said, "I just had the weirdest intake. I met with a new resident who looks just like my grandma. It felt like I was sitting with my grandma again; it was so neat. I love this new patient." The other social worker recognized that Katie's recollection of the event may be reflective of a countertransference response where Katie was placing her feelings of her grandmother onto the new patient. The social worker asked Katie about this and the two discussed the potential for countertransference and ways to ward against it. By the end of their conversation, Katie realized that maybe she was putting her own feelings onto the new resident and decided to reflect upon this interaction further and discuss this in her weekly supervision.

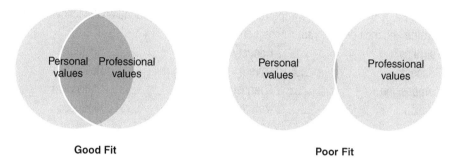

FIGURE 3.4 Professional goodness of fit: the overlap between personal and professional values.

Personal Values and Biases

A part of being a self-aware social worker is being aware of personal values and biases. It is important for social workers to routinely reflect upon their professional goodness of fit. Professional goodness of fit refers to the overlap between personal values and professional values. Figure 3.4 illustrates both good and poor fit between personal and professional values. Ideally, social workers find much overlap between their personal values and the values of the profession. As you may notice, in Figure 3.4, the circles that represent good fit do not totally overlap; that is intentional. Social workers do not need to be cookie-cutter professionals who all think, act, and believe the same things. Just as social workers value diversity and difference in client systems, the profession of social work values diversity and difference in the practitioners. The diversity among social work professionals lends itself to the richness of our ever-evolving helping profession.

▶ **Critical Thinking Questions**

Consider your professional goodness of fit. In what ways has your goodness of fit evolved during your social work education thus far?

After completing the value clarification exercise provided (Exhibit 3.1), how would you describe your professional goodness of fit? What values that are important to you align with the social work profession?

One tool that can be helpful to explore personal values is a value clarification exercise. We have included a value clarification exercise in Exhibit 3.1 to assist you in considering what you value personally. It is important to revisit your personal values periodically as they may change over time. Our values inform our worldview, and so it is important to be aware of what matters to us. That is why it is so important to continuously engage in self-reflection as a professional social worker.

EXHIBIT 3.1

VALUE CLARIFICATION EXERCISE IN SOCIAL WORK PRACTICE

Directions: Read through the list of the following 48 values. Then rank the values from 1 to 48, with 1 representing the value that means the most to you and 48 representing the value that means the least to you. If there is a value that is important to you that is not included on the following list, please add your value and include it in your ranking order.

_____ Fairness	_____ Honesty	_____ Solitude
_____ Success	_____ Love	_____ Rest
_____ Compassion	_____ Friendship	_____ Motivation
_____ Reason	_____ Nature	_____ Kindness
_____ Fun	_____ Adventure	_____ Fame
_____ Security	_____ Spirituality	_____ Equity
_____ Freedom	_____ Integrity	_____ Intimacy
_____ Prestige	_____ Safety	_____ Community
_____ Control	_____ Money	_____ Humor
_____ Diversity	_____ Character	_____ Trust
_____ Creativity	_____ Communication	_____ Autonomy
_____ Dependability	_____ Beauty	_____ Change
_____ Intelligence	_____ Competence	_____ Achievement
_____ Stability	_____ Challenge	_____ Ethics
_____ Connection	_____ Power	_____ Genuineness
_____ Flexibility	_____ Privacy	_____ Service

Social workers must also be aware of personal biases that may exist. A bias is prejudice or partiality to a particular group. Social workers are human and as a result may have personal experiences or beliefs that represent potential biases. It is important for social workers to be aware of this as they have the potential to interfere with the helping process and possibly harm the client. Even if a social worker possesses a bias of partiality, or what some might consider a "soft spot" for a particular group or population, that can be interfering and as equally detrimental to treatment as a bias of prejudice.

In order to explore potential biases regarding diversity and difference, it is important for social workers to be open to exploring their own cultural formulation. It is important to consider how you learned about your own culture. Mahler (2013) suggests that culture is relational and something that we learn and interact with throughout our lives. As we discussed related to self-awareness, social workers should reflect upon relational interactions that have informed their development. Social workers should seek out exposure to diversity and areas of difference. Something as simple as going to a cultural festival can assist in expanding one's worldview and exposing one to the richness of diversity.

Social workers need to be able to support any individual who needs their assistance. Social workers are called upon to serve all people; thus, social workers must be able to identify and challenge "personal prejudicial beliefs in a way that enables them to see each client as an individual and provide services to them without their personal values interfering" (Wahler, 2012, p. 1060). Self-awareness and reflection will provide an avenue to identify personal beliefs. Social workers should be honest with themselves regarding their self-appraisal of biases. Then social workers must seek to address such beliefs and attitudes. Challenging personal beliefs and attitudes can occur in a variety of ways including exposure to new experiences through readings, discussions, and interactions.

Constituents as Experts

The helping process is designed for the social worker to assist the client in enhancing his or her personal well-being. Social workers should always be mindful of their role in the helping relationship. The job of a social worker is not to do to or do for a client. Rather, social workers should strive to work with clients to address the mutually agreed-on goals. As a profession, we encourage and honor self-determination. Self-determination allows clients to make choices regarding their own lives. Self-determination is encouraged because clients understand their problems and needs better than anyone else. Social workers should be sensitive to what clients believe is best for themselves (Hepworth, Rooney, Rooney, & Strom-Gottfried, 2017). As a result, clients are the experts of their own experience. When considering diversity and difference, it is no different; clients are the experts of their own experiences as they relate to these aspects of their identity. Social workers should respect clients as the experts of their lives and approach clients with cultural humility.

Cultural Competence Standards

Social workers are ethically required to provide culturally competent practice to the clients they serve. Competence refers to having the knowledge and skills necessary to complete a prescribed task or activity. Social workers value competence. The professional value of competence asserts that social workers are continually learning and applying that information to their practice so that it is well-informed. The professional value of competence refers to all areas of social work practice. Cultural competence refers more specifically to being well-informed regarding culture, diversity, and difference. Ashford and Lecroy (2013) put forth that "the notion of cultural competence has been promoted for many years as a solution to the barriers to care and help encountered by ethnic, racial, and foreign-born groups in many of our service systems" (p. 15). Through cultural competence, social workers are aware of barriers that groups may experience in accessing, obtaining, or maintaining any needed social service supports. Social workers must advocate for solutions that provide opportunity for all.

A bit of caution must be applied to the idea of cultural competence. The word "competence" implies a set degree or level of knowing. Cultural competence, on the other hand, is not a position of "knowing it all" about culture. In fact, one can never really "know" everything there is to know about every culture (Walsh, 2013). Cultural competence encourages a level of understanding and recognizing that we do not know it all and appreciating between- and within-group differences that exist amid all cultures.

Social workers must demonstrate culturally sensitive practice. The *Social Work Dictionary* defines culturally sensitive practice as "the process of professional intervention while being knowledgeable, perceptive, empathic, and skillful about the unique as well as common characteristics of clients who possess racial, ethnic, religious, gender, age, sexual orientation, or socioeconomic differences" (Barker, 2003, p. 105). In order to better understand what is encompassed in culturally competent practice, we present 10 standards that have been developed by the NASW committee for racial and ethnic diversity. The NASW cultural competence standards are available online (www.socialworkers.org/LinkClick .aspx?fileticket=PonPTDEBrn4%3D&portalid=0).

Ethics and Values

At the start of this chapter, we explored the ethical standards and principles that were closely related to diversity and difference. The NASW *Code of Ethics* exists to safeguard the public and profession from unethical practice. Social workers must be familiar with all parts of the NASW *Code of Ethics*. In order to fulfill this standard, social workers must engage in ethical practice, practice cultural humility, promote social justice, and be able to professionally support vulnerable and oppressed groups during the helping process, considering barriers in place by the dominant culture (NASW, 2015).

Self-Awareness

Again, self-awareness is crucial for success as a social work professional. Just as social workers must understand the perspective of clients and the experiences that they have had, they must also be aware of their personal experiences and understand how these experiences have influenced their worldview. Social workers must not only be culturally aware but also culturally sensitive (NASW, 2015). By exploring their personal cultural identity, social workers are better prepared to practice cultural humility.

Cross-Cultural Knowledge

Social workers understand that culture is multidimensional and essential to the human experience. They are trained to understand the influences of culture at micro-, mezzo-, and macrolevels. Social workers are prepared to support systems across cultures. Social workers understand that culture is not static and, in turn, being a culturally competent social worker is an ongoing learning process (NASW, 2015).

Cross-Cultural Skills

Beyond cross-cultural knowledge, social workers possess cross-cultural skills. Social workers who demonstrate cross-cultural skills are able to communicate effectively in order to engage clients using tools such as warmth, authenticity, and genuineness (NASW, 2015). Social workers are required to ensure they are competent to meet the needs of their clients based on cultural differences.

Service Delivery

Social workers are not only concerned with their own cultural competence, but they are also concerned regarding the cultural competence of their organization (NASW, 2015). Social workers seek to remediate oppressive policies in order to ensure all persons have access to services. Social workers are uniquely prepared and qualified to monitor and evaluate agency systems, make appropriate recommendations based on the findings, and then implement and monitor the said recommendations.

Empowerment and Advocacy

Social workers are agents of change. They are leaders and advocates. Social workers must use these roles in order to stand up against oppression and discrimination in any form (NASW, 2015). Advocacy can occur at various levels including political advocacy at the community, state, and federal levels.

Diverse Workforce

Diversity should be represented in all aspects of the profession of social work. Social workers should strive to achieve a multicultural workforce and ensure policies that promote equity are in place. Within the workplace, social workers demonstrate the value of difference and encourage an open and welcoming environment (NASW, 2015).

Professional Education

Professional learning never ends for social workers. Ongoing training and education are necessary to be a competent social work professional (NASW, 2015). Social workers should ensure that they are adding to their cultural knowledge often. As we have stated, culture and experiences of culture are ever-changing, so it is important for social workers to be current on best practices in order to provide high-quality services to client systems.

Language and Communication

Self-determination is valued by social workers. Social workers honor the rights of clients to make their own decisions. The right to self-determination applies to the right to choose the preferred language in which to communicate. Legally, there are mandates that ensure individuals have access to supports such as a translator if necessary and deemed appropriate. To demonstrate this standard, social workers recognize the importance of language to a person's cultural identity and advocates for the rights of that person (NASW, 2015).

Leadership to Advance Cultural Competence

The final cultural competence standard set forth by NASW (2015) requires social workers to engage in the activity of leadership in order to promote practices and policies that are responsive to issues of diversity. Social workers use their power as professionals to advance cultural competence at all levels of practice. Leading social workers are at times in positions to have difficult conversations about difference but do not shy away from the mission to advance cultural competence.

Empowerment

Social workers strive to empower individuals, groups, and communities. Empowering systems gives them the tools and skills necessary to do something. Social workers may empower clients at the microlevel by helping enhance self-efficacy or boosting self-confidence in clients. Empowerment may flourish out of a positive helping relationship. At the macrolevel, the social worker may assist in community organizing in order to give the community members a chance to advocate for themselves.

Empowerment theory is an advocacy-based approach used by social workers to promote social justice and bring about change at various levels while addressing differences in social power (Congress & Chang-Muy, 2015). Payne (2016) asserts that empowerment is a process. Throughout the process of empowerment, social workers assist clients in identifying and ameliorating circumstances, conditions, and situations.

As we discussed earlier, we should not view individuals who have experienced oppression as less in any way. Social workers should strive to empower clients to advocate on their own behalf whenever possible. Furthermore, social workers can empower clients to bring about social change based on their experiences. The social worker can assist the client while letting the client lead the movement. Social workers should be open to learning from clients regarding their experiences.

Empathy

Social workers utilize empathy throughout the helping process with clients to help them feel felt by the worker. In addition to emotional empathy, social workers can display cultural empathy. Cultural empathy has been defined as "a deepening of the human empathic response to permit a sense of mutuality and understanding, across the great differences in value and expectation, that cross-cultural interchange often involves" (Ridley & Lingle, 1996, p. 22). Helpers with high levels of empathy may be more aware of the needs of client systems from diverse backgrounds (Lindsey, King, Hebl, & Levine, 2015). Cultural empathy is important in helping professions to ensure client systems feel heard and valued (Trimble, 2010).

Humility

Humility refers to being humble. When a person is humble, he or she is not self-important. Cultural humility is a way of approaching diversity and difference in a humble way to understand the experiences of others (Charles, Holley, & Kondrat, 2017). Cultural humility would be the opposite of ethnocentrism. Rosen, McCall, and Goodkind (2017) set forth that cultural humility is a "lifelong process with the attributes of openness, self-awareness, egolessness, self-reflection, and supportive interactions" (p. 291). Cultural humility is an ongoing process that:

> Encourages workers to take into account an individual's multiple identities and the ways in which their social experiences impact their worldview, particularly as it related to their expression of their culture. This perspective has the benefit of placing the worker in a learning mode as opposed to maintaining power, control and authority in the working relationship, especially over cultural experiences about which the client is far more knowledgeable. (Ortega & Faller, 2011, p. 33)

Culturally humble social workers seek to learn from clients about their cultural experiences, demonstrate standards of cultural competence, and value diversity and difference.

Rural Diversity

Often when one is considering diversity, they think of large metropolitan areas. It is also important to note that diversity exists within rural communities as well, and the experiences of diverse populations and rural communities can at times differ from same-group counter-parts who live in urban areas. Often, rural communities are assumed to lack diversity (Daley, 2015). Though there may be dominant or majority groups in rural areas, there are often other groups represented as well; furthermore, there is diversity between different rural areas (Ginsberg, 2005). Rural communities each possess their own patterns of communicating, making decisions, and relating to others (Johnson & Dunbar, 2005). Social workers must be mindful of the environment in which they are practicing to ensure that they are appreciating the nuances of the community, identifying strengths, and warding against potential barriers to services that may exist.

Rural social workers must be cognizant of the special needs of diverse populations in such settings. Often, rural social workers are faced with increased needs and decreased resources to meet those needs. With the lack of resources, it can at times be difficult to find services, providers, and resources to fit specific cultural needs. For example, in a rural area, it may be difficult to find a translator who speaks a specific rare dialect. In some areas, it can be diffi-cult to find a translator for any language. All social workers must be aware of such barriers and identify ways to combat them. Utilizing the translator example, the social worker may look into electronic or webpage translating services that are designed to support medical and social service workers (see Case 3.4).

Regarding rural diversity in small towns, there is often an array of diversity in regard to race, ethnicity, age, religion, and sexual orientation. At times, these differences are not "immediately apparent because the rural community does not always embrace difference" (Daley, 2015, p. 65). At times, minority groups are not actively engaged in the community due to this potential lack of acceptance. As a result, many groups at times remain hidden or closeted to avoid negative treatment (Daley, 2015).

CASE 3.4   DIVERSITY IN A RURAL AREA: CULTURAL COMPETENCY IN SOCIAL WORK PRACTICE

Anna is a hospice social worker in a rural community. She has many years of experience working in this field of social work. Recently, Anna was assigned to a new client, Mrs. Jones. As she does with all of her clients, Anna called the home of Mrs. Jones to schedule her first visit. The day arrived for Anna to go out and meet Mrs. Jones and her family. Anna was surprised when she opened the door and saw Mrs. Jones in a hospital bed that had been set up in her living room surrounded by what seemed like a dozen people. Often when Anna makes visits to her patients, there is family present but she has never seen that many at one time. Mrs. Jones welcomed Anna to her home; then she began introducing Anna to all of her children, grandchildren, nieces, and nephews who were present.

During the intake assessment, Anna learned that Mrs. Jones was from Haiti originally and came to the United States approximately 10 years ago to be closer to her children after her husband passed away.

(continued)

During the intake, it is customary for Anna to do a biopsychosocial–spiritual assessment. During the assessment, Anna learned that Mrs. Jones practiced Haitian voodoo. Anna had never met anyone who practiced voodoo. And really everything she knew about voodoo had been things she had seen on the television or in movies. All of her clients to this point had either been Christian or denied having any religious affiliation.

When Anna went back to the office, she began researching information on Haitian voodoo. Though Anna did not know about this specific religious practice, she did know that spiritual practices were often quite important in her line of work. She understood that spiritual practices often help the patient and their families deal with the death and dying experience.

Anna began with an Internet search, but that led her to several resources. After nearly an hour of perusing the web to learn about voodoo, Anna felt overwhelmed. So she stopped by her supervisor's office and shared with information about her new client.

The supervisor encouraged Anna to remember that the client is the expert regarding her own practices, and so it would make sense for Anna to just ask Mrs. Jones about what specific voodoo practices are important to her at this time in her life. Anna worried that if she had to ask Mrs. Jones, she would seem incompetent. But her supervisor reassured her saying, "Anna, no one expects you to know it all. It's impossible for you to know about every practice everywhere in the world. You are doing the right thing by reaching out and trying to learn about this practice but no book can teach you what Mrs. Jones wants in her life right now. You need to be open, curious, and culturally humble. I'm sure if you approach Mrs. Jones in a genuine and authentic way she and her family would be happy to share more about their practice of voodoo with you."

So, during her next visit with Mrs. Jones, when several extended family members were present, she did just that. She asked about Mrs. Jones's practices with voodoo and what would be important for her during the hospice experience.

From this experience, Anna learned that in order to provide culturally appropriate care, she is not expected to be an expert on every cultural practice that exists. Rather, she is called to practice cultural humility and honor the expertise of clients regarding their own cultural experiences.

■ Policy Issues

Social workers know that policy impacts all areas of practice. Related to diversity and difference, social workers must be mindful that policies are not discriminatory or oppressive. The NASW *Code of Ethics* calls for social workers to work on behalf of oppressed populations (NASW, 2017). Social workers must advocate against policies that oppress individuals and groups.

One such oppressive policy would be "Don't ask, don't tell," which was an official policy of the U.S. military since the mid-1990s. This policy discouraged military members from disclosing their sexual orientation in order to continue serving in the armed forces. This policy was repealed in 2011 by President Barack Obama and allowed service members to openly share their sexual orientation without fear of retaliation or discharge. In 2016, policies were expanded to provide protections to transgender people serving in the military. Despite this gain, concerns remain. First, there have been discussions to resume the "Don't ask, don't tell" policy. If this policy would be reenacted, it is unclear what would happen to service members who have openly shared their sexual orientation. Also, there remains controversy related to transgendered persons serving in the military. In 2017, President Trump tweeted that transgender persons would not be able to serve in the military. There have been several attempts to impede the president's ban by way of federal court injunctions.

In addition to fighting oppressive policies, social workers must also advocate for policies that provide protections to vulnerable and oppressed groups. In order to be an effective advocate for such groups, social workers must first recognize oppression and discrimination in all their forms against members of diverse groups. Social workers must attend to issues of racism, sexism, ageism, xenophobia, homophobia, and anti-Semitism. Social workers should champion policies that address these forms of oppression.

Religious discrimination and oppression, known as anti-Semitism, continues for many groups. In October 2018, a gunman entered a Jewish synagogue in urban Pittsburgh, Pennsylvania, and took the lives of eleven. The gunman was heard yelling anti-Jewish sentiments; even after the incident, when he taken to the hospital for the wounds he had received, his vile, hateful remarks continued. Unfortunately, this was not an isolated incident. In recent years, mass shootings have become nearly common occurrences in the United States. Vulnerable or oppressed groups are often targeted in such events. There has been an increase of 57% in anti-Semitic incidences in the past year alone, which is similar to an influx in all hate crimes across the United States (Gibbs, Benjamin, Graham, Meacham, & Lipstadt, 2018).

Hate crimes are criminal acts against a victim who is an identified member of an oppressed group (Chakraborti & Garland, 2015). There are varying levels or degrees to hate crimes, though most often media attention focuses on murder (Lewis, 2014). It is important to understand that the term hate crimes also includes lesser yet still deplorable acts against members of diverse groups.

In the rural town of Laramie, Colorado, in October 1998, Matthew Shepard was beaten, tortured, and left to die on a fence because he was an openly gay man. Matthew died as a result of the injuries he sustained that night. After his death, Matthew's parents established the Matthew Shepard Foundation (Sheerin, 2018). This foundation aided in expanding federal hate crime laws to include violence based on sexual orientation, gender, or disability (Chakraborti & Garland, 2015). Hate crime legislation was first signed by President Lyndon Johnson. The initial law addressed race, color, religion, or national origin.

■ Social Justice Issues

As we discussed at the start of this chapter, social workers value the principle of social justice. Related to diversity and difference, social workers are continuously striving to ameliorate conditions of injustice and inequality. Social workers must recognize that at present, many groups remain oppressed and marginalized. Some say we are in a post-racial society.

However, that discounts the experience of many groups that continue to face discrimination and prejudice based on an area of difference.

The Black Lives Matter movement exists in part to shine light on the continued discrimination and oppression of African Americans in the United States. Black Lives Matter uses marches and other means of protesting as well as online media platforms to spread their message and provide a forum for individuals to express their outrage (Edwards & Harris, 2016). What has evolved is a false dichotomy. Individuals feel there is a false choice to support the movement Black Lives Matter or the countermovement, in support of law enforcement, Blue Lives Matter, when in actuality, *all* lives matter. However, at present, all lives are not treated as such and that is why the Black Lives Matter movement is necessary. This movement raises awareness that the experience of Black people in the United States is different than that of those who identify as White. When dismissing the Black Lives Matter movement, people are dismissing the interactional and institutional discrimination and oppression that Black Americans have faced for decades. Some choose to believe that the Civil Rights Movement of the mid-20th century had addressed all issues pertaining to racial equality in the United States. That is not true. Though there were great strides during the Civil Rights Movements of the 1950s and 1960s, much more work remains to be done. Social workers can hold on to the eloquent words of Robert Frost, the American poet who wrote, "And miles to go before I sleep." We, as social workers, have miles to go before we sleep. We must not grow weary in our defense of social justice issues and must stand up against any efforts that diminish any group of people on the basis of any form of difference. Social workers are uniquely equipped with the knowledge and skills necessary to bring about change at all levels. We must never underestimate the power we hold as social workers. We are agents of change and must use this to live out the mission of our profession.

■ Summary

In this chapter, we explored the impact of diversity and difference. Social workers value and appreciate diversity and difference. Social workers also understand the intersectionality related to age, class, color, culture, disability and ability, ethnicity, gender identity and expression, immigration status, marital status, political ideology, race, religion/spirituality, sex, sexual orientation, and tribal sovereign status all impacts an individual's life experiences and identity formation. We explored various forms and mechanisms of oppression and discrimination at various levels (micro, mezzo, macro) as well as microaggressions. Theories were introduced to better understand diversity and difference. Cultural competence standards set forth by the NASW were shared. To demonstrate cultural competence, social workers must continuously be mindful of culture and diversity. Social workers are reflective and self-aware of their own personal values and biases and how they influence their practice. Furthermore, social workers should embrace cultural empathy and cultural humility as they seek to empower the client systems they are working with throughout the helping process.

CASE SUMMARY   "UNDOCUMENTED AND HOMELESS"

Practice Setting Description

Jackie is a first-year master of social work student completing an internship at an inner-city family service agency in the southwest. The agency is located in a section of the city that has a high crime rate, gang activity, and failing schools. The area has a diverse population with a large number of immigrants from Central and South America and a substantial African American population. The agency provides individual and family counseling services on a sliding fee scale. The agency also runs a number of educational and treatment groups as well as a temporary shelter for women and their children. Jackie has been assigned to work with the women and their children in the shelter. Her primary tasks are to provide concrete services and supportive counseling to the shelter residents.

Background Information

Elicia T and her daughter, Maria, are undocumented immigrants from Mexico. They have been in the United States for 5 years. Elicia and Maria fled to the area from another Southwestern city to escape her abusive husband approximately 2 months ago. Elicia is 25 years old and Maria 8 years old. Elicia has a 2-year-old daughter, Sarah, who was placed in foster care because of suspected abuse in the home. Sarah is in a foster home in a small rural community in the state hundreds of miles from Elicia's current residence. Since moving to the area, Maria has not been attending school.

Elicia and Maria are currently residing in the agency's temporary shelter for families. They have been at the shelter for 2 weeks, and the agency has a 90-day limit. It is viewed as temporary housing, and the residents are only allowed to stay for 3 months. Prior to arriving at the shelter, Elicia and Maria were homeless and living on the streets.

Elicia is a high-school dropout and was a stay-at-home mother prior to leaving her husband and moving to a different part of the state. She chose to move there because she has two female cousins living in the area who are also undocumented immigrants. Elicia's native language is Spanish. She speaks some English but is not as comfortable speaking in English. Her English comprehension appears to be good. Maria speaks both English and Spanish well. When communicating with the staff, Maria acts as Elicia's interpreter since none of the staff at the shelter speak Spanish.

Maria appears to be behind academically. She struggles reading simple children's books written in English. It is unknown if her ability to read in Spanish is better than her English reading skills.

Other than her two cousins, Elicia has no other sources of support in the community. Her cousins have young families and limited resources but are well established and connected to a Latino community in the city and the local Catholic church. Her cousins refused to let Elicia and Maria live with them while she was trying to find her own place and a job. They stated that they did not have enough room and are concerned they would get in trouble with their landlord if it was found out that they were letting people stay with them. They sent her to the local church for help and she was given the address for the agency's shelter by the priest.

(continued)

CASE SUMMARY

Elicia has been looking for housing in the Latino community. The housing market is tight with limited options, and she has been unable to find anything that she could possibly afford. The only affordable housing she found was a room in a rundown motel that rents by the hour or by the month. It is in an area of town known for drug dealing and sex work.

On arrival in the community, Elicia found occasional work for a house cleaning company. The company hires undocumented workers, pays them very low cash wages, and threatens to turn them in to Immigration and Customs Enforcement (ICE) if they complain. The job bosses also exploit their female workers sexually, threatening to turn them in if they do not comply. Elicia was fearful about applying for other jobs because of her illegal status. She considered turning to sex work to be able to take care of her children, but her Catholic upbringing and thoughts of how doing so would shame her family have kept her from doing so. She is in constant fear of being detained, separated from her children, and having them placed in foster care. She is also afraid that she will end up homeless again and forced to live on the streets or return to her abusive husband.

Elicia is extremely reluctant to sign up for any federally funded services, even those that she and her children are entitled to receiving. On the suggestion that she enroll for supplemental food through SNAP, Elicia became nervous and refused as she has heard that participation in SNAP services, and others like them, would draw the attention of ICE, and she had heard stories on the news of individuals being deported after signing up for such programs.

Presenting Problems

Elicia and her children are facing multiple obstacles. They need to find permanent, affordable housing and a job that pays enough to cover her housing and living expenses. In addition, Maria needs to be enrolled in school. Elicia also wants to regain custody of her youngest daughter in foster care.

Additionally, Elicia is experiencing an immense amount of stress, anxiety, and possibly post-traumatic stress disorder (PTSD). She described an instance where she could not calm down her breathing, and she felt lightheaded. She is very fearful of men and tries to avoid all contact with men in the community. She reports difficulty sleeping at night and feeling exhausted most of the time.

She is concerned about Maria. She has started acting out at the shelter, getting into fights with the other children, disobeying her mother, and being disrespectful and defiant to the staff and other adults. Elicia and Maria fight frequently, and when Elicia tries to discipline Maria, she throws a temper tantrum until Elicia gives up.

Elicia has many strengths. She had the strength to leave her abusive husband and move to a different city. She loves her daughters. She wants desperately to keep Maria with her and hopes to have Sarah returned to her custody. She is resilient and has managed to survive and keep her daughter safe despite not having a place to stay, a job, and a limited support network. Additionally, Elicia is highly motivated to find her own accommodations and support her children.

■ Discussion Questions

1. How can Jackie demonstrate that she is a culturally competent social worker during her work with Elicia and Maria?

2. How can conflict theory inform Jackie's practice with Elicia and Maria?

3. In what ways can Jackie utilize Elicia as a constituent expert? How would you present this to Elicia if you were the social worker?

4. Describe how Jackie can empower Elicia?

5. Describe Elicia's and Maria's individual intersectionalities.

6. Create a culturagram for Elicia and Maria.

■ References

Akhtar, F. N. (2013). *Mastering social work values and ethics.* London, UK: Jessica Kingsley Publishers.

Ashford, J. B., & Lecroy, C. W. (2013). *Human behavior in the social environment: A multidimensional perspective.* Belmont, CA: Brooks/Cole.

Barker, R. (Ed.). (2003). *The social work dictionary* (5th ed.). Washington, DC: NASW Press.

Bartos, O. J., & Wehr, P. E. (2002). *Using conflict theory.* Cambridge, UK: Cambridge University Press.

Beckett, C., & Maynard, A. (2013). *Values and ethics in social work* (2nd ed.). Thousand Oaks, CA: Sage.

Bubar, R., Cespedes, K., & Bundy-Fazioli, K. (2016). Intersectionality and social work: Omissions of race, class, and sexuality in graduate school education. *Journal of Social Work Education, 52*(3), 283–296. doi:10.1080/10437797.2016.1174636

Bulhan, H. (1987*). The constrained-strained theory: A general theory of deviance.* Boston, MA: Basic Health Management, Inc.

Chakraborti, N., & Garland, J. (2015). *Hate crime: Impact, causes and responses* (2nd ed.). London: SAGE Publications Ltd.

Charles, J. L. K., Holley, L. C., & Kondrat, D. C. (2017). Addressing our own biases: Social work educators' experiences with students with mental illnesses. *Social Work Education, 36*(4), 414–429. doi:10.1080/02615479.2017.1297393

Cho, S., Crenshaw, K. W., & McCall, L. (2013). Toward a field of intersectionality studies: Theory, applications, and praxis. *Signs: Journal of Women in Culture & Society, 38*(4), 785–810. doi:10.1086/669608

Congress, E. (1994). The use of culturagrams to assess and empower culturally diverse families. *Families in Society, 75*(9), 531–540. doi:10.1177/104438949407500901

Congress, E. P., & Chang-Muy, F. (2015). *Social work with immigrants and refugees: Legal issues, clinical skills, and advocacy* (2nd ed.). New York, NY: Springer Publishing Company.

Congress, E. P., & González, M. J. (2013). *Multicultural perspectives in social work practice with families* (3rd ed.). New York, NY: Springer Publishing Company.

Cox, L. E., Tice, C. J., & Long, D. D. (2016). *Introduction to social work: An advocacy-based profession.* Los Angeles, CA: Sage.

Crenshaw, K. W. (2012). From private violence to mass incarceration: Thinking intersectionally about women, race, and social control. *UCLA Law Review, 59*(6), 1418–1472.

Daley, M. R. (2015). *Rural social work in the 21st century.* Chicago, IL: Lyceum Books, Inc.

David, E. J. R. (2014). *Internalized oppression: The psychology of marginalized groups.* New York, NY: Springer Publishing Company.

David, E. J. R., & Derthick, A. O. (2017). *The psychology of oppression.* New York, NY: Springer Publishing Company

Edwards, S. B., & Harris, D. (2016). *Black lives matter.* Minneapolis, MN: ABDO.

Fisher, A. K., Moore, D. J., Simmons, C., & Allen, S. C. (2017). Teaching social workers about micro-aggressions to enhance understanding of subtle racism. *Journal of Human Behavior in the Social Environment, 27*(4), 346–355. doi:10.1080/10911359.2017.1289877

Fogler, S. (2008). Using conflict theory to explore the role of nursing home social workers in home- and community-based service utilization. *Journal of Gerontological Social Work, 52*(8), 859–869. doi:10.1080/01634370902914448

Gast, L., Wonnacott, J., & Patmore, A. (2012). *Mastering approaches to diversity in social work.* London, UK: Jessica Kingsley Publishers.

Gibbs, N., Benjamin, D., Graham, M., Meacham, J., & Lipstadt, D. E. (2018). Beyond hate. (cover story). *Time, 192*(20), 22–33.

Gil, D. G. (2013). *Confronting injustice and oppression: Concepts and strategies for social workers.* New York, NY: Columbia University Press.

Ginsberg, L. H. (2005). *Social work in rural communities* (4th ed.). Alexandria, VA: CSWE Press.

Hepworth, D. H., Rooney, R. H., Rooney, G. D., & Strom-Gottfried, K. (2017). *Direct social work practice: Theory and skills* (10th ed.). Boston, MA: Cengage.

Hutchinson, E. D. (2017). *Essentials of human behavior* (2nd ed.). Los Angeles, CA: Sage.

Johnson, M., & Dunbar, E. (2005). Culturally relevant social work practice in diverse rural communities. In Ginsberg, L. H. (2005). *Social work in rural communities* (4th ed., pp. 349–365. Alexandria, VA: CSWE Press.

Langer, C. L., & Lietz, C. (2014). *Applying theory to generalist social work practice.* Hoboken, NJ: Wiley.

Lewis, C. (2014). *Tough on hate?: The cultural politics of hate crimes.* New Brunswick, NJ: Rutgers University Press.

Lindsey, A., King, E., Hebl, M., & Levine, N. (2015). The impact of method, motivation, and empathy on diversity training effectiveness. *Journal of Business and Psychology, 30*(3), 605–617. doi:10.1007/s10869-014-9384-3

Liu, H. (2018). Re-radicalizing intersectionality in organization studies. *Ephemera: Theory & Politics in Organization, 18*(1), 81–101.

Mahler, S. J. (2013). *Culture as comfort.* Boston, MA: Pearson.

Marsiglia, F. F., & Kulis, S. (2016). *Diversity, oppression and change* (2nd ed.). Oxford, NY: Oxford University Press.

National Association of Black Social Workers. (2018). Mission statement. Retrieved from https://www.nabsw.org/page/MissionStatement

National Association of Social Workers. (2015). Standards and indicators for cultural competence in social work practice. Retrieved from https://www.socialworkers.org/LinkClick.aspx?fileticket=PonPTDEBrn4%3D&portalid=0

National Association of Social Workers. (2017). *Code of ethics.* Silver Spring, MD: Author.

Ortega, R. M., & Faller, K. C. (2011). Training child welfare workers from an intersectional cultural humility perspective: A paradigm shift. *Child Welfare, 90*(5), 27–49.

Payne, M. (2016). *Modern social work theory* (4th ed.). Oxford, NY: Oxford University Press.

Ridley, C. R., & Lingle, D. W. (1996). Cultural empathy in multicultural counselling: A multidimensional process model. In P. B. Pederson & J. G. Draguns (Eds.), *Counseling across culture* (4th ed., pp. 21–46). Thousand Oaks, CA: Sage.

Risberg, A., & Pilhofer, K. (2018). Diversity and difference research: A reflection on categories and categorization. *Ephemera: Theory & Politics in Organization, 18*(1), 131–148.

Rosen, D., McCall, J., & Goodkind, S. (2017). Teaching critical self-reflection through the lens of cultural humility: an assignment in a social work diversity course. *Social Work Education, 36*(3), 289–298. doi:10.1080/02615479.2017.1287260

Salem Press. (2014). *Sociology reference guide.* Pasadena, CA: Author.

Sheerin, J. (2018). Matthew Shepard: The murder that changed America. *BBC News.* Retrieved from https://www.bbc.com/news/world-us-canada-45968606

Stefancic, J., & Delgado, R. (2013). *Critical race theory: The cutting edge* (3rd ed.). Philadelphia, PA: Temple University Press.

Stovall, D. (2016). *Born out of struggle: Critical race theory, school creation, and the politics of interruption.* Albany, NY: SUNY Press.

Sue, D. W., Capodilupo, C. M., Torino, G. C., Bucceri, J. M., Holder, A. M. B., Nadal, K. L, & Esquilin, M. (2007). Racial microaggressions in everyday life: Implications for clinical practice. *American Psychologist, 62,* 271–279. doi:10.1037/0003-066X.62.4.271

Sue, D. W., Jackson, K. F., Rasheed, J. M., & Rasheed, M. N. (2015). *Multicultural social work practice: A competency-based approach to diversity and social justice.* Hoboken, NJ: Wiley & Sons.

Thyer, B. A. (2010). *Cultural diversity and social work practice* (3rd ed.). Springfield, MA: Charles C. Thomas.

Trimble, J. E. (2010). Bear spends time in our dreams now: Magical thinking and cultural empathy in multicultural counselling theory and practice. *Counselling Psychology Quarterly, 23*(3), 241–253. doi:10.1080/09515070.2010.505735

Wahler, E. A. (2012). Identifying and challenging social work students' biases. *Social Work Education, 31*(8), 1058–1070. doi:10.1080/02615479.2011.616585

Walsh, J. (2013). *Theories for direct social work practice* (3rd ed.). Stamford, CT: Cengage.

HUMAN RIGHTS AND JUSTICE IN A SOCIAL WORK PRACTICE ENVIRONMENT

Jackie was a second-year master of social work student doing her placement at a community action agency in a small Eastern city, which has high levels of poverty and a large minority population. A few months into her placement, Jackie began to hear complaints from her clients about health issues that were cropping up within families and the community. The school health nurse was raising concern about the number of children she was seeing who had asthma as well as the number of children with learning difficulties and exhibiting sluggishness and fatigue. The residents were concerned about the waste treatment plant that processed the garbage and waste for all the surrounding communities and about the presence of lead paint in most of the aging housing stock, which might be causing the health and behavioral issues with their children. Based on her clients' concerns, Jackie decided to do a little research to gather recent health data from the community to try and see if there was a link between the environmental issues and health problems in the community.

Jackie's initial research found some public health data that showed higher rates of asthma in the city than in the surrounding, more affluent communities. She also found data that indicated that a very large percentage of the residences in the city had been built in the 1940s, which pointed to the presence of lead paint in many of the homes. Jackie and her field instructor concluded that there was sufficient evidence that there was an environmental justice issue that needed to be addressed. They decided to begin organizing a community group of residents and service providers to address the community health concerns and their possible environmental causes.

LEARNING OBJECTIVES

This chapter focuses on Competency 3: Advance Human Rights and Social, Economic, and Environmental Justice. The chapter begins with a review of the National Association of Social Workers (NASW) ethical principle and standards that address human rights and social justice. This is followed by a discussion of Maslow's theory of motivation and hierarchy of need. We then review theories of justice and Rawls's theory of distributive justice. Discussion of universal human rights and human rights violations is followed by a review of the various forms of oppressions and the types and sources of power, social processes, and conflicts. The chapter concludes with a discussion of justice-informed practice, anti-oppressive practice (AOP), and a human rights policy issue. By the end of this chapter, you will be able to:

- Connect social justice issues with the NASW Code of Ethics
- Recognize the importance of advancing social, economic, and environmental justice
- Understand the conceptual theories and frameworks for social justice work
- Describe the various forms of oppressions
- Understand the facets of power and social aspects that contribute to injustices in these areas
- Utilize change strategies to implement social justice and anti-oppressive approaches in your social work practice

■ Competency 3: Advance Human Rights and Social, Economic, and Environmental Justice

Social workers understand that every person regardless of position in society has fundamental human rights such as freedom, safety, privacy, an adequate standard of living, healthcare, and education. Social workers understand the global interconnections of oppression and human rights violations, and are knowledgeable about theories of human need and social justice and strategies to promote social and economic justice and human rights. Social workers understand strategies designed to eliminate oppressive structural barriers to ensure that social goods, rights, and responsibilities are distributed equitably and that civil, political, environmental, economic, social, and cultural human rights are protected. Social workers:

- Apply their understanding of social, economic, and environmental justice to advocate for human rights at the individual and system levels
- Engage in practices that advance social, economic, and environmental justice

This chapter focuses on human rights issues, justice issues, and social work practice from a social justice perspective.

■ National Association of Social Workers (NASW) *Code of Ethics*

The NASW *Code of Ethics* (2017) has one ethical principle and one ethical standard that address human rights and social, economic, and environmental justice. The value is social justice and its associated ethical principle is challenging injustice (NASW, 2017). The ethical standard comes under responsibilities to the broader society and the call for social and political action (NASW, 2017).

The social and political action focuses on equal access to resources, employment, services and opportunities to meet basic human needs, expanding choice and opportunity for all people, promoting policies that safeguard peoples' rights, and preventing exploitation and discrimination against anyone based on his or her race, ethnicity, national origin, color, sex, sexual orientation, gender identity or expression, age, marital status, political belief, religion, immigration status, or mental or physical ability (NASW, 2017).

Clearly, the NASW *Code of Ethics* addresses the social work competency on advancing human rights and social, economic, and environmental justice. Social justice is a core social work value and an important component of social work practice.

■ Maslow's Theory of Motivation (Human Need)

Maslow's theory of motivation (1943) is applicable to any discussion of human rights and social, economic, and environmental justice. His hierarchy of human needs is shown in Figure 4.1.

There are five levels of need. The first four levels (lower order needs) are considered physiological needs, while the top (fifth) level of the pyramid is considered growth needs. The needs are hierarchical. Lower level needs must be satisfied before the next level need or needs can influence behavior. The two lowest levels of need are physiological and safety. Physiological needs include air, food, water, shelter, and sleep. Safety needs include security and stability. Security and safety include personal, emotional, and financial security as well as health and well-being. These two basic levels of need are survival needs and as such are fundamental human rights. People for whom these needs are not adequately met often face overwhelming social, economic, and/or environmental injustice. Not being able to satisfy these basic human needs is a violation of a person's human rights.

■ Theories of Social Justice

Social justice is a broad concept that encompasses fair and unbiased treatment of all individuals, eradication of discriminatory practices and institutionalized oppression, and

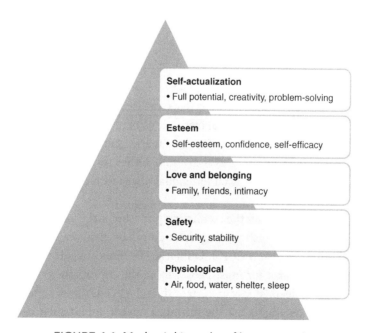

FIGURE 4.1 Maslow's hierarchy of human needs.

establishment of equality for members of historically marginalized and oppressed groups—achieved through the establishment of truly equal opportunity and access to resources (Barsky, 2010; Reisch, 2002; Young, 2001). The Council on Social Work Education (CSWE) addresses the social justice mandate by stating that "social work's purpose is actualized through its quest for social justice, the prevention of conditions that limit human rights, the elimination of poverty, and the enhancement of the quality of life for all persons" (2015, p. 5) and specifically calls upon all social workers to "understand the global interconnections of oppression and human rights violations; advocate for human rights [. . .]; and engage in practices that advance social, economic, and environmental justice" (2015, p. 8).

The meanings of social justice have wide implications, yet can be ambiguous, and interpretation into practice is challenging. It is important to remember that the concept of social justice is bound by context and history. Attempts to define the correct relationship among individuals, communities, states, and countries have been explored for centuries by philosophers, political theorists, and social workers (Finn & Jacobson, 2017).

The notion of social justice within the field of social work is generally based on Western ideologies and the Judeo-Christian religious tradition (Finn & Jacobson, 2017). Beliefs around social justice are generally abstract and are in line with what is moral and/or right—with a specific focus on the notion that all citizens are equal and have the right to meet their basic needs, the desire to share opportunities as equitably as possible, and the obligation to work toward eliminating unjustified inequalities. Caputo (2002) points out that while many notions of social justice within social work actually maintain the status quo, it still remains important as a goal of social work.

Some scholars examine social justice through the always-present tension that exists between individual liberty and the common good. These scholars would argue that social justice is endorsed to the degree that we can promote collective good without violating basic individual freedoms (Finn & Jacobson, 2017). Others contend that social justice incorporates fairness within fundamental rights and duties, economic opportunities, and social conditions (Miller, 1976).

Distributive Justice

A perspective often utilized by social work is that of a distributive approach of social justice—advocating for an organization of societal institutions that ensures human rights and access to meaningful social participation, as well as equitable distribution of resources. Distributive justice focuses on what society owes an individual. Other frameworks focus on what people owe society—legal justice—and what individuals owe one another—commutative justice (Reichert, 2003; Van Soest, 1995).

Social work generally addresses the conflicting philosophical frameworks used to explain choices in the realm of social justice using three dominant theories: utilitarian, libertarian, and egalitarian (Finn & Jacobson, 2017). Utilitarian theories consider decisions that result in greater good and less harm for most people to be the appropriate course of action. The right of the individual is deemed less important than the needs of the community or society at large, and as such, those rights may be infringed upon if a particular decision results in assisting the greater good (McCormick, 2003). Libertarian perspectives focus on individual freedom from external control or influence. This framework rejects the concept of equitable resource distribution, instead arguing that individuals have the right to any resources they acquire as long as no law is broken (Nozick, 1974). Clearly, this is in direct contrast to the utilitarian perspective as the obligation to society lies in the protection of individual freedoms. Finally, egalitarian theoretical frameworks argue that everyone should be guaranteed the same rights, opportunities, and access to goods and resources (Rawls, 1971). This approach advocates for the redistribution of resources to the vulnerable, oppressed, or disadvantaged in society to guarantee that unmet needs are rectified (Rawls, 1971).

Political philosopher John Rawls (2001) examines what would need to be present in a society that meets basic human needs, reduces excessive stress, encourages individuals' abilities, and reduces threats to well-being. Rawls advocates for an equal distribution of resources and burdens from tangible resources (good and services) and intangible resources (power and opportunity). Social justice comes down to two principles (Rawls, 2001, pp. 42–43):

- Each person has the same indefeasible claim to a fully adequate scheme of equal basic liberties; this scheme is compatible with the same scheme of liberties for all.

- Social and economic equalities are to satisfy two conditions: First, they are to be attached to offices and positions open to all under conditions of fair equality of opportunity, and second, they should provide the greatest benefit to the least advantaged members of society (the difference principle).

Distributive justice, as defined by Rawls, helps the field of social work to integrate social justice into both micro- and macropractice settings (Wakefield, 1988). This theoretical framework focuses on counteracting inequalities by advocating for unequal distribution of resources only if it is done to advance the least advantaged groups in society (Reisch, 1998).

■ Oppression and Human Rights Violations

Unfortunately, in the United States and throughout the world, there are large numbers of homeless people, people with insufficient food, people with inadequate and unsafe drinking water, and people living with dangerous air pollution and in environmentally unsafe areas. Also, large numbers of people are unsafe in their homes and neighborhoods, living in poverty with inadequate incomes as well as inadequate access to healthcare.

Article 25 of the *Universal Declaration of Human Rights* (UDHR) states that:

everyone has the right to a standard of living adequate for the health and well-being of himself and of his family, including food, clothing, housing and medical care and necessary social services, and the right to security in the event of unemployment, sickness, disability, widowhood, old age or other lack of livelihood in circumstances beyond his control. (United Nations, 2018a, Article 25, para. 1)

These fundamental human rights are not being met for a large number of people here and around the globe. This is a humanitarian and human rights crisis in the midst of unprecedented wealth and prosperity.

The best survey data show that the share of wealth held by the top 1 percent rose from just under 30 percent in 1989 to nearly 39 percent in 2016, while the share held by the bottom 90 percent fell from just over 33 percent to less than 23 percent over the same period (Stone, Trisi, Sherman, & Taylor, 2018, Wealth, para 1).

The income/wealth gap between the very wealthy and the rest of the population has widened, increasing inequality and social, economic, and environmental injustice.

In addition to the large numbers of people lacking the minimum standard of living, there are many other human rights violations occurring globally. Some examples from Amnesty International's 2009 World Report are shown in the following for five regions of the world:

- Armed conflict and insecurity in several African countries forced hundreds of thousands of people to flee from their homes, trying to find international protection across borders or some form of security within their own country. In some of the worst armed conflicts still affecting the region, government forces and armed groups completely disregarded the dignity and physical integrity of the population. The civilian population was routinely the object of attacks by parties to the conflict; rape and other forms of sexual violence remained widespread; children were often recruited to take part in hostilities; and humanitarian workers were targeted (p. 3).

- The Americas' laws to improve respect for women's rights and in particular the right to freedom from violence in the home, community, and workplace, exist in most countries in the region, with the notable exceptions of Haiti and some other Caribbean countries. Nicaragua and Haiti stood out in the region as two countries where more than 50% of all reported victims of sexual abuse were 18 years old or younger. In the vast majority of cases, the perpetrators were adult men, many holding positions of power. The sexual abuse of girls, some as young as 9 or 10, was intrinsically linked to poverty, deprivation, and exclusion, which left the girls at risk of sexual exploitation as their only means of survival. Despite the widespread nature of the problem, the stigma associated with sexual violence condemned many survivors to silence (p. 13).

- Even where ethnic discrimination did not give rise to armed conflict, it remained a common feature of the social landscape in the Asia-Pacific region, from the wealthiest societies to the most impoverished. For example, China's large ethnic minorities in the west of the country, in Tibetan-populated areas and the predominantly Muslim province of the Xinjiang Uighur Autonomous Region, continued to suffer systematic discrimination (pp. 26–27).

- In Europe and Central Asia, those already in poverty continued to lack access to many basic needs. Despite the festering economic crisis, Europe was home to some of the wealthiest countries in the world in 2008. It also, however, housed serious failings in the implementation of its inhabitants' rights to education, healthcare, secure housing, and livelihoods. Across the region, the divide between rich and poor remained gaping, and from either side of that divide, the experience of accessing human rights was markedly different (p. 31).

■ Middle East and North Africa women within the region faced additional insecurity, through discrimination under the law and in practice, and violence, often at the hands of their male relatives. At its most acute, such violence saw women killed in so-called honor crimes, as in Iraq, Jordan, the Palestinian Authority, and Syria. Women migrant domestic workers were particularly vulnerable to sexual and other abuse by employers as they were often unprotected by labor laws (p. 43).

In the United States, Amnesty International (2009, p. 348) reported that:

■ Racial, ethnic and national minorities, especially Latino and African American people, were disproportionately concentrated in poor residential areas characterized by sub-standard housing conditions, limited employment opportunities, inadequate access to healthcare facilities, under-resourced schools and high exposure to crime and violence.

■ Marginalized and poor women were at higher risk of death and complications from pregnancy and childbirth, with the maternal mortality rate among African American women three times higher than that of White women.

■ Native American and Alaska Native women continued to experience disproportionately high levels of sexual violence and inadequate access to support and justice. There were some welcome measures to address this issue.

The aforementioned examples are just a few of the many human rights violations that are occurring around the world. Most if not all human rights violations involve some form of oppression of vulnerable people at the hands of more powerful individuals or groups. It is beyond the scope of this textbook to detail all the types of human rights violations that occur on a daily basis in the United States and around the globe. The UDHR resolution was approved by the United Nations in 1948. Since its passage, the UDHR has

. . . spawn[ed] many other international treaties, including the **International Convention on the Elimination of All Forms of Racial Discrimination** (179 states); the **International Convention on the Elimination of All Forms of Discrimination Against Women** (189); the **United Nations Convention on the Rights of the Child** (196); and the **United Nations Convention Against Torture** (162). (United Nations, 2018b, 70th Anniversary, para. 4)

While there has been some progress during the past 70-plus years, human rights violations continue to be a significant issue for millions of people worldwide. The United Nations Human Rights Office's 70th Anniversary Report on the UDHR highlighted the following ongoing human rights challenges:

■ 880 million people today live in urban slums.

■ 1 in 10 children worldwide are still engaged in child labor.

■ 65 million men, women, and children were forced from their homes by war and persecution in 2015, which is 1 in every 113 people.

■ 101 journalists were killed in 2016: 1 death every 4 days.

- Almost 1 in 3 people in detention are held without being tried or sentenced for a crime.

- 59 million children were not in primary school in 2014. 52% of these were girls.

- Women represent only 24% of national parliaments.

- 700 million women today were married before age 18; 250 million were married before age 15. (United Nations, 2018b, 70th Anniversary, para. 5)

■ Global Interconnections

The world has become increasingly interconnected. Events that happen in one part of the world are known instantly throughout the rest of the world. Social media connects people in many different ways and platforms. The flow of news media is constant, going 24/7, and the number of media outlets is constantly expanding. However, in terms of human rights, the biggest threat comes from business and the global economy.

We live in a global economy. For the most part, countries trade with each other, and businesses can operate where they want. Many would agree that this globalized world has created jobs and helped grow the economy as a whole. However, certain economic decisions can violate human rights. For example, if a business decides to expand internationally and invest in projects that enforce child labor or utilize sweatshops with dangerous working conditions that do not pay workers a livable wage, that business is responsible for the violation of human rights. This situation is not uncommon, and many corporations have come under scrutiny for supporting unjust, unsafe working environments.

A key issue in globalization is who defines the goals and rules. If a company closes a factory in the United States and shifts production to China where it is cheaper to produce the product with fewer regulations, who benefits? The winners in this case are the company executives and shareholders and those in China who receive profits from the investment. The Chinese workers benefited from having jobs, but their working conditions might be hazardous. The factory operating with few regulations may be contributing to air and water pollution, which affects all the residents of the area. Also, the U.S. employees are losers in that they have lost their means of employment, healthcare, and other benefits. The closing of the factory also negatively impacted the economic and social well-being of the community.

On the question of who defines the goals or rules in this case, it is the Chinese government and the executives of the U.S. company. They define the goals and they are the beneficiaries of the decision to move the production operations. The workers from both countries do not play any role in the decision.

The human rights argument is that the globalization of the economy has created human rights violations. In the aforementioned example, the U.S. workers experience economic hardships and the community where the factor was located also experiences economic and social challenges. Articles 23 and 25 of the UDHR address the situation described. Article 23 states that "everyone has the right to work, to free choice of employment, to just and favourable conditions of work and to protection against unemployment" (United Nations, 2018a, Article 23, para. 1). Article 25 states that

> everyone has the right to a standard of living adequate for the health and well-being of himself and of his family, including food, clothing, housing and medical care and necessary social services, and the right to security in the event of unemployment, sickness, disability, widowhood, old age or other lack of livelihood in circumstances beyond his control. (United Nations, 2018a, Article 25, para. 1)

Both of these human rights would have been violated by the company's decision to close the U.S. factory and move its production facility to a country with lower wages and fewer regulations. Both articles also apply to the Chinese government's approval of the factory, the working conditions, and the negative impact the factory has on the environment and living conditions of the community.

The interconnectedness of the global economy has created numerous human rights violations worldwide. Another significant global human rights issue ishuman trafficking. Data on the extent of international trafficking of women and young girls is difficult to obtain. The United Nations Office on Drugs and Crime (UNODC) 2009 *Global Report on Trafficking in Persons* found that the most common form of human trafficking is sexual exploitation (79%) followed by forced labor (18%); about 66% of the victims were women and about 13% were girls (p. 11). "Much of the cross-border trafficking activity was between countries of the same general region, particularly between neighbouring countries. But there was also evidence of intercontinental trafficking" (UNODC, 2009, p. 11). Long-distance trafficking included:

> the trafficking of African victims to locations in Europe and North America; the trafficking of Latin American victims to North America and Europe; the trafficking of Central European, Eastern European and Central Asian victims to Europe and the Middle East; and the trafficking of South Asian victims to the Middle East. (p. 11)

In the United States, "in 2006 victims originated mainly from Latin America and the Caribbean (62%), Africa, Asia, Europe and the Pacific Islands. In 2007 certified victims originated mainly from Latin America and the Caribbean (41%), Asia (41%), Europe and the Pacific Islands" (UNODC, 2009, p. 137).

■ Forms of Oppression

As discussed earlier in the chapter, oppression is the result of inequities in power that allow groups in power to act out their biases, prejudices, and stereotypes in ways that deprive those not in power full access to resources, self-actualization, and autonomy (Thomas & Schwartzbaum, 2017).

There are many ways in which oppression, discrimination, and prejudice are seen in everyday life: prejudicial talk, avoidance of certain groups or individuals, segregation or exclusion in social systems (e.g., employment, education), violence to person or property, exploitation, marginalization (exclusion from social life), cultural imperialism (repressing the nondominant groups' norms and values), and organized extermination of a group of people based on their membership (Allport as cited in Thomas & Schwartzbaum, 2017; Young, 1990). Social workers will be able to identify the ways that these oppressive actions take place at micro-, mezzo-, and macrolevels. Daily microaggressions (common, regularly occurring humiliations—intentional or not, based on stereotypes and prejudices as defined by Sue et al., 2007), imbalances of power within interpersonal relationships, and systemic institutional and cultural discrimination and exclusions deny individuals the ability to be seen, and see themselves, as spiritually, mentally, and emotionally whole.

The damaging effects of oppression reach their height when individuals begin to internalize the negative stereotypes about the group they have membership in (Sue & Sue, 2012). Internalization of oppression can manifest itself in a variety of ways that can include self-hatred, engaging in self-harming behaviors, and acting in ways that are in accordance with the stereotypical messages they have received, among others. Kagan and Burton (2005) argue that the helplessness that many oppressed individuals feel is also a form of internalized oppression—they have internalized the dominance of those in power, and are rendered incapable, helpless, and powerless. While some are able to prevent this internalization through the coping skills they have developed, others are overwhelmed by the ongoing assault on their sense of self. Because of this, social workers must remember to utilize an ever-present lens of culture and oppression when working with clients. The next section defines the ways in which individuals are often targets for oppression—this list is not exhaustive.

Racism

Racism is pervasive, rooted in assumptions of superiority based on race, deeply infused in the history of the United States, and requires the critical attention of all social workers. As overt racism (legalized segregation, lynching, etc.) became less acceptable during the Civil Rights era, the acting out of racist ideologies evolved into a more concealed form of racism that is persistent in the institutions of society. The resulting policies create unequal outcomes for people of color including higher rates of incarceration; unequal access to financial, employment, and educational resources; inequity in representation, disparities in health outcomes; and more. A very important and often confusing concept is color-blind racism (Bonilla-Silva, 2003). Perhaps some of you reading this passage were even coached as children to "see people, not color." While regularly well-intentioned, claiming to not see people with regard to their race is actually an exceptionally damaging approach—not acknowledging and celebrating the differences in culture imposes the dominant (White) culture on everyone, robs people of color of their cultural uniqueness and pride, and assumes that everyone has the privilege of moving through the world in the same way, with a total disregard for the impact of discrimination, oppression, and ongoing microaggression (Bonilla-Silva, 2003). Very recently, the United States has been experiencing a significant increase in the expression of overt forms of racism, including the use of brazenly racist slogans, aligned with belief systems of the Ku Klux Klan and Nazism, with the intention of inciting violence and discrimination toward people of color (Siddique & Laughland, 2017).

Xenophobia and Ethnocentrism

Often fueled by racism, xenophobia is the fear or hatred of other countries and individuals from other countries. This is often seen in conjunction with ethnocentrism—the belief that one group (ethnic, religious, or specific culture) is superior to others, and often leads to prejudice and oppression based on ethnicity, religion, or country of origin (Sue & Sue, 2012). This greatly impacts beliefs and policies around immigration and globalization. Targeting immigrants as the cause of society's ills has long been a practice in the history of the United States. Which groups of immigrants are targeted and what those forms of discrimination look like fluctuate significantly based on political and economic factors (Thomas & Schwartzbaum, 2017). However, racism often plays a role in who is mostly often targeted, with people of color at a greater risk of discrimination due to racial profiling. An example of this is the ongoing targeting, since the attacks of September 11, 2001, of Arab individuals, Muslim individuals, and South Asian individuals for questioning related to immigration violations (American Civil Liberties Union, 2017).

Classism

Classism is the differential treatment based on (actual or perceived) social class. Lott and Bullock (2007) point out that classism occurs both individually and institutionally. Individual classism refers to the stereotypes and prejudices about individuals living in poverty, as well as working class individuals. Institutional classism refers to the social institutions that enact policies and procedures that negatively impact, marginalize, and harm individuals living in poverty. This can be seen in the education system, legal system, political system, and beyond. Additionally, denying the fact that class difference has systemic roots and blaming the poor for their poverty are additional forms of classism (Thomas & Schwartzbaum, 2017).

Religious Oppression

The pervasive oppression based on minority religious status is the product of the intersection of the historical tradition of Christian hegemony in the United States, the unequal power relationships of minority religious groups with the Christian majority, and the often-held belief of "One True Religion." Christian beliefs and norms are hegemonic in that they are assumed and are interwoven into society. Some examples are the addition of "In God We Trust" and the observance of Christian holidays by governmental agencies. Religious persecution based on these beliefs has resulted in violence and religious cleansing (systematic extermination of groups based on religious belief).

Sexism

Sexism is the discrimination on the basis of gender, most commonly occurring by men toward women. This form of discrimination is often rooted in a belief that women should be subservient to men, and that men are superior to women intellectually (Thomas & Schwartzbaum, 2017). Traditional notions of gender link behavioral, cultural, and social characteristics to an individual's gender. Sexism and gender-based discrimination and inequality includes violence, restricted access to education, economic, and governmental opportunities, resource restriction that results in health disparities, and others. Moral, religious, and cultural practices often reinforce traditional gender roles and attitudes. These beliefs are so strongly held that violence is perpetrated against those that violate them. Challenging traditional beliefs of gender and advocating for policies that decrease gender discrimination and sexual harassment are some of the ways that discrimination based on gender can be confronted (Littlefield et al., 2015).

Homophobia, Biphobia, and Heterosexism

Homophobia is the intense fear, hatred, or dread of homosexuals and homosexuality (Moses, 1982). Biphobia is an aversion to bisexuals and bisexuality. It is important to remember that individuals of any sexual orientation can hold homophobic and biphobic beliefs. Similar to other forms of oppression, homophobia and biphobia can manifest itself in a variety of ways, including violence, discrimination in education, employment, and housing. State-sponsored homophobia includes practices and policies that criminalize homosexuality, governmental figures engaging in hate speeches toward gay, lesbian, and bisexual individuals, and withholding certain rights and privileges (e.g., marriage, healthcare decision-making capacity) from same-sex couples. Often, many homophobic and biphobic beliefs are rooted in heterosexism (sometimes referred to as heterocentrism)—the systematic preference for opposite-sex sexuality and relationships (Jung & Smith, 1993). Heterosexism is pervasive in our majority customs and institutions. Some examples include denial that bisexuality and homosexuality exist, the assumption that sexual orientation can and should be changed, hostility toward same-sex relationships (with same-sex marriage only recently becoming legally recognized nationally), the existence of sodomy laws in a third of states, and resistance to the addition of sexual orientation to nondiscrimination statutes resulting in a lack of legal protection from discrimination based on sexual orientation. Additionally, social workers often unintentionally utilize heterosexist language in service delivery to clients, such as asking a female client if she has a boyfriend or husband. Evaluating service delivery for inclusion and making changes, such as moving away from exclusive language, takes intention and practice for social workers.

Transgender Oppression

Transgender oppressions refer to the devaluing, discrimination, stereotyping, and violence that individuals face when their appearance or identity does not conform to conventional beliefs of gender—namely, that only two genders exist, that they are fixed at birth, and are determined solely by the chromosomal and anatomical sex of an individual. Common beliefs tied to transgender oppression include that transgender individuals do not actually exist, individuals presenting as gender nonconforming are doing so for an ulterior motive (e.g., attention, political motivation), that transgender individuals are defying nature, and/or are acting against the will of God. These beliefs are tied to transphobia—the disgust, fear, hatred, and disbelief in the existence of transgender and gender nonconforming individuals (Chakraborti & Garland, 2009). Transgender oppression includes bullying, physical violence, harassment, false arrest, and sexual assault. Transgender and gender nonconforming individuals are often discriminated against in employment, education, and healthcare settings, and they face a lack of legal protection from discrimination based on the absence of gender identity in many nondiscrimination statutes. Data collected by the Federal Bureau of Investigation (FBI) concluded that lesbian, gay, bisexual, and transgender individuals are more likely to be targets of hate crimes than any other minority group—with transgender women of color being the most frequent targets of violence (Park & Mykhyalyshyn, 2016). Transgender oppression is further reinforced throughout the social systems in the United States, most notably through transgender and gender nonconforming invisibility. One obvious example is that most federal, state, institutional, organization, and agency forms only provide two options for gender or sex: male or female.

Ableism

Ableism is discrimination in favor of able-bodied people, the negative judgment about the capabilities of individuals with disabilities, the expression of hate for people with disabilities, and the denial of accessibility and resources (Smith, Foley, & Chaney, 2008; Thomas & Schwartzbaum, 2017). Smith et al. (2008) aptly point out that discrimination against individuals with disabilities is often characterized by the belief that they are abnormal, have some sort of deficit, need to be fixed, and cannot fully function in society. This framing of disability as deficient as opposed to difference has resulted in the ignoring of this dimension of cultural competence (Smith et al., 2008). Discrimination based on ableism manifests as discrimination in employment (most specifically, the rejection of disabled applicants for housing and jobs), failing to provide accessibility at all or beyond wheelchair ramps, using ableist language, individuals without disabilities utilizing resources allocated for those with disabilities (e.g., parking spaces, restrooms), making assumptions about an individual's disability status based on the visibility (or invisibility) of their disability, and policies and systems that, intentionally or not, keep people with disabilities in poverty.

■ Types and Sources of Power

In the preceding we discussed forms of oppression that exist due to inequities in power that allow groups in power to act out their biases, prejudices, and stereotypes in ways that deprive those not in power full access to resources, self-actualization, and autonomy (Thomas & Schwartzbaum, 2017). This section delves deeper into the types of power that exist as well as social dimensions that contribute to these power differences.

While power is a complex term with multiple meanings depending on context, the type of power we are focused on in regard to social justice refers to power within social structure and systems. Legitimately or otherwise, certain individuals and groups have power, and with that power utilize force (of varying types) to exploit others for their own gain. The purpose of focusing on power within social relationship and societal structures is to better understand social justice advocacy and how we, as social workers, can attempt to address the connections between privilege and exploitation.

There are three different types of power that exist (Dobratz, Waldner, & Buzzell, 2012):

1. Coercive and dominant power: Likely the most obvious use of power, coercive power uses the command of resources to dominate others into submission. For example, coercive power in the form of physical force could include military strength, brute force, violence, and so on.

2. Authority and legitimate power: Society creates order by acknowledging power based on tradition, norms, and laws. Authority and legitimate power is the form that arises from this acknowledgment. Members of society power accept that specific individuals or groups have power based on a sense of legitimacy and obedience or duty. This type of power is able to be obtained because individuals believe that placing power in states offers protection to members of society and preserves community interests.

3. Privileged and interdependent power: This type of power tends to be subtler, but still results in dramatic implications for social interactions and distribution of power in society. This type of power focuses specifically on the power relationship between two actors. Often, the actors do not realize exactly how much influence they have in a given situation. Piven and Cloward (2005) point out that people have potential power when others depend on them for the contributions they make to interdependent relationships that make up society. Johnson (2006) also points out that privilege links to the ways society makes differences important or significant. These include unearned advantages (one specific group rewarded) and conferred dominance (when one group pressures another group, or groups, into conforming to that privilege) as ways that privilege is created in society.

Framing societal power within your social work practice experience, it is important to recognize that power is the ability of individuals, groups, and/or structures to attain a plan through authority, influence, or even force (Dobratz et al., 2012). This is important because it recognizes that power exists on the microlevel as well as the macrolevel. When we are thinking about social justice and human rights, we are particularly concerned with the ways that dominant power, individually or collectively, is exploited by privileged individuals or groups. Often within the guise of preserving societal interests, certain groups end up marginalized, scapegoated, and exploited for the benefit of more powerful groups.

■ Social Processes

Originating from sociology theories, social processes refer to the various patterns of social interactions in which individuals and groups interact and establish social relationships. Examples of different forms of social interaction include competition, cooperation, conflict, assimilation, exploitation, accommodation, and others (Ginsberg, 1956). While there are a large number of social processes (e.g., education, political, religious, economic), Ruhela

(2005) argues that within the vast array of social processes there are really only two categories they can all fall under:

1. Integrative, conjunctive, or associative processes: social processes that bring the individuals and groups together to produce unity among members of a group or society. These processes take the interests of all members into account. Examples of this are cooperation and accommodation.

▶ **Critical Thinking Questions**

Advancing social justice requires practitioner transparency, collaboration, and respectful curiosity and humility in work with clients. It also requires that you consider the social justice implications of your interactions with clients. In reflecting upon your work with clients, describe an experience in which you identified a potential abuse of power, either by yourself, someone else, or the agency as a whole.

1. What were your affective reactions to this experience?
2. What ethical principles and standards apply to this situation?
3. How would you approach or respond to this situation if it were to happen again?

2. Disintegrative, disjunctive, or dissociative processes: social processes that produce hatred, tension, and bring disagreement among the members of a group or society. Competition, rivalry, and conflict are the main disintegrative processes.

Oppression and discrimination are embedded in the complexity of ever-changing and constant social processes.

■ Conflict

Conflict is an important social process that is a large part of society as a whole. It is a codified form of struggle that is deliberate in its attempt to oppose or resist the will of others. Conflict is universal, ever-present, and personal. While there are a multitude of theories on the origin of conflict, we do know that social change can be a direct cause of conflict, and conflict can result in social change. Conflict may seem overwhelmingly negative, due to the fact that it resists cooperation and can cause chaos; however, conflict can perform positive functions as well. It can result in a redefinition of circumstances by the conflicting individuals or groups. Generally, the groups in conflict have to give up outdated value systems and accept new value systems at the end of the conflict—this may result in new efforts of cooperation and accommodation.

There is perhaps no better known example of using conflict in the pursuit of social justice than that documented in a passage from Martin Luther King, Jr.'s *Letter from Birmingham Jail* (1963, p. 5) in which King states:

> You express a great deal of anxiety over our willingness to break laws. This is certainly a legitimate concern. Since we so diligently urge people to obey the Supreme Court's decision of 1954 outlawing segregation in the public schools, it is rather strange and paradoxical to find us consciously breaking laws. One may well ask, "How can you advocate breaking some laws and obeying others?" The answer is found in the fact that there are two types of laws: there are just laws, and there are unjust laws. I would agree with St. Augustine that "An unjust law is no law at all."

■ Justice-Informed Practice

So often, social justice is considered something that a social worker simply carves time out for (for instance, on something like an advocacy day), as opposed to being a framework for practice. It can be challenging to envision a practice philosophy that infuses these theories in an effort to have a human rights and social justice focus in daily work as a social worker. For example, traditional assessments in clinical practice often focus on problems, which a social construction framework will remind you are culturally and relationally bound. This opens up the possibility of seemingly endless interpretations with no one interpretation as the truth. However, the social worker can utilize collaborative approaches to seek to understand the client's theory of problem, which helps the social worker toward collaboration solutions.

Within practice, these lenses provide the social context necessary to recognize the impacts of oppression and economic disadvantages experienced by clients. Social justice requires practitioner transparency, collaboration, and respectful curiosity and humility in work with clients. Major (2011) emphasizes how social constructions are well-suited for practice with families in the child welfare system due to their emphasis on contextual meanings—so often families are judged according to the same standards as those with significantly more opportunities and resources.

Harrison, VanDeusen, and Way (2016) identify three strategies for implementing a social justice–infused practice framework even in microlevel social work practice. The first of these is increased self-awareness. Bonnycastle (2011) provides a helpful continuum for examining this critical theme of the self-awareness needed for effective justice-focused micropractice. This includes moving from a simple recognition that discrimination is bad to a full confrontation of the privilege the social worker holds, and the impact of the social worker's practice in relation to the social locations of the clients served. This process involves overcoming the social worker's denial and struggle to change.

The second strategy discussed by Harrison et al. (2016) is justice-informed engagement, assessment, and intervention. Because of the person-in-environment perspective, social workers are better prepared to infuse justice through their micropractice skills. This includes a focus on enhancing individuals' economic, psychological, and social conditions through collaborative approaches. The quest of social justice within micropractice can be infused into many theoretical approaches and intervention models. Examples of this include client-centered and collaborative approaches; strengths-based and empowerment approaches; biopsychosocial assessment that includes historic and political bases for social constructions; and a focus on the ways in which oppression, discrimination, and historical trauma can contribute to the development of individual difficulties.

The final strategy discussed by Harrison et al. (2016) is justice-informed policy and systems advocacy. Social workers must infuse social justice into their microwork by addressing social and organizational policies that perpetuate inequities. Similarly, social workers work in concert with their client toward social and economic justice, as they may begin to strive to address inequities in their own lives as their awareness of such inequities arises in their therapeutic experience (Moradi, 2012).

Reisch and Garvin (2016) stress the importance of utilizing social justice–infused approaches especially as it relates to processes and outcomes. While you are unable to deeply scrutinize every action you take, every facial expression, every word decision, and so on, it benefits you to critically self-reflect on the implications of these social interactions with clients. You need to consider the social justice implications of such a process, including how each part of the process reveals information about power differentials; how the actions reflect considerations for the empowerment of clients and oppressive social conditions; how you have informed your work through critical self-reflection on sources of injustice; what roles you are fulfilling in your social interactions with clients and whether those are reflective of the needs and rights of others; and finally, a critical self-reflection of the potential of abuse of power.

▶ **Critical Thinking Questions**

Concepts of social constructions encourage us to be critically self-reflective of our language usage with clients.

1. What problematic language have you heard used with clients? Why was it problematic?
2. How could have the situation been approached in a justice-informed way?

In thinking about social justice implications in mezzo- and macrolevels of practice, it is important to relate the personal and the political. The concerns that clients bring into their work with you are not due solely to individual shortcomings, but also to unjust policies and practices that occur within agencies and the larger society. The driving force for social justice–infused social work practice is the skill of challenging inequalities, which creates opportunities for change. You must understand that not every mezzo- and macro-challenge you attempt will be successful, and the process of challenging oppressive practices and policies can be uncomfortable and tedious for you as you attempt to institute the challenge. The most effective and appropriate challenges need to be person-centered; use an egalitarian value approach; use empowerment approaches to assist individuals in reducing unjust policies; and, like microwork, focus on process and outcome (see also Case 4.1).

As an example of challenging a potential abuse of power, consider this experience. In your placement with Child Protection Services, one of your clients, a 17-year-old foster youth, was denied a request to begin attending an after-school church youth group. The agency made this decision based on some bullying experiences the client had faced. Upon reflection, you recognize that the agency you are working with may have misused their power under the guise of "protecting" the client from harm. You decide to challenge this decision by approaching your supervisor and explaining that you appreciate the agency's concern for the client's safety; however, you are concerned about the organization taking away the client's right to self-determination. You share with your supervisor the importance of this client, who is approaching the age of 18, having the opportunity to make his own decisions, and not be denied the opportunity to attend an activity that may benefit him greatly. Using the NASW *Code of Ethics* as your guide, you would be able to challenge this decision in a constructive way and assert the client's right to self-determination and his right to nonoppressive service delivery from the agency.

CASE 4.1	IT'S A SHAME, REALLY: APPLYING THE JUSTICE-INFUSED APPROACH IN SOCIAL WORK PRACTICE

Bianca is a senior bachelor of social work student completing her field placement at Prairie View Middle School, located in a low-income area in a mid-Atlantic state. Bianca was pulled aside by Mrs. Iverson, a science teacher at the school. Mrs. Iverson has concerns about a student named Andrea, a seventh grader who is having a difficult time turning in her homework, even though she is one of the top performing students on the tests and in-class activities. Mrs. Iverson has tried to reach out to Andrea's parents by phone and email but has never gotten a response. Mrs. Iverson tells Bianca that she is pretty sure that Andrea's parents are unengaged and are not supporting her in her education. Mrs. Iverson says, "It's a shame really. We see it time and again. Really bright kids with parents that just don't care about education."

Bianca decides to reach out to other teachers who have Andrea in their classes—they report a similar pattern. Bianca decides to reach out to the teachers of Andrea's younger siblings and finds out that they do not have the same issue with turning in their homework. In fact, neither of them had any missing assignments.

Perplexed, Bianca sets up an appointment to chat with Andrea. Andrea insists that she has simply "dropped the ball" and "will do better on her upcoming assignments." Bianca is unconvinced and discusses the issue with her supervisor. Her supervisor suggests a home visit. Bianca attempts to contact the parents but does not have any luck. She receives permission to drop by the home over the weekend along with her supervisor.

Bianca and her supervisor learn that Andrea's father and mother both work multiple part-time jobs to support their family, and neither of them get home until after the children are asleep. Andrea has taken on the role of caretaker for her two younger siblings, which includes assisting them on their studies and getting them dinner. Andrea simply does not have time to complete nightly homework on top of her other responsibilities.

Bianca knows that a justice-infused approach to this situation is one that advocates for equitable approaches that consider the impact of the economic conditions for the student. Bianca sets up a meeting with Mrs. Iverson, Andrea's other teachers, and her supervisors to brainstorm alternative approaches for Andrea's learning. However, she does not stop there—Bianca recognizes that this situation is likely happening to other students. Bianca wants to know, on an institutional level:

- What biases might be stopping teachers from trying to improve the situation for other students? How can these biases be addressed?
- What opportunities exist to create more equitable policies?
- Who needs to be at the table when brainstorming these solutions?

■ Anti-Oppressive Practice

AOP is another justice-infused framework for micro-, mezzo-, and macropractice (Baines & Benjamin, 2011). Anti-oppressive social work addresses social divisions and structural inequalities in the work done by clients and workers (Strier & Binyamin, 2014). AOP focuses on a collaborative worker/client relationship, reducing inequalities in client's lives and reducing social hierarchies in how social workers and clients work together (Dominelli, 1996). The rationale for AOP is that social work and social services need to promote nonhierarchical relationships between workers and clients and adopt structural and contextual views of clients' social problems (Baines & Benjamin, 2011). AOP recognizes inherent inequalities and the power differentials of marginalized people and groups of people.

AOP is similar to strengths-based approaches and cultural competency approaches. What sets it apart from other approaches is an analysis of power and identification of the processes by which power imbalances occur simultaneously at an individual, organizational, and systemic level, resulting in the exclusion of social groups (Wong & Yee, 2010). The power analysis recognizes that in all relationships, power imbalances based on age, abilities, class, ethnicity, employment status, gender, geographic location, race, religion, sexual orientation, and so on exist and that the power imbalances are socially constructed (Wong & Yee, 2010).

A second distinguishing feature of AOP is a focus on social location. Social location is a way of expressing the core of a person's existence in the social and political world. Social locations are the groups people are a part of because of their place or position in history and society. Individuals all have a social location that is based on the intersection of all of their identities and group memberships (see Case 4.2). These identities include race, gender, ability, religion, sexual orientation, social class, age, actual geographic location, and more. Our identity, how we see the world, and how we are able to move through the world are greatly influenced by our group memberships. Specific roles, rules, power, and the existence or lack of privilege are a result of these memberships as well.

CASE 4.2   PUTTING ON A SHOW: THE AOP FRAMEWORK

Sara is a senior bachelor of social work student completing an internship at a local family service agency in a small city on the West coast. The agency provides individual and family counseling services on a sliding fee scale. Mrs. J, a 28-year-old Latina female, has three children, Brenda, Tasha, and Darren. Mrs. J's children were removed due to substantiated charges of neglect. The children are aged 12, 6, and 3. The children stayed with Mrs. J's sister after they were removed from Mrs. J's care. Mrs. J has been battling a drug addiction and she was unable to care for her children—their home was found to be squalid. After the removal of the children, Mrs. J began her third attempt at completing a drug treatment program. She was successful and was reunified with the children 2 months earlier.

Mrs. J comes to weekly sessions and reports that she is doing well to maintain her sobriety. Mrs. J and I spend a significant amount of time in our work discussing coping strategies for her stressors. She reports that the majority of her stresses include the demands of parenting three children with little support and financial stressors.

In a field seminar, one of Sara's peers, who is placed at a local middle school, shared a situation from her field placement that she was conflicted about. She stated that a student named "Jane (not her real name)" was expressing concerns about the fact that her mother had begun using marijuana

(continued)

CASE 4.2

at home. The personal use of marijuana is legal in our state, but it is not allowed under the conditions of the reunification agreement. This concerned "Jane" because she and her younger siblings had just barely moved back in with their mom. "Jane" is very stressed that someone is going to find out and she and her siblings will be forced to move back in with her aunt.

Sara recognized the similarities in the story with her client Mrs. J and knows that Brenda attends the same school as "Jane." It is clear that the young woman being described by Sara's peer is Mrs. J's daughter.

1. Based on the information provided, what issues related to human rights and social, economic, and environmental justice can you identify within this case?
2. Consider the case example in terms of social location. From the information provided, what are the different social identities that Mrs. J may inhabit? How might these locations be influencing Mrs. J's construction of reality?
3. Similarly, think about Sara's social identities and social locations. How might they impact Sara's construction of reality?
4. What are some of the areas that Sara should focus her self-reflection on using a justice-infused lens?

Social location can be defined as the groups that people belong to because of their place or position in society and history. All people have a social location that is defined by their gender, race, social class, age, ability, religion, sexual orientation, geographic location, etc. (Wong & Yee, 2010, pp. 8–9)

Those who are in the dominant group maintain privilege over marginalized groups. Each one of us has a social location, which determines where we are placed on a continuum of privilege or marginalization in society. In our society, able-bodied persons, males, Caucasians, employed, middle/upper income, heterosexuals, U.S. citizens, college-educated, English-speaking and Christians have dominant social locations of privilege. On the other hand, persons with disabilities, females, ethnic and racial minorities, gay, lesbian, bisexual and transgender persons, non–college educated persons, non–English speaking, immigrants and non-Christians have nondominant social locations and belong to marginalized groups that are subject to the norms and values of the dominant group.

The concept of social identities is closely related to social location. Kirk and Okazawa-Rey (2010) define identity as how we define ourselves at any specific instance in time that is a process of growth, change, and renewal. Identity may seem fixed, but over the course of the life span, it is more fluid. An interplay of individual choices, particular life events, community recognition and expectations, societal categorization, classifications, and socialization all comes into play in identity formation. Most definitions of identity point to the connections between us as individuals, how we are perceived by other people, and classified by social institutions. "Classifying and labeling human beings, often according to real or assumed physical, biological, or genetic differences, is a way to distinguish who is included and who is excluded from a group, to ascribe particular characteristics" and to prescribe social locations (Kirk & Okazawa-Rey, 2010, p. 52). In sum, social location determines power and privilege and social identity determines how one defines oneself.

At the microlevel, AOP strives to change clients' perceptions about their social identity, social location, and power in the helping relationship. In essence, AOP work involves those who have privilege becoming allies of those who do not, by sharing power and creating authentic collaboration (Wong & Yee, 2010). The following four self-reflection questions help incorporate AOP into micro social work practice with clients:

- In all interactions/situations, have I thought about power, privilege, and social location and how it impacts my actions?

- Have I questioned/challenged dominant ways of thinking to transform power toward equity?

- Have I ensured the actions I have taken are equitable, collaborative, and power sharing? How can I measure this?

- If yes, how can I promote these AOP actions at an institutional or systemic level? If no, what do I need to do differently? (Wong & Yee, 2010, p. 11)

These four questions can help you not take power imbalances for granted and as unquestioned norms. They will also prompt you to figure out ways you can incorporate AOP into your social work practice. Conducting power analysis in all situations and with all client interactions is the key component of effective AOP.

At the mezzolevel, AOP strives to change the culture of human service organizations to reduce power imbalances, identify processes that create or promote power imbalances, and develop a collective mind-set that consciously challenges and questions the status quo or the norms of the organization that foster inequalities. Change at the organizational/social service level is needed to effectively address social

> ▶ **Critical Thinking Questions**
>
> Charlotte is a bachelor of social work intern placed with a housing agency. Many of the clients in low-income housing face housing discrimination. Charlotte knows it is her duty to advocate for her clients both inside her agency and outside.
>
> 1. What are the potential injustice-infused microlevel practice steps that Charlotte can take?
>
> 2. What are the mezzolevel justice-infused practice steps that Charlotte can take?

injustices and eliminate oppressive barriers caused by social location and power imbalances of marginalized groups. The institutions that foster the marginalization of oppressed groups must be changed if change is to occur. One way to begin to create organizational change is to conduct an anti-oppression assessment. Conducting an organizational assessment from the lens of anti-oppression will help identify organizational strengths as well as areas that need improvement (Ouvertes, 2013). Key areas to address in an anti-oppression assessment include an organization's

- Vision, mission, purpose
- Identity, culture, values

- Governance structure (board of directors, bylaws, and administrative structure)

- Program evaluation and accountability

- Finance and fund development

- Hiring practices and staffing patterns (recruitment, retention, and promotion)

- Human resources policies and procedures (training, working conditions, and complaints)

- Physical environment (accessibility, location, and decorations)

- Programs and services

- Work with community groups

- Internal communications

- External communications

In each area of the organization, assess policies and procedures in terms of power balances and oppression. Identify areas that need to be changed and create anti-oppression action steps to begin to implement the needed changes. For change to happen, it has to be an organization-wide effect with a collective will to make the organization less anti-oppressive. Often, this requires a system-wide culture change in the organization's policies and procedures and in the mind-set of the administrative, support staff, and frontline workers. Wong and Yee (2010) identified the following four recommendations for anti-oppression organizational change:

> ▶ **Critical Thinking Questions**
> Consider some of the conflicts that Charlotte may encounter as she engages in the multilevel justice-infused practice you identified.
> 1. How might she work through those conflicts?
> 2. Is it Charlotte's role to bring justice-informed perspectives to her colleagues? Why or why not?

- Anti-oppression requires a change of culture reflected in the agency's work along with a focus on changes in the outcomes of child welfare

- Anti-oppression should not be an add-on to the organization; it should be embedded in the values, mission, policies, processes, and practices in the organization at all levels

- Anti-oppression is both a process and an outcome where progress is measurable as demonstrated change within the organization's work

- Agencies need to create a culture of openness and safety when implementing anti-oppression work (pp. 16–17)

The scenario in Case 4.3 demonstrates the AOP approach for caring for a child with special needs whose mother is terminally ill.

CASE 4.3   WHAT WILL HAPPEN TO JUAN? THE AOP APPROACH IN SOCIAL WORK PRACTICE

Jose is a first-year master of social work student completing his foundation field placement at the Hispanic Advocacy Center located in a predominately Spanish speaking community. A community resident, Anna, contacted the center for help in dealing with Child Protective Services. Child Protective Services had received a referral regarding Anna and her 11-year-old son, Juan. According to the referral information, the mother was in the last stages of terminal brain cancer, often confined to a hospital bed. The cancer had metastasized throughout her body and was not responding to treatment. Anna was becoming increasingly forgetful as a result of the repeated chemotherapy and radiation treatments, was physically weak, and emotionally overwhelmed.

Juan had been born with Fragile X syndrome and was diagnosed with mental retardation that presented intellectual as well as developmental challenges. He was recently withdrawn from school as the family had initially planned to move to Oregon to live with Anna's sister. These plans fell through after Anna's sister found out that Anna was using marijuana to combat the side effects of her medical treatment. In addition, due to her forgetfulness, Anna often failed to give Juan his prescribed medications.

Anna and Juan were left with no money, little family support, and were living in a one-room apartment with a known drug dealer. The most recent report stated that Anna had left Juan with a friend from church with a small bag of clothes asking that he care for Juan until her condition improved. Both Anna and her friend were advised by Juan's case manager from the county's mental retardation department to have Juan placed in a residential program.

Anna had been placed in a children's home as a child and remained there until she finished high school, craving contact with her extended family. After ending a physically abusive relationship with Juan's father, Anna raised Juan as a single mother. She was adamant that Juan not be placed in an institution. Fearing involvement of Child Protective Services and the very real potential that Juan would be removed from her care, Anna dodged the caseworker's attempts at contact for several weeks. During this time, her physical condition continued to deteriorate, but she also began to gain the support of neighbors and community members who learned of her plight. An informal support network slowly embraced both Anna and Juan. Her friends encouraged her to contact the Hispanic Advocacy Center for help as it became clear that more formal plans would need to be made for Juan's ongoing care in the future.

Jose met with Anna, and together they agreed that she needed to meet with Child Protective Services. Jose's supervisor suggested that they request a family group conference to plan for Juan's future that included other service providers in Anna's life as well as her friends and neighbors. Anna remained fearful of the intentions of the formal agencies, but strongly desired to be involved in planning for her son's future and agreed to the meeting with Jose's support. The visiting nurse, hospice social worker, and her attending physician advised against the meeting, due to Anna's compromised condition, but after being assured that the meeting would be kept within a 2-hour limit, they reluctantly agreed.

(continued)

CASE 4.3

Going against protocol, the family group conference was held in the mother's apartment rather than on "neutral ground." The family group conference consisted of Anna, Juan's caseworker from the Mental Retardation Case Management Unit, Juan's school social worker, a priest from Anna's church, and the Child Protective Services case worker. Also in attendance were Jose, Carol, and four other neighbors. Additionally, Jose arranged for an attorney from Legal Aid to be present.

Anna was placed on the couch by her hospice social worker and made as comfortable as possible. Her breathing was heavy and the nurse prepared an oxygen mask. Prior to the family group conference, it was agreed that the purpose of the meeting would be to develop a plan to provide a safe and stable home for Juan when his mother would no longer be able to do so herself. Almost immediately, some of the service providers expressed their concern that the purpose was unrealistic and that Child Protective Services would need to take custody of Juan in order for any plan to be successful. Anna was assured that while this was an option, she and her "family" could also plan around other options.

Wanting to save time, the nurse and hospice worker requested that the group forego the discussion about strengths and move directly into a discussion about the "grave" concerns facing both Anna and Juan. Jose who was facilitating the meeting asked Anna her preference, and the group followed the conference protocol and initiated a discussion about strengths. Throughout the discussion, the nurse and hospice worker continued to point at their watches, offering Anna medication and suggesting that she lie down. At the same time, Anna became more involved in the conversation, moving to a sitting position and became increasingly engaged in the discussion. She expressed her surprise that in her "hopeless" situation, the group was able to identify over 30 strengths.

When the discussion turned to concerns, the service providers quickly interjected that the situation could be quickly resolved if Anna simply allowed Child Protective Services to assume custody of Juan. Anna reminded the providers that according to the model, she would be given the opportunity to express her concerns first. Two main themes surfaced. Anna acknowledged that she was often unable to care for Juan and herself and identified that persons would need to be available to assist on a daily basis. Second, and just as important, an identified guardian had not been established for Juan, and clear steps would need to be taken to accomplish this task. The group was shocked at her honesty as well as the passion with which she expressed herself.

Although the first phase of the meeting lasted well over an hour and a half, Anna remained committed to the process over the objections of her nurse. After listening to the resources available through all of the formal systems, the service providers, with the exception of the hospice worker, the nurse, and the Legal Aid attorney, left the room while Anna and her friends along with Jose met together for another hour to address the concerns. After several interruptions regarding the length of the meeting, Anna asked her nurse and hospice worker to leave the room and wait in the hallway with the other service providers.

Unexpectedly, a detailed plan emerged, including an emergency contact list and a 24-hour schedule of support to maintain Anna in her home. It was agreed that Juan would remain in the family home as long as possible. When the need arose to move him, a family friend was identified as

(continued)

CASE 4.3

his permanent caretaker. Respite caregivers were also identified. The plan included detailed steps outlining how the legal transfer of custody would take place. In presenting their plan, it became apparent that Anna and her family had addressed almost all of the potential problematic issues that could arise in the future regarding Juan's care. At the end of the meeting, Anna addressed the group, thanking them for the opportunity to plan for her son's future. Anna explained the importance of being able to admit to herself that she was no longer able to care for Juan independently, a fact she refused to acknowledge when questioned in the past.

A month after Anna's death, Juan's mental retardation case manager contacted Child Protective Services requesting that the agency assume custody of Juan. The case manager was referred to the family group conference plan, which was being implemented. Juan's well-being was assured by Carol and other members of the "family group" as previously arranged. Over the next several months, similar calls were received. Each concern was addressed by referring back to the plan that continued to work well for Juan.

1. What aspects of Jose's handling of Anna's case were consistent with an AOP approach?
2. What could have Jose done to strengthen his work with Anna in terms of AOP strategies?
3. What do you think would have happened to Anna and Juan if Jose and the Hispanic Advocacy Center had not been involved?
4. Compare the motivations and concerns of the nurse and hospice social worker with Jose's motivations and concerns? How are they similar? How do they differ?

■ Policy Issue

A policy issue associated with the human rights and social, economic, and environmental justice competency concerns recent changes to the U.S. immigration policy. Early in 2018, the Trump administration implemented a new "zero-tolerance" policy to prosecute immigrants attempting entry into the United States. Part of this policy requires that children—including babies and toddlers—be separated from their parents; children are taken into temporary custody while their parents are jailed or deported. In many cases, neither party is informed of the whereabouts of the other—they are simply torn apart and taken to undisclosed locations (Center for the Study of Social Policy, 2018, para. 1).

Between May 5 and June 9 in 2018, over 2,300 children were separated from their parents at the United States–Mexican border and placed in detention centers (Huffington Post, 2018). The children have been held in over 100 facilities scattered over 17 states. Children get their own case in immigration court and are entitled to a full hearing by an immigration judge, a process that can take months. Their parents are either prosecuted or deported separately. Often the parents were deported without their children.

This policy is utterly inhumane both for the immediate pain that it inflicts on the families and also for the long-term harm it will cause for the children. Research makes clear that the experiences of traumatic events—like being forcibly separated from your parent, thrown into a makeshift encampment, and given zero information about your situation or your family's whereabouts—can have lifelong negative consequences. (Center for the Study of Social Policy, 2018, para. 2)

The U.S. practice of separating families through detention and deportation is at odds with its obligations under the International Covenant on Civil and Political Rights (ICCPR), which recognizes "family as the natural and fundamental group unit of society" and ensures protection of family rights and family unity. Its failure to consider the interests of the children of those facing deportation violates the right of the child to special protection, as guaranteed by the Convention on the Rights of the Child (CRC; Immigrant Defense Project, 2018).

A 2018 Department of Homeland Security (DHS) report on the "zero-tolerance" policy concluded that:

> ▶ **Critical Thinking Questions**
> 1. Which NASW ethical principles and standards conflict with the "zero-tolerance" policy?
> 2. How does the "zero-tolerance" policy fit with your personal values regarding immigration?
> 3. As a social worker, what could you do to help change U.S. immigration policy?

- The DHS was not fully prepared to implement the policy or deal with its after-effects.

- Customs and Border Protection (CBP) authorities broke the law and detained children for illegal amounts of time at facilities meant for short-term holding.

- A lack of communication between government agencies rendered officials unable to locate children's parents when they sought to reunite them.

- Parents were given misinformation about how (and if) they could reunite with their children.

- Policies at overwhelmed official ports of entry compelled many asylum seekers to attempt illegal border crossings (Office of the Inspector General, 2018).

The Trump Administration's zero-tolerance policy resulted in the United States breaking its own laws and in violating international human rights treaties. After a period of about 2 months, President Trump signed an executive order to end the practice of separating immigrant children from their parents. His compromise was to detain entire families together. U.S. immigration policies and enforcement procedures continue to raise serious concerns about the violation of basic human rights of immigrants and those seeking asylum.

■ Summary

As we already know, several of the issues facing your clients are rooted in far-reaching social, political, economic, and environmental conditions. Simultaneously, much of the assistance we as social workers are able to provide is done at an individual level. We must resist the urge to assume that the majority of problems are personal rather than a reflection of wider societal and structural problems. This chapter focused on different concepts related to injustices at multiple levels. First, conceptual and theoretical concepts around social justice were explored.

This section focused on how social justice calls for the fair and unbiased treatment of all individuals, eradication of discriminatory practices and institutionalized oppression, and establishment of equality for members of historically marginalized and oppressed groups.

Competency 3 focuses on advancing human rights and social, economic, and environmental justice. As a social worker, you are trained to keep the person-in-environment perspective as you engage with your clients. This uniquely positions you to maintain a justice-informed framework in your work. You must move beyond the understanding that discrimination is bad and move toward a full confrontation of your own power and privilege, and how it impacts the clients you wish to serve. You are also expected to recognize the impacts of oppression and economic disadvantages experienced by clients. Social justice requires practitioner transparency, collaboration, and respectful curiosity and humility in work with clients. An understanding that social constructions are well-suited for justice-informed practice due to their emphasis on contextual meanings is vital. It helps you to identify ways in which individuals, families, and groups are judged on unbalanced standards. Advancing human rights and social justice is an ongoing, intentional process that is actively infused in every aspect of practice, not simply something that the social worker does on the side with their free time.

The final section of this chapter explored strategies for you to infuse a justice lens into your practice in the field. All of these strategies require intentional, critical self-reflection on the choices you make, the language you use, and the ways you, and others, are potentially abusing your power. Multiple theoretical frameworks and intervention models lend themselves to justice-informed practice if you are intentional about applying them in such a way.

CASE SUMMARY   "UNDOCUMENTED AND HOMELESS"

Practice Setting Description

Jackie is a first-year master of social work student completing an internship at an inner-city family service agency in the southwest. The agency is located in a section of the city that has a high crime rate, gang activity, and failing schools. The area has a diverse population with a large number of immigrants from Central and South America and a substantial African American population. The agency provides individual and family counseling services on a sliding fee scale. The agency also runs a number of educational and treatment groups as well as a temporary shelter for women and their children. Jackie has been assigned to work with the women and their children in the shelter. Her primary tasks are to provide concrete services and supportive counseling to the shelter residents.

Background Information

Elicia T and her daughter, Maria, are undocumented immigrants from Mexico. They have been in the United States for 5 years. Elicia and Maria fled to the area from another southwestern city to escape her abusive husband approximately 2 months ago. Elicia is 25 years old and Maria 8 years old. Elicia has a 2-year-old daughter, Sarah, who was placed in foster care because of suspected abuse in

(continued)

CASE SUMMARY

the home. Sarah is in a foster home in a small rural community in the state hundreds of miles from Elicia's current residence. Since moving to the area, Maria has not been attending school.

Elicia and Maria are currently residing in the agency's temporary shelter for families. They have been at the shelter for 2 weeks, and the agency has a 90-day limit. It is viewed as temporary housing, and the residents are only allowed to stay for 3 months. Prior to arriving at the shelter, Elicia and Maria were homeless and living on the streets.

Elicia is a high-school dropout and was a stay-at-home mother prior to leaving her husband and moving to a different part of the state. She chose to move there because she has two female cousins living in the area who are also undocumented immigrants. Elicia's native language is Spanish. She speaks some English but is not as comfortable speaking in English. Her English comprehension appears to be good. Maria speaks both English and Spanish well. When communicating with the staff, Maria acts as Elicia's interpreter since none of the staff at the shelter speak Spanish.

Maria appears to be behind academically. She struggles reading simple children's books written in English. It is unknown if her ability to read in Spanish is better than her English reading skills.

Other than her two cousins, Elicia has no other sources of support in the community. Her cousins have young families and limited resources but are well established and connected to a Latino community in the city and the local Catholic church. Her cousins refused to let Elicia and Maria live with them while she was trying to find her own place and a job. They stated that they did not have enough room and are concerned they would get in trouble with their landlord if it was found out that they were letting people stay with them. They sent her to the local church for help and she was given the address for the agency's shelter by the priest.

Elicia has been looking for housing in the Latino community. The housing market is tight with limited options, and she has been unable to find anything that she could possibly afford. The only affordable housing she found was a room in a rundown motel that rents by the hour or by the month. It is in an area of town known for drug dealing and sex work.

On arrival in the community, Elicia found occasional work for a house cleaning company. The company hires undocumented workers, pays them very low cash wages, and threatens to turn them in to Immigration and Customs Enforcement (ICE) if they complain. The job bosses also exploit their female workers sexually, threatening to turn them in if they do not comply. Elicia was fearful about applying for other jobs because of her illegal status. She considered turning to sex work to be able to take care of her children, but her Catholic upbringing and thoughts of how doing so would shame her family have kept her from doing so. She is in constant fear of being detained, separated from her children, and having them placed in foster care. She is also afraid that she will end up homeless again and forced to live on the streets or return to her abusive husband.

Elicia is extremely reluctant to sign up for any federally funded services, even those that she and her children are entitled to receiving. On the suggestion that she enroll for supplemental food through SNAP, Elicia became nervous and refused as she has heard that participation in SNAP services, and others like them, would draw the attention of ICE, and she had heard stories on the news of individuals being deported after signing up for such programs.

(continued)

CASE SUMMARY

Presenting Problems

Elicia and her children are facing multiple obstacles. They need to find permanent, affordable housing and a job that pays enough to cover her housing and living expenses. In addition, Maria needs to be enrolled in school. Elicia also wants to regain custody of her youngest daughter in foster care.

Additionally, Elicia is experiencing an immense amount of stress, anxiety, and possibly post-traumatic stress disorder (PTSD). She described an instance where she could not calm down her breathing, and she felt lightheaded. She is very fearful of men and tries to avoid all contact with men in the community. She reports difficulty sleeping at night and feeling exhausted most of the time.

She is concerned about Maria. She has started acting out at the shelter, getting into fights with the other children, disobeying her mother, and being disrespectful and defiant to the staff and other adults. Elicia and Maria fight frequently, and when Elicia tries to discipline Maria, she throws a temper tantrum until Elicia gives up.

Elicia has many strengths. She had the strength to leave her abusive husband and move to a different city. She loves her daughters. She wants desperately to keep Maria with her and hopes to have Sarah returned to her custody. She is resilient and has managed to survive and keep her daughter safe despite not having a place to stay, a job, and a limited support network. Additionally, Elicia is highly motivated to find her own accommodations and support her children.

■ Discussion Questions

1. From the perspective of the Universal Declaration of Human Rights, what human rights violations has Elicia experienced?

2. What is Elicia's social location? How does her social location compare to Jackie's?

3. What can Jackie do to reduce the power differential between her and Elicia?

4. What form of discrimination has Elicia faced and what possible effects have they had on her ability to find permanent housing and employment?

5. How has discrimination impacted Elicia's mental health?

■ References

American Civil Liberties Union. (2017). *Racial profiling: Definition.* Retrieved from https://www.aclu.org/other/racial-profiling-definition

Baines, D., & Benjamin, A. (Eds.). (2011). *Doing anti-oppressive practice: Social justice social work* (2nd ed.). Nova Scotia, Canada: Fernwood Publishing.

Barsky, A. E. (2010). *Ethics and values in social work: An integrated approach for a comprehensive curriculum.* New York, NY: Oxford University Press.

Bonilla-Silva, E. (2003). "New racism," color-blind racism, and the future of whiteness in America. In A. W. Doane & E. Bonilla-Silva (Eds.), *White out: The continuing significance of racism.* New York, NY: Routledge Taylor & Francis.

Bonnycastle, C. R. (2011). Social justice along a continuum: A relational illustrative model. *Social Service Review, 85*, 267–295. doi:10.1086/660703

Caputo, R. K. (2002). Social justice, the ethics of care, and market economies. *Families in Society, 83*, 355–364. doi:10.1606/1044-3894.10

Center for the Study of Social Policy. (June 19, 2018). *Zero tolerance immigration policy is a cruel and immoral human rights violation*. Retrieved from https://cssp.org/about-us/connect/press-room/zero-tolerance-immigration-policy-is-a-cruel-and-immoral-human-rights-violation

Chakraborti, N., & Garland, J. (2009). *Hate Crime: Impact, Causes and Responses*. London, UK: SAGE Publications.

Dobratz, B., Waldner, L., & Buzzell, T. L. (2012). *Power, politics, and society: An introduction to political sociology*. Boston, MA: Pearson.

Dominelli, L. (1996). Deprofessionalizing social work: Anti-oppressive practice, competencies and postmodernism. *British Journal of Social Work, 26*, 153–175. doi:10.1093/oxfordjournals.bjsw.a011077

Finn, J. L., & Jacobson, M. (2017). *What is social justice?* Oxford University Press. Retrieved from https://blog.oup.com/2017/03/what-is-social-justice

Ginsberg, M. (1956). *On the Diversity of Morals*. London, UK: William Heinemann.

Harrison, J., VanDeusen, K., & Way, I. (2016). Embedding social justice within micro social work curricula. *Smith College Studies in Social Work, 86*(3), 258–273. doi:10.1080/00377317.2016.1191802

Huffington Post. (June 20, 2018). *Over 2,300 children separated from parents at U.S.-Mexican Border from May 5 to June 9*. Retrieved from https://www.huffingtonpost.com/entry/family-separation-at-border-reunification-process_us_5b29d9cfe4b05d6c16c8c48e

Immigrant Defense Project. (2018). *Deportation and human rights*. Retrieved from https://www.immigrantdefenseproject.org/issue-brief-deportation-and-human-rights

Johnson, A. (2006). *Privilege, power, and difference*. New York, NY: McGraw-Hill.

Jung, P. B., & Smith, R. F. (1993). *Heterosexism: An ethical challenge*. Albany, NY: State University of New York Press.

Kagan, C., & Burton, M. (2005). Marginalization. In G. Nelson & I. Prillenltensky (Eds.), *Community psychology: In pursuit of liberation and well-being* (pp. 292–308). New York, NY: Palgrave.

Kirk, G., & Okazawa-Rey, M. (2010). Living in a globalizing world. In G. Kirk & M. Okazawa-Rey (Eds.), *Women's lives: Multicultural perspectives* (pp. 371–392). New York, NY: McGraw-Hill.

Lott, B., & Bullock, H. E. (2007). *Psychology and economic injustice: Personal, professional, and political intersections*. Washington, DC: American Psychological Association.

Major, D. R. (2011). We mostly played whatever she chose. In S. Witkin (Ed.), *Social constructions and social work practice: Interpretations and innovations*. New York, NY: Columbia University Press.

Maslow, A. H. (1943). A theory of human motivation. *Psychological Review, 50*(4), 370–396. doi:10.1037/h0054346

McCormick, P. (2003). Whose justice? An examination of nine models of justice. *Social Thought, 22*(2/3), 7–25. doi:10.1080/15426432.2003.9960338

Miller, D. (1976). *Social justice*. Oxford, UK: Clarendon Press.

Moradi, B. (2012). Feminist social justice orientation: An indicator of optimal functioning? *The Counseling Psychologist, 40*(8), 1133–1148. doi:10.1177/0011000012439612

Moses, A. E. (1982). Counseling lesbian women and gay men. St. Louis, MO: The C.V. Mosby Company.

National Association of Social Workers. (2017). *Code of ethics*. Silver Spring, MD: National Association of Social Workers. Retrieved from http://www.socialworkers.org

Nozick, R. (1974). *Anarchy, state, and utopia*. New York, NY: Basic Books.

Office of the Inspector General. (2018). *Special review - Initial observations regarding family separation issues under the zero tolerance policy*. Department of Homeland Security. Retrieved from https://www.oig.dhs.gov/sites/default/files/assets/2018-10/OIG-18-84-Sep18.pdf

Ouvertes, P. (2013). Developing an anti-oppressive policy: Some things to keep in mind. Center for Community Organizations. Retrieved from https://coco-net.org/wp-content/uploads/2013/08/Anti-Oppression-Policy-for-Web.pdf

Park, H., & Mykhyalyshyn, I. (2016). L.G.B.T. People Are More Likely to Be Targets of Hate Crimes Than Any Other Minority Group. *The New York Times*. Retrieved from https://www.nytimes.com/interactive/2016/06/16/us/hate-crimes-against-lgbt.html

Piven, F. F., & Cloward, R. (2005). Rulemaking, rulebreaking, and power. In T. Janoski, R. Alford, A. Hicks, & M. Schwartz (Eds.), *Handbook of political sociology*. New York, NY: Cambridge University Press.

Rawls, J. (1971). *A theory of justice* (1st ed.). Cambridge, MA: Harvard University Press.

Rawls, J. (2001). *Justice as fairness: A restatement*. Cambridge, MA: Belknap Press of Harvard University Press.

Reichert, E. (2003). *Social work and human rights: A foundation for policy and practice*. New York, NY: Columbia University Press.

Reisch, M. (1998). *Economic globalization and the future of the welfare state. Welfare reform and social justice visiting scholars program*. Ann Arbor, MI: The University of Michigan School of Social Work.

Reisch, M. (2002). Defining justice in a socially unjust world. *Families in Society: The Journal of Contemporary Social Services, 83*, 343–354. doi:10.1606/1044-3894.17

Reisch, M., & Garvin, C. D. (2016). *Social work and social justice: Concepts, challenges, and strategies*. New York, NY: Oxford University Press.

Ruhela, S. P. (2005). *Introduction to sociology*. Gurgaon, India: Shubhi Publications.

Siddique, H., & Laughland, O. (2017). Charlottesville: United Nations warns US over "alarming" racism. *The Guardian*. Retrieved from https://www.theguardian.com/world/2017/aug/23/charlottesville-un-committee-warns-us-over-rise-of-racism

Smith, L., Foley, P. F., & Chaney, M. P. (2008). Addressing classism, ableism, and heterosexism in counselor education. *Journal of Counseling & Development, 86*, 303–309. doi:10.1002/j.1556-6678.2008.tb00513.x

Stone, C., Trisi, D., Sherman, A., & Taylor, R. (2018). *A guide to statistics on historical trends in income inequality*. Center on Budget and Policy Priorities. Retrieved from https://www.cbpp.org/research/poverty-and-inequality/a-guide-to-statistics-on-historical-trends-in-income-inequality

Strier, R. S., & Binyamin, S. (2014). Introducing anti-oppressive social work practices in public services: Rhetoric to practice. *British Journal of Social Work, 44*, 2095–2112. doi:10.1093/bjsw/bct049

Sue, D. W., Capodilupo, C. M., Torino, G. C., Bucceri, J. M., Holder, A. M. B., Nadal, K. L., & Esquilin, M. (2007). Racial microaggressions in everyday life: Implications for clinical practice. *American Psychologist, 62*, 271–286. doi:10.1037/0003-066X.62.4.271

Sue, D. W., & Sue, D. (2012). *Counseling the culturally diverse: Theory and Practice*. Hoboken, NJ: Wiley.

Thomas, A. J., & Schwartzbaum, S. (2017). *Culture and identity: Life stories for counselors and therapists*. Los Angeles, CA: Sage Publications.

United Nations. (2018a). *The universal declaration of human rights*. Retrieved from http://www.un.org/en/universal-declaration-human-rights

United Nations. (2018b). *The universal declaration of human rights 70th anniversary*. Retrieved from http://www.standup4humanrights.org/layout/files/proposals/UDHR70-MediaFactSheet.pdf

United Nations Office on Drugs and Crime. (2009). *Global report on trafficking in persons*. Retrieved from http://www.unodc.org/documents/Global_Report_on_TIP.pdf

Van Soest, D. (1995). *Incorporating peace and social justice into the social work curriculum*. Washington, DC: National Association of Social Workers.

Wakefield, J. C. (1988). Psychotherapy, distributive justice, and social work. II: Psychotherapy and the pursuit of justice. *Social Service Review, 62*, 353–382. doi:10.1086/644555

Wong, H., & Yee, J. Y. (2010). *An anti-oppressive framework for child welfare in Ontario*. Ontario Child Welfare Anti-Oppression Roundtable. Retrieved from http://www.oacas.org/wp-content/uploads/2017/01/Framework.pdf

Young, I. M. (1990). *Justice and the politics of difference*. Princeton, NJ: Princeton University Press.

Young, I. M. (2001). Equality for whom? Social groups and judgment of injustice. *The Journal of Political Philosophy, 9*(1), 1–18. doi:10.1111/1467-9760.00115

II

MICRO–SOCIAL WORK PRACTICE COMPETENCIES

ENGAGEMENT AND SOCIAL WORK PRACTICE

Nicole is a master of social work at a large children's hospital. She works in the emergency department. Nicole is often required to consult on cases for a variety of reasons. Sometimes, Nicole is paged to a room without knowing why she was paged. Today she was paged by the charge nurse to assist a family in identifying community resources. When Nicole entered the room, she saw the patient, Katie, a 6-year-old in the bed and her parents Joe and Lois by her side.

In order for Nicole to do her job effectively, she must engage with the clients quickly. As a hospital social worker, she must often build rapport quickly to work on the issues at hand. Nicole is also mindful that she must not only engage with the child but the parents as well. Engagement will vary for both as strategies to engage with children are different than strategies to engage with adults.

When she walks into the room, she warmly greets Katie with a smile and a hello and then extends her hand to introduce herself to Joe and Lisa. Nicole explains to the family that she is a social worker and she has been called in to assist the family in locating some resources. She shares that she is willing to help but asks if it would be okay for her to ask a few questions in order to be able to help them better. The family is agreeable, and Nicole can begin gathering information to start the helping process.

LEARNING OBJECTIVES

This chapter focuses on theories and skills related to Council on Social Work Education (CSWE, 2015) Competency 6, which asserts that social workers must be aware of how engagement influences the helping relationship throughout the helping process from the beginning to the end. Engagement is not simply a stage in the helping process that can be accomplished and then forgotten. Rather, good engagement is an ongoing process that evolves throughout the helping process, regardless of the level of practice. To engage with means to interact, participate, or become involved with. Social workers engage within their practice often in order to promote change. This competency requires social workers to recognize and be able to utilize theories that are related to human behavior and the social environment. Furthermore, social workers should be mindful of how their use of self can influence their ability to engage with clients at all levels of practice. Last, this competency asserts that social workers find worth and engage in collaboration and inter-professional relationships. Engagement across professions on behalf of client populations is often critical and necessary for client success. By the end of this chapter, you will be able to:

1. Identify and describe the National Association of Social Workers (NASW) principles and standards that relate to engagement
2. Describe how policy can influence engagement
3. Identify commonalities and differences related to engagement with differing client systems
4. Describe the stages of the helping process
5. Identify strategies that promote engagement and build relationships
6. Identify benefits and challenges to collaboration

■ Competency 6: Engage With Individuals, Families, Groups, Organizations, and Communities

Social workers understand that engagement is an ongoing component of the dynamic and interactive process of social work practice with, and on behalf of, diverse individuals, families, groups, organizations, and communities. Social workers value the importance of human relationships. Social workers understand theories of human behavior and the social environment, and critically evaluate and apply this knowledge to facilitate engagement with clients and constituencies, including individuals, families, groups, organizations, and communities. Social workers understand strategies to engage diverse clients and constituencies to advance practice effectiveness. They understand how their personal experiences and affective reactions may impact their ability to effectively engage with diverse clients and constituencies. Social workers value principles of relationship building and interprofessional collaboration to facilitate engagement with clients, constituencies, and other professionals as appropriate. Social workers:

- Apply knowledge of human behavior and the social environment, person-in-environment, and other multidisciplinary theoretical frameworks to engage with clients and constituencies
- Use empathy, reflection, and interpersonal skills to effectively engage diverse clients and constituencies

■ National Association of Social Workers (NASW) *Code of Ethics*

There are two ethical principles within the NASW *Code of Ethics* (2017) that closely relate to the concept of engagement. The principles of *importance of human relationships* and *dignity and worth of the individual* both illustrate the importance and necessity of engagement throughout the helping process (NASW, 2017). There are several ethical standards that relate to engagement including commitment to clients, informed consent, conflict of interests, privacy, and confidentiality. The NASW *Code of Ethics* is available online (www.socialworkers .org/About/Ethics/Code-of-Ethics/Code-of-Ethics-English).

The practice of social work is not something that a social worker does *to* or *for* another; rather, it is a collaborative process where the worker engages *with* the client to bring about change. In order to be able to effectively work with clients, social workers must be mindful of their ability to utilize engagement as a means to support the helping relationship.

Every single person has an inherent dignity and worth, and as a result, social workers treat every person as such. Social workers are called upon to treat all people with respect and dignity. When truly engaging with another, the social worker must first recognize the client's strengths, including his or her dignity and worth, in order to observe more clearly any concerns or problems.

Social workers are tasked with holding the needs of their clients as an utmost priority. Within the practice of social work, the work is not and should not be about social workers. Rather, the focus should always be on clients and what would best serve their needs at the present time. In order to demonstrate this commitment to the well-being of clients, social workers can be engaged and present with clients throughout all interactions. Engagement is not a task that can be completed in the first session; rather, successful engagement is an ongoing process that requires reflection and commitment on behalf of the social worker.

In order to ensure that the helping relationship is a true relationship between the social worker and the client, there must be informed consent. It is the responsibility of the social worker to ensure that the client is made aware of the purpose of his or her services, risks, limits, costs, and alternatives prior to starting (NASW, 2017). The social worker is tasked with sharing this information with the client in a clear and understandable way. Ensuring informed consent occurs early on during the process of engagement to ensure that the client is aware of his or her rights.

In order to ensure ethical practice, social workers should attempt to avoid dual relationships when possible. Dual relationships occur when the social worker and client have another relationship outside of the helping relationship. For example, a dual relationship would be if a social worker hired a client to do maintenance on his or her home. First, the social worker and client have a helping relationship; second, the social worker and client also have a business relationship in the form of the social worker hiring the client. Dual relationships often cause boundary confusion and could harm the client. The social worker is charged with establishing and maintaining boundaries. When engaging with clients, the social worker should be friendly; however, it is beyond the scope of ethical practice for social workers to become friends with their clients. Due to the work that we do as social workers, it is understandable that we as social workers must be mindful of boundaries throughout care. Also, when there is boundary confusion on the part of the client—maybe the client invites you to an event—it is the responsibility of the social worker to clarify his or her role and the purpose of their interactions. In situations such as this, when the social worker has well-established engagement with the client, conversations such as these often go easier.

Clients have a right to privacy and confidentiality. There are laws that have been established with the purpose of keeping personal information about clients private. Not only do social workers need to safeguard the information they have about their clients, they should also be respectful of the clients' rights to privacy.

Theories Related to Engagement

There are a variety of theories that can inform the dynamic process of engagement. Theories can provide a framework for understanding how to engage with client systems and can also provide insights into the benefits and potential barriers related to engagement. As with all aspects of social work practice, it is important to have a theoretical orientation and basis for your work with clients. The following theories can serve to provide you with a foundation to engage with clients.

Psychodynamic Theories

It is essential to consider theories of human behavior in order to effectively engage with client systems. The human experience is complex. As a result, it is necessary to draw upon a theoretical understanding of human behavior in order to assist you in your social work practice. Related to engagement, we consider attachment theory and personality theory.

Attachment Theory

Attachment is essential to the human experience. Humans are social animals. Unlike some species, humans must connect with others in order to continue to survive. Attachment refers to the connection that we have with other people; more specifically, we can explore the level of attachment or quality of the connection with others.

Many theories address attachments as they relate to the overall healthy development of young children. Brisch (2012) reports that attachment theory focuses on "the fundamental early influences on the emotional development of the child and attempts to explain the development of and changes in strong emotional attachments between individuals throughout the life cycle" (p. 14). Attachments serve to provide young children with a framework for understanding how the environment around them functions. As early as infancy, through dyadic relationships, children are able to produce "some sort of pattern out of chaos" (Winnicott, 1988).

The quality of the attachment need not be perfect, but rather a "good enough" child-rearing is sufficient to aid in healthy psychological development (Winnicott, 1988). The child does not need a perfect attachment, but rather a usually reliable and ready caregiver who is generally responsive to the needs of the child is a sufficient connection.

From these early attachments, children can begin to explore their worlds. Bowlby (1988) asserts that a secure base is necessary for children so that they can fully experience their world all the while knowing on their return to their caregiver:

> He will be welcomed when he gets there, nourished physically and emotionally, comforted when distressed, reassured if frightened. In essence this role is one of being available, ready to respond when called upon to encourage and perhaps assist, but to intervene actively when necessary. (p. 11)

Bowlby (1988) suggests that "attachment behavior is any form of behavior in a person attaining or maintaining proximity to some other clearly identified individual who is conceived as better able to cope with the world" (pp. 26–27). Attachment behaviors are present not only in children but in adolescents and adults of both genders as well (Bowlby, 1988). Bowlby (1988) asserts that attachment behaviors are evident "throughout the life cycle" especially during difficult times (p. 27).

The need for attachment is essential to the human experience; Bowlby (1988) puts forth "since it is seen in virtually all human beings (though in varying patterns), it is regarded as an integral part of human nature and one we share (to a varying extent) with members of other species" (p. 27). These healthy and appropriate attachments are necessary in life to safeguard the individual against negative experiences and risk factors that they may experience during their lifetime. Much research concurs that supportive relationships or attachments can serve as a buffer to life stress (Fraser, Kirby, & Smokowski, 2004).

Though the early roots of attachment theory focused on the relationship between mother and child, there is much evidence that other attachments such as fathers, grandparent-caregivers, and other stable adult models are just as beneficial to developing a healthy attachment style (Daniel & Taylor, 2001; Fraser et al., 2004). Uri Bronfenbrenner, a psychologist and key leader in the development of the national Head Start program, once stated that all children need just one person who is insanely in love with them. It is through this one quality attachment, this secure base, that individuals are given the resources and esteem to grow and flourish into thriving, productive, and well-adjusted resilient beings. The presence of another individual serves an instinctual human need to seek protection (Bowlby, 1988). The presence of simply one secure attachment can serve as a significant protective factor (Brisch, 2012).

Connections and attachments can be present at varying levels. Individuals can feel connected to another individual at the microlevel, or connected as a family at the mezzolevel, or even still connected to a community or culture at the macrolevel. Moreover, attachments do not exist within vacuums; but rather, they are often embedded within one another (Cain, 2006). For example, a parent–child attachment does not exist in isolation; rather, it exists within the context of a family system, a community system, and so on. The perceived quality of the connection and the meaning assigned to the attachment are much more important than the level at which the connection exists. Fraser et al. (2004) set forth that:

> In the middle part of the last century, experts interested in the genesis of social and health problems began to focus on the relationship between adversity and adaptation. Some scholars, for example, placed great emphasis on parent–child attachment, and disrupted attachments were thought to contribute to many kinds of childhood disorders. More recently, attention has shifted from, or perhaps a better word would be "broadened," to consider the characteristics of family life, schools, neighborhoods as factors that contribute to the development of social and health problems. (p. 13)

Attachment theory informed engagement with client systems by providing the social worker with a basis for understanding where the client is starting from. Within social work practice, it is commonly stated that we must "start where the client is" and in order to be able to do that, we need a theoretical foundation to understand how the person has been shaped into the who they are presentingcurrently. As with any theoretical orientation, we must be careful of overgeneralizations; however, the tenets of the theory allow us to formulate a case assessment and consider appropriate engagement styles.

■ Humanistic Theory

Humanistic theory centers around the person with whom you are engaging. Social work practice calls upon us to meet clients where they are in order to help them reach where they want to be. Social work has a long history of practice based on individualized humanistic principles including a nonjudgmental approach and an emphasis on strengths rather than on dysfunction (Misca & Unwin, 2016). A humanistic approach considers the "full range of human experiences and values human dignity" (Lonn & Dantzler, 2017, p. 65).

Maslow's Theory of Motivation

Maslow (1962) created a theory of motivation that was informed by a hierarchy of needs. Maslow set forth that for one to be able to meet goals and fulfill personal needs, there was a systematic (hierarchical) approach to do so (see Figure 5.1). Maslow ranked needs from the most basic to higher levels. In order for a person to be able to achieve success at a higher level need, all of the previous (lower level) needs had to be addressed first. For example, before someone could reach the highest level (self-actualization) where he or she could engage in such tasks as being creative and problem-solving, that person must first achieve the basic levels of feeling safe and having physiological needs for food and water met. At each level of need, individuals are motivated to have their needs meet; then once their need is met at that level, they can be motivated by the higher level need (Fisher, 2009).

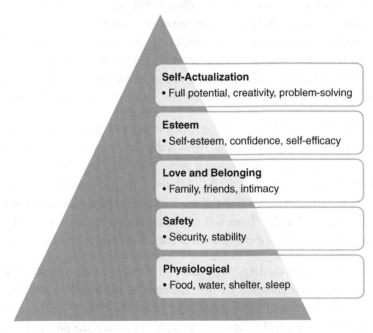

FIGURE 5.1 Maslow's hierarchy of needs.

During engagement, social workers should consider the client's current level of motivation and where he or she is regarding the hierarchy of needs. Considering where the client is can also serve as a means to address current strengths, in the form of currently accomplished or met needs, as well as areas for attention, in the form of the unmet needs.

Personality Theory and Client-Centered Therapy

Personality theory provides a humanistic approach to understanding the person. Carl Rogers believed that in order to thrive within their environments, people needed genuineness, acceptance, and empathy. Furthermore, he believe that people possessed the inner resources necessary to confront any challenges or problems that they were facing. Trust was also crucial to his theory. Rogers felt:

> Trust in the subjective experience and the belief in the essential trustworthiness of human nature went hand in hand. He discovered in the early years of his clinical practice that when he was able to commit himself to a deep understanding of his client's subjective world and was perceived as doing so by the client, then almost invariably the client would begin to behave in ways which were positive and forward moving. (Thorne et al., 2013, p. 26)

Genuineness refers to being authentic. When people are authentic, they are acting as their real self, not pretending or projecting to be viewed as anything other than who they are. Genuineness relates to being present, honest, and kind.

▶ **Critical Thinking Question**

As a social worker, how could you demonstrate genuineness, acceptance, and empathy toward the clients you are working with?

Acceptance, also considered unconditional positive regard, is the action of agreement with a client without confrontation. Individuals based on previous experiences often socially learned conditions of worth. The concept of unconditional positive regard is a counter to learned conditions of acceptance. Rather, regardless of performance or behavior, the person is accepted as is, simply for just being himself or herself.

Empathy, or the process of feeling with, is something that is often emphasized within social work practice. At the roots of empathy is compassion. Compassion is a fellow feeling or shared feeling. Empathy allows the social worker to demonstrate to the client a fellow feeling or understanding of what the client is expressing.

Self-concept is a central aspect of personality theory. Self-concept refers to the collective set of organized thoughts one has regarding his or her self. Related to this are self-esteem, self-image, and the ideal self. All of these are aspects of the person's internal representation of himself or herself.

Utilizing personality theory, or a Rogerian approach, can enhance engagement. This approach is aligned with the social work value of self-determination and client involvement. This approach to engagement can assist in fostering a therapeutic alliance between the client and social worker (Langer & Lietz, 2015). Understanding the person's inherent strengths, being genuine, providing unconditional positive regard, and expressing empathy are all strategies that can encourage a client to engage with you. Case 5.1 illustrates the use of this approach while engaging with a client.

CASE 5.1	BACK IN SERVICES AGAIN: UTILIZING THE PERSONALITY THEORY APPROACH IN SOCIAL WORK PRACTICE

Holly is a social worker at a local homeless shelter. She assists the residents in addressing their needs related to locating stable employment, housing, or other resources. Holly tries to meet with the residents at least a couple of times a week as they are often working on multiple goals at a time.

Macy had been at the shelter about 4 months ago. She had worked with Holly to find a full-time job and locate an apartment she could afford. Together they were able to locate resources to modestly furnish the apartment. Holly also helped Macy in linking to financial resources for energy assistance to assist with the utility bills.

Today as Holly was looking over the roster of residents in order to plan her meetings for the day, she saw Macy's name was on the list of new admissions. Holly stopped what she was doing in order to find Macy. When Holly walked up to Macy, Macy said "I know. I know. I know you must be so disappointed in me. I messed up. I lost my place. I'm sorry. Don't be mad." Holly smiled softly and said, "Macy, I am not upset at all. Actually, I am happy that you were able to return here so that we can assist you in getting back on your feet again." Macy asked, "Are you sure you are not mad?" "I'm sure, we all need some help from time to time. You were able to do this before and I am sure we can learn from what happened to better help you this time."

Later in supervision, Holly was discussing her interaction with her supervisor. Holly shared that she chose to use this approach while working with Macy because,

If I would have said I was disappointed she was back, that would not have helped the situation. Macy has a history of being emotionally neglected and told that she was never good enough. Why would I want to add to the idea that she messed up again. Instead, I am going to focus on her strengths and help her to try again.

■ Social Constructivism and Conflict Theories

Social constructivism refers to the idea that all reality (in social affairs) has been agreed on or constructed socially between people because it is beneficial to have a shared view in order to promote social order (Payne, 2016). In order to effectively engage with client systems, social workers must be aware of these social constructs. Furthermore, social workers must be aware that social construction changes over time and should be mindful about how that can impact client systems.

Conflict theories attempt to provide a framework for understanding the struggle among various groups. There are specific theories that relate to specific characteristics (race, class, gender). Regardless of characteristic, conflict theory suggests an inequality and the battle to obtain equality despite the characteristic of difference. Conflict theories often present a challenge to the status quo.

▶ **Critical Thinking Questions**
Identify current areas of conflict between two groups in society. Identify the current status quo as well as the positions of the two groups. What is the desired change by the oppressed group?

Feminist Standpoint Theory

Feminism refers to a wide range of beliefs that reflect the idea that inequality based on gender is oppressive and should be challenged and corrected. Often, feminism is used synonymously with women's rights; though that is in part what feminism is, it diminishes feminism to reduce it to simply that. At times, the concept of feminism is met with hostility or suspicion and often brings to mind negative views of women (Cree & Dean, 2015). There are many varieties of feminism.

▶ **Critical Thinking Questions**
1. How do you believe feminism is perceived by society?
2. How can this perception hinder or promote the quest for gender equality?

Feminist social work emerged in the 20th century through challenging several areas including clinical mental health frameworks, gender role divisions, and gender power differences (Eyal-Lubling & Krumer-Nevo, 2016). The social work profession has a long history of feminism, though at many times it was not labeled as such (Anyikwa, Chiarelli-Helminiak, Hodge, & Wells-Wilbon, 2015; Cree & Dean, 2015).

Standpoint feminism emphasizes giving a voice to and listening to women. This theory understands and values that women have cognitive styles that could promote equality and ameliorate oppression (Hartsock, 1983). At the heart of feminist standpoint theory is a "premise that the standpoint or position in society of women provides a vantage point from which to view women's social reality" (Van Wormer, 2009, pp. 108–109).

Related to engagement, social workers can utilize feminist standpoint theory as a reminder to consider the position of clients on the basis of their gender and in turn their perspective as it is influenced by culture and environmental factors. Social workers should be ever mindful that each person's experience is unique to that person, and it should not be generalized on the basis of any single characteristic. However, it is important to be considerate of views (current and historical) that may be influencing the client's perception of the current state.

Oppression Theory

Oppression is the "act or process of placing restrictions on an individual, group, or institution" (Hutchison, 2017, p. 323). Oppression can be intended or unintended. There are various common mechanisms of oppression. These mechanisms include such things as stereotyping, violence, blaming the victim, othering, and violence (Pharr, 1988). Mechanisms of oppression are used by the dominant group to maintain its position above the oppressed group.

Oppression theory, sometimes referred to as anti-oppressive theory, seeks to provide a framework for understanding the impact of oppression and can provide great insights to social work professionals as we are called to champion for oppressed groups. Related to engagement, social workers can use oppression theory to understand how members of historically oppressed groups may face barriers to engagement in the helping process. Social workers can be ready to address such barriers and advocate for anti-oppressive policies to promote engagement among such groups.

▶ **Critical Thinking Question**
Identify possible barriers to engagement for a member of a historically oppressed group.

Trauma Theory

The concept of trauma and trauma-informed practice has been burgeoning in the litera-ture in recent decades. In order to understand trauma theory, it is important to have an understanding of what trauma is and how it often presents. Trauma is an experience that overwhelms a person's ability to cope. Due to this definition of trauma, what is deemed to be traumatic is subjective, and varies from person to person. What may be traumatic to one individual may not necessarily elicit the same response in another individual. There are a variety of risk and protective factors that inter-play determining whether an individual is able to cope with an experience (see

> ▶ **Critical Thinking Questions**
>
> Describe how risk and protective factors can increase vulnerability to or buffer against a potentially traumatic experience. Are there any specific risk or protective factors that could be potentially more influential than others? If so, identify them and explain your rationale.

Table 5.1). Common traumatic experiences include single instances or ongoing exposures. Traumatic events could include such things as: verbal, physical, or sexual abuse; neglect; war; natural disasters (hurricanes, tornados, earthquakes); mass shootings; crime (rape, burglary, assault); transportation accidents (car, train, plane).

Regardless of whether the experience occurs once or over a period of time, the impact of the trauma is not varied. Trauma can impact an individual's emotions, behaviors, cognitions, and physiology. Just as responses to events are individualized, so are the impacts of trauma. Table 5.2 illustrates some examples of the ways that trauma can present within individuals. Trauma can change a person's worldview and how he or she perceives his or her environ-ment. For example, someone who has been the victim of a crime may, as a result, see the world as an unsafe or dangerous place.

One of the largest studies of the impact of trauma was the Adverse Childhood Experience (ACE) study. Throughout this large, longitudinal study, it was determined that adverse

TABLE 5.1 Risk and Protective Factors for Coping With Trauma

RISK FACTORS	PROTECTIVE FACTORS
Low self-esteem	Positive attitudes, values, or beliefs
Drug or alcohol use	Good mental, physical, spiritual, and emotional health
Poverty	
Homelessness	Positive self-esteem
Neighborhood crime	Success at school
Lack of positive role models	Parental supervision
Racism, discrimination, oppression	Strong social supports
Poor mental, physical, spiritual, and emotional health	Community engagement
	Problem-solving skills
Low literacy	Positive adult role models, coaches, mentors
Family violence	Positive peer group/friends
	Stable housing

TABLE 5.2 Cognitive, Behavioral, Emotional, and Physiological Symptoms of Trauma

COGNITIVE	BEHAVIORAL	EMOTIONAL	PHYSIOLOGICAL
Fear of going crazy	Hyperactivity	Anger, frustration	Pounding heart
Distractibility	Out-of-control behavior	Phobias	Sweating
Preoccupation	Sleep problems	Fear of recurrence	Nausea
Denial of the importance	Social withdrawal	Anxiety	Headaches
Problems setting priorities	Need to talk compulsively about the event	Oversensitivity	Muffled hearing
Difficulty problem-solving	Relationship problems	Depression	Fatigue
Time distortions	Flashbacks	Grief	More prone to illness
Orientation toward the past	Memory problems	Worry about physical health	Hyperarousal
Confusion		Shame/guilt	Startle response
		Resentment	

experiences in childhood have an impact on both physical and emotional health throughout the life span (Felitti et al., 1998). Adverse childhood experiences include the following events (prior to 18 years of age): physical abuse by a parent; emotional abuse by a parent; sexual abuse by anyone; growing up with an alcohol and/or drug abuser in the household; experiencing the incarceration of a household member; living with a family member experiencing mental illness; domestic violence; loss of a parent; emotional neglect; physical neglect. This study provided a better understanding of the prevalence of trauma. With a better understanding of how prevalent the experience of trauma is, the need for trauma-informed approaches to helping was seen as more important.

▶ **Critical Thinking Question**

Why do you think that adverse childhood experiences have such a detrimental impact on long-term functioning?

Trauma theory and trauma-informed care have been strongly informed by the work of Judith Herman. Herman (1998) suggests that trauma disconnects and disempowers individuals; in order to address trauma, it must occur via connection or in a relationship, and cannot occur in isolation. Trauma theory holds fast to a recovery model that promotes personal resilience and encourages healing through safety, stabilization, and reconnection (Herman, 1997).

Social workers who engage in trauma-informed practice "rely on their knowledge about trauma to respond to clients in ways that convey respect and compassion, honor self-determination, and enable the rebuilding of healthy interpersonal skills and coping strategies" (Levenson, 2017, p. 105). CSWE (2012) asserts that it is imperative for social work students to be prepared to provide trauma-informed care with all client systems. Related to engagement, social workers must be mindful that trauma can impact a client system's ability or willingness to engage. To that end, when using trauma theory to inform the practice of engagement, social workers should promote a trusting relationship "focusing on pacing,

---

BOX 5.1

TRAUMA-INFORMED ENGAGEMENT BEHAVIORS

- The trauma-informed social worker consistently demonstrates attention to nonverbal behaviors and cues, emotional dysregulation, and wariness of institutions that impede the establishment of a therapeutic alliance.

- The trauma-informed practitioner uses a range of interventions to address underlying motivations that influence help-seeking and help-rejecting behaviors, in a variety of contexts (e.g., from micro to macro) that affect engagement.

- The trauma-informed practitioner identifies, understands, respects, and addresses the range of coping strategies trauma survivors, mandated and voluntary, may demonstrate that create barriers to engagement.

- The trauma-informed social worker uses supervision and mentorship to reflect on effective use of self and affective self-regulation while navigating the engagement process, including issues such as the worker's own history of trauma, secondary traumatization, potential triggers (for both client and practitioner), and the worker's responses to those triggers.

- The trauma-informed social worker implements trauma-informed principles of engagement with services at the individual, organizational, and societal levels that are responsive to those underrepresented and oppressed in society.

Source: From Council on Social Work Education. (2018). *Specialized practice curricular guide for trauma-informed social work practice.* Alexandria, VA: Author.

---

empathetic responding, mirroring, attending, and awareness of nonverbal behavior" (CSWE, 2018, p. 111). The CSWE (2018) set forth trauma-informed engagement behaviors for social workers to support clients who have experienced trauma (see Box 5.1).

■ Person-in-Environment Perspective

Imagine that you are holding a single puzzle piece in your hand. Using that puzzle piece, can you describe the full picture of the puzzle? Of course it is impossible to describe the big picture because you are only looking at one small piece of the puzzle. The puzzle metaphor serves to underscore the importance of seeing as many pieces of the puzzle as possible in order to have the clearest, most accurate image of the entire picture. When engaging with clients, it is important not to reduce them to a single piece, but rather embrace all of the pieces of the environment that surrounds them.

The person-in-environment perspective is informed by systems and ecological theories and is a fundamental perspective for the social work profession (Langer & Lietz, 2015). It is a multidisciplinary theoretical framework that can be used with client systems at all levels of practice. When we consider a person's environment, we consider not only the physical environment, but also relationships, involvement with systems, both formally and informally, as well as resources that may or may not be available to the person.

This perspective asserts that people are complex beings and, furthermore, the environments within which these people exist are equally complex. This perspective requires a complete look at all of the complex dimensions of people and the environments, or systems, within which they find themselves belonging. Complex personal dimensions may include biological, psychological, social, or spiritual determinants, whereas complex environment dimensions may exist within families, groups, communities, organizations, culture, the physical environment, social movements, or social institutions (Hutchison, 2017).

Using this perspective, nearly all concerns or problems identified by the client can have "intervention implications that may include helping the client create an environment that is more 'conducive' to their particular needs" (Walsh, 2013, p. 26). A primary consideration when considering the person-in-environment perspective is the goodness of fit of the person within his or her environment at various levels—micro, mezzo, and macro (Steen, 2012). If there is a discrepancy between the current environment, at any level, and a client need, that can be an area for a social worker to focus attention to identify

▶ **Critical Thinking Question**
Consider the idea of goodness of fit within an environment. What may be some issues that are evidence of a poor goodness of fit in the environment?

appropriate resources to ameliorate the discrepancy and increase the goodness of fit. For example, if a client is homeless due to a lack of affordable housing options in the community, that could be an example of a poor goodness of fit between the person and his or her environment.

This perspective is closely related to early social work practice in the United States. The work of Mary Richmond in New York City used what could be considered a person-in-environment perspective though that label did not exist at that time. If we consider the work of Richmond and others, they sought to bring about change within the person by addressing the environments in which they existed.

■ Engagement With Different Client Systems

Regardless of the level of practice, engagement is a necessary and ongoing process. Social workers must be able to engage with client systems at the micro-, mezzo-, and macrolevels of practice. Engagement sets the foundation for other stages of the helping process including assessment and intervention. Just as a house with a shaky foundation is not secure and in risk of collapsing, success within the social work helping process is reliant on a good foundation built with quality engagement. Furthermore, engagement should be holistic, in that it is multilayered and multileveled (Adam & Pyles, 2016). The multilayered aspect of engagement refers to elements of the biopsychosocial–spiritual assessment that social workers are trained in. The multileveled aspect of engagement refers to the levels of social work practice with individuals (micro), families and groups (mezzo), or communities and organizations (macro).

Commonalities

Regardless of the population or level of practice, quality engagement begins with the social worker. The social worker is tasked with creating an environment or atmosphere that fosters authenticity and a space for genuine connection. In order to create such a place, the social worker must first be reflective and self-aware.

The social worker should not attempt to enact a persona; rather, the social worker should work on embracing his or her own style of practice. When engaging with clients, social workers should strive to be present and with clients, meet clients where they are, and be clear about their role and function as the worker in their interaction. Authenticity is an important element of

> ▶ **Critical Thinking Question**
> How can you tell if someone is being authentic? Give specific examples.

engagement. To be authentic is to be what one has said to be, to be real. Social workers place a special value on the principle of integrity. In a way, authenticity is a form of integrity, in that social workers hold themselves out in a way that is honest and forthcoming.

In addition to personal awareness, it is important that the social worker be well versed in interviewing skills. A good interview is not scripted or robotic; rather, it is a dynamic, evolving process that seeks to gather information necessary for the social worker to begin working with the client. We discuss some of these skills later in this chapter. However, though the skills we discuss are ways to improve the helping relationship and gather information, we encourage you to consider ways in which you already engage with others to connect. Most people who enter the social work profession consider themselves to be what is often referred to as a "people person" or as very social. Some of those skills that are used in everyday life can be transferable to engagement.

Differences

An effective social worker starts where the client is and goes from there. Engagement with clients is no exception. The social worker should begin where the client is to start the process of engaging. Where the client "is" may depend on many factors including, but not limited to, age, cognitive level, and culture. How a social worker would engage with a 5-year-old versus a 65-year-old would most likely look different due to the difference in age. Differing engagement based on the population you are working with is appropriate.

■ Building Relationships

Social workers build relationships and connections. As discussed earlier, social workers value the importance of human relationships. Taking that one step further, social workers value strong relationships. Through engagement, social workers can strive to create strong relationships with clients. Through strong engagement, or rapport, social work practice can occur. Much of the research available on the therapeutic process suggests that the number one predictor of success in treatment is the worker–client relationship. The quality of that relationship has been shown to be more indicative of success than the length of treatment or even treatment modality. Later in this chapter, we discuss ways to assess the helping relationship. First, let us explore ways to establish strong relationships.

Affective Reactions

There is an adage that goes "It is not what you said, but how you said it." Affective reactions are a part of the "how you said it" part of that expression. Nonverbal communication is powerful. Research suggests that nonverbal communication is more important than verbal communication. In addition to things such as body positioning and posture, what our face is doing is important nonverbal communication.

Social workers should not be robots; we should be able to express ourselves using our face. Responding to a client using facial expressions can be quite a helpful way to further the conversation with a minimal prompt. Despite the importance of being able to show expression, the social worker must be in control of the reactions given to the client at all times. The social worker must be able to express or show a reaction that is helpful in the helping process for the client. The term "poker face" is used to describe, when playing a game of poker, a facial expression that does not reveal the cards in one's hand. Consider having a "social work poker face" in that you do not reveal any reaction that comes to mind, but rather you present a controlled response that is helpful for the client. Case 5.2 illustrates the importance of appropriately managing facial expressions when working with a client. As with much of social work practice, there is a blend of art and science. Related to facial expressions and affective responses, we encourage you to be mindful of how you demonstrate expressions and to perhaps use a mirror or videotape yourself to have the opportunity to see what your face is saying when you are listening.

CASE 5.2   WHAT YOU SAY WITHOUT SAYING ANYTHING OUT LOUD

Maggie is a social worker at a community mental health setting. Her role is to conduct intake assessments with all new patients in order to determine the appropriate level of care. Due to the nature of her role, it is important for her to quickly engage with clients as she only has an hour and a half to complete a full biopsychosocial assessment and make treatment recommendations based on that information.

In a session with a new patient, Maggie asks about the patient's trauma history. The patient was hesitant at first, but Maggie was able to engage with the client and the client opened up. The client shared an extensive history of physical and sexual abuse that began during childhood lasting over a decade. Maggie felt bad for the client when listening to the recount of abuse. Without realizing it, Maggie's face was frowning and appeared quite sad. It was not until the client pointed out Maggie's facial expression and sharply said, "I don't need your pity. That not why I am here."

Maggie was initially taken aback by the client's response and quickly shook her head and said "Oh no, it's not that, I mean, I don't pity you, it's just, I feel bad that you had to experience that." As soon as Maggie said it, she realized that it did sound like she was pitying the client.

(continued)

CASE 5.2

Later, in supervision, Maggie was able to process the situation and how her facial expressions were not helpful to the client in this case. She had always thought that wearing her heart on her sleeve was a way to increase engagement. Maggie is now considering how she could better manage her affective responses in order to meet the needs of the patients she works with.

Self-Reflection and Biases

Self-reflection is an invaluable tool for professional social workers. Social workers should continuously use self-reflection as a means to enhance self-awareness related to practice. It is especially important for social workers to be aware of personal biases that may exist. It is necessary to be aware of these biases in order to ensure that they do not interfere with one's work with clients. Again, the work that social workers do is not about the worker; rather, it is about meeting clients where they are, supporting them, working with them, and assisting them in improving their well-being.

Though social workers must be able to work with anyone, it is necessary to understand and recognize that not all types of social work are for all people. It is important that social workers embrace the notion of being able to work with anyone. In some situations or settings, especially in rural areas, there may only be one social worker available, so the worker must be able to engage with anyone in order to meet the needs of clients. Social workers cannot discriminate care based on any biases. On the other hand, if a social worker finds that a particular area of practice is too personal for them, then it is mindful to avoid employment in such an area. For example, someone who grew up in a home with domestic violence may find it challenging or even triggering to work in a domestic violence shelter. Though the social worker recognizes potential limitations in his or her ability to be effective in such a setting, the social worker is aware that in his or her chosen area of practice, he or she may work with clients who have experienced domestic violence. The social worker will be required to provide the same level of care and support, regardless of personal experiences or biases.

Trust Building

Trust building is an important step to building strong relationships. Trust is also a cornerstone in the helping relationship. It is the responsibility of the social worker to build and maintain trust with the client. This should begin during the initial session during the process of informed consent. The social worker should always be honest, open, and forthcoming with all policies, expectations, as well as rights and responsibilities of both the worker and the client. During this initial discussion, the social worker should explicitly discuss privacy and confidentiality with the client. The social worker should clearly outline limits to confidentiality, such as a threat to harm oneself or another person, or child abuse.

▶ **Critical Thinking Questions**

1. How can trust improve the helping relationship between a social worker and client?
2. How would a lack of trust hinder the helping relationship between a social worker and client?

When establishing trust with a client, the social worker should always act with integrity. The social worker should keep all appointments and be on time for those appointments. Being on time and maintaining appointments is a way to demonstrate that you value clients and their time. This also demonstrates integrity, which will assist in building trust.

As with any relationship, when trust is lost, it is harder to gain it back. As a result, social workers should make great efforts to avoid diminishing the trust of their clients. However, there may be some legal or ethical limitations to the trusting relationship that you have with your clients.

The Helping Relationship Inventory

At the heart of social work practice is the relationship between the worker and the client system. As discussed previously, much research has been done across helping professions, which indicates the quality of the helping relationship is a greater predictor in client success. Knowing how important the therapeutic relationship is, it is necessary to examine and reflect upon the quality of the helping relationship in order to be a competent social worker.

In addition to self-reflection and supervision, social workers can utilize resources available to them to examine the quality

▶ **Critical Thinking Questions**

1. Why do you think that the quality of the helping relationship is the number one predictor of success?

2. What specific strategies or elements of the helping relationship can promote success in treatment?

of the helping relationships they currently have. One such tool is the Helping Relationship Inventory. This inventory was developed in order to assist helpers in examining the quality of their helping relationships with clients. This measure, developed by Poulin and Young (1997), was created in order to be specifically applicable to social workers across areas of practice, whereas many other helping relationship inventories are focused solely on clinical (therapeutic) practice. The inventory has two components, a structural component (see Box 5.2) and an interpersonal component (see Box 5.3). Each component can be reversed to a client version by replacing the word "social worker" with "client." The measure has been found to be effective and useful across domains of practice. This measure provides an easily accessible way to assess and improve the helping relationship (Young & Poulin, 1998).

BOX 5.2

HELPING RELATIONSHIP INVENTORY

Structural Component:

1. How much have you and your social worker discussed how you are going to approach your work together?

2. How clear are you about what is expected in your work together?

(continued)

(continued)

3. How clear are you about what is expected of your social worker and your work together?

4. How much input have you had in determining how the two of you will work together?

5. How much have you and your social worker discussed the specific problem(s) with which you want help?

6. How much input have you had in determining the specific problems you are addressing and your work together?

7. How clear are you about the specific problems that you and your social worker are addressing?

8. To what extent have you and your social worker discussed the specific goals you hope to accomplish in your work together?

9. How much input have you had in determining the goals you are working on?

10. How clear are you about the goals you hope to accomplish?

11. To what extent have you and your social worker discussed the specific actions you will take to add your difficulties?

12. To what extent have you and your social worker discussed the specific actions your social worker will take to address your difficulties?

13. How much input have you had in determining the actions you are taking to address your difficulties?

14. How clear are you about the actions you are expected to take?

15. How clear are you about the actions your social worker is taking?

16. How much have you and your social worker discussed how your progress is going to be assessed?

17. How much input do you have in determining how you and your social worker will assess your progress?

18. How clear are you about how you and your social worker are assessing your progress?

19. To what extent have you and your social worker discussed your progress?

BOX 5.3

HELPING RELATIONSHIP INVENTORY

Interpersonal Component:

1. Do you and your social worker work well together?

2. Do you feel your social worker pays attention to you?

(continued)

(continued)

3. Does your social worker explain to you his or her understanding of your difficulties?

4. Is your social worker's understanding of your difficulties similar to your own?

5. Does your social worker acknowledge your efforts to cope with your difficulties in addition to talking about your difficulties?

6. Does your social worker give you the impression that he or she enjoys meeting and talking with you?

7. Does talking with your social worker help you get more organized about resolving your difficulties?

8. Does talking with your social worker have a calming or soothing effect on you?

9. Is your social worker able to handle the emotional aspects of your difficulties?

10. Does talking to your social worker give you hope?

11. Does your social worker help you think more clearly about your difficulties?

12. Does talking with your social worker help you believe more in yourself in general?

13. Do you feel you and your social worker see things in similar ways?

14. Does your social worker help you to think more clearly about yourself?

15. Do you and your social worker talk about things you care about?

16. Do you feel that you and your social worker are alike in some ways?

■ The Helping Process

As social workers, we are called upon to help a variety of people in a variety of settings. Regardless of population or setting, the helping process often stays the same. The process of helping begins with engaging with the client. From the engagement, we are able to begin the assessment. Based on the assessment, we are able to determine how best to intervene. Following the intervention, we evaluate if the change efforts have been successful. To conclude the helping process, the final stage is termination. This five-step process should guide your social work practice.

Engage

Throughout this chapter, we have been exploring engagement in order to connect with clients. Initially, it is important to engage and build rapport. Rapport is the close relationship where the individuals understand one another and are able to communicate with each other. Rapport is helpful when trying to engage with clients.

Elaboration Skills

While engaging with clients, there will be times that we need to encourage the client to continue communicating with us. The ways in which we encourage the client to continue talking

TABLE 5.3 Verbal and Nonverbal Elaboration Skills

VERBAL ELABORATION SKILLS	NONVERBAL ELABORATION SKILLS
"Tell me more"	Nodding
"Go on"	Eye Contact
"Can you say more about that"	Leaning In
"Mm-hmm"	Facial Expressions
"I see"	

are called elaboration skills and are sometimes called furthering skills. The goal of these skills is to promote ongoing dialogue. Elaboration skills can be verbal or nonverbal. An example of a verbal elaboration skill would be statements that encourage the client to share more. In a similar way, nonverbal elaboration skills also set out to further the client's communication; however, they utilize nonverbal behaviors, not words. Table 5.3 provides several examples of verbal and nonverbal elaboration skills

Empathy Skills

Think about a time that you were talking to someone and you really felt heard. There is a good chance that the person was demonstrating empathy skills. When social workers use empathy skills, they are allowing the client to feel heard or understood. There are several empathy skills that social workers can employ including using active listening skills and validating. Active listening skills refer to being truly engaged in the receiving portion of communication. An active listener demonstrates nonverbal behaviors that demonstrate they are listening such as eye contact, open body position, leaning in, or perhaps even nodding along at times. An active listener is listening with the purpose to understand. When validating another person, you are recognizing and understanding their perspective. Validation can help someone feel understood.

Assess

Assessment is the process by which we collect data and, based on our clinical experiences, theoretical knowledge, and these data, make recommendations. Good assessment is ongoing assessment. Often agencies have a template for completing an assessment that must be finished within the first session or two. However, despite being done with formalized assessments, we encourage you to engage in ongoing assessment in order to monitor for new needs or other relevant information that may come to light at a later time. Assessments should also be comprehensive. Often social workers rely on biopsychosocial–spiritual assessments to guide their practice. These assessments seek to gain information about various aspects of the person's life in regard to biological, psychological, social, and spiritual determinants of behavior.

Contracting Skills

A contract is the formal agreement between the social worker and client related to treatment recommendations that were developed based on the assessment. Ideally, the contract is mutually constructed between the social worker and client. Utilizing engagement skills, the social worker should engage the client in the contracting process in order to establish mutually agreed-on goals and SMART objectives. When clients are a part of the contracting process, particularly the development of treatment goals, there is often a sense of increased buy-in which can lead to better results than if goals are just prescribed to clients without their input or insights.

Intervene

Social workers intervene by engaging in an intervention that is designed to address the issues identified in the assessment phase. Throughout the intervention, social workers are continually engaging with clients. Often the interventions selected are evidence-based practice, meaning they are the researched best approach for a specific situation or issue.

Intervention Skills

Though intervention skills will vary from intervention to intervention, there are a few general skills that are common across interventions. One common intervention skill that social workers must possess is the ability to clearly communicate throughout the intervention process. The social worker should explain in a clear way the expectations of the intervention to the client. These expectations include, but are not limited to, how long to expect the intervention to last as well as client requirements or responsibilities during this phase. Another common skill is ongoing assessment during the intervention implementation. The social worker should be monitoring changes that are both observed and reported during this phase of treatment.

Evaluate

Evaluation is the process by which social workers determine whether or not the intervention has been successful. Evaluations can occur throughout the intervention or at the end of the intervention. Evaluations sometimes use formal methods such as scales or assessments. Sometimes evaluations are more informal based on observations and client self-reports.

Evaluation Skills

Social workers are required to be research-informed professionals. When social workers engage in evaluating their practice, they are undertaking practice-based research. When evaluating, skills that the social worker should possess are good critical thinking skills and organization.

Good critical thinking skills are necessary for social workers engaging in evaluation because the social worker needs to decide how and when to evaluate based on the work he or she is doing. Further, the social worker must also be able to critically weigh or assess the data that are received during the evaluation process in order to make clinical determinations. Organization is important for research-informed social workers because they need to know when to evaluate and at times keep track of data over a period of time.

Terminate

At the end of the social work helping process is the phase of termination. Planning for termination should begin from the first session. Termination planning should also include discharge plans including possible alternative services and resources and a plan for follow-up. Research suggests that termination can be a time filled with a myriad of emotions for both the client and the social worker (Baum, 2007; Knapp, 2010). Ideally, termination is planned and prepared for; however, under some circumstances, termination occurs abruptly. Early planning for termination is particularly helpful in cases in which an abrupt termination occurs.

Ending Skills

As throughout the helping process, the social worker should remain engaged with the client throughout the termination or ending phase. Engagement can help to diminish negative or worried feelings the client may be experiencing in response to termination.

During the termination phase, the social worker and client are in essence ending their contract together. The social worker should be sure to share gains with the client regarding progress made during their time working together. The social worker should also be clear about continued areas of focus and how those can and will be addressed in the discharge plan.

■ Interprofessional

Just as no person is an island, no social worker is an island. In turn, no social worker is a lone helper. Since there are often a variety of helpers in the lives of the clients we serve, it is necessary for social workers to be skilled at working interprofessionally both within an agency as well as outside of it. There are a variety of ways that social workers can work interprofessionally including collaboration, building professional relationships, and working on a team.

Collaboration

Social workers must ensure that clients receive continuity of care. Continuity of care refers to the seamless or consistent integration of care across providers, time, and/or setting. Continuity of care requires collaboration among professionals. Collaboration is the professional action of working together on a common task or project. For the purposes of this text, we define collaboration as the professional action of working with other professionals in order to provide continuity of care on behalf of a client. Good, clear, consistent collaboration is necessary for competent social work practice. Social workers are well-positioned to participate in collaboration. According to Parris (2012):

> The multidisciplinary nature of modern social work involves joint working and information-sharing between professionals and agencies, and it is vital that this is done effectively in the interests of service users, so that the appropriate actions are taken and services put in place. Failure to communicate effectively between agencies can lead to profound and sometimes tragic consequences. . . . Effective multi-agency communication is important in working with all service users because social workers intervene at times of crisis or difficulty in people's lives and their input can have far-reaching consequences. (p. 107)

Social workers have an ethical responsibility to engage in interprofessional collaboration on behalf of clients. The NASW *Code of Ethics* (2017) puts forth that:

> Social workers who are members of an interdisciplinary team should participate in and contribute to decisions that affect the well-being of clients by drawing on the perspectives, values, and experiences of the social work profession. Professional and ethical obligations of the interdisciplinary team as a whole and of its individual members should be clearly established. (2.03 Interdisciplinary Collaboration, para. a)

Collaboration Challenges

Though collaboration is necessary within social work practice for the benefit of our clients, at times, challenges related to collaboration can arise. Some challenges related to collaboration include lack of engagement with other professionals, lack of emphasis on continuity of care, and legal considerations.

Just as social workers must engage with clients, social workers must also engage with other professionals in order to collaborate. At times, engaging with other professionals can be difficult. When engaging in interdisciplinary collaboration, or collaboration with individuals from a variety of professions or disciplines (e.g., teacher, nurse, psychiatrist, pediatrician, school counselor, case manager), each professional may be approaching the case from a different perspective based on their professional orientation. Just as social workers must be aware of their role and function when engaging with a client, it is helpful for the social workers to be clear regarding the roles and functions of the other professionals with which they are engaging in order to benefit the most from the collaborative process. Social workers should strive to engage and collaborate with all appropriate service providers to ensure continuity of care for the client. In order to suc-

▶ **Critical Thinking Questions**

As a social worker, how would you promote interdisciplinary collaboration with other professionals?

cessfully do this, the social worker must be able to be clear regarding the reason and need to collaborate for the other professionals. At times, a lack of emphasis on continuity of care exists. Within some areas of practice, collaboration is a nonreimbursable task and as a result, sometimes a forgotten task. We caution against this. Collaboration that is helpful to the client should always be a priority to maintain, even amid discouraging situations. Related to this, the social worker may need to be proactive and seek out collaborative relationships. In order to seek out or engage in collaborative relationships, the social worker should be mindful of legal considerations. One legal consideration is having clients sign a document allowing you permission to contact other professionals and share information related to their treatment. Clients have the right to refuse to sign releases of information, in which case, collaboration cannot exist. However, if collaboration would be beneficial for the client, the social worker should share the potential benefits and risks with the clients before honoring the client's right to self-determine whether or not to sign the release of information. Though the social worker may feel collaboration would be helpful, without a signed release of information, any communication with another professional would be a breach of privacy and confidentiality, which has serious implications and ramifications for the professional.

Building Professional Relationships

Valuing the importance of human relationships for social workers also extends to the value placed on other professionals. Professional relationships and collaborations are an integral part of the helping process in order to ensure continuity of care and promote the best outcomes possible for clients, all the while trying to avoid duplication of services.

Roles and Responsibilities

Just as it is necessary for social workers to be clear on their role with clients early on in the engagement process, it is equally necessary for social workers and other professionals to be clear on each other's roles as well. Social workers can wear a variety of hats. Due to this, it is important not to assume that by simply identifying yourself as a social worker, another professional will accurately understand your role. It is necessary to consider that social workers may have a variety of different roles, including, but not limited to, counselor, mediator, broker, case manager, researcher, supervisor, organizer, and educator. Depending on the role in which the social worker is acting, it is important to be clear with other professionals what your functions are in regard to the scope of practice with the shared client. Furthermore, collaborating professionals should be clear on responsibilities related to various tasks, assessments, and interventions regarding mutual cases.

Working on a Team

Working on a team can be very rewarding but can also have some challenges. When you are working as a part of a team, you have the benefit of a variety of perspectives and experiences that can inform the discussion. Team brainstorming can lead to creative ideas that someone may not have thought of on their own. Also, when working on a team, there can be a sharing of tasks and there is less likely to be a duplication of services for the consumers as all of the providers are working together and on the same page. Challenges that may arise when working on a team include a conflict of

> ▶ **Critical Thinking Questions**
> Describe your experiences working on a team.
> 1. What elements of being on a team have been positive?
> 2. What elements of being on a team have been difficult?

personalities or perspectives. Sometimes team members do not agree. As social workers, we must find a way to have conversations and reach an end agreement that is best for the client.

■ Policy Issues

Policy issues influence all social workers in all areas of practice and can play a significant role in the engagement process. In order to be able to engage with clients, you must first have access to clients. Policies can serve to attract or deter potential clients from seeking support from a social worker.

Policies can serve to promote engagement. For example, policies that have been established to ensure that individuals have equal access to resources, services, and opportunities can enhance the likelihood of an individual reaching out for services. One such policy would be the Patient Protection and Affordable Care Act of 2010, which provides access to mental health and drug and alcohol related services to more people than ever before through insurance coverage. Due to this Act, individuals who had been previously uninsured or underinsured were given access to services and resources to meet their needs.

On the other hand, some policies can hinder engagement with certain groups. For example, current U.S. policies are viewed by many to be unwelcoming to individuals who are considered refugees or have an undocumented status. An individual who has an undocumented status may be hesitant to engage with a social worker out of fear that his or her immigration status may be uncovered and that he or she may be reported. The NASW has set forth that social workers are called to serve all individuals, regardless of their immigration status.

▶ **Critical Thinking Questions**

1. As a social worker, do you need to know if your client has documentation? Why or why not?

2. Would your answer change based on your social work role? If so, describe.

However, despite this decree on behalf of the social work profession, there are many legal and government departments that will refuse services or report individuals based on this. Social workers must be mindful of such policy issues that could serve as a barrier to engagement with clients and reflect upon ways to meet clients where they are in order to engage and provide resources, services, and supports (see Case 5.3).

CASE 5.3   **AFRAID TO ASK FOR HELP: UNDOCUMENTED CLIENTS IN THE SOCIAL WORK PRACTICE**

Rose is a social worker at a small nonprofit charity-based organization that is connected to several local churches in the community. The organization is Christian-based but nondenominational. At the agency, donated clothes are sold at an extreme discount or even given away to people who demonstrate financial need. The agency also has access to its own food pantry and a small furniture store to provide housewares and home goods to individuals with financial need. They also have an allotted monthly allowance to be able to assist individuals in paying bills that may be too large or in danger of having a utility shut off. Rose's job is to meet with individuals coming in who are requesting assistance of some kind whether it be for clothes, food, furniture, or help with bills. Sometimes people have appointments to meet with Rose. However, the agency has a policy that no one is turned away; so if someone shows up, it is Rose's responsibility to see them and assess their need.

During these meetings, Rose asks demographic data information on finances and spending habits. Rose knows that sometimes people feel uncomfortable coming in and asking for help. In order to help people, Rose strives to engage with people early on so that the interview process can go smoothly. Rose makes sure that when she leaves her office, she is smiling and polite to all customers as any one of them may be there for an interview. Rose found that by being friendly, it often helps people feel more comfortable speaking with her. During meetings, Rose tries to display empathy,

(continued)

CASE 5.3

she monitors her affective responses, and uses elaboration skills in order to keep the interview running smoothly. Rose knows that if she does not get people to engage with her, it may be difficult to determine their full level of need and in turn provide them with the services to meet their needs.

Carla recently traveled to America in order to escape the horrific violence in her home country in South America. Carla came to the United States with very little, only what she could carry for both herself and her 7-year-old daughter Anna who accompanied her on her journey. After months traveling to the United States, Carla and Anna were able to connect with cousins who had been in the United States for some time. Soon after settling in the same community as her cousins, Carla was able to find housing. However, since Carla has yet to find a steady, good-paying job, she and her daughter have been sleeping on the floor of the apartment. Carla remains private, but through discussion with the priest at her Catholic church, she learned about a local agency that could assist her in getting some furniture for the home. She was told she could just show up at the agency and they would give her furniture, "no questions asked."

At the agency, Rose was having a busy day with back-to-back appointments. After what she thought was her last appointment of the day when she stepped out of her office, she saw a woman and her daughter sitting in her waiting area. Though Rose was tired, she took a deep breath, smiled, and greeted the pair in the waiting area. She smiled, reached out her hand, and said, "Hello, I am Rose. I am a social worker. Can I help you?" Carla softly said "I am here for furniture." Rose said, "Ok, great, please come in my office so we can get started on the paperwork." Carla's face looked confused and worried all at once. She said, "No. No, paperwork, I just need furniture. I was told 'no questions asked.' I just need furniture." Carla was worried that if she needed to complete paperwork, the social worker would find out that she and her daughter are undocumented, and she is in fear of deportation. Rose could tell that Carla was concerned about completing paperwork, but she needs to have documentation for all of the goods she gives away. Rose thought for a moment. She did not know what the big deal was; it was just a couple of forms that people fill out every day. But Rose could tell that something was bothering Carla, so she did not want to push it because she wanted to find a way to help.

Rose considered her role and the purpose of meeting with Carla. Rose knew that the NASW promotes supporting clients regardless of their documentation status. Rose also knew that the paperwork she completed at her agency was used to tally the types of services provided. Thinking about all of this, Rose considered what she could do to promote engagement with Carla, who was visibly nervous. Then, Rose remembered that during her initial training at the agency she was told that clients who are reluctant to share personally identifiable data (such as name, address, or phone number) were allowed to not disclose such information. In the training, they emphasized that due to the nature of this agency, paperwork could include an alias or even initials. Rose asked Carla if she would like to use an alias on the paperwork. Rose shared with Carla that the purpose of this paperwork is to demonstrate that the agency is helping community members and that she could use an alias if that would help her feel more comfortable. Carla seemed to be more at ease after moving past the personally identifiable information. In fact, by the end of the intake session, Carla was smiling and nodding along with Rose as she continued the interview.

In order to fully meet clients where they are, social workers must be respectful of diversity. The NASW *Code of Ethics* (2017) asserts that social workers must be culturally aware and "should understand culture and its function in human behavior and society." Social workers should recognize that the process of engaging and engagement ought to be based on culture.

Social workers must appreciate differences in diversity and be mindful of how the engagement process may need to be modified in order to be culturally sensitive. For example, though the social worker may be comfortable and used to greeting clients with a handshake and lengthy eye contact, the social worker should appreciate that in some cultures, that would be a very offensive or off-putting introduction.

▶ **Critical Thinking Question**
How can you ensure that you are appreciating diversity when engaging with a client or client system?

We encourage cultural humility regarding identifying what works best to engage with each client. Though there are some generalizations related to interaction based on culture, social workers should not assume that their clients ascribe to those beliefs. Utilizing a culturally humble approach to engagement may be as simple as asking clients how they would like to be referred to by you.

■ Social Justice Issues

Social workers are required by the NASW *Code of Ethics* (2017) to challenge social injustice and to fight on behalf of poor, vulnerable, and oppressed populations. Social workers are called to be a voice for those who need their assistance the most. There can be struggles when engaging with the groups mentioned previously. For example, when a social worker is engaging with an individual without economic means or resources, the social worker must be aware of how this will influence their time together. If the client does not have the money or means to have access to food, shelter, or other basic needs, it could be quite difficult to conduct therapy. According to Maslow's hierarchy of needs (see Figure 5.1), individuals must first have their basic needs met and feel safe before conquering tasks related to esteem, belonging, or self-actualization. Many schools across the United States now offer breakfast for students and have anti-bullying policies in place. These two examples would show how schools are attempting to address the two most basic needs of the students: first, the physiological need for food to ward against hunger, and second, the safety needed to decrease bullying. By addressing these

▶ **Critical Thinking Question**
How can a social worker use Maslow's hierarchy of needs to enhance engagement with a client?

two needs, students would be in a better state to be able to learn. In the same way, we as social workers must be mindful of the lower level needs in the hierarchy that may be barriers to our work with clients and resources, which we can identify to support our clients. Through good engagement, we can assess each level of need and discuss ways to ameliorate each area as well.

We must be considerate of vulnerable populations when considering engagement. Earlier in this chapter when we discussed policy issues, we explored policies that may hinder populations from seeking out services or being resistant to engaging with a social worker. In addition to the example provided earlier, other vulnerable populations may include children, older adults, and prisoners. Social workers who are serving children need to be mindful of the age of consent laws in their jurisdiction. However, regardless of the age of consent, social workers should make every effort possible to discuss with the child in an age-appropriate manner the role and purpose of the services being provided. Including the child in as many aspects of the informed consent process as possible is an important consideration.

When considering engagement with elderly populations, the social worker should be cognizant of issues related to consent, ensuring that the individual can adequately hear what the social worker is explaining as well as read the print on the initial paperwork. Also, social workers, as with any population, should be sure to explain the purpose of their services clearly in an understandable way. Furthermore, social workers should be considerate of potential limits in the availability or use of technology by some seniors. The NASW *Code of Ethics* (2017) sets forth that social workers must be aware of limits related to technology that clients may present with to ensure this will not be a barrier to their care. Engaging older adults by utilizing their strengths has been found to promote the outcome of client empowerment (Vishal, 2018). Social workers are well-positioned to utilize the strengths perspective with all clients, including older adults.

Last, when considering engagement with individuals who find themselves incarcerated, it is important to be mindful of potential issues related to informed consent, perceived coercion, and privacy. When engaging with someone who is incarcerated, it is understandable that he or she may be hesitant to fully open up and engage. With populations such as this, the social worker should be aware how the setting in which the interactions are occurring may be tempering the information gathered. For example, it is not uncommon for a prisoner to remain guarded during a session as a result of the prison setting. When considering engagement, the social worker should strive to provide as safe an environment as possible in which the individual feels like he or she has the ability to genuinely engage.

■ Summary

Throughout this chapter, we explored the process of engagement. Engagement is a dynamic and ongoing process between the social worker and the client systems. Engagement is the necessary foundation upon which later processes such as intervention and assessment are built upon. We explored how attachment theory, personality theory, feminist standpoint theory, trauma theory, humanistic theory, and the person-in-environment perspective can all be utilized to inform engagement with client systems. We reviewed the phases of the helping process while underscoring the importance of the helping relationship in predicting client success. The Helping Relationship Inventory was provided as a tool to assist social workers in monitoring the quality of their helping relationships with clients. Last, we explored the benefits and challenges related to interprofessional collaboration and working on a team, which are necessary aspects of competent social work practice.

CASE SUMMARY   "UNDOCUMENTED AND HOMELESS"

Practice Setting Description

Jackie is a first-year master of social work student completing an internship at an inner-city family service agency in the southwest. The agency is located in a section of the city that has a high crime rate, gang activity, and failing schools. The area has a diverse population with a large number of immigrants from Central and South America and a substantial African American population. The agency provides individual and family counseling services on a sliding fee scale. The agency also runs a number of educational and treatment groups as well as a temporary shelter for women and their children. Jackie has been assigned to work with the women and their children in the shelter. Her primary tasks are to provide concrete services and supportive counseling to the shelter residents.

Background Information

Elicia T and her daughter, Maria, are undocumented immigrants from Mexico. They have been in the United States for 5 years. Elicia and Maria fled to the area from another southwestern city to escape her abusive husband approximately 2 months ago. Elicia is 25 years old and Maria 8 years old. Elicia has a 2-year-old daughter, Sarah, who was placed in foster care because of suspected abuse in the home. Sarah is in a foster home in a small rural community in the state hundreds of miles from Elicia's current residence. Since moving to the area, Maria has not been attending school.

Elicia and Maria are currently residing in the agency's temporary shelter for families. They have been at the shelter for 2 weeks, and the agency has a 90-day limit. It is viewed as temporary housing, and the residents are only allowed to stay for 3 months. Prior to arriving at the shelter, Elicia and Maria were homeless and living on the streets.

Elicia is a high-school dropout and was a stay-at-home mother prior to leaving her husband and moving to a different part of the state. She chose to move there because she has two female cousins living in the area who are also undocumented immigrants. Elicia's native language is Spanish. She speaks some English but is not as comfortable speaking in English. Her English comprehension appears to be good. Maria speaks both English and Spanish well. When communicating with the staff, Maria acts as Elicia's interpreter since none of the staff at the shelter speak Spanish.

Maria appears to be behind academically. She struggles reading simple children's books written in English. It is unknown if her ability to read in Spanish is better than her English reading skills.

Other than her two cousins, Elicia has no other sources of support in the community. Her cousins have young families and limited resources but are well established and connected to a Latino community in the city and the local Catholic church. Her cousins refused to let Elicia and Maria live with them while she was trying to find her own place and a job. They stated that they did not have enough room and are concerned they would get in trouble with their landlord if it was found out that they were letting people stay with them. They sent her to the local church for help, and she was given the address for the agency's shelter by the priest.

Elicia has been looking for housing in the Latino community. The housing market is tight with limited options, and she has been unable to find anything that she could possibly afford. The only

(continued)

CASE SUMMARY

affordable housing she found was a room in a rundown motel that rents by the hour or by the month. It is in an area of town known for drug dealing and sex work.

On arrival in the community, Elicia found occasional work for a house cleaning company. The company hires undocumented workers, pays them very low cash wages, and threatens to turn them in to Immigration and Customs Enforcement (ICE) if they complain. The job bosses also exploit their female workers sexually, threatening to turn them in if they do not comply. Elicia was fearful about applying for other jobs because of her illegal status. She considered turning to sex work to be able to take care of her children, but her Catholic upbringing and thoughts of how doing so would shame her family have kept her from doing so. She is in constant fear of being detained, separated from her children, and having them placed in foster care. She is also afraid that she will end up homeless again and forced to live on the streets or return to her abusive husband.

Elicia is extremely reluctant to sign up for any federally funded services, even those that she and her children are entitled to receiving. On the suggestion that she enroll for supplemental food through SNAP, Elicia became nervous and refused as she has heard that participation in SNAP services, and others like them, would draw the attention of ICE, and she had heard stories on the news of individuals being deported after signing up for such programs.

Presenting Problems

Elicia and her children are facing multiple obstacles. They need to find permanent, affordable housing and a job that pays enough to cover her housing and living expenses. In addition, Maria needs to be enrolled in school. Elicia also wants to regain custody of her youngest daughter in foster care.

Additionally, Elicia is experiencing an immense amount of stress, anxiety, and possibly post-traumatic stress disorder (PTSD). She described an instance where she could not calm down her breathing, and she felt lightheaded. She is very fearful of men and tries to avoid all contact with men in the community. She reports difficulty sleeping at night and feeling exhausted most of the time.

She is concerned about Maria. She has started acting out at the shelter, getting into fights with the other children, disobeying her mother, and being disrespectful and defiant to the staff and other adults. Elicia and Maria fight frequently, and when Elicia tries to discipline Maria, she throws a temper tantrum until Elicia gives up.

Elicia has many strengths. She had the strength to leave her abusive husband and move to a different city. She loves her daughters. She wants desperately to keep Maria with her and hopes to have Sarah returned to her custody. She is resilient and has managed to survive and keep her daughter safe despite not having a place to stay, a job, and a limited support network. Additionally, Elicia is highly motivated to find her own accommodations and support her children.

■ Discussion Questions

1. What barriers may Jackie encounter when attempting to engage with Elicia and Maria? How can Jackie address these barriers?

2. How can Jackie utilize her understanding of trauma-informed practices to assist her in engaging with Elicia and Maria?

3. Considering the theories presented in this chapter, select two and describe how Jackie could use those theories to inform her engagement with Elicia and Maria.

4. How could interprofessional collaboration aid Jackie in helping Elicia and Maria?

■ References

Adam, G., & Pyles, L. (2016). *Holistic engagement: Transformative social work education in the 21st Century*. Oxford: Oxford University Press

Anyikwa, V. A., Chiarelli-Helminiak, C. M., Hodge, D. M., & Wells-Wilbon, R. (2015). Women empowering women. *Journal of Social Work Education, 51*, 723–737. doi:10.1080/10437797.2015.1076283

Baum, N. (2007). Therapists' responses to treatment termination: An inquiry into the variables that contribute to therapists' experiences. *Clinical Social Work Journal, 35*(2), 97–106. doi:10.1007/s10615-006-0066-0

Bowlby, J. (1988). *A secure base: Parent-child attachment and healthy human development*. New York, NY: Basic Books Inc.

Brisch, K. H. (2012). *Treating attachment disorders: From theory to therapy* (2nd ed.). New York, NY: Guilford Press.

Cain, C. (2006). *Attachment disorders*. Lanham, MD: Jason Aronson Publishing.

Council on Social Work Education. (2012). *Advanced social work practice in trauma*. Alexandria, VA: Author.

Council on Social Work Education. (2015). *Educational policy and accreditation standards*. Alexandria, VA: Author.

Council on Social Work Education. (2018). *Specialized practice curricular guide for trauma-informed social work practice*. Alexandria, VA: Author.

Cree, V. E., & Dean, J. S. (2015). Exploring social work students' attitudes towards feminism: Opening up conversations. *Social Work Education, 34*(8), 903–920. doi:10.1080/02615479.2015.1081884

Daniel, B., & Taylor, J. (2001). *Engaging with fathers: Practice issues for health and social care*. London, UK: Jessica Kingsley Publishers.

Eyal-Lubling, R., & Krumer-Nevo, M. (2016). Feminist social work: Practice and theory of practice. *Social Work, 6*(3), 245–254. doi:10.1093/sw/sww026

Felitti, V. J., Anda, R. F., Nordenberg, D., Williamson, D. F., Spitz, A. M., Edwards, V., . . . Marks, J. S. (1998). Relationship of childhood abuse and household dysfunction to many of the leading causes of death in adults. *American Journal of Preventive Medicine, 14*(4), 245–258. doi:10.1016/S0749-3797(98)00017-8

Fisher, E. A. (2009). Motivation and leadership in social work management: A review of theories and related studies. *Administration in Social Work, 33*(4), 347–367. doi:10.1080/03643100902769160

Fraser, M. W., Kirby, L. D., & Smokowski, P. R. (2004). Risk and resilience in childhood. In M. W. Fraser (Ed.), *Risk and resilience in childhood: An ecological perspective.* (pp. 13–66). Washington, DC: NASW Press.

Hartsock, N. (1983). The feminist standpoint. In S. Harding & M. Hintikka (Ed.), *Discovering reality* (pp. 283–310). Dordrecht, The Netherlands: D. Reidel.

Herman, J. L. (1997). *Trauma and recovery*. New York, NY: Basic Books.

Herman, J. L. (1998). Recovery from psychological trauma. *Psychiatry & Clinical Neurosciences, 52*, S145–S150. doi:10.1046/j.1440-1819.1998.0520s5S145.x

Hutchison, E. D. (2017). *Essentials of human behavior: Integrating person, environment, and the life course* (2nd ed.). Thousand Oaks, CA: Sage Publications, Inc.

Knapp, H. (2010). *Introduction to social work practice: A practical workbook*. Los Angeles, CA: SAGE Publications, Inc.

Langer, C. L., & Lietz, C. A. (2015). *Applying theory to generalist social work practice*. Hoboken, NJ: Wiley.

Levenson, J. (2017). Trauma-informed social work practice. *Social Work, 62*(2), 105–113. doi:10.1093/sw/swx001

Lonn, M. R., & Dantzler, J. Z. (2017). A practical approach to counseling refugees: Applying Maslow's hierarchy of needs. *Journal of Counselor Practice, 8*(2), 61–83.

Maslow, A. (1962). *Toward a psychology of being*. New York, NY: Viking.

Misca, G., & Unwin, P. (2016). *Psychology and social work: Applied perspectives*. Malden, MA: Polity.

National Association of Social Workers. (2017). *Code of ethics*. Silver Spring, MD: National Association of Social Workers.

Parris, M. (2012). *An introduction to social work practice: A practical handbook*. Maidenhead, UK: McGraw-Hill Education.

Payne, M. (2016). *Modern social work theory* (4th ed.). New York, NY: Oxford University Press.

Pharr, S. (1988). *Homophobia: A weapon for sexism*. Inverness, CA: Chardon Press.

Poulin, J., & Young, T. (1997). Development of a helping relationship inventory for social work practice. *Research on Social Work Practice, 7*(4), 463–489. doi:10.1177/104973159700700403

Steen, J. A. (2012). The human rights philosophy as a values framework for the human behavior course: Integration of human rights concepts in the person-in-environment perspective. *Journal of Human Behavior in the Social Environment, 22*, 853–862. doi:10.1080/10911359.2012.707917

Thorne, B., Sanders, P., Oven, A., Wharton, K., Burrows, R., & Bury, S. (2013). *Carl Rogers* (3rd ed.). London, England: SAGE Publications Ltd.

Van Wormer, K. (2009). Restorative justice as social justice for victims of gendered violence: A standpoint feminist perspective. *Social Work, 54*(2), 107–116. doi:10.1093/sw/54.2.107

Vishal, M. V. (2018). Strengths-based social work: Proposing protective and engagement practice with older adults. *Journal of Social Work Education and Practice, 3*(3), 46–53.

Walsh, J. (2013) *Theories for direct social work practice* (3rd ed.). Stamford, CT: Cengage Learning.

Winnicott, D. W. (1988). *Human nature*. New York, NY: Schocken Books.

Young, T., & Poulin, J. (1998) The helping relationship inventory: A clinical appraisal. *The Journal of Contemporary Social Services, 79*(2), 123–133. doi:10.1606/1044-3894.3613

MICROSYSTEMS ASSESSMENT: INDIVIDUALS, FAMILIES, AND GROUPS

Nicole is a social worker at a large urban facility that provides both mental health and substance use support services. The agency provides treatment at a variety of levels of care from outpatient to more intensive services including partial hospitalization programs. Nicole's job title is "intake counselor." As an intake counselor, Nicole sees all individuals who are seeking services for either mental health or substance use and decides the appropriate level of care necessary to meet the client's needs.

Nicole's appointments are scheduled every 90 minutes. During that time, she must engage with the client, review intake paperwork including informed consent and confidentiality policies, and complete a biopsychosocial–spiritual assessment. Nicole must gather a lot of information during this initial meeting to be sure that her assessment is thorough and complete. The assessment serves as the basis to determine what types of services are most appropriate for the client; so it is critically important to be sure the assessment is as full and accurate as possible.

Nicole relies on her background in social work to guide her through the assessment process. She starts where the client is and makes sure to establish a rapport quickly to help the client feel at ease. Nicole attempts to be authentic and genuine while engaging with clients. While engaging in the assessment process, Nicole gathers information both from client self-reporting and her own clinical observations during the meeting. Nicole also works to identify other possible sources of information that would be necessary to support the client assessment. When she identifies such a source, she asks the client to sign a written release of information in order to gather that collateral information. Nicole understands how important assessments are in the helping process; so she tries to be as diligent as possible to be sure that the assessment is comprehensive and accurately reflects the client's current needs.

LEARNING OBJECTIVES

This chapter explores assessment with individuals, families, and groups. Assessment is a stage within the helping process. However, good assessment is ongoing assessment, not limited to an intake that gets recorded and stuffed in a client chart. Assessment begins with the first encounter with clients and continues through termination. As social workers, when we are assessing clients, we are gathering and examining information from a myriad of sources. Assessments should be thorough and comprehensive. Assessments should aim to get a complete snapshot of clients, their history, and their current functioning. Social workers should assess impacts on the clients at the micro-, mezzo-, and macrolevels. By the end of this chapter, you will be able to:

1. Review theories that inform assessment

2. Recognize the stages of human development proposed by Erikson and how they inform assessment

3. Understand how an ecomap can be used to assess client systems

4. Understand how a genogram can be used to assess client family systems

5. Identify policies that impact assessment

■ Competency 7: Assess Individuals, Families, Groups, Organizations, and Communities

Social workers understand that assessment is an ongoing component of the dynamic and interactive process of social work practice with, and on behalf of, diverse individuals, families, groups, organizations, and communities. Social workers understand theories of human behavior and the social environment, and critically evaluate and apply this knowledge in the assessment of diverse clients and constituencies, including individuals, families, groups, organizations, and communities. Social workers understand methods of assessment with diverse clients and constituencies to advance practice effectiveness. Social workers recognize the implications of the larger practice context in the assessment process and value the importance of interprofessional collaboration in this process. Social workers understand how their personal experiences and affective reactions may affect their assessment and decision-making. Social workers:

- Collect and organize data and apply critical thinking to interpret information from clients and constituencies

- Apply knowledge of human behavior and the social environment, person-in-environment, and other multidisciplinary theoretical frameworks in the analysis of assessment data from clients and constituencies

- Develop mutually agreed-on intervention goals and objectives based on the critical assessment of strengths, needs, and challenges within clients and constituencies

- Select appropriate intervention strategies based on the assessment, research knowledge, values, and preferences of clients and constituencies

■ National Association of Social Workers (NASW) *Code of Ethics*

The NASW *Code of Ethics* serves as a guide throughout the helping process including during and throughout the assessment process. Assessments can be complex yet must be ethical in all aspects. The ethical principles that relate to assessment include importance of human relationships as well as competence. The related ethical standards are privacy and confidentiality, clients who lack decision-making capacity, and referral for services. The NASW *Code of Ethics* is available online (www.socialworkers.org/About/Ethics/Code-of-Ethics/Code-of-Ethics-English).

When assessing a client, social workers recognize that human relationships are vitally important to the human experience. Clients do not exist in isolation. They are often involved in a variety of relationships, both formal and informal. Formal relationships would reflect formalized or professional supports in place in the client's life. For example, a social worker would be a formal support or relationship in a client's life. Informal relationships refer to supports such as friends, family, and community. At times, social workers must better understand, or assess, relationships that are present in the lives of their clients. The NASW *Code of Ethics* (2017) sets forth that social workers must seek to strengthen human connections and relationships. In order for social workers to be able to strengthen relationships, they should first have a clear understanding of their functioning, which can occur via a complete assessment.

Professional social workers must be competent. Competence is at the heart of ethical social work practice. Social workers must be aware of how to conduct assessments and use them appropriately within their practice. Social workers should not use assessment tools that they have not been trained to implement. Social workers should seek out training and support to be sure that their assessment practices are competent in order to best meet the needs of the clients.

Self-determination refers to a client's right to make his or her own choices regarding treatment goals. Social workers strive to promote client involvement in all aspects of treatment. However, at times, social workers must limit or restrict clients' right to self-determination when clients put themselves or others at risk.

Social workers value the privacy of their clients and practice safeguards to ensure client privacy and confidentiality are maintained. Social workers cannot share client information without the written permission of the client. Social workers cannot seek information about a client without written permission as well. Though an assessment could be greatly benefited by other reports or supportive documentation, if a client refuses consent, the social worker is bound to respect the wishes of the client.

Social workers must determine or assess if a client is able to make decisions regarding his or her personal circumstances. Social workers must follow legal mandates regarding decision-making capacity. Though someone may be limited in his or her ability to make decisions, he or she should be included as much as possible in the assessment process.

Competent social workers know the limits of their practice expertise. As professionals, social workers value competence and recognize limitations. If, during the course of the assessment process, the social worker learns that the client is in need of more specialized services, the social worker should refer the client to such appropriate services. Whenever referring a client, social workers should try to provide as much continuity of care as possible.

■ Human Development Theories

Humans are constantly developing. From infancy through late adulthood, there are a variety of physical and psychological stages and milestones. During typical development, humans progress through these stages and milestones in a predictable pattern. However, at times, stages and milestones may be delayed or unattended to due to a variety of causes. Theories of human development assist social workers in better understanding the progression of stages and milestones that are a part of maturation.

> ▶ **Critical Thinking Questions**
>
> Considering typical human development, identify physical milestones that humans progress through throughout the life span from infancy to late adulthood. Why is it important for social workers to have a clear understanding of typical developmental milestones?

Social workers recognize that there are various forms of development: physical, psychological, social, and cognitive. Physical development refers to such things as biological milestones and growth. Physical development can also refer to things such as gross motor skills like sitting up, walking, or running. Fine motor skills including the ability to write and manipulate objects are also a part of physical development. Psychological development includes the transition from egocentric to being able to take on the perspectives of others and even moral development. Social development includes interacting with friends and family and play. The legendary children's show host Mister Rogers is credited with saying that "play is the work of childhood." As children engage in play with others, they are developing socially as they move through the stages of play from parallel play onto cooperative or even reciprocal play. Last, cognitive development includes the ability to think and reason, beginning with concrete, tangible thoughts onto more complex, abstract reasoning. Social workers understand that despite these orderly progressions of typical development, not all individuals will progress through each type of development the same way. Some may have an advanced physical development and a delayed cognitive development. Others may have extremely advanced cognitive development and delayed social development. This is why social workers must assess each individual regarding each area of human development. Social workers must assess where the person is in his or her development and how this influences participation in the person's environments.

Psychosocial Theories

Psychosocial theories set out to address psychological stages and milestones throughout the life span. These theories attempt to explore how social interactions influence psychological growth and development at various ages or stages. Much of this work is based on the initial works of Sigmund Freud, who is often considered the father of modern psychology. Freud initially put forth his stages of psychosexual development as an attempt to explain how children progress through orderly stages, facing a crisis or task at each stage. As you will read, many of the stage theorists we introduce have built their work upon Freud's initial proposals. These theories focus on the process of psychological aging that occurs while individuals physically age. Psychological aging refers to developments in regard to personality, mental reasoning, and functioning, as well as the creation of a sense of self, or personal identity (Morgan & Kunkel, 2016).

Theory of Motivation

In Chapter 5, Engagement and Social Work Practice, we introduced Maslow's hierarchy of needs (see Figure 5.1). Maslow's theory of motivation can inform assessment by determining client levels of motivation in treatment. Social workers should assess client motivation to change. Maslow provides a foundation for considering client assessment in regard to their needs including their physiological needs, safety, love and belonging, esteem, and self-actualization. It is important to assess client needs and functioning across each area of need. Considering Maslow's work, it is critically necessary to understand where there are areas of need so that they can be attended to in order for the client to be able to address higher levels of needs.

Psychosocial Development Theory

Erik Erikson set forth a theory for understanding the human experience, utilizing stages from infancy to late adulthood and "at each stage, the rational mind deals with a maturational crisis presented by the social circumstances of our life" (Payne, 2016, p. 107). Each of the stages is outlined in Table 6.1. In each stage, the individual is faced with a crisis that must be addressed. Should the individual come through the crisis in a positive manner, the individual will gain a core strength that aids inongoing development. Erikson's theories can be quite useful during the helping process as each stage has a:

> Specific kind of existential search or quest for "something missing." In this regard, clients come to therapy because they feel uncomfortable about something in their lives and have a vague sense that something is missing or is not right. They want to feel better about themselves and be "all right" in the world. They are often unaware that this sense of something missing or wanting to feel better is often the same thing. The

TABLE 6.1 Stages of Psychosocial Development in the Individual From Infancy to Adulthood

AGE	CRISIS OR CONFLICT
Infancy	Trust vs. mistrust
Toddlerhood	Autonomy vs. shame and doubt
Early childhood	Initiative vs. guilt
Middle childhood	Industry vs. inferiority
Adolescence	Identity vs. role confusion
Early adulthood	Intimacy vs. isolation
Middle adulthood	Generativity vs. stagnation
Late adulthood	Integrity vs. despair

search for something missing is experienced differently at the different life cycle stages, and thus the nature of the search is stage-related and developmental. The resolution of the search at one stage of therapy often leads to the development of another search, which implies that the therapy process comprises a series of searches as clients progress through their therapy. (Knight, 2017, p. 1048)

Through a comprehensive biopsychosocial–spiritual assessment process that explores all aspects of human development, social workers can work with clients to explore areas of concern that may be related to a conflict or crisis at a particular stage of development. Social workers must be good critical thinkers and use their professional judgment in order to assist clients in identifying previous conflicts with current concerns. Social workers who are aware of these eight stages can be mindful during the assessment process to address potential issues that may have arose throughout development and then be in a better place to move forward in the helping process.

Trust Versus Mistrust

During infancy, human babies are totally dependent on others to have their needs met. When infants have a need, whether it be to eat or have a diaper change, they vocalize their needs through their cry. Infants who have their needs consistently attended to are able to develop a sense of trust in others, knowing that their needs will be met. On the other hand, infants who do not consistently have their needs met begin to establish mistrust. This mistrust couples with a feeling that others may be unpredictable, undependable, or even dangerous. In extreme cases, when infants find that their cries are not responded to, they may even stop crying. In cases when children have stopped crying to have their needs met, there can be various concerns related to development. At times, parental concerns from physical or mental illnesses, including postpartum depression, can be common barriers to providing consistent care during infancy. Case 6.1 illustrates such an example.

CASE 6.1   OVERWHELMED: CLIENTS WITH POSTPARTUM DEPRESSION IN SOCIAL WORK PRACTICE

Ava recently gave birth to her first child, a son, Tyler. Ava is a single mother and has limited supports. Her mother and grandmother have both offered to help, but Ava does not want to inconvenience anyone and does not want to seem like she cannot take care of the baby on her own. Ever since coming home from the hospital after the birth, Ava has not felt like herself. She has felt really overwhelmed, tired, and sad. She often finds herself crying in her bed with little energy to get up. She has no appetite and does not even want to eat. She has Tyler in a bassinet in her bedroom, but sometimes she is just too exhausted to pick him up when he starts to cry. Ava feels like something is not right, but she is not sure what it is. Ava feels like maybe she is just a bad mother and does not have what it takes to be there for Tyler. At her checkup with her obstetrician, Ava started to cry and shared some of how she has been feeling. The doctor was very understanding and reassuring with Ava. He said

---

(continued)

CASE 6.1

that it sounds like she may be experiencing postpartum depression. The doctor also shared how it is really important for Ava to reach out to supports so that Tyler has his needs attended to regularly in a consistent and timely manner. The doctor shared how detrimental it can be for the baby to have inconsistent care during infancy and how that can have long-standing negative impacts on the child's physical and psychological growth. After this appointment, Ava realized that she did need help, not just for herself but for Tyler as his needs should be addressed consistently.

Ava began seeing a social worker and taking an antidepressant medication prescribed by her doctor. She also had her mother and grandmother over much more to help her with the day-to-day household tasks and caring for Tyler. Ava began to recognize that as she was starting to feel better and with the help of her family, Tyler was becoming more engaging and was able to be comforted more easily. She realized that it was less important to appear to be able to do it all on her own and more important to give Tyler the consistent support he needs to develop into a healthy and happy baby.

When this stage is successfully addressed and the child develops trust in the world, the strength of hope is instilled with the child. Hope is often thought of as a feeling; rather, some theorists have suggested that hope is not an emotion but a way of thinking (Snyder, 2002). Hope is defined as a motivational state based on a sense of successful goals, pathways, and agency (Snyder, 2002). Hope is important for future personal psychological success. Hopelessness is a strong predictor of low levels of resilience across the adult life span (Gooding, Hurst, Johnson, & Tarrier, 2011). Brown (2010) suggests "in order to learn hopefulness children need relationships that are characterized by boundaries, consistency, and support" (p. 66).

When conducting an assessment, it is important for social workers to ask questions about early childhood experiences. Most comprehensive biopsychosocial–spiritual assessments include questions about early development, including information about the pregnancy. Though social workers are not medical professionals, it is important to gather such information because social workers understand that physical development can impact psychological and social development throughout the life span. Also, competent social work professionals understand that, at times, medical conditions can cause psychological and/or social impairments. In such cases, social workers should refer the client for a medical examination to rule out any underlying medical conditions that may be the source of impairment.

Social workers who have an understanding of human growth and development throughout the life span can assist clients in identifying possible areas of concern that the client may be unaware of. Case 6.2 illustrates such an example. It is important to be cautious, however, when considering the etiology of concerns. Theories can be extremely beneficial in providing a framework for understanding a myriad of phenomena related to human growth and behavior. However, theories cannot provide evidence of direct causation in all cases. For instance, an individual may have experienced inconsistent caregiving during his or her infancy; this does not mean that person will have a pathological distrust of all others and will be unable to have long-term relationships. Social workers should be ever mindful not to overly pathologize individuals. Theories, such as Erikson's stages of development, provide an opportunity to better understand how development occurs and in turn explain some behaviors that may occur as a result of various influences throughout the life span.

CASE 6.2   RELATIONSHIP PROBLEMS: APPLYING ERIKSON'S THEORY OF DEVELOPMENT IN SOCIAL WORK PRACTICE

Shelly recently ended a 1-year relationship and is seeking the support of a social worker to help her deal with feelings related to the breakup. During the first session, the social worker, Gina, began engaging with Shelly and building a rapport. Gina began conducting a biopsychosocial–spiritual assessment with Shelly. Shelly, though she stated she was interested in having a long-term relationship and interested in getting married one day, also shared that she is hesitant to engage in relationships because she knows they usually do not work out. Throughout the interview, Shelly makes several references to a history of poor relationships she has had and shares that she has a hard time opening up and feeling close to others. When asking about her early childhood, Gina learned that Shelly spent her first 2 years of life in the child welfare system due to neglectful living conditions in her family of origin.

Gina asked Shelly about her early experiences, which included multiple foster care placements and inadequate care on the part of her parents. Shelly shared that she has not really thought much about it because she was so young she does not remember any of it. As the assessment continued, Gina was able to identify several examples where Shelly has been closed off to others and at times distrustful of people, which has hindered her ability to be fully engaged in relationships with family, friends, and romantic partners. Gina recognized that Shelly may be having relationship difficulties due to an early imprinting of mistrust since her needs were not met consistently during her infancy.

Gina shared information with Shelly about early development, including the tasks of development suggested by Erikson. At first, Shelly felt overwhelmed and worried that she missed this milestone and now there was no hope for her. Gina reassured Shelly that this was something that they could work on together in treatment. Gina and Shelly discussed how they could develop treatment goals in order to increase trust in others and mend Shelly's current worldview.

Autonomy Versus Shame and Doubt

As toddlers, children are beginning to explore their world in new ways. As children become more ambulatory, they are able to experience their world through their senses and have a greater sense of independence than they did as toddlers. A critical task for children during this stage is often toilet training. During this stage, when children are validated for their experiences interacting with their environment, they can develop a sense of autonomy. Autonomy refers to an independence or free will of one's own actions. At this stage of a child's life, they are learning if it is okay to be themselves and explore their world. Children who successfully master this stage will freely explore their world as they continue to learn and grow. To be autonomous, it is important for young children to have the opportunity to be in control of their body and make choices. Conversely, children who are not allowed to explore their environment or are harshly criticized for their explorations will develop shame and doubt. This shame and doubt will begin to permeate throughout their experiences, and they will not freely explore their environment.

Children who can successfully gain autonomy develop the strength of will. Will relates to a personal drive or determination. Children with strong will do not give up easily, even in the face of adversity or challenge. This strong will can be closely linked to the concept of grit. Tough (2012) puts forth that grit is "a passionate commitment to a single mission and an unswerving dedication to achieve that mission" (p. 74).

Initiative Versus Guilt

In early childhood, children become much more active. Children who are promoted to play, act, imagine, and engage with their world can become creative and develop a sense of initiative. On the other hand, children who are not encouraged to do such things often develop a sense of guilt. They may feel that they are wrong and not explore their world. When children are able to achieve initiative at this stage, they inherit the strength of purpose. Purpose relates closely with having intention or drive for a particular task.

When conducting an assessment, social workers should inquire about schooling experiences. Formalized schooling is a large part of childhood. Children spend a significant amount of time in school from the age of 6 to 18. Understanding how this experience was perceived by the client is important. It is essential to ask about what was positive as well as what was disliked about these experiences. School serves as a critical environment that children engage in on a regular basis. During the school year, many children spend just as much if not more time in school with their teachers and friends than at home. These relationships can extremely impact the development of a child.

> ▶ **Critical Thinking Question**
> Consider how can school relationships (with peers and staff including teachers, school social workers, etc.) impede or promote development during childhood.

Industry Versus Inferiority

As childhood progress, children often enroll into formalized schooling. As a part of this process, children begin to create work products frequently. When a child feels praise or proud of their productive work, they can develop a sense of competence. When this occurs, the child experiences industry. However, if a child feels inadequate, he or she may develop a sense of inferiority, feeling less than, or incapable.

When this stage is successfully addressed and industry is achieved, children develop the strength of competence. Competence refers to one's capacity to do something effectively and efficiently to the best of one's ability. Children with the strength of competence believe in their own ability to complete a task. This coupled with the previous strengths of will and purpose allows for youth to become quite productive.

Identity Versus Role Confusion

During adolescence, young people are seeking out an identity and trying to answer the questions, "Who am I?" and "Who do I want to be?." This stage of life is a transition between childhood and adulthood. When youth feel they are able to belong and develop a personal image of their self, they develop identity. When youth feel unable to develop their own identity or lack peer relationships or future plans for their self, they may develop a sense of confusion related to their role in this world. Case 6.3 illustrates a common search for personal identity that adolescents experience.

CASE 6.3   WHO AM I? DEVELOPING A SENSE OF IDENTITY IN ADOLESCENCE

Brian is a high-school sophomore. Growing up, he had always enjoyed playing sports. He tried out for the high school basketball team, but unfortunately he did not make the team. Brian was crushed. He always thought of himself as a "jock," but now that he did not make the team, he did not know who he was. Making matters worse, his two best friends did make the team. Within a few weeks, Brian found he was not spending much time with his best friends because they were busy every day after school with practices and conditioning. Brian found himself alone and with nothing to do. Brian started coming home from school and going straight to his room and going to sleep.

Brian's parents recognized that he was not acting himself and talked to him about what was going on. Brian did not want to talk to his parents about what was going on because he did not think that they would understand. He felt all alone and lost. His parents suggested he invite his friends over, and they hang out. This was proof to Brian that his parents just did not get it because he felt like he did not have any friends right now.

The next week at school, there was a club fair. Brian was not interested in joining any clubs because he was only ever interested in basketball. But as he walked through the hall, he noticed a group of people laughing and having fun together. He wondered what was going on over there and he slowed down to get a closer look. As he slowed down, someone at the table said hi to him and asked him how he was. Brian stopped to exchange introductions. The club representative, Len, asked Brian if he was interested in theater. Brian smirked and said, "nah." Len said they have something for everyone, "not everyone goes on stage, there is actually a lot of guys who build and move the sets around." Brian was not sure if he wanted to be in the theater club, but he did like how everyone was getting along and he wanted to be a part of something. Within a few weeks, Brian found he really enjoyed being a part of the stage crew for the theater department. He was meeting lots of new people and making new friendships.

As the school year progressed, Brian realized that though basketball had been an important part of his life, and something that he still enjoyed, there were many parts to himself that he could explore. Brian was becoming more engaged with others and more confident in his own skin again. Brian felt like he belonged to a group and liked who he was becoming.

At this stage, youth sometimes experience an identity crisis in the midst of trying to find themselves. It is not uncommon for youth to try out a variety of social identities when attempting to find which one best fits them. When adolescents are able to successfully develop a sense of identity and avoid identity confusion, they are able to develop the strength of fidelity. Fidelity refers to the ability of the adolescent to be true to his or her own self, identity that he or she has developed.

Intimacy Versus Isolation

In early adulthood, the primary task is to seek out close intimate relationships with others. Intimacy refers to a deep closeness. Sometimes this occurs via romantic relationships but can also exist through friendships. When young adults feel that they are able to care about and share experiences with others, they develop a sense of intimacy and in turn strong relationships. When a person does not experience the closeness of others, they can feel uncared for and alone, which leads to isolation. When individuals are able to achieve intimacy, they also achieve the strength of love.

When assessing intimacy, social workers should be mindful to explore various types of relationships. There may be a tendency to overly focus on romantic relationships, but it is also important to consider other close relationships during the assessment process. Social workers value human relationships and understand how important they are for individuals. Understanding this, social workers seek to assess all relationships present in a client's life. Social workers also seek to enhance client awareness of

▶ **Critical Thinking Question**

Why is it important for social workers to assess the types of relationships or supports available for clients?

personal relationships. It is important for social workers to explicitly identify personal supports present for clients. At times, clients may have difficulty identifying informal supports or relationships. Tools, such as genograms, which we discuss later in this chapter, can be beneficial in assisting clients in identifying personal supports during the assessment process.

Generativity Versus Stagnation

The task of middle adulthood is making life count. When adults experience a sense that they are productive and contributing to future generations, they can develop generativity. When adults do not feel productive or involved in contributing to the future, they may experience stagnation. Stagnation refers to experiencing no movement or growth. When an adult is able to achieve generativity, he or she is able to obtain the strength of care. Care refers to the concern or interest shown in something. Care at to this stage relates to the care of others and future generations.

Integrity Versus Despair

During late adulthood, the final task of development is to reflect back upon life and determine if it has been a good life. When people look back on their life with fond feelings, they experience integrity. However, when one has many regrets or bitterness, this can lead to despair. At this point in the life span, "dying is the final developmental stage, with its own central crisis, potential, and pitfalls. Successful handling of the crisis leads to the development of a special potential or virtues" (Zalenski & Raspa, 2016, p. 804). Death is a natural part of the life cycle; however, in some cultures, death is avoided or minimized and as a result not considered until it is imminent. Reflecting upon one's life when death is near can be either rewarding and fulfilling or filled with despair and regrets. At times, individuals experience the phenomenon of death anxiety. Schwarz (2017) puts forth that death anxiety is the anxiety that arises as individuals age and reflect upon their life and ultimate death, which can be compounded by the loss of other loved ones, particularly for individuals who are alone.

When this stage is able to be successfully addressed through the attainment of integrity, the strength of wisdom is achieved. Wisdom relates to having awareness, judgment, and insights. Wisdom is closely related to a sense of inner peace and acceptance (see Case 6.4).

CASE 6.4   WANTING TO SHARE WISDOM: PSYCHOSOCIAL DEVELOPMENT IN LATE ADULTHOOD

Lily is an 84-year-old female who lives alone in an assisted living facility. She has been in this facility for the past 2 years, ever since her husband of 50 years passed away. Lily and her husband had five children, but as the children grew up, they each moved away and now live out of town. Lily's children try to visit a couple of times a year and call every now and then. Lily feels lonely. She has fond memories of her childhood and young adult life. She was lucky to meet her husband at a young age and live what she calls a "fairy tale" with him. Lily and her husband had a great relationship and were together all of the time. Since his passing, Lily does not do any of the things she used to enjoy doing like shopping, playing bingo, or going to church. Lily spends most of her time sitting in her living room watching TV. The staff at the facility have noticed that Lily is increasingly becoming isolated and not engaging in the group activities that happen regularly at the facility. The facility social worker, Ashley, was notified about Lily and decided to set up a visit to talk with Lily.

When Ashley arrived at Lily's room, Lily was eager to invite her in and had a plate of cookies ready for the social worker to enjoy. Ashley sat with Lily in the living room, and Lily was eager to speak with her. Ashley realized early on that Lily was lonely. She had a lifetime of memories but no one with whom to share her stories and reflect back on her memories. Ashley asked Lily if she would like to meet more regularly to chat. Lily said she would very much like that. Ashley began to meet with Lily once or twice a week. Lily would share stories from throughout her life with Ashley and was able to identify that she was sad that she did not have the chance to share her stories with anyone before meeting with Ashley.

Ashley understood the importance for older adults to be able to share their personal experiences with others. It is important for them to reflect on their lives and to share their cumulative wisdom with others. By meeting with Ashley, Lily was able to share her experiences and feel a sense of pride in the life that she lived.

Stage Theory

John Piaget was a cognitive theorist who developed a stage theory to better understand how children are able to think, reason, and in turn learn. Piaget set out to further the understanding of cognitive development in children. Cognition refers to the ability to acquire or learn new information. Piaget believed that the cognition, or mental processes, of a child evolved

TABLE 6.2 Piaget's Theory of Cognitive Development

Sensorimotor	Birth to age 2	Children experience the world through their senses (touch, taste, see, hear, smell).
Preoperational	2–6 years	Children begin to use words and images to represent items in their world.
Concrete Operational	7–11 years	Children are able to begin thinking logically about concrete events.
Formal Operational	12+ years	Children are able to begin thinking abstractly about events and scenarios.

in an orderly logical progression. Table 6.2 outlines the four stages of cognitive develop-ment that Piaget identified: sensorimotor, preoperational, concrete operational, and formal operational. Throughout these stages, Piaget set forth that individuals developed via their thought processes and how they were able to understand and interact with the environment around them (Misca & Unwin, 2016). Piaget's stages demonstrate that children begin learn-ing through very tactile experiences, and as they grow and develop, they are able to think in more complex ways.

Piaget believed that all information received by people would be categorized into schema. Schemas are mental representations or structures. The information would either be assimilated or accommodated based on previous experiences. Assimilation involves incorporating new information with existing schema. Accommodation involves creating a new schema or mod-ifying an existing schema. Case 6.5 provides an example of assimilation and accommodation.

CASE 6.5   SORTING NEW INFORMATION: ASSIMILATION AND ACCOMMODATION IN SOCIAL WORK PRACTICE

Assimilation

Riley is a 6-year-old girl. Riley is about to start kindergarten. She had attended preschool for 2 years so when her parents shared with her that she would be going to kindergarten and likened it to preschool, Riley had a preexisting schema to incorporate this information. Because Riley has expe-rienced preschool, she has an existing idea of what to expect from kindergarten. Though there will be some differences, overall this information was able to be assimilated into the existing schema.

Accommodation

Benet is a 3-year-old boy. At home, Benet lives with his parents and two cats. One day while out for a walk with his parents, they pass a dog park. Benet sees the furry, four-legged animals. He points and says "kitty cats." His mother smiled and said, "no, those are dogs." Benet had never seen a dog before. Prior to this experience, all furry, four-legged creatures with tails were cats. This is new information that does not fit into the existing schema of cat, so Benet must accommodate this infor-mation by creating a new schema for the category of dogs.

Psychodynamic Theories

Psychodynamic theories are approaches that are derived from the work of Freud that attempt to understand human development through exploring the role of the ego, drives, and structures of the personality. To understand these approaches, it is necessary to be familiar with the levels of consciousness that Freud proposed: conscious, preconscious, and unconscious. The conscious mind is that which you are readily aware of at any given moment. Right now, you may be conscious of what you are reading or how you are feeling. The preconscious refers to that which can be called into the unconscious quite easily. For example, if you were asked to recall the name of your favorite elementary school teacher, you are most likely able to readily remember the teacher's name and maybe even some other fond memories of that classroom experience even though you had not been thinking about it prior to being asked about it. The unconscious mind refers to thoughts that we are generally unaware of that may be suppressed as a defense mechanism.

Another Freudian concept that is important to understand is how Freud viewed the structures of the mind: id, ego, and superego. These structures are not actual parts of the brain like the limbic system or prefrontal cortex; rather, these are conceptual structures to help understand personality and internal drives that influence personality and behavior. The id represents the instinctual drives that are present at birth. The primary concern of the id is having wants and needs met. The id is sometimes referred to as the pleasure seeker. The ego is the representation of the self that is most in touch with reality. The superego is the ideal self that is interested in following the rules and being moral. The ego must mediate between the id and superego.

Ego Psychology

Ego psychology derives closely from Freud's work on the structures of personality. Heinz Hartmann, the founder of ego psychology, believed that conflicts were part of the human condition and it is the role of the ego to mediate conflicts. It is noteworthy though that he believed that there were conflict-free times as well. Hartmann set forth that the ego and id were continuously interacting with the environment influencing each other.

Hartmann explored not only pathological development but also typical development. He set forth the notion of an "average acceptable environment" that was necessary for children to grow within. This environment includes parental involvement and interactions between the parent and child. Hartmann's work was influential as it set out:

> ... focusing on healthy and adaptive development. In contrast to others before him who saw ego development as dominated by conflict, Hartmann saw it as a progression. The ego develops along parallel tracks. One is in conflict, the other in conflict-free capacities within the id and ego. These capacities include perception, memory, motor coordination, language, gifts, and talents. As long as there is a predictable environment, these conflict-free capacities develop into ego functions, which function independently from id drives. (Danzer, 2012, p. 10)

When social workers are conducting assessments, it is important to be mindful not only of conflicts but also of the typical progression of client development free from conflict. This approach is much aligned to the strengths-based approach of social work assessment, which we discuss later in this chapter.

Object Relations Theory

Melanie Klein established object relations theory based on the previous works of Freud. This theory explores the relationships between infants and their primary caregivers. The caregivers are considered the objects. This theory explores the relationship between the infant and the object, or caregivers. It is then, based on this relationship, that the child develops and creates a sense of self with his or her world. The term "object" was used to describe others in part to "convey the fact that sometimes people do not perceive others as they really are, but rather as they imagine them to be" (Frankland, 2010).

Klein was a pioneer in analyzing children, whereas previous psychoanalytic theorists, like Freud, had focused their work on adults. Klein suggested that children fluctuated between periods of pleasure, when their needs are being met, and pain, when needs are unmet. As children grow, they can eventually understand that there is a combination of both pleasure and pain, which is defined as "ambivalence." Ambivalence relates to understanding that there is both good and bad, positives and negatives, in an object or situation. Through reality testing, children are able to grow from a primitive state to this depressive position that supports ambivalence (Polat, 2017).

Another key concept that Klein set forth was that of the depressive position. This is a stage where children recognize the existence of ambivalence in many aspects of life. The depressive position holds that there is uncertainty, contradiction, and at times inconsistency within the world. Klein notes that not all children will come to the place of the depressive position, and may never fully accept this state of ambiguity. When children do not reach the depressive position, she set forth that they were stuck in a stage where they cannot tolerate these ambivalences, which she called the paranoid-schizoid position. Within this position, individuals fluctuate between positive or negative without holding a position or space in the middle. Whereas an individual with a depressive position can understand that a person can have positive qualities that they love and some negative qualities that may, at times, be annoying, they can still love the person. An individual with a paranoid-schizoid position, on the other hand, cannot embrace the juxtaposition of the two opposing qualities and either loves or hates the person.

When considering Klein's theory and assessment, social workers can explore how individuals interact and view their relationships with others. In fact, there may be patterns of interactions that social workers can assess for during this process. Clients who come forth with a limited ability to tolerate the ambiguity of others may need the assistance of the social worker to assist them in more accurately identifying the positives and negatives that exist within most. Social workers understand that very little can be described by all-or-nothing thinking. Rather, social workers appreciate that instead of black or white, there is much gray. Social workers can assess if clients possess all-or-nothing thought patterns and if these interfere with their functioning.

Self-Psychology

Heinz Kohut was a theorist who was highly influenced by the work of Sigmund Freud. Kohut recognized the necessary importance of empathy related to human development. He set forth concepts such as mirroring and healthy narcissism. Previously narcissism had been viewed as pathological. Kohut set forth that healthy narcissism is a healthy sense of self, even a component of self-efficacy. Self-efficacy is the belief in one's own ability to complete a task or mission.

Social workers should assess clients for healthy narcissism, or their sense of self. Social workers should consider if the clients view themselves as inflated, deflated, or relatively accurate. In cases of an inflated sense of self, some may recognize this as more closely fitting with traditional views on narcissism. An inflated sense of self can, at times, be damaging or problematic for clients and their relationships with others. On the other hand, a deflated sense of self may be evidenced by poor self-esteem or self-concept. This view of oneself can be equally damaging and problematic for clients and should be assessed by the social worker.

Furthermore, considering self-psychology can also be a beneficial approach for social workers as many individuals from time to time may experience copious amounts of stress or some other trial or tribulation. As put forth by Cooper and Randall (2012), "every one of us, even the most self-secure, even those with highly empathic self-objects in our past, can lose our self-cohesion and begin to fragment to some degree when burdens and injuries become too heavy" (p. 7). Self-psychology provides a framework for addressing such concerns.

Systems Theory

A system is a set of things that work together. Systems theory seeks to understand the interactions of people and the systems in their lives. Systems often exist in order to achieve a mutual purpose; common systems that social workers engage with are families, communities, and organizations (Langer & Lietz, 2015). When considering systems theory, there are several key concepts to understanding the relationship of systems.

Homeostasis is a systems concept that refers to the desire to avoid change. Humans desire homeostasis. Homeostasis is a state of normal order or being. Homeostasis is not equivalent to optimal functioning but rather the typical or common state of functioning that a system is accustomed to. Inputs and outputs influence the system and impact homeostasis. Inputs and outputs occur via a feedback loop where energy is brought in and taken away from the system. Equifinality is a systems concept that suggests that there are multiple ways to achieve or reach a desired outcome. Multifinality asserts that there are multiple outcomes that can be reached via the same paths.

Systems theory can be useful for social workers who are engaging in assessment. If you consider this theory while examining the interrelated workings of various parts during the assessment, the social worker can explore not only how each part is functioning independently but also consider how they are functioning or working together. This is a practical approach to assessment. Though independently one aspect of an individual's life may not be of concern, when you consider it in combination or relationship to the other parts present, there may indeed be room for growth and remediation.

Family Systems Theory

Families are a special type of system or group. The work of Bowen on family systems was based on the work of systems theorists (Langer & Lietz, 2015). Families have long been studied by social workers and other helping professionals. Understanding the family unit is important.

Social workers recognize that all human relationships, including families, are important. Regardless of family composition (nuclear, blended, multigenerational, etc.), it is important to appreciate that every family is unique. In order to best understand the family of a client, it is best to ask the client to describe his or her family. Assumptions based on personal experiences of families should be avoided as they may bias your work with client systems.

Bowen set forth a specific family theory to assist helping professionals in better understanding family systems.

Bowen's work observing and working with families allowed him to set forth that families had predictable patterns of interactions. This organized, predictable pattern of interaction is a family's homeostasis. His view of families was that they are an "emotional unit that governs the biology and behavior of each member. Everyone plays a part when symptoms occur for any family member. Any symptom is a function of common factors." (Harrison, 2018, p. 167). Bowen also set forth other concepts such as differentiation of self and triangles that assist in assessing and understanding families better.

Differentiation of self refers to the need or desires of each individual to be an individual as well as a part of the family group. Differentiation explores how close and separate members of a family system are to one another. Humans experience two drives, or needs, for closeness and connection and another for individualization, and the concept of differentiation from one's family illustrates these two drives (Frederick, Purrington, & Dunbar, 2016). Differentiation and the development of one's self outside of the family is a healthy piece of development; however, differentiation may occur abruptly or not at all, which can lead to areas of concern. In order to assess the degree to which people have differentiation themselves, the Differentiation of Self Scale provides a metric that ranges from 0 to 100, where higher scores represent a higher level of "solid self" and low scores represent a "pseudo self" (MacKay, 2017). This scale can be a helpful assessment tool for social workers when assessing individuals and families.

Just as a triangle has three sides, triangles within families are dynamic relationships among three persons where there is tension. At times there are "insiders" and at other times there are "outsiders" when considering triangulation within family systems. Sometimes these present via alliances, which are overt relationships within the family or as collations, which are covert relationships within the family. Case 6.6 illustrates a family triangle that is problematic and impeding optimal functioning in a multigenerational family system. Triangles and triangulation are not unique to family systems but can occur in a variety of other group contexts as well as it is often common for individuals who are experiencing conflict to seek out the support of a third party (Crabtree-Nelson & Kohli, 2017).

■ Person-in-Environment Perspective in Assessment

As we have discussed throughout this text, people are complex. It is impossible to understand people fully without considering the full context of their lives including the environments in which they exist. The person-in-environment perspective explores all systems or environments in which a person exists. Social workers should also explore the physical environment in which a person resides (Akesson, Burns, & Hordyk, 2017).

CASE 6.6   ADDRESSING FAMILY TRIANGLES IN SOCIAL WORK PRACTICE

Quinn is a social worker who works as an in-home family therapist. Quinn received a referral for a new client, Amy, a 10-year-old female who lives with her mother, Sheri, and grandmother, Elizabeth. Amy has been acting out at school and is in danger of expulsion. At home, she fights with her mother verbally and has threatened to hit her. Quinn sets up a time to visit the home and meet with Sheri while Amy is at school.

At the house during the intake, Quinn meets both Sheri and Elizabeth. Quinn notices that Sheri seems quite distraught with Amy's current behaviors and at her wit's end, not sure what to do next. She also notices that Elizabeth seems to minimize Amy's behaviors and at times even blames Sheri for inconsistent parenting that causes the problems in the home. Quinn completed all of the required paperwork and reviewed policies and procedures for the services she would be able to provide, including confidentiality and informed consent. Quinn set up her next appointment with the family for the following day in the evening when she could meet Amy.

When Quinn got back to the office after the first visit, she completed all of her paperwork and created a genogram based on the information she had collected thus far. She gathered some materials that she would take out to the home during her next visit with the family as well.

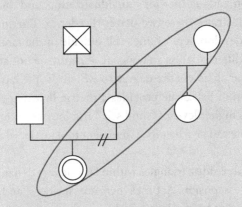

The next day, Quinn returned to the family home for her first visit with Amy. Amy was reluctant to meet with Quinn. Sheri told Amy that Quinn was there to help the family and to help Amy stay in her school, which is something she wants. Amy was still hesitant to engage with Quinn. Then grandma jumped in and said, "Come on baby, come and sit with me, we can talk to this nice lady." Quinn noticed that Amy responded much more favorably to her grandmother, even cuddling up next to her on the couch. Grandma then continued, "Go ahead, tell her about what a good softball player you are. You are my shining star." Amy's face lit up. Quinn could obviously see that Amy and her grandmother had an especially close relationship.

As the session progressed, Quinn noticed how, though Amy and her grandmother were quite close, Sheri seemed to not be close with either of them. It appeared she was left out of many of the special things that Amy and her grandmother shared. Actually, though Sheri would try to engage with them, either Elizabeth or Amy would often dismiss Sheri and return to only interacting with each other.

(continued)

CASE 6.6

As Quinn continued to assess while working with the family, she began to notice patterns of inter-action and was better able to understand the triangulation occurring in the home between Amy and her grandmother that left Sheri, as the mother, out of the loop. Because she felt like an outsider, Sheri was often in conflict with her mother and with her daughter. Quinn was able to depict the family's pattern of interaction using the following triangle. During a session with Sheri and Elizabeth, Quinn shared about how the concept of triangulation can impact families and provided examples of how it can hinder family functioning. Quinn asked the family to depict how they felt their family functioned in relationship to triangulation. Sheri was able to express to her mother how she often feels like an outsider and how that is difficult for her. Elizabeth was receptive to what Sheri was saying. Quinn was able to then teach Sheri and Elizabeth some strategies that could assist them in co-parenting Amy and ways to avoid the conflicts of triangulation in the future.

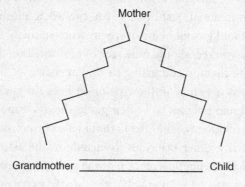

When assessing the person and his or her environments, the social worker must first be aware of all of the environments within which the person exists. This requires a good, comprehensive, ongoing assessment. Social workers must be thorough during the assessment process and ask follow-up questions for clarification whenever necessary. Social workers must use good interviewing skills as well as good nonverbal communication strategies to engage clients so that they can share the information that is necessary for social workers to conduct a thorough assessment.

■ Assessment Process

The assessment process is a key phase in the helping relationship. Assessment involves gathering information necessary to provide services to the client. As a result, assessment serves as a foundation for the future step of intervening with client systems. Formal assessments typically begin during the initial meeting with clients and occur concurrently while engaging with clients. Most formal assessments are completed in the first few initial meetings. It is important to address assessment early in the helping process since it does serve to inform future work with clients.

It is important to distinguish between assessment and diagnosis. These terms are different, though at times, some attempt to use them interchangeably. Diagnosis is the process of identifying the appropriate condition that represents the presenting symptoms and concerns. Many social workers do in fact participate in the diagnosis process. Social workers, more than all other types of helping professionals combined, provide the majority of mental health services in the United States (Dziegielewski, 2015). In order to provide mental health services, a *Diagnostic and Statistical Manual of Mental Disorders* (5th ed.; *DSM-5*; American Psychiatric Association, 2013) diagnosis is often required in order to meet eligibility requirements or to seek reimbursement for services from insurance companies. In order to provide an accurate and appropriate diagnosis, social workers must conduct a thorough and comprehensive assessment. So, in fact, all social workers who diagnose do conduct assessments. However, not all social workers who complete assessments diagnose clients.

Social workers should be mindful of the scope of information needed and should limit their assessment to such material. Just because you can ask a question does not mean you should. Social workers should avoid being overly instructive solely for the sake of curiosity or interest. Rather, social workers should only seek out information that informs the helping relationship and assist the client in addressing treatment goals.

The assessment process depends on the type of services the social worker is providing. Furthermore, organizational policies will often guide the assessment process. In addition to those factors, the expectations of the clients should also be considered when conducting an assessment. Additionally, other priorities to include in the assessment process include such things as identifying the client perception of the problem/concern, any legal mandates that may direct treatment, as well as specific health and safety concerns (Hepworth, Rooney, Rooney, & Strom-Gottfried, 2017).

Use of Self

All professions have tools of the trade. One social worker tool is the self. Social workers must be able to effectively use their self to bring about change throughout the helping process. Social workers must be able to attend to clients and demonstrate good verbal and nonverbal communication skills during the interview process that will promote the client sharing the information needed to conduct the assessment.

> ▶ **Critical Thinking Questions**
> 1. What are some specific verbal and nonverbal behaviors that could enhance the assessment process?
> 2. What are some specific verbal and nonverbal behaviors that could hinder the assessment process?

The social worker must be aware of how to ask sometimes difficult or personal questions. Preparing a client for such questions can often be helpful. Simply acknowledging that the questions you are able to ask may seem personal can be enough to provide ease in such a situation. Also, asking the client if you may ask about such things promotes the client's role in the assessment process and honors his or her right to determine what information he or she would like to share with you.

Affective Reactions

When conducting an assessment, paying attention to affective responses can be useful. Social workers should be aware of not only what the client is saying, but how they are saying it, as well as what they are not saying. That may sound like a lot to pay attention to during the assessment and it is, but as a developing social worker you will have the opportunity to practice these skills in order to be able to be fully attuned to clients.

At times, clients will be sharing information verbally and their affect will be incongruent to what they have said. For example, if a client says that he or she is "fine" but you see that he or she is teary-eyed and has flat affect, this would be an example of incongruence. Social workers can use a clarification response to address such incongruence to seek further clarification. The social worker may say, "You say that you are fine, but I noticed that you are teary-eyed. Can you tell me more about that?" It may be that the person is indeed fine and just suffering from allergies that have their eyes watering. Or it may be a sign of something else. Social workers are not tasked to be mind readers and are encouraged to seek clarification from clients when it is needed.

Value Conflicts

Values are important within professional social work practice. Social workers must be aware of personal and professional values and recognize when value conflicts arise. During the assessment process, social workers seek to better understand the values of the client. It is important to recognize what is important for the client. As we have stated, it is critical that social workers start where the client is, and with assessment it is no different. In order to be able to start where the client is, social workers must know what clients value. Social workers should directly ask clients what they value and what is important for them. Social workers recognize that successful treatment may look different for different clients and respect the rights of clients to determine their own definition of success whenever possible.

Once social workers are aware of what the client values, then they are better positioned to identify potential value conflicts when they arise. Social workers can use the skill of confrontation to address any potential value conflicts that they have identified with clients. Sometimes clients do not recognize when there is a conflict between their stated values and current actions, so a social worker illuminating this can be a helpful tool in the helping process. A sample confrontation response related to a value conflict could be, "You have shared that it is important for you to earn your GED. However, you haven't been attending the necessary classes that are required to take the exam." You will notice in the sample response there are two parts. First, the social worker states the value the client shared. In the second part of the statement, the social worker identifies the contradictory actions that are in conflict with the value in the first part of the response.

■ Strengths-Based Assessment: Individuals and Families

Social workers are trained to identify strengths. Social workers understand that though problems and concerns may exist, so do strengths. Sometimes clients are able to identify their own strengths; other times, the social worker must assist clients in viewing their own strengths. At times, society operates from more of a deficit-based perspective. In order to receive many social services, individuals must be able to identify problems, issues, or needs. Rarely are people called to identify personal strengths. Since this is not the customary approach or orientation of all social services, social workers must be sure to assist clients in recognizing and honoring personal strengths as this can be a source of empowerment. Danzer (2012) sets forth that the goal of strengths-based social work practice is to help clients "explore and re-claim their natural talents and abilities, cultural, creative, and spiritual practices" adding that these internal resources have allowed clients to "survive a lifetime of stress and oppression and can be mobilized to facilitate positive coping in the present" (p. 10).

During the assessment process, social workers should directly address and assess client strengths. Sometimes social workers must reframe client conditions as strengths; for example, if a client believes that he or she is unable to do so. Social workers should recognize that it can at times be very difficult for clients to engage in treatment, so by the very nature that they are working with you, the clients have demonstrated a commitment to addressing the concern that brought them to you. Case 6.7 illustrates a strengths-based approach to client assessment.

CASE 6.7   THE SOCIAL WORKER'S ROLE IN HELPING CLIENTS FIND THEIR STRENGTHS

Nadine is seeking the support of a clinical social worker to address her current stress levels. Nadine is married to John. Nadine and John met while both attending Narcotics Anonymous (NA) meetings. They found that they were able to be supportive to each other as they were both in the early stages of recovery. John had a history of using cocaine and Nadine a history of using opioids.

Two years ago, Nadine and John experienced a second-trimester miscarriage. Nadine recalls that was a very difficult time for her because not only did she suffer the miscarriage but only 1 month earlier her father passed away suddenly. As a result of all of the stress, Nadine relapsed after 15 months clean. Nadine blamed herself for the miscarriage thinking that her past drug use may have been the reason she lost the baby. After going to treatment for her drug use again, Nadine has been clean for about 11 months.

Two months ago, Nadine and John had a son, Leo. Leo was born 6 weeks early, so he had to spend time in the neonatal intensive care unit (NICU) at the hospital. Nadine did not want to leave Leo's side, so she stayed in the hospital room with him during his stay. Again, Nadine began blaming herself for the baby being born early. Though she did not use during her pregnancy, she feared that her past use was at fault. Nadine felt immense guilt.

Since Leo's release from the hospital, Nadine has been staying home with him while John has returned to work. John works as a truck driver and has not been home much since Leo's birth because he is trying to earn as much overtime as possible to pay for the medical bills from the birth and NICU stay.

Nadine's mother, Bev, has offered to help Nadine and John out financially, but John is reluctant to accept the help. John says "family shouldn't borrow money from family." Nadine's younger sister,

(continued)

CASE 6.7

Susan, has offered to help by babysitting, but Nadine worries at the thought of leaving Leo. Also, Nadine does not really have anywhere to go if she did leave the house. Part of her recovery was to change the people she used to hang out with and the places she used to go in order to avoid a relapse. Nadine knows she is safest when she is home with baby Leo.

Nadine had been close to her mother-in-law, but since she passed away the past year, she has not had much contact with her father-in-law or John's older brother or sister. Nadine feels overwhelmed managing her household and new baby all by herself. At the same time, she is having a hard time accepting support from others. Nadine thinks that a social worker may be able to help give her some perspective. She had always enjoyed working with the counselors at the drug and alcohol facility, so she thought she would look into talking to someone.

During the initial meeting with Nadine, the social worker asked about her strengths. Nadine was not sure how to answer that question. She had never really thought about that before. Nadine still viewed herself as an addict and did not really have anything positive to say about herself. The social worker talked with Nadine and began offering possible strengths, such as she is a good mother, as evidenced by how she makes sure Leo is always fed and changed when he cries. After hearing it from the social worker, Nadine nodded in agreement. The social worker added, "I think it is a strength that you knew you needed someone to talk to and reached out to make your appointment here today." Nadine had not thought of it that way, "I guess I do have some strengths." After the start from the social worker, Nadine was able to identify other strengths, including her supportive family and commitment to her recovery.

Strengths Perspective Principles

A strengths-based approach may seem to be an obvious hallmark of the social work profession as social workers often explore strengths, resources, and talents available at micro-, mezzo-, and macrolevels of the client's environment. In order to better understand the strengths-based perspective as it relates to assessment, it is helpful to consider the six strengths perspective principles. These principles set forth by Saleebey (2013) assist social workers in incorporating strengths-based approaches in all areas of the helping process. Box 6.1 lists the six principles.

At the heart of these principles is the inherent belief that strengths exist within every individual, every group, every family, and every community. Despite what may appear as adversity, resilience exists. Further, the capacity for resilience is limitless and social workers must allow clients to identify their own hopes, goals, and desires for their future during the helping process.

Strengths and Obstacles Worksheet

At times, it can be helpful to have a resource or tool to support you in identifying strengths across various domains. One such tool is the strengths and obstacles worksheet that is illustrated in Exhibit 6.1. When possible, the client should complete this worksheet and it should be reviewed by the social worker. This worksheet can serve to inform the assessment process by attempting to provide a comprehensive look at what may hinder or promote client success and progress during the helping process.

BOX 6.1

STRENGTHS-PERSPECTIVE PRINCIPLES IN SOCIAL WORK PRACTICE

Principle 1: Every individual, group, family, and community has strengths.

Principle 2: Trauma, abuse, illness, and struggle may be injurious, but they may also be sources of challenge and opportunity.

Principle 3: Assume that you do not know the upper limits of the capacity to grow and change, and take individual, group, and community aspirations seriously.

Principle 4: We best serve clients by collaborating with them.

Principle 5: Every environment is full of resources.

Principle 6: Caring, caretaking, and context are important.

Source: Data from Saleebey, D. (2013). *The strengths-perspective in social work practice* (6th ed.). London, UK: Pearson.

EXHIBIT 6.1

INDIVIDUAL AND FAMILY STRENGTHS AND OBSTACLES WORKSHEET

Client: _____   **Worker:** _____   **Date:** _____

Instructions: Briefly describe to the best of your knowledge as many items on the worksheet as possible. Base your assessment on information you have obtained directly from your client, indirectly by your observations, case records, contacts with collaterals, and any other sources of information. The first page focuses on a description of the client's concerns/problem situation. The remaining pages comprise an assessment of personal, family, and environmental factors. For each relevant factor, describe potential obstacles, strengths, and their impact on the problem situation.

Concerns/Problem Situation

Briefly summarize client concerns and/or problems that the client wants to address.

List concerns or problems in order of priority from the highest to the lowest.

INDIVIDUAL FACTORS			
SUBSYSTEM	**OBSTACLES**	**STRENGTHS**	**IMPACT PROBLEM**
Motivation and Commitment			
Coping and Resourcefulness			
Values and Beliefs			
Developmental Life Stage			
Mental Health Status			
Health Status			
Employment/Economic Status			
Interpersonal Relationships			

FAMILY FACTORS			
SUBSYSTEM	**OBSTACLES**	**STRENGTHS**	**IMPACT PROBLEM**
Family Structure			
Power and Authority			
Family Life-Cycle Stage			
Family Values and Beliefs			
Family Rules and Myths			
Emotional Climate			
Communication Patterns			
Boundaries			

ENVIRONMENTAL FACTORS			
SUBSYSTEM	**OBSTACLES**	**STRENGTHS**	**IMPACT PROBLEM**
Work/School			
Clubs, Churches, and Associations			
Community/Neighborhood			
Service Organizations			
Other Factors and Considerations			

Source: From Poulin, J., Matis, S., Witt, H. (2019). *The social work field placement: A competency-based approach.* New York, NY: Springer Publishing Company.

Ecomaps

Ecomaps are visual representations of the systems present in a client's environment. Ecomaps assist in gathering information and assessing the relationship between clients and other systems present in their lives. Social workers can use an ecomap to measure progress or change over time with clients when conducting ongoing assessment.

Ecomaps should be individualized to address the individual experiences of the client. Based on this, ecomaps may need to contain various domains that are pertinent to the life of the client. For example, if a client is in college, higher education would be included on the ecomap, whereas if a client has no involvement or engagement with formalized education systems, then education would not need to be listed as a domain. Domains that are often included on ecomaps include family, community, employer, education and training, friends, formal service, providers, and social welfare. Ecomaps are often depicted using circles. At the center of the ecomap is the client. Radiating around the client are circles that include the various applicable domains (see Figure 6.1 for a sample image of an ecomap).

When conducting assessments, social workers should be comprehensive in exploring the various domains that are influencing the client. We suggested several domains to explore when creating an ecomap. First, when considering the domain of family, social workers should consider immediate and extended familial relationships. Families are complex systems; social workers are aware of this and must assess it as such. Social workers should not make assumptions about relationships but rather gather information throughout the assessment process. Regardless of the nature of the relationships, whether it be positive, neutral, or negative, social workers can use this information to inform their work with clients, and it provides insights into the clients' current environments.

When considering community, social workers should explore various communities and cultural experiences that the client engages in. Community can include the physical community in which clients reside but may also include ethnic, racial, religious, or social

FIGURE 6.1 Sample ecomap domains present in the client's environment.

communities. For example, belonging to a religious organization or church community should be depicted on a client ecomap. Other types of community may include groups where a client feels a sense of belonging.

▶ **Critical Thinking Questions**
Consider your life and the environments in which you engage. Create an ecomap that represents you currently.

Domains related to employment, education, and training are also important to explore when constructing an ecomap. Even if a client is currently unemployed, but hoping to obtain employment, this domain can be depicted on the ecomap noting the current strain. In the event that the domain is not applicable, meaning it is not present or sought after in the client's life, it is not necessary to include that domain on the ecomap.

As we have discussed, relationships are important. Social workers should consider friendships and other informal supports available to clients. Informal supports may include friends, neighbors, work colleagues, or school peers. In addition to informal supports, social workers should assess for formal service providers such as social workers, medical professionals, caseworkers, or other professionals who are providing a service of some sort in the life of the client. Closely related to formal providers is the domain of social welfare. Sometimes there are professionals related to social welfare present in the client's life. Other social welfare considerations may include medical assistance or supplemental nutrition assistance programs.

Ecomaps not only include the domains applicable to the client but also represent the type or quality of relationship present between the client and each domain. Ecomaps can visually depict relationships that are positive, neutral, negative, and even cut off. As with any type of map, it is important to include a key with your ecomap to represent interactions. This is important as there are various methods to illustrate the quality of relationships. This ensures that the ecomap is as clear as possible in order to avoid misinterpretation. Figure 6.2 illustrates common symbols to denote the type or quality of relationship present between clients and their various domains.

Genograms

A genogram is a visual representation of a client's family system. In some ways, genograms are like a family tree, but they are able to represent so much more. Genograms are great assessment tools that assist in building rapport and joining with clients. Genograms are also a practical tool that can be used to keep track of family systems and patterns of interactions. There is the old adage that a picture is worth a thousand words. A genogram is a picture that represents family systems that, at times, can be quite complex. See Case 6.8 for a discussion of multiple families within one family.

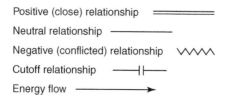

FIGURE 6.2 Ecomap interactional symbols.

CASE 6.8	MULTIPLE FAMILIES IN ONE FAMILY

Katie is a 16-year-old female who resides with her father Howard, paternal grandmother Gloria, her older sister Kelly, and Kelly's paramour Greg. Also residing in the home with Katie is her 3-month-old daughter Ashley. Howard and Katie's mother Mary Ann separated when Katie was only 4 years old. During that same year, Katie's paternal grandfather passed away and an aunt with whom Katie was close moved to another state. Howard recognizes that at that time, Katie became much more introverted and, as he describes, "clingy."

Throughout her youth, Katie has participated in community activities such as softball and soccer. She reports having very few close friends even though she was actively involved in social activities. The family denies any current affiliation with a religious organization or church though on several occasions Katie has attended teen nights at a local Baptist church, which she reports enjoying.

Two years ago, Katie met Roger at school. Shortly after the couple began dating, Katie became pregnant. Katie decided she wanted to keep the baby and raise it on her own, with Roger's help. Roger has a history of mental health issues and aggressive behaviors. Roger has abused Katie in several domestic violence instances, including hitting Katie with a fan on her stomach, which induced labor. Since baby Ashley's birth, Roger has continued his domestic violence tendencies and has sprained Katie's wrist during an argument.

Howard is seeking help for his daughter, and Katie agrees that she needs help managing her depression and admits having someone to talk to would be helpful. During the first meeting, the social worker began the assessment process.

Consider that you are the social worker in this case:

- How can you implement the strengths perspective principles in your work with this client system?
- What systems would you include in the ecomap for this client system?
- Create a genogram for this family.

Within a genogram, people are represented by shapes. Typically squares represent males and circles represent females. When considering individuals who identify as a gender other than that assigned to them at birth, you can represent that within the genogram by having their identified gender as the outer shape. When creating a gen-ogram, relationships are evidenced by

> ▶ Critical Thinking Question
> Consider your family. Create a genogram to represent you.

horizontal lines and children are evidenced by vertical lines that are drawn off relationship lines. Figure 6.3 illustrates common genogram symbols.

When constructing a genogram, there are general rules that should be followed. For example, when drawing a relationship, men are typically on the left and women are typically on the right. Children should be ordered from oldest to youngest from left to right. Similarly, relationships should be shown from first to the most recent, again from left to right. Deceased

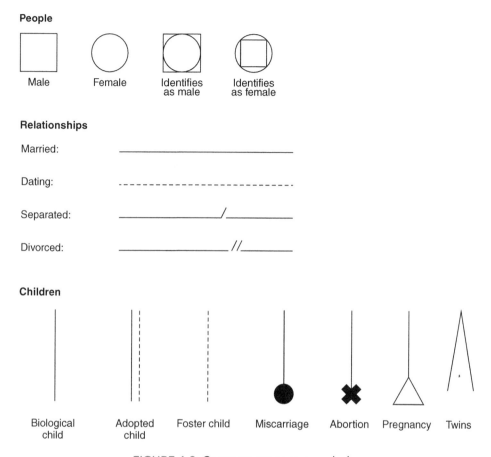

FIGURE 6.3 Common genogram symbols.

family members should be included in genograms. To indicate that a person is deceased, an "X" can be drawn over their shape. Clients are identified on the genogram by doubling their gender symbol. After adding all of the individuals to a genogram, use a circle to identify who resides in the home together. See Figure 6.4 for an example of a genogram.

■ Strengths-Based Assessment: Groups

Social workers often practice at the mezzolevel or group level. Working with groups can be challenging but also can be quite rewarding. It is necessary to be clear that all groups are inherently unique as they are composed of unique individuals. Based on this, every group will have their own strength and obstacles. As a social worker, it may be helpful to reflect on the group as a whole as well as the members of the group to assist in assessing the group.

Assessment at the group level is much like microassessment and family assessment. Social workers approach group assessment from the same strengths-based perspective and apply the same six strengths-perspective principles to this process. At times, social workers assess the group as a whole, whereas other times social workers assess the individual members of the group.

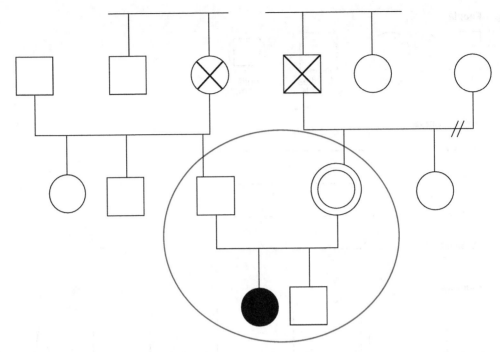

FIGURE 6.4 Sample genogram of a client's family system. This genogram depicts the family described in Case 6.6.

Assessing the Group as a Whole

Sometimes during the assessment process, social workers must assess groups as a whole. One such way to assess groups as a whole is to assess at what stage the group is functioning. There are various stages of group functioning. These stages are often referred to as forming, storming, norming, performing, and adjourning. It can be helpful to assess what stage at which the group is functioning to ensure that the group is developing through the stages appropriately and at the desired rate based on the anticipated length of the group. This can be useful for a variety of different reasons, including practical concerns. For example, if a social worker is running a 6-week long group and at week 3 assesses that the group is still in the forming stages, the social worker recognizes that the group is delayed in formation and as a result of limited time, may not be able to complete the other stages in the remaining 3 weeks. The social worker can then encourage the group to move on to the next stage.

Assessing Individual Group Members

Sometimes it is necessary for social workers to assess individual members of a group. When assessing individual members of the group, often the assessment may look like a typical microassessment. However, sometimes the social worker may be assessing an individual in relationship to the group. In such cases, the social worker would be exploring the individual's relationship with other members of the group or the individual's participation in the group process.

It is important for social workers to recognize that power exists within all groups. Social workers must assess in an ongoing manner the power dynamics of a group. It is important to be mindful of the group purpose and be sure that individual members or alliances within the group are not disrupting the purpose or process of the group. When it is interfering with the group, the social worker should take action to ameliorate such conditions and assist the group to get back on track.

▶ **Critical Thinking Questions**

Reflect upon your experiences working in groups.

1. How were you assessed (as an individual or as a group)?

2. Did the way you were assessed accurately reflect the group? How or how not?

Strengths-Based Group Assessment

Strengths-based group assessment recognizes and honors that strengths exist in the group as a collective and within each member of the group. When operating from a strengths-based perspective when assessing groups, it is important for social workers to be aware that self-determination still exists. Groups have the right to self-determine. The way in which they decide what determination to reach is in fact an example of just that. As we have stated, all groups are unique and as a result, social workers must allow space for groups to come together and work on, and at times, through issues.

■ Policy Issues

Social workers must be mindful of policy issues in all areas of practice. At the level of assessment, social workers should be aware of potential policy issues that may arise based on the information gained during the assessment process. Social workers hold tightly to the value of self-determination. However, there are times when a social worker must limit a client's right to self-determination in order to protect the client or others from harm.

One such example may be if a client is expressing suicidal ideation with an intent to hurt self. If a client is a threat to self, social workers must ensure client safety by seeking a higher level of care. After conducting a suicide assessment, if the client is deemed to be a threat to self, the social worker should follow organization and state policies. In the United States, there are policies established by each state regarding specific criteria for voluntary and involuntary mental health commitments. Voluntary commitments refer to when a client is willing to sign himself or herself into the psychiatric facility. Involuntary commitments refer to when a client is refusing to agree to treatment in a psychiatric facility, but due to the imminent danger he or she poses, a delegate can determine that the client must be committed regardless of his or her wish not to be.

In addition to policies that relate to commitment for clients likely to commit suicide, many states have policies in place regarding requirements of social workers and other helping professionals to receive continuing education on suicide assessment. In 2012, the state of Washington passed the Matt Adler Suicide Assessment, Treatment, and Management Act (House Bill 2366), the first statewide law to require ongoing suicide training. The bill is named after Matt Adler who completed suicide in 2011. Matt, a lawyer, was experiencing a great deal of stress in his life. He sought out a counselor; however, when he told the professional that he was thinking about suicide, the professional did not take him seriously and refused to provide further treatment (Volk, 2014). His wife, Jenn, has championed for legislation to address suicide assessment. Since 2012, several other states have adopted policies, many named after Matt Adler, regarding suicide assessment including Pennsylvania, Indiana, Kentucky, California, New Hampshire, Nevada, Tennessee, Washington, and West Virginia (Graves, Mackelprang, Van Natta, & Holliday, 2018).

Sometimes clients can present as a harm to others. When a client expresses a direct threat to harm another person or group of people, social workers and other helping professionals have an obligation or duty to warn the identified victim. Policies surrounding a helping professional's duty to warn are often influenced by the Tarasoff ruling. Tarasoff policies are named after Tatiana "Tanya" Tarasoff, a college student in California who was murdered in 1969 by a fellow student who had previously stated his desire to kill her in a counseling session (Rothstein, 2014). When assessing the dangerousness of a client and the likelihood of imminent risk to others, social workers must consider a variety of factors including such things as age, gender, intellectual ability, family and community experiences, peer culture, coping patterns, and history of violent acts (Kagle & Kopels, 1994).

From the Tarasoff ruling, social workers and other mental health helping professionals have the obligation to address threats. Tarasoff imposed a legal duty to

> ... warn a person who was the potential targeted victim of a violent act by their patient. The duty to warn ruling triggers action on the part of the health care provider when a patient reveals an intent to inflict physical or bodily harm on an identified victim(s). Once triggered, providers can institute any one or more of the following actions to fulfill the duty: warning the intended target of the threat, alerting law enforcement, or initiating the process of having the patient confined voluntarily or involuntary. (Henderson, 2015, p. 193)

■ Social Justice Issues

When considering social justice issues that relate to assessment, social workers must consider issues related to drug and alcohol use by clients. Since the war on drugs was initiated by President Richard Nixon, there have been massive incarcerations for low-level drug crimes but little progress in reducing the drug epidemic in the United States. It is important to recognize that although drugs are used across racial and ethnic divides, the war on drugs has disproportionately criminalized minority groups (Bowen & Redmond, 2016).

Due to the pervasive nature of drug abuse, it is likely that regardless of the type of practice, social workers will encounter someone directly impacted by drug abuse. Social workers must be aware of current drug trends in their regions and how it can impact their clients. Currently, the opioid epidemic is crippling much of the United States. Though issues related to opioid use are global, the United States has the highest rates of opioid overdoses internationally (Vakharia, 2014). When considering the opioid epidemic, social workers can utilize a systems perspective as it:

... provides an ideal frame through which to view the current opioid overdose crisis because it can help students to view this seemingly individual-level phenomenon as one that is actually dynamically impacting (and impacted by) interpersonal and family systems, health care delivery systems, human service agencies, the criminal justice system, the pharmaceutical industry, local/national drug policy, and local/national public health policy. (Vakharia, 2014, p. 695)

Training to utilize the lifesaving opioid Narcan can be a simple way to address the opioid epidemic while maintaining the dignity and worth of all people, even those currently struggling with addiction. Social workers must champion for policies and procedures that promote the value of life for all people.

■ Summary

Throughout this chapter, we explored the topic of assessment at the micro- and mezzolevels of practice. Social workers must employ comprehensive assessment practices in order to ensure that they are best serving their clients. Good assessment is ongoing assessment and can be a tool used throughout the helping process as new information arises or greater details are learned. Social workers and clients mutually work together throughout the assessment process. The social worker is careful not to overpathologize clients based on their experiences but rather utilize critical thinking skills and their best clinical judgment when making assessments. Effective social work professionals have knowledge of a variety of theoretical approaches, orientations, and frameworks to assist them in better conceptualizing client wants and needs while addressing clinical concerns, all of which are identified during the assessment process.

CASE SUMMARY   "UNDOCUMENTED AND HOMELESS"

Practice Setting Description

Jackie is a first-year master of social work student completing an internship at an inner-city family service agency in the Southwest. The agency is located in a section of the city that has a high crime rate, gang activity, and failing schools. The area has a diverse population with a large number of immigrants from Central and South America and a substantial African American population. The agency provides individual and family counseling services on a sliding fee scale. The agency also runs a number of educational and treatment groups as well as a temporary shelter for women and their children. Jackie has been assigned to work with the women and their children in the shelter. Her primary tasks are to provide concrete services and supportive counseling to the shelter residents.

Background Information

Elicia T and her daughter, Maria, are undocumented immigrants from Mexico. They have been in the United States for 5 years. Elicia and Maria fled to the area from another southwestern city to escape

(continued)

CASE SUMMARY

her abusive husband approximately 2 months ago. Elicia is 25 years old and Maria 8 years old. Elicia has a 2-year-old daughter, Sarah, who was placed in foster care because of suspected abuse in the home. Sarah is in a foster home in a small rural community in the state hundreds of miles from Elicia's current residence. Since moving to the area, Maria has not been attending school.

Elicia and Maria are currently residing in the agency's temporary shelter for families. They have been at the shelter for 2 weeks, and the agency has a 90-day limit. It is viewed as temporary housing, and the residents are only allowed to stay for 3 months. Prior to arriving at the shelter, Elicia and Maria were homeless and living on the streets.

Elicia is a high-school dropout and was a stay-at-home mother prior to leaving her husband and moving to a different part of the state. She chose to move there because she has two female cousins living in the area who are also undocumented immigrants. Elicia's native language is Spanish. She speaks some English but is not as comfortable speaking in English. Her English comprehension appears to be good. Maria speaks both English and Spanish well. When communicating with the staff, Maria acts as Elicia's interpreter since none of the staff at the shelter speak Spanish.

Maria appears to be behind academically. She struggles reading simple children's books written in English. It is unknown if her ability to read in Spanish is better than her English reading skills.

Other than her two cousins, Elicia has no other sources of support in the community. Her cousins have young families and limited resources but are well established and connected to a Latino community in the city and the local Catholic church. Her cousins refused to let Elicia and Maria live with them while she was trying to find her own place and a job. They stated that they did not have enough room and are concerned they would get in trouble with their landlord if it was found out that they were letting people stay with them. They sent her to the local church for help, and she was given the address for the agency's shelter by the priest.

Elicia has been looking for housing in the Latino community. The housing market is tight with limited options, and she has been unable to find anything that she could possibly afford. The only affordable housing she found was a room in a rundown motel that rents by the hour or by the month. It is in an area of town known for drug dealing and sex work.

On arrival in the community, Elicia found occasional work for a house cleaning company. The company hires undocumented workers, pays them very low cash wages, and threatens to turn them in to Immigration and Customs Enforcement (ICE) if they complain. The job bosses also exploit their female workers sexually, threatening to turn them in if they do not comply. Elicia was fearful about applying for other jobs because of her illegal status. She considered turning to sex work to be able to take care of her children, but her Catholic upbringing and thoughts of how doing so would shame her family have kept her from doing so. She is in constant fear of being detained, separated from her children, and having them placed in foster care. She is also afraid that she will end up homeless again and forced to live on the streets or return to her abusive husband.

Elicia is extremely reluctant to sign up for any federally funded services, even those that she and her children are entitled to receiving. On the suggestion that she enroll for supplemental food through SNAP, Elicia became nervous and refused as she has heard that participation in SNAP

(continued)

CASE SUMMARY

services, and others like them, would draw the attention of ICE, and she had heard stories on the news of individuals being deported after signing up for such programs.

Presenting Problems

Elicia and her children are facing multiple obstacles. They need to find permanent, affordable housing and a job that pays enough to cover her housing and living expenses. In addition, Maria needs to be enrolled in school. Elicia also wants to regain custody of her youngest daughter in foster care.

Additionally, Elicia is experiencing an immense amount of stress, anxiety, and possibly posttraumatic stress disorder (PTSD). She described an instance where she could not calm down her breathing, and she felt lightheaded. She is very fearful of men and tries to avoid all contact with men in the community. She reports difficulty sleeping at night and feeling exhausted most of the time.

She is concerned about Maria. She has started acting out at the shelter, getting into fights with the other children, disobeying her mother, and being disrespectful and defiant to the staff and other adults. Elicia and Maria fight frequently, and when Elicia tries to discipline Maria, she throws a temper tantrum until Elicia gives up.

Elicia has many strengths. She had the strength to leave her abusive husband and move to a different city. She loves her daughters. She wants desperately to keep Maria with her and hopes to have Sarah returned to her custody. She is resilient and has managed to survive and keep her daughter safe despite not having a place to stay, a job, and a limited support network. Additionally, Elicia is highly motivated to find her own accommodations and support her children.

■ Discussion Questions

1. Consider Erikson's stages of psychosocial development. At what stages are Elicia and Maria currently? How does their current stage and experiences at past stages influence your approach as a social worker?

2. Utilizing a family systems theory approach to assessing Elicia and Maria, how does the concept of "differentiation of self" relate to this case and your work with both of them, individually and together?

3. Create an ecomap that represents the systems currently involved in Elicia and Maria's lives.

4. Create a genogram for Elicia and Maria.

■ References

Akesson, B., Burns, V., & Hordyk, S.-R. (2017). The place of place in social work: Rethinking the person-in-environment model in social work education and practice. *Journal of Social Work Education, 53*(3), 372–383. doi:10.1080/10437797.2016.1272512

Bowen, E. A., & Redmond, H. (2016). Teaching note—No peace without justice: Addressing the United States' war on drugs in social work education. *Journal of Social Work Education, 52*(4), 503–508. doi: 10.1080/10437797.2016.1198296

Brown, B. (2010). *The gifts of imperfection: Let go of who you think you're supposed to be and embrace who you are.* Center City, MN: Hazelden.

Cooper, T. D., & Randall, R. L. (2012). *Grace for the injured self: The healing approach of Heinz Kohut.* Cambridge, UK: Lutterworth Press.

Crabtree-Nelson, S., & Kohli, S. (2017). Navigating a murky landscape: The application of Bowen family systems to field office ethics. *Journal of Social Work Values and Ethics, 14*(1), 30–39.

Danzer, G. (2012). Integrating ego psychology and strengths-based social work. *Journal of Theory Construction & Testing, 16*(1), 9–15.

Dziegielewski, S. F. (2015). *DSM-5 in action* (3rd ed.). Hoboken, NJ: Wiley.

Frankland, A. G. (2010). *The little psychotherapy book: Object relations in practice.* Oxford, UK: Oxford University Press.

Frederick, T., Purrington, S., & Dunbar, S. (2016). Differentiation of self, religious coping, and subjective well-being. *Mental Health, Religion & Culture, 19*(6), 553–564. doi:10.1080/13674676.2016.1216530

Gooding, P. A., Hurst, A., Johnson, J., & Tarrier, N. (2011). Psychological resilience in young and older adults. *International Journal of Geriatric Psychiatry, 27*, 262–270. doi:10.1002/gps.2712

Graves, J. M., Mackelprang, J. L., Van Natta, S. E., & Holliday, C. (2018). Suicide prevention training: Policies for health care professionals across the United States as of October 2017. *American Journal of Public Health, 108*(6), 760–768. doi:10.2105/AJPH.2018.304373

Harrison, V. (2018). The difference Bowen theory makes in clinical practice: Challenges and choices. *Family Systems: A Journal of Natural Systems Thinking in Psychiatry & the Sciences, 13*(2), 165–183.

Henderson, E. (2015). Potentially dangerous patients: A review of the duty to warn. *Journal of Emergency Nursing, 41*(3), 193–200. doi:10.1016/j.jen.2014.08.012

Hepworth, D. H., Rooney, R. H., Rooney, G. D., & Strom-Gottfried, K. (2017). *Direct social work practice: Theory and skills* (10th ed.). Boston, MA: Cengage.

Kagle, J. D., & Kopels, S. (1994). Confidentiality after Tarasoff. Social workers believe that they have a duty to warn. *Health & Social Work, 19*(3), 217–222. doi:10.1093/hsw/19.3.217

Knight, Z. G. (2017). A proposed model of psychodynamic psychotherapy linked to Erik Erikson's eight stages of psychosocial development. *Clinical Psychology & Psychotherapy, 24*(5), 1047–1058. doi:10.1002/cpp.2066

Langer, C. L., & Lietz, C. A. (2015). *Applying theory to generalist social work practice.* Hoboken, NJ: Wiley.

MacKay, L. M. (2017). Differentiation of self: Enhancing therapist resilience when working with relational trauma. *Australian & New Zealand Journal of Family Therapy, 38*(4), 637–656. doi:10.1002/anzf.1276

Misca, G., & Unwin, P. (2016). *Psychology and social work: Applied perspectives.* Malden, MA: Polity.

Morgan, L. A., & Kunkel, S. (2016). *Aging, society, and the life course* (5th ed.). New York, NY: Springer Publishing Company.

National Association of Social Workers. (2017). *Code of ethics.* Silver Spring, MD: Author. Retrieved from https://www.socialworkers.org/About/Ethics/Code-of-Ethics/Code-of-Ethics-English

Payne, M. (2016). *Modern social work theory* (4th ed.). Oxford, UK: Oxford University Press.

Polat, B. (2017). Before attachment theory: Separation research at the Tavistock clinic, 1948-1956. *Journal of The History of The Behavioral Sciences, 53*(1), 48–70. doi:10.1002/jhbs.21834

Poulin, J., Matis, S., & Witt, H. (2019). *The social work field placement: A competency-based approach.* New York, NY: Springer Publishing Company.

Rothstein, M. A. (2014). Tarasoff duties after Newtown. *Journal of Law, Medicine & Ethics, 42*(1), 104–109. doi:10.1111/jlme.12123

Saleeby, D. (2013). *The strengths-perspective in social work practice* (6th ed.). London, UK: Pearson.

Schwarz, J. E. (2017). *Counseling women across the life span: Empowerment, advocacy, and intervention.* New York, NY: Springer Publishing Company.

Snyder, C. R. (2002). Hope theory: Rainbows of the mind. *Psychological Inquiry, 4*, 249–275. doi:10.1207/S15327965PLI1304_01

Tough, P. (2012). *How children succeed: Grit, curiosity, and the hidden power of character*. New York, NY: Houghton Mifflin Harcourt Publishing Company.

Vakharia, S. P. (2014). Incorporating substance use content into social work curricula: Opioid overdose as a micro, mezzo, and macro problem. *Social Work Education, 33*(5), 692–698. doi:10.1080/026154 79.2014.919093

Volk, D. (2014). Hope after heartache. *Columns Archive: The University of Washington Alumni Magazine*. Retrieved from https://www.washington.edu/alumni/columns/pdf/columns_march_2014.pdf

Zalenski, R. J., & Raspa, R. (2016). Facing death: Palliative care, Erik Erikson, and the final stage of life. *Journal of Palliative Medicine, 19*(8), 804–805. doi:10.1089/jpm.2016.0154

MICROSYSTEMS INTERVENTION: INDIVIDUALS, FAMILIES, AND GROUPS

Janet is a social worker at a children's partial hospitalization program. Janet's duties include monitoring the classroom behavior of her clients, conducting individual therapeutic sessions, and facilitating group sessions. Janet must determine the appropriate interventions for her clients in the classroom as well as in individual sessions and in groups. Janet is well aware of the importance of selecting evidence-based practices to drive intervention decisions. Furthermore, Janet takes into consideration the individualized needs of each client when selecting intervention strategies.

Janet has recently noticed that the children in her classroom are having trouble staying on task during class. She has conducted an assessment that has given her insights into the motives of their behaviors. It appears that the children are being positively reinforced for their off-task behavior by getting personalized attention from a member of the staff in the room. Janet proposed to the staff an intervention designed to target the off-task behaviors. She hopes that by implementing this intervention, she will be able to change the negative problem behavior in the classroom.

LEARNING OBJECTIVES

In this chapter, we explore the role of intervention in the social work helping process. We focus on intervention with individuals, families, and groups. During the intervention phase of treatment, we often are working on bringing about some sort of change with our clients. The type of intervention selected is dependent on practice setting, expertise, and client presentation. As with most aspects of social work practice, selecting an intervention depends on the role and goal of the social worker. If we are in the role of broker, our selected intervention may be quite different from that of an advocate or even a mediator who are all working with the same client. As social workers, we must be able to recognize where our clients are regarding the change process. Some clients seek out the support of a social worker to assist them with a change for which they have already identified a desire to address. On other occasions, clients may be mandated to treatment or reluctant to pursue change for a variety of reasons. In such cases, it is the duty of the social worker to recognize this and address it with the client directly. By the end of this chapter, you will be able to:

- Identify the various stages related to the stages of change model
- Describe generalist practice and identify various generalist practice techniques
- Explain various clinical practice models that are commonly used in intervention
- Recognize the importance of planning for transitions and endings with clients

■ Competency 8: Intervene With Individuals, Families, Groups, Organizations, and Communities

Social workers understand that intervention is an ongoing component of the dynamic and interactive process of social work practice with, and on behalf of, diverse individuals, families, groups, organizations, and communities. Social workers are knowledgeable about evidence-informed interventions to achieve the goals of clients and constituencies, including individuals, families, groups, organizations, and communities. Social workers understand theories of human behavior and the social environment, and critically evaluate and apply this knowledge to effectively intervene with clients and constituencies. Social workers understand methods of identifying, analyzing, and implementing evidence-informed interventions to achieve client and constituency goals. Social workers value the importance of interprofessional teamwork and communication in interventions, recognizing that beneficial outcomes may require interdisciplinary, interprofessional, and interorganizational collaboration. Social workers:

- Critically choose and implement interventions to achieve practice goals and enhance capacities of clients and constituencies

- Apply knowledge of human behavior and the social environment, person-in-environment, and other multidisciplinary theoretical frameworks in interventions with clients and constituencies

- Use interprofessional collaboration as appropriate to achieve beneficial practice outcomes

- Negotiate, mediate, and advocate with and on behalf of diverse clients and constituencies

- Facilitate effective transitions and endings that advance mutually agreed-on goals

■ National Association of Social Workers (NASW) *Code of Ethics*

When social workers are engaging in interventions with client systems, they must be mindful of the NASW *Code of Ethics* (2017) and how that mandates their professional and ethical duties to clients. Social workers must ensure that they are providing an unwavering commitment to what is best for the client. Recognizing the importance of the work that they do with clients, social workers also recognize that at times, difficulties can arise during the intervention stage of treatment. For example, maybe the client needs another level of care and a referral or termination in services are warranted. In such a case, social workers must follow the guidelines set forth within the *Code of Ethics* in order to ensure that the client istaken care of during this transition.

Social workers value human relationships. We understand that people do not exist in isolation. Humans exist within the context of their relationships with others. The work that social workers do with clients is important work. Social workers must be mindful of the importance of this therapeutic relationship and at all times do their best to support the client, demonstrating commitment above all else. Social workers must also abide by the *Code of Ethics* regarding all aspects of intervention. When we are intervening with client systems, we must be mindful of the relationships that exist. Both informal and formal relationships are important to note when intervening with families and groups. It is particularly important to monitor the nature and quality of all relationships as you proceed through the helping process.

Especially as it relates to intervention, human relationships is vital. As we explore in this chapter and have noted previously throughout this text, the quality of the therapeutic relationship is a strong predictor of treatment success. The quality of the therapeutic relationship between social workers and clients is dependent on many factors. The relationship can begin, being enhanced early in the treatment process by establishing rapport and enhancing engagement. Social workers should strive to help clients feel heard. Social workers should be present for clients and attend to their needs. Our profession values a commitment to our clients. When clients feel this commitment to them, that can enhance the therapeutic relationship.

All people have value. Throughout the intervention process, we must never forget that. Social workers must be mindful to respect the dignity of all people during the intervention phase; we must tirelessly work to reduce stigma related to interventions. Unfortunately, many who need the help of social workers do not seek it out because of the stigma that still exists around mental health treatment in the United States,.

Throughout the intervention process, social workers must be mindful to never make clients feel less inferior or inadequate. Even amid adversity and challenge, clients have dignity. Social workers must treat all clients in a humane and dignified manner. This relates back to the importance of the therapeutic relationship and how social workers can help clients fill a part of the service. We should never attempt to do for clients; rather, we should make every effort to work with clients in order to increase their self-determination, empowerment, and overall self-efficacy.

Social workers must demonstrate a continuous commitment to their clients. Demonstrating their commitment to clients, social workers should strive to avoid interruptions of services; however, there may be times when interruptions of services are unavoidable. During such a time, social workers should make reasonable efforts to provide service continuity (NASW, 2017). Reasonable effort means different things based on the area of practice and type of social work that is being performed. The spirit of the standard is that in the event of an interruption of service, the client is taken care of. Interruptions can include things such as staff unavailability, relocations, or illness.

At times, a referral becomes clinically necessary. Sometimes a referral is necessary if a client needs specialized treatment or expertise that the social worker does not have. In such a case, the ethical principle of competence would come into play. It is important that social workers recognize limitations to their professional competence and make referrals when necessary. In the event that it is necessary to make a referral to another provider, social workers must make every attempt to provide continuity of care. Continuity of care refers to the process of collaborating with the new provider so that the transition can be as smooth as possible for the client.

Just as referrals for services may be necessary, at times clients may need to be transferred. A transfer of care may be warranted in situations when a conflict of interest arises, or when a worker is leaving his or her current position. Like the previous standard, it is important for social workers to ensure continuity of care and do whatever is possible to support the client during the transfer.

Throughout the helping process, social workers should be mindful to consider if the client continues to need services. Should a client no longer need services, or the services no longer fit the client's needs, the social worker should take the steps necessary to terminate the helping relationship. Social workers should not continue helping relationships that are not in the best interests of the client. When a termination must occur, for whatever reason, social workers should not abandon clients. When appropriate, social workers should provide continuity of care to other service providers. Should the client not need another service provider, the social worker may provide the client with resources or share who to contact should the client need future assistance. Termination is something that should be planned for and addressed in session. Planning for termination should begin early in treatment and should evolve as necessary. By addressing termination during treatment, it is preparing clients for the final phase of the helping process.

■ Stages of Change

Intervention is all about change. In order to fully understand intervention, it is necessary to be familiar with the stages of change model presented by Prochaska and Clemente (Figure 7.1). This model was initially developed to address stages of change related to health behaviors; it is a good framework for understanding most types of change social workers will undertake with clients. This model has also been found to be highly useful in both clinical and nonclinical settings (Abel & O'Brien, 2014). Their model for understanding change has six stages: precontemplation, contemplation, preparation, action, maintenance, and relapse. We explore each stage and discuss how each could influence your intervention with a client.

The initial stage of this model is the precontemplation stage of change. At this stage, there are no active thoughts regarding the need or desire to change. If clients have sought out social work services on their own, they have often considered or contemplated change. Contemplation is the second stage in this model. You may be wondering how a person could be meeting with a social worker if he or she has not even considered change. Well, this could happen in several ways. For example, a client may have sought out the support of a social worker for another issue and upon meeting and assessing, the social worker has noticed an area to address. Another example would be if the person did not initially seek out the social worker but rather

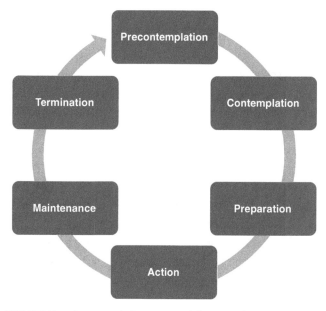

FIGURE 7.1 Stages of change model in social work practice.

the social worker sought out the client. This often happens in hospital settings when the medical staff page social work for a consultation. It could also happen when a child welfare agency receives a report and as a result must initiate services with a family. If a client is in the precontemplation stage, the goal of the intervention is to bring the condition or problem into the client's awareness.

▶ **Critical Thinking Questions**

1. As a social worker, how would you work with clients who are in the precontemplation stage of change and did not seek out your services?

2. How would your work with such a client differ from your work with a client who sought out your services?

3. How would your work with both clients be alike?

Once the client is aware of the issue that would benefit from change and is considering change, the client would be in the stage of contemplation. In this stage, the client is aware of the need for a change but is not actively changing or preparing to change. At this time, the intervention would focus on addressing the idea of change. At this stage, there are several variables including the person's beliefs about the problem, their insight into how the problem is impacting them and others, as well as the amount of energy the person has available to address the issue (Cooper, 2012).

Following contemplation, the next stage is preparation. At this stage, the client has recognized the desire to change and is taking steps to prepare to make changes. The actual change efforts have not yet begun. Rather, the planning for them is underway. This stage can be likened to buying exercise equipment in order to later work out and get in shape. Buying the equipment itself does not change the individual's health status, but it is a way to prepare to address personal fitness. In the realm of social work interventions, preparations can be quite varied. Case 7.1 illustrates a social worker assisting a client through the various stages of change.

CASE 7.1   INTERVENING AT THE VARIOUS STAGES OF CHANGE IN SOCIAL
WORK PRACTICE

Stephanie is a hospital social worker. She is often called in on consult by the medical staff in order
to support the emotional, behavioral, and social needs of patients. Stephanie was called in for a consult when an adolescent female presented to the emergency department with alcohol intoxication.
Before entering the room, Stephanie reviewed the patient's electronic medical records in order to
have a better understanding of what she was walking in on.

Upon arriving at the patient's room, Stephanie knocked on the door and introduced herself lightly;
identifying herself as the social worker, she asked the patient, Michelle, if she would be willing to talk to
her. Michelle agreed. Stephanie asked Michelle about what brought her into the hospital today. Michelle
shared that she did not understand what the big deal was as in her words, "I had some drinks with my
friends, this whole thing is being blown out of proportion." Stephanie ask Michelle if it would be okay
to talk about her use of alcohol. Michelle reluctantly agreed, adding that they can talk about it but reassuring Stephanie that she does not have a problem. Stephanie began to ask Michelle about her typical
alcohol use and ways that it impacts her life. Though having multiple hospitalizations for alcohol intoxication, being in danger, failing her current grade, and having conflict with her family, Michelle denies
having a problem and due to this denial is not even considering the need or possibility for change.

Stephanie recognizes that Michelle is in the precontemplation stage of change. Based on this
recognition, she realizes that in order to have an effective intervention with Michelle, she will need to
help her begin considering the possibility of change.

Later in her shift, Stephanie received another page. This time Stephanie was paged for a consult
to support a 38-year-old male who was in the hospital for a medical procedure but while there shared
with the staff that he has been depressed. Again before going into the room, Stephanie reviewed the
patient's chart to prepare for their meeting.

Again, Stephanie knocked on the door and introduced herself warmly. She was welcomed in by
the patient, Charlie. Stephanie ask Charlie if it would be okay to talk about how he has been feeling
lately emotionally. Charlie agreed. Charlie shared that he has long been considering getting help for
his depression, and he had even made an appointment once or twice but never followed through
and attended.

Stephanie recognized the Charlie had contemplated making a change in the past and had even
attempted to engage in the preparation stage of change by making an appointment for himself.
However, the breakdown occurred in the action stage exchange. Based on this information, Stephanie
knows where to begin her intervention with Charlie.

The next stage in the model is the action stage. It is at this point that the actual change efforts
begin to occur. During the action stage, the client initiates behaviors that are designed to bring
about change. The following stage is maintenance where the action stage is sustained long term.
For some clients who are able to sustain their change, termination is the final stage of the model.

It is important to note that the stages of change model, though circular, is not always completed in this orderly way. For example, a client can just move from contemplation directly
into action, skipping the preparation stage of the model. A client can move through this cycle

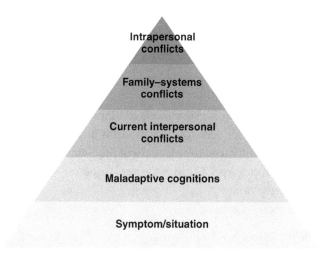

FIGURE 7.2 Levels of change in social work practice.

numerous times while working on the same issue or condition. It is noteworthy that each time a stage in the circle is revisited, there is now a history of experiences that can serve to inform client behaviors on the next attempt to bring about change.

▶ **Critical Thinking Questions**

Consider a common problem or condition that social workers often work with clients to address. Utilizing the stages of change model, identify how a client may be presenting at the various stages. Identify how you, as the social worker, would intervene at each stage of change with the client.

In addition to the stages of change, Prochaska and Clemente also put forth the process of change as well as levels of change. The levels of change are seen as hierarchical (see Figure 7.2). At the lowest level is the symptom that the client is presenting with. At this level of change, it is important to consider what brought the client to treatment as well as how these symptoms are being impacted by other goings on within the client's system. At the level of maladaptive cognitions, clients may have problematic thoughts related to their problem, need for change, or another aspect of their life. Interpersonal conflicts can sometimes occur as a result of the problem of concern. If that is what has brought the client to treatment, this and the lower levels of change would all need to be addressed. For example, if clients who have been dealing with addiction are seeking out services because their employer has required them to do so, that would be an example of an interpersonal conflict. The next level is that of family–systems conflicts. This is similar to the previous level; however, in the previous level, conflicts were with friends and colleagues, whereas at this level, conflicts are with family members. At the highest level of change are intrapersonal conflicts, which are conflicts that exist within the person.

■ Generalist Practice Interventions

Generalist practice requires that social workers have a skill set that can be generalized across settings and populations to provide support. Social workers who have a generalist background are well versed in a variety of ways to help or intervene with client systems. In this chapter, we introduce a variety of approaches that can be utilized to support clients. Generalist practice models provide a guide for social workers to support clients at various levels (micro, mezzo, macro) in various practice settings. This model is often a problem-solving approach that seeks to assess and then intervene to reduce client problems. Generalist practitioners are often trained in the areas of casework (or management), one-on-one work, and group work. We explore these three areas now.

> ▶ **Critical Thinking Question**
> Why do you think it is beneficial for social workers to have generalist skills?

Case Management

Social work has a long tradition in casework, which is now often referred to as case management. Case management involves identifying client needs and linking the client to appropriate services that can address those needs. A case manager does not address each of the client needs directly, but rather acts as a broker to coordinate services. Case managers remain open and supportive of the client as a formal service provider. Case managers are tasked with ensuring continuity of care and do a great deal of collaboration with other formal service providers present in the client's life.

Social work case managers support clients in a variety of ways including such things as education and advocacy. The case manager does not simply prescribe services for the client but rather works together with the client to identify appropriate needs that are areas to target. Over time, there has been a shift from considering the work of case management to that of case coordination (Blundo & Simon, 2016). In some areas, this language has already transitioned to be more inclusive of the process and less hierarchical. Whether called case management or case coordination, the involvement of social workers to ensure appropriate interventions for clients is an important role.

Supportive Counseling

Supportive counseling refers to the intervention that is often used in a variety of social work practice settings. Supportive counseling is not the same as talk therapy. Supportive counseling often involves comfort and guidance. In this intervention, clients are able to express their thoughts and feelings with a social worker. This may seem similar to therapy, but in supportive counseling, the social worker is not seeking to address specific psychological causes of distress. If an issue related to a specific psychological stressor would arise, the social worker would refer the client to another professional, such as a clinical social worker who specializes in such therapeutic treatment. Supportive counseling is common in settings such as child welfare organizations, community organizations, hospitals, and schools. This can occur in individual or family sessions. Supportive counseling, as its name implies, offers support to the client. The therapist will often listen and provide feedback. Authenticity and empathy are extremely important in this intervention.

Group Interventions

Social workers often work with groups across types of practice. Social work with groups involves individuals joining together to work on a particular goal. There are numerous types of groups (therapeutic, education, etc.). Regardless of the group type, it is important for social workers to be able to support groups as a whole while simultaneously supporting the individual members of the group. The social worker must be mindful of group objectives, membership, decision-making, atmosphere, and action (Dominelli, 2012). Group objectives refer to the needs to be considered during the group planning process. It is important for the social worker to properly plan out the structure of the group prior to implementation. It is often helpful for the social worker to consider the type of group and what the purpose of the group is. Social workers should clearly identify what the group is designed to achieve. Another factor to contemplate during the planning process relates to membership. The social worker should determine the ideal size of the group. It is important to know who will (and will not) be granted access to the group. These are important considerations prior to starting the recruitment process. Also, the social worker must consider whether the group will have open or closed membership. Group decision-making is a dynamic process. Social workers should be aware of the ways in which groups make decisions and how groupthink can influence group members. Furthermore, social workers should determine if there will be leadership roles within the groups and if so, how those roles will be assigned. The atmosphere of the group is another component of group work that social workers must attend to. Social workers seek to help clients feel comfortable; that goal is the same within the group setting. Furthermore, because of the nature of group work, the social worker should be mindful as to how to intervene should conflict arise. The final consideration is action. Group action refers to tasks and activities of the group. It is important to determine how group success will be measured. Within the field of social work, success can mean a variety of different things depending on the practice setting.

■ Clinical Practice Models

Clinical practice models can be used in an array of social work practice settings. Clinical practice models provide an approach to treatment. Each model, which is based on a theoretical orientation, provides a direction to take in supportive counseling. Social workers provide the majority of mental health services in the United States (Dziegielewski, 2014). Knowing this, it is important for social workers to be familiar with various clinical practice models.

Ecosystem Perspective

The ecological perspective seeks to assist social workers in understanding the complex dynamics of the human-in-environment experience. As social workers, we study human behavior in the social environment because we understand the importance of recognizing interactions that influence people. When we are considering the social environment, we are not only examining the physical environment but also considering conditions and relationships as well. Social environments are multifaceted. Understanding the way in which clients exist within the contexts of their social environments is a necessary function of our profession.

The ecosystem perspective to intervention seeks to bring attention to the principles of the ecological and systems theories. This theory focuses on various principles including the interconnection of systems, the importance of goodness of fit, boundaries, and patterns of relationships. Social workers find that "consistent with ecological and system theories, the intervention seeks to enhance the functioning of a system by improving the goodness of fit between the client and the systems with which she interacts" (Langer & Leitz, 2015, p. 42).

Life Model

The life model has a long tradition in the profession of social work. From the earliest days of social work in the United States, during the time of the Settlement House movement, the life model is evident. The term was officially coined during the mid-20th century based on the idea of social work practice resembling life itself. Gitterman and Germain (2008) put forth that "such a life-modeled practice fits the social work profession's purpose of releasing the potential for growth and satisfying social functioning of individuals, families, and groups, while increasing the responsiveness of their environment to people's needs, rights, and aspirations" (p. 71). As you can see, within the life model it is critically important to consider the client's social environment holistically. By focusing on the transactions between clients and their environments, the social worker can identify means of coping that clients already possess. By exploring these existing coping mechanisms, social workers can encourage and enhance clients' overall functioning.

This model requires that social workers learn from clients and join them in the process of life. Life can be difficult and, at times, messy. As professionals, we must recognize this reality. As a profession, we often say that we must meet clients where they are. In order to do so fully, we must recognize where the client is within his or her life. Throughout life, people grow, develop, and change. We must recognize where the client has been and where he or she is now. Equally important, we must understand where it is that the client seeks to go. One way that the social worker can gain these insights is through listening to the client tell his or her life story. The client's life story is the personal narrative of his or her experiences.

The life model is characterized by the 10 features outlined in Table 7.1. The model has four phases: preparatory, initial, ongoing, and ending. During the preparatory phase of the life model intervention, the social worker must be prepared to be empathetic to the client and his or her life story. We have discussed in previous chapters the importance of empathy within social work practice. Without empathy, clients may not open up and share their experiences with the worker. If clients do not feel that they can be open and honest, this will detrimentally hinder the intervention.

During the initial phase of this model, the social worker seeks to create a supportive relationship with the client. This relationship creates an accepting environment in which clients can share their experiences and social workers can use empathy and curiosity to elicit more information from clients. In this phase, there is an emphasis on defining stressors and degree

TABLE 7.1 Life Model Features in Social Work Practice

Professional function	The role of the social worker in this model is to ameliorate client stressors and improve coping strategies. Social workers seek to match client needs with available resources.
Ethical practice	Social workers view ethical principles within a hierarchy to determine priority. From the highest to the lowest priority: protection of life, equality and inequality, autonomy and freedom, least harm, quality of life, privacy and confidentiality, truthfulness, and full disclosure.
Diversity-sensitive	Social workers respect all clients and engage in culturally competent practice. Furthermore, social workers honor individual differences.
Empowerment	Empowerment and addressing social justice issues are central to this model.
Integrated methods	There are numerous modalities and methods that are utilized in this approach to address change.
Partnership	The relationship between the social worker and client is viewed as a partnership rather than a hierarchical relationship.
Mutual agreement	Shared definitions are a critical piece of this model. These shared definitions must be mutually agreed on.
Strengths	This approach is inherently strengths-based.
Significance of culture and environment	Social workers appreciate the role of culture and environment on the individual.
Evaluation	Various methods exist that can assist in determining if the approach was successful.

Source: From Gitterman, A., & Germain, C. B. (2008). *The life model of social work practice: Advances in theory and practice* (3rd ed.). New York, NY: Columbia University Press.

of choice. At this stage, the social worker and client must clearly identify all stressors that are of concern. As with many social work interventions, it is very important that the client and social worker are on the same page related to what are the identified problems. Not only should problems be stated; when problems are defined as clearly as possible will ensure that both the worker and client are on the same page.

The degree of choice refers to the client's choice of services. As we have discussed at the start of this chapter, at times, clients seek out social work support for concerns whereas at other times, social workers are made available to clients due to a referral of some sort. When clients have not sought out the service for themselves but are rather offered, or in some cases mandated, social work support, there may be a reluctance to participate. Social workers should acknowledge this and address any feelings the client may have regarding this from an empathetic stance.

Other tasks that occur during this stage include obtaining the client's informed consent for treatment as well as reviewing agency policies and procedures. The social worker and client also work together to develop goals for treatment. It is important that goal setting is a mutual process. The social worker and client also discuss expectations for their work together.

The next phase of treatment is the ongoing phase. Within this phase, the social worker is intervening, utilizing a variety of modalities. Social workers seek to clarify client responses and encourage further exploration. Social workers identify client strengths that can be used to address areas of concern. Supporting clients as they move through the problem-solving process is another way in which social workers support clients during this phase of treatment.

The final phase of this model is the ending phase. The social worker must plan for this stage with the client in order to avoid negative feelings related to the termination of services. The social worker reflects with the client upon their work together and assists the client in identifying areas of growth and progress gained throughout the process.

Family Interventions

Social workers recognize that working with families is important. Working with families can be challenging, but it can also be quite rewarding. There are several different clinical approaches to supporting families that we will cover. Regardless of the approach, social workers must recognize that families are complex groups. Social workers must also understand that all families have strengths. The strengths perspective can, and should, be applied to family systems. While working with families, social workers should consider who within the family system should be participating in treatment. Furthermore, it is important to recognize that it may not always be appropriate to have all members of the family present at all times. For example, there may be times when it would be inappropriate to have the children present during some conversations between the parents and the social worker. Social workers must utilize their professional judgmentin regard to such decisions.

Family Systems Therapy

Family systems therapy, which we introduced in Chapter 6, Microsystems Assessment: Individuals, Families, and Groups, is an intervention approach that involves the whole family to address problems within the family system. This approach was developed by psychiatrist Murray Bowen and is sometimes called Bowenian therapy. This approach relies on the premise of interconnection from systems theory. Based on this, the approach puts forth that a change in one family member will impact everyone in the family.

Key concepts related to this approach include patterns of familial interaction, differentiation, and triangulation (all of which can be viewed in Chapter 6, Microsystems Assessment: Individuals, Families, and Groups).

When considering a family systems intervention, social workers should consider how systems are influencing the family. It is important to consider how systems influence the family as a whole and how they influence members of the family individually as well. Completing an ecomap with each member of the family can be a strategy to identify such systems. Creating a family ecomap follows the same process as you would when creating an individual ecomap. However, instead of having the individual client at the center, you would include the identified family members. Figure 7.3 shows a sample family ecomap. When constructing a family ecomap, you can indicate both relationships between outside systems and individuals within the family and the relationship between outside systems and the family as a whole system.

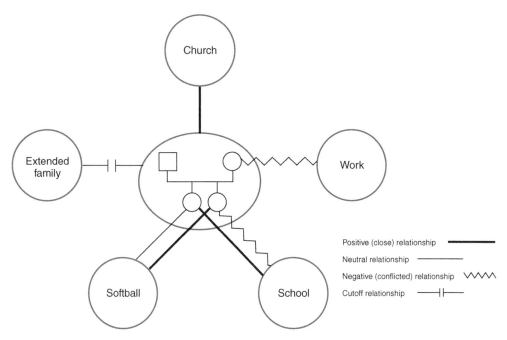

Positive (close) relationship
Neutral relationship
Negative (conflicted) relationship
Cutoff relationship

FIGURE 7.3 Family ecomap: diagram illustrating the relationship between the family and
outside systems.

Functional Family Therapy

Functional family therapy (FFT) is a short-term treatment model designed to support families with children who are identified as at-risk. FFT combined both systems theory and cognitive behavioral theory to create this intervention approach (Robbins, Alexander, Turner, &
Hollimon, 2016).

FFT is a manualized evidence-based practice. There are five phases of FFT: engagement,
motivation, relational assessment, behavior change, and generalization (Robbins et al., 2016).
During the engagement phase, the social worker is tasked with engaging the family to the
extent that they will continue treatment. According to Hartnett, Carr, Hamilton, and Sexton
(2017), "the goal of the engagement and motivation phase of treatment is the reduction of
negativity and blame between family members and the development of a more family-fo-
cused view of their presenting problems" (p. 83). During the motivation stage, the social
worker seeks to support the family in developing a congruent motivation for change. At
times, things such as blame, alliances, and conflicts need to be addressed. The third stage of
FFT is relational assessment, which involves exploring the functional behaviors and interactions among the family. It is important to recognize that all behavior fulfills some function.
Though the person engaging in the behavior is not aware of the functions of the behavior at
present, the social worker can assist in bringing such things to light. The next stage of the
intervention involves the social worker teaching skills and strategies to address the identified
problem(s). The goal is to diminish dysfunctional behaviors and interactions within the family system. During the final stage, generalization occurs when the family is able to take what
they have learned in therapy and apply it outside of the therapeutic environment.

Multisystemic Therapy

Multisystemic therapy (MST) is an evidence-based practice that has been shown to be effective at addressing severe behavioral and antisocial problems and reducing out-of-home placements for youth. MST seeks to support caregivers and increase their abilities to parent as the "ultimate goal is to create a context that supports adaptive, rather than deviant, youth and parent behavior" (Henggeler & Schaeffer, 2016, p. 515).

MST is a brief intervention designed to support youth with severe psychosocial or behavioral issues. This is a home- and community-based treatment program. As the name implies, the MST intervention seeks to engage all of the systems involved in the youth's life to provide support. Various systems that could be involved in treatment include mental health providers, child welfare, juvenile justice or probation, and school. A critical target of MST is to empower caregivers in order to bring about change within the family system (Fox, Bibi, Millar, & Holland, 2017).

In this specific intervention, the caregiver is viewed as the "main facilitator of change" (Fox et al., 2017, p. 244). The social worker is tasked with supporting families and empowering the caregivers of the identified child. This intervention seeks to address and improve family functioning in order to then have an impact on the other systems in the life of the child. There are nine MST treatment principles that guide this intervention (Table 7.2).

Brief Structural Family Therapy

Brief structural family therapy was developed by Salvador Minuchin. This form of family therapy occurs in the home and community setting. Services are often delivered by a team of two clinicians (one at the master's level and the other at the bachelor's level). The team works intensively with the family to bring about change within the structure of the family. Originally developed as an alternative to traditional talk therapies, structural family therapy seeks to address family systems and subsystems to improve functioning (McAdams et al., 2016).

This intervention approach requires that the social worker assist the family in addressing issues related to family structure. This may include family roles, rules, boundaries, and subsystems. Roles refer to the assigned positions that each person in the family fulfills. There are a variety of family roles that are appropriate; for example, the role of caretaker for a parent. However, there may be dysfunctional roles, such as the scapegoat, which can disrupt family functioning. Rules are another important focus of structural family therapy. All family systems have rules. Some rules are explicit, whereas others are not overtly stated but are still just as powerful. Boundaries reflect the parameters of the relationships within the family system. Healthy boundaries are clear. However, at times, boundaries may be unclear or diffused. When there are unclear boundaries, this can negatively impact the family structure. Subsystems within this approach refer to the minisystems present within the family system. For example, mother and father make up the parent subsystem. Subsystems can be positive and healthy. Some subsystems are not helpful and may create issues related to triangulation.

TABLE 7.2 MST Principles in Social Work Practice

Finding the fit	The social worker must conduct a complete assessment in order to fully understand how the problems fit within the family system.
Focusing on positives and strengths	The social worker utilizes a strengths-based approach throughout treatment.
Increasing responsibility	A goal of MST treatment is to increase responsibility for the identified child as well as other members of the family, including caregivers.
Present-focused, action-oriented, and well-defined	The social worker is primarily concerned with present functioning of the family. The social worker and family together strive to identify specific action steps to address treatment goals.
Targeting sequences	Treatment addresses all systems of the child's life including home, school, and community.
Developmentally appropriate	This treatment is client-specific. There is no MST manual or scripting. This flexibility allows for the services to be tailored to the specific developmental needs of the clients.
Continuous effort	This is an intensive service that requires the child and family to do a significant amount of work. Families must be engaged and working on treatment for this model to succeed.
Evaluation and accountability	Progress (or lack thereof) is measured frequently to determine how treatment is going. If treatment is not progressing, the social worker explores how they can make changes to improve outcomes. Families cannot fail at MST; rather, social workers have not tailored the treatment to reach the family.
Generalization	The intervention of MST is driven by the caregiver with the assistance of the social worker. As a result, the caregiver has realized his or her ability to address family needs, which can be used in future situations.

MST, multisystemic therapy.

Source: From Henggeler, S. W., & Schaeffer, C. M. (2016). Multisystemic therapy® : Clinical overview, outcomes, and implementation research. *Family Process, 55*(3), 514–528.

Strengths Perspective

The strengths perspective seeks to identify the strengths present within our clients. As social workers, we believe in the inherent worth of all people. The strengths perspective seeks to have us identify these strengths. Strengths may be internal or external. Examples of internal strengths include things such as "a sense of humor, insight, and flexibility that help people cope with challenges they face" whereas external strengths include things such as "resources outside of the person . . . extended family, connection to a faith community, services available in a client's local geographic area" (Langer & Leitz, 2015, p. 61).

During the assessment process, social workers should begin identifying client strengths. These identified strengths can inform the intervention process and support the ongoing work between the client and social worker. At times, it may be

▶ **Critical Thinking Question**

As a social worker, how would you help clients identify personal strengths?

difficult for clients to identify their own personal strengths. In such cases, it is the role of the social worker to identify the strengths. Case 7.2 illustrates a social worker utilizing the strengths perspective to assist a client.

Some critique this perspective noting that it is conceptually vague and overly emphasizes the strengths of the clients and in turn diminishes the problems the client is presenting with (Simmons, Shapiro, Accomazzo, & Manthey, 2016). Simmons et al. (2016) goes on to state that due to the lack of clarity, "a strength may be defined entirely different in every intervention stage" (p. 149). Social workers should recognize these critiques but not allow them to hinder efforts to identify strengths. Yes, it is important to recognize and address problems. However, social workers must not become consumed by a deficit-based approach. Rather, we must seek to identify strengths as a way to inform our interventions and empower the client systems we work with.

A key concept related to the strengths perspective is the concept of resilience. Resilience is often considered the ability to bounce back from difficulty. Graham (2013) defines resilience as "the capacity to respond to pressures and tragedies quickly, adaptively, and effectively"

CASE 7.2 FINDING STRENGTHS: UTILIZING THE STRENGTHS PERSPECTIVE IN SOCIAL WORK PRACTICE

Megan is a social worker who is a case manager at a drug rehabilitation center. A part of Megan's job is to meet with the patients at the facility and work with them to find education or job opportunities. This requires Megan spending time getting to know the patients and their interests. It is also important for Megan to pay attention to what the patient strengths are and try to find a good match between their strengths and the skills and requirements needed for various educational and job opportunities.

Today Megan met with Jack, a patient who has been at the facility for approximately 3 months and is looking to be discharged soon and is in need of finding employment. During their meeting, Megan asked Jack what he thought his strengths were. Jack did not know how to answer the question. Megan rephrased the question and asked him again to tell her about the things he was good at; again, Jack did not have a response. Nevertheless, Megan persisted asking in another way. Finally, Jack said, "I'm not good at anything, I've never had a real job. I don't know what I would even be able to do." Megan asked Jack what he did to make money before coming into rehab. Jack shared that he had always made ends meet by hustling on the streets. Then, Megan said, "Well, there you have it; that is one of your strengths." Jack was surprised; so he said to Meghan, "What do you mean? There is no way that I can go back to hustling on the streets and stay clean." Megan agreed, but she helped Jack to see that some of the skills he used in order to hustle would help him in the job market. She pointed out to Jack that he dealt with many people; this translates into good people skills. Those people skills would be helpful in a customer service position. She pointed out to Jack that he often had to manage his money and keep track of money in and money out. Those are great financial skills. Megan and Jack went on to identify other strengths that he had based on his previous experiences that would be helpful in future endeavors. By the end of the session, Jack was proud of his strengths and had a new confidence about himself.

(p. xxv). According to Rutter (2006), resilience is an "interactive concept" that must be considered in relation to both risk and protective factors (p. 3). Resilience is often influenced by factors that are external from the individual (Luthar, Cicchetti, & Becker, 2000). Within a social work framework, influences at the micro-, mezzo-, and macrolevels affect the development of resilience. Luthar et al. (2000) set forth that attributes of the individual, the family system, as well as the wider social environment influence resilience. Factors influencing resilience include such things as support systems, coping skills, and resources available.

▶ **Critical Thinking Question**

Identify how the strengths perspective and the concept of resilience align with social work values.

Many researchers have identified protective factors as well as risk factors in an attempt to classify the influences on resilience at the micro- and mezzolevels. Protective factors refer to a set of characteristics that are often shared by individuals who are considered to be resilient (Earvolino-Ramirez, 2007). Protective factors can include, but are not limited to, such things as: healthy relationships, quality educational opportunities, healthy self-esteem, and a good sense of humor. Studies from different countries demonstrate that some factors are universally experienced as protective (Gunnestad & Thwala, 2011). Canavan (2008) asserts that protective factors serve to diminish the likelihood of impaired development as the result of experiencing one or multiple risk factors. Within the literature, protective factors include such things as:

> Good natured, easy temperament, positive relationships, communicates effectively, sense of personal worthiness, sense of control over fate, effective in work, play, love, positive social orientation, assertive, asks for help, above average social intelligence, informal social support network, ability to have close relationships, healthy expectations and needs, use of talents to personal advantage, delays gratification, internal locus of control, flexible, believes in her or his self-efficacy, desires to improve, interpersonal sensitivity, problem-solving ability, decision-making ability, future oriented, trusts in others, hope for the future, sense of humor, productive critical thinking skills, manages range of emotions, adaptive distancing, high expectations. (Earvolino-Ramirez, 2007, p. 75)

Narrative Therapy

Every person has a story. As social workers, we are invested in hearing those stories. We are invested in honoring those stories. Narrative therapy is a technique where the client's story is the focus of the intervention. The premise of this technique is that individuals are constantly engaged in constructing their personal narrative or life story (Walsh, 2013). The self-narratives that are constructed in narrative therapy provide a sense of identity for the client (Allen, 2011). This relatively newer technique was developed by Michael White and David Epston. White and Epston (1990) put forth:

> In striving to make sense of their lives, persons face the task of arranging their experiences of events in sequences across time in such a way as to arrive at a coherent account of themselves and the world around them. (p. 10)

During the fluid process of human development, stories may change. These stories are extremely powerful as they do not only account for our experiences but can shape our experiences as well. These stories can be a focus in treatment. This technique has been found effective with individuals as well as with couples (White, 2009).

Within narrative therapy, there is an emphasis on understanding personal meaning. Much research and theory have been dedicated to the necessity of meaning making in human life. Frankl (2006) sets forth that "man's search for meaning is the primary motivation in his life . . . it must and can be fulfilled by him alone" (p. 99). Frankl (2006) asserts that nothing exists that "would so effectively help one to survive even the worst conditions as the knowledge that there is meaning in one's life . . . he who has a why to live for can bear almost any how" (p. 104).

Hauser and Allen (2006) set forth that "personal meaning and meaning making can foster unexpected pathways from adolescent misfortune to young adult competence in friendships, marriage, and parenting" (p. 574). Research suggests that making positive meaning from negative life events can assist the individual in reframing the adversity and in turn buffering the impact of the adversity on the mind and the person's overall well-being (Lightsey, 2006; O'Connor, 2003). Some view meaning making as a necessary human experience (Brown, 2015).

Within narrative therapy, the personal story is deconstructed by the social worker and the client. Deconstructed refers to the critical analysis that occurs by the social worker and client when exploring the personal narrative. Assumptions are addressed and challenged when appropriate. Another aspect of narrative therapy includes reconstruction. During the stage of reconstruction, the client creates a new, more functional, personal narrative. The social worker is often very active in assisting the client in identifying options for the new narrative. However, as with most elements of social work practice, the construction of a new narrative relies on the self-determination of the client. The final stage of narrative therapy is connecting. During this stage, the client integrates the new personal narrative into his or her life and engages with others. This is also a stage of celebrating the new narrative (see Case 7.3).

CASE 7.3   FINDING THE STORY: THE IMPORTANCE OF THE PERSONAL NARRATIVE IN SOCIAL WORK PRACTICE

Paige is a social worker who works at a counseling center. In her role, she provides individual counseling services. She just began meeting weekly with a client, Denise. Denise sought out services to deal with her low self-esteem. Paige and Denise have been exploring the personal story Denise has about herself. Denise has been able to identify that she long had a personal narrative that she is a screwup and no one will ever love her.

Together Paige and Denise work to recreate her personal narrative. Paige asks Denise what she would rather her story be. Denise recognizes she wants to feel good about herself and acknowledges she has talents and close friends who do love her.

Over time, Paige and Denise work together to solidify this personal narrative. Eventually comes the time to celebrate Denise's new personal narrative. Denise feels like a new person and wants to celebrate her vibrant self with her friends. Denise feels more comfortable being herself and living her new narrative.

Task-Centered Practice

Task-centered practice is a problem-solving approach that can be utilized as a social work intervention with clients. This is a highly adaptable model that can be used in a variety of practice settings. It is a short-term model that emphasizes taking action to address the problem rather than ruminating on the problem (Langer & Leitz, 2015). This approach emphasizes completing specific tasks in order to address the problem. The problems are the wants and needs of the clients. Within this approach, problems are viewed as an inevitable piece of the human experience. In practice, the problem selected to be addressed during the intervention is called the target problem. It is important to note that a client may present with numerous problems and it may not be within the scope of your practice to be able to address all problems. Or it may not be feasible to address all of the problems at once. In such a case, it is important to work with the client to prioritize problems so that the most urgent problem can be addressed first. Again, considering client self-determination is important. Once a target problem has been identified, target tasks, or the tasks necessary to ameliorate, or lessen, the problem are identified. There are three phases of treatment in the task-centered approach, which are illustrated in Table 7.3.

Solution-Focused Brief Therapy

Solution-focused brief therapy was designed based on both the task-centered approach and the strengths perspective. In this short-term intervention, the focus is on solutions. This approach is very much future-oriented. The social worker builds rapport through joining with the client. The social worker assists the client in seeking change, starting where the client is. A key component of this approach is the notion that "people possess all of the skills and strengths necessary to solve their problems" (Langer & Leitz, 2015, p. 212). The social worker must at times assist the client in recognizing these skills and strengths. Although in other

TABLE 7.3 Phases in the Task-Centered Model

Initial phases	The social worker engages with the client in order to establish rapport. The social worker then begins the assessment in order to identify problems and their contexts. Target problems are discussed in specific detail. Once the target problem has been clearly specified, the social worker and client develop a contract including goals with specific steps to address the target problem.
Intervention	During this stage, the client is completing the goals outlined in the contract to reduce the target problem. The social worker and client often work together in order to identify various possibilities to meet the specified goals. During meetings together, the social worker and client review progress toward achieving goals. If goals have not yet been achieved, the social worker and client discuss the reasons for this and make changes as necessary.
Termination	This is the final stage of the task-centered model. Termination is the overarching goal of this brief treatment approach and as a result should be discussed early in treatment. The social worker and client reflect upon accomplishments and plan for ongoing maintenance.

Source: From Langer, C. L., & Lietz, C. A. (2015). *Applying theory to generalist social work practice.* Hoboken, NJ: Wiley.

models there is an emphasis on the social worker teaching new skills, this approach relies on what the client already has available to him or her.

In order to set appropriate goals for this approach, the miracle question is a technique that is often utilized. The miracle question requires clients to consider their future without their current problem. Through this question, social workers can gain insights into how clients envision their future through a hopeful perspective. This can provide the social worker with ideas regarding possible skills and resources that can be useful in this approach. Another important technique is the scaling question. This question asks the client to rate, often on a scale of 1 to 10, how present the problem is in their lives: 1 represents no problem, whereas 10 represents the problem is fully present. This question can be helpful in evaluating progress throughout your work with the client.

Social Learning Theory

Albert Bandura sought out to better understand how individuals learned. He conducted the famous Bobo doll experiment. In this experiment, Bandura had a Bobo doll, a clown-like punching toy. It was in a room with other toys. Children were invited into the room to play. Children were then shown a video of adults playing roughly, punching and knocking down the toy. After watching this video, the children emulated the behaviors of the adult models that they had seen in the videos. As a result of this experiment, Bandura put forth that children learn through the observation of models. Furthermore, he asserted the experience of vicarious learning. Vicarious learning refers to the ability to learn solely through the observation of others.

Social learning theory can inform social work intervention as it also directs social workers to use models for clients to learn new behaviors. This can be particularly helpful for individuals with social skill deficits. The use of modeling to teach appropriate social skills is a common intervention that utilizes vicarious learning. This approach is grounded in both behavioral theory and cognitive theory.

When considering learning, it is important to understand reinforcement and punishment, which are important aspects of behavioral theory (Figure 7.4). Social workers often rely on intervention strategies that address these two behavior change principles. Reinforcement is used when we want to have a behavior increase. However, on the other hand, punishment is used when we want to have a behavior decrease. We can use the terms positive and negative to describe types of reinforcement and punishment. These terms can sometimes become confusing. When we consider the terms positive and negative, we are not using them to describe good or bad; rather, we are using them to describe the addition of or removal of some stimuli. Positive reinforcement occurs when a stimulus is added in the hopes of increasing a behavior. An example of a positive reinforcement would be praising a child who used appropriate social skills. The praise was added in the hopes of reinforcing the appropriate social skill behaviors. Negative reinforcement occurs when a stimulus is removed in the hopes of increasing a behavior. Positive punishment occurs when a stimulus is added with the intention of decreasing a behavior. An example of positive punishment would be if a child talks back to his or her parent, the child must then write an apology note. Negative punishment occurs when a stimulus is removed with the intention of decreasing a behavior. An example of negative punishment is when a child is throwing a tantrum and the parents send

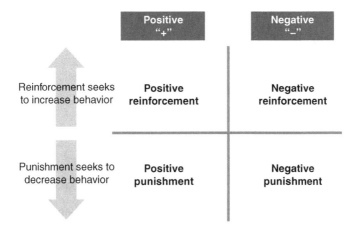

FIGURE 7.4 Reinforcement and punishment in cognitive behavioral therapy.

the child to his or her room. In this case, the parents want the tantrum behavior to decrease. In an attempt to reduce the tantrums, the parents have the child removed from the current environment and placed in his or her room.

Cognitive Behavioral Therapy

Cognitive behavioral therapy (CBT) is an evidence-based practice with roots in both cognitive and behavioral theories that was developed by Aaron Beck. This is an evidence-based practice that is often used in talk therapy interventions. It is popular due to its transferability across settings, populations, and problems. CBT is rooted in the premise that our thoughts, feelings, and behaviors are interconnected (see Figure 7.5). CBT asserts that individuals have control of what thoughts they choose to believe and which, in turn can shape their outlooks. González-Prendes and Brisebois (2012) find that the intervention of CBT is congruent with social work values, asserting that:

> CBT does this by promoting self-respect through the development of unconditional self-acceptance; adopting a strength perspective that recognizes clients' abilities to change and the expertise that they have about themselves; promoting a collaborative therapeutic relationship that respects and seeks out clients' input and participation in every step of the process; empowering clients to become active agents in the resolution of their problems; and acknowledging the impact of one's social context on core beliefs and schemas, as well as the oppressive nature of internalized biases and stigmas. (p. 29)

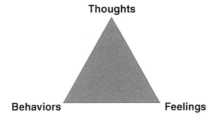

FIGURE 7.5 The cognitive behavioral therapy triangle.

With such good alignment, social workers should at the least be aware of intervention of CBT and when appropriate, consider this intervention with clients. Skill training is a key piece to the CBT intervention (Fisher & O'Donohue, 2012). In skill training, it is the obligation of the social worker to provide the client with the skills necessary to combat the problem at hand. Case 7.4 illustrates the use of CBT as an intervention.

CASE 7.4   CONNECTING THOUGHTS, BEHAVIORS, AND FEELINGS IN SOCIAL WORK PRACTICE

Giada is a school social worker. She is working with a high school freshman, Nicole, who has been experiencing school anxiety. After a thorough assessment, Giada finds that the best method of intervention is cognitive behavioral therapy (CBT). She believes that the student will strongly benefit from recognizing the relationship among thoughts, behaviors, and feelings. In a session, Giada shared with Nicole the CBT triangle. She explained the triangle by saying, "Our thoughts, feelings, and behaviors are all interrelated. If we can change our thoughts, we can change what we feel, and in turn change how we behave, or react. Let me give you an example. Imagine you see a couple of friends down the hall and you see them talking to each other. You cannot hear what they are saying, but you see them laugh. What might you think?" Nicole thinks for a moment, "Well, maybe they are talking about me." Giada then asks, "How would you feel if you thought your friends were talking about you?" "I would be upset." Nicole responded quickly. "Ok, if you were upset with your friends, how might you behave or react to them?" Giada asked. Nicole thought, "Well, I probably would not even want to talk to them, so I would turn around and walk the other way." Giada then said, "Ok, let's try something different. What if instead of thinking your friends were talking about you, you thought to yourself, that they must be laughing because they told a funny joke?" Nicole responded, "Well, I would probably be curious about what they are talking about." "And how might that change how you behave?" Giada asked. Nicole was quick to say "I would probably walk up to them and ask what they are talking about."

After discussing the hypothetical situation, Giada felt that Nicole had a good understanding of the interrelationship among thoughts, behaviors, and feelings. Giada then began to work with Nicole to apply the CBT triangle to her current problem. Giada asked, "So, Nicole, what are the thoughts that you usually have about school that upset you?" Nicole thought, "Well, I worry about all of the work I am going to have to do throughout the day and worry I might forget something for class, and I worry that I might get bullied. I just worry that it is going to be an awful day." Giada asked, "And how does that make you feel?" "Anxious, worried, upset!" Nicole was quick to respond. "And how do you behave as a result?" Giada asked. "Sometimes I avoid school, other times, when I am here I am quieter than usual because I am wrapped up in my thoughts in my head." Giada then encouraged Nicole to think about things that could be different if she would change her thoughts. Nicole was able to recognize that if she changed her thought

---

(continued)

CASE 7.4

to "today is going to be a good day at school," she would probably feel neutral, or maybe even excited. She also realized that if she felt excited to be at school, she would probably want to go to school and be more engaged while there.

Giada was excited to see Nicole's insight into the situation. The intervention was not over; they would still have work to do. However, today they made a good first step in addressing the problem at hand. Giada plans to utilize other CBT tools and techniques such as the thought record to help Nicole continue to see the impact of her thoughts and encourage her to challenge negative automatic thoughts.

Motivational Interviewing

Motivational interviewing (MI) is a short-term, evidence-based practice. It seeks to build motivation and focus on change-oriented talk to promote change (Dix, 2016). This is a non-confrontational approach to bringing about change with clients. According to Miller and Rollnick (2013):

> Motivational interviewing is a collaborative, goal-oriented style of communication with particular attention to the language of change. It is designed to strengthen personal motivation for and commitment to a specific goal by eliciting and exploring the person's own reasons for change within an atmosphere of acceptance and compassion. (p. 29)

MI is practical in its focus. The strategies of MI are more persuasive than coercive and more supportive than argumentative. The five general principles of MI are:

1. Express empathy through reflective listening.

2. Develop discrepancy between clients' goals or values and their current behavior.

3. Avoid argument and direct confrontation.

4. Adjust to client resistance rather than opposing it directly.

5. Support self-efficacy and optimism. (Miller & Rollnick, 2013, p. 51)

Empathy "is a specifiable and learnable skill for *understanding* another's meaning through the use of reflective listening" (Miller & Rollnick, 1991, p. 20). An empathic style:

- Communicates respect for and acceptance of clients and their feelings
- Encourages a nonjudgmental, collaborative relationship
- Allows you to be a supportive and knowledgeable consultant
- Sincerely compliments rather than denigrates
- Listens rather than tells

- Gently persuades, with the understanding that the decision to change is the client's

- Provides support throughout the recovery process. (Substance Abuse and Mental Health Services Administration [SAMHSA], 1999)

Empathic MI seeks to create a safe and open environment to examine issues and elicit personal reasons for change. A fundamental component of MI is understanding each client's unique perspective, feelings, and values while conveying acceptance, but not necessarily approval or agreement.

Motivation for change is enhanced when clients perceive discrepancies between their current situation and their hopes for the future. The work involves helping clients see how their current behavior differs from their desired behavior. Separate the behavior from the person and help your client explore how important personal goals (e.g., good health, marital happiness, financial success) are being undermined by current behaviors. If the client shows concern about the effects of personal behavior, highlight this concern to heighten the client's perception and acknowledgment of discrepancy (SAMHSA, 1999).

Avoid arguments about your clients' behavior. You may occasionally be tempted to argue with a client. However, trying to convince a client that a problem exists or that change is needed could precipitate even more resistance. When it is the client, not you, who voices arguments for change, progress can be made. The goal is to "walk" with clients (i.e., accompany clients through treatment), not "drag" them along (i.e., direct clients' treatment; SAMHSA, 1999). Accusing clients of being in denial or resistant is more likely to increase their resistance than to instill motivation for change.

Common to MI are scaling questions, including utilizing a readiness ruler. The readiness ruler utilizes a 0 to 10 scale that seeks to have clients rate their motivation to change. When using the ruler in practice, if the patient would select a 6, as the social worker, you would probe the client to determine why they selected a 6 versus a lower or higher number. The rationale for their selection can be helpful in providing you insights into the client's current state. In addition, MI entails asking open-ended questions, listening reflectively, summarizing, affirming, and eliciting self-motivational statements. The goal is to help motivate client change. It is not to create change but help clients self-identify the need and desire for change.

Rational Emotive Behavioral Therapy

Rational emotive behavioral therapy (REBT), previously referred to as rational therapy, is a short-term intervention approach that emphasizes challenging irrational thoughts by replacing them with more rational, or productive, thoughts. This intervention was developed by Albert Ellis. This approach draws on a variety of theories including humanistic, cognitive, and behavioral.

The intervention of REBT is viewed to be one of the main pillars of CBT (David, Cotet, Matu, Mogoase, & Stefan, 2018). Though there are many similarities between REBT and CBT, there are some distinct differences. REBT places emphasis on unconditional self-acceptance. Clients are encouraged to accept themselves rather than rate themselves in any way. Another distinction is that REBT asserts that some negative emotions are actually helpful or appropriate. For example, grief would be viewed as an appropriate negative emotion.

There are six principles of REBT. The first principle is that all people have both rational and irrational thoughts. This is human nature. The second principle is that experiences may increase irrational thinking. These experiences may include elements related to family and culture. The third principle is that people think, feel, and behave at the same time, and these functions are interrelated. The fourth principle is that the social worker must at times be critical and provide confrontation to the client in order to address concerns. The fifth principle is that a variety of strategies can be used to promote rational thinking. The final principle is that irrational beliefs cause emotional problems.

Empowerment Therapy

Empowerment therapy is a clinical approach that is closely aligned with social work values. Social workers often seek to empower client systems. Within this approach, social workers engage with clients to increase empowerment. Langer and Leitz (2015) set forth:

> Empowerment is both a concept and a practice model. Social workers empower individuals to create change on their own behalf, taking personal responsibility for change, by identifying personal strengths, recognizing and removing structural barriers, or through various other methods, such as advocacy. (p. 168)

When considering the empowerment approach, it is important to consider self-efficacy. Self-efficacy is the belief in one's self to be able to succeed or accomplish a task. Self-efficacy can increase as a result of increased empowerment. Specific techniques to empower a client include honoring the client's position so that the client feels heard, believed, and valued. It is then important for the social worker and client to identify strengths. It is important to then consider power dynamics including unequal distributions of power that are present in the client's system. The social worker then provides skills, tools, and resources to the client. It is important that this stage occurs through mutual participation. The social worker does not simply pass down this information but facilitates this learning with the client. During the final phase, the client is able to use the new skills, tools, and resources.

Conflict Theory

As we discussed in Chapter 3, Diversity and Difference, conflict theory seeks to understand the tensions between groups. Key points related to conflict theory is the competition for resources and an unequal treatment or lack of opportunities for one group in comparison to another. There are several intervention approaches that are derived from this theory.

Feminist Therapy

Feminist therapy involves "a collaborative relationship between social worker and client is critical as there should be a focus on breaking down power differentials and imbalances and fostering positive, healthy relationships" (Teater, 2014, p. 96). Furthermore, goals of feminist therapy often involve addressing symptoms of presenting problems, self-esteem and body image, relationships, diversity, and social action (Teater, 2014).

This approach developed to provide a feminist-informed approach to therapy. Also, it provides a means by which to explore problems from a feminist perspective. This approach acknowledges socialization based on gender as well as issues related to gender inequality or discrimination that may impact the client. This approach can integrate a variety of techniques and clinical practice approaches.

It is important to note that feminist therapy is not only an intervention for women. Men can benefit from feminist therapy as well as they often "experience negative consequences due to societal expectations of their gender role" (Teater, 2014, p. 96). This approach can also assist men in addressing issues related to gender stereotyping. It can also be helpful to address issues related to intimacy and vulnerability.

Anti-Oppressive Practice

Anti-oppressive practice is a social work intervention approach that seeks to address and end oppressive practices. This intervention approach is closely connected to the social work value of social justice. The approach seeks to reduce inequalities and enhance opportunities. Social workers who engage in anti-oppressive practice can utilize this approach at all levels of practice. Anti-oppressive practice, much like feminist therapy, utilizes a variety of other techniques and intervention strategies to bring about change while considering the role of oppression on the client.

Focus within anti-oppressive practice could be related to systemic issues of oppression or issues related to internalized oppression. Individuals and groups who have experienced oppression often feel devalued or marginalized. These concerns often need to be attended to within anti-oppressive practice.

■ Transitions and Endings

There will come a time when our work with a client will transition or end. We, as social workers, must be prepared for this. More importantly, we must make every effort to ensure our clients are prepared for this as well. Change, including transitions and endings, can be difficult. As a result, it is important for social workers to discuss plans for this early on and often with clients. Planning for termination is often called discharge planning. Discharge planning should begin early in treatment, even during the initial meeting whenever possible. Discharge planning will require individualized planning (just like treatment planning). Sometimes discharge planning involves referrals to lower levels of care. In such an event, when other formalized services are still required by the client, the social worker should make every effort to provide continuity of care so that the transition can be as seamless as possible and as supportive as possible of the client.

For many clients who are working with a social worker, it is important to have a positive ending. Unfortunately, they may have had disruptions and negative endings and transitions in the past. It is important that, as the social worker, you provide a positive experience related to an ending.

> ▶ **Critical Thinking Questions**
>
> Consider a transition or ending that you have experienced.
>
> 1. What things influenced how you felt about the transition or ending?
> 2. What can you take from your experience and apply to future transitions and endings?

■ Policy Issue

A policy issue related to intervention that requires social work attention relates to insurance coverage and access to services for clients. Unfortunately, at times, decisions related to length of stay in treatment are not made by the frontline clinicians working with the client directly; rather, they are often made by insurance companies and managed care organizations. Because of this, social workers must be prepared to advocate for clients to receive the level and amount of care that is clinically appropriate for them. Social workers can advocate for specific clients during collaborative contacts with their insurance but also on a larger scale. Social workers are policy advocates. Social workers should be sure to use their policy skills to promote change at the state and federal levels related to insurance coverage language.

■ Social Justice Issue

Throughout this chapter, we have explored a variety of intervention techniques that can be extremely beneficial within the context of the helping relationship. However, regardless of how successful or evidence-based an intervention approach is, if an individual in need of services does not reach out for services, social workers are unable to assist. A social justice issue that social workers must address is the lack of utilization of some types of services based on population. For example, it is well-documented that men seek out interventions for mental health problems at a much lower rate than females. The numbers are even lower for men of color seeking mental health services. Social workers recognize that there is not a decreased prevalence within these populations, so we must critically consider the reasons for this underutilization of services. Perhaps, stigma is a barrier to treatment for males to seek out mental health support. Despite advancements in attempting to reduce stigma made by numerous groups, it does still exist. Also, as we noted earlier in this chapter, societal expectations are different based on gender. The expectation of strength and invulnerability placed on men may be another contributing factor to the lack of service utilization.

■ Summary

Throughout this chapter, we explored the role of the social worker during the intervention process. We explored the stages and level of change models. Social workers recognize that it is important to identify where clients are regarding the stage of change in order to ensure intervention efforts are tailored to meet the clients where they are. The generalist perspective model was introduced as well as case management, supportive counseling, and group work. We reviewed a variety of clinical practice techniques that can be useful strategies for intervention. Last, we discussed the importance of attending to transitions and endings in the helping relationship. It is important for the social worker to prepare and support the client throughout the final phases of treatment just as the social worker demonstrated support throughout the rest of the helping process.

Practice Setting Description

Jackie is a first-year master of social work student completing an internship at an inner-city family service agency in the Southwest. The agency is located in a section of the city that has a high crime rate, gang activity, and failing schools. The area has a diverse population with a large number of immigrants from Central and South America and a substantial African American population. The agency provides individual and family counseling services on a sliding fee scale. The agency also runs a number of educational and treatment groups as well as a temporary shelter for women and their children. Jackie has been assigned to work with the women and their children in the shelter. Her primary tasks are to provide concrete services and supportive counseling to the shelter residents.

Background Information

Elicia T and her daughter, Maria, are undocumented immigrants from Mexico. They have been in the United States for 5 years. Elicia and Maria fled to the area from another southwestern city to escape her abusive husband approximately 2 months ago. Elicia is 25 years old and Maria 8 years old. Elicia has a 2-year-old daughter, Sarah, who was placed in foster care because of suspected abuse in the home. Sarah is in a foster home in a small rural community in the state hundreds of miles from Elicia's current residence. Since moving to the area, Maria has not been attending school.

Elicia and Maria are currently residing in the agency's temporary shelter for families. They have been at the shelter for 2 weeks, and the agency has a 90-day limit. It is viewed as temporary housing, and the residents are only allowed to stay for 3 months. Prior to arriving at the shelter, Elicia and Maria were homeless and living on the streets.

Elicia is a high-school dropout and was a stay-at-home mother prior to leaving her husband and moving to a different part of the state. She chose to move there because she has two female cousins living in the area who are also undocumented immigrants. Elicia's native language is Spanish. She speaks some English but is not as comfortable speaking in English. Her English comprehension appears to be good. Maria speaks both English and Spanish well. When communicating with the staff, Maria acts as Elicia's interpreter since none of the staff at the shelter speak Spanish.

Maria appears to be behind academically. She struggles reading simple children's books written in English. It is unknown if her ability to read in Spanish is better than her English reading skills.

Other than her two cousins, Elicia has no other sources of support in the community. Her cousins have young families and limited resources but are well established and connected to a Latino community in the city and the local Catholic church. Her cousins refused to let Elicia and Maria live with them while she was trying to find her own place and a job. They stated that they did not have enough room and are concerned they would get in trouble with their landlord if it was found out that they were letting people stay with them. They sent her to the local church for help, and she was given the address for the agency's shelter by the priest.

(continued)

CASE SUMMARY

Elicia has been looking for housing in the Latino community. The housing market is tight with limited options, and she has been unable to find anything that she could possibly afford. The only affordable housing she found was a room in a rundown motel that rents by the hour or by the month. It is in an area of town known for drug dealing and prostitution.

On arrival in the community, Elicia found occasional work for a house cleaning company. The company hires undocumented workers, pays them very low cash wages, and threatens to turn them in to Immigration and Customs Enforcement (ICE) if they complain. The job bosses also exploit their female workers sexually, threatening to turn them in if they do not comply. Elicia was fearful about applying for other jobs because of her illegal status. She considered turning to prostitution to be able to take care of her children, but her Catholic upbringing and thoughts of how doing so would shame her family have kept her from going down that path. She is in constant fear of being detained, separated from her children, and having them placed in foster care. She is also afraid that she will end up homeless again and forced to live on the streets or return to her abusive husband.

Elicia is extremely reluctant to sign up for any federally funded services, even those that she and her children are entitled to receiving. On the suggestion that she enroll for supplemental food through SNAP, Elicia became nervous and refused as she has heard that participation in SNAP services, and others like them, would draw the attention of ICE, and she had heard stories on the news of individuals being deported after signing up for such programs.

Presenting Problems

Elicia and her children are facing multiple obstacles. They need to find permanent, affordable housing and a job that pays enough to cover her housing and living expenses. In addition, Maria needs to be enrolled in school. Elicia also wants to regain custody of her youngest daughter in foster care.

Additionally, Elicia is experiencing an immense amount of stress, anxiety, and possibly post-traumatic stress disorder (PTSD). She described an instance where she could not calm down her breathing, and she felt lightheaded. She is very fearful of men and tries to avoid all contact with men in the community. She reports difficulty sleeping at night and feeling exhausted most of the time.

She is concerned about Maria. She has started acting out at the shelter, getting into fights with the other children, disobeying her mother, and being disrespectful and defiant to the staff and other adults. Elicia and Maria fight frequently, and when Elicia tries to discipline Maria, she throws a temper tantrum until Elicia gives up.

Elicia has many strengths. She had the strength to leave her abusive husband and move to a different city. She loves her daughters. She wants desperately to keep Maria with her and hopes to have Sarah returned to her custody. She is resilient and has managed to survive and keep her daughter safe despite not having a place to stay, a job, and a limited support network. Additionally, Elicia is highly motivated to find her own accommodations and support her children.

■ Discussion Questions

1. Consider the stages of change. How would you determine Elicia and Maria's stages of change?

2. As the social worker, which of the several models that were presented in this chapter would you select for your work with Elicia and Maria? Justify your selection.

3. Utilizing the strengths perspective, identify strengths for both Elicia and Maria.

4. How would you prepare Elicia and Maria for termination of services?

■ References

Abel, N., & O'Brien, J. (2014). *Treating addictions with EMDR therapy and the stages of change.* New York, NY: Springer Publishing Company.

Allen, M. (2011). Narrative therapy for women experiencing domestic violence: Supporting women's transitions from abuse to safety. London, UK: Jessica Kingsley Publishers.

Blundo, R. G., & Simon, J. K. (2016). *Solution-focused case management.* New York, NY: Springer Publishing Company.

Brown, B. (2015). Rising Strong: The reckoning, the rumble, and the revolution. New York, NY: Spiegel & Grau.

Canavan, J. (2008). Resilience: Cautiously welcoming a contested concept. *Child Care in Practice, 14*(1), 1–7. doi:10.1080/13575270701733633

Cooper, S. (2012). *Change: Models and processes.* Springfield, IL: Charles C Thomas.

Earvolino-Ramirez, M. (2007). Resilience: A concept analysis. *Nursing Forum, 42*(2), 73–82. doi:10.1111/j.1744-6198.2007.00070.x

David, D., Cotet, C., Matu, S., Mogoase, C., & Stefan, S. (2018). 50 years of rational-emotive and cognitive-behavioral therapy: A systematic review and meta-analysis. *Journal of Clinical Psychology, 74*(3), 304–318. doi:10.1002/jclp.22514

Dix, H. (2016). Motivational interviewing and social work education: The power of relationship based practice. *Journal of Practice Teaching & Learning, 14*(1), 59–72.

Dominelli, L. (2012). Group work: A critical addition to the social work repertoire. In C. Glisson, K. M. Sowers, & C. N. Dulmus (Eds.), *Social work practice with groups, communities, and organizations: Evidence-based assessments and interventions* (pp. 41–58). Hoboken, NJ: Wiley.

Dziegielewski, S. A. (2014) *DSM-5 in action* (3rd ed.). Hoboken, NJ: Wiley.

Fisher, J. E., & O'Donohue, W. T. (2012). *Cognitive behavior therapy: Core principles for practice.* Hoboken, NJ: Wiley.

Fox, S., Bibi, F., Millar, H., & Holland, A. (2017). The role of cultural factors in engagement and change in multisystemic therapy (MST). *Journal of Family Therapy, 39*(2), 243–263. doi:10.1111/1467-6427.12134

Frankl, V. E. (2006). A man's search for meaning. Boston, MA: Beacon Press.

Gitterman, A., & Germain, C. B. (2008). *The life model of social work practice: Advances in theory and practice* (3rd ed.). New York, NY: Columbia University Press.

González-Prendes, A. A., & Brisebois, K. (2012). Cognitive-behavioral therapy and social work values: A critical analysis. *Journal of Social Work Values & Ethics, 9*(2), 21–33.

Graham, L. (2013). Bouncing back: Rewiring your brain for maximum resilience and well-being. Novato, CA: New World Library.

Gunnestad, A., & Thwala, S. (2011). Resilience and religion in children and youth in Southern Africa. *International Journal of Children's Spirituality, 16*(2), 169–185. doi:10.1080/1364436X.2011.580726

Hartnett, D., Carr, A., Hamilton, E., & Sexton, T. L. (2017). Therapist implementation and parent experiences of the three phases of functional family therapy. *Journal of Family Therapy, 39*(1), 80–102. doi:10.1111/1467-6427.12120

Hauser, S. T., & Allen, J. P. (2006). Overcoming adversity in adolescence: Narratives of resilience. *Psychoanalytic Inquiry, 26*, 549–576. doi:10.1080/07351690701310623

Henggeler, S. W., & Schaeffer, C. M. (2016). Multisystemic therapy: Clinical overview, outcomes, and implementation research. *Family Process, 55*(3), 514–528. doi:10.1111/famp.12232

Langer, C. L., & Lietz, C. A. (2015). *Applying theory to generalist social work practice.* Hoboken, NJ: Wiley.

Lightsey, O. R. (2006). Resilience, meaning, and well-being. The Counseling Psychologist, 34(1), 96–107. doi:10.1177/0011000005282369

Luthar, S. S., Cicchetti, D., & Becker, B. (2000). The construct of resilience: A critical evaluation and guidelines for future work. *Child Development, 71*(3), 543–562. doi:10.1111/1467-8624.00164

McAdams, C. R., III, Avadhanam, R., Foster, V. A., Harris, P. N., Javaheri, A., Kim, S., . . . Williams, A. E. (2016). The viability of structural family therapy in the twenty-first century: An analysis of key indicators. *Contemporary Family Therapy: An International Journal, 38*(3), 255–261. doi:10.1007/s10591-016-9383-9

Miller, W. R., & Rollnick, S. (2013). *Motivational interviewing: Helping people change.* New York, NY: Guilford Press.

Miller, W. R., & Rollnick, S. (1991). Motivational interviewing: Preparing people to change addictive behavior. New York: Guilford Press.

National Association of Social Workers. (2017). *Code of ethics.* Silver Spring, MD: Author. Retrieved from https://www.socialworkers.org/About/Ethics/Code-of-Ethics/Code-of-Ethics-English

O'Connor, M. F. (2003). Making meaning of life events: Theory, evidence, and research directions for an alternative model. *Omega: Journal of Death and Dying, 46,* 51–75. doi:10.2190/0CKD-PVQ0-T260-NTXU

Robbins, M. S., Alexander, J. F., Turner, C. W., & Hollimon, A. (2016). Evolution of functional family therapy as an evidence-based practice for adolescents with disruptive behavior problems. *Family Process, 55*(3), 543–557. doi:10.1111/famp.12230

Rutter, M. (2006). Implications of resilience concepts for scientific understanding. In B. M. Lester, A. Masten, & B. McEwen (Eds.), *Resilience in children.* (pp. 1–12). Boston, MA: New York Academy of the Sciences.

Substance Abuse and Mental Health Services Administration. (1999). *Treatment Improvement Protocol (TIP) Series, No. 35.* Rockville, MD: Center for Substance Abuse Treatment. Retrieved from https://www.ncbi.nlm.nih.gov/books/NBK64964

Simmons, C. A., Shapiro, V. B., Accomazzo, S., & Manthey, T. J. (2016). Strengths-based social work: A social work metatheory to guide the profession. In N. Coady & P. Lehmann (Eds.), *Theoretical perspectives for direct social work practice: A generalist-eclectic approach* (3rd ed., pp. 131–158). New York, NY: Springer Publishing Company.

Teater, B. (2014). *An introduction to applying social work theories and methods* (2nd ed.). Maidenhead, Berkshire: McGraw-Hill Education.

Walsh, J. (2013). *Theories for direct social work practice* (3rd ed.). Stamford, CT: Cengage.

White, M., & Epston, D. (1990). Narrative Means to Therapeutic Ends. W. W. Norton, New York.

White, M. (2009). Narrative practice and conflicts dissolution in couples therapy. *Clinical Social Work Journal, 37*(3), 200–213. doi:10.1007/s10615-009-0192-6

RESEARCH-INFORMED SOCIAL WORK PRACTICE

Ron A, who is in his second year of a 3-year part-time master of social work program, has a field placement at an Area Agency on Aging. Ron had worked as the case manager for 3 years in a small community agency. As part of his field placement duties, Ron is charged with completing clients' assessment and evaluation plans. His regular job approaches case management much more informally than does his field placement agency.

Ron met with his first field placement client twice and is working on completing the agency's comprehensive assessment and evaluation plan. He is comfortable about completing the assessment component and believes that he has a good handle on his client's needs, strengths, and challenges. Ron is less sure about completing the evaluation component of the plan. He has never been involved in systematically evaluating client progress. He is unsure how to measure progress on the goals they had set up. He is also unsure how his clients will react to filling out forms and questionnaires.

LEARNING OBJECTIVES

In this chapter, we explore how research is an integral component of professional social work practice. Often, social work students doubt their competence related to research much more than the other content areas of the social work curriculum. Research can seem intimidating, but we encourage you to view research as approachable. Research is infused in many aspects of the social work profession. Carey (2012) puts forth that "research is not merely about gathering information or describing facts in detail and, in social work especially, should also not be too detached from practical and professional life" (p. 5). The practice of social work is both an art and a science. Research supports the science component of practice. Research allows social workers to make important decisions at the micro-, mezzo-, and macrolevels. It guides us in determining what is effective and what is not. It can also support us in identifying the best ways to support client systems. By the end of this chapter, you will be able to:

1. Acknowledge the necessity for social workers to engage in research

2. Understand the importance of research-informed practice

3. Identify methods by which to disseminate research findings

4. Identify social workers' ethical responsibilities related to evaluating practice effectiveness

5. Conduct informal evaluations of your practice effectiveness

6. Construct self-anchored rating scales and goal attainment scales

7. Use client logs and behavioral observation in measuring client system progress

8. Locate standardized measures that are appropriate for use with social work client systems

9. Interpret the reliability and validity of standardized measures

10. Design a single-system evaluation to monitor client system progress

■ Competency 4: Engage in Practice-Informed Research and Research-Informed Practice

Social workers understand quantitative and qualitative research methods and their respective roles in advancing a science of social work and in evaluating their practice. Social workers know the principles of logic, scientific inquiry, and culturally informed and ethical approaches to building knowledge. Social workers understand that evidence that informs practice derives from multidisciplinary sources and multiple ways of knowing. They also understand the processes for translating research findings into effective practice. Social workers:

- Use practice experience and theory to inform scientific inquiry and research

- Apply critical thinking to engage in analysis of quantitative and qualitative research methods and research findings

- Use and translate research evidence to inform and improve practice, policy, and service delivery

■ Competency 9: Evaluate Practice With Individuals, Families, Groups, Organizations, and Communities

Social workers understand that evaluation is an ongoing component of the dynamic and interactive process of social work practice with, and on behalf of, diverse individuals, families, groups, organizations, and communities. Social workers recognize the importance of evaluating processes and outcomes to advance practice, policy, and service delivery effectiveness. Social workers understand theories of human behavior and the social environment, and critically evaluate and apply this knowledge in evaluating outcomes. Social workers understand qualitative and quantitative methods for evaluating outcomes and practice effectiveness. Social workers:

- Select and use appropriate methods for evaluation of outcomes

- Apply knowledge of human behavior and the social environment, person-in-environment, and other multidisciplinary theoretical frameworks in the evaluation of outcomes

- Critically analyze, monitor, and evaluate intervention and program processes and outcomes

- Apply evaluation findings to improve practice effectiveness at the micro-, mezzo-, and macrolevels

■ National Association of Social Workers (NASW) *Code of Ethics*

The NASW *Code of Ethics* (2017) serves to orient social workers to engage in professional social worker practice that is ethical. The *Code of Ethics* serves to safeguard clients, communities, and the profession as a whole. It is imperative that social workers are familiar with all aspects of the *Code of Ethics* regarding what it puts forth for all types of social work practice. In the following sections, we will be looking specifically at how the NASW *Code of Ethics* applies to research-informed practice. It is necessary that social workers only engage in research that is ethical. Throughout history, there have been egregious violations of human rights in the name of "research." An example of this would be the medical experiments conducted by Nazi doctors during World War II. During wartime, medical doctors used prisoners of concentration camps to conduct research. Some of their experiments were designed to provide insights into ways to support Nazi soldiers. One such way was to examine the use of anticoagulant medications in order to determine the best means to support a soldier who suffered an amputation. The experimenters would test their theories by amputating limbs from the war camp prisoners. This is just one example of the heinous experiments that were done in the name of science. As a result of these experiments, the Nuremberg Trials began in the mid-1940s to address the blatant disregard for human rights. The Nuremberg Code, a document that addresses ethical research, was derived from these trials. This code established a set of standards and practices that were necessary when research would involve human subjects.

▶ **Critical Thinking Questions**
Why is it important to learn about past unethical research experiments? How can this inform present research endeavors?

Unfortunately, the development of this code did not stop unethical research on human participants. Another example of unethical research practices on human subjects is the infamous Tuskegee Experiments that were conducted in the southern United States in the 20th century. During the Tuskegee Experiments researchers purposely injected low income Black subjects with syphilis in the hopes of better understanding the disease and its treatment. This experiment continued for decades, long after a known cure for the disease (penicillin) was found. This experiment was deceptive and prevented participants from accessing the lifesaving medication that was known to be beneficial for this condition.

As a result of these experiments, the Belmont Code was established to address ethical research practice. This code sets forth three core values, which include respect for the person, beneficence, and justice. These three values are well aligned with social work values. Respect for the person requires researchers to honor the autonomy of the person and protect those with diminished autonomy (Belmont Report, 1979). Social workers understand the importance of the value of each person through their value of dignity and worth of the person as well as the importance they place on the right to self-determination. The second value of

▶ Critical Thinking Question

How can a social worker try to minimize harm when conducting research?

beneficence refers to the necessity to have participants' welfare considered. In medicine, the term "do no harm" is often used to describe this principle. Within the confines of research, researchers should seek to minimize harm whenever possible. It is understood that some research may possess potential harm; it is the duty of the researcher to ensure that undue harm is not inflicted and that there are adequate and appropriate resources and supports to address any potential harm. The final value of the Belmont Report is justice. Justice in the Belmont Report encouraged equality.

Based on these advancements to protect human participants, institutional review boards (IRBs) have been established to ensure that research participants are protected from undue harm. Researchers who will be using human subjects must go through the IRB review process. This process involves sharing all materials involved with the research experience with this board. The purpose of the board is not to examine the efficacy of the research design but solely focuson protecting human subjects.

In all aspects of social work practice, social workers should be trustworthy and ethical. Regarding research, social workers must be aware of agency policies and procedures surrounding collecting and analyzing data. Furthermore, social workers must be aware of legal and ethical mandates related to research in their field of practice. As we have discussed, there have been numerous ethical violations conducted in the name of research or science; social workers must not allow this to continue. Social workers must be able to recognize unethical research practices and stand against them.

Social workers should not only seek to understand professional knowledge but should also make efforts to contribute to the body of professional knowledge. Within the social work profession, practitioners and researchers had historically been siloed apart from one another. This is not conducive to good social work practice. It makes sense that research should inform practice and, conversely, practice should inform research. As a result of this, social workers have sought to encourage research-informed practice and practice-informed research. There is much to be gained from this integrated perspective of social work. Social workers should consciously attempt to be a part of this practice.

Social workers have ethical responsibilities to their profession. In order to maintain the integrity of the profession, social workers must consistently uphold the values of the profession in all areas of practice, including research. Research is an important component of your social work education. As one of the main content areas of the profession, research should not be viewed as an isolated endeavor. Rather, social workers must diligently seek out ways in which to infuse research in all other areas of practice. Research should also inform all parts of the social work helping process—engagement, assessment, intervention, and evaluation.

As discussed, social workers are strongly encouraged to share contributions of knowledge with the profession. There are many great social workers doing many great things with a variety of client systems in a variety of settings. Social workers should share what they have found to be effective with others in order to spread those good outcomes. The social work profession has a long history of sharing means and methods with others. Consider the early works of Mary Richmond and her casework manual. This book was a piece of disseminated research sharing what she had found to be effective in working with her clients. We must continue this in order to continually advance our profession.

We can share this knowledge in a variety of ways, including publications and presentations. Social workers should endeavor to disseminate their findings with other professionals to promote the ongoing integrity and evolution of the profession of social work. Without sharing our results, we are not fulfilling our ethical obligation to the social work profession.

The evaluation and research standard of the NASW *Code of Ethics* (2017) has more subpoints than any other standard in the *Code of Ethics*. You can review all of the subpoints of the *Code of Ethics* online (www.socialworkers.org/About/Ethics/Code-of-Ethics/Code-of-Ethics-English).

As you are aware, social workers are called upon to engage in various aspects of evaluation and research. This standard not only outlines the need for social workers to be engaged in research but also addresses the need to protect human rights during research. Social workers must obtain consent from research participants that is voluntary and informed. Social workers must be mindful of their position of power that could potentially be seen as coercive to some research participants. Furthermore, social workers often find themselves working with vulnerable and oppressed populations. It is important that the rights of these individuals are attended to during the consent and research process.

In addition to ensuring ethical consent procedures, social workers should also be sure that research participants understand their rights related to withdrawing from research as well. Participants who chose to begin participating in a research project have the right to discontinue their involvement at any time. Social workers must be sure to share with participants in the informed consent what will occur if participants withdraw from the study. For example, if the research is being done as an anonymous electronic survey, if a participant chooses to stop, there may not be a way to remove his or her previous answer selections from the data set.

Social workers should seek to minimize harm and not expose participants to any unnecessary harm or distress. This standard is clearly aligned with both the Nuremberg and Belmont codes we previously noted. Harm could be physical or emotional. For example, asking about sensitive topics, such as past traumatic experiences, could potentially bring up disturbing thoughts in the research participants. That is not to say that we should never ask about things that could bring up emotional discomfort. As social workers, we are often concerned with sensitive topics and so it is important to know more about such topics. Before we ask about such things, we need to clearly outline that in the informed consent and provide adequate resources and supports to participants who experienced distress. For example, you could provide information for a crisis hotline or other community supports.

Social workers should be clear whether their research is anonymous or confidential. At times, these terms are incorrectly used interchangeably. Anonymous participation refers to collecting no identifiable information on the participants. On the other hand, confidential participation is when the identities of the participants are known to the researcher but not shared in the findings or with others outside the research team. Social workers have a duty to share with clients if their identity will be known during the research process. Social workers should inform clients how their data will be used.

■ Positivism

The theory of positivism has had many contributors. However, a main contributor was Auguste Comte, who is considered to be one of the fathers of sociology. Positivism sets forth to be objective and fact-based. It holds tightly to the scientific method, and there is an emphasis on empirical observation. It suggests that in order to truly know, or understand, something, it must be observable through one or more of the five senses (sight, touch, hearing, taste, and smell). Positivism holds to the "verifiability principle," which sets forth "that a statement was meaningful only if it was empirically verifiable"; furthermore, it is "critical of ideas that could not be tested" (Walsh, 2013, p. 173). This form of thinking has deep roots in empiricism, which can be traced back to the time of Aristotle.

> ▶ **Critical Thinking Questions**
> 1. What are the potential benefits and limitations to a positivist approach that relies solely on the five senses?
> 2. What would be potential limitations to relying solely on the five senses?

From a positivism perspective, it is impossible to know anything if you cannot tangibly observe them. This can be troublesome for social scientists. For example, social workers are often concerned with feelings and emotions. However, some argue that these things cannot be empirically observed based on the truest standards of positivism. On the other hand, social work can benefit greatly from the theory of positivism regarding many quantitative designs including various single-subject designs that are quite common in social work practice. Furthermore, Dybicz (2015) put forth that related, to the person-in-environment model, "the strength of positivism in explaining cause-and-effect mechanisms contains the inherent shortcoming of emphasizing causal determinism when seeking to explain human behavior" (p. 237). As you can see, there are both benefits and limitations to utilizing this theory to inform social work practice and social work research.

Social worker Bruce Thyer has been a champion for logical positivism within the social work profession. Though some assert "that a focus on observable behavior runs contrary to the profession's increasingly holistic perspective, Thyer has eloquently demonstrated its utility for promoting positive outcomes with a variety of client populations" (Walsh, 2013, p. 148). It is important for social work to hold to both the objective and the subjective—the tangible and the intangible—in order to fully understand the client system.

Empiricism

Empirical evidence is evidence that is verifiable. Willis (2007) posits that "the broadest meaning of the term empiricism is that what we know about the world comes from experience" (p. 36). There is an assumption with positivism and empiricism that phenomena regarding humans and human behavior can be discovered if it is well studied by an objective and scientific method (Willis, 2007). This puts forth "the existence of an objective reality that is knowable, however imperfectly, to outside observers" (Kirk & Reid, 2002, p. 15). By the nature of our profession, social workers serve as outside observers and are thus able to examine evidence and make observations. Many believe that social work is best served by a pursuit of "knowledge building, incorporating philosophy, theory, and methods that are congruent with empiricism" (Caputo, Epstein, Stoesz, & Thyer, 2015, p. 645).

Scientific Inquiry

A systematic, logical approach to understanding problems and providing answers is science. At some point in your schooling, you have most likely been introduced to the scientific method. The scientific method at its simplest starts with an observation that leads to a research question as well as a tentative hypothesis or educated guess. The scientific method is simply a standardized step-based approach to collecting information to gain knowledge. The scientific method can be applied to more than just laboratory or clinical science. Social sciences including social work, psychology, and sociology all utilize the scientific method to better understand people, experiences, and social phenomena.

Sometimes social work and other helping professions including psychology and sociology, are referred to as the "soft sciences" because, due to the nature of what we are researching, we at times may have less strict measurement and intervention criteria as we would be able to have if we were working in a lab and able to control all conditions. With humans, we are unable to control some variables. Not being able to control all variables is part of the reason for referring to social work as a soft science. This term, which is slightly derogatory toward our profession, undermines the rigor and credibility that social workers strive to have in their research. Though it is true that social work research and science is different than laboratory research and science, it is not less credible. Good research is good research just as poorly designed research is poorly designed research.

The scientific method has a long history within the social work profession. There have been movements that have encouraged a clinical scientist or scientifically based practice paradigm (Kirk & Reid, 2002). Social workers have long been aware of the necessity to explore their practice from the lens of science. Social workers must attempt to provide known and effective methods to address client needs whenever possible (Case 8.1).

▶ **Critical Thinking Question**
Why do you think it is important for social workers to consider their practice a "practice of science?"

■ Role of Research in Social Work Practice

We have discussed that social workers are called upon by the NASW *Code of Ethics* to engage in research in order to demonstrate commitment to the profession of social work. Social workers must engage in research-informed practice and practice-informed research. We explore both of these concepts throughout this text. Social workers must integrate research information into their practice in order to be sure they are providing the best possible care for the clients they serve.

CASE 8.1   APPLYING POSITIVISM IN SOCIAL WORK PRACTICE RESEARCH

Bella is a social worker at a community food bank. The food bank operated much like a grocery store where clients could come in and select the items that they wished to have. The agency strongly values the rights of the clients to determine what kinds of food they like and want rather than just giving a box of food to them. Bella loves that her agency values self-determination. She is interested in better understanding the needs of the clients serviced by her agency. Bella decided that she was going to use the theory of positivism to inform her quest for more knowledge about her clients. Bella understood that positivism is rooted in empirical evidence and scientific inquiry. Bella felt that this would be a good theoretical approach to guide her research as it is often considered fact-based and objective. She believed this would be an excellent source of data for her to share with the agency board of directors.

Bella believed that fresh foods (vegetables, fruits, dairy, and meat products) were more desirable than the typical nonperishable items typically available at the food bank. Bella decided to use a quantitative design where she would keep track of how many clients selected these items versus clients who did not select any of these items. Bella felt this was the best way to gain understanding about these items as she can simply observe when these items are selected by clients. Furthermore, she worried that if she interviewed clients, their responses would be biased based on what they thought she wanted to hear.

As a result of Bella's positivist study, she was able to share with the board of directors that these perishable items were highly desired by clients. Based on these findings, the board decided to establish ongoing partnerships with other agencies in order to provide more of the desired perishable foods to the clients they serve.

The profession of social work has a long history of providing a systematic approach to helping. The social work pioneer Mary Richmond, in her early writings, spoke to the need to support individuals on the basis of facts. As the profession evolved over time, we have seen an influx of research to influence our practice. Research has helped us better understand the individuals, families, communities, and organizations that we work with. Research has helped us better understand development and growth. Research has also helped us regarding how we can intervene and support these client systems.

As research has evolved across time to this point, research will continue to evolve. We continue to make advancements in what we know about client systems and how to best support them. Additionally, new conditions or concerns arise, and we must use research to determine the best means of support. We caution social work students to not consider their education done at the time of graduation. You must never stop learning. The knowledge of the profession is ongoing and professional social workers must be continuous, lifelong learners.

Research-Informed Practice

As we have discussed, social workers must rely on science to inform their practice. It is important that social workers speak out regarding research in order to be sure they are providing the best possible services to their clients. What we know is constantly evolving as we learn more and find better ways to address social problems. As social workers, we must be ready and willing to continually reflect back on and go to research to determine if there are new, better ways to address client conditions. Furthermore, social workers must identify when there are gaps in our research knowledge and assist to close the loop and provide feedback on their professional experiences related to such matters. Social work practitioners should be active contributors to the professional body of knowledge of the social work profession.

Some social workers cite barriers to incorporating research into their professional practice. Table 8.1 outlines several barriers that have been identified as potential barriers to research-informed practice (Case 8.2).

▶ **Critical Thinking Question**

Think about the barriers to research-informed practice presented in Table 8.1. Identify strategies to address each barrier.

Critiquing Existing Research

It is not enough that social workers find research that relates to their area of practice; they must be sure that the research they are finding is valuable. Not all research is created equal, and social workers must recognize this before they begin fusing research into their practice. Before allowing research to inform one's professional practice, they should

TABLE 8.1 Barriers to Research-Informed Social Work Practice

BARRIER	DESCRIPTION
Busyness	Social workers are often busy. Increasingly, social workers are being called upon to do more with less. It may be difficult for social workers to find time to seek out relevant research that can inform their practice. Furthermore, some social workers may worry that if they are seen looking for research during their work day, others may think that they are not busy enough and in turn give them more duties or cases.
Lack of access	It can, at times, be difficult to locate reliable, valid research that is relevant to a specific area of practice. While in college, social work students often have access to library resources including sophisticated search engines that are reliable in regard to finding pertinent research. Social workers must know where to look in order to find the appropriate information that is required to inform their practice. Thankfully, there are increasingly more and more avenues to find good quality research through internet search engines designed to specifically disseminate information to professionals.
Difficult to interpret	For some, interpreting research can feel daunting. When social workers are insecure in their ability to read, interpret, and infer from the research they have found, it is difficult to integrate research into practice. Sometimes statistics can be quite complicated and overwhelming. For this reason, some avoid looking for scholarly research.

Source: Based on McLaughlin, H. (2012). *Understanding social work research* (2nd ed.). Los Angeles, CA: Sage.

CASE 8.2   AN EXAMPLE OF RESEARCH-INFORMED PRACTICE

Tony is a social worker at a behavioral health rehabilitation service provider. He has recently been assigned a case with a 3-year-old child who is diagnosed with autism. Tony's role is to serve as the behavior specialist consultant, and he needs to develop a treatment plan to address the needs of his client. Tony has worked with children diagnosed with autism previously. However, they were typically school-age children; he has no experience working with a child this young. Also, this child is currently nonverbal; all of Tony's other clients have been able to speak. Tony seeks out supervision from his supervisor to assist him in formulating a plan to work with this client. Tony and his supervisor discuss what practices are deemed evidence-based for young children diagnosed with autism. Tony learns that applied behavioral analysis, which is grounded in behavioral theory, is a common approach to support such clients. Tony is familiar with behavioral theory and concepts related to applied behavior analysis from his schooling and ongoing training. Tony recognizes that it is important to brush up his skills, and so he seeks out a local training opportunity that will be happening next week. He also finds several journal articles related to using this modality with young children. Tony also makes it a point to schedule follow-up supervision with his supervisor weekly.

critically analyze and critique the source. Unfortunately, bad research is out there. It is the duty and obligation of professional social workers to ensure that this research does not infiltrate their practice. One way that social workers can be sure they are not incorporating bad research into their practice is by applying critical thinking skills to the analysis of research. Critical thinking is a necessary piece of professional practice. To successfully integrate research into social work practice, it is necessary that social workers become critical thinkers and are able to critique existing research. It is important to not simply accept information without first considering several factors. First, where is this information coming from? It is important to consider who is authoring or supporting this research.

Another important consideration when critiquing existing research is to examine where the information was found. Information from peer-reviewed journals is typically held to a higher degree of scrutiny and thus can be relatively trustworthy. With that being said, not all journals are equal. It is important to consider the source.

Another place where social workers must use good critical judgment is when finding research online. The Internet can provide exceptionally valuable research. Unfortunately, it can also provide useless research. It is important to critique where the information is found. We live in an age where information is more readily available than ever before. We are lucky that with a few clicks of the mouse, we are able to peruse a myriad of source material. Additionally, we are able to connect with other professionals more rapidly than ever before. These benefits are truly astounding and can assist us in enhancing our professional practice. However, we must be mindful that, as with most great advancements, there are potential drawbacks. Again, it is important for the social worker to consider who is putting this information forth and what their motivations may be to do so. Box 8.1 provides five points—accuracy, authority, objectivity, currency, and coverage—to consider when evaluating online sources. Furthermore, these guidelines to evaluating online material may be helpful to consider should you wish to present your own material online for others.

▶ **Critical Thinking Question**

You need to find information online for an area of social work practice that interests you. Identify three online sites that would be trustworthy sources of information.

Evidence-Based Practice

Evidence is a collection of facts that demonstrate a position to be true. Evidence-based practices (EBPs), which began flourishing in the late 20th century, are professional practices and strategies that have a basis in research, which indicates the method is successful to address a

---

BOX 8.1

EVALUATING ONLINE SOURCES

When evaluating resources, consider the following five criteria:

1. Accuracy: It is important to consider if the information being presented is accurate. If there is a reference list, you can critically analyze the source material utilized. If there is no reference list of source material, you can verify the information on your own utilizing another source to check for accuracy.

2. Authority: Consider if the authors or contributors are listed on the site. If there are listed authors and contributors, you can look at their credentials to determine if they have the knowledge base to put forth the material you are reviewing. In addition to the person posting the information, you should notice if there are any organizational or institutional affiliations as well.

3. Objectivity: Objectivity refers to being based on facts not opinions. In order to determine if the material is objective, you want to pay close attention to the language utilized in the material. Language can often provide clues as to whether the author is subjective (sharing opinion) or objective (presenting facts).

4. Currency: It is important to be mindful that the information you are gathering is currently relevant and not outdated. Looking for dates on a website can assist in determining when the material was posted or updated.

5. Coverage: It is important to consider if the source is comprehensive regarding its stated purpose.

Source: From Western Connecticut State University. (2015). *Guide to evaluating web sites.* Retrieved from http://people.wcsu.edu/reitzj/res/evalweb.html

specific condition or with a particular population. EBPs are utilized by helping professions to provide the best practices.

EBP serves to ground the social work profession in empiricism (Okpych & Yu, 2014). There is a generally accepted process of EBP, which begins with identifying the need for information. That need for information must then be translated into a question. Evidence to answer this question is then sought. After finding evidence, it is then critically analyzed or critiqued to determine its validity. If the evidence is valid and applicable for the current need, it is then incorporated with the clinician's expertise. The clinician should also be mindful of the goodness of fit with the client system. If it is a good fit, the evidence is integrated into the social worker's practice with the client. The social worker monitors this implementation and seeks out additional evidence as necessary. Case 8.3 illustrates a social worker going through the process of EBP.

CASE 8.3   THE EVIDENCE-BASED PRACTICE PROCESS IN SOCIAL WORK

Melody is a social worker at a child welfare organization. She very much enjoys her job and support-ing families. Melody was recently transferred to a new unit within the organization. As Melody was familiarizing herself with the new requirements of this position, she began to notice that many of the children on her new caseload have had multiple disrupted placements. Disrupted placement is when an out-of-home placement must be terminated and the child must be placed in a new home. Melody thought that this must be difficult for the children. Melody wondered what she could do to support placements in order to avoid multiple disruptive placements.

Melody began searching scholarly material to find research on how to best support placements in order to avoid disruption. Melody found several articles and reports that address this issue. Of the practices that were found to be beneficial were those that provided additional support for foster fam-ilies as well as respite care. Melody spoke with her supervisor about these recommendations to pos-sibly improve placements. Both support and respite care were services that the organization already had available but were often underutilized. Melody and her supervisor discussed ways to share this information with families including having the caseworkers speak with the family members about resources available to them. Melody began incorporating this into her practice. Over time, Melody noticed fewer and fewer disrupted placements.

EBP encourages social workers to be considerate of the importance of outcomes in prac-tice, whether client situations are improving, staying the same, or worsening. As we have discussed related to assessment, good assessment is ongoing assessment. Social workers must be particularly thoughtful in recognizing changes in the client system when incorpo-rating an EBP. Furthermore, social workers must be cautious in assuming causation between their EBP and client changes. This underscores the importance of a thorough assessment in order to determine if there are other changes occurring that could account for the change in client presentation.

The process of EBP involves finding the "best available evidence to support clinical decision making that also considers a social worker's clinical judgment and professional ethics and the client's personal and cultural preferences" (Langer & Lietz, 2015, p. 13). Social workers must be aware that clients are not "passive recipients of social work practice" and therefore, EBP should be selected in consideration of the clients' rights to self-determination (McLaughlin, 2012). We must continuously be aware that clients come to us with their own unique histories and experiences, and we as professionals must meet the clients where they are. It is our job to begin where the client is.

Multiple Ways of Knowing

How do you know what you know? This may seem like quite a philosophical question, but it is an important one to consider. There are multiple ways of knowing, each coming with benefits and limitations. It is important that social workers be critical thinkers. In order to be a critical thinker, one must consider from where the information one is receiving originates. It is important for social workers to consider such things because social workers are often called upon to make many decisions every day that have implications for clients, communities, and the profession itself.

▶ **Critical Thinking Questions**

Consider how you know what you know. Think about current events in the United States.

1. How do you get most of your information? How do you know this information is true?
2. Why is it necessary to critically analyze how you are getting information and whether or not it is coming from a trusted source?

Social workers must be aware that it is easy to make errors in logic. Common errors in reasoning include overgeneralization, selective observation, illogical reasoning, resistance to change, and adherence to authority (Engel & Schutt, 2014). Overgeneralization refers to the tendency of individuals to take what they know to be true in one case and apply it in all situations. This is a simplistic error that does not allow for individual experiences. As we know, most issues that social workers deal with are quite complex and multifaceted. Overgeneralizations do not take into account individual differences or experiences. Social workers must be cautious to avoid this error in logic. Selective observation occurs when an individual seeks out only information that is confirmatory to already held beliefs. For example, if a person believes that boys are more aggressive for girls, they may only notice situations in which boys are engaging in aggression as that fits their predetermined belief. Illogical reasoning happens when an individual holds on to untrue assumptions or jumps to conclusions without support. Many timesindividuals always think a certain way about something and as a result, they may be resistant to changing their beliefs. This is an error in logic as the person is not open to new information. This error in logic is sometimes referred to as tradition. Social workers must recognize that at times people hold tightly on to traditionally held beliefs even when presented with evidence to the contrary. Adherence to authority refers to when a person believes something simply because he or she was told about it by a person in a (real or perceived) place of authority (Case 8.4).

| CASE 8.4 | WHY DO WE DO IT THIS WAY? THE IMPORTANCE OF RESEARCH-BASED SOCIAL WORK PRACTICE |

Tran is a new social worker who was recently hired at an outpatient facility that provides various services to veterans including assistance in finding housing and employment in addition to providing on-site mental health and drug and alcohol counseling. Tran is very excited about her new position because she has always wanted to work with the military population. As a part of being a new hire, Tran is assigned to a mentor who is someone who has been with the agency and can show her the ropes. Tran will shadow her mentor for the first week at the agency. On the first day, Tran met her mentor, Kelly. Kelly has been with the agency for almost two decades.

Throughout the day, Tran was secretly observing Kelly work with other colleagues as well as with clients. Tran kept notes on questions she had to ask Kelly about the way in which she was doing things so that she could better understand organizational expectations. Over lunch, Kelly asked Tran if she had any questions, Tran consulted her notebook and began to ask about the group session she observed Kelly facilitate that morning. She asked Kelly about how the group was run. Kelly shared that when she started at the agency all those years ago, that was the way the group was run and that is why she does it the way she does. This answer surprised Tran because she expected that the group was based on research or evidence related to the best practices with this population. As the training went on that week, Tran noticed more and more that things were just done the way they had always been done without a researched rationale as to why.

This concerned Tran. During her supervision, she directly asked her supervisor how clinical decisions such as what modalities to use in group or individual sessions are made. The supervisor shared with Tran that the agency follows a trauma-informed care model and relies heavily on cognitive behavioral approaches. Tran felt better after talking with her supervisor about how researched practices inform their organization. Tran was then able to seek out readings and source material regarding the specific perspectives that inform this agency. Throughout her first few months at the agency, Tran found that her weekly supervision was extremely helpful to review research related to the population and interventions. Her supervisor was also quite impressed with Tran's initiative to seek out research to inform and improve her practice.

Social workers must also be on the lookout for pseudoscience. Thyer and Pignotti (2015) put forth that "pseudoscientific practices are practices that give the superficial appearance of being derived from science and yet lack an actual scientific basis" (p. 6). Believing pseudoscience can be an additional error in logic. In order for social workers to distinguish between true science and pseudoscience, they must have a basic understanding of good research methods in order to detect issues with a research design. Social workers must have a critical eye when evaluating research in order to determine if it is truly good science.

Practice wisdom is something that is valued in many professions, including social work. The capstone of the social work educational experience is a field experience where social work students are placed with competent social work professionals who guide students, many times with practice wisdom, toward becoming competent professionals themselves. Practice wisdom is complex and requires reflection and analysis that brings together various learning sources and contexts in order to encapsulate or understand better how things work (Shaw, 2016). Though practice wisdom is an integral part of our profession, we encourage social workers to not rely solely on practice wisdom. Practice wisdom based on best practices and sciences is best. As a result, social workers must be critical thinkers and evaluate and not just blindly accept or conform to faulty logic (Rubin & Bellamy, 2012).

There are various forms of research knowledge that are available for social workers. Three types of research knowledge include descriptive, predictive, and prescriptive knowledge (Yegidis, Weinbach, & Myers, 2018). Descriptive knowledge, as its name implies, seeks to describe how things are. This type of knowledge may describe things currently and as they change over time. Predictive knowledge attempts to predict what will happen in the future. This type of knowledge is possible when we have enough descriptive knowledge in order to be able to make reasonable inferences about future occurrences. Prescriptive knowledge provides insights into the intervention to address a current condition. Yegidis et al. (2018) set forth that "in EBP, social workers use prescriptive knowledge, along with their experience, client preferences, and so forth, to decide what intervention should be used to address an existing problem or to prevent one that they predict will occur" (p. 14).

Translating Findings Into Practice

Research findings are only beneficial if they can be used and applied to practice. As we discussed at the start of this chapter, it is unreasonable to separate research and practice from one another. Research must be integrated into practice in order to be of any value or use. When thinking about integrating research findings into professional practice, social workers should thoroughly learn about the proposed methods. Furthermore, social workers must be critical thinkers in order to determine if these new methods would be a good fit for their client population. Social workers must be considerate of cultural limitations regarding some findings. For example, some EBPs have only been researched on specific populations (age, gender, race/ethnicity, etc.). Also, it is necessary that social workers only implement EBP and other findings in their practice only if they have been sufficiently trained and are competent in the EBP. If a social worker is not trained in a specific EBP, it would be unethical to administer that EBP. Social workers should also be mindful of their limits of competence and seek out ongoing learning opportunities to enhance their practice skills related to innovative methods.

■ Evaluating Micropractice Effectiveness: Informal

This section focuses on the practice effectiveness component of the evaluating practice competency. It addresses methods or approaches to determine the effectiveness of your social work practice with individuals, families, and groups. It is about evaluating micro–social work practice using informal approaches. The following section reviews more formal methods of evaluating micro–social work practice.

Supervision and Self-Reflection

One approach to evaluating the effectiveness of your social work practice with clients is through supervision. As noted in Chapter 2, Ethical and Professional Behavior, social work supervision entails three components: administration, education, and support. It is the educational component that can be used to evaluate your practice effectiveness.

Also noted in Chapter 2 was that an important part of the supervisory process is the willingness to share and be vulnerable. Sometimes we may not want to share certain things because they make us feel at risk. Vulnerability refers to a state of being open or exposed to criticism or judgment. It can be scary especially within the context of your supervisory relationship. Despite that, being vulnerable is if you are engaged in a process of self-reflection and discussion of your social work practice and practice effectiveness with your supervisor.

Effective use of supervision to assess your social work practice effectiveness is dependent on the establishment of a trusting worker/supervisor relationship. A key to developing a strong positive worker/supervisor relationship is establishing some level of trust. The social worker must be able to trust the supervisor. Relationships cannot be built in the absence of trust. A certain degree of trust must be established between the worker and the supervisor for the workers to engage in the process of self-evaluation and the evaluation of his or her practice effectiveness.

Trust is essential for relationships to develop and grow between social workers and their supervisors. A strong relationship requires the absence of fear and suspicion and the presence of feelings of acceptance, support, and affirmation. Building trust with supervisors is an interactional process. Trust cannot be built in the absence of interpersonal interactions between the worker and the supervisor. It is built upon a sequence of trusting and trustworthy interactions. The worker must act in a trusting manner and the supervisor must respond with trustworthy actions.

Within each interaction, three conditions are required for trust to develop. First, the worker must take a risk (make a choice) where the potential harmful consequences outweigh the potential benefits associated with the risk. Second, the worker must realize that the beneficial or harmful consequences associated with the risk depend on the supervisor's actions (response) as the helping professional. Third, the worker must experience the supervisor's actions as beneficial (Fong & Cox, 1983). All three conditions must be present for the interaction to contribute to the trust-building process.

The bond of trust is built over time through a series of trusting actions (risks) and trustworthy responses (confirmations). Although it takes time for trust to be established, it can be destroyed through a single worker risk and supervisor disconfirmation (nontrustworthy) response (Fong & Cox, 1983).

The critical element in developing trust is risk. The supervisor is an active partner in the search for understanding and insights. This cannot happen if the worker is unable to take a risk by being open and honest about his or her social work practice with clients. Social workers have to be willing to share their thoughts, insights, feelings, and questions about their practice to be able to use the supervisory relationship to access their practice effectiveness. The primary task for the supervisor is to facilitate risk taking. The worker's task is to be self-reflective and to be willing to share information about his or her successes, mistakes, and ongoing challenges to assess client progress and possibly needed adjustments in their work together.

Ongoing Client Feedback

The social work value of competency discussed earlier implies that ethical social work practice involves an ongoing assessment of practice effectiveness throughout the helping relationship. This type of informal practice evaluation is based on the subjective responses of the clients. It is a joint and collaborative effort. Both the worker and the client have roles in this type of practice evaluation.

Ongoing informal evaluation is a relatively easy way for social workers to evaluate the effectiveness of their work with clients. In keeping with the principles of collaboration and empowerment in which the client is the expert about his or her progress, subjective assessments play a prominent role in strengths-based social work practice and other practice models. Clients' subjective assessments of their situations are the primary basis for evaluating the effectiveness of the helping process. The critical factor is whether the issues or concerns for which they are seeking help have, in their view, improved. It also helps the social worker and client identify what is working and what is not.

▶ **Critical Thinking Questions**

1. What is the parallel between building trust in the supervisory relationship and trust in the work/client relationship?

2. What is the connection between supervision and self-reflection in evaluating your practice effectiveness?

Informal evaluation is an ongoing process. The client and worker begin by exploring the client's person-in-environment system and life experiences in order to identify concerns and factors that potentially affect them. During this and later stages, the social worker makes sure that his or her interpretations of the client's experiences are consistent with the client's perceptions. This approach to practice emphasizes listening to the client's story and understanding the client's perceptions of experiences. The worker needs to continually evaluate the extent to which his or her understanding of the client's experiences is consistent with the client's.

As work continues, informal evaluation techniques identical to the process described earlier play a role. The social worker has to make a conscious effort to ensure that there is agreement about the identified goals and specifics of the helping contract. The worker and client need to evaluate the client's commitment to the plan. Is it genuine? How strong is it? What can the social worker do to help the client maintain or strengthen his or her commitment to change?

The key to ongoing assessment of client progress and practice effectiveness is persistently and relentlessly following through on the intervention plan. It is checking in with your client between meetings. It is regularly monitoring progress and exploring why or why not progress is being made. In addition to providing feedback, seeking ongoing client feedback helps create expectations for success and for making the identified changes. It communicates that you care and that you are committed to helping your clients overcome the challenges they are facing. The following section describes some measurement tools that can be used in your practice to informally evaluate client progress and practice effectiveness.

Measurement Tools

There are a number of measurement methods that involve clients, are easy to construct and implement, and are appropriate for social work practice evaluations. The more frequently used measurement tools are:

- Client logs
- Behavioral observations
- Rating scales
- Goal attainment scales

Client Logs

Having clients prepare narrative accounts of their activities, thoughts, and feelings is an effective method of monitoring progress. Client logs or journals help clarify the nature of client problems and the circumstances that contribute to the problem situation. Clients often find that keeping a log helps them increase their understanding and awareness of the factors that contribute to the identified problem situation. It enables them to "track the antecedents and consequences, or the feelings and thoughts, surrounding the occurrence of a specific event" (Berlin & Marsh, 1993, p. 99). Client logs allow a client to systematically take notes on the occurrence of a target problem and the events surrounding each occurrence. Doing so prevents distortions and misperceptions caused by faulty memory (Bloom, Fischer, & Orme, 2009).

Client logs also are an excellent source of baseline data on the frequency of the target problem. Baseline data obtained from logs serve as clinical measurements of client thoughts, feelings, and behaviors. These recordings help the client gain insight and help the practitioner to monitor clinical progress during treatment (Jordan & Franklin, 2015).

Client logs are easy to construct. Most are divided into columns, with the types of information the client should record listed at the top of each column. The columns should record the incident or behavior, when it occurred, and how the client responded to it (Bloom et al., 2009). Information on circumstances just prior to and just after the problem event may also be included in client logs.

Two decisions need to be made regarding the completion of logs. The first is when to record the information, and the second is what to record. Clients can record at preset time periods or immediately following the occurrence of the target event. Recording at preset time periods works if you have narrowed down the occurrence of a target event to a specific period, that is, if you know in advance approximately when the target problem is likely to occur. For example, a family might complain about sibling fights after school and during dinner. The client log then might cover the time period of 3:00 p.m. to 7:00 p.m. in the evening. The client keeping the log would record all the sibling fights that occurred during this time period.

The second option is to use open time categories. This method is sometimes referred to as critical incident recording (Bloom et al., 2009). With this type of log, the client decides whether to record an event. The client decides if the event is related to the problem or target and then records it as soon as possible after it occurs. This method works best when you need information about events that are likely to be spread out over the entire day.

TABLE 8.2 Sample Client Log for Use in Social Work Practice Evaluations

CLIENT LOG				
DATE AND TIME	EVENT (THOUGHTS, FEELINGS, OR BEHAVIOR)	CIRCUMSTANCES BEFORE EVENT	CIRCUMSTANCES AFTER EVENT	REFLECTION ON EVENT

In addition to specifying when the recording will take place, you also need to clarify in advance what will be recorded. By design, client logs give the client control over the content. Clients choose which of the many thoughts, feelings, and behaviors they experience daily to include and exclude. They employ a great deal of subjective judgment in completing logs. Information recorded on the log should be limited to what the client believes is important (Bloom et al., 2009). Thus, you and the client need to be clear about what constitutes a critical incident. Discuss with the client the types of events that would be appropriate for inclusion in the log. In the beginning, encourage clients to be inclusive rather than exclusive in their recordings. Review the first logs together with an eye toward the appropriateness of the entries as well as events that the client did not record but should have. Table 8.2 shows a sample client log.

Behavioral Observations

Behavioral observations are direct client behavior (Jordan & Franklin, 2015). The frequency and duration of specific client behaviors can be observed and recorded (Bloom et al., 2009). Behavioral observation can provide detailed information on the occurrence of client behaviors and the context of those behaviors. It represents one of the most reliable and valid methods of measuring client change.

Typically, the first step in using behavioral observation is to operationally define the target behavior. An example would be specifying the types of disruptive behavior a child displays in the classroom, such as getting out of his or her seat or talking with classmates while the teacher is talking. The target problem must be clearly defined in behavioral terms and must be observable. Observation cannot be used to measure target problems that focus on feelings or thoughts. It is limited to measuring the frequency, duration, and context of behaviors.

The second step is to select the observer or observers. Often, the observers are significant others, family members, or other professionals who have access to the client's person-in-environment interactions. For example, a young child having a problem controlling his or her temper can be observed at home by a parent and at school by a teacher or teacher's aide.

The third step is to train the observers. Observers must know in advance exactly what behavior to look for and how to recognize the behavior when it occurs (Jordan & Franklin, 2015). In addition, they have to be trained to conduct the observations. "Deciding how to sample the behaviors is the fundamental question in conducting a structured observation" (Berlin & Marsh, 1993, p. 107). You must decide whether to record all instances of the behavior or a sample. Continuous recording involves recording every occurrence of a target behavior every time it occurs (Bloom et al., 2009). A simple form can be created that includes at a minimum the date, time, location, and brief description of the behavior. The continuous recording approach requires the observer to be willing and available, and it works best when the target behavior does not occur with great frequency. Often, these conditions cannot be satisfied, and a sampling strategy is used.

Time sampling is appropriate when events occur continuously or frequently. "Time sampling requires the selection of specific units of time, either intervals or discrete points, during which the occurrence or nonoccurrence of a specific behavior is recorded" (Berlin & Marsh, 1993, p. 107). The assumption is that the sample behavior would be the same if all occurrences of it were recorded (Haynes, 1978). There are two types of time sampling: interval and discrete. Interval sampling involves selecting a time period and dividing it into equal blocks of time. The observer records the occurrence or nonoccurrence of the behavior during each interval. The behavior is recorded once for each interval regardless of how many times it occurs (Bloom et al., 2009).

Discrete time sampling involves selecting specific time periods and recording all instances of the target behavior that occur during the selected periods. The key issue in this type of recording is to select periods that are representative in terms of the target behavior. If the behaviors occur often and regularly, you would need fewer periods to obtain a representative sample of them (Bloom et al., 2009). If the behaviors occur during certain time periods, for example, during meals, then the selected periods must correspond to the behavioral patterns of the client.

Overall, direct observation is an excellent method for assessing client outcomes. It is one of the most effective tools we have for measuring behavior. When it is used with two or more observers, it can provide reliable and valid outcome data. It also has the potential to provide valuable clinical information on the context within which target problems occur. Direct observation should be seriously considered when a target problem is behavioral in nature, the situation allows for direct observation, and implementing direct observation is feasible. Exhibit 8.1 is a sample behavioral observation form.

EXHIBIT 8.1

SAMPLE BEHAVIORAL OBSERVATION FORM IN SOCIAL WORK PRACTICE

Client's Name _____ Recorder's Name _____

Target Behavior _____

Location _____

Date & Time	Description of Behavior and Context

Rating Scales

Individualized rating scales are measures of client problems that are created by the client and the social worker together (Bloom et al., 2009). These types of measures are also referred to as self-anchored rating scales (Jordan & Franklin, 2015). The major advantage of an individualized rating scale is that it measures the specific problem or concern that you and your client have identified as the focus of intervention. Thus, a rating scale is directly linked to the feeling, thought, or event that is being addressed in the helping process.

Another advantage of individualized rating scales is that they are based on the client's unique experiences and perceptions. The anchor points of the scale are defined by the client. The low, middle, and high points of the scale are labeled with short, succinct terms. The labels (anchors) describe what the numbers represent (e.g., behaviors, thoughts, and feelings that the client would experience at various points along the scale). Having the client define the anchor points gives the measure great relevance for the client. It becomes a unique measure of the client's feelings, thoughts, or behaviors. It represents his or her perceptions and experiences.

Individualized rating scales usually have 5 to 10 points. Scales that have more than 10 points are difficult for clients to score and are therefore not recommended (Bloom et al., 2009). For example, if a self-esteem scale had 1 to 100 points, it would be very difficult to determine the difference between ratings of 70 and 75. Scales with seven points are considered ideal (Jordan & Franklin, 2015). An example of an individualized rating scale is shown in Exhibit 8.2.

Individualized rating scales are easy to construct. Identify with the client the behavior, thought, or feeling that is targeted for change. A wide range of characteristics of the target can be rated (Bloom et al., 2009). It is important for the target to be clearly articulated and for each rating scale to measure only one aspect or dimension of the target (Gingerich, 1979). Bloom et al. (2009) warn against using different dimensions at each end of the scale, such as happy at one end and sad at the other. People often experience contradictory feelings and can feel happy and sad at the same time. It is preferable to develop two measures, a sadness scale and a happiness scale, rather than one scale on which both dimensions are rated. They also recommend that the target and its measurement be worded positively, something the client wants to achieve not just something eliminating a negative (Bloom et al., 2009). For example,

EXHIBIT 8.2

SAMPLE INDIVIDUALIZED RATING SCALE IN SOCIAL WORK PRACTICE
Comfort in social situations

1	2	3	4	5	6	7
Terrified, overwhelmed, completely unable to engage in conversation with strangers			Somewhat anxious, yet able to respond when spoken to		Relaxed, confident, able to initiate conversations with strangers	

if the problem is feelings of sadness, the goal might be to increase feelings of happiness, and the rating scale would measure the level of happiness.

The next step is to decide on the number of scale points and develop anchor descriptions for the two end points and possibly the middle point. Scales with seven or nine points are popular because they have a clear midpoint. The numbers on the scale represent gradations for the target problem from low to high. The higher the score, the more frequent, serious, important, or problematic the target problem. The end points of the scale are defined by the client, as are the descriptions or examples of the low, middle, and high numbers. These anchor descriptions define the meaning of the numbers on the rating scale. Begin by asking the client to describe what it would be like at one end of the scale for the given target problem. Repeat the process for the other end of the scale and for the midpoint. Anchors should describe the behaviors, thoughts, or feelings the client would experience along the continuum of the scale (Bloom et al., 2009).

After you and your client construct the scale, make sure that the anchors fit the client's perception of the situation and that both of you are clear about what constitutes a low or high score. This is best accomplished by practicing using the scale and asking the client to retrospectively complete a rating for different points in his or her life. This will increase the client's comfort in using the scale and provides an opportunity to determine whether the anchor points provide adequate differentiation of the target problem.

An important point to keep in mind in constructing individualized rating scales is that they must be truly *individualized*. The anchors reflect images and pictures of what the situation is like for the client. Your job is to help the client put those images into words. Make sure the words are the client's, not yours or someone else's. The strength of individualized rating scales is that they are client defined and derived directly from the identified target problem.

An alternative to individually constructed anchors is general anchor descriptions. Rating scales with general anchors can be used for different client situations. For example, a general rating scale that measures feelings of connectedness could be used to measure a client's relationships with each member of his or her family. The disadvantage of general anchors is that they are more ambiguous and less precise than individually tailored anchors (Coulton & Solomon, 1977). Exhibit 8.3 shows two general rating scales.

EXHIBIT 8.3

SAMPLE GENERAL RATING SCALES

Amount of anxiety

1	2	3	4	5	6	7
Little or no anxiety			Moderate anxiety			Extreme anxiety

Frequency of feeling lonely

1	2	3	4	5	6	7
Never			Sometimes			All the time

Individualized and general rating scales are excellent tools for measuring client progress and change on identified target problems. They have a high level of face validity because they are derived directly from client problems or concerns. There is some evidence that the validity of single-item rating scales is comparable to that of standardized measures (Nugent, 1992). However, the validity and reliability of individualized rating scales cannot be readily established, because they are designed for use with individual clients (Berlin & Marsh, 1993). Rating scales do, however, have a high level of clinical applicability and are excellent tools for measuring client target problems and assessing progress.

Goal Attainment Scales

Goal attainment scaling (GAS) was developed in the field of mental health during the 1960s (Royse, Thyer, & Padgett, 2016). It has been used in a large number of settings and with a wide range of client populations. GAS is similar to individualized rating scales in that the client develops and defines the scale anchors or descriptors. The two methods differ, however, in that goal attainment scales are based directly on the client's goals rather than on behaviors, thoughts, or feelings. A strength of GAS is that it can be used to monitor your client's perception of progress toward the identified treatment goals (Jordan & Franklin, 2015). Thus, GAS has been effective in assessing client change related to the identified goals (Corcoran, 1992).

To use GAS, you and your client need to have specified change goals. A question that arises is which goals or how many should be measured (Seaburg & Gillespie, 1977). In general, the number of goals measured should correspond to the number of goals being addressed in the helping relationship. The number of goals being addressed at any given time should be limited. As discussed earlier in this chapter, the goals selected should be those most significant to the client that intervention is most likely to change (Royse et al., 2016).

In conjunction with the client, list each goal on a five-point scale ranging from 0 to 4. The scale categories are:

(4) Optimal progress

(3) Major progress

(2) Moderate progress

(1) Some progress

(0) No progress

Work with the client to develop anchors for each scale point. The anchors should represent potential outcomes related to each category and should be as specific as possible. Avoid vague, general outcome statements. Table 8.3 shows a sample goal attainment scale that was developed with an 80-year-old woman who was caring for her 55-year-old mentally retarded son. The social worker was helping the women address her anxiety and concern about her son's future.

GAS is a client-focused method of measuring progress. It is a direct extension of the goal-oriented approach to practice and is easily incorporated into

▶ **Critical Thinking Questions**

1. What are the strengths of the various client measures discussed here? What are their weaknesses?

2. With what kinds of cases or clients are they appropriate to use? Why?

TABLE 8.3 Sample Goal Attainment Scale in Social Work Practice

LEVEL	GOAL 1 INCREASE ABILITY TO DEAL WITH PANIC ATTACKS	GOAL 2 MAKE PLANS FOR SON'S FUTURE
No progress (0)	Unable to calm myself down, unable to catch breath, heart racing, extreme anxiety	Unable to discuss with son his future needs and plans
Some progress (1)	Limited ability to calm myself down, some difficulty breathing, pacing the floor, moderate anxiety	Discussed son's future with other members of the family
Moderate progress (2)	Able to calm down using breathing/relaxation techniques, maintain composure, low anxiety	Discussed with son his future needs
Major progress (3)	Able to verbalize feelings, remain calm in stressful situations, almost no anxiety	Discussed with son his future needs and involved family and outside agencies in assessing son's needs
Optimal progress (4)	Able to deal with stressful situations without experiencing panic attacks, very low anxiety, calm and relaxed	Working with son, family, and outside agencies and services to prepare son to care for himself in the future

generalist social work practice with a diverse range of client populations. GAS also empowers clients by placing responsibility for defining and monitoring progress with them. The client is viewed as the expert on what constitutes progress and on determining the extent to which progress is being made. In these respects, GAS is useful as a clinical measurement tool for engaging clients in the helping process.

■ Evaluating Micropractice Effectiveness: Formal

This section focuses on formal approaches to evaluating micropractice effectiveness. It begins with a discussion of measurement guidelines and standardized measures. Designing single-system evaluation and analyzing single-systems data are then reviewed.

Measurement Guidelines

Social workers engaged in practice evaluation need to follow established research guidelines regarding measurement (Poulin, 2010). Berlin and Marsh (1993) suggest that the data collection effort will be enhanced if you:

- ■ Specify the client's problems and goals clearly;
- ■ Use multiple measures for each objective;
- ■ Collect information that is relevant rather than convenient;

- Collect information early in the course of the work with the client;

- Use good and accurate measures;

- Organize the data; and

- Obtain the client's cooperation and consent. (p. 93)

Clearly Specify Problems and Goals

This guideline is fundamental to the measurement process. As noted earlier, client problems and expected outcomes must be specific and stated in clear, unambiguous terms. Measurable objectives related to each goal must be developed. Collecting client data is impossible without specific and observable indicators attached to each objective (Poulin, 2010).

Use Multiple Measures

The use of more than one measure to assess a single phenomenon is a basic research strategy referred to as triangulation (Royse et al., 2016). The assumption behind this strategy is that all measures are to some extent flawed or imperfect. Because any one measure may not be accurate, it is necessary to use more than one measure to assess client progress. The logical assumption is that if two or more imperfect measures indicate change, there is more reason to be confident that change has occurred than if only one imperfect measure is used. Relying on a single measure of client progress is risky. The problems addressed by generalist social workers and their clients are too complex to be assessed with a single imperfect measure.

The inaccuracy of measurement strategies should not discourage you from using quantitative measures in your practice. Crude indicators of progress are preferable to no indicators. What is important is to be aware of the limitations of measurement tools. The data alone will not provide you and your clients with definitive answers. The data will, however, provide you and your clients with helpful information that can be incorporated into your work together. Analyzing the data with your clients will facilitate the helping process and provide a basis for ongoing assessment of your work together (Poulin, 2010).

Collect Relevant Information

Berlin and Marsh warn that "one of the most frequent mistakes that clinicians make is to track something that is not very important" (1993, p. 94). Typically, the client's problem is reconceptualized to fit an existing measure or instrument. The convenience factor is high, but the relevance factor is low. If you cannot specify the expected changes, the problem may not have been conceptualized accurately or the terms may not be specific enough. Relevant measures should flow directly from clearly conceptualized problems and objectives.

Collect Information Early

There are a number of reasons to begin the process of collecting data early in the helping process. The first reason is that measuring the target problem or objective prior to implementing the intervention provides baseline data, which are a basis for future comparisons. Change must be evaluated comparatively. Without some sort of comparison, it is impossible to assess the extent to which the desired changes have occurred. Collecting assessment data early in the helping process will allow you to periodically evaluate the effectiveness of the work throughout the helping relationship (Poulin, 2010).

A second reason to begin collecting data early in the helping process is to communicate to clients that you are interested in understanding their situation and that you are committed to helping them successfully address their concerns or problems. Measurement is an active and concrete process. Developing measures communicates that you take their concerns seriously and that their concerns are important enough to warrant the effort required to develop measures and collect data.

A third reason to start the measurement process early is that it engages the client in a collaborative activity. You and the client define the target problem, develop the objectives, and develop the measurement plan. You and your client may even develop many of the measures used. The client becomes an active participant in the process. This communicates expectations about how you will work together as well as the idea that the client is the expert on his or her situation (Poulin, 2010).

Use Good and Accurate Measures

Every effort should be made to use the best measures available. According to Berlin and Marsh (1993), four criteria are useful in judging the adequacy of different measures: relevance, sensitivity to change, reliability, and validity.

Relevance refers to the extent the measure is directly related to the targeted outcomes. Is there a good fit between the measure and the expected changes? The relevance of any measure is a function of the identified target problem or the specific change objectives. Make sure the measure you choose matches what the client hopes to change.

Sensitivity to change is the second criterion of a good measure. Not all measures are capable of capturing change. Some are more sensitive than others. It may be possible to use measures that have shown change in previous evaluations and have thus been proved useful. A measure's track record of detecting change is one of the best indicators of its sensitivity to change (Bloom et al., 2009). Often, however, information on a measure's sensitivity is not available; thus, it is not always possible to know in advance whether a measure will be sensitive to change. Berlin and Marsh (1993) suggest that global measures are usually less sensitive to change than measures directly related to specific behaviors targeted for change. Measures of behaviors that occur more frequently are likely to be more sensitive than measures of behaviors that occur less frequently. High-frequency behaviors are more responsive to small changes while low-frequency behaviors may only respond to major changes (Bloom et al., 2009).

Reliability refers to the consistency of measurements. When measuring client change, you want to be reasonably confident that the differences among the first measurement and subsequent ones relate to changes in the client and not to problems with the measure. An instrument that can do this is said to be reliable. "Every type of measure involves some kind of error, and the measure is reliable to the extent that the error is minimal" (Berlin & Marsh, 1993, p. 97). The two most common ways of testing the reliability of a measure are to assess its internal consistency and its test–retest characteristics. Internal consistency reliability is the extent to which the individual items that make up a scale or index are correlated with one another. Test–retest reliability refers to the extent to which the same result is obtained when the same measure is administered to the same client at two different points in time. Both types of reliability are important. However, in evaluating client change, test–retest reliability is critical. To the extent possible, use at least one measure that has been tested for reliability and has a reliability coefficient of .80 or higher (Poulin, 2010).

Validity refers to the extent to which an instrument measures what it is supposed to measure and not anything else (Royse et al., 2016). For example, if you are assessing a client's self-confidence, the instrument should measure self-confidence, not a related concept such as self-esteem. Because concepts in social work tend to be complex, no measure will be entirely valid, only more or less so (Royse et al., 2016).

There are various ways to determine the validity of an instrument. The least rigorous kind of validity is face validity. Does the instrument appear to measure the concept? A measure is said to have face validity if knowledgeable persons agree that it measures what it is intended to measure (Poulin, 2010).

Another type of validity is content validity. This method also relies on expert opinion. In this case, experts are asked to review it to see if the entire range of the concept is represented in the sample of items selected for the scale (Royse et al., 2016). For example, a scale designed to measure stress should have items that represent the different components of stress, such as feeling tense, feeling pressured, having difficulty sleeping, and being short-tempered.

Neither content nor face validity empirically demonstrates a scale's validity. This can be done in a number of ways.

A scale's concurrent validity is demonstrated by comparing its results with another scale that has previously been determined (proven) to have validity when administered to the same group of subjects (Royse et al., 2016). If the two scales are highly correlated, at .80 or above, the new scale has demonstrated concurrent validity.

Construct validity refers to the extent to which an instrument actually measures the concept in question. Construct validity is established by demonstrating convergent validity and discriminant validity. A measure is said to have convergent validity if it is correlated in a predicted manner with other measures with which it theoretically should correlate (Bloom et al., 2009). For example, a measure of the strength of a helping relationship should correlate positively with measures of trust and openness. Those who are more trusting and open are more likely to develop strong helping relationships with their social workers than those who are less trusting and open.

A measure's discriminant validity is demonstrated by a lack of correlation with measures with which it theoretically should not be correlated. This indicates that the measure can discriminate between concepts. For example, there is no theoretical basis for predicting how certain client problems will correlate with the development of a helping relationship with the social worker. Clients with high self-esteem are as likely to develop a strong helping relationship as those with low self-esteem. Similarly, a client's level of depression is not associated with the strength of the helping relationship (Poulin, 2010).

Construct validity is demonstrated when a measure is correlated with other measures that it theoretically should be related to (convergent validity) and not correlated with measures with which it theoretically should not be correlated (discriminant validity). When selecting measures to evaluate client change, look for some evidence of the validity of the measure. At the very least, the measure should have face validity. Empirical verification of the measure's validity is preferable.

Organize the Data

For data to be useful, they have to be organized in some systematic way. It is difficult to interpret or draw meaning from unorganized raw data. Data need to be presented in a way that makes sense to both you and your client. Typically, data obtained to evaluate client change can be easily computed and presented in simple graphs.

The basic graphic presentation of change data is a line graph on which the client's scores are plotted over time. A visual inspection of the data points provides feedback on client progress. Time is plotted on the horizontal (*x*) axis, and scores measuring the target problem on the vertical (*y*) axis. The time dimension reflects the number of times the measure of the target problem is completed and the time period between measurements. The time unit selected depends on the nature of the target problem. Typically, measures of the target problem are completed on a daily or weekly basis. Figure 8.1 is a sample line graph on which a client's level of self-esteem is plotted over an 11-week period.

An important component of the helping process is reviewing the data on the graphic displays with clients. In collaborative social work, the clients are actively involved in inspecting the organized data and interpreting the patterns and results. Most clients are interested in examining graphs of their progress and in providing interpretations of what is happening. Involving clients in this process can be a powerful tool. It keeps your work focused on the change objectives, and it provides an opportunity for you and the client to review progress, tasks, and effort as well as the appropriateness of

▶ **Critical Thinking Question**
1. Why do social workers need to understand research measurement guidelines?

goals and objectives. If strides are being made, it can motivate further efforts. If progress is not forthcoming, you and the client can assess the situation and make adjustments as needed.

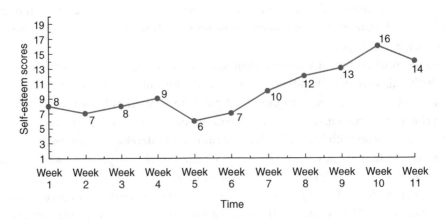

FIGURE 8.1 Client's weekly self-esteem scores.

Obtain Client Cooperation and Consent

Naturally, the process of selecting and incorporating measurement strategies into social work practice requires the full cooperation of clients. Most models of social work practice are based on the assumption that clients are full partners in the helping process. Measuring client progress without their full cooperation is a waste of time. Clients need to have ownership of the measures and willingness to engage in a process of self-assessment and change. Their commitment to the data collection and evaluation process reflects their commitment to achieving the changes they are seeking.

Standardized Measures

Standardized measures are instruments developed following empirical scale construction techniques with uniform administration and scoring procedures (Jordan & Franklin, 2015). Their reliability is known, and their validity has usually been empirically tested.

Standardized measures are available for a wide range of client behaviors, including marital satisfaction, self-esteem, anxiety, and family relations. Some standardized measures assess global behaviors, such as generalized contentment, while others assess specific behaviors and problems, such as fear, depression, or sexual satisfaction. Standardized measures are available in rapid assessment formats with up to 25 scale items, as well as in lengthy, comprehensive formats with hundreds of scale items. Rapid assessment instruments are easy to use and to incorporate into a generalist social work practice.

"Standardized measures represent the most useful quantitative clinical measurement tools that are available to practitioners" (Jordan & Franklin, 2015, p. 53). There are numerous sources of standardized measures. *Measures for Clinical Practice* by Corcoran and Fischer (2013) is an excellent two-volume collection of rapid assessment instruments. Volume 1 contains measures for use with couples, families, and children, and Volume 2 contains instruments for individual adults. The two-volume set contains more than 300 different brief assessment instruments, with supporting information on each instrument's purpose, scoring, reliability, and validity. Another great source of rapid assessment instruments is *Measures of Personality and Social Psychological Attitudes* (1991) by Robinson, Shaver, and Wrightsman. In this book, measures are organized by clinical topic (e.g., self-esteem, depression, anxiety).

A useful list of commercially available measures can be found in *Clinical Assessment for Social Workers* by Jordan and Franklin (2015). The WALMYR Publishing Company is also an excellent source for commercially available measurement instruments designed specifically for use in social work practice. WALMYR sells a number of individual and family adjustment scales as well as comprehensive multidimensional assessment instruments.

Standardized measures, especially the rapid assessment variety, are well-suited for use in social work practice. If you can locate one that closely corresponds to identified client problems or concerns, standardized measures offer several advantages. They have known psychometric properties, that is, their reliability and validity have been established. They are also efficient, do not require extensive training, and are easy to administer and score (Corcoran & Fischer, 2013).

Designing the Evaluation

Having established measurable goals and selected measurement strategies, the next step is to determine how you are going to implement the evaluation process. The term *evaluation design* is often used to describe how practitioners plan to evaluate progress and case outcomes (Bloom et al., 2009). One of the most widely used ways to evaluate practice effectiveness in social work is the single-system design (Miley, O'Melia, & DuBois, 2013). Single-system designs are used in formal case-levels evaluations. They involve the study of one client involving repeated measurements over time in order to measure change (Bloom et al., 2009).

Single-system designs hold great promise for social workers. The requirements for using them fit well with social work practice. Single-system designs require clear specification of the target problem, development of measurable goals, selection and implementation of an intervention, and continued monitoring of the client's progress on the identified target problem. All these requirements are consistent with the requirements of sound social work practice.

Bloom et al. (2009) provide a comprehensive and detailed description of numerous types of single-system designs. However, the designs that are likely to be used as part of a social worker's ongoing practice are more limited. The single-system design selected depends primarily on what questions you are attempting to answer (Berlin & Marsh, 1993). Two questions appropriate for social work practice evaluations are: Is the intervention working? and Is the intervention causing the change?

More complex experimental designs provide information on the causal effect of the intervention. Did the client system improve because of the intervention? What aspects of the intervention are most important in causing the change? Answers to such questions contribute to social work knowledge. They help document the effectiveness of various interventions with different types of clients and target problems. However, answering questions about causality and implementing experiential type designs are beyond the level of evaluation expected for most social work practitioners. They are better addressed through research than through ongoing social work practice with clients.

As noted earlier, social workers have a responsibility to promote the well-being of clients and provide services competently (NASW, 2017). This entails, in part, assessing the effectiveness of our interventions. Is the client making progress? Does the intervention appear to be working? Is the target problem improving, getting worse, or staying the same? This section focuses only on designs that provide information on client progress. Such designs best fit social work practice. They are easy to implement with client systems, and they provide important information on the effectiveness of the work.

Components of Single-System Designs

There are a number of single-system evaluation designs. Some components are common to all of them. The basic components of single-subject designs are:

- Specifying the target problem
- Developing quantitative measures of the target problem
- Establishing baseline measures of the target problem before intervention

- Measuring the target problem repeatedly throughout the intervention

- Displaying the data on a graph

- Making comparisons across phases

Specifying the target problem, developing measures, and displaying data on graphs were discussed earlier.

Establishing a Baseline

The **baseline** is the measure of the target problem before the worker begins the intervention. Repeated measurements prior to the intervention are necessary to establish a baseline. The baseline allows you to compare the client's target problem before and after the intervention (Bloom et al., 2009).

There are two types of baselines: concurrent and retrospective. For a concurrent baseline, data are collected while other assessment activities are taking place. Repeated measures of the target problem are collected before you implement an intervention within the client system. For a retrospective baseline, the client reconstructs measures of the target problem from an earlier time period, using his or her memory. In many situations, delaying the intervention while a concurrent baseline is obtained is unacceptable. For example, it would be unethical to delay providing counseling services to people who experienced a traumatic event, such as a school shooting, in order to obtain baseline information on the victims' levels of traumatic stress. In such cases, using a retrospective baseline is an acceptable alternative.

A common question is how many data points or measurements are needed for the baseline. The answer is that it depends. For meaningful comparisons to be made between the preintervention (baseline) and the intervention phases, the baseline has to be stable. That is, there has to be an observable pattern of measurement scores during the baseline period. A stable baseline is one that does not contain obvious cycles or wide fluctuations in the data (Bloom et al., 2009). Fluctuations are acceptable only if they occur with some regularity (Marlow, 2011). Thus, ideally, the baseline phase does not end until the baseline is stable. How long it takes is influenced, in part, by the amount of variation among the data points. The greater the variation (range of scores), the more the data points needed to achieve stability. Conversely, if the variation among points on the baseline is relatively small (similar scores), fewer data points are needed to achieve stability (Poulin, 2010).

Using an unstable baseline is problematic. If the measures of the target problem fluctuate widely and no pattern exists, it is difficult to determine what factors are affecting changes in the target problem and whether change has occurred once the intervention starts (Bloom et al., 2009). In other words, it is unclear whether changes between the baseline and the intervention phases are due to usual fluctuations in the target problem or if change has actually taken place.

Making Comparisons

Assessing change requires making some sort of comparison. In traditional experimental evaluation designs, a treatment group is compared with a control group that does not receive treatment. In case evaluations using single-system designs, the client provides the basis for comparison. In essence, the client serves as his or her own control group. Is the client better after getting help than before? Without comparisons, it is impossible to assess change.

Work with clients can be divided into phases (Marlow, 2011). During the first few contacts, baseline data on the target problem may be collected; this is the assessment phase. The second phase is the next series of sessions, in which an intervention is implemented. If the first intervention did not achieve the desired results, a second intervention may be tried; this would be the third phrase.

Single-system evaluations use letters to label the different phases. The letter *A* is used to designate the baseline phase. "Successive interventions are represented by successive letters: B for the first, C for the second, D for the third, and so on" (Royse et al., 2016). A single-system design that consists of a baseline phase followed by an intervention is called an AB design. An evaluation that does not have a baseline and only one intervention is called a B design. An ABA design is one in which a baseline (*A*) phase is followed by an intervention (*B*) phase and a second baseline (*A*) period. The various phases of a single-subject design are usually labeled on the line graph and represented by dashed vertical lines. Figure 8.2 is a line graph of an AB design.

The AB design is the most frequently used single-system design in service settings (Marlow, 2011). In this design, repeated measurements of the target problem are taken during the baseline (*A*) and intervention (*B*) phases. Measures of the target problem are taken before the intervention is implemented and throughout the intervention. As with all single-system evaluations, the findings are analyzed by plotting the data points on a chart.

The advantage of the AB design is its simplicity (Marlow, 2011). One must merely identify or develop an appropriate measurement of the target problem and then take repeated measurements during the first baseline phase and the intervention phase. This design can easily be incorporated into social work practice. It is consistent with normal practice procedures in that an assessment data-gathering phase is followed by an intervention phase (Poulin, 2010). The design usually does not compromise or hinder the development of a helping relationship and the provision of service. It fits well into most practice models, and it provides evidence of whether the intervention is working or not.

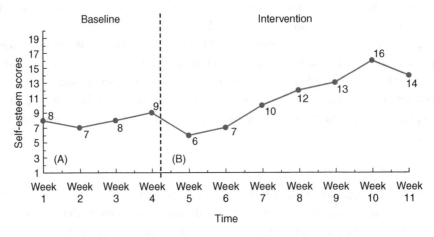

FIGURE 8.2 Sample AB design.

The one area of potential difficulty with the AB design is obtaining a baseline. This is a problem with all single-system designs used to evaluate ongoing practice with client systems (Poulin, 2010). Delaying the intervention while baseline data are collected is problematic when the situation warrants immediate attention. Obtaining measures of the target problem over a prolonged period of time often is not feasible or desirable. In these situations, developing a retrospective baseline is best. You and the client construct a baseline from the client's recollection of the target problem in the recent past. Although it is a compromise, a retrospective baseline provides a basis of comparison to answer the fundamental question: Is the intervention working?

The B design is the preferred option when it is necessary to intervene immediately, as in a crisis situation, without collecting baseline information or retrospective baseline information (Berlin & Marsh, 1993). It consists solely of an intervention (*B*) phase. Repeated measures of the target problem are taken throughout the intervention. This design is weaker than the AB design because pre-intervention comparison data are not available. It does, however, provide information on client progress, whether the target problem is improving, and whether the goals of the intervention have been achieved.

A third design that can be used to evaluate client progress is the ABC design. This design is an extension of the AB design. It involves the introduction of a second intervention (*C*) phase. If additional interventions are added beyond the second (*C*), they are labeled *D, E,* and so on. The ABC design is used when the first (*B*) intervention is modified or when the first intervention does not appear to be working. It does not provide information on which intervention caused change in the target problem, nor does it allow for separation of the effects of the successive interventions. It does, however, provide information on client progress.

Other single-system design options are shown in Table 8.4.

Analyzing Single-System Data

Single-system design data are plotted on line graphs similar to those in Figure 8.2. Three types of significance can be used to judge change in the target problem: clinical, visual, and statistical. Clinical and visual significance are reviewed here. A review of the various approaches to calculating statistical significance is beyond the capabilities of this chapter. For a detailed discussion of the different approaches to calculating statistical significance, see Nugent's (2009) book, *Analyzing Single System Design Data*.

Clinical Significance

Clinical significance, also known as practical significance, is based on the client and the social worker believing that there has been meaningful change in the problem (Bloom et al., 2009). Clinical significance is achieved when the specified goal of the intervention has been reached (Marlow, 2011). Determining clinical significance is generally a subjective process that requires discussion and negotiation among the involved parties. If everyone involved agrees that the target problem has been resolved, clinical significance has been achieved.

Determining clinical significance when a goal has not been fully achieved is more difficult: How much change is clinically meaningful? There are no criteria for establishing the clinical significance of partial change in the target problem. Client change can be considered clinically significant if those involved in the helping process agree that meaningful change has occurred.

TABLE 8.4 Other Single-System Designs

DESIGN TYPE	DESCRIPTION OF DESIGN
B	Measurement occurs during the intervention phase. There is no baseline data collection phase. Example: A client enters an inpatient drug and alcohol rehabilitation program. Upon entry into the program, he immediately begins receiving medication to treat his physical symptoms of withdrawal and begins individual cognitive behavioral therapy with a social worker. Since the social worker did not have a period of baseline prior to starting her therapeutic work with this client, all of the data collected while providing the therapy would be considered the treatment phase (B).
ABA	There is a period of baseline data collection where no intervention is given. Following the baseline phase, the intervention is administered, and data are then collected. After a period of time, the intervention is withdrawn, and another period of baseline data collection occurs. It is noteworthy that treatment carryover effects can interfere with the second baseline in this type of design. Example: A child with behavioral outbursts begins BHRS. During the intake process the treatment team collects data in the forms of observations, interviews, and scales in order to determine current needs and to establish goals. This is the baseline phase (A). After collecting the baseline data, the team implements a behavior modification plan that includes reinforcements and punishments in an attempt to increase positive behaviors and eliminate undesired behaviors. While the behavior modification plan is being implemented, data are collected (B). Once the child has met the treatment goals, before discharging the child from services, the treatment team stops implementing the behavior modification plan and tracks rates of behaviors. While data are being collected after the intervention has been removed is a second baseline phase (A).
BAB	Measurement occurs during the intervention phase. The intervention is then withdrawn to collect baseline data. Following collection of baseline data, the intervention is reintroduced. Example: A woman with anxiety comes to a community mental health clinic for support. During her first session, the treatment begins with the social worker teaching her techniques to calm down, focus on her breath, and engage in mindfulness. The therapist asks the client to continue this intervention. Since there was no baseline period before the intervention was introduced, this case starts with the treatment phase (B). After several successful weeks using the intervention, the social worker stops the intervention and continues to collect data. Since there is no intervention being delivered, this is a baseline phase (A). The social worker eventually reintroduces the intervention, and data are collected during the second treatment phase (B).

BHRS, behavioral health rehabilitation services.

Visual Significance

Visual analysis is used for data that has been collected over time. It focuses on the trend and direction of the data. A trend occurs when data points move directionally in a relatively steady manner. A trend can be a steady increasing pattern, steady pattern of no change, or a steady decreasing pattern. Data in which there are no discernible trends or patterns are considered unstable. Unstable data show wide fluctuations in the measurement of the target problem. The interpretation of unstable data is difficult. Little can be said beyond the fact that there is no pattern and the scores vary widely (Poulin, 2010).

The visual analysis of single-system data is based primarily on a comparison of the baseline and intervention phases. For meaningful comparisons to be made, the baseline data must be stable. If they are not, interpretation of the effect of the intervention is impossible. Interpretation is also difficult if the baseline data are moving steadily in a direction that would represent improvement on the target problem. For example, if a decrease in occurrence of the target problem represents client improvement and the baseline trend shows a steady decline on the measure, it would be difficult to attribute the improved scores to the effectiveness of the intervention, because the data were already moving in the desired direction (Krishef, 1991).

Calculating a celeration line helps to visually determine a trend in the data (Bloom et al., 2009). A celeration line connects the midpoints of the first and second halves of the baseline phase and extends into the intervention phase (Figure 8.3). The basic idea is that the trend established during the baseline phase is an estimate of what would happen if the baseline pattern were to continue and there were no intervention. The steps involved in calculating a celeration line are as follows:

1. Plot the baseline and intervention data on a line graph.

2. Divide the baseline section of the line graph in half, drawing a vertical line. If there are an even number of data points in the baseline, draw the line between the data points; if there are an odd number of points, draw the line through the midpoint number.

▶ **Critical Thinking Questions**

1. How would incorporating formal practice evaluation methods affect your social work practice with clients?

2. What are the advantages and disadvantages of doing so?

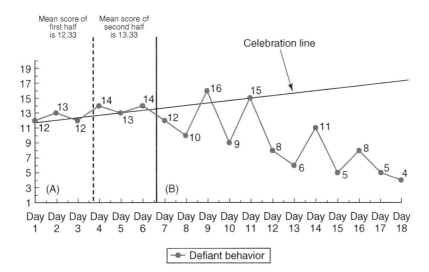

FIGURE 8.3 Line graph with celeration line.

3. Divide each half into half by drawing dashed vertical lines on the chart.

4. Determine the mean score of the first half of the baseline by adding the scores in the half and dividing by the number of scores in the half. For baselines with an odd number of scores, omit the middle number.

5. Determine the mean score of the second half of the baseline by adding the scores in the half and dividing by the number of scores in the half. For baselines with an odd number of scores, omit the middle number.

6. Mark the dashed vertical line at the mean point for each half.

7. Draw a solid line connecting the two marks in the baseline and extend the line through the intervention phase.

The evaluation of program and intervention outcomes is typically associated with social work practice with organizations and communities. The evaluation methods used for both client systems are the same. The two types of program and intervention evaluations are formative (process) evaluations and summative evaluations (outcome). Both types of evaluations begin with the logic model discussed in Chapter 10, Mezzointerventions in Social Work: Organizations and Communities, on mezzosystem assessment. The program's logic model sets the stage for its formative and summative evaluation. In the following, we revisit the logic model from the evaluation perspective.

Social Justice Issues

Social workers understand that social justice issues are present across all areas and levels of practice. Related to research, social workers must practice with integrity and ensure that human participants are treated in an ethical and respectful manner. The mission of the social work profession calls for social workers to support vulnerable and oppressed populations. Social workers should ensure that research practices related to all populations are ethical and humane with particular attention to these vulnerable and oppressed groups. Research that targets vulnerable populations should be particularly cautious to ensure adequate safeguards are in place to ensure ethical conditions.

Social workers must address a myriad of social justice issues including such things as "health disparities, mass incarceration, the interrelationship between substance use and incarceration, unemployment and education, and racial and ethnic inequalities in the juvenile and criminal justice systems" while "relying on social innovation to increase health and well-being among vulnerable populations" (Maschi & Leibowitz, 2017, p. 4). Furthermore, Maschi and Leibowitz (2017) underscore that social workers must be "data driven and apply the empirical literature and the evidence from scientific research to address the most pressing social problems" (p. 4). In order to be data driven, research must be conducted with these vulnerable populations and shared with the profession. Let us explore social justice that would arise looking at the issue of racial and ethnic inequalities in the juvenile and criminal justice systems (see Case 8.5).

This population is vulnerable on the basis of their complex intersectionality. First, they are juveniles (under the age of 18). Though ages of consent vary from state to state, in general

CASE 8.5   PRACTICE-INFORMED RESEARCH WITHIN A JUVENILE DETENTION CENTER

Angela is a social worker at a juvenile detention center in an urban community. The facility has 100 beds, and it is always at capacity. Angela is one of two mental health social workers. Her role in the facility is to provide mental health counseling individually and in groups. At any given time, Angela has approximately half of the population on her caseload to support. She loves her job and is continually looking for ways to improve her clinical skills so that she can provide better services to the youth she works with.

Angela often runs an anger management group with the youth, many of whom can benefit from learning how to better cope with intense emotions in an acceptable manner. Angela had been to a social work conference recently where she was learning about new strategies to address anger issues utilizing mindfulness and breathing exercises. She thought that it was a very interesting presentation and wants to incorporate it into her next group. Angela wants to be able to measure if this new intervention will be more successful than her previous intervention. Angela talks to her supervisor about having the youth complete an anger rating scale at the start of the anger management group and then repeat the measure at the end of the group. Angela was excited about this idea and could not wait to share it with her supervisor.

During supervision, Angela shared her idea with her supervisor, Penelope. Penelope listened intently to Angela, noticing her excitement regarding her idea for practice informed research. After Angela finished explaining her idea she asked Penelope what she thought. Penelope smiled and acknowledged that Angela was very passionate about her job and this new idea. However, she recognized a few concerns regarding this proposed research plan. Penelope shared with Angela that she was concerned regarding the lack of informed consent. Angela brought up that her anger management group is a voluntary group and wondered if that would be enough to proceed. Penelope shared that in order to conduct research, there are specific steps that must be followed to protect the participants. Penelope then pulled out her copy of the NASW Code of Ethics to share with Angela. Angela was almost offended thinking that Penelope was suggesting that what she was doing was unethical. Penelope quickly assured Angela that she recognized that Angela was not intentionally being unethical, however, there are specific ethical guidelines for conducting research that she had missed in the creation of her plan. Together Angela and Penelope reviewed the applicable portions of the Code of Ethics and decided to come up with a plan to be able to introduce these new techniques and measure their effectiveness in a way that was fully aligned with the NASW Code of Ethics.

18 years old is deemed the age at which a person can provide full informed consent for a research study. In this case, the youth would need to complete an assent form and parents or guardians would need to be contacted in order to gain written informed consent.

As the youth are in the criminal justice system, if they are in custody, they would be considered prisoners, or individuals who are incarcerated. This population has special protections in addition to those for other human participants (Christopher et al., 2017). There are only four categories of research that can be conducted on incarcerated individuals which include:

. . . minimal-risk studies on possible causes, effects, and processes of incarceration and of criminal behavior; minimal-risk studies of prisons as institutional structures or of prisoners as incarcerated persons; research on conditions particularly affecting prisoners as a class; and research on practices that are intended and deemed likely to improve the health or well-being of participants. (Christopher et al., 2017, p. 21)

Due to the inherent power imbalance in such a situation, social workers must be extra cognizant in order to avoid coercion. Coercion can occur, even if it was not intended. Intentions are important, but intentions of good will are simply not enough to safeguard vulnerable populations. Social workers must consider how the participant will perceive the experience as well in order to ensure that best efforts are made to protect participants.

A final area of intersectionality would relate to their racial or ethnic minority status. In the United States, there is disproportionate incarceration of people of color. African American and Hispanic American males are incarcerated at much higher rates than any other group. Some minority juveniles who are incarcerated may not speak English as their first language. Special consideration must be paid in such a case to ensure informed consent and appropriate translation of study materials.

■ Summary

Throughout this chapter, we introduced the importance of research for social workers. We particularly focused on the importance of research-informed practice. Social workers must be able to integrate science into their professional practice in order to ensure best outcomes for client systems. It is necessary for social workers to be critical thinkers regarding the information they are receiving, recognizing that there are multiple ways of knowing. When considering how to critically analyze information, social workers seek to understand the strengths and limitations related to various types of knowing. Professional social workers recognize that research-informed practice is necessary to support clients and the profession as a whole. Throughout this chapter, we talked about how research can inform all aspects of social work practice at all levels: micro, mezzo, and macro. We have reviewed the importance of using evidence to inform practice and utilize EBPs whenever possible to ensure the best outcome for clients.

CASE SUMMARY   "UNDOCUMENTED AND HOMELESS"

Practice Setting Description

Jackie is a first-year master of social work student completing an internship at an inner-city family service agency in the Southwest. The agency is located in a section of the city that has a high crime rate, gang activity, and failing schools. The area has a diverse population with a large number of immigrants from Central and South America and a substantial African American population. The agency provides individual and family counseling services on a sliding fee scale. The agency also

---

(continued)

CASE SUMMARY

runs a number of educational and treatment groups as well as a temporary shelter for women and their children. Jackie has been assigned to work with the women and their children in the shelter. Her primary tasks are to provide concrete services and supportive counseling to the shelter residents.

Background Information

Elicia T and her daughter, Maria, are undocumented immigrants from Mexico. They have been in the United States for 5 years. Elicia and Maria fled to the area from another southwestern city to escape her abusive husband approximately 2 months ago. Elicia is 25 years old and Maria 8 years old. Elicia has a 2-year-old daughter, Sarah, who was placed in foster care because of suspected abuse in the home. Sarah is in a foster home in a small rural community in the state hundreds of miles from Elicia's current residence. Since moving to the area, Maria has not been attending school.

Elicia and Maria are currently residing in the agency's temporary shelter for families. They have been at the shelter for 2 weeks, and the agency has a 90-day limit. It is viewed as temporary housing, and the residents are only allowed to stay for 3 months. Prior to arriving at the shelter, Elicia and Maria were homeless and living on the streets.

Elicia is a high-school dropout and was a stay-at-home mother prior to leaving her husband and moving to a different part of the state. She chose to move there because she has two female cousins living in the area who are also undocumented immigrants. Elicia's native language is Spanish. She speaks some English but is not as comfortable speaking in English. Her English comprehension appears to be good. Maria speaks both English and Spanish well. When communicating with the staff, Maria acts as Elicia's interpreter since none of the staff at the shelter speak Spanish.

Maria appears to be behind academically. She struggles reading simple children's books written in English. It is unknown if her ability to read in Spanish is better than her English reading skills.

Other than her two cousins, Elicia has no other sources of support in the community. Her cousins have young families and limited resources but are well established and connected to a Latino community in the city and the local Catholic church. Her cousins refused to let Elicia and Maria live with them while she was trying to find her own place and a job. They stated that they did not have enough room and are concerned they would get in trouble with their landlord if it was found out that they were letting people stay with them. They sent her to the local church for help, and she was given the address for the agency's shelter by the priest.

Elicia has been looking for housing in the Latino community. The housing market is tight with limited options, and she has been unable to find anything that she could possibly afford. The only affordable housing she found was a room in a rundown motel that rents by the hour or by the month. It is in an area of town known for drug dealing and sex work.

On arrival in the community, Elicia found occasional work for a house cleaning company. The company hires undocumented workers, pays them very low cash wages, and threatens to turn them in to Immigration and Customs Enforcement (ICE) if they complain. The job bosses also exploit their female workers sexually, threatening to turn them in if they do not comply. Elicia was fearful about

(continued)

CASE SUMMARY

applying for other jobs because of her illegal status. She considered turning to sex work to be able to take care of her children, but her Catholic upbringing and thoughts of how doing so would shame her family have kept her from doing so. She is in constant fear of being detained, separated from her children, and having them placed in foster care. She is also afraid that she will end up homeless again and forced to live on the streets or return to her abusive husband.

Elicia is extremely reluctant to sign up for any federally funded services, even those that she and her children are entitled to receiving. On the suggestion that she enroll for supplemental food through SNAP, Elicia became nervous and refused as she has heard that participation in SNAP services, and others like them, would draw the attention of ICE, and she had heard stories on the news of individuals being deported after signing up for such programs.

Presenting Problems

Elicia and her children are facing multiple obstacles. They need to find permanent, affordable housing and a job that pays enough to cover her housing and living expenses. In addition, Maria needs to be enrolled in school. Elicia also wants to regain custody of her youngest daughter in foster care.

Additionally, Elicia is experiencing an immense amount of stress, anxiety, and possibly post-traumatic stress disorder (PTSD). She described an instance where she could not calm down her breathing, and she felt lightheaded. She is very fearful of men and tries to avoid all contact with men in the community. She reports difficulty sleeping at night and feeling exhausted most of the time.

She is concerned about Maria. She has started acting out at the shelter, getting into fights with the other children, disobeying her mother, and being disrespectful and defiant to the staff and other adults. Elicia and Maria fight frequently, and when Elicia tries to discipline Maria, she throws a temper tantrum until Elicia gives up.

Elicia has many strengths. She had the strength to leave her abusive husband and move to a different city. She loves her daughters. She wants desperately to keep Maria with her and hopes to have Sarah returned to her custody. She is resilient and has managed to survive and keep her daughter safe despite not having a place to stay, a job, and a limited support network. Additionally, Elicia is highly motivated to find her own accommodations and support her children.

■ Discussion Questions

1. If you were working with Elicia and Maria, what research would you need to locate and review to inform your practice? How would you go about finding this research?

2. As the social worker working with Elicia and Maria, how would research inform your practice? Provide two specific examples.

3. Identify a micropractice issue that you would address with Elicia and/or Maria. How would you informally evaluate your practice effectiveness for one of your identified issues? What client measure would you use?

4. Identify a second micropractice that you would address in your work with Elicia and/or Maria. How would you formally evaluate your practice effectiveness? What standardized measure would you use? What single-system design would you choose? What type of baseline would be appropriate and why?

■ References

Belmont Report. (1979). Retrieved from https://www.hhs.gov/ohrp/sites/default/files/the-belmont -report-508c_FINAL.pdf

Berlin, S., & Marsh, J. (1993). *Informing practice decisions.* New York, NY: Macmillan.

Bloom, M., Fischer, J., & Orme, J. (2009). *Evaluating practice: Guidelines for the accountable professional* (6th ed.). New York, NY: Pearson.

Caputo, R., Epstein, W., Stoesz, D., & Thyer, B. (2015). Postmodernism: A dead end social work epistemology. *Journal of Social Work Education, 51*(4), 638–647. doi:10.1080/10437797.2015.1076260

Carey, M. (2012). *Qualitative research skills for social work: Theory and practice.* Farnham, UK: Routledge.

Christopher, P. P., Garcia, S. L. G., Stein, M., Johnson, J., Rich, J., & Lidz, C. (2017). Enrolling in clinical research while incarcerated: What influences participants' decisions? *Hastings Center Report, 47*(2), 21–29. doi:10.1002/hast.686

Corcoran, K. (1992). Practice evaluation: Setting goals, measuring and assessing change. In K. Corcoran (Ed.), *Structuring change: Effective practice for common client problems* (pp. 28–47). Chicago, IL: Lyceum.

Corcoran, K., & Fischer, J. (2013). *Measures for clinical practice: A sourcebook* (Volumes 1 and 2, 5th ed.). London, UK: Oxford University Press.

Coulton, C. J., & Solomon, P. L. (1977). Measuring outcomes of intervention. *Social Work Research and Abstracts, 13,* 3–9. doi:10.1093/swra/13.4.3

Dybicz, P. (2015). From person-in-environment to strengths: The promise of postmodern practice. *Journal of Social Work Education, 51*(2), 237–249. doi:10.1080/10437797.2015.1012923

Engel, R. J., & Schutt, R. K. (2014). *Fundamentals of social work research* (2nd ed.). Los Angeles, CA: Sage.

Fong, M. L., & Cox, B. G. (1983). Trust as an underlying dynamic in a counseling process: How clients test trust. *Personal and Guidance Journal, 62,* 163–166. doi:10.1111/j.2164-4918.1983.tb00176.x

Gingerich, W. (1979). Procedure for evaluating clinical practice. *Health and Social Work, 4,* 104–130. doi:10.1093/hsw/4.2.104

Haynes, S. N. (1978). *Principles of behavioral assessment.* New York, NY: Gardner.

Jordan, C., & Franklin, C. (2015). *Clinical assessment for social workers: Quantitative and qualitative methods* (4th ed.). London: Oxford University Press.

Kirk, S. A., & Reid, W. J. (2002). *Science and social work: A critical appraisal.* New York, NY: Columbia University Press.

Krishef, C. H. (1991). *Fundamental approaches to single subject design and analysis.* Malabar, FL: Krieger Publishing Company.

Langer, C. L., & Lietz, C. A. (2015). *Applying theory to generalist social work practice.* Hoboken, NJ: Wiley.

Marlow, C. R. (2011). *Research methods for generalist social work* (5th ed.). Belmont, CA: Cengage Learning.

Maschi, T., & Leibowitz, G. S. (2017). *Forensic social work: Psychosocial and legal issues across diverse populations and settings* (2nd ed.). New York, NY: Springer Publishing Company.

McLaughlin, H. (2012). *Understanding social work research* (2nd ed.). Los Angeles, CA: Sage.

Miley, K., O'Melia, M., & DuBois, B. L. (2013). *Generalist social work practice: An empowering approach* (7th ed.). Boston, MA: Pearson.

National Association of Social Workers. (2017). *Code of ethics.* Silver Spring, MD: Author. Retrieved from https://www.socialworkers.org/About/Ethics/Code-of-Ethics/Code-of-Ethics-English

Nugent, W. R. (1992). Psychometric characteristics of self-anchored scales in clinical application. *Journal of Social Service Research, 3,* 137–152. doi:10.1300/J079v15n03_08

Nugent, W. R. (2009). *Analyzing single system design data*. London, UK: Oxford University Press.

Okpych, N. J., & Yu, L. H. U. (2014). A historical analysis of evidence-based practice in social work: The unfinished journey toward an empirically grounded profession. *Social Service Review, 88*(1), 3–58. doi:10.1086/674969

Poulin, J. (2010). *Strengths-based generalist practice: A collaborative approach* (3rd ed.). Belmont, CA: Cengage Learning.

Robinson, J. P., Shaver, P., & Wrightsman, L. S. (1991). *Measures of personality and social psychological attitudes*. San Diego, CA: Academic Press.

Royse, D., Thyer, B. A., & Padgett, D. K. (2016). *Program evaluation: An introduction to an evidence-based approach* (6th ed.). Boston, MA: Cengage.

Rubin, A., & Bellamy, J. (2012). *Practitioner's guide to using research for evidenced-based practice* (2nd ed.). Hoboken, NJ: Wiley.

Seaburg, J. R., & Gillespie, D. F. (1977). Goal attainment scaling: A critique. *Social Work Research and Abstracts, 13*, 43–56. doi:10.1093/swra/13.2.4

Shaw, I. (2016). *Social work science*. New York, NY: Columbia University Press.

Thyer, B. A., & Pignotti, M. (2015). *Science and pseudoscience in social work practice*. New York, NY: Springer Publishing Company.

Walsh, J. (2013). *Theories for direct social work practice* (3rd ed.). Stamford, CT: Cengage.

Western Connecticut State University. (2015). *Guide to evaluating web sites*. Retrieved from http://people.wcsu.edu/reitzj/res/evalweb.html

Willis, J. W. (2007). *Foundations of qualitative research: Interpretive and critical approaches*. Los Angeles, CA: Sage.

Yegidis, B. L., Weinbach, R. W., & Myers, L. L. (2018). *Research methods for social workers* (8th ed.). New York, NY: Pearson.

MEZZO- AND MACROPRACTICE
COMPETENCIES

MEZZOSYSTEMS ASSESSMENT: ORGANIZATIONS AND COMMUNITIES

JOHN POULIN | STEPHEN KAUFFMAN | MARINA BARNETT

John's foundation master of social work field placement is with a large nonprofit agency providing residential placement and foster care services to abused and neglected children and their families. The agency has a professional staff of about 200 social workers providing a wide range of services. During his first month, John worked closely with his field instructor to learn the agency's operating procedures and began his work with his caseload of foster children, biological parents, and foster families. He liked his field instructor, his team, and the work.

Over the next few months, John began to notice some concerning organizational issues. The first was that staff morale was very low. The vast majority of the social workers were unhappy, and many were looking for other jobs. The staff were distrustful of the administration, and a number of the social workers advised John to never admit any mistake and to be very careful in what he said to supervisors and administrators. John also began to realize that many of the social workers made disparaging comments and jokes about their clients. They seemed to view them as failures incapable of change and with almost no compassion or empathy.

As members of the staff left, the caseloads of the remaining staff were increased. Staff morale continued to plummet. By the end of his first semester, there were a number of unfilled positions and the workers' caseloads continued to increase. John found the atmosphere in the office depressing. There was very little interaction among the staff with most working behind closed doors. The staff were angry at the administration. The administration distrusted the staff, and neither the staff nor the administrators appeared to care about the clients.

LEARNING OBJECTIVES

This chapter focuses on assessing organizations and communities. This is the mezzo-component of Competency 7: Assess Individuals, Families, Groups, Organizations, and Communities. The chapter focuses on conducting ethical organizational and community assessments. By the end of this chapter, you will be able to:

- Identify the ethical principles and standards related to organizational and community assessment

- Describe five theories related to assessing organizations
- Design an organizational assessment
- Describe three theories related to assessing communities
- Design a community assessment

■ Competency 7: Assess Individuals, Families, Groups, Organizations, and Communities

Social workers understand that assessment is an ongoing component of the dynamic and interactive process of social work practice with, and on behalf of, diverse individuals, families, groups, organizations, and communities. Social workers understand theories of human behavior and the social environment, and critically evaluate and apply this knowledge in the assessment of diverse clients and constituencies, including individuals, families, groups, organizations, and communities. Social workers understand methods of assessment with diverse clients and constituencies to advance the practice effectiveness. Social workers recognize the implications of the larger practice context in the assessment process and value the importance of interprofessional collaboration in this process. Social workers understand how their personal experiences and affective reactions may affect their assessment and decision-making. Social workers:

- Collect and organize data, and apply critical thinking to interpret information from clients and constituencies
- Apply knowledge of human behavior and the social environment, person-in-environment, and other multidisciplinary theoretical frameworks in the analysis of assessment data from clients and constituencies
- Develop mutually agreed-on intervention goals and objectives based on the critical assessment of strengths, needs, and challenges within clients and constituencies
- Select appropriate intervention strategies based on the assessment, research knowledge, and values and preferences of clients and constituencies

This chapter focuses on the knowledge, skills, and values associated with assessing organizations and communities.

■ National Association of Social Workers (NASW) *Code of Ethics*

The NASW *Code of Ethics* (2017) has four ethical standards that are related to organizational and community assessment. The NASW *Code of Ethics* has ethical standards related to organizational assessment contained in the ethical responsibilities to the practice setting domain. The first is about advocating for adequate resources to meet client needs. The second is about ensuring adequate resources to provide staff supervision and the third is about ensuring a work environment that encourages compliance with the NASW Code of Ethics

(NASW, 2017). Compliance with these ethical standards requires some sort of organizational assessment in order to determine if the organization is meeting the resource needs of clients, providing adequate resources for staff supervision, and creating an organizational environment that is consistent with and encourages compliance with the *Code of Ethics*.

▶ **Critical Thinking Questions**

Based on the opening chapter case example:

1. What ethical standards potentially apply to the functioning of the agency?

2. As a social work intern, what could have John done to address possible ethical violations?

A fourth ethical standard related to organizational assessment is about improving agency policies and procedures to improve client services. Again, accomplishing this requires some kind of organizational assessment to identify policies and procedures that need to be improved.

The NASW *Code of Ethics* (2017) has two ethical standards under the ethical responsibilities to the broader society, which are relevant to assessing communities. The first ethical standard is about advocating for improved living conditions and the second is about facilitating public participation in the development of social policies and institutions. Compliance with both of these ethical standards requires some type of community assessment to identify community needs and resources.

■ Organizational Theories

This section focuses on a review of five widely used theories of organizations that are associated with the rational systems perspective. The rational systems perspective is the idea that an organization is a tool for achieving a definable goal or set of goals. A rational organization uses a formal structure to define the role of each member of the organization. The two main characteristics of rational systems are goal specificity and formalization. In an organization, where roles and goals are clearly defined, the process of management should be rational and predictable. The rational system theories reviewed in this chapter are scientific management, administrative theory, bureaucratic theory, rational decision-making theory, and organizational development theory. These five organizational theories are reviewed from the perspective of assessing organizational functioning.

Scientific Management

Fredrick Taylor published *The Principles of Scientific Management* in 1911. Taylor proposed a scientific approach to management aimed at deploying workers as efficiently as possible. He studied the use of the workforce and ways to improve production through activity analysis and time studies.

> Through the activity analyses, he was able to identify what activities workers had to perform when carrying out their tasks. He also conducted time measurements for all kinds of activities that were carried out by workers during the production process. In the methodology studies, he evaluated which working method could best be used to ensure maximum productivity. (Mulder, 2015, para 2)

Activities for administrators and workers were analyzed.

Taylor's activity analyses led him to conclude that certain people could work more efficiently than others. And that matching the right person with the right job tasks was an important aspect of organizational efficiency. Taylor developed four principles of scientific management. The four principles are as follows: use the most efficient way to perform work tasks, assign workers based on their skills, supervise work tasks, and allocate work so that managers plan and supervise (Fredrick Taylor and scientific management, 2019, para. 3).

Critics of Taylor's scientific management theory argue that it promotes the idea that there is "one right way" to do something and that it undervalues the social needs of people such as appreciation and recognition. Decisions are purely made on rational grounds in which performance measurement is a central component and that it is at odds with models stressing individual responsibility, autonomy, and shared decision-making (Mulder, 2015). Nevertheless, Taylor's ideas and principles have relevance for assessing agencies and organizations.

His principle for matching workers to their job based on capacity and motivation is critical in the delivery of social work services. People have different skill sets and not matching workers to jobs that fit their skill sets can have negative effects on worker morale and the delivery of client services. Social workers who are very effective in providing direct services to clients may not be well-suited to becoming a supervisor or team leader. "Getting people on the right bus and getting them in the right seat" (Collins, 2001) is a key to an effective organization. In the previous example, the social worker might have been on the right bus (human services) but not in the right seat (supervisor). Organizational assessments conducted by social workers and social work administrators that analyze the organization's workforce in terms of the fit between employees and their job tasks and responsibilities can contribute to more effective delivery of social work services to clients and constituencies (Case 9.1).

Taylor's use of time studies still has great relevance for social work organizations. Assessing how social work line staff, supervisors, and administrators spend their time on various job tasks can help improve organizational functioning and service delivery. This type of organizational assessment can be easily conducted by social workers and social work administrators.

Administrative Theory

Administrative theory was proposed by Henry Fayol in the early 1900s. Fayol studied the organizational problems from the manager's viewpoint. While Taylor's scientific management looked at production from the worker's perspective, administrative theory looked at productivity improvements from the manager's perspective. Fayol identified five functions of management and 14 management principles. The five basic elements of management are planning, organizing, commanding, coordinating, and controlling ("Note on Fayol's Administrative Management Theory," 2019). The 14 principles are employee specialization, manager authority, upholding discipline, employees have one supervisor, teams have one manager, general interests over individual interests, fair pay for employees, centralized decision-making, employees follow the chain of command, organized work environment, practice fairness to employees, minimize employee turnover, employee initiatives encouraged, and promoting team spirit and unity ("Henri Fayol's Principles of Management," 2019).

| CASE 9.1 | TOO MUCH PAPERWORK: USE OF TIME STUDIES TO IMPROVE ORGANIZATIONAL FUNCTION IN SOCIAL WORK PRACTICE |

In the opening case example, John found himself interning at a child welfare agency that was facing several organizational issues. Staff morale was low, and there appeared to be tension and distrust between the social workers and the agency's supervisors and administrators. The social workers voiced complaints about being overworked, underappreciated, and not heard. John, who needed a research project for his research and program evaluation class, proposed to his supervisor that he conduct a time study of the social work staff to get a better understanding of their work pressures and time demands. His supervisor liked the idea, and the project was approved by the agency administrators. The project was approved by his university institutional review board and was implemented at the beginning of his second semester of placement.

In short, a data collection form was designed. It required the workers to keep track of their activities and how much time they spent on each activity on a daily basis for a period of 3 weeks. The form contained a list of all the activities the social workers were expected to complete. The results were interesting and informative. The social workers on average only spent about 20% of their time in direct client contact. Most of the workers' time was spent doing paperwork (45%), followed by attending meetings (25%), and trying to figure out agency policies and procedures (10%). Based on the time study finding, the agency set up an agency task force to examine and review agency policies and procedures in the hope of simplifying them to reduce the amount of time the social workers spend on administrative functions and to increase client contact hours. Conducting the time study and creating a task force in themselves appeared to increase staff morale.

Administrative theory and Fayol's management functions and principles have relevance for assessing the organization of the managerial functions of human service organizations and performance of social work managers and administrators. The identified functions and principles provide a structure or components for an organizational assessment of the administrative functioning of the agency. It helps identify what should be assessed. The social worker and/or social work administrators determine how the assessment will be carried out.

Bureaucratic Theory

In the early 1900s Weber coined the term "bureaucracy" to describe organizations characterized by many rules, standardized processes, procedures, and requirements. Weber believed that bureaucracy was the most efficient way to set up an organization. "Bureaucracy is the basis for the systematic formation of any organization and is designed to ensure efficiency and economic effectiveness. It is an ideal model for management and its administration to bring an organization's power structure into focus" (Mulder, 2017, para. 4).

Weber identified six bureaucratic management principles: task specialization, hierarchical authority, formal selection, rules and requirements, impersonal, and career orientation. Each is briefly described in the following.

1. **Task specialization.** Tasks are divided into simple, routine categories on the basis of competencies and functional specializations. Every employee knows exactly what is expected of him or her and what his or her powers are within the organization. Every employee has a specific place within the organization and is expected to solely focus on his or her area of expertise. Going beyond your responsibilities and taking on tasks of colleagues is not permitted within a bureaucracy.

2. **Hierarchical authority.** Managers are organized into hierarchical layers, where each layer of management is responsible for its staff and overall performance. The hierarchy of authority is a system in which different positions are related in order of precedence and in which the highest rung on the ladder has the greatest power. The bottom layers of bureaucratic organizational structures are always subject to supervision and control of higher layers. This hierarchy reflects lines of bureaucratic communication and the degree of delegation, and clearly lays out how powers and responsibilities are divided.

3. **Formal selection.** All employees are selected on the basis of technical skills and competences, which have been acquired through training, education, and experience. One of the basic principles is that employees are paid for their services and that the level of their salary is dependent on their position.

4. **Rules and requirements.** Formal rules and requirements are required to ensure uniformity, so that employees know exactly what is expected of them. All administrative processes are defined in the official rules. By enforcing strict rules, the organization can more easily achieve uniformity and all employee efforts can be better coordinated.

5. **Impersonal.** Regulations and clear requirements create distant and impersonal relationships among employees. Decisions are made solely on the basis of rational factors, rather than personal factors.

6. **Career orientation.** Employees of a bureaucratic organization are selected on the basis of their expertise. The right division of labor within a bureaucratic organization also allows employees to specialize themselves further, so that they may become experts in their own field and significantly improve their performance. (Mulder, 2017, para. 6–11)

A benefit of bureaucracy is that large organizations can become structured and work effectively. The establishment of hierarchies, rules, and procedures allows for high efficiency and consistent execution of work by all employees. A major disadvantage of bureaucracy is characterized by a large amount of red tape, paperwork, and slow bureaucratic communication due to its many hierarchical layers. Another disadvantage is that it restricts innovation and problem-solving from nonadministrative employees. Nevertheless, bureaucratic theory can help shape organizational assessments in the same way as scientific management and administrative theory can. It identifies key organizational components for inclusion in an organizational assessment.

Rational Decision-Making Theory

Herbert Simon recognized that administration is largely a process of human decision-making with the publication of *Administrative Behavior: A Study of Decision-Making Processes in Administrative Organizations* in 1947. Administration is the behavioral and cognitive process of making rationale choices or decisions. Rational decision-making is a multistep process, from problem identification through solution, for making logically sound decisions. It is a multistep process for making choices among alternatives. The steps in the decision-making process include:

1. Formulating a goal(s)
2. Identifying the criteria for making the decision
3. Identifying alternatives
4. Performing an analysis
5. Making a final decision

Rational decision-making favors objective data and a formal process of analysis over subjectivity and intuition. The model of rational decision-making assumes that decision makers have full or perfect information about alternatives; it also assumes they have the time, cognitive ability, and resources to evaluate each choice against the others. This model assumes that people will make choices that will maximize benefits for themselves and minimize any cost and that measurable criteria exist for which data can be collected and analyzed. The rational decision-making model does not consider factors that cannot be quantified, such as ethical concerns or the value of altruism. It leaves out consideration of personal feelings, loyalties, or sense of obligation.

Critics of rational choice theory—or the rational model of decision-making—claim that this model makes unrealistic and oversimplified assumptions. The model assumes that people have full (or perfect) information. This is rarely the case. Often the information is not available, the person might not be able to access it, or it might take too much time or too many resources to acquire. Additionally, individual rationality is limited by a person's ability to conduct analysis and think through competing alternatives. The more complex a decision, the greater the limits are to making completely rational choices (Rational and Non-Rational decision Making, 2019).

In response to the limitations of rational decision-making theory, Simon proposed the idea of bounded rationality (1994). Bounded rationality recognizes that individuals' rationality is limited by the information they have, the cognitive limitations of their minds, and the finite amount of time they have to make a decision. While acknowledging that decision-making is a rational process, it recognizes that people act on the basis of limited information. Because decision makers usually lack full information, they instead apply their rationality to a set of choices that are bounded by the more satisfying (rather than maximizing or optimizing) choices in complex situations.

Collaborative decision-making is an alternative to a hierarchical approach to decision-making. It applies a group decision-making model to the rational decision-making process. Collaborative decision-making is an inclusionary process that promotes lateral communication and shared decision-making. Its strength is that it fosters a greater buy-in to the decisions and increased stakeholder participation in the decision process. Collaboration can offer members full responsibility for achieving change. By enhancing members' roles in governance and decision-making, buy-in to implementation and the outcomes will be strengthened.

Collaborative decision-making is a process with 11 guiding principles. The guiding principles are: people need a reason to participate, involve all those with a significant interest, educate all the participants, participation is voluntary, everyone has an opportunity to participate in the design of the collaborative process, the process is flexible, egalitarian, respectful, time-limited, accountable, and achievable (Principles of Decision Making, 2019).

When implementing a collaborative decision-making approach, organizations need to determine the method that will be used. The two most common approaches are the consensus and democratic approaches. The consensus approach involves the entire group in the decision-making process. The goal of consensus decision-making is to find common ground, exploring issues and opinions from everyone's perspective. Discussions leading to consensus aim to bring the group to mutual agreement by addressing all concerns. Consensus does not require unanimity. Rather, everyone must agree they can "live with" the decision.

Democratic decision-making involves discussing options fully so that members are informed as to the decision's consequences. Decisions are then made by majority vote. The important ground rule here is that the "losing" side agrees to support the decision, even though it was not their first choice.

Decision-making theory, the concept of bounded rationality, and collaborative decision-making models help inform the assessment of organizational decision-making and communication. The decision-making function in human service organizations can profoundly impact the availability and quality of service delivery to clients. It can also significantly affect the organizational climate, the work environment, and morale of the agency's direct service workers as well as its supervisors and managers.

Organizational Development Theory

Lewin is generally considered the founder of organizational development theory in the 1940s and 1950s. Organizational development focuses on expanding the knowledge and effectiveness of people to accomplish more successful organizational change and performance. It is a comprehensive strategy for organizational improvement, particularly through a more effective and collaborative management culture.

The objectives of organizational development are:

1. To increase the level of trust and support among organizational members
2. To increase the incidence of confrontation of organizational problems, both within groups and among groups, in contrast to "sweeping problems under the rug"
3. To create an environment in which designation of assigned roles is augmented based on knowledge and skills
4. To increase the openness of communication laterally, vertically, and diagonally
5. To increase the level of personal enthusiasm and satisfaction in the organization

6. To find synergistic solutions to problems with greater frequency. Synergistic solutions are creative solutions in which 2 + 2 equals more than 4, and through which all parties gain more through cooperation than through conflict

7. To increase the level of self and group responsibility in planning and implementation (French & Bell, 1999)

Lewin identified three key areas of organizational functioning: organizational climate, organizational culture, and organizational strategies. The organizational climate is the mood or unique "personality" of an organization. The administrators' and managers' attitudes and beliefs about organizational practices help create organizational climate and influence members' collective behavior. Climate features and characteristics may be associated with employee satisfaction, stress, service quality and outcomes and successful implementation of new programs. Climate features and characteristics include leadership, openness of communication, participatory management, role clarity, conflict resolution, leader support, and leader control.

The organizational culture is the deeply seated norms, values, and behaviors that members share. The elements of an organization's culture include assumptions, values, behavioral norms, behavioral patterns, and organizational artifacts. These elements help shape the organization's behavior and the decision-making process. Organizational strategies on the other hand are the actions taken to create organizational change and improvement. Change strategies usually involve four action steps. The first is diagnosis. Diagnosis is done to identify problem areas and underlying causes. An organizational development approach to diagnosis seeks to identify problems by examining the organization's mission, goals, policies, structures, and technologies; climate and culture; environmental factors; desired outcomes; and readiness to take action (French & Bell, 1999).

The second action step is planning. Organizations need to formulate change plans and strategies. The planning step involves identifying options and assessing feasibility. At this stage, the preferred strategy or strategies are identified as are the goals and objectives of the planned intervention strategy. The third action step is intervention. This results in the identified plan being put into action to address the identified need and diagnosed problem(s). The final and fourth action step is evaluation. This involves assessing the planned change efforts by tracking the organization's progress in implementing the change and by documenting its impact on the organization.

Organizational development theory has great relevance for organizational assessment. Organizational development theory identifies three major components of organizations that greatly impact an organization's ability to achieve its goals and objectives. Organizational climate, culture, and the strategies employed to improve an organization's performance impact the delivery of services to clients as well as the job satisfaction, commitment, and motivation of the professional staff and administrators.

■ Organizational Assessment

There are a number of possible reasons to conduct an organizational assessment. An organizational assessment can be useful in identifying an organization's strengths and weaknesses. They are often used to:

■ Provide stakeholders with information about the organization's performance and generate information that will be useful in planning and decision-making

■ Identify resources (human and otherwise) that the organization can use to effectively improve its performance

■ Identify needs that should be addressed through specific actions

■ Respond to a need or desire to change an organization's performance

Organizational assessments can also be used to help make strategic decisions. Should the organization grow or change its mission? An organizational assessment can also be helpful in making program decisions. Should you expand your programs? Should you offer new services? Organizational assessments can also help with funding decisions as well as staffing considerations.

The key to a good assessment is knowing what represents optimal functioning of the organization. Yet, at the same time, there is no "one best way" to construct an organization to meet all desired ends. Organizations may be structured in any one of a number of ways, each of which may be effective at achieving the goals of the organization under some conditions but at the same time may be problematic under other conditions. Various groups or "constituencies" make up an organization. These may include line staff, supervisors, support staff, administration, clients, and external collaborators. Each typically has their own set of needs and perceptions about the organization, and thus each will have something valuable to contribute to the assessment (Kauffman, 2010).

Table 9.1 shows the organizational components that are covered by the five organizational theories reviewed in this chapter. Taken together, the five organizational theories cover almost all functions of an organization. When designing an organizational assessment, the organizational dimensions shown in Table 9.1 provide the beginning of a list of the basic organizational components to include in the assessment.

TABLE 9.1 Organizational Theories and Organizational Assessment in Social Work Practice

THEORY	ORGANIZATIONAL DIMENSION
Scientific management	Worker tasks and functions Worker/task fit
Administrative theory	Manager effectiveness Administrative functioning
Bureaucratic theory	Task specialization Hierarchical authority Formal selection Rules and requirements Impersonal Career orientation
Rational decision-making theory	Decision-making process
Organizational development	Organizational climate Organizational culture Organizational strategies

Social service organizations, like all organizations, have the dimensions or components listed in Table 9.1. These dimensions can be classified into two broad groups: internal and environmental characteristics. From each of these groupings is found many elements that strengthen and support the organization, or act as stressors or obstacles to optimal functioning. The characteristics within each group contribute to organizational functioning and are important components of an organizational assessment.

Internal Organizational Characteristics

Beyond the issues of identity, a large number of elements are associated with the internal characteristics of the organization that need to be included in an assessment. These characteristics can be placed into three groupings: foundation policies, internal structure, and internal processes. Elements from each grouping must be examined for their possible usefulness as strengths to the organization or serving as an obstacle or stressor to the organization (Kauffman & Barnett, 2019).

Foundation Policies

Foundation policies refer to the documents and guidelines (generally written) that give meaning and guidance to the agency. Organizations exist for a purpose, and these policies express both this purpose and a description of the overarching structure and processes of the organization. At the same time, simply because something is written does not mean it is followed, and it may be that this disconnect between what is written and what is real may cause some of the organizations' difficulties. The most important types of foundation policies are the constitution and bylaws, vision, mission, goals, and strategic plans.

Organizational Mission and Vision

Organizations are guided by a set of principles outlined in their mission. Mission statements specify the fundamental purpose of the organization. The mission statement documents the needs that the organization seeks to address (purpose), specifies how the organization addresses those needs (business), and states the principles or beliefs (values) of the organization. According to Kettner, Moroney, and Rettman (2017), the mission statement "should focus on what lies ahead for its clients and or consumers if the agency is successful in addressing their problems and meeting their needs" (p. 110).

Organizations also have vision statements. Vision statements are statements of the future. They are statements about what the organization hopes to become. The values and philosophy of the organization determine the priorities of the mission and the design and implementation of programs and activities. The organization's mission and vision statements set the stage to identify programs and activities.

An assessment of an organization's mission and vision would involve examination of the statements themselves to determine clarity of content as well as the extent to which the mission and vision statements are consistent with the organization's programs and services. Are the mission and vision statements guiding the organization's programs and services, initiatives, and the operation of the organization? To what extent are the mission and vision statements guiding the direction and functioning of the agency?

Organizational Goals and Objectives

Much of what has been stated about microsystem client goals and the goal setting process applies to mezzosystems as well. Organizational goals are the statements of the desired qualities in human and social conditions. Goals suggest intended outcomes, provide organizational direction, and provide standards or criteria for evaluation and legitimacy (Coley & Scheinberg, 2017). Goals are broad, nonmeasurable statements that describe a "desired state."

Goals are often confused with objectives, but these are not interchangeable concepts. While goals provide the direction for the organization's focus, objectives establish precise expectations of what the organization is attempting to achieve, including a time frame (Kettner et al., 2017). Objectives are the means by which the goals are achieved. While goals are broad statements of what we would like to see, objectives should be specific, measurable, achievable, realistic, and time-bound.

In assessing an organization's goals and objectives, first determine if the goals are written in terms of a broad desired end state. Are the goals broad statements about what the organization hopes to achieve? Are the goals nonmeasurable statements of a desired positive outcome? On the other hand, are the organization's objectives specific and measurable? Do they describe in very concrete terms exactly what will be accomplished? Are they measurable and achievable? Are the organization's objectives time-limited and related to a single result? Box 9.1 includes examples of two organizational goals and their associated objectives.

BOX 9.1

SAMPLE ORGANIZATIONAL GOALS AND OBJECTIVES

Goal 1: Seven Arrows Center will provide a variety of effective, evidence-based substance abuse treatment services, both inpatient and outpatient, to all persons in need in the North Hills region.

> *Objective 1.1*: To provide inpatient, residential treatment services to a minimum of 250 clients per year.

> *Objective 1.2*: To provide methadone maintenance services for a maximum of 500 clients per year.

> *Objective 1.3*: To provide outpatient counseling services for a maximum of 1,000 clients per year.

Goal 2: Seven Arrows Center will achieve the highest standards of quality through support of staff, nondiscriminatory practices, and community involvement.

> *Objective 2.1*: Seven Arrows Center will provide a minimum of 100 hours of advanced training to each staff member each year.

> *Objective 2.2*: Staff satisfaction will be maximized by establishing a benefits package, customized for each employee, that will include health and dental care, retirement plans, and rotating sabbaticals for all full-time employees.

> *Objective 2.3*: To establish a Community Advisory Board to assist the agency in developing policies that help the agency better meet community needs.

Internal Structure

The structure of an organization varies dramatically by the purposes of the organization, but there are some commonalities that crosscut most types. Simply stated, these are the administration, frontline workers, as well as a large variety of support staff. The central questions that an assessment should focus on here relate to the qualifications and skills of each of the positions in these structural components, as well as how staff are supported and/or how the work responsibilities create burdens for the staff (Kauffman, 2010).

Thus, most social workers are in administrative, middle-line, or frontline positions. These are the workers who are most concerned with the primary tasks of the organization, whatever they may be. Generally, administrators are concerned with the overall functioning of the organization. This often includes policy development, planning, personnel, resource development and acquisition, compliance with external (and legal) requirements, as well as leadership and setting the tone of the organization. In other words, the administration sets the informal climate of the organization. A climate where workers feel supported can go a long way in overcoming the stress that is created by clients or the environment that the organization rests. On the other hand, a climate that feels oppressive and uncaring may make even pleasant work tasks feel stressful.

Supervisors (the middle line), on the other hand, serve as intermediaries between the administration and the frontline worker. Their task in the human service organization is to translate policies from the administration to the frontline, communicate information both up and down the chain of command, oversee job function, and provide guidance to the frontline worker. The quality by which these functions are carried out may be a source of either serious problems for the organization and/or its greatest successes. The assumption is that the supervisor understands both the needs and problems of the frontline worker, while also understanding the work requirements of the administration.

Finally, the frontline represents the employee who is most responsible for carrying out the primary tasks of the organization. In social service agency settings, this usually applies to working with people in some form. The tasks of the frontline staff are vastly different depending on the agency's function, so it is somewhat difficult to provide any generalities. It is, however, critical to consider frontline workers' training, education, preparedness, and support. The quality of their work is a function of their ability, resources, and workload.

Internal Processes

How the staff and structure operate represent the final element of the internal organizational considerations. These are what are called the processes, and how they function often proves to be the most problematic concerns for an organization. Among these, the most well-known are power (and its manifestations as authority and leadership) and information (and its manifestation as communication).

Every organization demonstrates some degree of applied power. It is this applied power that ensures that the right work is done in the right amount at the right time. This form of power is what people refer to as authority, or the degree and type of control exerted within the organization.

How this authority is applied, in what settings, and to what degree need to be considered. Authority that is used correctly and judiciously will be positive for the organization, while incorrectly applied authority may damage or hurt the organization. Most particularly, authority is necessary to motivate staff to move the organization in the desired direction. This is a function of leadership. Staff may work to achieve organizational goals without some form of external authority, but the odds of success are greatly improved in the presence of an effective leader. Organizational assessments very often find that the problems that exist in the social service agency are closely connected to the quality of the leadership provided, and how well the leader manages the agency. Thus, a good assessment will spend time examining the quality of leadership.

Along with authority, a second internal process is information and how this information is communicated. An organization cannot function without the free flow of information both up and down the structure. A number of obstacles can affect the flow of communication, and as with leadership, a major focus of an organizational assessment should be on communication.

Organizational Environmental Considerations

From the standpoint of assessment, there are a number of direct variables that might be included. For example, a major potential barrier to any organization is access to resources. Resources for different organizations may mean different things—people, technology, and information are examples. But few, if any, social service organizations can continue to exist for very long without one critically important resource—money.

The methods and degree of success by which the agency is able to fund its services affect almost all aspects of the agency, from the quality of services provided to the level of employee satisfaction. The key questions relating to resources are simple enough—Is funding adequate, has there been a change in the funding source, and/or is the method effective? In any case, funding shortages or even the possibility of changes in funding can be enough to cause significant fear and disruption to the agency.

Technology has and continues to change at impressive rates. In brief, technology is how the organization does what it does. It may be counseling, or methadone maintenance, or community organization, or use of computers. The big issue associated with technology that any assessment should consider is its effectiveness.

Organizational Assessment: How to Assess and What Tools to Use

Burke and Litwin (1992) developed a performance and change model that identifies the primary variables that need to be considered to understand an organization's functioning. The model is shown in Figure 9.1.

The Burke–Litwin model is a helpful tool in structuring an organizational assessment. One of its strengths is that it shows the interrelationships among the various organizational variables. Table 9.2 lists the model's 12 organizational variables and some sample assessment questions for each variable.

Conducting an organizational assessment allows an agency to evaluate whether it is meeting its mission and its goals. The first step in designing an assessment is to identify the variables or components of the organization that will be assessed. The second step is to determine how to assess and what tools to use. What methodology will be used to collect the data?

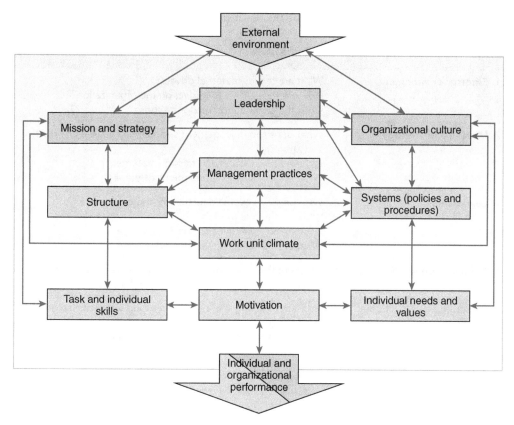

FIGURE 9.1 Burke–Litwin model of organizational performance and change.

Almost any research methodology can be used. Two of the more common organizational assessment methods are given in the following.

Focus Groups

Focus groups are a wonderfully flexible method that may be used to gain a large amount of data quickly under almost any set of conditions—with the exception of a constituency that is unable to carry on a conversation. At its most general, a focus group is a group of six to 15 (usually) similar persons who are led through a series of open-ended questions with the purpose of finding consensus answers. Focus groups are very helpful in understanding the why question. A major limitation is the lack of representativeness of the findings. Another limitation is the inability to provide descriptive data on the magnitude and scope of the issue being assessed.

Observational Performance Ratings

A second approach toward assessment involves observation of the functioning of the organization, and then rating what is seen. There are a large number of organizational assessment tools that can be used. Many of them are either in the public domain or may be used with the permission of the persons who hold the copyright.

TABLE 9.2 Organizational Variables of the Burke–Litwin Model

DIMENSIONS OF MODEL	KEY QUESTIONS
1. External environment	■ What are the key external drivers? ■ How are these likely to impact on the organization? ■ Does the organization recognize these?
2. Mission and strategy	■ What does top management see as the organization's mission and strategy? ■ Is there a clear vision and mission statement? ■ What are employees' perceptions of these?
3. Leadership	■ Who provides overall direction for the organization? ■ Who are the role models? ■ What is the style of leadership? ■ What are the perspectives of employees?
4. Organizational culture	■ What are the overt and covert rules, values, customs, and principles that guide organizational behavior?
5. Structure	■ How are functions and people arranged in specific areas and levels of responsibility? ■ What are the key decision-making, communication, and control relationships?
6. Systems	■ What are the organization's policies and procedures, including systems for reward and performance appraisal, management information, human resources, and resource planning?
7. Management practices	■ How do managers use human and material resources to carry out the organization's strategy? ■ What is their style of management, and how do they relate to subordinates?
8. Work unit climate	■ What are the collective impressions, expectations, and feelings of staff? ■ What is the nature of relationship with work unit colleagues and those in other work units?
9. Task and individual skills	■ What are the task requirements and individual skills/abilities/knowledge needed for task effectiveness? ■ How appropriate is the organization's "job–person" match?
10. Individual needs and values	■ What do staff members value in their work? ■ What are the psychological factors that would enrich their jobs and increase job satisfaction?
11. Motivation	■ Do staff feel motivated to take the action necessary to achieve the organization's strategy? ■ Of factors 1 through 10, which seem to be impacting motivation the most?
12. Individual and organizational performance	■ What is the level of performance in terms of productivity, customer satisfaction, quality, and so on? ■ Which factors are critical for motivation and therefore performance?

Some useful examples of these types of tools include the Checklist of Nonprofit Organizational Indicators (Greater Twin Cities United Way, 2019) developed by Minneapolis United Way to help clarify organizational strengths and weaknesses. The rating is a very simple "Needs Work," "Met," or "Not Met" in several areas, including performance indicators in legal issues, governance, human resources, planning, financial, and fundraising (Greater Twin Cities United Way, 2019). The form can even be completed online for free (www .surveymonkey.com/s.asp?u=3754722401).

■ Community Theories

Community Development Theory

Community development theory has taken a number of forms. Schiele (2005) defines community development collective problem-solving, self-help, and empowerment. Paiva (1977) identified four major concepts of community development: structural change, socioeconomic integration, institutional development, and institutional renewal. What the various definitions have in common is a focus on the capacity building and empowerment of the local community in order to bring socioeconomic, political, and environmental changes to the community.

> The goal and substance of social development is the welfare of the people, as determined by the people themselves, and the consequent creation or alteration of institutions (including people's values, individual behavior, and motivation) so as to create a capacity for meeting human needs at all levels (especially those at the lower levels) and for improving the quality of human relationships and relationships between people and societal institutions. (Paiva, 1977, p. 329)

Tan's influential 2009 paper on community development theory and practice incorporated Perkins's (1982) three Rs of community development: relocation, redistribution, and reconciliation. Relocation refers to the physical relocation of the social worker or another change agent into the community he or she seeks to serve. Relocation highlights the collaborative and empowering aspects of community development theory. In this model the social worker is a community partner and not an outside expert.

> Relocation allows for the social worker to develop shared experiences with his or her clients. It allows for a more authentic ability to build rapport with clients and, especially in diverse and oppressed communities, can serve as a tremendous and powerful catalyst in establishing trust. (Tan, 2009, pp. 9–10)

In addition to physically relocating to the community, relocation in community development theory also refers to the relocation of power back to the community. This entails collaboration with community members, a belief in people's abilities to solve their own community's problems, and the development of indigenous leadership.

Redistribution refers to the acquisition or redistribution of resources. "Redistribution, from a framework of Community Development, requires first the identification of issues of injustice and gaps in resources and then the collective advocacy of the community to secure those resources" (Tan, 2009, p. 11). Oppressed communities by definition lack resources.

Community development theory emphasizes the importance of increasing available resources to strengthen and improve community well-being.

Reconciliation in community development is the process of acknowledging roles of the oppressed and oppressors in the hopes of creating a new or changed relationship. The emphasis is on the oppressor's awareness of his or her role in the oppression. Thus, an important tenet of community development theory and community development practice is the reconciliation between the social worker and the community members. "Reconciliation calls into account the past or present hurt and oppression individual clients or entire communities bring into the helping relationship" (Tan, 2009, p. 12).

Some of the core principles of community development theory include:

- *Community participation.* All members of the community can make valued contributions and are invited to participate in the change process.

- *Community ownership.* Community members have ownership and control of the decision-making process and the community change efforts.

- *Empowerment.* Power is vested in the community and its members. Change occurs through empowering individuals and communities.

- *Indigenous leadership.* Sustained community change can only occur when the knowledge, skills, and expertise of the community members are strengthened, and leadership is in the hands of community members.

- *Social action.* Factors that negatively impact the community are analyzed and addressed through collective action.

- *Structural change.* Structural change is critical to community development. Without it, there can be no significant impact on the community and peoples' well-being.

A community development theory places the social worker firmly in the role of facilitator, not expert. The social worker's job is to help the development of community leadership, mobilization and development of community change strategies. It is about helping organize self-help rather than providing expertise and leading change efforts.

Conflict Theory

Conflict is a relationship where two or more parties want the same resources, power, status, or control and both parties act on their desire (Hardcastle, Powers, & Wenocur, 2011). Conflict theory has its roots in classical Marxism and Marx's theory of dialectical materialism, which provides a basis for understanding and distinguishing power differentials in relationships (Langer & Lietz, 2015). Marx identified four principles or assumptions of conflict theory. They are:

1. Conflict is inevitable.

2. There is an unequal distribution of power in relationships.

3. There is an ongoing struggle for scarce resources.

4. Whoever has the most power controls the distribution of resources. (Langer & Lietz, 2015, p. 102)

Dahrendorf (1959) viewed social systems as dynamic systems in a constant state of change resulting in ongoing conflict. Dahrendorf, as well as Marx, believed that social systems systematically generate conflict and that conflict is a pervasive feature of society. He also postulated that conflict is dialectical in that the resolution of one conflict creates a new set of opposed interests, which creates further conflict (Hardcastle et al., 2011). In short, unequal distribution of scarce resources and power among dominant and subordinate groups creates conflict.

Conflict theory helps explain how power structures and power disparities impact people's lives. Power is unequally divided in every society. Structural inequalities contribute to and maintain various forms of oppression and social, economic, and environmental injustices. Dominant groups maintain social order through manipulation and control. But social change can be achieved through conflict—that is, interrupting periods of stability. In this theory, life is characterized by conflict (either open or through exploitation) instead of consensus. By addressing these asymmetric power relationships and the distribution of resources, social workers can help disadvantaged and oppressed communities improve the well-being of individuals, families, and communities. Conflict theory helps social workers empower communities and community members to create change. Rather than helping people adjust to the "status quo," social work practice from a conflict theory perspective seeks transformative change through a redistribution of power and resources.

▶ **Critical Thinking Questions**
1. What are the similarities between community development theory and conflict theory?
2. How are they different?

In terms of community assessment, conflict theory highlights the need to assess community power structures, decision-making processes, and the allocation and distribution of resources to the community. Social workers conducting community assessments can also use conflict theory to help assess a community's willingness and readiness to engage in the struggle to increase power and obtain needed resources through personal and social change.

Structural Functionalism

Structural functionalism theory sees society as a complex system whose parts work together to promote solidarity and stability. Two theorists, Herbert Spencer and Robert Merton, were major contributors to this perspective. Important concepts in functionalism include social structure, social functions, manifest functions, and latent functions.

Social Structure

Society is viewed as having interrelated parts or structures designed to meet the biological and social needs of the individuals in that society. These structures are relatively stable patterns of social behavior. They give shape to our lives. Social structures are the social patterns through which a society is organized and can be horizontal or vertical. Horizontal social structure refers to the social relationships and the social and physical characteristics of communities to which individuals belong, while vertical social structure refers to ways in which a society or group ranks people in a hierarchy.

Social structures at the macrolevel are the major social institutions and patterns of institutionalized relationships. The major social institutions include family, religion, education, media, law, politics, and economy. These are understood as distinct institutions that are interrelated and interdependent and together help compose the overarching social structure of a society.

At the mezzolevel, social structure refers to the experiences of groups and the interactions among groups. It is the social networks that have been organized by the social institutions and institutionalized social relationships. The social networks act as structuring forces by shaping the opportunities that may or may not be available, and by fostering particular behavioral and interactional norms that determine social relationships. For example, sexism fosters discrimination against women, which results in male-dominated social networks and interaction patterns.

At the microlevel, social structure refers to everyday interactions among people in the forms of norms and customs. Micro–social structures are what we expect from others, how we expect to be seen by them, and how we interact together. It is the way we interact with others based on institutionalized norms and customs of behavior.

Social Functions

Structural functionalism theory postulates that all social structures have social functions. Social functions serve as the purposes of social structures. For example, education serves several important social functions in society, such as socialization, learning, and social status. Social functions can also be divided into manifest and latent functions.

Manifest and Latent Functions

Manifest functions are those that are intended and recognized. Latent functions are unrecognized and unintended. A manifest function of college education, for example, includes gaining knowledge, preparing for a career, and finding a good job that utilizes that education. These are the intended purposes of the social process of education. Latent functions of education could be questioning your values and beliefs, meeting people from diverse backgrounds, and finding new and unexpected interests and activities. Latent functions can be beneficial, neutral, or harmful. Social processes that have undesirable consequences for the operation of society are called **dysfunctions.** In education, examples of dysfunction include getting bad grades, truancy, dropping out, not graduating, and not finding suitable employment.

A major criticism of structural functionalism theory is that it supports the status quo. Structural functionalism does not account for the possibilities of social change. It is an equilibrium model based on assumptions of consensus. Conflict situations have been neglected. Social institutions, because they are considered to be functional, cannot be changed or abolished without endangering the social system. Social change is not addressed by structural functionalism theory.

Structural functionalism theory can contribute to designing a community assessment. One of its contributions would be in the social structures in the community and their interrelationships. The structures and their relationships impact the functioning of the community. Assessing their manifest and latent functioning can help identify areas of dysfunction that can lead to recommendations for improved functioning and change.

■ Community Assessment

One approach Tina could pursue in Case 9.2 would be to use a community development and/ or conflict theory approach in conducting the needs assessment. Both theoretical approaches focus on building relationships with community members in assessing community needs. With these perspectives, the community is viewed as capable of identifying and addressing its own issues. As a social worker, you are a partner in the assessment process. You provide technical assistance and support to the community members and constituent groups. The following section describes the steps in conducting a community needs assessment (Barnett, 2010).

CASE 9.2   IT'S NOT JUST ME, IT'S A COMMUNITY PROBLEM: CONDUCTING A NEEDS ASSESSMENT IN SOCIAL WORK PRACTICE

Trina is a first-year master of social work student placed in an inner-city school district as a school social worker intern. She has been working with Adia, a fifth-grade girl who has been skipping school. Sessions with Adia reveal that she does not like coming to school because she is being teased by other students in the class. Trina schedules a home visit with Adia's parents to discuss the truancy issue. Adia's parents both work at the local university. Adia's mother is an administrative assistant, and her father is a security guard.

"I don't know what to do with that girl." Adia's mother states dispiritedly. "I take her to school every day and drop her off myself. She won't stay. Those kids down there are so mean to her. We've tried to help her lose weight, her doctor says that she is 25 pounds overweight now and it seems to be getting worse. She has gained 10 pounds in the past 3 months since this mess all started." "We try to keep the junk out of the house," said Adia's father, "but she sneaks it. And that cafeteria is the worst! Hot dogs, hamburgers, pizza, hot wings! Soda machines in the cafeteria and candy galore in the school store. The homemade lunches we send with her every day can't compete with that. Not to mention that they just got rid of another gym period at the school in order to give more time to preparing for the achievement tests. We can't keep up."

Trina asks the parents if they are members of the home and school associations. Both parents indicate that their schedules are hectic and that they do not have time to attend the meetings. Trina lets them know that there is a meeting scheduled every third Wednesday at 7:30 p.m. The meetings only last an hour, and Trina encourages them to come to the meeting to discuss their concerns about the nutrition and exercise program at the school. Adia's mother attends the meeting and brings up the issues. At the meeting, she meets several parents who have the same concerns. They form a committee to investigate the issue further.

(continued)

CASE 9.2

The next day, Trina receives a call from Adia's mother. Several of the parents are getting together to discuss a strategy for addressing obesity among their children, and she invites Trina to attend. Trina asks if it is okay to invite her supervisor and the school nurse to the meeting. At the meeting, the school nurse indicates that their last round of health screenings indicated that as many as 20% of the youth in the district are overweight.

Trina is excited about the possibility of helping the parents with their concerns about the health of their children. Her field instructor discusses the possibilities and decides to suggest conducting a needs assessment to the group to gather data on the extent of obesity in the school district and possible causes and consequences.

Community Needs Assessments

Community needs assessments help to empower community residents to create services and programs that respond to their challenges, concerns, and opportunities. It is a systematic way to identify the resources and needs of residents by gathering data, soliciting the perspectives of residents and leaders, and surveying service providers and other community resources (Samuels, Ahsan, & Garcia, 1995, p. 8).

The social worker and the community partners develop a community profile that incorporates the use of quantitative statistics, demographic indicators, focus groups, and key informant interviews that provide information on political and sociocultural factors. Needs assessments can be used to:

1. Determine if an intervention exists in a community

2. Determine if there are enough clients with a particular problem to justify creating a new program

3. Determine if existing interventions are known or recognized by potential clients

4. Determine what barriers prevent clients from accessing existing services

5. Document the existence of an ongoing or exacerbating social problem (Royse, Thyer, Padgett, & Logan, 2005, p. 53)

Regardless of how the needs assessment will be used, the process entails the identification and documentation of issues identified by the community that represent an issue, problem, or gap in services that needs to be addressed. The following outlines the steps to completing a needs assessment and the activities associated with each stage (Philadelphia Health Management Corporation, 1997).

Stages and Activities in Conducting Needs Assessments
Step 1: Define the Goal

When conducting a needs assessment, it is important to understand how you want to use it. Generalist social workers utilize needs assessments to provide information to mobilize for social action, identify potential partners, and to develop "buy-in" for the community. The key to conducting an assessment from the empowerment perspective is to have the needs defined by the community, not by the social worker.

Step 2: *Define the Community*

As stated earlier, communities encompass various geographic localities, interests, and a diversity of people. It is necessary to define the boundaries of the community in which you are working. Examples of community definitions may include physical boundaries (counties, zip codes, neighborhoods where the agency provides services) or may include a specific population (immigrants from Vietnam, Spanish-speaking residents). It is important to involve the community members in the needs assessment process. Often indigenous residents are able to uncover issues that may not be known to the professional community.

Step 3: *Identify and Collect Existing Data*

In documenting the needs of a community, multiple sources of information and a variety of research methodologies are available to you. A mixed methods approach to analyzing needs will allow for a balanced presentation of the information that not only describes phenomena in a community, but also may provide information on the history of the phenomena and potential explanations for causes or contributing factors. You can find information about a social problem in a variety of places. A good place to start is with your clients and professionals in the field who may know something about the existence of the problem that you are trying to address. You will also need to obtain data from the research literature as well as from existing sources of secondary data.

Effective needs assessments must be grounded in the research literature. In conducting analyses of the literature, we want to consider the following questions: What do we know about the causes and consequences of the problem? What is the magnitude and scope of the problem? What has worked? What has not worked? How does the target community or population vary from those reported in the literature?

Answers to these and other questions place your needs assessment within a context and provide a basis for comparing the significance of the problem being studied and the relevance of the proposed solution with the problem in general and in other communities.

The use of multiple population-based and resource-based information is needed to provide a demographic assessment of the community. Population-based information includes the use of census data, public health vital statistics data, and community surveys conducted by either professionals or community residents. These data are generally available from government agencies at the federal, state, and local levels. Census data are available online (www.census.gov) and can be analyzed by state, county, municipality, and census track. A wealth of population and neighborhood data are contained within the census data. In addition to federal data, "every state maintains a wealth of useful data for planners and evaluators" (Royse et al., 2005, p. 59). Most states have databases of crime and arrest statistics, health indicators, teen pregnancy rates, educational statistics, and many other kinds of information that can be helpful in conducting needs assessments. Other types of government data from over 70 federal government agencies can be accessed on the Internet (https://www.usa.gov/statistics).

Resource data are government reports that are available on a specific topic. Data from published reports and from private foundations can also be used to document needs. Secondary data sources are excellent resources for needs assessments. These reports are available from service providers or private vendors, are relatively cheap to access, and provide a wealth of quantitative and qualitative data on many social and community problems.

There are a number of Internet sites where you can access demographic data and reports. "Research Navigator Guide: The Helping Professions" is an excellent reference for social workers (Kjosness, Barr, & Rettman, 2004). You might also check with the reference librarian at your university. Often academic departments have designated library liaisons that create specialized reference listings of resources on the Internet that are discipline specific. The categories are usually listed on the library's website. Websites such as PolicyMap.com utilize the census to compile all of the relevant data in a complete report. PolicyMap also offers easy-to-use online mapping with data on demographics, real estate, health, jobs, and more in communities across the United States.

Conducting an assessment of the population and resource data will provide you with information regarding age, race, ethnicity, educational attainment, population size, marital status, morbidity and mortality, income inequality and socioeconomic status, wages, population mobility, employment trends, and community and academic definitions of social problems and previous attempts to address them.

Step 4: *Analyze Data*

Once you have collected the appropriate data, you can now prepare a profile of the community that describes the population (socioeconomic, demographic, health, crime, etc.). You have conducted an assessment of who lives in the community, what it looks like, and what some of the health or economic issues that may need to be addressed are.

Step 5: *Identify Data Needs*

The quantitative analyses tell us what the conditions are, but not necessarily what caused the conditions or why they continue to exist. The analysis may also not give us an accurate picture of the composition of the community. In many communities, disenfranchised populations do not necessarily show up in census data. Many minorities go undercounted and unnoticed. Accurate measures of, say, the number of gay or lesbian Spanish-speaking residents in a community are not likely to be documented in a report or on the web. This information can often only be discovered through discussion with community partners. In Step 5, it is necessary to determine what information you still need to collect in order to accomplish your needs assessment goals.

Step 6: *Collect New Data*

There are many ways to collect the data that you need for your community assessment. Observation, surveys, and focus groups provide three options. **Observation data** focuses on documenting behavior as it occurs. The observation may be conducted independently from the group being observed or as a participant. Observation includes going out into the community, walking the streets, interacting with community members, or attending meetings. This allows you to get to know the people and the environment.

Survey data uses questionnaires and/or interview schedules. Both tools are excellent ways of "checking the pulse of the community and getting specific and current information from a cross section of residents in a timely manner" (Andranovich & Howell, 1995, p. 1). When developing a community survey, it is important to consult with community partners to understand the purpose for conducting the survey. Reaffirm the need or problem that they seek to address. What information do they want to know in the end? How will the information be used? Who are the best people to interview? How can interviewing these people help the community to achieve its goals? What is your time frame for completing the analysis? The three most common types of community assessment surveys are key informant surveys, community surveys, and client satisfaction surveys.

Key informant surveys obtain data from those who are informed about a given problem because of training or work experience—usually because they are involved in some sort of service with that population (Royse et al., 2005). Typically, they are the community residents, block captains, organizational leaders, local politicians, ward leaders, local business owners, law enforcement officers, school officials, and human services professionals who work with the client population whose need is being assessed.

"Snowball" sampling techniques are often used to generate a list of key informants. One begins with a few key informants and asks them to identify other persons knowledgeable about the problem or population being studied. Depending on the size of the key informant list, the key informants can be interviewed by telephone, in person, or by a mailed questionnaire. The interview or questionnaire obtains their perceptions of the community issue being studied as well as information about possible solutions. Survey research methods are used to construct the questionnaire and to conduct the data analysis. Key informant surveys are a relatively inexpensive and convenient way to obtain subjective (expert opinion) needs assessment data.

Community surveys of households or community residents is another approach for assessing needs. Typically, these types of surveys are more expensive and require a high level of survey research expertise to carry out. Community surveys can provide information on residents' perceptions of their needs and community conditions as well as empirical data that can be extrapolated to the community or population being investigated. The benefit of a well-executed community survey is that the findings are representative and can be generalized with a specified degree of confidence to the community or population being studied. The downside is cost and difficulties in carrying them out.

Client satisfaction surveys are similar to community surveys except that current or past recipients of a service or program are queried instead of community residents in general. Obtaining a sample of former or current clients tends to be easier than community surveys because the study population is known, defined, and more limited. Client satisfaction studies can provide useful information for needs assessments. Clients are in a unique position to provide feedback on how well the service or program is meeting their needs, additional unmet needs, and the operation of the service or program.

Focus groups, described earlier, are another approach to documenting needs using key informants, community members, or clients. The social worker facilitating the focus group uses open-ended questioning and elaboration skills to obtain in-depth information on the topic under investigation. Focus group participants are selected based on their knowledge of the problem as well as how representative they are of the population group.

Step 7: *Identify Needs*

The needs statement should define the issues and problems that face the community. This would include, but would not be limited to, home, school, work, services, businesses neighborhoods/streets, psychosocial, and recreational activities.

The needs statement should be supported by evidence gathered from your community assessment including: your own experience, quantitative data/statistics, and qualitative data from persons or organizations that are knowledgeable about the community. The statement should be clearly related to the goals articulated by the community, clear and concise, and stated in terms of those who will benefit in the community rather than the needs or problems faced by your organization.

Step 8: *Inventory Resources*

One of the functions of social work is that we often act as resource managers. In order for us to provide adequate services to our clients, we must be knowledgeable about what resources, assets, or opportunities exist in our community. Resource mapping requires us to leave our offices to look around the community to see what is out there and available to our clients. There are various sources of resource data. These include personal observation, existing resource manuals, and the Internet. Useful tools for identifying resources include the Individual Capacity Assessment and the Organizational Assessment. A more detailed explanation of these tools follows in the next section on asset assessment.

Step 9: *Identify Gaps in Services*

This stage involves the use of critical analysis skills to compare problems and needs that have been identified to existing resources. Here it is necessary to determine whether you have the resources available in the community to actually address the social problem. Social workers engage community members in a discussion to decide which problems they would like to address first. This is not an easy process. We all have our own conceptions about which problem we think is the most important. Addressing the problems is a collaborative process that will involve all of the community partners. The challenge is to encourage buy-in and to keep partners engaged throughout.

Step 10: *Plan Interventions*

Program planning is the development, expansion, and coordination of social services and social policies. It involves activities that "address the development and coordination of community agencies and services to meet community functions and responsibilities and to provide for its members" (Hardcastle et al., 2011, p. 2). Program planning can be conducted at the individual agency level, by a consortium of human service agencies, or by regional or state human service planning agencies (Weil & Gamble, 1995). Generalist social workers typically become involved in program planning activities that seek to improve the operation of existing services and programs and to develop new services and programs at the agency and community levels by working with agency task forces, professional task forces, or community coalitions.

Community-Based Participatory Research

Community-based participatory research (CBPR) is an approach to conducting community needs assessments that is based on conflict theory. It is an empowering approach to assessing community needs and change in oppressive community structures. CBPR has increasingly been used for eliminating racial and ethnic health disparities through engaging community members as partners in research design, collaborative discourse about knowledge, and in intervention development and health policy making (Belone et al., 2016). CBPR emphasizes joining with the community as full and equal partners in all phases of the research process.

Community-based action research recognizes the importance of involving members of a study population as active and equal participants, in all phases of the community needs assessment, if the process is to be a means of facilitating change. CBPR is used to assess social, structural, and physical environmental inequities through the active involvement of community members, organizational representatives, and researchers in all aspects of the research process (Holkup, Tripp-Reimer, Salois, & Weinert, 2004).

Implementing a community needs assessment following the CBPR model is similar to the steps followed in a traditional needs assessment where the researcher is the expert. The difference, however, is in the process and the roles community members play in the needs assessment. Throughout the process, community members are equal partners in (a) identifying the research question or target problem to be assessed, (b) identifying the community stakeholders and participants, (c) designing the needs assessment and data collection methods, (d) implementing the data collection process, (e) analyzing the data, (f) interpreting the results, and (g) the dissemination of results.

Asset Assessment

Asset assessment is the process of determining the amount of social capital within the community. The solutions to community challenges are seen as residing within the community residents themselves. Community assets, as defined by Kretzmann, McKnight, Dobrowolski, and Puntenney (2005), refer to those strengths that exist in a community. These strengths include individual, economic, institutional, and organizational resources that are available to community residents. Additionally, a strengths-based assessment reveals the existing opportunities for residents to both access needed resources and contribute their individual "gifts" toward the betterment of the communities in which they live. Components of an asset assessment may include:

1. Local residents: their skills, experiences, passions, capacities, and willingness to contribute to the project, with special attention paid to residents who are sometimes "marginalized"

2. Local voluntary associations, clubs, and networks: for example, all of the athletic, cultural, social, faith-based, and so on, groups powered by volunteer members, which might contribute to the project

3. Local institutions: for example, public institutions such as schools, libraries, parks, police stations, and so on along with local businesses and nonprofits, which might contribute to the project

4. Physical assets: for example, the land, the buildings, the infrastructure, transportation, and so on, which might contribute to the project

5. Economic assets: for example, what people produce and consume, businesses, informal economic exchanges, barter relationships, and so on

An excellent resource for organizers seeking to understand asset-based community development is the Asset-Based Community Development (ABCD) Institute at DePaul University (https://resources.depaul.edu/abcd-institute/Pages/default.aspx). The three basic steps of ABCD are (a) discovering the strengths in our communities, (b) connecting with each other and our community, and (c) coming together to build on our knowledge and skills. The ABCD website provides a detailed description of ABCD, tools and instruments for conducting assessments, and case examples of the use of ABCD.

Asset Mapping

A useful community assessment tool is the development of an asset map. Asset maps are visual representations of a community's resources. Organizers use capacity assessment instruments to determine the strengths and skills of individual residents (individual capacity assessment) and opportunities and resources available to residents through the provision of social service programs offered by agencies or organizations (organizational capacity assessment). Once information is collected regarding community resources, community social workers use geographic information system (GIS) mapping to represent the special relationships of the existing resources and the community residents. Simple asset maps can be created by conducting a community resource assessment and plotting the addresses of the resources found on a map. The community resource assessment allows the social worker to identify potential assets and resources that are available to the client.

Some resources can be found by conducting a simple Internet search. Many resources in low-income communities may still not be documented. In order to uncover hidden assets, walk the neighborhood in which your agency resides. Often, services exist in faith-based organizations, hospitals, within fraternal and sorority organizations, or even in recreation centers. Social workers can provide a helpful resource to their agencies and their clients by collecting this information and geographically plotting it on a map. These asset maps allow clients to see where resources exist and how far they are from their homes, as well as identify gaps or under-resourced areas.

Programs that use GIS software are available at ESRI.com. Mapping for 200 addresses or less can be plotted using free programs such as Batchgeo.com. Both of these programs interface with Excel spreadsheets. Be sure to read licensing agreements to determine charges for your organization or personal use. A helpful guide to community asset mapping can be found online (www.communityscience.com/knowledge4equity/AssetMappingToolkit.pdf).

Community Members' Capacity Assessment

This type of assessment is designed to measure the skills of individual residents in the community and to determine what resources they have available to address a particular social problem. Community members respond to questions that assess their vocational, interpersonal, and associational capacities. The goal is to ascertain not only the individual's personal assets, but also to determine the amount of interaction that person has in the community. Often community members belong to or have connections with organizations or associations that can be helpful in addressing a problem. The inventory also asks residents to identify skills they would like to learn or that they could teach.

Community Organizational Capacity Assessment

This type of assessment involves bringing together the various organizations, agencies, and associations in a given area to determine who can provide what services to your client population or who can contribute to the elimination of the identified social problem. Organizations are asked to provide a description of the services they provide, the population they serve, and their level of community involvement.

Resource Mapping

Resource mapping is a visual representation of the data that allows you to see where the resources in a community are in relation to your client population. Data can be mapped using a variety of tools that are available either through purchase or by using free resources on the Internet. Programs like Microsoft's MapPoint are relatively inexpensive and are fairly easy to learn. It is necessary to develop a database of information to categorize your resource findings prior to mapping.

Social Justice Issue

A social justice issue related to community assessment concerns conducting cross-cultural research with minority populations. Researchers working on cross-cultural research have been criticized for the exploitation of ethnic and minority participants, community damage, and inaccurate findings (Loff & Black, 2000). A key issue in conducting community needs assessments in low-income communities is the power imbalance between the expert researcher or social worker representing the dominant culture and the research subjects who are poor and members of marginalized groups. Although the researcher or social worker might be approaching the needs assessment with good intentions and a desire to help, a lack of awareness of the power imbalance can lead to negative experiences and/or outcomes for the community members and possibly the community.

Not understanding the power imbalance can lead the social worker and/or researcher to adopt the dominant culture's perspective and worldview in assessing the minority community. The perceptions and experiences of the minority community are usually very different from those of the dominant culture. This can lead to findings and interpretations that do not reflect the cultural values, experiences, and perceptions of the research subjects.

Another potential issue in conducting community needs assessments using the traditional expert model is having the academic exploitation of community data, stigmatization of communities, and violation of privacy. This leads to feelings of being exploited by the "outside" researchers. Community members feel they are being studied for the benefit of the researchers and that their participation in the community needs assessment does not result in any community change or improvement (Ponic & Frisby, 2010).

Social workers involved in community needs assessments should be critically aware of power differentials in the process and cultural differences between the majority culture and the values, beliefs, and perspectives of community members in marginalized minority communities. Case 9.3 illustrates the distrust that members of a low-income predominately African American community felt about having a university-based research team conducting a community needs assessment.

CASE 9.3 COME ONLY IF YOU ARE WILLING TO STAY: CONDUCTING NEEDS ASSESSMENTS IN COMMUNITIES THAT HAVE NEGATIVE EXPERIENCES WITH RESEARCHERS

The social work faculty of a university located in a disadvantaged low-income minority community decided that the social work program needed to help the local community address its many pressing social problems. The faculty felt that, as social workers concerned with social justice issues, the varied expertise of the faculty members could be used to help address community needs and strengthen the capacity of local grassroots community-based organizations. Doing so would be consistent with the mission of the program and with the values of the profession. A faculty task force was established to explore this idea and identify possible strategies.

The task force members decided that the first step would be to schedule meetings with the directors of the human service organizations located in the community to discuss interests and identify possible partners. These meetings identified three themes. The first was that the need for additional resources in the community was great. The unmet needs in terms of employment, housing, food availability, education, drug use, and gang activity were great. The second theme was that faculty expertise and university resources were viewed as an asset that could potentially benefit the community. The third theme was that the community did not trust the university. The existing relationship between the community and the university was viewed negatively by most community leaders. Nevertheless, the consensus was that the proposed project by the social work faculty should be explored further.

With the help of the directors of the community organizations, a community meeting was scheduled. Local community members, religious leaders, and professionals working in the community were invited. The message given by the directors was reinforced in the meeting. Many of those in attendance were angry at the university for past indifference and past promises that were not fulfilled. The residents did not trust the university and were suspicious of the social work faculty's proposed initiative. The message was clear. We can use your help, but only come if you plan to stay. Many community members felt that outside experts had come making promises, did their research studies, left, and nothing changed. Too often, expectations had been raised but not realized. The social work faculty heard the community members and made a commitment to partner with the community in addressing the social problem impacting the community. More importantly, they made a commitment to implement community change efforts as an ongoing part of the program's mission.

■ Summary

This chapter focused on the social work competency related to the assessments of organizations and communities. Conducting organizational assessments is guided by the ethical responsibilities to the practice settings. Compliance requires some sort of organizational assessment in order to determine if the organization is meeting the resource needs of clients, providing adequate resources for staff supervision, and creating an organizational environment that is consistent with and encourages compliance with the *Code of Ethics*. Social workers also have an ethical responsibility to work to improve agency policies and procedures to increase the efficiency and effectiveness of their services. Accomplishing these ethical responsibilities requires some kind of organizational assessment. Conducting community assessments is associated with the ethical responsibilities to the broader society. Social workers have an ethical responsibility to promote the welfare of communities and to facilitate informed participation in shaping social policies and institutions.

We also reviewed five organizational theories that help inform organizational assessments, all of which fall under the systems perspective. The rational system theories reviewed were scientific management, administrative theory, bureaucratic theory, rational decision-making theory, and organizational development theory. Organizational assessment methods were then reviewed. This included a discussion of internal and external organizational considerations and a review of common organizational assessment tools.

The chapter then reviewed three community theories that can be used in a community assessment. The two theories derived from a social constructivism perspective were community development theory and conflict theory. The third community theory reviewed was structuralism functionalism, which falls under the systems perspective. The three theories can be used to help inform the design and implementation of a community assessment. The discussion of community theories was followed by a review of community assessment methods and tools. The chapter concluded with a discussion of a social justice issue related to conducting community needs assessments.

CASE SUMMARY   "UNDOCUMENTED AND HOMELESS"

Practice Setting Description

Jackie is a first-year master of social work student completing an internship at an inner-city family service agency in the Southwest. The agency is located in a section of the city that has a high crime rate, gang activity, and failing schools. The area has a diverse population with a large number of immigrants from Central and South America and a substantial African American population. The agency provides individual and family counseling services on a sliding fee scale. The agency also runs a number of educational and treatment groups as well as a temporary shelter for women and their children. Jackie has been assigned to work with the women and their children in the shelter. Her primary tasks are to provide concrete services and supportive counseling to the shelter residents.

(continued)

CASE SUMMARY

Background Information

Elicia T and her daughter, Maria, are undocumented immigrants from Mexico. They have been in the United States for 5 years. Elicia and Maria fled to the area from another southwestern city to escape her abusive husband approximately 2 months ago. Elicia is 25 years old and Maria 8 years old. Elicia has a 2-year-old daughter, Sarah, who was placed in foster care because of suspected abuse in the home. Sarah is in a foster home in a small rural community in the state hundreds of miles from Elicia's current residence. Since moving to the area, Maria has not been attending school.

Elicia and Maria are currently residing in the agency's temporary shelter for families. They have been at the shelter for 2 weeks, and the agency has a 90-day limit. It is viewed as temporary housing, and the residents are only allowed to stay for 3 months. Prior to arriving at the shelter, Elicia and Maria were homeless and living on the streets.

Elicia is a high-school dropout and was a stay-at-home mother prior to leaving her husband and moving to a different part of the state. She chose to move there because she has two female cousins living in the area who are also undocumented immigrants. Elicia's native language is Spanish. She speaks some English but is not as comfortable speaking in English. Her English comprehension appears to be good. Maria speaks both English and Spanish well. When communicating with the staff, Maria acts as Elicia's interpreter since none of the staff at the shelter speak Spanish.

Maria appears to be behind academically. She struggles reading simple children's books written in English. It is unknown if her ability to read in Spanish is better than her English reading skills.

Other than her two cousins, Elicia has no other sources of support in the community. Her cousins have young families and limited resources but are well established and connected to a Latino community in the city and the local Catholic church. Her cousins refused to let Elicia and Maria live with them while she was trying to find her own place and a job. They stated that they did not have enough room and are concerned they would get in trouble with their landlord if it was found out that they were letting people stay with them. They sent her to the local church for help, and she was given the address for the agency's shelter by the priest.

Elicia has been looking for housing in the Latino community. The housing market is tight with limited options, and she has been unable to find anything that she could possibly afford. The only affordable housing she found was a room in a rundown motel that rents by the hour or by the month. It is in an area of town known for drug dealing and sex work.

On arrival in the community, Elicia found occasional work for a house cleaning company. The company hires undocumented workers, pays them very low cash wages, and threatens to turn them in to Immigration and Customs Enforcement (ICE) if they complain. The job bosses also exploit their female workers sexually, threatening to turn them in if they do not comply. Elicia was fearful about applying for other jobs because of her illegal status. She considered turning to sex work to be able to take care of her children, but her Catholic upbringing and thoughts of how doing so would shame her family have kept her from doing so. She is in constant fear of being detained, separated from her children, and having them placed in foster care. She is also afraid that she will end up homeless again and forced to live on the streets or return to her abusive husband.

(continued)

CASE SUMMARY

Elicia is extremely reluctant to sign up for any federally funded services, even those that she and her children are entitled to receiving. On the suggestion that she enroll for supplemental food through SNAP, Elicia became nervous and refused as she has heard that participation in SNAP services, and others like them, would draw the attention of ICE, and she had heard stories on the news of individuals being deported after signing up for such programs.

Presenting Problems

Elicia and her children are facing multiple obstacles. They need to find permanent, affordable housing and a job that pays enough to cover her housing and living expenses. In addition, Maria needs to be enrolled in school. Elicia also wants to regain custody of her youngest daughter in foster care.

Additionally, Elicia is experiencing an immense amount of stress, anxiety, and possibly post-traumatic stress disorder (PTSD). She described an instance where she could not calm down her breathing, and she felt lightheaded. She is very fearful of men and tries to avoid all contact with men in the community. She reports difficulty sleeping at night and feeling exhausted most of the time.

She is concerned about Maria. She has started acting out at the shelter, getting into fights with the other children, disobeying her mother, and being disrespectful and defiant to the staff and other adults. Elicia and Maria fight frequently, and when Elicia tries to discipline Maria, she throws a temper tantrum until Elicia gives up.

Elicia has many strengths. She had the strength to leave her abusive husband and move to a different city. She loves her daughters. She wants desperately to keep Maria with her and hopes to have Sarah returned to her custody. She is resilient and has managed to survive and keep her daughter safe despite not having a place to stay, a job, and a limited support network. Additionally, Elicia is highly motivated to find her own accommodations and support her children.

■ Discussion Questions

1. Identify two organizational (agency) issues that are impacting Elicia and her daughter. What theory or theories would you use to conduct an organizational assessment of the identified issues?

2. For the preceding organizational assessment, what organizational variables would you assess? What assessment methods would you use to collect the assessment data?

3. Identify two community issues that are impacting Elicia and her daughter. What theory or theories would you use to conduct a community assessment of the identified issues?

4. For the preceding community assessment, what community variables would you assess? What assessment methods would you use to collect the assessment data?

■ References

Andranovich, G., & Howell, R. (1995). *The community survey: A tool for participation and fact-finding*. Pullman, WA: Western Regional Extension Publication WREP0132.

Barnett, M. (2010). Generalist practice with communities. In J. Poulin (Ed.), *Strengths-based generalist practice: A collaborative approach* (pp. 322–371). Belmont, CA: Cengage.

Belone, L., Lucero, J. E., Duran, B., Tafoya, G., Baker, E. A., Chan, D., . . . Wallerstein, N. (2016). Community-based participatory research conceptual model: Community partner consultation and face validity. *Qualitative Health Research, 26*, 117–135. doi:10.1177/1049732314557084

Burke, W. W., & Litwin, G. H. (1992). A causal model of organizational performance and change. *Journal of Management, 18*, 523–545. doi:10.1177/014920639201800306

Coley, S. M., & Scheinberg, C. A. (2017). *Proposal writing: Effective grantsmanship for funding* (5th ed.). Thousand Oaks, CA: Sage.

Collins, J. (2001). *Good to great; Why some companies make the leap and others don't*. New York, NY: HarperCollins Publishers.

Dahrendorf, R. (1959). Class and class conflict in industrial society. Stanford, CA: Stanford University Press.

Fredrick Taylor and scientific management: Understanding Taylorism and early management theory. (2019). Retrieved from https://www.mindtools.com/pages/article/newTMM_Taylor.htm

French, W. L., & Bell, C. H. (1999). *Organization development: Behavioral science interventions for organization improvement* (6th ed.). London, UK: Pearson.

Greater Twin Cities United Way. (2019). Retrieved from https://managementhelp.org/organizational performance/nonprofits/index.htm

Hardcastle, D. A., Powers, P. R., & Wenocur, S. (2011). *Community practice: Theories and skills for social workers* (3rd ed.). New York, NY: Oxford University Press.

Henri Fayol's principles of management: Early management theory. (2019). Retrieved from https://www .mindtools.com/pages/article/henri-fayol.htm

Holkup, P. A., Tripp-Reimer, T., Salois, E. M., & Weinert, C. (2004). Community-based participatory research: An approach to intervention research with a Native American community. *Advances in Nursing Science, 27*, 162–175. doi:10.1097/00012272-200407000-00002

Kauffman, S. (2010). Generalist practice with organizations. In J. Poulin (Ed.), *Strengths-based generalist practice: A collaborative approach* (pp. 254–321). Belmont, CA: Cengage.

Kauffman, S., & Barnett, M. (2019). Mezzo assessment: Organizations and communities. In J. Poulin, S. Matis, & H. Witt (Ed.), *The social work field placement: A competency-based approach* (pp. 259–284). New York, NY: Springer Publishing Company.

Kettner, P. M., Moroney, R. M., & Rettman, S. (2017). *Designing and managing programs: An effectiveness-based approach* (5th ed.). Thousand Oaks, CA: Sage.

Kjosness, J., Barr, L., & Rettman, S. (2004). *Research navigator guide: The helping professions*. Boston, MA: Allyn & Bacon.

Kretzmann, J., McKnight, J., Dobrowolski, S., & Puntenney, D. (2005). Discovering community power: A guide to mobilizing local assets and your organization's capacity. Retrieved from https://resources .depaul.edu/abcd-institute/publications/publications-by-topic/Documents/kelloggabcd.pdf

Langer, C. L., & Lietz, C. A. (2015). *Applying theory to generalist social work practice*. Hoboken, NJ: John Wiley & Sons, Inc.

Loff, B., & Black, J. (2000). The Declaration of Helsinki and research in vulnerable populations. *Medical Journal of Australia, 172*, 292–295.

Mulder, P. (2015). *Scientific management and Taylorism*. Retrieved from ToolsHero https://www .toolshero.com/quality-management/scientific-management

Mulder, P. (2017). *Bureaucratic theory by Max Weber*. Retrieved from ToolsHero https://www.toolshero .com/management/bureaucratic-theory-weber

National Association of Social Workers. (2017). *Code of ethics*. Silver Spring, MD: Author. Retrieved from https://www.socialworkers.org/About/Ethics/Code-of-Ethics/Code-of-Ethics-English

Note on Fayol's administrative management theory: Concept and principles. (2019). Retrieved from https://www.kullabs.com/classes/subjects/units/lessons/notes/note-detail/4439.

Paiva, J. F. X. (1977). A conception of social development. *Social Service Review, 51*, 327–336. doi:10.1086/643500

Perkins, J. (1982). *With justice for all*. Ventura, CA: Regal Books.

Philadelphia Health Management Corporation. (1997). *Doing the right thing: Community-based program planning and evaluation*. A Community Health Database Seminar for the William Penn Youth Violence Prevention Grant Program.

Ponic, P., & Frisby, W. (2010). Unpacking assumptions about inclusion in community based health promotion: Perspectives of women living in poverty, *Qualitative Health Research, 20*, 1519–1531. doi:10.1177/1049732310374303

Principles of decision making. (2019). Retrieved from https://www.gdrc.org/decision/fs-2.html

Rational and non-rational decision making. (2019). Retrieved from https://courses.lumenlearning.com/boundless-management/chapter/rational-and-nonrational-decision-making

Royse, D., Thyer, B., Padgett, D., & Logan, T. (2005). Program evaluation: An introduction (4th ed.). Stamford, CT: Brooks Cole.

Samuels, B., Ahsan, N., & Garcia, J. (1995). *Know your community: A step-by-step guide to community needs and resources assessment* (2nd ed.). Family Resource Coalition. Retrieved from http://eric.ed.gov/ERICDocs/data/ericdocs2sql/content_storage_01/0000019b/80/15/c3/fc.pdf

Schiele, J. J. H. (2005). Maggie Lena Walker and African American community development. *Affilia, 20*, 21–38. doi:10.1177/0886109904272012

Tan, A. (2009, October). *Community development theory and practice: Bridging the divide between "micro" and "macro" practice*. Paper presented at the North American Association of Christian Social Workers. Indianapolis, IN.

Taylor, F. (1911). *The principles of scientific management*. New York, NY: Harper and Brothers Publishers.

Weil, M., & Gamble, D. (1995). Community practice models. In R. Edwards (Ed.-in-Chief), *Encyclopedia of Social Work* (19th ed.). Silver Spring, MD: NASW Press.

MEZZOINTERVENTIONS IN SOCIAL WORK PRACTICE: ORGANIZATIONS AND COMMUNITIES

STEPHEN KAUFFMAN | JOHN POULIN | MARINA BARNETT

James is a first-year master of social work student placed in a community-based program that provides consultation services to grassroots human service programs in an economically disadvantaged community with numerous social problems. The agency's mission is to increase the number of services available to community residents as well as to strengthen the capacities of the local service organizations. The after-school program serves low-income families, many of whom also need social work and case management services. Many of the children in the after-school program are struggling in school because of issues and challenges that are occurring in their homes and with their families. The two agencies have agreed to explore the possibility of developing a new service that provides case management and counseling services to the children's families. James has been tasked with helping develop the new family service.

James is excited about his field assignment and the opportunity to help families overcome the challenges of poverty and to help low-income children to become more successful in school. James knows that his first step is to learn all he can about the community and the experiences of the low-income residents who will use the new program. He also has many unanswered questions that he will need to address: How will he partner with the community members? What professional and community groups need to be involved in the planning process? What are the families' needs? What kinds of services and assistance will best address those needs? How will they fund the new program? How best to prepare a grant proposal?

LEARNING OBJECTIVES

This chapter addresses Competency 8: Intervene With Individuals, Families, Groups, Organizations, and Communities. It focuses on mezzointerventions with organizations and communities. By the end of this chapter, you will be able to:

- Understand the purposes of mezzo–social work practice
- Identify mezzo–social work practice interventions

- Identify social work values and ethics related to mezzo–social work practice with organizations and communities
- Use change theory to create organizational change
- Develop goals and measurable objectives
- Create a program logic model
- Prepare a grant proposal
- Research external program funding opportunities
- Describe three approaches to community development
- Understand the process of coalition building

■ Competency 8: Intervene With Individuals, Families, Groups, Organizations, and Communities

Social workers understand that intervention is an ongoing component of the dynamic and interactive process of social work practice with, and on behalf of, diverse individuals, families, groups, organizations, and communities. Social workers are knowledgeable about evidence-informed interventions to achieve the goals of clients and constituencies, including individuals, families, groups, organizations, and communities. Social workers understand theories of human behavior and the social environment, and critically evaluate and apply this knowledge to effectively intervene with clients and constituencies. Social workers understand methods of identifying, analyzing, and implementing evidence-informed interventions to achieve client and constituency goals. Social workers value the importance of interprofessional teamwork and communication in interventions, recognizing that beneficial outcomes may require interdisciplinary, interprofessional, and interorganizational collaboration. Social workers:

- Critically choose and implement interventions to achieve practice goals and enhance capacities of clients and constituencies
- Apply knowledge of human behavior and the social environment, person-in-environment, and other multidisciplinary theoretical frameworks in interventions with clients and constituencies
- Use interprofessional collaboration as appropriate to achieve beneficial practice outcomes
- Negotiate, mediate, and advocate with and on behalf of diverse clients and constituencies
- Facilitate effective transitions and endings that advance mutually agreed-on goals

This chapter focuses on the knowledge, skills, and values associated with intervening with organizations and communities.

■ National Association of Social Workers (NASW) *Code of Ethics*

The NASW *Code of Ethics* (2017) value of service is related to intervening with organizations and communities. Its associated ethical principle is that social workers' primary goal is to help people in need and to address social problems. The social justice value is also related to intervening with organizations and communities. Its associated ethical principle is that social workers challenge social injustice. Organizational and community interventions in social work are designed to help those in need and to address social problems as well as social justice issues.

The NASW *Code of Ethics* (2017) ethical standards are related to organizational and community interventions. One is the ethical responsibility to clients. The ultimate aim of social workers engaged in organizational and community interventions is enhancing the well-being of clients served by the organizations and the community members.

Three ethical standards under the ethical responsibilities to the broader society are relevant to the organizational and community interventions (NASW, 2017). The first is about promoting the general welfare of communities. The second ethical standard is about informed participation and the third is about social and political action. Addressing the issues identified in the NASW *Code of Ethics* requires social work interventions at the mezzolevel designed to address the larger systemic issues impacting people and their communities.

■ Mezzointervention Theories

The theories reviewed in this chapter on assessing organizations and communities are also applicable to mezzolevel interventions. This chapter reviews one additional theory that can help inform the development and implementation of organizational change.

Change Theory

Lewin's change theory (1947) is useful in creating organizational change. Social service organizations, both not-for profit and government agencies, like any other organization, are resistant to change. They develop set ways of doing things, and creating change even if it is beneficial, is challenging. To overcome resistance, people need to let go of old habits and structures. This is a difficult assignment because change leads to a disruption of a stable situation. People like to keep the old situation as it is, because it is safe and predictable. People are only capable of accepting change when they know what this change will bring them. Lewin's change model conceptualizes change in a three-step process. The steps in this model are the unfreeze stage, the change stage, and the refreeze stage.

> ▶ **Critical Thinking Questions**
> Based on the chapter opening case example:
> 1. What ethical principles and standards apply to James's field placement project?
> 2. Why do they apply and what will James need to do to be compliant with the ethical principles?

Unfreezing

This is the preparing for change stage. It is preparing the organization and its members for change. It involves breaking down the old way of doing things and changing peoples' mind-set about how the organization functions. The key is showing people that the current way cannot continue, and that change will lead to improved outcomes for clients and/or the organization. Unfreezing means getting people to open up to new ways of reaching their objectives. Basically, the current practices and processes have to be reassessed before organizational change can take place. During the unfreezing stage, you need to determine what needs to be changed. A number of different methods can be used to identify areas that need to be changed. Possible methods include outcome studies, consumer surveys, employee surveys, and focus groups. The greater the level of participation in identifying the change targets, the greater the likelihood that the change goals will be achieved (Schein, 1996). It is also important to create a clear message about why change has to occur. The "why" needs to be tied to the organization's vision and mission. Finally, during the unfreezing stage, it is important to address doubts and concerns. Being open to employee concerns and addressing them from the perspective of the need to change will help overcome stakeholder concerns (Schein, 1996).

Change

This is the implementation stage. Once the organization members have accepted that change is needed, then change can start. It is important that the change is implemented within a short time. The longer the change process takes, the more likely employees will relapse into old habits and behaviors (Schein, 1996). By acting quickly and implementing the change within a short time, the stakeholders will accept the importance of the change effort more quickly. After the uncertainty created in the unfreeze stage, the change stage is where the uncertainty is replaced with new ways to do things. People start to believe and act in ways that support the new direction. Time and communication are the two keys to the changes occurring successfully. People need time to understand the changes,

> ▶ **Critical Thinking Questions**
> Compare Lewin's change theory with Simon's rational decision-making theory.
> 1. How are the different?
> 2. How are they alike?
> 3. What are the strengths of change theory compared to rational decision-making theory?

and they also need to feel highly connected to the organization throughout the transition period. During the change stage, it is important to communicate often to prepare people for the change and to dispel rumors that can undermine the change process. It is also important to empower action and provide lots of opportunities for employee involvement.

Refreeze

The refreeze stage is where the changes become internalized and incorporated into the overall functioning of the organization. It is about solidifying the change. Employees need to feel comfortable and confident with the new ways of working. The refreezing stage is important. Without it, employees are not sure how things should be done, so nothing ever gets done to full capacity. It then becomes a short-term change, and people revert to the old ways of doing things. During the refreezing stage, the goal is to anchor the changes into the culture of the organization as well as identify what supports the change and what the barriers are that need to be overcome to support long-term change (Schein, 1996).

■ Mezzointerventions

Mezzo–social work practice is an intervention with organizations and communities or neighborhoods. The purpose of mezzolevel practice is to improve organizational functioning and service delivery and community well-being for vulnerable populations. Macrolevel practice involves change efforts at the municipality, county, state, national, or international level. The purpose of macrolevel practice is to help vulnerable populations indirectly through policy change, program development, and advocacy.

Table 10.1 lists social work practice interventions related to organizations and communities. Intervention tasks are categorized by practice at the mezzosystem level (organizations and communities) and client systems. Social work practice often requires simultaneous interventions at multiple levels. In any case, situation, or practice setting, you might be involved in a number of interventions at different practice and system levels.

Mezzolevel interventions focus on organizational and community change. As shown in Table 10.1, typical client systems at the organizational level are organizational leaders, task forces, and committees. The system level is the organization, and the client systems that the social worker engages are the decision makers and decision-making structures of the organization. The worker usually participates in formally organized work groups, such as agency task forces or committees, often to develop new services or improve existing services. The client system might also be the organization's decision makers, that is, administrators and supervisors. Thus, a social worker seeking to change an organization may view the decision makers or the decision-making structures as the client system to improve how decisions are made or how the organization communicates about decisions, activities, or services. Addressing these client systems is often of the greatest importance, because organizations are often where microsystems (individual clients) turn to for help. An organization that does not function well may not serve its clients or even the very staff that work within those organizations. Thus, at the organizational level, the purpose of mezzolevel practice is to improve the

TABLE 10.1 Mezzolevel Interventions With Organizations and Communities

SYSTEM LEVEL	CLIENT SYSTEM	MEZZOLEVEL INTERVENTIONS
Organization	Administrators Task forces Committees Advisory boards	Education and training Planning and program development
Community/ neighborhood	Professional task forces Community coalitions Neighborhood groups	Models of community practice Community development Coalition building

functioning of the organization, improve services and service delivery, or develop new services through program development and/or grant writing. All three purposes involve change of the organization or agency. Social workers tend to be agency based and work within an organizational framework.

Typical client systems at the community level are professional task forces, community coalitions, and neighborhood or community citizens' groups. Often the purpose of community practice is to improve community or neighborhood conditions, empower residents, develop resources, increase community awareness of social and economic problems, and mobilize people to advocate for needed resources and changes. Social workers engaged in community change usually work with professional or community groups. Some groups have both professional and citizen members. Social workers engaged in community practice may view the group they are working with as the client system. In other words, the client system is the professional task force, neighborhood group, or community coalition that is seeking to change or improve the community. But the client system may also be the residents of the community as a whole.

Importantly, all of the microlevel skills generalist social workers develop may well be needed when working with mezzo- and macrolevel client systems. Effective communication, goal setting, and sensitivity to the needs of individuals in some ways become even more important when working with the (often) large and complex client systems that are found at the organizational and community levels.

When thinking about mezzointerventions, remember that microlevel skills are almost always needed when working with mezzolevel client systems. In many cases, basic social work practices, such as simply opening up lines of communication with others, being respectful, or being sensitive to differences, will be critical and essential to ensuring effective outcomes. Social workers at the organizational level intervene using education and training, planning and program development, grant writing, and coalition building. At the community level, social workers intervene using social planning, locality development, and social action.

After the organizational or community assessment is completed, the identified problems/issues need to be prioritized and a plan of action developed. This includes developing goals and objective, action steps, and an evaluation plan

Setting Goals and Objectives

Goals serve a variety of critical purposes in the overall intervention. As well as serving as positive outcomes to the intervention activity, they help provide meaning and definition to the agency and giving direction and helping to keep everyone focused. Goals may also serve as an internal source of motivation and commitment. Commonly, goals are viewed as the desired end states of the activity or intervention. As such, it is essential that the goal is linked to a problem, or more specifically, to the "resolution" of the problem. Note the examples in Table 10.2.

But, importantly, there is an issue that requires our attention here. Very often, end states have different "dimensions" or qualities, and as such it may be a bit difficult for us to really be certain that we have achieved that end state. For example, common organizational problems like "staff morale," "high-quality services," or even "client satisfaction" may each have two, three, or even more aspects, each of which must be addressed if we are to be certain that we have achieved the goal.

TABLE 10.2 Examples of Agency Goals in Mezzolevel Interventions

PROBLEM	GOAL RESPONSE
Low staff morale	*Goal 1.* The agency will achieve a high level of employee morale.
Financial difficulties	*Goal 2.* The agency will achieve complete financial solvency.
Poor client satisfaction	*Goal 3.* The agency will achieve a high level of customer satisfaction
Communication problems	*Goal 4.* The agency will achieve a high level of quality of communication, both inside and outside of the organization.

Building on the goal examples in Table 10.2, Table 10.3 presents some of the different dimensions associated with some common organizational goals. To consider this issue in a slightly different way, it may be useful to think of the various dimensions of the problem/goal as possible indicators of the problem, and on the flip side, as indicators of goal attainment. As such, each of the indicators in Table 10.3 may be used for an indicator of goal attainment.

So, if goals have multiple dimensions, and each of these dimensions may serve as an indicator of goal attainment, how do we organize the information for planning purposes? The answer is to break the goals down into three stages: *goals, objectives,* and *tasks* (or action steps or activities), with each stage presenting an increasingly specific level of information. The goals, again, are the first level and are the desired end states, again often with different dimensions. The objective, or the next level, now becomes an indicator of goal attainment, and it contains a single dimension of the goal. Indeed, for complex goals, we may choose to select two, three, or even more indicators, each of which focuses on one of the dimensions of the goal. The final level, the task or activity, speaks to the specific responsibilities of the staff

TABLE 10.3 Examples of Problem Dimensions of Goals That May Be Used as Goal Attainment Indicators

LOW STAFF MORALE	AGENCY FINANCIAL DIFFICULTIES	POOR CLIENT SATISFACTION	COMMUNICATION PROBLEMS
Staff retention	Number of authorized client admissions	Client retention	Number of missed meetings by staff due to failure to inform
Worker satisfaction ratings	Supplies available to staff	Client satisfaction ratings	Worker level of reported satisfaction with communication ratings
Level of conflicts between workers	Travel reimbursements' disbursement time	Treatment compliance	Number of conflicts between workers with communication identified as cause
Worker absenteeism	Number of successful grant applications	Client absenteeism	

or client in carrying out the intervention. More on tasks/action steps is provided later on as we conceptualize the interventions a bit more thoroughly.

In the meantime, using the problem indicators in Table 10.3, the following examples of objectives may be developed from the aforementioned goals. Notice the difference between the measurability and specificity of the goals in Table 10.2 (examples of agency goals) and those in Table 10.4 (examples of measurable agency objectives).

TABLE 10.4 Examples of Measurable Agency Objectives in Mezzolevel Interventions

PROBLEM	GOAL AND OBJECTIVE RESPONSE
Low Staff Morale	**Goal 1.** The agency will achieve a high level of employee morale.
Objective 1.1	The agency will improve staff retention, as measured by employees with more than 2 years of service, by 50% by March 2021.
Objective 1.2	Employee's satisfaction with employment, as measured by quarterly satisfaction surveys, will increase by 80% from current levels by March 2021.
Objective 1.3	The rate of employee's daily absenteeism will fall by 75%, from current levels, by March 2021.
Financial Difficulties	**Goal 2.** The agency will achieve complete financial solvency.
Objective 2.1	The number of authorized client admissions will increase by 30% from current levels by March 2021.
Objective 2.2	The time between submission and payment of staff travel reimbursements for all employees will reduce from 90 days to 14 days by December 2021.
Objective 2.3	The number of successful grant applications written by the agency will increase by 100% from current levels by March 2021.
Poor Client Satisfaction	**Goal 3.** The agency will achieve a high level of customer satisfaction.
Objective 3.1	The agency will improve client retention, as measured by clients completing treatment, by 50% by March 20211.
Objective 3.2	The agency will improve client treatment compliance, as measured by the percentage of clients who meet monthly task assignments, by 75% by December 2021.
Objective 3.3	The rate of client's daily absenteeism will fall by 75% from current levels by March 2021.
Communication Problems	**Goal 4.** The agency will achieve a high level of quality of communication, both inside and outside of the organization.
Objective 4.1	The number of missed meetings by staff due to failure to inform will fall by 75% from current levels by March 2021.
Objective 4.2	Worker level of reported satisfaction with communication, as measured by quarterly satisfaction surveys, will increase by 80% from current levels by March 2021.
Objective 4.3	The number of conflicts between workers with communication identified as cause will fall by 75% from current levels by March 2021.

The next level, the objectives, as defined earlier, are the indicators of goal attainment, and these indicators are the measurable dimensions of the problem (and goal) at hand. Unlike goals, therefore, objectives must be highly specific in every way. Any ambiguity may potentially misconstrue the meaning of the objective. But by enhancing the measurability of the objective, demonstration of objective attainment becomes easier.

Surprisingly, there is no mystery in writing good objectives; a few guidelines will greatly assist you in creating sharp and useful objectives. Indeed, the acronym "SMART" will help. SMART stands for statements that are:

- **S**pecific

- **M**easurable

- **A**ttainable

- **R**elevant

- **T**ime-bound

The characteristics of each of these terms have been nicely described (Cothran, Wysocki, Farnsworth, & Clark (2019):

- Specific means that the statement has fully addressed four questions.

    - Who is to be involved?

    - What is to be accomplished?

    - Where is it to be done?

    - When is it to be done?

- Measurable means that the statement has fully addressed three questions.

    - How much?

    - How will you know when it is accomplished?

    - How many?

- Attainable means that the statement has a real chance of success.

- Relevant means the statement is consistent with the mission of the organization.

- Time-bound means the statement has a beginning and an ending point.

Now, following the aforementioned example, using the same problem indicators and goals, the following objectives may be written. Look at the examples in Table 10.4 and notice how measurable and specific each one is.

One final question remains as far as goals and objectives are concerned, and that is: How many goals and objectives are necessary in a plan? The short answer is as many as necessary. But a somewhat better answer is to at least *consider* adding a new goal each time (a) your problem area changes, (b) the target group changes, or (c) the major thrust of the intervention changes. Then, consider adding a new objective for each problem indicator you select. An example of a goal planning form is shown in Table 10.5.

With assessment completed, and agency goals and objectives firmly in place, the time for the actual intervention is at hand. As with any system, from single individuals to families,

TABLE 10.5 Agency Goal Planning Form for Mezzolevel Interventions

Problem Area 1:		
	Define the problem here from the ssessment. Include specific indicators in the description.	
	Goal and Objective Response: In the space below, write a goal to address problem area 1. Follow the goal with objectives as needed. For each objective, be sure to include problem indicator, amount of desired change in the indicator, and time for completion of objective. Use additional pages if more than 5 objectives per goal.	
	Goal 1:	
	Objective 1.1	
	Objective 1.2	
	Objective 1.3	
	Objective 1.4	
	Objective 1.5	

all the way to communities, a number of interventions are always available. The first guiding principle with an organizational intervention, and most similar to any other system, is to keep your eyes on the literature. Evidence-based practice is increasingly the norm and the expectation. Therefore, watching the changes in empirical and theoretical knowledge will only help you to select the tools that will best serve you and your client. Regardless of the intervention you ultimately choose, you will need to develop an intervention and evaluation plan.

Developing the Intervention Plan

The intervention plan lays out the tasks/action steps and responsibilities for all parties in the change process. Essentially, this is an action plan and a contract that provides a great amount of detail for the successful implementation of the intervention. In other words, it again presents the tasks/action steps for the project.

Tasks/action steps, as initially discussed, come from your goals and objectives, but they are also closely connected to the intervention. They are, very simply, the specific activities that each person involved in the intervention must carry out if the intervention is to be successful. They are statements of the "who, what, when, and where" of the plan. Questions such as what needs to be done, who will do what, and when does it need to be completed should be addressed.

TABLE 10.6 Mezzolevel Intervention Planning Form

Goal 1:					
	Objective 1.1				
	Task/Action	Responsibility	Completion Date	Comments	Completed?

Generally, the more detail and specificity within the plan, the more successful it will be. The specifics, however, are again linked to the objectives and the interventions. The following are some examples of organization and community interventions. Table 10.6 shows an example of an intervention planning form. The intervention planning form is used in conjunction with the goal planning form.

Another component of the intervention plan is how it will be evaluated. Each of the objectives identified needs to be evaluated or measured. The program goals are not evaluated; the more specific objectives are. Thus, for each objective, identify the measure that will be used, the data source for the measure, a time frame, a baseline, and the benchmark for the objective. The first objective in Table 10.4 is "the agency will improve staff retention, as measured by employees with more than 2 years of service, by 50% by March 2021." For this objective, the measure is staff retention. The data source is the employment records. The time frame is by March 2021. The benchmark is a 50% increase in retention. A baseline is not specified in the objective as written but to be able to calculate the percentage increase, the number of employees with 2 or more years of service would need to be measured at the beginning of the intervention and again at the target date.

Education and Training

One application of education as a mezzointervention that is widely used is structured trainings, often through workshops. Trainings may be designed to be short and narrowly targeted events, or they may be designed to take place over a longer period of time and address a large variety of issues. Among the kinds of issues that many social workers confront and which trainings may be useful include improving productivity and the use of technology.

Trainings to Enhance Productivity and Technology

One common issue that social workers confront is how to improve a group's productivity. Productivity refers to the output of work relative to the effort involved. Often, it is the case that a group may have to "to do more with less." Indeed, groups and organizations may be otherwise effective, but service demands exceed the resources necessary to address those demands. In these situations, the problems of the group or organization may be improved by enhancing or correcting the procedures already in place (Brody, 2014). In other words, work to improve the productivity of the group by focusing on the strengths of the group. Rarely are organizations so lost that everything must be changed. Commonly, it only requires some element of reform or enhancement.

Technology, for example, is a common tool for enhancing productivity. The NASW *Code of Ethics* (2017) provides some guidance in the use of technology in the provision of social work services. The guidelines cover the competent use of technology and the second is about complying with the laws governing the use of technology. The specific language of these ethical standards can be found online (www.socialworkers.org/About/Ethics/Code-of-Ethics/Code-of-Ethics-English).

In recent years, a variety of technological applications have become available that have aided everything from communication to diagnosis to service provision. Consider for a moment the difficulties associated with agency paperwork. With the development and application of some simple programs and perhaps an intranet, many routine tasks such as case notes, internal communication, and even diagnosis may be improved. A generalist social worker can convene or coordinate work groups to help choose and then train group members to use the proper technology.

The problem of group communication processes also serves as a case in point. It is not that difficult to greatly enhance communication through very simple processes. These may include selecting a better method of communication through matching the needs and purposes of the communication with the technique (Brody, 2014). Meetings, important as they are, do not need to be held if information can be more effectively passed on through individual contacts or electronic means.

Technology resources such as videoconferencing, online scheduling, and cloud document management can increase collaboration and productivity in organizations.

These resources make more time available to staff, while reducing some complexity for administrators and clients. Again, the generalist social worker can convene or coordinate work groups to help select the appropriate solution, and then train group members in how to use it.

Trainings to Improve Group Skills

Trainings may also be used to enhance other needed skills. Many of us, for example, have benefited from trainings to address issues as broad as diversity and culture, or as narrow as the application of a particular counseling technique. The question to address in planning for this intervention is whether the need may be corrected in a single event, or if the need is for a multievent, long-term set of trainings. The social worker can facilitate the training and/or coordinate the planning for the training.

Case 10.1 illustrates the beginning steps in developing a staff workshop. This example highlights the importance of getting input from members of the target group before implementing a training program. The probation officers' perceptions of what they were interested in were very different from their director's perceptions. The workshop turned out to be a success and was well received by the probation officers, even though it was not exactly what the director originally envisioned. If the training team had proceeded without any input from the participants, it would most likely have been less well received. The workshop would have been a trying experience for both the training team and the participants.

CASE 10.1   EARLY STEPS IN STAFF WORKSHOP DEVELOPMENT

Christiana, Laurie, and Pat all were graduate social work students doing their second-year field placements at Social Work Consultation Services (SWCS). SWCS provided generalist social work learning experiences for student interns and social work and capacity-building services for residents and organizations of an economically disadvantaged community. The Director of Adult Probation in the county contacted SWCS about conducting a staff development workshop for her probation officers. Christiana, Laurie, and Pat took on the project under the supervision of a school faculty member.

The training team scheduled a meeting with the Director of Adult Probation to get a better understanding of the agency's needs and her expectations about the purpose and objectives of the workshop. The director felt that her staff could benefit from a workshop on relationship-building skills and on how to engage reluctant, resistant, or hostile clients in a collaborative working relationship. She felt that many of the probation officers were showing signs of burnout and a lot of frustration with their clients and the legal system. Many seemed to have given up trying to make a difference in their clients' lives and were not making any efforts to connect with them. The team left the meeting with a clear understanding of what the director wanted. They felt it was something that they would be able to put together and deliver effectively.

With the approval of the director, the training team scheduled a pre-workshop meeting with the probation officers who would be attending the workshop. The purpose of the meeting was to get an understanding of their training needs and interests. The meeting did not go as expected. The probation officers had absolutely no interest in learning "soft" relationship skills and were totally against the idea of having to attend a workshop on how to connect with reluctant or hostile clients. They felt that such training would be a total waste of time. They used the meeting to vent their feelings about the system and working with clients who lied and were manipulative.

The team struggled to find some common ground between the director's and staff's perceived needs. Because the probation officers were so clear about the frustrations of their job, Pat asked if they would be interested in a workshop that focused on coping strategies and burnout prevention. This, too, was rejected as a waste of time. Most of the group members claimed not to have any problems in that area and said they could take care of themselves just fine.

Having struck out making suggestions to this group, Christiana asked them what would be helpful. After quite a bit of back-and-forth discussion among the probation officers, it was decided that a workshop on the link between mental health and substance abuse would be helpful. All of their clients were substance abusers, and the workers felt that for many, mental health issues compounded their difficulties with substance abuse and the law. The team agreed to the proposed focus, pending approval by the probation officers' director.

Trainings to Enhance Leadership

Social workers are called upon to be leaders in the fight against social injustice. Leadership development is a critical component that may require focus in training activities. Many people mistakenly consider leadership to be of concern only to managers or administrators. But in reality, everyone can benefit from enhanced leadership skills. It is very difficult for any mezzolevel group to function well without effective leadership.

While leadership has been widely studied, recent studies have resulted in a number of important breakthroughs in understanding the concept. Research by Elpers and Westhuis (2008) finds that organizational performance in the human services is enhanced by utilizing a transformational leadership style accompanied by participatory decision-making (Gellis, 2001; Fuller, Morrison, Jones, Bridger, & Brown, 1999). Transformational leaders are proactive, positive, and are able to motivate and influence others. Participatory leadership styles allow employees to engage in the problem-solving process. All members of the organization are viewed as having individual skills, abilities, and talents that can enhance the functioning of the organization or the community.

Emotional intelligence (the ability to accurately interpret emotional states and needs) is also a critical element of leadership (Ovans, 2015). Consisting of such attributes as self-awareness, self-regulation, empathy, and solid social skills (Goleman, 1998; Goleman & Boyatzis, 2017), the idea is that a leader who understands people will help improve many workplace conditions. Emotional intelligence can be improved through training.

Trainings to Address Organizational and Group Trauma

In recent years, the concept of "trauma" has taken root as an effective way to understand the causes and consequences of problems within group, organizational, and community systems. The problem of how to address trauma in groups can be addressed through trainings developing knowledge and skills as related to trauma. Why? Trauma implies disruption, and how well the system can cope with disruption should be of major concern to any system. For example, trauma affects communication, power and empowerment, emotions, conflict, and cognitions, and these are closely linked to trust and the capacity to form and support human bonds and relationships. As such, trauma may create disruption in a variety of ways. Clients may come to the agency with personal trauma. Workers can experience this as vicarious trauma by working closely with such clients. But further, the organizations may in fact be trauma-producing themselves! Because of ongoing issues of under-resourcing or poor (or traumatized) leadership or stressful environments, the organization may become maladapted. Indeed, many social service organizations are functioning as trauma-organized systems (Bloom & Sreedhar, 2008). Consequences include authoritarian and punitive administrators, and workers become more aggressive and exhibit passive-aggressive behavior. The entire organizational environment may become progressively more unjust (Bloom & Sreedhar, 2008).

Community Education

The value of education and training does not stop with small groups and organizations. Often, larger mezzogroups, such as communities can benefit from education and training activities. In recent years, for example, social workers have created or participated in community education programs to address issues as disparate as sexually transmitted disease (STD) prevention, violence reduction, health education, cultural sensitivity, and environmental concerns.

Developing the appropriate education program is often complex. A number of issues as diverse as how to choose the best model all the way to how to effectively communicate in a small group has to be taken into consideration. Further, social media provides useful tools for both identifying and contacting potential target groups, as well as actually distributing informational content.

Ideally, community education seeks to empower and build internal capacity among the members or residents. As with organizational training and education, it is important for the members of the target community to be involved in the definition of the problems and the structuring of interventions. Education and training at the community level tend to focus on increasing community awareness and understanding of social issues and community problems (DuBois & Miley, 2008). Social workers make formal presentations at community meetings, serve as panelists at public forums, and conduct community workshops and seminars. The two examples in Case 10.2 illustrate how social workers may use education and training as a mezzolevel practice intervention.

CASE 10.2   EDUCATION AND TRAINING INTERVENTIONS FOR SOCIAL WORKERS

Marcus W

Marcus W is the social worker with the Chester Community Improvement Project, a grant-funded agency that provides community residents with information to assist them in home ownership. The project seeks to address the needs of families through its rehabilitation project, new housing construction project, mortgage counseling, and job training for youth. Marcus designed a series of workshops for local residents to educate them about financial literacy, saving for the first home, and understanding mortgages. Marcus discussed the current condition of the local neighborhood and cited statistics showing that the neighborhood could be stabilized by increasing home ownership among the residents.

Sharon D

Sharon D is a second-year student placed with the local charter school. The past year the school was in jeopardy of not making the Annual Yearly Progress benchmarks. Significant numbers of students scored below grade level in reading and math.

In consultation with parents, students, and staff, Sharon and a staff member from the school developed a homework after-school project for parents. The program is designed to tutor parents in upper-level math and science so that they will be able to provide assistance to their children. In addition to the classes, Sharon has developed a monthly newsletter to communicate to parents about school events and provide tips on subjects such as time management and reducing stress.

Planning and Program Development

Generalist social workers may also find planning and program development as a necessary mezzolevel intervention. Many of the problems identified by the target system may best be addressed by creating new programs and services. Sometimes, an organization may choose to provide a new service. But communities as well may benefit from programs that target the entire community. Planning, like education and training, has many dimensions and considerations. But there are two broad types: strategic planning and planning for program development.

Strategic Planning

Strategic planning focuses on giving the client system longer term direction and identifies the steps to achieve the identified outcomes. Both organizations and communities may benefit from the development of strategic plans. Such plans can help identify concerns, assess and identify group values, create and operationalize goals, articulate specific steps, and help to characterize challenges and opportunities. Further, external funding may be enhanced through strategic planning. Often, funders require strategic plans. The funder may see the plans as evidence that the group has adequately examined the need for certain programs, as well as the strengths and weaknesses of the system. Showing alignment between a strategic plan and a grant proposal will greatly improve the system being funded.

While what specifically goes into a strategic plan should be dictated by the group's needs, it usually describes the goals, needs, problems, and tasks for the group over the intermediate to longer term future. While it makes total sense that having a plan is a critical element for an organization or community, it is often the case that plans are old, out of date, and no longer relevant to the realities in which a group may find itself. A generalist social worker can help in the development or updating of a strategic plan.

In some ways, the strategic plan should be a priority concern for an organization or community. As such, it can become not just a guide, but a real review of what is relevant or what is not. Brody (2014) presents a series of steps and questions that can guide the strategic planning process. These include:

1. Carefully examine the purposes for the plan

2. Determine the level of commitment of major constituencies

3. Establish a committee to oversee the effort

4. Assess the problems, opportunities, and strengths of the organization

5. Analyze and/or recreate the organizational vision

6. Examine/revise and/or draft a mission statement

7. Prioritize the challenges to the organization

8. Develop mid- and long-term goals

9. Submit a draft of the plan for multiple reviews by different constituencies

10. Implement the plan

11. Update annually (p. 35)

SWOT Analysis

One model to assist in this process is called a SWOT analysis, which stands for strengths, weaknesses, opportunities, and threats. The results of the data analysis are organized into a four-component framework, which is divided into two internal analysis components (strengths and weaknesses) and two external components (opportunities and threats). Strengths and opportunities are helpful to the organization, whereas weaknesses and threats are those things that may be harmful to the organization. This perspective is shown in Table 10.7.

Program Funding

Program development is not only a strategic activity, but also a necessary activity at the level of the program. The "program" is one of the central organizing units of social work practice. A program is defined as a coordinated service or set of services, often with its own set of resources, workers, and administrators. It is here that planning often connects with the issue of resources for the system. Resources and money are often the source of a group's problems. At the very least, creating new programs often requires newly developed funds. As such, identifying and/or developing resources is often an essential concern of the social worker.

There are many ways a program may enhance its resources. A description of each type of funding is provided in Table 10.8, with a short description of the considerations needed for each.

TABLE 10.7 SWOT Analysis

STRENGTHS	WEAKNESSES
▦ What do we do best?	▦ What could we improve?
▦ What unique knowledge, talent, or resources do we have?	▦ What knowledge, talent, skills and/or resources are we lacking?
▦ What advantages do we have?	▦ What disadvantages do we have?
▦ What do other people say we do well?	▦ What do other people say we don't do well?
▦ What resources do we have available?	▦ In what areas do we need more training?
▦ What is our greatest achievement?	▦ What complaints have we had about our service?
OPPORTUNITIES	**THREATS**
▦ How can we turn our strengths into opportunities?	▦ What obstacles do we face?
▦ How can we turn our weaknesses into opportunities?	▦ Could any of our weaknesses prevent our unit from meeting our goals?
▦ Is there a need in our agency that no one is meeting?	▦ Who and/or what might cause us problems in the future? How?
▦ What could we do today that isn't being done?	▦ Are there any standards, policies, and/or legislation changing that might negatively impact us?
▦ How is our field changing? How can we take advantage of those changes?	▦ Are we competing with others to provide service?
▦ Who could we support? How could we support them?	▦ Are there changes in our field or in technology that could threaten our success?

SWOT, strengths, weaknesses, opportunities, and threats.

Source: From SWOT analysis: Questions for conducting an analysis with your team. Retrieved from http://www.civilservice.louisiana.gov/files/divisions/Training/Job%20Aid/Supervisor%20Toolbox/Questions%20for%20Professional%20SWOT.pdf

TABLE 10.8 Methods of Program Funding in Social Work Practice

FUNDING METHOD	DESCRIPTION	ISSUES
Fee for service	Client pays for service provided	Requires enough clients who have disposable income to support agency. Client numbers change, making planning difficult.
Third-party payments, insurance reimbursements	Payments made by insurer for services	Limited types of services covered. Requires certification/licensure. Services may require preauthorization by insurance company.
Loans—commercial source	Loans provided at market rates	Market rates fluctuate—rates based on agency credit rating.
Loans—government or noncommercial source	Loans provided at nonmarket rates, often by government agencies	Eligibility often linked to specific policy/problem areas.
Contract with governmental source	Governmental source (federal, state, county) preselects types of services/clients, and chooses and contracts with agency to provide services	Dependent on political and legislative action. Agency must meet eligibility criteria. Contracts are competitive. Time-limited. Applies only to limited types of services or clients.
Grants—governmental source	Agency writes grant proposal for funds to underwrite program. Government source evaluates and chooses among submitting agencies.	Dependent on political and legislative action. Requires grant-writing expertise. Long application period with no guarantee of funding. Time-limited funding. Many limits on use of funds.
Grants—foundation source	Agency writes grant proposal for funds to underwrite program. Foundation source evaluates and chooses among submitting agencies.	Dependent on foundation attention to problem area. Requires grant-writing expertise. Long application period with no guarantee of funding. Time-limited funding. Most funding sources are small. Many limits on use of funds.
Grants—general source (United Way, Walmart)	Agency writes grant proposal for funds to underwrite program. Foundation source evaluates and chooses among submitting agencies.	Dependent on foundation attention to problem area. Requires grant-writing expertise. Long application period with no guarantee of funding. Time-limited funding. Many limits on use of funds.
Direct solicitation fundraising	Bake sales, direct mail requests, employee contributions	Unless the organization is well-known or "in the public spotlight," contributions tend to be small. Usually very undependable.

Grant Writing

While having knowledge about all of these areas is often necessary, the one resource development skill set that all generalist social workers should develop is grant writing. Many organizations supplement or expand their resources through grant writing; it is easy to see why. Americans have a long history of giving, and between federal, state, and local governmental sources and the vast number of grant-making foundations, there are literally thousands of sources with billions of dollars. Indeed, in 2016, statistics show that American's total charitable contributions exceeded $390 billion (IUPUI Lilly Family School of Philanthropy, 2017). Although most of this funding (71%) came from individuals, 68 foundations donated more than $75 million each in 2013 (Philanthropy Roundtable, 2018) and many dozens more giving $1 million or more. Berlin (2017) reports that in 2016, the U.S. government allocated approximately $666 billion in federal grants to support state and local programs.

The process of writing a grant can range from an endeavor that is very short and simple —typically for small, community grants—to complex and exhaustive. But in general, the process of applying for and organizing most grant proposals is more or less done the same way. The general steps are: (a) develop a clear project or problem; (b) select the grant source; and (c) write the proposal. Each of these steps is described in detail.

Step 1: Develop a Clear Project or Problem

This part of the process is not really very different from planning for any intervention, with perhaps two important differences. First, in many cases, the focus of the project now may expand beyond the needs of a specific agency to possibly include other system client needs as well. Often effective interventions will be strongest if many "partners" are a part of the process. While you might consider seeking funding for what is known as "capacity building," enhancement of skills, or agency infrastructure, you might also consider writing a grant to address an unmet client need through partnerships with other organizations as well. In doing so, the funding may be of value in addressing the organization needs at the same time as it is helping the clients.

A second difference that may apply here is that most successful grants depend on a grounding in the literature. An empirical basis for any project, as drawn from the literature of social work, sociology, psychology, or similar fields, will have a much greater chance of success than one that is based on anecdotes or practice wisdom alone. Funders, especially for larger grants, want to provide money to projects that are likely to succeed. And the empirical basis may provide the evidence needed to support that sense.

Overall, you can think about the types of project or problems as one of several types. You will want to identify the type that is closest to your intent. Doing so will make searching for grants a bit easier and will improve the chances of being funded. The various types of projects and problems include the following:

- Research or planning projects/problems: funds provide money for projects designed to help the agency examine a problem and/or plan for new services

- Demonstration projects: projects designed to implement new or untested services

- Operating expenses and services support: projects designed to raise funds for existing services

- Endowment development: projects designed to help build the endowment and long-term assets of the agency

- Construction projects: projects designed to help the agency build a new physical plant or renovate the physical plant

- Capacity building: projects designed to enhance the skills or knowledge of the staff or to improve the agency's infrastructure

While there are grants available for all of these types of projects, some are more available than others. Typically, funding will be somewhat more available for research or planning, demonstration projects, or capacity building than for construction or endowment development. Operating expenses and service support, commonly an ongoing need in any organization, are fairly easy to find funding for, but rarely in large amounts or in the amounts necessary to do anything more than partially support a major project. To put this another way, funding is an ongoing activity, and grant writing, while of unquestionable value, is also an ongoing process.

Step 2: Select the Grant Source

To begin, you must find out who (what organization) is providing funding. This is, at least "on paper," actually fairly easy, as organizations that give away money must notify the public that funds are available, although finding the right source might be more difficult. The notifications you will be seeking are variously known as an RFP (Request for Proposals), NOFAs (Notice of Funding Availability), FOAs (Funding Opportunity Announcements), or SUPER NOFAs (groups of NOFAs). Table 10.9 shows the content RFPs typically describe.

Make sure you review these sections carefully. Many grant sources receive hundreds of applications, so you must prepare the right proposal for the right source. Although individuals may provide grant funds, most conceptualizations of grant funding sources focus on government (federal, state, local), or a foundation. There are advantages and disadvantages to the different grant sources. Government sources are often considered to be more prestigious and high-dollar, but very competitive, restrictive, and extremely complex to write. Foundations, on the other hand, are more varied. With literally thousands of different sources, it is possible to find everything from large, high-dollar, complex grants to small, essentially noncompetitive microgrants.

Where does one find an RFP, or learn about grant sources? From the federal government, the *Catalog of Domestic Federal Assistance* was the standard until the opportunities provided by the Internet. Now, almost every government agency provides information about sources at their websites. And even easier source is www.grants.gov, which collects information across agencies.

For foundations, comprehensive information is harder to find simply because of the number of foundations that exist. Yet again, several websites exist that can help, although they are often fee or subscription based. Table 10.10 presents some useful sites for government and foundational supports.

TABLE 10.9 Components of RFPs in Social Work Practice

SECTION	INFORMATION PROVIDED
Information about funder	Name of program Name of organization and auspice
Funding amounts and time frames	Minimum, maximum, and average grant size Duration of grant (typically 1 to 3 years, sometimes renewable) Expected match amount
Selection criteria—what may be funded	This could involve 　Discipline(s) 　Problem area(s) 　Client characteristics 　Geography 　Intervention approach, methods, or activities
Selection criteria—what may not be funded	Commonly seen 　Limitations on overhead (indirect costs), administration, travel, etc. 　Construction, lobbying, endowments
Application process	Due dates Contact information Where to get application forms (if necessary) Grant/technical assistance advisor

RFPs, request for proposals.

Step 3: Write the Proposal

Writing the proposal may seem complex, but in many ways it really only involves drawing together information that may already exist, albeit it must be put together in a clear, concise,

TABLE 10.10 Grant Search Engine Websites

WEBSITE	AGENCY/FOUNDATION
www.grants.gov	Grants Learning Center: Your gateway to the federal grants world. The Grants Learning Center is where you can learn more about the federal grants life cycle, policies on grants management, and profiles on grant making.
www.foundationcenter.org	The Foundation Center is the leading source of information about philanthropy worldwide. Maintains a comprehensive database about U.S. and global grants.
www.grantspace.org	A database maintained by the Foundation Center, GrantSpace provides easy-to-use, self-service tools and resources to help nonprofits worldwide become more viable grant applicants and build strong, sustainable organizations.
https://grantwatch.com	Website for international, Canada, and U.S. federal, state, local, foundation, and corporation grants

and logical way. While every proposal *must* be specific to the RFP and *must* follow all of the directions perfectly, it is also the case that the components of most proposals are similar. These components are shown in Table 10.11 (Coley & Scheinberg, 2008, p. 4).

Each of these sections should be logically connected to the others. This means that every section of the proposal builds on what has gone before and prepares for what comes after. While this might seem evident and obvious, the lack of logical connection is a common flaw. One way to avoid this is to remember that that the strongest proposals will have a clear relationship between indicators of need, your outcome objectives, and the degree of change in outcomes you seek to demonstrate in your evaluation. Do not identify and

TABLE 10.11 Common Grant Proposal Sections

GRANT SECTION	INFORMATION PROVIDED
Title or Cover Page	Often supplied by funder. Includes contact information for submitting organization.
Abstract	Short overview of proposal. Typically, 100–150 words.
Introduction/Summary	One- to three-page summary of the project. Introduces the project and the agency to the funder. Includes the mission and vision of the agency.
Needs Statement (Problem Statement)	The Statement of Need describes what the problem/issue is that the grant wants to address. Typically, includes a problem definition, statistics describing the community setting, the size of the problem, and some evidence about the seriousness of the problem (such as a comparison statistic of your target group to other groups).
Project Description	Identifies the project goals and objectives and provides details about the implementation plan, including the timeline to complete project activities. This section often includes a scope of work grid of the project delivery plan.
Evaluation Plan	Explains the measurement procedures that will be used to determine if the goals and objectives have been met.
Budget Request	Itemizes the expenditures of the project and includes a rationale or budget justification for the expenses.
Applicant Capability	Demonstrates the applicant's past performance and ability to accomplish the proposed project. Often includes an organizational chart.
Organizational Sustainability	Indicates the plan to continue the project beyond the requested funding period.
Letters of Support	Letters reflecting support for the proposed project from program recipients, community leaders, partnering agencies, coalitions, religious organizations, universities, or political leaders.
Memoranda of Understanding	A written agreement from each of the partners or co-applicant agencies on how they will cooperate to implement the grant.
Appendix Materials	These may include an audited financial statement, insurance documentation, or any other documentation required by the funder.

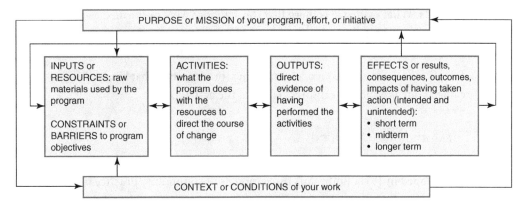

FIGURE 10.1 Logic model for the grant development process.

Source: From Milstein, B., Chapel, T. (n.d.). Developing a logic model or yheory of change. Retrieved from https://ctb.ku.edu/en/table-of-contents/overview/models-for-community-health-and-development/logic-model-development/main

measure a need one way, while focusing your objectives and evaluation criteria some-where else.

One tool that is commonly used as part of the grant development process is a logic model. The logic model serves a number of useful purposes, both to the organization that is submitting it and for the funders, who are increasingly requiring these with grant sub-missions. A logic model presents a picture of how your effort or initiative is supposed to work. It explains why your strategy is a good solution to the problem at hand. Effective logic models make an explicit, often visual, statement of the activities that will bring about change and the results you expect to see for the community and its people. A logic model keeps participants in the effort moving in the same direction by providing a common lan-guage and point of reference; see Figure 10.1 (University of Kansas Center for Health and Development, 2017a).

While there a number of useful resources as to what is included in a logic model, and everything else related to grant development, you should follow the explicit directions given by a potential funder. A logic model typically provides a table that describes:

- **Purpose**, or mission. What motivates the need for change? This can also be expressed as the problems or opportunities that the program is addressing.

- **Context**, or conditions. What is the climate in which change will take place? How will new policies and programs be aligned with existing ones? What trends com-pete with the proposed program?

- **Inputs**, or resources or infrastructure. What raw materials will be used to conduct the effort or initiative? Inputs can also include constraints on the program, such as regulations or funding gaps, which are barriers to your objectives.

- **Activities**, or interventions. What will the initiative do with its resources to direct the course of change? Your intervention, and thus your logic model, should be guided by a clear analysis of risk and protective factors.

- **Outputs**. What evidence is there that the activities were performed as planned? Indicators might include the number of mentors trained and youth referred, and the frequency, type, duration, and intensity of mentoring contacts.

- **Effects**, or results, consequences, outcomes, or impacts. What kinds of changes came about as a direct or indirect effect of the activities?

Models of Community Practice

Rothman (1995) identify three models of community organization and macropractice. Originally developed in 1970, Rothman's three models of community practice have probably been one of the most influential conceptualizations of community social work practice. The three approaches are:

- Locality development

- Social planning

- Social action

The locality development model is referred to as a bottom-up approach because it is a self-help, participatory model of change. It is based on the premise that for change to occur, it is necessary to include the broadest possible participation of community citizens in the planning implementation and evaluation process (see Case 10.3). It places a great deal of emphasis on self-determination and the democratic process. Professionals cannot change the community for the people; they must do that themselves (Models of Community Practice, 2019). The overall goal of locality development is to enhance the relationship between the community power structure and its citizens. This approach assumes that all parties have, or can come to have, common interests, and any differences are reconcilable through rational discussion and interaction (Hyman, 1990). Considerable attention is given to group dynamics, participation in the planning, implementation, and evaluation process, democratic procedures, self-help, the development of community leaders, and education. This model places great emphasis on consensus and cooperation.

Social planning is referred to as a top-down model of community change. It emphasizes the technical aspects of solving problems. Professionals who have specialized expertise guide and control the change process through the use of technical skills such as sophisticated data collection and analysis. The model provides little opportunity for citizen input into the planning process.

Rothman's social action model assumes one segment of the community is being overlooked or bypassed. The focus of this model is on organizing those segments of the community to stand up for their rights, to demand that their needs and concerns be addressed (Models of Community Practice, 2019). This model emphasizes social advocacy to bring about change in communities or community practices, and to redistribute power, resources, and decision-making processes in the community. This model brings issues of social justice, equity, oppression, and discrimination to the forefront of the community's consciousness.

CASE 10.3   EXAMPLE OF A LOCALITY DEVELOPMENT MODEL: THE PRESTON ARTISTIC HISTORY

Preston, Pennsylvania, has a long history of participation in the arts, and although neither its size nor its wealth would suggest it, many famous musicians and artists lived or worked in Preston throughout the 20th century. Famous artists such as Bill Haley, John Coltrane, and many others had connections to, or lived in, Preston in earlier times. Many visual artists and dancers also lived and performed in Preston in the years immediately preceding and closely following World War II.

Sadly, however, major economic changes affected the city from the 1960s onward. Indeed, Preston lost its tax base and virtually all of its manufacturing jobs, as well as a vibrant commercial community. These events, as well as a period of political corruption, decimated the artistic community. All of the organizations and institutions that supported the arts (except for two small community groups) were forced to close. And to make matters even worse, the arts and music programs in the local school district were dramatically cut back and even eliminated for many grades. By the early 1990s, no art galleries existed in Preston and no clubs of any type supported music, (again) except for a small school program and small programs offered by the YWCA and one other group.

At the same time, a core of artists and musicians continued to exist in the city. And thanks to one very dedicated city resident who was able to form a 501c(3) nonprofit organization, a small art gallery was established in 1993 for the first time since the 1960s. The agency, called the Irving Fine Arts Center, grew quite fast under the direction of its founder, Elise Irving. Within just a few years, the agency had established a number of programs, including a gallery, several children's art programs, a Visiting Artist in Residence program, a Friday night local music series, and an annual Children's Art Show at the local University Social Work Program.

Assessment

Over time, however, the director and the organization began to experience tensions. The director had a staff of three to five all-volunteer employees. Materials for the children's programs were chronically short, and after three very successful years, funding to support the visiting artist program ran short. One of the visiting artists, a longtime friend of the director, left in the middle of the season, with no reason given. Further, the volunteers seemed to be staying for shorter times.

To make matters more complicated still, many of the funding sources used to establish the programs were no longer available, either for reasons of state art program cutbacks or changes in foundation priorities. Some additional grants were available, but accessing them in the time available required information that the art center did not have. This information included a full description of the numbers served through the various programs, ages and other characteristics of their students, and benefits that the programs were providing for their students and the larger community.

Intervention

Due to the relationship that already existed between the art center and the local university social work program, the art center director contacted the dean and asked for help. As luck would have it,

(continued)

the social work program had recently redesigned a course in Social Work Practice with Organizations and Communities, and the primary assignment for that course was working with an organization. The course instructor asked the class to complete the following tasks: (a) to conduct a thorough collaborative assessment of the strengths and challenges facing the organization, (b) to collaboratively develop goals and objectives for the organization, and (c) to develop an intervention plan. Due to the semester time frame, the actual intervention and its assessment would have to be implemented by others, but this did not appear to be a problem for any of those involved.

The assessment the students developed and carried out was quite extensive. Using a combination of focus groups and surveys to examine the perspectives of the various constituencies (staff/volunteers, students, advisory board, and community residents), and an examination of the records the organization maintained, the assessment determined that the primary strengths of the organization were Elise (her energy and love of the project), community need and interest, and the relationship with the social work program. Challenges, on the other hand, included Elise (excessive micromanagement and fear of delegation of tasks), finances and lack of a financial /strategic plan, and no system for tracking services and clients.

The students then followed up this assessment with goal planning conversations with Elsie and members of the advisory board. They came up with two goals for the organization, subsequently as objectives and the intervention plan. The two goals and objectives were:

Goal I: To strengthen the long- and short-term financial health of the Irving Fine Arts Center.

Objective 1.1: To develop a comprehensive, 5-year strategic plan by July 2021.

Objective 1.2: To identify and apply for a minimum of five grant proposals each year between 2021 and 2026.

Objective 1.3: To establish a fundraising committee, composed of members of the advisory board and community volunteers who will develop and implement fundraising activities on an ongoing basis.

Goal II: To establish a flexible and user-friendly data management system for the Irving Fine Arts Center.

Objective 2.1: To develop and implement a computer information management system for data tracking by December 2021.

Objective 2.2: To identify and develop goals, objectives, and an evaluation plan for each program of the Irving Fine Arts Center by November 2021.

Objective 2.3: To select and train an evaluation committee, composed of members of the advisory board and community volunteers who will oversee evaluation activities on an ongoing basis.

Beyond these goals and objectives, the action steps and responsibilities in the intervention plan were laid out in a way that *reduced* the workload on Ms. Irving. Her micromanagement style, it seemed to all, was more of a response to a small organization that grew faster than the number of employees, rather than any intrinsic issues with the director. As such, it was hoped that time, along with the removal of many fundraising duties from Ms. Irving, would correct the problem of micromanagement.

(continued)

CASE 10.3

Further, several students and faculty of the social work program took it upon themselves *after* the end of the semester to work as volunteers to assist with some of the objectives. Two of the students, for example, wrote the software program for the data management objective, and then taught volunteers how to use it. In addition, one of the members of the faculty developed evaluation tools, and then analyzed data as it was needed. These results were used for assistance in writing several grants over the next 2 years,

Finally, programs were developed over time that enlisted social work students to provide case management services to families and individuals associated with the programs.

Evaluation

While the center continues to face many problems, and Preston itself is undergoing changes that have unclear results, it appears that the center is making progress in overcoming its difficulties. Several grant proposals have been successfully funded, volunteers are staying longer, and Ms. Irving now has a funded, part-time assistant. In addition, two venues for music performance have opened in the city, and two charter schools have implemented arts programs. There is hope that all of these efforts will reawaken the artist spirit that once permeated the community, but only time will tell.

Community Development

Rothman's models of community organizing significantly impacted the field of community social work. Current community practice, referred to as community development, incorporates all various aspects of his three models. Community development involves the participation of community members in developing a capacity and consensus in identifying and solving their own problems (Fellin, 2001). Social work interventions are often aimed at improving community conditions and empowering residents to seek community change. Community development also has a social action component, which includes activities aimed at challenging inequalities, confronting decision makers, and empowering people to change unjust conditions (Zastrow, 2009; Zastrow & Kirst-Ashman, 2009; Rubin & Rubin, 2008). Recognizing that power/disempowerment is often at the core of many social problems, social action focuses on social, political, and economic justice for the disadvantaged and disenfranchised (Weil & Gamble, 1995; Zastrow, 2009; Zastrow & Kirst-Ashman, 2009).

Community development strategies seek to improve community conditions, empower residents, develop resources, and mobilize citizen groups. To achieve these purposes, the generalist social worker organizes constituent groups, builds community coalitions, conducts community needs assessments, lobbies political and government leaders, and advocates on behalf of constituent groups. Community development activities may also involve economic development projects, installation of public facilities, establishment of community centers, recruitment of new businesses, code enforcement, and developing homeowner assistance programs.

To achieve the varying ends of community development, almost every social work practice skill is necessary. Social workers involved in organizing constituent groups often take responsibility for convening and facilitating meetings. They do the planning and the legwork to get participants to attend. This requires skill in managing groups and conducting meetings. An empowering approach to the process focuses on having community residents assume control and leadership of the development effort. The social worker helps get the process going, but the ultimate responsibility for the effort rests with participants and indigenous leadership.

Coalition Building

Both as an independent activity or as a component of community development, coalition building occurs when representatives of diverse community groups join forces to influence external institutions on one or more issues affecting their constituencies (Mizrahi & Rosenthal, 2001). The process may be intended as short or long term, but the idea is that there is strength in numbers; often the problems to be addressed are larger and more intractable than a single individual or group can effectively address—in other words, a "common goal" exists (University of Kansas Center for Health and Development, 2017b). A coalition, then, has as its goal to build a power base sufficient to influence decision-making and the allocation of resources (Weil & Gamble, 1995).

Unfortunately, coalitions are difficult to create and hold together. Often, there is inherent tension between the coalition members' interest in maintaining the autonomy and power of their constituent groups and the need to share power and resources to make the coalition successful. Additionally, a number of barriers often exist to a successful coalition. These may include issues of turf ownership, history, attempted dominance by one group or professionals over the larger public, inadequate leadership, or real or perceived costs (University of Kansas Center for Health and Development, 2017b). With such difficulties, all of a social worker's micro- and mezzoskills may be needed. Social workers need well-developed mediation and negotiation skills to effectively build coalitions, as well as skills in interorganizational relations and planning (Gamble & Weil, 2010).

■ Social Justice Issue

The social, economic, and environmental justice issues associated with mezzo–social work practice are too numerous to list here. The various justice issues facing many communities in this country are staggering. Never has the need for social work interventions been greater. One long-standing issue has been disparities in educational opportunities between wealthy communities and communities with large numbers of low-income and minority families. The quality of the school systems, the availability of resources, and the educational outcomes in low-income communities are significantly below those in more affluent communities.

Racial differences in educational achievement have increased over the past 40 years (Reardon, 2011). Garcia and Weiss (2017) report that

> ... extensive research has conclusively demonstrated that children's social class is one of the most significant predictors—if not the single most significant predictor—of their educational success. Moreover, it is increasingly apparent that performance gaps by

social class take root in the earliest years of children's lives and fail to narrow in the years that follow. That is, children who start behind stay behind—they are rarely able to make up the lost ground. (p. 1)

Garcia and Weiss found large performance gaps between high and low socioeconomic status (SES) children and that the gaps persisted over time. Low educational achievement leads to lower economic prospects in later life and the lack of social mobility (Garcia & Weiss, 2017).

Educational inequality is also related to race. A Brookings Institute study found "that on every tangible measure—from qualified teachers to curriculum offerings—schools serving greater numbers of students of color had significantly fewer resources than schools serving mostly White students" (Darling-Hammon, 1998, p. 1). Great disparities still exist. *The New York Times* reported that schools with mostly students of color receive less funding but employ more inexperienced teachers (Yin, 2017). See Case 10.4 for an example of two social workers' intervention to improve computer literacy in an economically disadvantaged school.

CASE 10.4   MOMS AND KIDS AFTER-SCHOOL COMPUTER LITERACY PROGRAM

Grace and Krystin are first-year master of social work students doing their field placement in a community-based program that focuses on educational issues. The agency is located in an economically disadvantaged community that is almost 100% people of color. The public school system is ranked the lowest in the state on most academic performance measures. It is a failing school system.

Grace and Krystin were asked by the agency director to identify a project that would help address an educational issue in the community. After talking with the agency staff and a parent group, they identified two issues. The first was computer literacy. Most of the families in the community do not have computers in their homes and this was creating a computer literacy gap between the children and their peers in more affluent communities. The second issue they identified was that many of the parents had challenges when they were in school and many, even if they graduated from high school, were not comfortable or able to help their children with their homework.

After brainstorming together, Grace and Krystin decided on their intervention project. The idea was to create a twice-a-week 10-week after-school program for mothers and their elementary school children. The program would have three components. During the first hour or so, the moms would help their children with their homework. Grace and Krystin would support the mothers as needed and encourage positive interactions. During the second hour working with their children, the mothers would receive basic computer instruction on word processing, use of the Internet, and email. During the final half hour or so, the children could do free play, do arts and crafts, or play games on a computer. The mothers used the time as a support group to discuss concerns and/or parenting issues.

The agency director liked their proposed project and encouraged Grace and Krystin to apply for grant funding. They identified a community foundation that supported computer literacy projects. They applied for $10,000 to hire a computer repair expert to upgrade used computers donated by a local university. They were successful with the grant application, and on completing the 10-week after-school program, each family was given a slightly used and upgraded computer.

■ Summary

Social work values and ethics utilize organization and community interventions to address social, economic, and environmental justice issues. Social workers engage in a partnership to work collaboratively with organization and community members and to identify assets and resources to improve services and the well-being of communities. At the mezzolevel, social workers engage in education and training, program planning, and community development–type interventions. The purposes of these mezzolevel interventions at the organizational level are to improve the functioning of organizations, to improve the delivery of existing services, and to develop new services. Their purposes at the community level are to improve community conditions, empower residents, develop community resources, increase citizen awareness of community issues, and mobilize citizens to work for change.

In planning interventions at the community level, social workers utilize a problem-solving strategy. Once the community has identified an issue they want to address, social workers engage with the community to conduct an assessment, set goals, develop interventions, and evaluate their efforts. Community development and education and training activities involve the participation of community members in developing capacity and consensus in identifying and solving their own problems. Social workers' activities include program development, advocacy, and coalition building.

CASE SUMMARY   "UNDOCUMENTED AND HOMELESS"

Practice Setting Description

Jackie is a first-year master of social work student completing an internship at an inner-city family service agency in the Southwest. The agency is located in a section of the city that has a high crime rate, gang activity, and failing schools. The area has a diverse population with a large number of immigrants from Central and South America and a substantial African American population. The agency provides individual and family counseling services on a sliding fee scale. The agency also runs a number of educational and treatment groups as well as a temporary shelter for women and their children. Jackie has been assigned to work with the women and their children in the shelter. Her primary tasks are to provide concrete services and supportive counseling to the shelter residents.

Background Information

Elicia T and her daughter, Maria, are undocumented immigrants from Mexico. They have been in the United States for 5 years. Elicia and Maria fled to the area from another southwestern city to escape her abusive husband approximately 2 months ago. Elicia is 25 years old and Maria 8 years old. Elicia has a 2-year-old daughter, Sarah, who was placed in foster care because of suspected abuse in the home. Sarah is in a foster home in a small rural community in the state hundreds of miles from Elicia's current residence. Since moving to the area, Maria has not been attending school.

(continued)

CASE SUMMARY

Elicia and Maria are currently residing in the agency's temporary shelter for families. They have been at the shelter for 2 weeks, and the agency has a 90-day limit. It is viewed as temporary housing, and the residents are only allowed to stay for 3 months. Prior to arriving at the shelter, Elicia and Maria were homeless and living on the streets.

Elicia is a high-school dropout and was a stay-at-home mother prior to leaving her husband and moving to a different part of the state. She chose to move there because she has two female cousins living in the area who are also undocumented immigrants. Elicia's native language is Spanish. She speaks some English but is not as comfortable speaking in English. Her English comprehension appears to be good. Maria speaks both English and Spanish well. When communicating with the staff, Maria acts as Elicia's interpreter since none of the staff at the shelter speak Spanish.

Maria appears to be behind academically. She struggles reading simple children's books written in English. It is unknown if her ability to read in Spanish is better than her English reading skills.

Other than her two cousins, Elicia has no other sources of support in the community. Her cousins have young families and limited resources but are well established and connected to a Latino community in the city and the local Catholic church. Her cousins refused to let Elicia and Maria live with them while she was trying to find her own place and a job. They stated that they did not have enough room and are concerned they would get in trouble with their landlord if it was found out that they were letting people stay with them. They sent her to the local church for help, and she was given the address for the agency's shelter by the priest.

Elicia has been looking for housing in the Latino community. The housing market is tight with limited options, and she has been unable to find anything that she could possibly afford. The only affordable housing she found was a room in a rundown motel that rents by the hour or by the month. It is in an area of town known for drug dealing and sex work.

On arrival in the community, Elicia found occasional work for a house cleaning company. The company hires undocumented workers, pays them very low cash wages, and threatens to turn them in to Immigration and Customs Enforcement (ICE) if they complain. The job bosses also exploit their female workers sexually, threatening to turn them in if they do not comply. Elicia was fearful about applying for other jobs because of her illegal status. She considered turning to sex work to be able to take care of her children, but her Catholic upbringing and thoughts of how doing so would shame her family have kept her from doing so. She is in constant fear of being detained, separated from her children, and having them placed in foster care. She is also afraid that she will end up homeless again and forced to live on the streets or return to her abusive husband.

Elicia is extremely reluctant to sign up for any federally funded services, even those that she and her children are entitled to receiving. On the suggestion that she enroll for supplemental food through SNAP, Elicia became nervous and refused as she has heard that participation in SNAP services, and others like them, would draw the attention of ICE, and she had heard stories on the news of individuals being deported after signing up for such programs.

(continued)

CASE SUMMARY

Presenting Problems

Elicia and her children are facing multiple obstacles. They need to find permanent, affordable housing and a job that pays enough to cover her housing and living expenses. In addition, Maria needs to be enrolled in school. Elicia also wants to regain custody of her youngest daughter in foster care.

Additionally, Elicia is experiencing an immense amount of stress, anxiety, and possibly post-traumatic stress disorder (PTSD). She described an instance where she could not calm down her breathing, and she felt lightheaded. She is very fearful of men and tries to avoid all contact with men in the community. She reports difficulty sleeping at night and feeling exhausted most of the time.

She is concerned about Maria. She has started acting out at the shelter, getting into fights with the other children, disobeying her mother, and being disrespectful and defiant to the staff and other adults. Elicia and Maria fight frequently, and when Elicia tries to discipline Maria, she throws a temper tantrum until Elicia gives up.

Elicia has many strengths. She had the strength to leave her abusive husband and move to a different city. She loves her daughters. She wants desperately to keep Maria with her and hopes to have Sarah returned to her custody. She is resilient and has managed to survive and keep her daughter safe despite not having a place to stay, a job, and a limited support network. Additionally, Elicia is highly motivated to find her own accommodations and support her children.

■ Discussion Questions

1. Identify an organizational (agency) or community intervention that would help Elicia and/or her daughter deal with their current situation. Discuss why you think your new intervention would be helpful?

2. For the preceding intervention, create a logic model. What components of your logic model were challenging to complete? Why?

3. Identify a potential funding source for your intervention. What are the funding requirements of your identified funding source?

4. How would you evaluate the effectiveness of your intervention?

■ References

Berlin, L. (2017). Money on the Table: Why Cities Aren't Fully Spending Federal Grants. Retrieved from https://www.lincolninst.edu/publications/articles/money-table

Bloom, S. L., & Sreedhar, S. Y. (2008). The sanctuary model of trauma-informed organizational change. *Reclaiming Children and youth from Trauma to Trust, 17*(3), 48–53.

Brody, R., (2014). *Effectively managing human service organizations* (4th ed.). Thousand Oaks, CA: Sage.

Coley, S., & Scheinberg, C. (2008). *Proposal writing effective grantsmanship*. Los Angeles, CA: Sage Press.

Cothran, H., Wysocki, A., Farnsworth, D., & Clark, J. L. (2019). Developing smart goal for your organization. Food and Resource Economics Department, UF/IFAS Extension. Retrieved from https://edis.ifas.ufl.edu/pdffiles/FE/FE57700.pdf

Darling-Hammon, L. (1998). *Unequal opportunity: Race and education.* Washington, DC: Brookings Institute. Retrieved from https://www.brookings.edu/articles/unequal-opportunity-race-and-education

Dubois, B., & Miley, K. (2008). *Social work: An empowering profession* (6th ed.). Boston, MA: Allyn & Bacon.

Elpers, K., & Westhuis, D. (2008). Organizational leadership and its impact on social workers' job satisfaction: A national study. *Administration in Social Work, 32*(3), 26–43. doi:10.1080/03643100801922399

Fellin, P. (2001). *The community and the social worker* (3rd ed.). Belmont, CA: Brooks/Cole Cengage Learning.

Fuller, J. B., Morrison, R., Jones, L., Bridger, D., & Brown, V. (1999). The effects of psychological empowerment on transformational leadership and job satisfaction. *Journal of Social Psychology, 139,* 389–391. doi:10.1080/00224549909598396

Gamble, D., & Weil, M. (2010). *Community practice skills: Local to global perspectives.* New York, NY: Columbia University Press.

Garcia, E., & Weiss, E. (2017). *Educational inequalities at the school starting gate: Gaps, trends and strategies to address them.* Washington, DC: Economic Policy Institute. Retrieved from https://www.epi.org/files/pdf/132500.pdf

Gellis, Z. D. (2001). Social work perceptions of transformational and transactional leadership in health care. *Social Work Research, 25*(1), 17–25. doi:10.1093/swr/25.1.17

Goleman, D. (1998). What makes a leader? *Harvard Business Review, 76,* 93–102. doi:10.1002/ltl.40619981008

Goleman, D., & Boyatzis, R. (2017). Emotional intelligence has 12 elements. Which do you need to work on? *Harvard Business Review.* Retrieved at https://hbr.org/2017/02/emotional-intelligence-has-12-elements-which-do-you-need-to-work-on

Hyman, D. (1990). Six models of community intervention: A dialectical synthesis of social theory and social action. *Sociological Practice, 8,* 32–47. Retrieved from http://digitalcommons.wayne.edu/socprac/vol8/iss1/5

IUPUI Lilly Family School of Philanthropy. (2017). *Giving USA.* Retrieved from https://givingusa.org/giving-usa-2017-total-charitable-donations-rise-to-new-high-of-390-05-billion

Lewin, K. (1947). Frontiers in group dynamics. *Human Relations, 1,* 5–41. doi:10.1177/001872674700100103

Mizrahi, T., & Rosenthal, B. (2001) Complexities of effective coalition-building: A study of leaders' strategies, struggles and solutions. *Social Work, 46*(1), 63–78. doi:10.1093/sw/46.1.63

Models of Community Practice. (2019). Retrieved from https://canvas.du.edu/courses/22997/files/1179222/download?wrap=1

National Association of Social Workers. (2017). *Code of ethics.* Silver Spring, MD: Author. Retrieved from https://www.socialworkers.org/About/Ethics/Code-of-Ethics/Code-of-Ethics-English

Ovans, A. (2015). How emotional intelligence became a key leadership skill. *Harvard Business Review.* Retrieved from https://hbr.org/2015/04/how-emotional-intelligence-became-a-key-leadership-skill

Philanthropy Roundtable. (2018). *Statistics.* Retrieved from http://www.philanthropyroundtable.org/almanac/statistics/#a

Reardon, S. F. (2011). The widening academic achievement gap between the rich and the poor: New evidence and possible explanations. In G. J. Duncan & R. J. Muranc (Eds.), *Whither opportunity?: Rising inequality, schools and children's life chances* (pp. 91–116). New York, NY: Russel Sage Foundation.

Rothman, J. (1995). Approaches to community intervention. In J. Rothman, J. L. Erlich, & J. E. Tropman (Eds.), *Strategies of community intervention* (5th ed., pp. 26–63). Itasca, IL: F. E. Peacock Publishers, Inc.

Rubin, H., & Rubin, I. (2008). *Community organizing and development* (4th ed.). Boston, MA: Pearson/Allyn & Bacon.

Schein, E. H. (1996). Kurt Lewin's change theory in the field and in the classroom: Notes toward a model of managed learning. *Systems Practice, 9,* 27–47. doi:10.1007/BF02173417

University of Kansas Center for Health and Development. (2017a). *The community toolbox.* Retrieved from https://ctb.ku.edu/en/table-of-contents/overview/models-for-community-health-and-development/logic-model-development/main

University of Kansas Center for Health and Development. (2017b). *The community toolbox.* Retrieved from https://ctb.ku.edu/en

Weil, M., & Gamble, D. (1995). Community practice models. In R. Edwards (Ed.-in-Chief), *Encyclopedia of social work* (19th ed.). Silver Spring, MD: NASW Press.

Yin, A. (2017). Education by the numbers. *The New York Times*. Retrieved from https://www.nytimes.com/2017/09/08/magazine/education-by-the-numbers.html

Zastrow, C. (2009). *The practice of social work: A comprehensive worktext*. Belmont, CA: Cengage Learning.

Zastrow, C., & Kirst-Ashman, K. (2009). *Understanding human behavior and the social environment*. Belmont, CA: Cengage Learning.

POLICY PRACTICE: HOW POLICY IS MADE

STEPHEN KAUFFMAN

Shortly after moving to her first job as a newly minted licensed social worker at the middle school, Kylie began to notice some unusual behaviors in the students that did not fit into any patterns she normally saw. Several students with histories of strong academic achievement were complaining of being unable to concentrate on their schoolwork, and indeed many had trouble staying awake in class. Following up with the parents of these children, she began to understand that the community flooding last summer may have had much to do with what she was seeing. She heard that the flooding had also affected a number of poultry and farm waste ponds (locally known as lagoons or slop pits), and that several chemical by-products were deposited around her community as the result of the flooding. These chemicals could well be the cause of what she was seeing in her students.

Unfortunately, the state would not release any funds to investigate the problem and help to clarify any relationship among the floods, waste, and symptoms. To address the funding issue, she heard that the state had considered enacting a new law to provide communities like hers with funds and expertise to look into this and similar problems. But the law seemed to be stalled. It had come up for votes twice, but both times it was tabled and sent back to the committee for further review. The local state representative seemed to be supportive, based on comments published in the local newspaper, but she found out he had voted to table the bill both times, and without his efforts, the bill had no chance of becoming a new law. She began to wonder why. What was affecting this process? Why was the representative, who seemed so supportive, apparently doing nothing to further the legislation? And what was this process that was slowing down the system? What did tabling even mean? She knew she had to investigate further.

LEARNING OBJECTIVES

This chapter focuses on Competency 5: Policy Practice, with emphasis on the policy formation and structural aspects of social welfare policy. The chapter begins with a review of the National Association of Social Workers (NASW) ethical principle and standards that address policy and social justice. This is followed by a definition of policy and the difference from norms. Then the chapter discusses the major characteristics and components of social welfare policy. The chapter then examines major social, political, economic, and historical factors that affect policy choices. Subsequently, we examine how policies are made, with primary focus on the legislative, executive, and judicial roles. By the end of this chapter, you will be able to:

1. Define policy, social welfare, and social welfare policy
2. Understand the centrality of policy in the NASW Code of Ethics
3. Understand the role of policy in addressing social welfare and social justice needs
4. Describe major historical, economic, organizational, environmental, and global influences affecting current social policies and services
5. Articulate major structural components of social policies and services
6. Articulate the ways policies are made

■ Competency 5: Engage in Policy Practice

Social workers understand that human rights and social justice, as well as social welfare and services, are mediated by policy and its implementation at the federal, state, and local levels. Social workers understand the history and current structures of social policies and services, the role of policy in service delivery, and the role of practice in policy development. Social workers understand their role in policy development and implementation within their practice settings at the micro-, mezzo-, and macrolevels, and they actively engage in policy practice to effect change within those settings. Social workers recognize and understand the historical, social, cultural, economic, organizational, environmental, and global influences that affect social policy. They are also knowledgeable about policy formulation, analysis, implementation, and evaluation. Social workers:

- Identify social policy at the local, state, and federal levels that impacts well-being, service delivery, and access to social services
- Assess how social welfare and economic policies impact the delivery of and access to social services
- Apply critical thinking to analyze, formulate, and advocate for policies that advance human rights and social, economic, and environmental justice

■ National Association of Social Workers (NASW) *Code of Ethics*

The NASW *Code of Ethics* (the "Code") is a policy document that addresses concerns about social policy throughout. And the importance of policy is clear from the Preamble onward. Indeed, the very first sentence in the Preamble lays out the basic guiding statement.

The primary mission of the social work profession is to enhance human well-being and help meet the basic human needs of all people, with particular attention to the needs and empowerment of people who are vulnerable, oppressed, and living in poverty. (NASW, 2017, p. 1)

As you will see in the following narrative, the NASW *Code of Ethics* is itself a policy document! And from it, the profession draws its interpretation of what social welfare policies should do, and why.

The Ethical Principles that guide our understanding of policy are clearly articulated in the Code. While all of the Principles have applicability in terms of policy, two are very clear. The first is about helping people in need and to address social problems. The second is about challenging social injustice (NASW, 2017). The specific language of these two principles can be found online (www.socialworkers.org/About/Ethics/Code-of-Ethics/Code-of-Ethics-English).

Further, these two principles are expanded in several places in the Code through the Standards. As with the Principles, virtually all have applicability, but perhaps the most direct statements are found under Social Workers' Ethical Responsibilities to the Broader Society. Here, the Standards are very clear. Social workers should promote the general welfare of society, they should facilitate public participation in the policy process, and they should engage in social and political action (NASW, 2017).

■ Social Welfare Policies: What Are They and Why We Care

Definition of Policies: What Are Policies?

The formal definition of a policy is conceptually straightforward, although there is no absolute, perfect universal definition. As Merriam-Webster Dictionary defines the term, a policy is a plan, a course of action, or a guideline to help address current or potential issues (Merriam-Webster, 2018a). On the other hand, the Centers for Disease Control and Prevention (2011) defines a policy "as a law, regulation, procedure, administrative action, incentive or voluntary practice of governments and other institutions" (p. 1). However, as the dictionary suggests, in the simplest terms, a policy is really nothing more than a rule or plan of action. But from here on, things get interesting!

Why? Every group, from a family to organizations representing everyone on the planet, wants or needs to regulate or change the behaviors of its members. This can be done in several ways. Sometimes, there are formal rules or methods, or sometimes there are just unspoken expectations. Sometimes there are agreed-on ways that the rules or methods are made, but sometimes the expectations "just sort of show up." Sometimes, these rules address earth-changing issues like global climate change or the rights of refugees. Sometimes the rules affect just persons residing in the United States, such as who may receive heating or housing assistance, or perhaps who and how a person may become a resident of the United States. Or sometimes the rules might address whether a state provides healthcare to persons above 180% of the poverty line or the cost a person must bear to go to college. And other times, the rules might simply determine the acceptability of the name of the fashion designer on our sneakers, or the kind of music we listen to, or even where we sit in a classroom.

Are all of these examples policies? Well yes, and no. It largely depends on how the rule came about in the first place. To understand the differences between things that are policies and things that are not, the place to start is with the distinction between two major ways groups try to control behaviors or achieve desired outcomes (and stop undesired outcomes)—policies and norms.

Policies Versus Norms

Groups, such as societies, have a variety of tools at their disposal to control behaviors or achieve desired outcomes (and stop undesired outcomes). Think about this for a moment. What influences how you act in a social context? While there are many possible answers, one powerful set of "influencers" are the rules set by others. While these rules can address major issues (murder and the killing of others, for example), they can also address very minor things, such as the foods on your plate. How do they influence? Part of it is the use of reward and punishment; if you follow the rule, you are rewarded (or at least you are not sanctioned), but if you do not, there are costs.

Both policies and norms are rules, and both have rewards and punishments associated with them, but there are important differences. The single biggest difference between a "policy" and a norm is the source. A policy is *formal and legitimate*, whereas a norm is *nonformal and nonlegitimate*. Now, that does not mean that a policy is good or real and a norm is bad or "fake." We all know there are plenty of bad, even stupid policies. Similarly, there are plenty of norms that are useful and desirable, while others are of questionable value. For our purposes, what legitimate and formal means is that a policy has been created by a legal, authoritative source, using legal, authoritative procedures. A Congressional law, for example, is legit-

> ▶ **Critical Thinking Questions**
> 1. What are some examples of behaviors you participate in that might be norms?
> 2. What happens when you violate norms? Are the consequences as serious as with a policy?

imate and formal. Our Congress has the authority to make a law, and generally speaking, people accept both the law and the right of Congress to make the law. That results in something we would call a policy. The acceptability of a fashion designer, on the other hand, has not been determined by a legitimate source that everyone accepts as authoritative. Some folks would not be caught dead in a pair of sneakers without a name brand. But others will wear anything as long as it keeps their feet warm and safe.

Oh, and as for where you sit in the classroom? My guess is that in the first grade, your teacher assigned you a seat (using the dreaded seating chart). That was in fact a policy, as your teacher had the legitimate authority to assign your seat. Now? Probably not.

One further difference between a policy and a norm is the power of the reward or punishment. In most cases, the reward for following a norm is acceptance by the group. The punishment is typically little more than a strange look, albeit over time these "strange looks" can lead to exclusion from the group, and as we see from the number of teenage suicides in America, exclusion can be very painful.

On the other hand, the punishments/rewards for following or not following a policy can be quite costly. Consider the fines of a speeding ticket or the years a person may lose in prison for even minor drug offenses. Groups indeed have power.

What Are Social Welfare Policies?

Policies, as you might conceive, affect many areas of our lives. We have policies that affect how fast we can drive on roads (think about speed limits), or what kinds of products are acceptable to sell in stores (when was the last time you saw plutonium at the grocery?), or how many ships our navy should have, or what our field placement considers appropriate dress (as presented in the Employee Handbook, if your agency has one). While a good argument can be made that all of these are incredibly important, social work tends to be more concerned with the policies affecting some life domains more than others. Many of these policies address human need, and are what are called *social welfare policies*. Most directly, social welfare policies are policies that target human need or quality-of-life concerns.

But the kinds of problems or issues that such policies may include are an open question. Some narrow perspectives suggest that it only includes policies designed to help the disadvantaged (Merriam-Webster, 2018b), while others suggest more expansive domains, such as social services in general (Dictionary.com, 2018). And some are thought of even more broadly.

The difference in how inclusive we interpret social welfare policies to be is based on how one defines social welfare, and how extensive, broadly, or even how important one sees the role of social welfare activities in the society in question. In the broadest sense, any organized activity seeking to meet human need or improve quality of life is "social welfare." This may include the domains identified by Maslow in his famous hierarchy of needs (Maslow, 1954). These include physiological needs, safety needs, belonging, esteem, self-actualization, and, added in later years (Maslow, 1971), self-transcendence. Another, more recent perspective, looks at the problem from the perspective of well-being, with dimensions including objective well-being (health) and subjective well-being (happiness; Harvard University, T. H. Chan School of Public

> ▶ **Critical Thinking Questions**
>
> 1. Why do you think the United States rates 18th in world happiness and not higher?
> 2. How do you define happiness? Are there any policies you can think of that would directly influence your level of happiness?

Health, 2017). Such a perspective has enabled the construction and application of a *World Happiness Report* (Helliwell, 2018), as well as the measurement of national happiness. Using this approach, in 2018, Finland, Norway, Denmark, Iceland, and Switzerland ranked as the world's happiest countries. The United States ranked 18th, and is dropping in the measures (Hetter, 2018)!

Interestingly, it may not be a coincidence that all of the countries with the highest rankings (except, arguably Switzerland) have the most expansive systems of social welfare policies. Is there a connection? What do you think?

One other way to conceptualize what might comprise social welfare policies looks at the aspects of a society that are critical for its survival. Warren (1987) identified what he called the five critical functions of a community—the things that any community must do to survive, which he labeled:

- Production–distribution–consumption (an economic system to help people meet basic needs)

■ Socialization (an educational system to teach the rules)

■ Social control (a system to protect members)

■ Social participation (a system to integrate members)

■ Mutual support (a system to help those in need)

Although Warren focused these on communities, it is clear they may apply to a nation as well as a community. Every society must create and support the systems necessary to meet human need and the quality of life that are associated with each of these domains. And this creation and support almost always takes place through the use of policies and norms. Indeed, history is rife with societies that fail to correctly implement one or more of these systems, and as a result, decay and sometimes even social collapse result.

There are a couple of interesting historical examples that might show how important these become. The ancient Chinese empires often talked about the "mandate of heaven," meaning that a leader (an emperor usually) could only lead as long as the "mandate of heaven" applied. Evidence that the mandate was in danger, or was lost, came about as famine, wars, or other social strife that affected the society. And many societies have collapsed because they could no longer feed their people. Not to project too far without supportive evidence, but one wonders what the effects of climate change will do to social order in a few decades!

Thus, for our purposes of definition, policies that affect all of these domains might be considered social welfare policies. But there are distinctions—relative priorities are often assigned to domains in different societies, resulting in some policies clearly considered social welfare policies, while other policies may not be so called. But what might determine the distinction? Here is a hint. Consider the word "welfare."

> ▶ **Critical Thinking Questions**
> 1. What does the word welfare mean to you?
> 2. How do you think most Americans define the word welfare?

There are actually conceptual categories that are used to clarify how we think about the centrality of social welfare in general to the society. As suggested in the preceding discussion, social welfare policies may or may not be at the core of what the society sees as important. So ask yourself, should social welfare include all (or perhaps most) of the social functions within its domain, or is it a bit of an afterthought? How you answer that question will classify your distinction as either having an institutional perspective or a residual perspective.

How a society classifies its thinking about the difference has some pretty significant consequences. For one thing, it has critical effects on how social policies are structured. For example, do policies address everyone or just some people? The *residual* perspective is the name we give to policies that target just some recipients, generally those who are most vulnerable to poverty—for example, Food Stamps (Supplemental Nutrition Assistance Program [SNAP] or electronic benefits transfer [EBT]), welfare cash assistance (Temporary Assistance for Needy Families [TANF]), and Medicaid are provided to only a part of the population. Indeed, most American social welfare policies are targeted in such a way.

It is useful to examine the assumptions people make to support the residual perspective (see Table 11.1). Perhaps the most important of these is that the primary justification for any request for assistance is that welfare needs are not the norm in a society. Rather,

TABLE 11.1 Types of Social Welfare Policies

CHARACTERISTICS	INSTITUTIONAL APPROACH	RESIDUAL APPROACH	
Role of social welfare	Central function of government—replaces or highly regulates the market to ensure needs are met	Secondary function of government— limited replacement of market functions (to address temporary market failures or support those unable to function in the marketplace)	
Assumption of need	Everyone	Only those unable to function in the market	
Service mind-set	Proactive and preventive	Reactive	
Service eligibility	Universal (eligibility open to all)	Selective (eligibility based on assessment of need)	
Methods for determining eligibility	Citizenship or presence	Means testing (income and assets)	Demographics (family composition, disability, employment status)
Justifications	▨ Some needs are ubiquitous ▨ Costs of meeting needs are high for everyone ▨ Concern about stigmatization of recipients	▨ Needs are best filled by market ▨ Focus on the truly needy ensures adequate resources for those in need ▨ Keeps taxes low	
Consequences of choice	▨ Everyone has care ▨ Tax rates tend to be higher ▨ Generally strong political support ▨ No stigma on recipients	▨ Some "fall through" cracks and get no/little care ▨ Tax rates tend to be lower ▨ Political support varies ▨ May be anger/stigma directed at recipients ▨ Encourages cheating	
Examples	Universal health insurance (UK, France, Norway, etc.) Family support, cash benefits (France, Sweden)	Temporary Assistance for Needy Families Medicaid (Medical assistance for low-income Americans)	

it is assumed that most people are adequately cared for by their own efforts and through market mechanisms (like having a job) and only in cases of market failure and temporary hardship should government step in and provide benefits. Generally, this implies the society has a limited and reactive mind-set about social problems. This is what is often called "the safety net."

On the other hand, some societies believe that meeting human needs is one of the central and most important roles for government. Such societies implement what is called the *institutional* approach. In these societies, the assumption is that personal efforts and the market are unable to address needs because of cost, market limitation (such as consistent unemployment), and historical factors like racism or sexism. Almost all of the so-called "developed" nations of the world except the United States maintain such a position. In consequence, a preventive mind-set and sense of social care are dominant. Again, Table 11.1 shows the assumptions underlying the institutional perspective.

What Are the Important Components of Social Welfare Policies?

Whether a society follows a residual or institutional approach to social welfare, there are important questions or components associated with any social welfare policies. This means what does the policy actually do, and how does it do it. To a degree, these can be thought of as the "who, what, how, and why" of social welfare policies. And how these questions are answered in a given society is often linked to that initial difference between the residual and the institutional approaches.

Eligibility: Selective Versus Universal Programs

Take the question of "Who is eligible?" for example. This question affects every single policy, and often a clue for how it may be answered is found by knowing how central social welfare is to a society. In other words, who is allowed to receive the benefit? There are a range of possible answers, although what is commonly found in societies with a residual approach are programs where eligibility is narrowly targeted, that is, some people are eligible but not others. These types of social welfare policies are called *selective* because the recipients are, well, selected based on some criteria. Most often, this selection is based on a combination of a person's demographic characteristics (such as gender, disability, employment, and/or family composition) and their economic status (usually their income and assets). Importantly, this can mean that every single person who seeks the benefit must be closely reviewed to see if they meet all of the eligibility criteria. How this is done differs from country to country, and even policy to policy. But the demographic criteria are usually examined by either self-report or some referral based on some previous examination. On the other hand, the name given to the examination of their economic status is *means testing*. This requires a close review of the person's ability to support himself or herself—their "means." It may involve everything from looking at a person's bank accounts, credit scores, and tax returns all the way to a visit and review of where the person lives and what he or she owns.

There are justifications that have been made to support selective eligibility. As shown on Table 11.1, these justifications range from value assumptions held by the society as a whole, to beliefs about human psychology, all the way to the cost of the policy. But overwhelmingly, the strongest assumptions are that selective policies will ensure sufficient resources are available to those most in need, with greater efficiency and lower cost (and therefore lower taxes) and better controls over cheating.

Some societies however—including mainly those who most generally follow the institutional approach—acknowledge other factors largely ignored by selective applications to justify a different level of eligibility—everyone! These types of policies are said to have universal eligibility. First among these is that some types of needs, like the need for healthcare, are experienced by everyone and the costs of addressing those needs are high enough that even higher income persons have difficulty affording care. Second, greater efficiencies are found by including everyone as there are always problems when making distinctions between people as to benefit or no benefit. For example, the line drawn between those who may receive the benefit and those who do not may result in a number of persons deemed ineligible who only earn a few dollars more than those who get the benefit. As a consequence, the ineligible may feel angry, frustrated, or cheated. And further, they may feel resentment toward those persons who received the benefit even though they are in essentially the same situation. Or those potentially ineligible may feel inclined to lie or cheat in order to pass the means test. Finally, many in the society as a whole may attach stigma to those who receive the benefit.

Thus, the alternative to selectivity is to provide the benefits to everyone in the society. These types of policies have been called universal because eligibility is open to everyone (sometimes only to citizens, but sometimes anyone who is in the country has at least some access). Worldwide, the most common example is healthcare, where again, as seen in many developed countries, the benefit is available to everyone in the society—not just to those who can pay or those who are poor enough for assistance (see Case 11.1).

Benefits: Hard Versus Soft Benefits

Another distinction in social welfare policies is what people get—what comprises the benefits. If you think about all of the different types of things that you need to live, you can guess that benefits can be many different things. Indeed, the range of items or services that could go on this list is as long as the range of items or services that are needed for a person's quality of life or happiness.

That said, the list is typically much narrower. Instead, it focuses on the kinds of things relevant to a more or less normal life in the country in question. And there are distinctions. For example, one distinction sometimes used is between "hard" benefits, which are things having some materiality, and things that are intangible, which are "soft," such as a right or opportunity. Similarly, there is a distinction often made between cash and what are called "in-kind" benefits, which means pretty much anything that is not cash. But these distinctions are only the start, for each type has a large variety of possibilities. Table 11.2 describes each and shows

---

CASE 11.1   YOU'RE COVERED OVER HERE: SOCIAL BENEFITS IN SWEDEN

Recently, William returned from a trip to Sweden. While he was there, his aunt, who lived there and whom he was visiting, had a very serious illness. For part of the illness, she lapsed into a coma for about 6 days. William was prepared to stay as long as necessary to care for his aunt. But on the third day after she came out of the coma, a social worker visited and explained what would happen during the course of his aunt's treatment and recovery. Putting William's mind at ease, the social worker told William that with Sweden's social insurance system, his aunt would receive care in the hospital for as long as medically necessary. Then, she would receive care in a nursing facility with full vocational and occupational rehabilitation for as long as needed. And when she returned home, she would have a home health aide for as much of the day as needed. She would also receive her needed medications and a cash support stipend for as long as needed.

All of this sounded wonderful to William, but he knew his aunt was far from wealthy. He asked what the cost would be and how much he might need to contribute. The social worker simply smiled.

TABLE 11.2 Types of Social Service Benefits in the United States

TYPE OF BENEFITS	STRENGTHS, ADVANTAGES	WEAKNESSES, DISADVANTAGES	COMMON EXAMPLES
HARD BENEFITS			
Cash (or checks)	■ Allows recipient to determine use ■ Administrative costs low	■ Recipient must apply ■ Concern about improper use/diversion ■ No/little external control over recipient	■ TANF ■ Social Security Old Age Pensions ■ Unemployment insurance
Vouchers (including targeted EBT transfers)—generally allows choice of vendor but within a category	■ May be moderate choice by recipient over selected vendor ■ Less concern about improper use than cash ■ Some external control over recipient	■ Recipient must apply ■ May be limited number of qualified vendors ■ Administrative costs moderate to high	■ Food Stamps ■ WIC vouchers ■ Vouchers for school choice
Commodity distributions (food, clothes, etc.)	■ High external control over recipient ■ Ensures commodity gets "in hands" of recipient	■ Recipient must apply ■ Recipient has little/ no choice over quality, quantity, or type ■ Administrative costs moderate to high	■ Bread, cheese commodities ■ Heating assistance
SOFT BENEFITS			
Tax deductions	■ High external control over recipient ■ Encourages desirable behaviors	■ Applies only if tax return filed ■ Applies only if tax paid ■ Requires high degree of knowledge by recipient ■ Administrative costs moderate to high	■ Bread, cheese commodities ■ Childcare deduction ■ Deduction for college loan interest
Tax credits/ deductions	■ High external control over recipient ■ Encourages desirable behaviors	■ Applies only if tax return filed ■ Requires high degree of knowledge by recipient ■ Administrative costs moderate to high	■ Earned income tax credit
Services	■ High external control over recipient ■ Use of services provides interface with experts/ professionals	■ Recipient may have little choice over provider or service ■ May be wait lists for service	■ Most counseling programs ■ Most educational programs
Rights	■ Generally widest impact ■ Makes powerful statements	■ Hard to measure ■ Often debates over meaning	■ Civil rights laws ■ Right to know acts

EBT, electronic benefits transfer; TANF, Temporary Assistance for Needy Families; WIC, Supplemental Nutrition Program for Women, Infants, and Children.

the strengths and weaknesses of each general type, which typically form the common justifi-cations for/against their use.

Overall, the issue of any given benefit selection comes down to a debate about a number of factors. Among these are degree of recipient control, degree of external (public) control, administrative cost and complexity, and the influence of external interests. Looking at the question by type of participant, while there are plenty of discrete exceptions, recipients prefer maximum control and choice while the public prefers some degree of control to ensure the benefit is used as a benefit. What is interesting, however, is the role that some external inter-ests (including social workers) beyond policy makers and recipients may play in the selection and support for given choices. Take SNAP or EBT, once known as Food Stamps, for example. There is huge support for this program from America's agricultural and commercial sectors due to the amount of money it pours into commercial activity. Even when there are calls to cut benefits for the poor, SNAP is often reasonably free from such cuts for this reason.

Why Should We Care: The Social Work Role in Policy and Policy Practice

Why any person should care about the social welfare policies in the society they live in should be coming clearer. Every society must concern itself with meeting needs. Social welfare poli-cies are one of the most important tools a society has for addressing needs and quality of life. Imagine for a moment living in a society that did not care for or had no systems to care for older adults, the sick or disabled, the hungry, or youth seeking an education? Or living in a society that did not have adequate clean water or had bad air quality? Or living in a society that allowed just a few people—perhaps those of only a certain skin color, age, or ethnic-ity—to own everything and make all decisions affecting a person's occupation? These are the kinds of questions a person, family, community, nation, or even the collective population of the planet must be able to answer and that will tell us why we should care about our policies.

But what about a social worker in particular? Why is it important to our profession? The simplest answers here are probably the most correct ones. On the one hand, as several pre-vious chapters have articulated, our profession is deeply rooted in values and ethics. At the core, the answer is both straightforward and profound. As articulated in both the NASW *Code of Ethics*, and the Council on Social Work Education (CSWE) Educational Policy and Accreditation Standards (EPAS), work on and for social welfare policies plays a central role in our profession.

There are many different ways our profession can implement these positions, many of which will be described throughout Chapter 12, Policy Practice: How to Conduct Policy Practice. But here are two ways as a sort of introduction—one is a method (policy practice), and the other is through commitment to our guiding principles (social justice and environ-mental injustice).

Policy Practice

Chapter 12, Policy Practice: How to Conduct Policy Practice, will more deeply discuss policy practice and will describe many of the methods that may be appropriate to a policy practi-tioner, but as a way of definition and introduction, policy practice is a desired aspect of social work practice. As with many of the concepts we are examining, there are multiple definitions and models (Wyers, 1991), but in most cases, it involves the application of social work skills directed toward policy change with the goal being enhanced social justice. For example, Jansson (2003) defined the concept as "efforts to change policies in legislative, agency and community settings whether by establishing new policies, improving existing ones or defeating the policy initiatives of other people" (Jansson, 2003, p. 10).

And as will be discussed in a following section, the role of social justice is central to our work with policy. The social work profession is a profession that basks in values and ethics, and our work with policy is essential in achieving such values across the society.

> ▶ **Critical Thinking Questions**
>
> 1. What are some examples of social welfare policies that have directly affected your quality of life?
>
> 2. What are some examples of social welfare policies that directly affect the clients in your field placement?

Summary

What are social welfare policies and why do we care? Every society must concern itself with meeting needs. While societies have different tools available to address needs and improve the quality of life of their members, social welfare policies have emerged as one of the most versatile and effective. As we have seen, there are a wide variety of approaches that policies may apply. And such variety allows policy makers to adapt different approaches to different needs and goals. As social workers, being well versed in the different approaches allow us to participate in policy work and to meet our ethical obligations to our clients, our neighbors, and indeed our planet. But, as will be seen in the following section, there are a wide variety of factors to examine when we say something is a "social welfare policy."

■ Policy Formation: Why Do We Choose the Social Welfare Policies We Do?

As you might suspect from what has already been stated, there are any number of different problem areas that could be targets for social welfare policies. There are also a number of different ways policies could be focused to address need. But importantly, all social policies are constructs of the entity (nation, state, organization) that creates them. Other countries may have very different policies—or even no policy at all—that affect the same problem or need. Consider the problem of healthcare. Some countries, like France, Norway, or Sweden have a system by which all healthcare is provided by government employees and all services are paid by tax revenues. The United States has a very different model, where healthcare services are overwhelmingly done by independent, private individuals. But even different states in the United States have different policies that address the need. You may have heard of the "Medicaid Expansion" that came as a part of the Patient Protection and Affordable Care Act (ACA). Some states have chosen to participate, while others have not.

The big question is why? Why do some countries or states have social welfare policies to address healthcare needs, while others do not? Why do some countries like the United States have a patchwork approach, while others fully centralize it? Why do some countries pay virtually all healthcare costs through tax revenues, while others, like the United States, have much of the cost borne by individuals and businesses? And why might some countries have little or no healthcare social welfare policies'?

There is no simple answer. But there are important clues drawn from economics, political science, sociology, and other academic disciplines. This section will hopefully illuminate the "why" problem.

Let us begin with a series of a discussion questions. These might help to clarify the kinds of issues that make policy choices the complex processes that they are. For each of the following examples, consider four questions. First, would you say the statement is "possible" or "not possible?" Second, would you say it is "highly likely to be true" or "highly unlikely to be true?" Third, would you say achieving the statement is "desirable" or "not desirable?" And finally, explain why you answered the way you did.

▶ **Critical Thinking Questions**

Are these likely to be achieved? Are they desirable? Why do you think so?

- Poverty in the United States could be eradicated within 6 months.

- Every American family could have good healthcare—as least as good as Medicare—within 1 year.

- Humanity could cut its carbon and other greenhouse gas emissions by 75% within 5 years.

- Religion should be a factor when determining the rights of immigrants to the United States.

- Merchants may refuse to serve persons for any reason, including sexual or gender identity.

Policy Foundational Concepts

How you—or how a nation—considers these statements is in part similar to the way you thought about your answer to the discussion questions. There are at least three important sets of factors (or concepts) that might be called *policy foundational concepts* (PFDs) that affect your answers. These PFDs might be thought of as groups of situational or belief factors that influence how people in a group think about many aspects of their lives, including what they see as important, what they are willing to pay for, what they believe government should do or not do, and how people should act toward one another and the world in which they live. The three PFD groupings are *Resources, Values and Ideology,* and *Social Relationships (including social structure and power relationships)*, and altogether they influence policy in many ways. Further, historical precedent plays a major role. How a society conceptualized a problem or a policy in the past will often provide important clues for how it is currently addressed.

Before we launch into a full discussion of each, there are some important assumptions or caveats to be stated. These include:

- PFDs are not static. They change, grow, and are altered over time. What is "true" about a society now may in fact be false in the past or future. For example, the United States did not "believe in" or provide much social welfare from the federal government prior to the 1930s. After the 1930s, however, federal efforts became the norm.

TABLE 11.3 Definitions and Examples of Policy Foundational Concepts

RESOURCES		BELIEFS/VALUES/IDEOLOGY		SOCIAL STRUCTURE AND POWER	
Resources are what the group has to work with (may be called "capital"		Beliefs/Values/Ideology (what the group believes)		Social Structure and Power addresses how the group organizes itself; who has power and wealth and who does not	
	Types of capital		Examples of beliefs/values/ideology		Examples of components of power and social structure
	Financial capital Capital goods Natural capital Social capital Instructional capital Human capital Public capital		Personal values Instrumental values (freedom, equality, justice, and solidarity) Operational (guiding process)		Class Gender Race Age Income Wealth

■ PFDs influence, and are strongly influenced by each other. For example, there is much evidence to suggest that a person's beliefs about money and social responsibility change as income and wealth levels change.

Table 11.3 shows the definition of the three PFDs and gives examples of each.

Resources

The simplest way to think about *Resources* and social welfare policies is to think about your own life. There are likely many things you would like to do but are unable because you may not have the money, time, or skills to do those things. On the other hand, there are some things that you must do regardless of your resource situation. In the latter case, not doing the thing causes some form of suffering, loss, or legal consequence. Therefore, you either must dedicate some resources to do these things, develop new resources to help to do those things, or suffer the consequence. Thus, in the domain of social welfare policies, the simplistic way of thinking about resources is that the more resources you have, the more you *can* do, but not necessarily will do.

What do we mean by resources? There are many kinds of things that can be thought of as resources that are available to a society, as well as different ways of organizing such resources. But here we will defer to economists who over the centuries have spent extensive time in analyzing the types of things that might apply here. And from them, perhaps the most useful classification approach is to talk about resources as capital, of which an extensive typology has been created. For example, there are different types including *financial capital*, which is money, wealth, or other securities. There is also a grouping called *capital goods*, which are produced assets that are used to produce other goods (like a factory that produces materials). *Natural capital* is what might be called raw materials or land. *Social capital* is a way of thinking about human interrelationships, while human capital is the capacities of people. There is also *instructional* capital (what can be taught) and *public capital*, or what we hold in common in terms of infrastructure.

Put a bit more simply, a society can draw upon wealth and income, natural resources, knowledge, technology, or people. Given a problem or need, the group needs to allocate resources to address the issue. If the United States, or any country, wishes to provide benefits through social welfare policies, there are costs. And those costs can be economic, increased taxation, social, or other. In some cases, those costs can be quite large. According to the United Nations (Organization for Economic Co-operation and Development, n.d.), across the globe in 2016, countries spent about 21% of their gross domestic product (GDP), which is a measure of the aggregate economic wealth of a country, on social welfare. For comparison, 20 countries spent a higher percentage than the United States, which spent about 19%. In real dollars, these numbers may be huge. In 2016, Social Security—the largest federal social welfare policy—paid out $916 billion, while all federal healthcare spending amounted to $1 trillion (Center on Budget and Policy Priorities, 2017), and the total cost from all sources was somewhere around $3.24 trillion. This total makes up about 17% of U.S. GDP, even with something like 10% of the population underinsured (Pollin, 2018). Education is similarly quite costly. According to the National Center for Education Statistics, the total cost for primary and secondary education in the United States in 2014–2015 was $668 billion. This amounts to $13,119 per pupil (U.S. Department of Education, National Center for Education Statistics, n.d.).

As a society, we have generally (though not unquestionably) agreed that these costs are worth the money. But what about what *we could* do? To help clarify the importance of resources here, let us return to the preceding Critical Thinking Questions for a moment. Consider the statements about poverty, healthcare, and greenhouse gas emissions. Believe it or not, all three of the stated outcomes are completely possible! We *could* eliminate poverty, provide high-quality healthcare, and curtail huge percentages of greenhouse gasses in a very short amount of time. But it would be very costly in resources. Income poverty might serve as a good starting point. Although good measures of poverty are fraught with problems (including large differences from actual need), and thus completely accurate cost estimates are difficult, some general calculations suggest the size of the problem. Poverty is currently defined as an income below $25,100 for a family of four in the 48 contiguous states (U.S. Department of Health & Human Services, 2018). Across the United States, the average income deficit of a family, meaning income necessary to reach the poverty line was $10,819 among 7,758,000 families in 2017 (Fontenot, Semega, & Kollar, 2018). The dollar amount needed to simply, over and above what we already spend, bring them up to the poverty line is approximately $84 billion per year, and this does not include individuals or, again, actual need (as opposed to poverty as defined by the poverty line, a concept discussed later). This is a possibly, but with a large cost.

But more dramatic might be the cost of health for all Americans. Medicare for all—one model that is being discussed—has current cost estimates of between $1.38 trillion per year and $2.8 trillion a year (Jacobson, 2017). Again, quite large, but still possible—especially considering how much we have already spent. But now, consider the final example—the cost to address climate change. Since climate change is a global problem, while completely agreed-on dollar values do not exist, all estimates are large. The latest National Climate Assessment (U.S. Global Change Research Program, 2018) puts the costs in stark language.

> With continued growth in emissions at historic rates, annual losses in some economic sectors are projected to reach hundreds of billions of dollars by the end of the century— more than the current gross domestic product (GDP) of many U.S. states. (U.S. Global Change Research Program, 2018)

Across the planet, this amounts to *trillions* of dollars.

Before you throw up your hands, move to a corner, and begin to cry, however, remember a few things. First, what choice do we really have? But second, remember resources are not only dollars—they include people, technology, and the opportunities that we create. Given those considerations, the next question is "Why don't we expend resources on such critical concerns?" Or a follow-up, "Why have we expended so many resources on some social welfare policies, but little or nothing on others?"

Beliefs: Values and Ideology

The answer to these last questions moves us toward the second set of PFDs—our beliefs, driven largely by values and ideology. Specifically, this second group addresses what the group believes. Like resources, this topic moves us well into a number of domains outside of social work. Most importantly, it moves us into questions of philosophy, religion, and psychology. Why? Because values and ideology address the big questions about life, the relationship between individuals and the groups they are a part of, and what kind of life we want to live. In other words, what is important? In

> ▶ **Critical Thinking Questions**
> What social problems concern you most due to their possible impact in your life? Why?

policy, they serve at least three critical purposes. First, they guide our thinking about the kind of society we want to create and support. Second, they provide guiding principles for how to make and implement policy. And third, they provide measures for success.

There are several somewhat similar terms that are used as people discuss these ideas; beliefs, values, ideology, and ethics. Values—a commonly used term—is the name we give to concepts, beliefs, or ideas that a person or group holds as important. Now, it is important to remember that values, like other beliefs, are concepts, and as concepts or ideas, they are without materiality, meaning it is difficult or perhaps impossible to hold values in your hand. But as ideas we see as important, they can motivate us to act, provide guidance as we think about a problem or course of action, and they can provide "benchmarks" (sometimes referred to as normative standards) to which we can compare actions or outcomes.

Values can be organized in many ways. For example, values can be classified as personal, meaning they guide our individual choices, or social/cultural, meaning they apply to social relationships and the organization of a society. Or values can be instrumental versus operational. Instrumental values are the "high-level" outcomes we seek as members of a group, while operational goals are guides we may use to get us there.

Ethics is the more specific name we give to the general or specific guides for action that derive from values. Sometimes ethics are referred to as applied values. But they face the same basic limitations as values—they are concepts and again cannot be held in one's hand. But what is important about ethics is they often guide behavior in many domains in a society. Think, for example, about, the NASW (2017) *Code of Ethics*. The Principles and Standards presented here are critical for making judgments about our actions.

Ideology, the last of the terms, is a bit more complex. It is a system of interlocking concepts or ideas—some purely conceptual and some drawn from experience—that form a conceptual structure for understanding the world, or what may be called a worldview. Often, these worldviews are associated with a political or economic culture (Oxford English Dictionary, 2019).

But where do our values, ethics, and ideologies come from? The simplest and most direct answer to this question is our history and experience. But beyond that answer, much complexity exists. It could have a behavior basis in our evolutionary history. But certainly, as humanity has evolved, as religions have arisen, and as our understanding of the meaning of being an individual or the member of a group has developed, so have our values, ethics, and ideology. Unfortunately, space does not allow a full discussion of this rich history to go here. And as the ethics of social work have been fully discussed in earlier chapters, here the focus is on the social/cultural beliefs that are important to our social welfare policies. Three types of values and ideologies are examined here: the instrumental values of freedom, equality, justice, and solidarity; beliefs affecting poverty policies; and beliefs affecting minorities including individual rights.

The Instrumental Values of Freedom, Equality, Justice, and Solidarity

Almost any discussion of social welfare policies begins with an examination of the major instrumental beliefs that have governed political and economic thinking in the modern world since the so-called Age of Enlightenment of 17th and 18th century Europe. As a point of comparison, with very few exceptions, for most of human history, very few individuals in any society were ever granted much in the way of freedom—certainly political freedom, but individual freedom as well. For us, living in the 21st century, this might not make much sense. After all, we can and do make choices about our lives all the time. But this ability is in fact rather new. For almost all of the history of our species, our choices and actions were profoundly constrained by the whims of a king, or the dictates of our religions, or the limitations of our caste, community, or family.

Something, however, dramatic began with the philosophical movement of the Enlightenment. Specifically, the individual increasingly was believed to be autonomous— both capable of personal choices and having the right to express those choices through action in the individual's relationship with thecommunity. This philosophical change gave rise to what I call the instrumental values of freedom, equality, justice (or equity), and solidarity. These are instrumental in some ways because they are among the most important political and economic values in the very construction of our political and economic systems, and therefore the policies that govern much of our modern life. What do these terms that we use so commonly now really mean? Are there parts of our lives where these ideas may come into conflict with one another?

Freedom

Freedom really has two different major meanings. When we think of freedom, we think of freedom to do something, as well as the freedom from some form of oppression or constraint. Within these two interpretations are vast ranges of possibilities and worlds of nuance. But in practice, this has generally meant that people may make economic and political choices (freedom "to") with minimal external political coercion (freedom "from"), although it is not too difficult to find lots of exceptions to this perspective!

Think of all the times you use this term on a near daily basis. Well, that is an important part of the story. But in our political and economic world, the term has profound purposes. The concept sits in a central place in our Republic's founding documents—the Declaration of Independence and the Constitution. Indeed, many of the statements comprising the Bill of Rights speak to the issue of freedom. The first amendment serves as a case in point.

> Congress shall make no law respecting an establishment of religion, or prohibiting the free exercise thereof; or abridging the freedom of speech, or of the press; or the right of the people peaceably to assemble, and to petition the Government for a redress of grievances. (National Archives, 2018)

Further, what was true at the time of the Constitution still carries weight today. We believe that freedom enhances our quality of life and our happiness. Many studies have examined this relationship and indeed many believe that personal freedom and choice should be valued above virtually everything else in our society (Markus & Schwartz, 2009). And the effects of this value on policy cannot be downplayed. Consider the debate over reproductive rights. What are the two primary opposing positions here? One of them speaks directly to freedom to choose what happens to one's body, and indeed this position has been embodied in policy initiatives such as the H.R.1964—Freedom of Choice Act (U.S. House of Representatives, 2008). Similarly, initiatives attempting to enhance freedom are found with the right to same-sex marriage and the rights of individuals to serve in the military, regardless of sexual orientation or identity.

One very important derivative value from this perspective relates to assumptions of personal responsibility. For most of American history, social policies placed much of the blame for one's plight on one's own choices. With our improved understanding of the ways that economies work, this rather hard assumption has somewhat been downplayed in recent decades. But there is still a significant strain of belief in our society that people suffer because of bad choices. Similarly, one of the goals often found in many of our policies, and indeed one of the measures of success in many of our policies is how the policy enhances personal responsibility.

Equality

The second instrumental value, and again one embodied in the founding documents of the republic, is the concept of equality. Like freedom, equality has different meanings. While formally, equality generally means equal treatment, just what equal treatment means can vary widely across the domains of life. Consider differences in what it might mean politically, or economically to treat everyone the same. And would such equal treatment even be desirable?

One such complication is found between the ideal of equal treatment or opportunity versus the ideal of equal results. Most Americans support the idea of equal treatment, while somewhat less agree with the idea of equal opportunity, and there is little support for the idea of equal outcomes. These differences have played out over the past century in the quest, through policy, to promote civil rights for various minorities.

From the time of the earliest settlements in North America until late in the 20th century, demographic groups other than White males experienced serious forms of systematic oppression and exclusion from American life. Such oppression and exclusion ranged from what was essentially genocide in the case of native peoples, to slavery in the case of African Americans, to limited or nonexistent rights and opportunities for persons of Asian descent, sexual minorities, and women.

As our collective understanding of equality confronted these serious injustices, a huge number—perhaps hundreds—of policy initiatives were proposed to expand the rights and opportunities for these groups. For example, a very partial list, beginning with the 13th Amendment to the Constitution, enacted in 1865, identifies 21 discrete policy actions affecting expansions of rights for African Americans in some way (U.S. House of Representatives Historian, n.d.). A different, more expansive compendium lists 70 separate actions addressing expanded rights for individuals who have experienced oppression or discrimination between 1865 and 2014 (U.S. Library of Congress, n.d.). Many of these policies—particularly those in the years after the passage of the 1965 Civil Rights Act—address a specific tool for achieving greater equality, affirmative action. Affirmative action is defined as

> a set of procedures designed to eliminate unlawful discrimination among applicants, remedy the results of such prior discrimination, and prevent such discrimination in the future. Applicants may be seeking admission to an educational program or looking for professional employment. In modern American jurisprudence, it typically imposes remedies against discrimination on the basis of, at the very least, race, creed, color, and national origin. (Cornell University, n.d.)

Yet, despite significant support for expanding equality and tools like affirmative action, the issue of both the meaning of equality and how to achieve it are still serious policy problems for the United States. Consider the legal treatment associated with sexual/gender identity. The LGBTQ (lesbian, gay, bisexual, transgender, and queer) in our population have only recently been winning more equal rights with majority groups. This includes the striking of antisodomy laws (U.S. Supreme Court, 2003), equal participation in military service with PL 111-321 in 2010 (U.S. Government Publishing Office, n.d.), and marital equality with the 2015 Obergefell v. Hodges Supreme Court decision (Supreme Court of the United States, 2015).

Despite such critical policy decisions, the inequalities remain. Many states have various discriminatory laws on the books. And many states are also attempting to limit the scope of LGBTQ rights, often through the use of "religious exemption" arguments (Human Rights Watch, 2018). Further, laws against the LGBTQ exist around the world, and recently, President Trump indicated a push to at least decriminalize homosexuality (Lederman, 2019). As promising and desirable as this is, however, some of President Trump's other initiatives regarding LGBTQ rights appear less satisfying. Among these are his 2017 directive ordering the military to prohibit accepting transgender persons from service. In early 2019, the Supreme Court upheld at least parts of the ban, based primarily on his authority as commander in chief (Williams, 2019).

Thus, achieving equality as a valued end in our nation shows evidence of forward motion, but with serious difficulties along the path. But Americans do support enhancing equality. As recently as February 2019, public polling from Gallup (Norman, 2019) shows new highs in percentages of Americans who support affirmative action programs for women (65%) and minorities (61%).

Justice/Equity

The third of these instrumental values is equity, or in application, the idea of just treatment or justice. For this discussion, I primarily focus on the idea of justice, for as with the other instrumental values, equity and justice have different meanings. But as social workers, we are interested in the application. And here, the commonality of meanings is all rooted in the idea of fairness or fair treatment, or as Aristotle wrote "equals should be treated equally and unequals unequally." But societies are complex, and the issues of past treatment, differing opportunity access, and even how a society differentially values personal characteristics like race, gender, gender identity, or age affects how justice is applied.

Generally, most Americans believe in and support the concept of fair treatment. Consider for a moment how we compensate people for their work efforts. Our economic system tends to value (perhaps overvalue?) and therefore reward people who have rare skills or talents, as well as those who spend long periods of time in educational efforts and/or work hard. Yet the model is not perfect. There are plenty of examples of people who study for years or work endless hours who in fact struggle to get by. Is that fair? Is that just?

Broadly speaking, justice is often divided into three types in our contemporary world. Distributive justice, for example, is concerned with how fairly the costs and benefits of life are shared. Retributive or corrective justice addresses problems of crime and punishment. And compensatory justice addresses how well people are compensated for past losses. There are many examples of how distributive justice impacts our clients directly and through our policy choices.

To that list, we also want to add a term with particular meaning for social workers and much of the work we do—*social justice*. Social justice is essentially fairness/fair treatment applied to the societal domain. One definition puts it this way:

> Social justice encompasses economic justice. Social justice is the virtue which guides us in creating those organized human interactions we call institutions. In turn, social institutions, when justly organized, provide us with access to what is good for the person, both individually and in our associations with others. Social justice also imposes on each of us a personal responsibility to collaborate with others, at whatever level of the "Common Good" in which we participate, to design and continually perfect our institutions as tools for personal and social development. (Center for Economic and Social Justice, 2019)

▶ **Critical Thinking Questions**
Does something called the "common good" exist? Why or why not? If so, what does it mean?

One of the most interesting aspects of this definition, but unfortunately one we do not have the time to explore, is the concept of the "common good." Does such a thing exist?

And what does it look like? Finding a fully agreed-on answer to those questions would go far toward eliminating conflict in our society! Unfortunately, we do not have a common definition.

But we do have some understanding (although not universally shared) of what social justice might mean in the policy domain. This vision also often incorporates the idea of economic justice as well. Again, drawing on the work of the Center for Economic and Social Justice (2019), economic justice means:

> Economic justice, which touches the individual person as well as the social order, encompasses the moral principles which guide us in designing our economic institutions. These institutions determine how each person earns a living, enters into contracts, exchanges goods and services with others and otherwise produces an independent material foundation for his or her economic sustenance. The ultimate purpose of economic justice is to free each person to engage creatively in the unlimited work beyond economics, that of the mind and the spirit.

The point in this definition, as with social justice, is that participation in a society ought to ensure a fair balance between what a person contributes to his or her society, and what a person gets back. In so many areas of our collective life, the returns for our efforts are not anywhere near commensurate with what we put into it. Consider the problem of wealth. From 1963 to 2013, the difference in percentage of income earned by the lowest and highest 10% of income earners grew dramatically. In 1963, the difference in average income between the two groups was about 700%.In 2013, it had grown to about 1,200% (Urban Institute, 2017). Similarly, during the same period, huge differences grew in wealth. In 1963, families near the bottom of the wealth distribution (those at the 10th percentile) went from having no wealth on average to being about $1,000 in debt, while families at the top of the distribution experienced a 500% increase (Urban Institute, 2017).

Why do such differences exist? Well, while a number of important factors are at play, among them are the relative growth in wages at the top and bottom of the distribution, the loss of protections by labor unions, and tax law changes that have all benefited people at the top of the distribution. But factors outside of economics are also critically important. Race (Conley, 2010; Oliver & Shapiro 2006), gender (Correll, Bernard, & Paik, 2007; Fortin, 2005; Matsumoto 2001; Nakdimen 1984; Weichselbaumer 2004; Young, 2009), age (c.f. Petit, 2007), and similar demographic factors have impacts. Such factors exist. Now, the question is: Are these differences acceptable? Are they just?

One area where the problem of social justice serves as a case in point that clearly shows the issues of distributive and compensatory justice is the problem of environmental justice. This concept, little understood before the 1980s, is focused on how the consequences and benefits of environmental actions have been unequally shared across society. Often, the benefits—such as profit—from manufacturing, development, mining, or waste disposal accrue to a small number of people (or even sometimes society at large), while the consequences—such as a polluted environment—fall heavily on a different group. This different group commonly includes the poor, minority groups, children, and/or indigenous peoples (c.f. Bullard, 1990; Chavis, 1994; Gray, Edwards, & Miranda, 2013; Hicken et al., 2012; Hornberg & Pauli, 2007; Nesmith & Smyth, 2015; U.S. Environmental Protection Agency, 2016). And the negative consequences can include very serious health impacts, as well as decreased property values, and a variety of mental health issues. And to make the problem even worse, this unequal distribution of costs and benefits often includes barriers to meaningful participation by such groups about environmental actions (Nesmith & Smyth, 2015; U.S. Environmental Protection Agency, 2016).

Social work has come to the realization of this important domain rather late, even as issues of lead poisoning and occupational health issues were among the earliest concerns of our Settlement House ancestors and the connection among health, poverty, and environment is better understood all of the time. Poor and minority children exposed to environmental risks have greater likelihood of fetal death, birth defects, being small for gestational age, preterm birth, clinically overt cognitive, neurologic, and behavioral abnormalities, subtle neuropsychological deficits, cancer, asthma, other respiratory diseases, obesity, and acute poisoning. And many chemical exposures lead to intelligence deficits, antisocial behavior, violence, and substances abuse, all of which result in burdensome costs to individuals, families, and society.

And it is quite likely that some of our greatest challenges in the next few decades are associated here. Children exposed to traumatic events such as natural disasters, exacerbated by climate change, can suffer from posttraumatic stress disorder. The number and type of problems associated with climate change are only now beginning to be seen.

Evidence for all of these environmentally linked issues, and their effects on humans, in general, and disenfranchised populations, in particular, grows literally by the hour. Population alone serves as a starting point for understanding the issue. Three very basic human activities—production/consumption, reproduction, and waste creation—although essential for life, are overwhelming the natural world's capacity to keep up. The number of humans on the planet has exploded in the past two centuries, from about 1 billion in 1800 to 7.5 billion today. And by the end of the 21st century, we could add as many as 3 billion more. Some areas, like Africa, are expected to double in population over the next century.

Whether the raw numbers are a "problem" or not is an open question, but even basic consequences such as how to feed, clothe, house, and provide clean water to these increasing populations are already acute. And when you add the issues of environmental impacts, especially differentiated by such constructs as class, color, gender, and others (discussed in the following), the problems quickly inflate. Two examples of such impacts—one global and one local—highlight these concerns.

Globally, climate change may well be the critical issue humans confront during the next several decades. Climate affects everything from temperature, weather, and coastlines to what crops can be grown, what species live or die, and where it is or is not comfortable to live. For all of the history of the planet until at least the agricultural age, climate was exclusively driven by natural processes. Changes occasionally happened quickly (such as when volcanoes erupted or meteors struck the earth), but generally change was slow, taking centuries or millennia. But with the increasing human population, the actions of production/consumption and waste creation have become critical factors. In particular, the burning of fossil fuels, the use of refrigerants, production of methane, and the transitioning of forests to other uses have caused the planet to warm. This temperature increase (likely between 2°C and 7°C) makes some areas of the earth warmer (such as Arctic areas and the oceans) and provides extra energy for weather. Anticipated and actual effects of this heat and energy include rising sea levels (as glaciers and sea ice melt), warmer oceans (with changes to ocean life), stronger and more frequent storms, and changes in weather leading to changes in agricultural zones. Recent research suggests that how we treat the planet, even in the past, has huge impacts. For example, just the effects of European colonization of the Americas, with the corresponding decimation of native peoples (from 60.5 million at the time of Columbus to just a few million by the end of the 19th century) dropped the planet's temperature enough to cause a global cooling (Koch, Brierly, Maslin, & Lewis, 2019). How? Native peoples had cleared much of the land for agriculture, and as they died off, the natural vegetation returned and absorbed significant amounts of carbon from the atmosphere.

While these issues will affect all of us, poor and minority populations will suffer the greatest effects. Although humans are reasonably good at adapting to environmental changes—even climate changes (Jacobs, 2019) across the planet—the poor and disenfranchised around the world will find it difficult to impossible to adapt. Migrant farmworkers, for example, will find it difficult to work in oppressive heat and therefore find it difficult to feed their families. Pacific Islanders will become migratory as islands sink (Thompson, 2019). Poor individuals and communities across the planet will face the greatest degree of hardship in assessments in Liberia (Front Page Africa, 2019). Fishing stocks and costs will be harmful to fisherman across the world (Daileda, 2019). And these poor counties are leading the call for action (Beam, 2019).

> ▶ **Critical Thinking Questions**
> Have you seen evidence of climate change in your life? In your client's lives? What do those changes mean for you and your clients?

Process Values

While the aforementioned instrumental values guide policy making at the highest conceptual levels, there are a number of other values that are important in how policies are implemented. In our capitalistic economy, one of the most important of these is *efficiency*. Efficiency—usually defined in economic terms—refers to the greatest output with the least cost. The idea here is that policies that keep waste to a minimum are the most desirable.

The second of these process values is personal responsibility. While the idea of personal responsibility was addressed earlier, closely related to that is the value of *work*. Work is viewed as a valuable end in itself, and as such many of our policies seek to require work, work training, or education as a requirement of the benefit, as well as one of the ways we measure success.

Another process value that also is connected to freedom, but also efficiency, is the idea of *minimal government influence*. For America's first 150 years, very few of our social welfare policies were federally funded or implemented. Indeed, with just a few (but important) exceptions, government involvement in most forms of social welfare policies was generally limited to state or local actions. The general assumption is to try and keep the response as close to the problem as possible. And even assuming that some government assistance was to be provided, the overall bias favored family or private charity rather than any governmental action. Case 11.2 provides an example of a family whose choices encompass these process values. Table 11.4 shows the general flow of thinking that guided social welfare policies' responsibility before the 1930s and after the 1930s.

CASE 11.2   CHOICES: PROCESS VALUES IN SOCIAL WELFARE POLICIES

Dequan loved his parents, but he had a hard time understanding some of their choices. Lifestyle and economic decisions that they were making seemed to be exactly wrong for this point in history. They were quite well off economically, and they had worked very hard all of their lives to achieve their high degree of economic stability. But what they were choosing to do with their money seemed to Dequan, well, wrong. They bought a beautiful large piece of property with a number of 200-year-old trees, and they were planning to cut them all down for the development of a new home—a home, by the way, that was big enough for several families to live in. Further, the property was located along an area that at various times in recent years had been declared off limits to development because of wetland status (although a recent ruling by the Environmental Protection Agency [EPA] under President Trump had rescinded that status). Dequan was quite torn over how to talk to his parents about this. On the one hand, they worked hard and earned the money to make such a choice a possibility. But on the other hand, was the action, solely beneficial to his parents, really in the best interest of, well, everyone else? Dequan had recently read about a First Nation tribe that considered seven generations forward when evaluating an action. Dequan believed in that perspective.

TABLE 11.4 Changing View of Personal Welfare Responsibility

SOCIAL LEVELS	PRE-1930s	POST-1930s
Person	Very clear distinction between "worthy" and "unworthy" of assistance. Individual *generally* held responsible for personal welfare needs with few exceptions for some groups (veterans, primary education in Northern states, some orphans as examples).	Distinction between "worthy" and "unworthy" of assistance generally eliminated (at least on paper—many people still hold belief). Individual *primarily* responsible for personal welfare, but with many exceptions (single women with children, elderly, K–12 education in all states as examples).
Family	First line of support—many intergenerational families with expectation of care for older adults, disabled, and otherwise needy.	Parents responsible for minor children (but often with governmental oversight). All other situations generally "optional."
Private/ religious charity	Important second line of support, particularly if family unavailable or unable. Level of support very uneven.	Important second line of support, particularly if governmental assistance unavailable or inadequate to need.
Local/state government	Third line of support. Most states (often through counties) provided residential care facilities, workhouses, and/or prisons. But funding and quality of care very uneven. These were viewed as a last resort and to be avoided.	Critical partner with federal government. For many forms of assistance, local and state governments provide the interface with services as well as funding.

(continued)

TABLE 11.4 Changing View of Personal Welfare Responsibility (*continued*)

SOCIAL LEVELS	PRE-1930S	POST-1930S
Federal government	Extremely limited role. Exceptions included veterans, some policy mandates (such as in the Northwest Ordinance which required set-asides for education), limited help for native people, and land giveaways (for homesteads, railroads, timber, and mining).	Critical partner with states and private entities. Provides most funding, policy direction, and oversight. Very few areas where federal government not involved.

A further example is the belief that the governmental response should be as close to the problem as possible. Like minimal government, this ideal is old and one that predates the founding of the Republic. Why is it so powerful of an idea? Well, historically, if a local government would have responsibility, it could bring all of its knowledge about local problems, conditions, needs, and potential recipients into its decision-making. Historically, it could even argue that government officials know the actual recipients. Thus, it could help to assess local needs and conditions; at the same time, it could keep an eye on the recipients of aid to make sure they were not cheating the system.

Social Structure and Power

Now, suppose there was some social problem that, although expensive, we could afford to resolve, and that virtually everyone agrees should be provided. Under these conditions, there is a fair chance the policy would exist. But in many cases, the policy still remains unenacted. Why? What is stopping the society from having the policy? The answer in many situations is because of the last set of PFDs—what we call the social or power structure of a society. In other words, who in a society has the power to ensure a need is addressed through a policy. The point is that in some societies, some policies have greater opposition than others. But like beliefs, social and political structures must be examined through a complex and broad set of concepts that come from sociology, political science, economics, and others. All these concepts, however, "boil down" to a couple of straightforward observations that feed off each other.

First, all societies have an unequal distribution of power and resources. Different groups and individuals have different levels of wealth, power, rights, and control over their lives. Depending on the society, this may be due to relatively desirable differential awards (think here of justice), or it might be due to a range of other things such as religious beliefs, past political values and choices, beliefs about occupational status, economic theory, beliefs about the relative value of personal characteristics (like gender, age, race, or ethnicity), how wealth and power are transferred from one generation to the next, or even just luck. Often, these differences are labeled as differences of class. The two major ways a status or class is gained are ascription, whereby an individual receives the status involuntarily (at birth or later in life), and by achievement and some degree of individual effort (Parsons 1951/1991).

But a person's status/position may be helped through policy. The truth of the matter is that all policies have winners and losers. A law raising or lowering tax rates or inheritance taxes or outlawing certain kinds of discrimination are examples. All of these will enhance or detract from an individual's status and power. Note that an extended discussion of power is provided in Chapter 12, Policy Practice: How to Conduct Policy Practice. For our purposes here, status refers to a person's position in society, and power refers to the capacity to influence decisions.

Making this last statement a bit more ominous, however, is that power can be leveraged. This means the more resources and power a person or group has, the more influence they have over the policy-making process and over policies selected. Chapter 12, Policy Practice: How to Conduct Policy Practice, examines this particular issue in a bit more depth. But the final important observation will hopefully drive this home. Once an individual or group starts winning, the more likely they are to continue to win, meaning as you amass power and influence, it is possible to use it to achieve even more!

As important as it is to examine these last statements and their influence in the United States may be, time does not allow a deeper discussion here. Instead, we look at who the winners and losers are in the United States, particularly, why we have major differences in power and what this means for policy and quality of life.

The Historical Roots of Social Structure and Power in the United States

The seeds of our current social and power structures are found in our history. Historically, most of the countries that Americans emigrated from had quite rigid social and power structures. Most European countries had systems where one or a very few persons held all of the political and economic power. Ownership of land, generally the main form of wealth until the 19th century, was generally narrow, and few people held skills or occupations that would allow a person to build wealth. Political power was even more tightly held. Almost no one in most countries had the right to vote or meaningfully express their desires. In Africa, the other primary source of early Americans, as with most Native American tribes, land and property ownership, as well as political voice, were more widely distributed (often through common ownership). But for these groups, such structures were destroyed with European settlement.

Several assumptions of belief, codified in early social policy, reinforced these early structures in North America. And though altered through time, greater access to land, and intentional policy, the consequences remain to this day. Perhaps the most important of these were beliefs associated with race and ethnicity (the supposed superiority of certain White European groups), gender (the supposed superiority of males), and religion (the supposed superiority of Christians [primarily Protestants] over other groups). Indeed, from the earliest days, the United States placed barriers in the way of many groups based on such characteristics from full participation and upward mobility. A full discussion of how these factors have worked through American history is not possible here, but Table 11.5 gives an overview of some of the major historical ways that the factors have worked to create our understanding of those in poverty, and therefore on social welfare responses.

The ways we have conceptualized poverty have resulted in many groups being marginalized even today. The policies that we have in place now have helped us make progress, but there is still a long way to go. Just a few statistics show this. First, how wealth is distributed.

TABLE 11.5 Historical Views of Poverty

Poverty as a cosmic consequence	**Poverty is the result of existential forces, beyond any control of humanity.**
	Poverty results from vindictive deities (ancient Greece).
	Poverty is "God's will"—sometimes negatively (as some early forms of Calvinism), sometimes positively (as in early forms of Christianity), or neutral (as with caste systems).
	Poverty is genetic (as with Social Darwinism).
Poverty as an individual consequence	**Poverty is the result of individual choices.**
	Poverty is the result of moral failure (as with early capitalism).
	Poverty is a result of laziness (many contemporary capitalists).
Poverty as a social consequence	Poverty is the result of social choices/actions.
	Poverty is the result of discrimination (such as Jim Crow policies).
	Poverty is due to unintentional social/economic choices (poor school, economic change).
	Poverty is an intentional social/economic choice; Marx's surplus capital, for example, or economic choice.
Poverty as the result of mixed causes	Poverty has multiple causes, often interacting with one another.
	Culture of poverty (conservative models).
	Culture of poverty (liberal models).

In 2014, if wealth were equally distributed across families in the United States, families would have a net worth of over $750,000. Yet the actual distribution shows that for the poorest 50% of families, the average wealth is just $11,000 (Yellen, 2014). In terms of income, just 1% of families in 2015 took home 26.3 times as much income as the bottom 99% (Sommeiller & Price, 2018). In 2017, the difference in wage growth between the highest 1% of wage earners and the bottom 90% was the highest ever recorded (Mishel & Wolfe, 2018).

Relationship Between Social Welfare Policies and Labor Market (Surplus Labor Theory; Trickle-Down Economics)

A further important factor impacting the social and power structure of persons is how the economic system is organized. There is a very long history of the relationship between our Western economic systems and employment and poverty in Western societies. As early as 1351, this relationship was recognized and addressed through policy in the "English Statute of Labourers." The law intended to ensure low wages and adequate workforce for employers in the years after the "black death" (Cohn, 2007; Trattner, 1999). This law was only the beginning. Labor regulation has long been associated with governmental action in capitalist societies. Indeed, one of Karl Marx's most useful observations is how low wages to the benefit of employers are built into modern economics through a reserve army of the unemployed (Marx, 1867). There is little evidence that there is intentional macroeconomic actions to create this surplus army, but having a ready supply of low wage workers has long been a goal of many policy choices. For example, some of the debate around contemporary immigration revolves around the importance of low skill, low wage workers in our economy. Business interests want such workers, while low skill workers may not.

A further manifestation of the power held by the commercial and business interests in the United States to affect employment is the effects of the use of the tax code. Although income taxes have been used to raise revenue for government off and on since at least the Civil War, the constitutionality of the approach was settled with the ratification of the 16th Amendment to the Constitution (Pollack, 2013). For most of the years afterward, our tax system has been defined as progressive, meaning that the higher the income, the greater the rate paid. Beginning in the late 1970s, however, an economic theory proposed by Arthur Laffer argued that tax rates may in fact get so high that they discourage investment. This resulted in a move to dramatically cut taxes through the 1980s and to the present day. Variously dubbed "supply side economics" and "trickle-down" economics, the assumption was that by putting more money in the hands of the investment class, greater economic activity would result, and everyone would benefit.

Whether the theory is ultimately true or not is a bit of an open question. But one major consequence is the explosion in government debt and deficits as revenues to government have decreased.

■ How Do We Fund the Social Welfare Policies We Choose?

With all of the complex factors and this evidence that groups are excluded from participation in our system, funding the social services is really as complex as the interplay of the factors themselves. In the broadest sense, funding exists and is drawn from both private and public sources, and then a mix of both on somewhat of a continuum from the client themselves, all the way to the overall society. Table 11.6 briefly shows the complex interplay, strengths, and all of the sources we use.

As you can see from Table 11.6, there are several different approaches that we use, but within these approaches are some fundamental distinctions affecting which is selected. The primary types of distinctions that have evolved through time and guided our thinking about funding can be organized into five major assumptions. They are:

- The individual or family has primary responsibility to pay for one's needs.
- The distinction between those determined to be worthy to receive assistance (those in need through no fault of their own) and the less worthy. The less worthy may receive assistance, but at low levels and only temporarily.
- If a need exists, private sources of charity are desirable because it maximizes a person's choice as to provide assistance or not, as well as to provide an opportunity to meet religious obligation and to receive the sense of good feeling that charitable action provides.
- But charitable funding is not always adequate, so it is acceptable for the government to step in and use tax revenues to assist.

TABLE 11.6 Methods of Funding the Social Services in the United States

METHOD	PUBLIC OR PRIVATE SOURCE	STRENGTHS, ADVANTAGES	WEAKNESSES, DISADVANTAGES
Self-pay/fee for service	Private, but sometimes supplemented through "sliding scales"	Close connection to service; client choice maximized; might limit unnecessary use	Service might be unavailable if no funds
Charity (wide range including charitable giving, larger endowment cost sharing, competitive grants)	Private, but sometimes "giver" is public organization	"Giver" gets good feeling of helping others	May not be enough support for unpopular problems or in times of high service use
Third-party payment (insurance)	Private, but source may be an individual, an organization, or both	Small payments on regular basis protects from catastrophic or unexpected costs	Insurer sets rules making exclusion from benefit possible; ability to make even small payments might be difficult; high administrative costs
Social insurance (third-party payment from public source)	Public, but individuals and organizations provide substantial contribution through dedicated taxes	Small payments on regular basis protects from catastrophic or unexpected costs. Large pool of contributors keeps costs low; low administrative costs	Types of things covered fairly narrow; political instability (at times); incentive to use money for unintended purposes
Legislative appropriation—three main types (direct services, contracted services, competitive grants)	Public, funded by general revenues— typically taxation. May be federal, state, local, or a combination	May ensure ongoing source of funds; public admission of problem need	Politically unstable

- But taxation should be kept low and wherever possible, the source of both the funds and determinations of who is eligible should remain close to those in need.

These assumptions have resulted in some important consequences for our social welfare system. First is the distinction between private and public funding. Our country has a long history of mixing the two sources, although for most of our history (until the past century), private funding was by far and away the most common source. Generally, the guiding assumption was that an individual or family would be responsible for payment for most needs. Or if the family could not provide, some form of charitable assistance, such as private charity would step in and take care of the person in need. Religious organizations were among the first systems of private charity, but these were supplemented at various times and ways by increased funds from voluntary contributions. Indeed, as some Americans created significant wealth in the 19th and the early 20th century, substantial funds were allocated for various types of need.

But it has been recognized for some time that these sources would be inadequate for all situations—especially for groups deemed "worthy" of assistance or for special projects. And in these situations, the government would step in and provide assistance using tax revenues to care for those in need. This recognition has its roots in what were called the Poor Laws in Europe but were brought to the new world and implemented early.

In fact, the basic structure of the Poor Laws governed the structure of social welfare for most of the history of the United States until the 1930s. There are only a few substantive exceptions in the United States where federal aid became normalized. Veterans and their families, native peoples (subject to all kinds of limitations), and (for a few years after the Civil War) newly freed slaves received aid (Trattner, 1999). Otherwise, the basic structure of the Poor Laws remained generally intact, with local and states the only governmental structures providing aid, and typically in very restricted ways.

Beginning with the New Deal of the 1930s, however, the payment structure began to bend toward the federal government. In the years since then, funding has become much more complex, with significant sources drawn from both governmental and nongovernmental funds. An extended discussion of this complexity is provided in Chapter 12, Policy Practice: How to Conduct Policy Practice.

■ Policy Formation: How We Make Policy

All of the complexity discussed earlier about the types of policies, benefits, and issues relating to the foundational conceptual areas comes together when examining how policies are actually created. Returning for a moment to the differences between policies and norms, the focus here is exclusively on how policies are made. For, as policies are "formal," our discussion here will target the formal systems we use to create policies. Likewise, this discussion is limited to governmental policy-making systems. As any formal organization can make policy, and although many of the processes are very similar, what follows may or may not apply to organizations in the private market due to some important differences that we will not examine here. Unfortunately, norms will have to wait until a future opportunity, for sometimes major social changes take place through normative reassessments, such as the #MeToo movement or greater acceptance of nonbinary gender identities, but as these are not, strictly speaking, policies (although they lead to changes in policies), we do not discuss them here.

Formal Authoritative Policy Structures: The Legislative, Executive, and Judicial Branches

Now, it is critically important to understand that the policy-making systems in use in the United States are based on what are essentially past policy-making choices. And the most important policy-making systems receive their basic structure from the U.S. Constitution. Today, virtually all policy-making authority derives from that document, and most of the basic structure for how to make policy is either in the document or from subsequent documents evolving from it.

These evolutions include amendments, state constitutions, congressional decisions, and legal decisions. It is from this document that the basic structure for policy making is established in the United States as manifestations of two implicit concepts intended to widely disperse political power. These are known as federalism and the so-called three branches of government. The Constitution itself contains policies that attempt to implement these concepts.

Federalism, for example, refers to the idea that power is to be distributed vertically between the federal government, state governments, and individuals. In the Constitution are a number of powers that are given to the federal government (making treaties, for example), but it specifically also says that any power not enumerated for the federal government is reserved for the states. One commonly cited example of this is school curricula, which is usually determined by state (or local) boards of education. But a further, and powerful example of this idea of the vertical separation of powers is the policies articulated in the Bill of Rights, the first ten amendments to the Constitution. As articulations of rights, these statements provide important protections for Americans and (presumably) set up a bulwark beyond which certain actions of government cannot generally go.

The Three Branches (and a Fourth and Fifth as Well!)

The horizontal distribution of powers is most clearly articulated in the U.S. Constitution as it describes what might be called "policies about how to make policies" through the well-known three branches of government: the legislative, executive, and judicial branches. The Constitution lays out the basic structure and process of each, areas in which their policy-making authority applies, as well as some basic statements about the relationship of a branch to other branches of government.

There is far too much detail for a discussion of all of the important content from this document here. Some very good basic sources of information that describe what the Constitution says are found at www.law.cornell.edu/constitution and the National Constitution Center (constitutioncenter.org). For now, what remains are several distinct ways in which policies are made, with three primary ways (legislation, executive orders, and judicial decisions) as well as at least two other methods that are also commonly used. Importantly, all three are subject to review and varying degrees of change from the others, as well as a rich context of other forces we discuss in Chapter 12, Policy Practice: How to Conduct Policy Practice. Briefly, the three types—each associated with one of the branches of government—are described in the following.

- Legislative laws, created by the legislative branch (Congress). This is the source of most policies through what are known as "public laws." At the federal level, the process requires the approval of both the House of Representatives and the Senate, and is subject to review (and to a high degree) approval of the other two branches (the executive and the judicial). Almost no area of policy can be fully free of the effects of Congress. Even areas that are carved out for the executive and judicial systems require at least some level of support from Congress through funding appropriations or enforcement mechanisms. All states/commonwealths have similar (though not identical) structures.

  - Importantly, legislative processes are complex. Generally, it involves a formalized process of bill introduction, review, and vote that can take years (subject to electoral limitations). And in this process, individual legislators can be incredibly powerful. Often, a given bill can be approved, rejected, amended, or tabled (essentially meaning ignored). And in the case of the U.S. Congress, the proposed legislation has to pass both the House and Senate if it is to become law. And even then, the President has to sign the legislation post passage for it to become law.

- ▪ Executive Orders, created by the Executive branch. At the federal level, the executive branch of government refers to the President and the President's Cabinet (Vice President, Secretary of State, Secretary of the Treasury, Secretary of Defense, etc.; see www.whitehouse.gov/administration/cabinet). In this structure, the President has the authority to issue unilateral policies called "Executive Orders." There are generally two sources of authority at play. First are orders that are rooted directly in powers granted by the Constitution (such as military actions or those that affect the activity of the executive branch) and second are based on powers granted by Congress. Again, states/commonwealths have similar procedures.

- ▪ Judicial decisions, created by the courts. The judicial branch of government is highly complex and has many levels (Supreme Court, Courts of Appeals, and District Courts), each of which has the power to issue decisions. Of these, the most powerful is the Supreme Court. Its decisions cannot be overturned by lower courts, but it may overturn its own decisions.

- ▪ The fourth type, administrative decisions and regulations, is actions taken by an agency or organization in the federal or state bureaucracy that has been created by legislative or executive actions. While this is not one of the constitutionally driven methods, in some cases, the results of such decisions can be monumental. The Federal Reserve, for example, determines interest rates and as such can have huge effects on the economy. On the other hand, most of these decisions/actions are what are called regulations. Regulations are the specific actions that are used by the bureaucracy to implement the policy actions of the legislature, the executive branch, and the courts. This generally falls under a branch of what is called administrative law. And we have an extended discussion on this in Chapter 12, Policy Practice: How to Conduct Policy Practice.

- ▪ Finally, the United States is a part of a large number of global and international organizations. From time to time, these organizations create international agreements, often called treaties. To a degree, treaties are still connected to the legislative and executive branches, as these units must ratify the documents. But there is a significant difference here. These agreements form binding relationships across nations. There are a number of important examples that apply here, but many deal with transnational issues such as environmental problems (ozone depletion, climate change, fisheries, whaling, etc.), trade, weapons (nuclear weapons, chemical weapons, etc.), and aspirational rights (rights of children, women, refugees, etc.). A good list is found online (en.wikipedia.org/wiki/List_of_treaties_by_number_of_parties).

With all of the complexity in how these various systems operate, a review may be useful. The U.S. Congress has published a comprehensive discussion of the legal processes (U.S. Library of Congress, 2019). For those of you who actually need to look at the implemented policies from across these domains, there fortunately is a shortcut, at least at the federal level, with states having similar codifications. At the federal level, this codification is called the United States Code of Federal Regulations (U.S. Government Publishing Office, 2019). The document is continually updated as policies change, but it is invaluable to access for critical information about policy.

Relationship Between the Federal Government and the States

With all of the various sources and types of social welfare policy factors and actors, there is in fact a complexity to the American social welfare system that is a bit unique in the world.

Here, we consider the relationship that federalism creates. For it includes and encourages participation from every level of government. The federal government, or individual states, may serve to be the source of a policy. For the first few decades of U.S. history, most innovative social welfare policies (to the degree there were any) were usually introduced at the state level. In part, that was due to the constitutional interpretation that a power not specifically enumerated for the federal government was reserved for the states. Things like care for the poor, the mentally ill, and the nonveteran disabled were almost exclusively state policies. At the same time, there were aspects of both the Constitution and history that pulled policy toward the federal government. Among these were the supremacy clause indicating that the federal government had powers that were "supreme" when disputes occurred with states, the necessary and proper clause, which gives the federal government significant discretion over policy domains, the commerce clause, and of course, major events like the U.S. Civil War. But perhaps the most immediate justification came with the Great Depression of the 1930s that overwhelmed states and private charity.

As such, much of the social welfare policies changed in the 1930s with the "New Deal." This leaves us today with some important comments relating to the relationship. First, the general path of social welfare policies usually starts with a federal action (although there are a number of really important exceptions, like marijuana legalization or paid family leave, which are state initiatives). In the case of a piece of federal legislation, the following characteristics are quite typical.

- The law passed will very often provide mandated directives for states to carry out, while providing much of the funding. This typically means that the states have to carry out some minimum activities defined in the law (often in the form of direct services) but some or all of the funding to do so comes from the federal government. Often, states may supplement services and funding based on their own needs.

- The law passed will often be essentially a "shell of intent," but much of the actual details will be written by the bureaucracy through the regulatory process. There are actually laws that define how this is to happen.

Executive Orders and court decisions are somewhat different. Neither the executive nor the judicial branch has the authority to allocate funding. Funding allocations are the exclusive domain of Congress. Further, there are fairly substantial limits on the domains in which policies can be made. For example, an Executive Order usually applies to the activity of the bureaucracy, or to areas where Congress has granted power.

The courts are in some ways more flexible but also more constrained. First off, court decisions carry no power of implementation. The courts depend on the executive branch or states to carry out their will. Second, courts may not independently act—they depend on someone bringing a case to them, and most are not taken up by the Supreme Court. About 7,000 to 8,000 new cases are filed in the Supreme Court each year (www.supremecourt.gov/about/justicecaseload.aspx) and they choose to listen to only about 80. And the actions may be very, very slow! From the time someone brings a case until a Supreme Court decision is made can take years.

■ Summary

This chapter focused on Competency 5: Policy Practice. In this chapter, we examined Competency 5 and the NASW *Code of Ethics* as they describe the perspective of social work about policy. We examined the critical definitions associated with policy, with the major historical economic, organizational, environmental, and global influences on policy, and finally with the way the legislative, executive, and judicial roles create policy. In Chapter 12, Policy Practice: How to Conduct Policy Practice, we more closely examine how you, the social worker, can engage in policy practice.

CASE SUMMARY   "UNDOCUMENTED AND HOMELESS"

Practice Setting Description

Jackie is a first-year master of social work student completing an internship at an inner-city family service agency in the Southwest. The agency is located in a section of the city that has a high crime rate, gang activity, and failing schools. The area has a diverse population with a large number of immigrants from Central and South America and a substantial African American population. The agency provides individual and family counseling services on a sliding fee scale. The agency also runs a number of educational and treatment groups as well as a temporary shelter for women and their children. Jackie has been assigned to work with the women and their children in the shelter. Her primary tasks are to provide concrete services and supportive counseling to the shelter residents.

Background Information

Elicia T and her daughter, Maria, are undocumented immigrants from Mexico. They have been in the United States for 5 years. Elicia and Maria fled to the area from another southwestern city to escape her abusive husband approximately 2 months ago. Elicia is 25 years old and Maria 8 years old. Elicia

(continued)

CASE SUMMARY

has a 2-year-old daughter, Sarah, who was placed in foster care because of suspected abuse in the home. Sarah is in a foster home in a small rural community in the state hundreds of miles from Elicia's current residence. Since moving to the area, Maria has not been attending school.

Elicia and Maria are currently residing in the agency's temporary shelter for families. They have been at the shelter for 2 weeks, and the agency has a 90-day limit. It is viewed as temporary housing, and the residents are only allowed to stay for 3 months. Prior to arriving at the shelter, Elicia and Maria were homeless and living on the streets.

Elicia is a high-school dropout and was a stay-at-home mother prior to leaving her husband and moving to a different part of the state. She chose to move there because she has two female cousins living in the area who are also undocumented immigrants. Elicia's native language is Spanish. She speaks some English but is not as comfortable speaking in English. Her English comprehension appears to be good. Maria speaks both English and Spanish well. When communicating with the staff, Maria acts as Elicia's interpreter since none of the staff at the shelter speak Spanish.

Maria appears to be behind academically. She struggles reading simple children's books written in English. It is unknown if her ability to read in Spanish is better than her English reading skills.

Other than her two cousins, Elicia has no other sources of support in the community. Her cousins have young families and limited resources but are well established and connected to a Latino community in the city and the local Catholic church. Her cousins refused to let Elicia and Maria live with them while she was trying to find her own place and a job. They stated that they did not have enough room and are concerned they would get in trouble with their landlord if it was found out that they were letting people stay with them. They sent her to the local church for help, and she was given the address for the agency's shelter by the priest.

Elicia has been looking for housing in the Latino community. The housing market is tight with limited options, and she has been unable to find anything that she could possibly afford. The only affordable housing she found was a room in a rundown motel that rents by the hour or by the month. It is in an area of town known for drug dealing and sex work.

On arrival in the community, Elicia found occasional work for a house cleaning company. The company hires undocumented workers, pays them very low cash wages, and threatens to turn them in to Immigration and Customs Enforcement (ICE) if they complain. The job bosses also exploit their female workers sexually, threatening to turn them in if they do not comply. Elicia was fearful about applying for other jobs because of her illegal status. She considered turning to sex work to be able to take care of her children, but her Catholic upbringing and thoughts of how doing so would shame her family have kept her from doing so. She is in constant fear of being detained, separated from her children, and having them placed in foster care. She is also afraid that she will end up homeless again and forced to live on the streets or return to her abusive husband.

Elicia is extremely reluctant to sign up for any federally funded services, even those that she and her children are entitled to receiving. On the suggestion that she enroll for supplemental food through SNAP, Elicia became nervous and refused as she has heard that participation in SNAP

(continued)

CASE SUMMARY

services, and others like them, would draw the attention of ICE, and she had heard stories on the news of individuals being deported after signing up for such programs.

Presenting Problems

Elicia and her children are facing multiple obstacles. They need to find permanent, affordable housing and a job that pays enough to cover her housing and living expenses. In addition, Maria needs to be enrolled in school. Elicia also wants to regain custody of her youngest daughter in foster care.

Additionally, Elicia is experiencing an immense amount of stress, anxiety, and possibly post-traumatic stress disorder (PTSD). She described an instance where she could not calm down her breathing, and she felt lightheaded. She is very fearful of men and tries to avoid all contact with men in the community. She reports difficulty sleeping at night and feeling exhausted most of the time.

She is concerned about Maria. She has started acting out at the shelter, getting into fights with the other children, disobeying her mother, and being disrespectful and defiant to the staff and other adults. Elicia and Maria fight frequently, and when Elicia tries to discipline Maria, she throws a temper tantrum until Elicia gives up.

Elicia has many strengths. She had the strength to leave her abusive husband and move to a different city. She loves her daughters. She wants desperately to keep Maria with her and hopes to have Sarah returned to her custody. She is resilient and has managed to survive and keep her daughter safe despite not having a place to stay, a job, and a limited support network. Additionally, Elicia is highly motivated to find her own accommodations and support her children.

■ Discussion Questions

1. What are the primary federal policy issues that are evident from Elicia's experience?

2. Can you identify any possible normative cultural and historical factors that might explain some of Elicia's concern with seeking formal help? What about the effects of the present political climate?

3. How might Elicia's concerns about programs like SNAP change if SNAP had universal eligibility?

4. Do you think Elicia and her family would be better served by cash-based policies or by specific services? Why or why not?

■ References

Beam. (2019). *The least developed countries call for urgent action at UN climate talks*. Retrieved from https://cleantechnica.com/2019/02/26/the-least-developed-countries-call-for-urgent-action-at-un-climate-talks

Bullard, R. (1990). *Dumping in Dixie: Race, class, and environmental quality*. Boulder. CO: Westview Press.

Centers for Disease Control and Prevention. (2011). *Brief 1: Overview of policy evaluation*. Retrieved from https://www.cdc.gov/injury/pdfs/policy/brief%201-a.pdf

Center for Economic and Social Justice. (2019). *Defining economic justice and social justice*. Retrieved from http://www.cesj.org/learn/definitions/defining-economic-justice-and-social-justice

Center on Budget and Policy Priorities. (2017). *Policy basics: Where do our federal tax dollars go?* Retrieved from https://www.cbpp.org/research/federal-budget/policy-basics-where-do-our-federal-tax-dollars-go

Chavis, B. (1994). *Unequal protection: Environmental justice and communities of color*. San Francisco, CA: Sierra Club Books.

Cohn, S. (2007). After the black death: Labour legislation and attitudes towards labour in ate-medieval Western Europe. *Economic History Review, 60*(3), 457–485. doi:10.1111/j.1468-0289.2006.00368.x

Conley, D. (2010). *Being black, living in the red: Race, wealth, and social policy in America*. Berkeley, CA: University of California Press.

Cornell University. (n.d.). *Affirmative action*. Retrieved from https://www.law.cornell.edu/wex/affirmative_action

Correll, S., Bernard, S., & Paik, I. (2007). Getting a job: Is there a motherhood penalty? *American Journal of Sociology, 112*(5), 1297–1338. doi:10.1086/511799

Daileda, C. (2019). *Warming waters heat up fishing costs along India's Malabar Coast*. Retrieved from http://news.trust.org/item/20190225015410-xjr1b

Dictionary.com. (2018). *Social welfare*. Retrieved from https://www.dictionary.com/browse/social-welfare

Fontenot, K., Semega, J., & Kollar, M. (2018). *Income and poverty in the United States: 2017*. Retrieved from https://www.census.gov/content/dam/Census/library/publications/2018/demo/p60-263.pdf

Fortin, N. (2005). Gender role attitudes and the labour market outcomes of women across OECD countries. *Oxford Review of Economic Policy*, 21, 416–438. doi:10.1093/oxrep/gri024

Front Page Africa. (2019). *Findings on gender and social impact of climate change in Liberia presented to stakeholders*. Retrieved from https://frontpageafricaonline.com/environment/findings-on-gender-and-social-impact-of-climate-change-in-liberia-presented-to-stakeholders

Gray, S. C., Edwards, S. E., & Miranda, M. L. (2013). Race, socioeconomic status, and air pollution exposure in North Carolina. *Environmental Research*, 126, 152–158. doi:10.1016/j.envres.2013.06.005

Harvard University, T.H. Chan School of Public Health. (2017). *Measurement of well-being*. Retrieved from https://www.hsph.harvard.edu/health-happiness/research-new/positive-health/measurement-of-well-being

Helliwell, R. L. (2018). *World happiness report. Sustainable development solutions network for the United Nations*. Retrieved from http://worldhappiness.report

Hetter, K. (2018, March 15). *CNN travel*. Retrieved from https://www.cnn.com/travel/article/worlds-happiest-countries-united-nations-2018/index.html

Hicken, M. T., Gee, G. C., Morenoff, J., Connell, C. M., Snow, R. C., & Hu, H. (2012). A novel look at racial health disparities: The interaction between social disadvantage and environmental health. *American Journal of Public Health, 102*(12), 2344–2351. doi:10.2105/AJPH.2012.300774

Hornberg, C., & Pauli, A. (2007). Child poverty and environmental justice. *International Journal of Hygiene and Environmental Health*, 210, 571–580. doi:10.1016/j.ijheh.2007.07.006

Human Rights Watch. (2018). *All we want is equality: Religious exemptions and discrimination against LGBT people in the United States*. Retrieved from https://www.hrw.org/report/2018/02/19/all-we-want-equality/religious-exemptions-and-discrimination-against-lgbt-people

Jacobs, T. (2019). *As the climate changes, are we all boiling frogs?* Retrieved from https://psmag.com/environment/as-the-climate-changes-are-we-all-boiling-frogs

Jacobson, L. (2017). *How expensive would a single-payer system be?* Retrieved from Politifact https://www.politifact.com/truth-o-meter/article/2017/jul/21/how-expensive-would-single-payer-system-be

Jansson, B. (2003). *Becoming an effective policy advocate* (4th ed.). Pacific Grove, CA: Brooks/Cole.

Koch, A., Brierly, C., Maslin, M., & Lewis, S. (2019). Earth system impacts of the European arrival and great dying in the Americas after 1492. *Quaternary Science Reviews, 207,* 13–36. doi:10.1016/j.quascrirev.2018.12.004

Lederman, J. (2019). *Trump administration launches global effort to end criminalization of homosexuality*. Retrieved from https://www.nbcnews.com/politics/national-security/trump-administration-launches-global-effort-end-criminalization-homosexuality-n973081

Markus, H., & Schwartz, B. (2009). Does choice mean freedom and well-being? *Journal of Consumer Research, 37*, 344–355. Retrieved from http://www.jstor.org/stable/10.1086/651242

Marx, K. (1867). *Capital: A Critique of Political Economy.* Translated by Samuel Moore and Edward Aveling, edited by Frederick. Progress Publishers, Moscow, 1969

Maslow, A. (1954). *Motivation and personality.* New York, NY: Harper.

Maslow, A. (1971). *Farther reaches of human nature.* New York, NY: Viking Press.

Matsumoto, D. (2001). *The handbook of culture and psychology.* London, UK: Oxford University Press.

Merriam-Webster. (2018a). *Merriam-Webster dictionary.* Retrieved from https://www.merriam-webster.com/dictionary/policy

Merriam-Webster. (2018b). *Definition of social welfare policy.* Retrieved from https://www.merriam-webster.com/dictionary/social%20welfare

Mishel, L., & Wolfe, J. (2018). Top 1 percent reaches highest wages ever—Up 157 percent since 1979. *Working Economics* (Economic Policy Institute blog), October 18, 2018.

Nakdimen, K. A. (1984). The physiognomic basis of sexual stereotyping. *American Journal of Psychiatry, 141*(4): 499–503. doi:10.1176/ajp.141.4.499. PMID 6703126

National Archives. (2018). *The Bill of Rights: A transcription.* Retrieved from https://www.archives.gov/founding-docs/bill-of-rights-transcript

National Association of Social Workers. (2017). *Code of ethics.* Silver Spring, MD: Author. Retrieved from https://www.socialworkers.org/About/Ethics/Code-of-Ethics/Code-of-Ethics-English

Nesmith, A., &. Smyth, N. (2015). Environmental justice and social work education. *Social Work Education, 34*(5), 484–501. doi:10.1080/02615479.2015.1063600

Norman, J. (2019). *Americans' support for affirmative action programs rises.* Retrieved from https://news.gallup.com/poll/247046/americans-support-affirmative-action-programs-rises.aspx?utm_source=alert&utm_medium=email&utm_content=morelink&utm_campaign=syndication

Oliver, M., & Shapiro, T. (2006). *Black wealth, white wealth: A new perspective on racial inequality.* New York, NY: Routledge.

Organization for Economic Co-operation and Development. (n.d.). *Social Expenditure - Aggregated data.* Retrieved from https://stats.oecd.org/Index.aspx?DataSetCode=SOCX_AGG

Oxford English Dictionary. (2019). *Definition of ideology in English.* Retrieved from https://en.oxforddictionaries.com/definition/ideology

Parsons, T. (1951/1991). *The social system.* London, UK: Routledge. Retrieved from http://home.ku.edu.tr/~mbaker/cshs503/talcottparsonssocialsystem.pdf

Petit, P. (2007). The effects of age and family constraints on gender hiring discrimination: A field experiment in the French financial sector. *Labour Economics, 14*(3), 371–391. doi:10.1016/j.labeco.2006.01.006

Pollack, S. (2013). Origins of the modern income tax, 1894-1913, Tax Lawyer, 66, 323–324.

Pollin, J. H.-L. (2018, November 30). *Economic analysis of Medicare for all.* Retrieved from https://www.peri.umass.edu; https://www.peri.umass.edu/publication/item/1127-economic-analysis-of-medicare-for-all

Sommeiller, E., & Price, M. (2018). The new gilded age: Income inequality in the U.S. by state, metropolitan area, and county. *Economic Policy Institute.* Retrieved from https://www.epi.org/publication/the-new-gilded-age-income-inequality-in-the-u-s-by-state-metropolitan-area-and-county

Supreme Court of the United States. (2015). Obergefell v. Hodges. Retrieved from https://www.scotusblog.com/case-files/cases/obergefell-v-hodges

Thompson, A. (2019). *To save themselves from sea level rise, the Marshall Islands want to raise the land.* Retrieved from https://www.popularmechanics.com/science/environment/a26541069/marshall-islands-raise-land-sea-level-rise

Trattner, W. (1999). *From poor law to welfare state: A history of social welfare in America* (6th Ed.). New York, NY: Free Press.

Urban Institute. (2017). *Nine charts about wealth inequality in America (Updated).* Retrieved from http://apps.urban.org/features/wealth-inequality-charts

U.S. Department of Education, National Center for Education Statistics. (n.d.). *Fast facts.* Retrieved from National Center for Education Statistics, US Department of Education https://nces.ed.gov/fastfacts/display.asp?id=66

U.S. Department of Health and Human Services. (2018). *Poverty guidelines*. U.S. Department of Health and Human Services, Office of the Assistant Secretary for Planning and Evaluation: Retrieved from https://aspe.hhs.gov/poverty-guidelines

U.S. Environmental Protection Agency. (2016). *Learn about environmental justice*. Retrieved from www.epa.gov; http://epa.gov/environmentaljustice/learn-about-environmental-justice

U.S. Global Change Research Program. (2018). *Fourth National Climate Assessment, Volume II —* Impacts, Risks, and Adaptation in the United States. Retrieved from https://nca2018.globalchange.gov/downloads/NCA4_Ch01_Summary-Findings.pdf

U.S. Government Publishing Office. (2019). United States Code of Federal Regulations. Retrieved from https://www.govinfo.gov/app/collection/cfr

U.S. Government Publishing Office. (n.d.). Public Law 111 - 321 - *Don't ask, don't tell repeal act of 2010*. Retrieved from https://www.govinfo.gov/app/details/PLAW-111publ321

U.S. House of Representatives. (2008). *H.R.1964 -Freedom of choice act*. Retrieved from https://www.congress.gov/bill/110th-congress/house-bill/1964

U.S. House of Representatives Historian. (n.d.). *Constitutional amendments and major civil rights acts of congress referenced in black Americans in congress*. Retrieved from https://history.house.gov/Exhibitions-and-Publications/BAIC/Historical-Data/Constitutional-Amendments-and-Legislation/

U.S. Library of Congress. (2019). *How our laws are made*. Retrieved from https://www.congress.gov/resources/display/content/How+Our+Laws+Are+Made+-+Learn+About+the+Legislative+Process

U.S. Library of Congress. (n.d.). The Civil Rights Act of 1964: A Long Struggle for Freedom. Retrieved from https://www.loc.gov/exhibits/civil-rights-act/legal-events-timeline.html

Warren, R. L. (1987). *The community in America* (3rd ed.). State College, PA: Pennsylvania State University.

Weichselbaumer, D. (2004). Is it sex or personality? The impact of sex stereotypes on discrimination in applicant selection. *Eastern Economic Journal, 30*(2), 159–186.

Williams, P. (2019). *Supreme Court allows Trump administration to enforce transgender military ban*. Retrieved from https://www.nbcnews.com/politics/supreme-court/supreme-court-declines-take-daca-transgender-cases-n961196

Wyers, N. (1991). Policy-practice in social work: Models and issues. *Journal of Social Work Education, 27*, 241–250. doi:10.1080/10437797.1991.10672196

Yellen, J. (2014). *Speech by Chair Yellen on perspectives on inequality and opportunity from the Survey of Consumer Finances*. Board of Governors of the Federal Reserve System.

Young, L. (2009). *The motherhood penalty: Working moms face pay gap vs. childless peers*. Bloomberg Businessweek. (June 5, 2009), Retrieved from http://www.businessweek.com/careers/workingparents/blog/archives/2009/06/the_motherhood.html.

POLICY PRACTICE: HOW TO CONDUCT POLICY PRACTICE

STEPHEN KAUFFMAN

Devon, a second-year master of social work student, realized that the opiate addiction problem in his community was serious when his younger brother Felix overdosed. Felix survived, but only due to an extremely fortunate set of circumstances. But 93 others (by Devon's count) had not been so lucky over the past year. Something had to be done, and now.

The problem was how to build support for two very effective harm reduction strategies: greater naltrexone availability and funding a new methadone maintenance center. But his community and state were quite conservative, and drugs were viewed as evil. So Devon began to build awareness about the problem and to attempt to gain supporters at the state capitol. Because he was in school and had virtually no economic resources to draw upon, he needed to develop a plan to achieve his goals. But what should he do first? Who should he turn to for support?

Devon did, however, know that he needed to start with research about the problem. He worked with a number of community groups in the area. Among these groups, he found past users, some providers, and first responders were in agreement with his efforts. Further, many family members were willing to provide information to him. On the other hand, some groups that provided traditional substance abuse treatment were wary. Devon wondered about that wariness—why? It would appear that services for some would be a plus for all. But overall, Devon gathered some impressive statistical information on the community issue. Now, what to do with it—where to go?

LEARNING OBJECTIVES

This chapter focuses on Competency 5: Policy Practice, with the primary emphasis on the ways social workers may participate in the policy process. The chapter begins with a review of the National Association of Social Workers (NASW) ethical principle and standards that address policy and social justice (these are essentially the same as shown in Chapter 11, Policy Practice: How Policy Is Made). This is followed by a definition of policy practice. Then, we examine the policy process and the associated primary tasks. And the bulk of the chapter looks closely at ways that social workers may participate in policy through various forms of policy practice. In particular, we examine problem identification and characterization, political mobilization and political advocacy, policy implementation, and then policy analysis. At each of these stages, a close analysis of how the social worker can participate and affect policy is examined. By the end of this chapter, you will be able to:

1. Describe the role of practice and the practitioner in policy development

2. Understand how to actively engage in policy practice to effect change

3. Know how to evaluate policies

4. Apply critical thinking to analyze, formulate, and advocate for policies that advance human rights and social, economic, and environmental justice

■ Competency 5: Engage in Policy Practice

Social workers understand that human rights and social justice, as well as social welfare and services, are mediated by policy and its implementation at the federal, state, and local levels. Social workers understand the history and current structures of social policies and services, the role of policy in service delivery, and the role of practice in policy development. Social workers understand their role in policy development and implementation within their practice settings at the micro-, mezzo-, and macrolevels, and they actively engage in policy practice to effect change within those settings. Social workers recognize and understand the historical, social, cultural, economic, organizational, environmental, and global influences that affect social policy. They are also knowledgeable about policy formulation, analysis, implementation, and evaluation. Social workers:

- Identify social policy at the local, state, and federal levels that impacts well-being, service delivery, and access to social services

- Assess how social welfare and economic policies impact the delivery of and access to social services

- Apply critical thinking to analyze, formulate, and advocate for policies that advance human rights and social, economic, and environmental justice

■ National Association of Social Workers (NASW) *Code of Ethics*

The NASW *Code of Ethics* (2017) principles and standards related to policy practice are the same as those discussed in Chapter 11, Policy Practice: How Policy Is Made. To review the *Code of Ethics* online, go to www.socialworkers.org/About/Ethics/Code-of-Ethics/Code-of-Ethics-English.

■ What Is Policy Practice?

In reality, almost everything we as social workers do has a connection to policy practice, although we may not see the connections. Formally, "policy practice encompasses the professional efforts to influence the development, enactment, implementation, modification, or assessment of social policies, primarily to ensure social justice and equal access to basic social goods" (Barker, 2003, p. 330). From a slightly different perspective, what this means is we take our social work skills, theories, and beliefs and apply them to the policy domain. It may involve what we normally consider to be macropractice, with a focus on such activities as advocacy, policy analysis, lobbying, community work, and administrative practice. But it also involves "bringing the macro to the micro"— bringing important policy change tools into our daily direct contact with and for clients.

▶ **Critical Thinking Questions**

1. What micropractice skills do you think might have applicability in policy work?

2. Why do you think these skills might apply?

This chapter picks up from where we ended in Chapter 11, Policy Practice : How Policy Is Made, and turns our focus to the practice skills of this work. As a structure for doing this, we begin by presenting a path for the flow of policy implementation from the first indication that a need exists through the selection of a policy response to the direct practice resulting from that policy and beyond. This flow is what is known as the "policy process." Over the years, many different models of the policy process have been constructed, but the model we use is shown in Table 12.1. Somewhat different social work skill sets are applicable at each step of the process, although some overlap exists. These too are shown in Table 12.1. This chapter examines these steps and some useful policy practice skills.

TABLE 12.1 Policy Process and Social Worker Policy Practice Activities

POLICY STAGE	PRIMARY TASK	SOCIAL WORKER ROLES/ ACTIVITIES
Problem identification and characterization	▦ Social problem identified from direct practice experience ▦ Social problem defined and characterized (includes how problem is constructed and measurement of size and scope)	▦ Research: Monitor client's experience, identify patterns, collect data
Political mobilization and political advocacy	▦ Develop support for policy response ▦ Selection of policy-making domain and policy alternatives ▦ Advocate for policy and apply pressure on policy makers ▦ Advocate for adequate budget	▦ Social problem identified from direct practice experience ▦ Social problem defined and characterized (includes how problem is constructed and measurement of size and scope)
Policy implementation	▦ Develop regulations from enacted policy ▦ Organizational capacity developed	
Evaluation and policy improvement	▦ Review and critique policy and implementation	

Stages of the Policy Process and the Associated Primary Tasks

As is shown in Table 12.1, our model of the policy process is composed of four stages, each of which has associated primary tasks. As you examine the table, note that this model is not the only such model, and that different models may organize the stages somewhat differently. Further, while the stages are generally sequential and chronologically connected, the model is dynamic, with purposes and activities at one stage informing and influencing other stages of the model. Moreover, all of the content discussed in Chapter 6, Microsystems Assessment: Individuals, Families, and Groups, informs (and is informed by) what occurs in this model, meaning you need to be aware of the concepts discussed in the earlier chapter. Similarly, skills examined throughout this entire book are applicable at many places in the policy practice model, and the needed skills at any one stage are also needed at other stages. Thus, like many models, this should serve as a starting point for understanding and conducting policy practice—not as a complete and perfect model.

In our model, the four stages are (a) problem identification and characterization, where the primary tasks are identification of the problem, definition of the problem, and establishing the scope of the problem (including measuring and mapping the problem); (b) political mobilization and political advocacy, where the primary tasks are related to building support for a policy; (c) policy implementation, where the primary tasks are to ensure the best and most successful policy implementation; and (d) evaluation and policy improvement, where the primary tasks are to review and critique policy and implementation.

■ Policy Stages: Problem Identification and Characterization

Problem Identification

No issue was ever addressed by a policy or even by direct practice that was not first identified as a problem. In our practice, the closeness we maintain with client systems places us in a unique position to see emerging situations in our clients' lives early in and/or throughout the treatment process. This requires ongoing observation of the domains of our clients' lives. Social work can and does plays a critical role in this stage, and in "transforming private troubles, such as unemployment, domestic violence, homelessness, and mass incarceration, into public issues" (Reisch, 2017, p. 4). This means we must observe, document, and articulate what we see.

Interestingly, some professional fields maintain this observational perspective as a matter of standard practice, and have even developed institutions to support it. For example, in the medical and public health world, there is a system known as "surveillance" designed to catch emerging health issues while they are still small and manageable. This system is so well developed that it includes virtually every hospital and physician on the planet, and organizations as large and well-funded as the World Health Organization (WHO) and the Centers for Disease Control and Prevention (CDC) in the United States have created a system that ideally catches emerging problems anywhere on the planet. How is it done? Well, according to the CDC, the system is designed with several goals in mind. The system is designed to be inclusive, to provide timely information, to provide an accurate representation of the problem, to be sensitive to problem characteristics, and to be specific to the disease in question (CDC, 2018). Consider the attention given to recent outbreaks of the Ebola virus or the annual flu shot campaign. Both of these are the results of knowledge developed through surveillance.

Even now, there are a number of emerging policy areas where social workers will serve on the front line of problem identification. For example, as the effects of climate change come more to the fore, the ways it affects clients become more and more evident. The number and type of problems associated with climate change are beginning to be seen in the very communities we work with. In part, this is because it creates a shock to our systems and is creating disequilibrium throughout our world, but such trauma may look different in different localities (see Case 12.1). For example, food production shocks are becoming more common, new diseases and forms of trauma, and differential effects on different client groups and communities are likely to come to the fore. You, as a social worker, can identify and publicize the need for responses where you find them.

▶ **Critical Thinking Questions**

1. What comprises "good evidence" when thinking about a problem?

2. What methods do you think can be used to gather information that will carry the greatest weight in an argument?

Thus, at this early stage, no particularly unique set of policy skills are required other than vigilance. But this is not an unimportant task. Think about it. Who first identified the needs of persons with the HIV/AIDS virus? Or large numbers of persons overdosing from opiates?

CASE 12.1   TIRED AND SCARED: SOCIAL WELFARE POLICY PRACTICE FOR WORKING WITH REFUGEES

Salya enjoyed working with refugees. Overwhelmingly in the 4 years she had worked at the facility, she had found the clients kind, but scared. All had been traumatized, and had spent significant time getting here. But what she was hearing on the news, and even from some of her coworkers, was frightening. She had never met a refugee who was anything other than honestly in need, and never showed any criminal intent.

Knowing how the problem was being talked about in the media, she decided to do research on her own. As her clients overwhelmingly spoke Spanish, and the few who did not spoke a local language that she knew, she began to conduct interviews with the clients. She wanted the "real" stories from the clients, and as such she decided to use primarily open-ended, qualitative surveys. She did have some questions about the proper methodological approach, because she wanted the data to be as robust as possible. So she contacted a former professor from her master in social work program. But beyond those issues, she found the clients willing to tell their stories. And what she heard, particularly from young women, was frightening. And she could not help growing more and more angry with her coworkers and the folks telling these stories.

Or changes in the characteristics of the homeless population in the 2010s? I cannot guarantee that in all of these cases, it was a social worker, but it may well have been!

Problem Characterization

As this stage continues, better evidence needs to be developed about the problem. Who is affected? How many persons? What are the parameters of the problem in question? And how shall we define it and talk about it?

The answers to the questions are important, as social problems do not appear as fully formed, discrete, easily understood issues. Indeed, the way we understand a social problem is the result of persons like yourself who examine, define, and characterize the issue. From a purely intellectual perspective, this in some ways is one of the most interesting but perhaps difficult aspects of the policy process. There are two somewhat different processes here—the problem of social construction and definition, and the problem of measurement (application of how the problem is constructed to measurement of size and scope). Social workers have clear policy practice opportunities during this phase.

Social Constructions and Definition

To attempt to better understand these two processes, let us first think about the construction and definition. Consider the following questions. First, if you were to ask any 100 Americans, "What is the problem with immigration?" you likely would get a variety of answers. Among some of the answers might be:

- There are too many immigrants of all types coming into the United States.
- There are too many low skilled immigrants coming into the United States.
- There are too many Muslim (or non-European, or Asian, or. . .) immigrants coming into the United States.
- There are not enough legal immigrants coming into the United States to meet the needs of business.
- Our immigration laws are discriminatory to persons of color.

Now consider a second question, also asked of any 100 Americans. The question "Who should be able to serve in the U.S. military?" Here, you would likely get answers as diverse as:

- Anyone who meets the necessary physical and mental criteria
- Any able male, but not any female
- Anyone, but only if their current gender identity matches their birth gender (meaning no transgender persons)
- Only persons with a heterosexual sexual orientation

Or finally, consider the question "What is the problem of money and politics?" Here, you would likely get answers as diverse as:

- There should be no government restrictions! Money is speech and regulating it violates free speech.

- There should be limited government restrictions! Money is speech, but the public has the right to know who is spending it to influence their choices.

- There should be limited government restrictions! Money is speech, and money from foreign sources should not be allowed.

- There should be extensive government restrictions! Money may or may not be speech, but this is a case where it is in society's best interest to limit it.

The answers to these questions show the range of positions the questions evoke. Why? What is important about the differences? The answer is that each response leads to a different understanding of what the problem means to the person responding. And depending on how the person answered, the possible solution to the problem at hand is constrained. Take the immigration case for a moment. Virtually everyone agrees that the United States is a nation of immigrants; everyone is either an immigrant or in a family whose line includes immigrants. Even today, the numbers are large. According to the U.S. Census Bureau (2017), from 2012 to 2016, over 13% of the U.S. population was foreign-born. In terms of what are called legal immigrants, in 2017, over 700,000 foreign nationals were either granted lawful permanent residence, were admitted on a temporary basis, applied for asylum or refugee status, or were naturalized (U.S. Department of Homeland Security [DHS], 2019).

But despite the numbers and the history, immigration is not without controversy. A large number of Americans want to limit immigrants (Fussell, 2014) for a variety of reasons, from a general fear of outsiders (Critchley, 2007) to national security to the effects on low-income workers and salaries (Borjas, 2003) and the general risk they bring to the society (Tan, 2015). At the same time, many people believe that immigrants bring benefits to a society (Faver, 2004).

A similar example in recent years is how our understanding about "the problem of drugs" has changed. In the lifetime of many of the people reading this chapter, marijuana has gone from an evil substance subverting the youth of America and causing depraved behavior, to a somewhat more benign substance but that might serve as a "gateway" to the use of other drugs, to a drug that is fully legal in 10 states and at least partially legal for medical purposes in 47 states. That is a dramatic change! And to some degree, many people would no longer include marijuana in a conversation talking about the problem of drugs.

At the same time, opiates are now the central part of a discussion about the problem of drugs. A few current statistics show how opiates have become the core of the discussion.

- 130 persons die from opioid overdose every day in the United States (U.S. Department of Health and Human Services, Centers for Disease Prevention, 2018).

- The economic "burden" of prescription opioids alone in the United States is $78.5 billion a year (Florence, Zhou, Luo, & Xu, 2016).

- Opioid overdoses increased 30% in 18 months from 2016 through 2017 in many areas in the United States (Vivolo-Kantor et al, 2018).

- Drug overdose deaths are the leading cause of death of persons under 50 in the United States (National Institutes of Health, 2019).

Why the problem of drugs has changed so dramatically is one of the clearest examples of changes in what is seen as important and how the problem definition has evolved. Importantly, the definition is associated with what is called the social construction of the problem. The idea of social construction is, at the same time, fairly easy and immensely complex to understand. Formally, it is the process by which humans attach meaning to things or events. The point to these different perspectives is that the way the problems are conceptualized leads to important distinctions in our understanding of the causes, or how serious it is, or what we believe the solutions could be. And this points to an important "truth" about a problem—that definitions of the problem are not fixed, permanent, concepts with clear boundaries. Instead they are socially constructed. As one writer states, "a social construct is something that exists not in objective reality, but as a result of human interaction. It exists because humans agree that it exists" (Bainbridge, 2018).

Does this mean that our world is not real? Well, I would prefer to defer that question to another time, but it does mean that our experience with the world (and everything in it) depends on how we think about it. Consider the word "family." Ask an American in the 1950s what a family is and they would likely say something like father, mother, and 2 to 4 children. Ask instead what a family is to a member of the Ogallala Sioux and they would likely name dozens of persons, some not at all blood related. The term "family" has different social constructions.

A second quick example. Consider the thing we call "shoes." Shoes are simply products made with leather, cotton, or synthetic materials to protect our feet. But now consider two pairs that are exactly alike, made with the same materials, by the same people in the same factory. One pair costs $15 and the other costs $300. Why? Most likely simply the name that is attached to the shoes. If the name on one is considered a luxury brand, worn by celebrities, and advertised in high profile magazines, videos, or social media sites, it is likely the more desirable. Indeed, in recent years, people have even been killed to obtain the higher cost pair. Some people do not care; other people "would not be caught dead" wearing the less expensive off-brand.

Everything in our lives is affected by the same general phenomena. We value, fear, or seek some items, people, or experiences, while we dislike, undervalue, or avoid almost identical phenomena. And the only difference is what meanings we attach and how we think about the thing. In other words, the meanings we attach are the critical difference!

▶ **Critical Thinking Questions**
1. What factors define quality to you?
2. Do you believe these factors are widely shared by your peers? Why or why not?

Now, how is this useful? We can participate in this process. Our understanding of the problem—what we see and what our clients tell us—can be useful in shaping the discussion around a problem.

Research Skills

The major skill set associated with problem characterization is research skills. They are the tools we use to "capture" and frame a problem. And such data are useful in shaping and understanding the size and scope of a given problem. All social work practitioners, even those who do not engage in research as a part of their job description, need to develop various skills in research. And one policy practice domain where this comes to the fore is in our efforts to understand a problem. Several types of research skills are useful here.

Tools for Assessing Need

At this phase, understanding the scope of the problem is critical. There are any number of excellent "how to" guides that will help you in this process. But for our purposes, we will focus on the kinds of information that will be useful to know. What you want to focus on are a series of questions that, if answered, will help you to better understand the problem. The following questions serve as useful starting points.

- What is the etiology of the condition? In other words, how and/or where did it begin? So data about the history would be useful.

- Where and when was it first seen?

- Who first identified it?

- What are its causes? Are there identifiable, possible antecedents?

- What are the characteristics of those who can be defined as having the condition?

- How many people are affected?

- How quickly is the problem expanding?

- How severely are people affected?

- In what ways are people affected?

- Can they be located geographically? Consider looking at comparative geographic areas as a way of showing severity or change.

- How widely is the condition recognized?

- Are there unique, identifiable characteristics?

As with any research, how you collect the data matters. But a variety of methods may be appropriate. Likewise, both qualitative data (narrative, nonstatistical information) and quantitative statistical data may be useful. Qualitative data, in the form of first-person accounts, are excellent ways to tell the clients' stories, while statistical data show the extent of the experiences.

A further and highly valuable approach at this stage of the process is mapping, as mapping the physical extent of an emerging problem is of great value as we try and understand the scope of the problem. One recent example where mapping has been used to examine an emerging problem is mapping areas of vulnerability to climate change. For example, many areas in North Carolina were identified as highly at risk from hurricane damage (Mock, 2018), and by such knowledge, prevention and remediation were more possible in 2018. Several excellent online mapping tools are now available, with accessible data at a variety of geographic levels, from entire states all the way down to neighborhoods and streets (c.f. ejscreen.epa.gov/mapper/index.html; or through sources at Climate Central sealevel.climatecentral.org/maps).

Political Mobilization and Political Advocacy

Once the problem has been identified and characterized, the concern turns to building support for the policy response, as well as using appropriate forms of pressure on policy makers to ensure that action is taken. This phase, in many ways, is the one that requires both the greatest creativity from the social worker, but also best fits the entire range of social worker skills. And there have been some major successes over the years. These include women's suffrage, the Civil Rights movement, the Gay Rights movement, or resistance against apartheid (Schwartz & Sanchez, 2016). But here is the critical point. Not one of these changes took place because of social workers alone. In every case, it took broad pressure from across the societies in question. And this "broad pressure" is the fruit of mobilization!

By necessity, political mobilization involves organizing and advocacy. Policy makers and the public need to be made aware of what the problem is, who is affected and how, what options are available, and which is the preferred option and why. There are several themes that affect these needs. But before examining the specific themes, the issue of power will be examined.

Why power? What is power? Here, we are largely talking about power as social or political power, and in the political world power is just about the whole ball game. Politics and social change depend on its application. And unfortunately, many of the things we, as humans, care about—friendship, love, and personal growth—matter much less than the medium of power. So let us begin with an understanding of what power is, and what power does.

As a starting point, power is not easy to define, despite (or perhaps, because of) the fact that power is one of the most studied phenomena in the social sciences. For our purposes, power means the ability to exert social and political influence. The sources of power are many and varied. Among some of the identified aspects are personal charisma, authority, position, status, expertise (knowledge and skills), wealth, numbers of followers, technology, and more (French & Raven, 1959; Weber, 1978/1914; Fiske & Berdahl, 2007). But regardless of the source/basis of power used, the point is that power is the one critical tool that forms the core of virtually all effective organizational activities—one that must be developed and used for effective policy work.

How? Well, digging a bit deeper, Fiske and Berdahl (2007), in an attempt to understand the phenomena, suggest that there are three categories of definitions that apply here. They are power as influence, power as potential influence, and power as outcome. Thinking about our purposes of creating or changing policy, there is value in all three categories. Power as influence refers to the direct application to achieve a result. A vote in a referendum is an example, or conversely a large cash contribution to a candidate given along with an expressed desire about how to vote on a piece of legislation. Power as potential influence has many contemporary examples. Until very recently, all a politician needed to hear was the expressed desire about how to vote on a piece of firearm legislation from the National Rifle Association (NRA) and the candidate would know that if he or she voted differently, large numbers of persons would work against his or her re-election.

Finally, power as outcome means empowerment. This is a goal of almost all advocacy efforts to at least some degree.

One other definitional aspect of power should be acknowledged. Power can be implied and quiet, or it can be coercive and overt. As social workers, we generally prefer the more quiet and implied forms. But history has shown that sometimes the application of power can be loud and messy. So how loud and

▶ **Critical Thinking Questions**

1. Is violence ever acceptable on behalf of social change? Why or why not?
2. When working to change a policy, sometimes it is necessary to change your strategy and tactics. What would suggest to you that it is necessary to change your approach?

messy should the effort to influence be? Is there a role for conflict, and if so, is there a role for violence? Well virtually everyone would say that violence is out of the question. But the broader answer is that applying power should be as loud as it needs to be to get people involved, to continue to stay involved, and to have policy makers act. This suggests at least some need for balance. You need to activate and motivate enough of the public (or the right people) but not alienate people because of your tactics. In Dr. Martin Luther King's famous letter from Birmingham jail (King, 1963), he talks about the flow of effort that leads to the direct actions employed. In this case, the direct actions occurred because nothing else worked. In his words:

> As the weeks and months unfolded, we realized that we were the victims of a broken promise. The signs remained. As in so many experiences of the past, we were confronted with blasted hopes, and the dark shadow of a deep disappointment settled upon us. So we had no alternative except that of preparing for direct action, whereby we would present our very bodies as a means of laying our case before the conscience of the local and national community. We were not unmindful of the difficulties involved. So we decided to go through a process of self - purification. We started having workshops on nonviolence and repeatedly asked ourselves the questions, "Are you able to accept blows without retaliating?" and "Are you able to endure the ordeals of jail?" We decided to set our direct-action program around the Easter season, realizing that, with exception of Christmas, this was the largest shopping period of the year. Knowing that a strong economic withdrawal program would be the by-product of direct action, we felt that this was the best time to bring pressure on the merchants for the needed changes. (King, 1963).

And overall, in many cases, some types of direct action are needed to bring focus and attention to the problem. A large variety of such actions are possible. They range from the generally quiet activities of letter writing, emails, calls, or text campaigns to policy makers, or direct in-person meetings with policy makers to much larger and more powerful events, such as lawsuits and boycotts. Often, as is the case described by Dr. King, there will be a "ratcheting up" of efforts.

So what are some of the effective methods that can be used in the process of mobilization? As indicated, here, we will address a few important aspects of the process of mobilization—lobbying, campaign funding, and public mobilization. But before examining a few domains in depth, it is worthwhile to consider a much longer list of ways that social workers may influence the policy maker. Among the methods that are available are:

- Networking with other organizations
- Providing training to key people

- Commenting on draft policy documents

- Organizing policy seminars

- Publications on policy issues

- Providing services

- Articles in the media

- Pilots of alternative policy approaches

- Insider lobbying

- Websites

- Newsletter to policy makers

- Work on projects commissioned by policy makers (modified from Kornsweig Osborne, Hovland, & Court, 2006)

Lobbying

One form of attempts to change policy that is ubiquitous in our political system is what is called "lobbying." Formally, lobbying is defined as any individual or private interest group attempting to influence the actions, policies, or decisions of legislators or members of regulatory agencies. Although the actual etymology of the term is somewhat lost in history, it does appear to have a connection with the presence of persons attempting to influence legislation in areas such as lobbying.

What is important, however, is that it is generally accepted in our political world. Indeed, our Constitution protects persons' rights to free speech, peaceable assembly, and the right to petition lawmakers. And with these rights, there is a long history of persons and interest groups attempting to change/bend legislation and other policies in ways that help them. What is more problematic is what kinds of lobbying work, what kinds of lobbying are legal, and what kinds of lobbying are otherwise illegal or unethical?

Effective Forms of Lobbying

There are a great variety of ways to lobby, each with strengths and limitations. For example, lobbying can be thought of as inside (direct) lobbying or outside (indirect) lobbying. Inside lobbying is largely composed of direct contact with policy makers, while outside is more typically mobilizing the public to bring numbers or attention to an issue (Kollman, 1998). Inside lobbying may include one-on-one meetings with policy makers or their staff. But it also includes the general or policy-specific meetings that policy makers often hold with constituents.

Now, when many of us think of lobbying, we have a narrow and sometimes negative view of the activity. Often, it is associated with professional lobbyists, and the scope of such lobbying activity across America is huge. Indeed, the numbers of lobbyists and lobbying organizations are great (in Washington, DC, there is an area called K Street, where hundreds of lobbyists are located) and both the states and the federal government have laws that govern how lobbyists may operate. To give an idea of how large the industry is, between 1998 and 2018, 18 organizations (corporations and trade organizations) spent over $200 million each on lobbying, and one entity, the U.S. Chamber of Commerce spent over $1.5 billion (Center for Responsive Politics, 2019a).

Importantly, this number of lobbying organizations, while overwhelmingly from the business world, is not exclusively so. The profession of social work has professional lobbying organizations, and many of the advocacy and issue groups associated with the profession and allies do likewise (c.f. AARP, Boys & Girls Clubs, NEA etc.). Indeed, most social workers either through an advocacy organization or on their own will have at least some opportunity to participate in lobbying in one form or another. In what follows are some of the types of lobbying we are likely to experience and use. A nonexhaustive list of methods (World Animal Net, 2017) may include:

- Working with policy makers ("Insider Advocacy")—many lobbyists develop direct relationships with policy makers through volunteering and participation in advisory groups

- Consultations—often based on direct outreach from policy makers

- Face-to-face meetings with policy makers

- Presentations to policy makers

- Presentations at conferences, seminars, public meetings, and so on

- International conferences

- Articulating written materials about problems and possible solutions—such as through policy briefs (discussed in the following)

- Legal challenges—many times, citizens and groups may bring lawsuits to ensure governments act as needed

If you have the opportunity to meet with policy makers and/or their staff to directly lobby, a few general guidelines will help to maximize the effectiveness of the effort (Case 12.2). First of all, you are more likely to talk to a staff person than to the actual policy maker. That is okay. You are not being ignored (in most cases!) but rather you are attempting to talk to a person (the policy maker) with many demands on his or her time. And generally, the staff person is good at reporting what his or her constituents are saying. Indeed, the same applies to calling a policy maker and talking by phone. The staff member will pass the information on. Now, would we rather talk to the actual policy maker? Sure. But in our system, that opportunity often comes with strings attached (see Campaign Funding).

CASE 12.2   WASHINGTON! MEETING WITH POLICY MAKERS

David and his fellow students were going to Washington to meet with both of his senators about the new bill to expand college access. But neither senator had yet to "sign on" to the legislation, and in fact both had a history of opposition to college student support. So what should he say? What kind of evidence would make an effective argument? Or further, how could the students, as students, apply the kinds of pressure needed to influence a senator? What tools made sense, and would be available so that the Congress would act?

Importantly, policy makers usually set the rules about who they will talk to, what they will/will not talk about, as well as for how long and under what conditions. As you may recall, in the past few years, many public meetings with lawmakers became quite heated over the Patient Protection and Affordable Care Act (the ACA or Obamacare). Congress itself has established some basic ethical standards for constituent meetings (U.S. House of Representatives, n.d.), but many congresspersons have established their own rules. Often, being a constituent in a group of constituents is a high priority (Bowman, 2014). Further, being a contributor to a politician is a serious plus (see campaign funding in the following), with one study finding it 231% more likely a politician will meet with you if you contributed to his or her campaign (Kalla & Broockman, 2016).

However, regardless of which type of lobbying you choose, there are a few general rules/skill sets you want to consider. First, do your research. You need to know the subject, but also the individuals you will be interacting with. Often, you will not be seeing the actual politician, but one of the staff. Knowing their names is a plus (Florida Education Association, n.d.a.). In your remarks, be brief, direct, and clear. You may be as passionate as you feel, even angry, but not vulgar. And never, ever, ever be threatening or violent. And acknowledge and thank the politician (Florida Education Association, n.d.a.).

Campaign Funding

One of the most commonly used ways to try and influence politicians is to give money to politicians to help fund their campaigns. Why? In our democratic republican form of government, we elect politicians to represent us. And not surprisingly, politicians want our support as they run for election. At its base, running for office is very inexpensive—only a few dollars to file papers and voila, a person becomes a candidate.

On the other hand, *successfully* running for office can be incredibly expensive. Candidates need to mobilize the public, hire staff, do research, establish plans, and engage the media. To do these things, money is necessary. How much? Well, the numbers are a bit frightening. The estimated cost of the 2018 midterm elections was over $5 billion (Center for Responsive Politics, 2018), which was the most in history for a midterm. Similarly, the 2016 election (president and Congress combined) cost $6.5 billion (Ingraham, 2017). And in the 2018 election, the average senator seeking reelection spent $13,460,873 (Center for Responsive Politics, 2019b). In practical terms, this means that the typical successful senator over his or her 6-year term has to raise over $43,000 every single week he or she is in office!! That's a lot of money!

So giving money to politicians is desirable. But there are important caveats. First, it is illegal everywhere to "buy" a vote. You cannot make a deal with a politician saying, "I will give you $1,000 if you vote for/against this bill." And the reverse is also true; a politician cannot promise to vote a certain way based only on a contribution. Similarly, there are currently a number of restrictions on how much money a person can give to any politician during a calendar year or election. Generally, most individual donors are limited to a few thousand dollars per cycle (see the Federal Election Commission at FEC.gov for the limits). But there are also a number of ways people attempt to get around these restrictions. For example, the individual limits are easily multiplied by the number of persons in a family (so if a limit is $2,800, but there are six people in a family, then the contribution is as much as $16,800).

More importantly, restrictions are lessened by giving money to political parties rather than individuals, or by creating special types of organizations that are exempt from many regulations. Among these are what are known as political action committees (PACs), which can bundle monies from many sources, or certain types of 501(c) organizations whose primary function is issue advocacy (as opposed to political advocacy), or 527 organizations (called Super PACs) that intend to publically educate on issues. Again, these organizations have a number of exemptions related to contribution limits and/or donor disclosure.

Further, as the result of some important Supreme Court decisions, the ability of the government to regulate political spending has been diminished. In 2010, the court decided in Citizen's United *v.* FEC that corporations could spend money for political advocacy, on the basis of their free speech rights. A second case, SpeechNOW.org *v.* FEC (2010), took this a step further and basically removed all contribution limits from certain kinds of nonprofit organizations as long as the spending organization did not coordinate with a candidate.

But the biggest issue, and thus one to remember is rarely will "the little person" have enough funds to compete on this field. Think of it this way. If Bill Gates and you both call your senator and leave a message, who is the senator more likely to call back? Probably not you. But that is perhaps not as bad as it sounds. First, in recent years, it has become clear how important small campaign contributions can be. The 2016 and 2020 campaigns of politicians like Bernie Sanders, Kamala Harris, and others have demonstrated that enough small donations can quickly grow large sums.

Further, we need instead to utilize other tools to influence politicians. Thus, the expanded forms of mobilization are critical.

Educating, Mobilizing, and Organizing the Public

While both lobbying of policy makers and contributing money to campaigns are necessary, unfortunately limits to time and cash resources restrict how much effect these methods have among practicing social workers. In part, we can address these restrictions by joining advocacy organizations. By doing so, we bring the power of numbers to our efforts. Numbers are often (though unfortunately not always) the key to almost any effective application of power. But whether it is through participation in such an organization, or on our own, one very critical tool we have at our disposal is a more general mobilization of the public. As that theme is more fully covered in Chapter 10, Mezzointerventions in Social Work: Organizations and Communities, only a few words on the subject are presented here. (Note: A wonderful resource guide that covers all aspects of organizing may be found at the *Community Toolbox* from University of Kansas (2015), which gives a virtual step-by-step description of the organizing process.)

Here, instead, we will focus on one set of skills that has wide utility in policy work—educating policy makers and the public. Three types of written educational materials are particularly valuable, as they can be developed and applied by individual social workers, as well as the creation of YouTube© videos. In other words, joining a group is not necessary to develop and apply these materials.

The reality and importance of this activity is weighty. In our complex and highly stimulating world, both policy makers and the general public typically have limited information about any given problem or possible solutions. Like any human knowledge area, these limitations are influenced by things like personal interest and time. No one can know everything. Interestingly, sometimes the knowledge limitations of policy makers are associated with the very positions the policy maker holds. For example, one common observation about Congress is that differences in policy knowledge exist by body (Edwards & Lippucci, 1998; O'Connor, Sabato, Haag, & Keith, 2004). Senators tend to be "policy generalists," meaning that because they serve entire states, they need to know at least a little bit about a lot of policy areas, but not necessarily a lot about any specific policy problem. On the other hand, members of the House of Representatives tend to be "policy specialists" and perhaps quite knowledgeable about the areas important to their district but perhaps ignorant of less relevant issues.

But regardless of the level of knowledge about any given problem, you bring important perspectives and evidence that should be presented. So you as an individual social worker or as a member of an advocacy organization can help to address these problems. The "inside" perspective of a one-on-one conversation with the policy maker (or more likely, the staff of a policy maker) is only one way to educate and inform. Other ways are equally important. These may include testifying before policy makers in a hearing of one form or another and writing policy briefs.

Giving Testimony

Social workers are often asked to present testimony in what are called "hearings." These times are great opportunities to carry your "on the ground" expertise, and to present valuable alternatives. Unfortunately, these will not always be pleasant activities—sometimes the events are used to kill policies that are desirable from our perspective (Florida Education Association, n.d.a.), or to give the illusion of community input, but our voices and the information we provide can be invaluable.

The opportunities come as policy makers seek testimony from persons like yourself in any one of several types of hearings. These may include legislative hearings that seek information about policies, oversight hearings that review existing programs and agencies, investigative hearings that look into allegations of wrongdoing by persons in the government, and confirmation hearings that address appointees to government positions (Heitshusen, 2018). If it is an area you know something about, you may ask or be asked to provide testimony, and this could be either or both written and in person (Heitshusen, 2017).

What you say is up to you. You may bring statistics, anecdotes from the field, or stories heard from clients. As a social worker, you are (hopefully) well trained in public communication. But always be brief, to the point, factual, and know the committee members. There will be some participants who are friendly to you, and others who are not.

Unfortunately, not all hearings are the same. The hearing may be an event for "show" with little chance it will influence policy. Or you might find yourself presenting your testimony to an empty room (congresspersons are not obligated to attend), or you might find you are facing one or more hostile politicians who ask questions that are more like diatribes with little opportunity for you to respond. But always be polite even as you are assertive. Congresspersons have been known to respond quite testily even if they agree with you if you "impugn" a member. Overall, this is a fabulous opportunity to get information to the people who make the decisions.

Policy Briefs

While the testimony is quick and ephemeral, putting the material "on paper" allows the wider distribution of information. Indeed, it is a nearly critical aspect of almost all mobilization efforts. In particular, the form called the "policy brief" is very useful. It is a written presentation of written facts associated with a policy or problem. While there is no one format universally defined as the policy brief, there are some characteristics associated with most forms. A good brief will be, well, brief. One model is shown in the following. But in general, the information should include a strong title, problem/policy background and significance, your position and desired steps or outcomes, and reputable references (Domingo, 2015). A number of excellent examples and step-by-step models are found online (www.slideshare .net/search/slideshow?searchfrom=header&q=policy+briefs).

Here is one format that is "tried and true," although the content in a policy brief is, to a degree, up to you and what it is that you hope the audience will take from it. Generally, but not always, a good policy brief will include the following.

A description of the problem you are hoping to resolve. This should include a definition, a few powerful statistics, and perhaps a very quick history of previous attempts to resolve the problem. Or if the brief is attempting to inform the reader about failings in existing policy, you will want to describe the policy currently in place and the reasons the policy is not adequate. It should include:

- A description of the goals of the policy response.

- A description of the necessary components of the policy response. At a minimum, this could include such things as who needs the potential benefit and what the potential benefit should be.

- A statement of what you are asking the reader to do. This could include contacts, names of organizations that advocate for the policy, and governmental committees or individuals that need to hear from the reader.

- Information about who is responsible for this brief.

These briefs may then be distributed in person, through email, or through social media. As a final thought, in the experience of the author, you will find that the audiences who read these briefs vary widely. As such, you might consider two or three different formats, each written slightly differently to address the needs and concerns of a given group.

> ▶ **Critical Thinking Questions**
> 1. What "catches your attention" when you are reviewing the news or a website?
> 2. What kinds of information might you include to maximize interest in a Letter to the Editor?

Letters to the Editor

If the goal of your written work is to reach a wide audience, few methods/formats are as effective as the Letter to the Editor. Of course, we assume this means in newspapers, but very similar components and formats apply to any number of online opportunities, such as blogs or other social media posts. As with the policy brief, a number of appropriate structures exist, but the general content areas are similar with just a couple of differences. The major differences relate to the difference in audience. Newspapers and social media posts are usually seen primarily by people with some commonality, for instance, they live in the same town or have the same interests. Therefore, when you write such a letter, make sure you have written it in such a way to address that commonality. As the National Education Association (2019) states, "Newspaper readers care about how an issue will impact them or their families locally. Including brief information on the economic or other impacts of an issue in the community will draw readers' interest."

YouTube Videos

Our informational universe has been transformed by technology and its democratization. Cell phones and the Internet place, without much exaggeration, the entire knowledge base of humanity at our finger tips. Further, the ease and availability of digital cameras and easy-to-use editing software and "cloud" storage have made video production and distribution a common activity.

For social workers, this educational medium is almost too good to ignore. How widely does this format reach? YouTube reports that more than 1.9 billion users log in each month and watch over one billion hours of videos (YouTube, 2019). Many of these videos are created by users like yourselves, and in just a few hours, you can create a video with the potential for a worldwide distribution and impact. Of course, just creating and posting is no guarantee that people will watch and will act on what they see. Fortunately, there are a number of YouTube videos (!) that can help you develop an effective presence. But like the policy brief and the Letter to the Editor, direct, uncluttered information is best. There is, however, one technique that seems to be very important with effective videos—start with a story. In our work life, we undoubtedly hear interesting, insightful, and powerful stories all the time. As long as you are respectful of the ethical aspects of a client's life and maintain confidentiality and anonymity, feel free to use these stories. They will help to get the message across.

■ Policy Implementation

One of the real shocks to many people who interact with the policy world is that even when a policy is enacted at the federal, state, or local level, a whole process of implementation begins. Generally stated, policy implementation runs the gamut of activities that occur from the time a given law becomes law, through the regulatory process, and on through the final activities that take place between the social worker and client. And such a process can enhance but also undermine the actual law. Importantly, policy itself often lays out little more than statements of intention, a budget, and directed bureaucratic control through an agency or department. With those limited components, a system "kicks in" to write the rules or regulations associated with the policy. It is at this point that the phrase "the devil is in the details" makes sense. Choices about these details can affect the whole domain of policy issues about the who, what, where, and how of the policy. Two domains in particular are important here—regulations (often called rulemaking) and organizational or administrative practice.

Regulatory Actions

Many of the choices affecting policy come out in the regulatory process. The process may be long and complex, but it is governed by laws that set the parameters of the regulatory flow, with virtually every unit of federal and state departments and agencies having unique procedures that govern how this works. But there are some general principles that we examine in what follows. Further, for more details on many of the unique elements of the process, a useful overview has been published by the U.S. Office of the Federal Register (n.d.) that goes into greater specificity. The general steps include:

1. Initiating events—some specific action initiates the regulatory process, such as passage of a law or a court decision

2. Determination whether a rule is needed—the lead agency makes a determination if a rule should be put in place

3. Preparation of proposed rule—the lead agency is required to draft a proposed regulation

4. Office of Management and Budget (OMB) review of proposed rule—the OMB examines the proposed rule to see if it aligns with all relevant federal laws

5. Publication of proposed rule—the lead agency is required to notify the public that a proposed rule is being examined

6. Public comments—the public is given a 30-, 60-, or 90-day period to make comments about the proposed regulation

7. Preparation of final rule, interim final rule, or direct final rule—after the comment period ends

8. OMB review of final rule, interim final rule, or direct final rule

9. Publication of final rule, interim final rule, or direct final rule

Within this process, there are several important points of access and opportunities for social workers to participate. This points are largely related to the opportunities to comment on the proposed rules. What is of particular importance is knowledge about the opportunities, as well as procedures that must be used for the comments. In reality, both can be overwhelming. And this is one of the times when connection to an advocacy group is critical. Most of the advocacy organizations social workers work with have established methods to keep track of relevant regulations under development and review. Thus, connection with these organizations will provide access to strong supportive action.

Organizational Practice

But even the regulatory decision process is not the end of the implementation stage. For the services/actions determined by the regulation still need to be provided! This moves us into the realm of organizational practice. While organizational theory and practice are generally outside of the frame of this chapter, it is critical to understand how organizations work as virtually all policies are implemented—not to mention created—by organizations. They provide the primary medium for our work, and it is no exaggeration to say that all we do with and for clients takes place through our, and their, connection to organizations, whether they be government departments, county services offices, or small, local agencies.

One way this can be understood is by examining what is sometimes classified as organizational or administrative practice. Birkenmaier and Berg-Weger (2007) provide a useful listing of the knowledge and skills associated with this practice. This listing includes:

- Budgeting and financial management
- Working with the board of directors
- Resource development
- Program evaluation
- Organizational design, development, assessment, and diagnosis
- Computer information systems and technology
- Leadership and personnel management
- Networking
- Fundraising
- Media and marketing (Birkenmaier & Berg-Weger, 2007)

Chapter 9, Mezzosystems Assessment: Organizations and Communities, and Chapter 10, Mezzointerventions in Social Work: Organizations and Communities, discuss organizations in much greater detail. But the point cannot be downplayed here. Organizations are where the action takes place! And as such, participation in policy often means working to maximize the effectiveness of organizations.

Policy Evaluation

The last area of policy practice we examine is the area commonly known as policy evaluation or policy analysis. Formally defined, "Policy evaluation applies evaluation principles and methods to examine the content, implementation or impact of a policy. Evaluation is the activity through which we develop an understanding of the merit, worth, and utility of a policy" (CDC, 2011, p. 1). Policy analysis provides the opportunity to examine and provide informed critical analysis of existing policies. And as such, this form of analysis may have value at any point in the policy process, but it is listed here because it implies the policy has been enacted. And with that in mind, one of the most useful aspects of the policy analysis is that it can be used to provide feedback to change and improve policy if needed.

Indeed, policy analysis can serve a variety of purposes, and a wide variety of approaches and methods can be used. In part, this is due to the fact that policies are complex, and in part this is because a wide variety of different questions can be asked about a policy. In addition, policy analysis does not belong to any unique academic discipline, and as such the various paradigms of the different disciplines may affect the project.

With these provisos in mind, there are a number of general types of issues to consider in a policy analysis. These include the purpose of the analysis (why it is being done), what the policy does (the policy description), and how the analysis is done. Exhibit 12.1 goes over several types of policy analysis and the questions the analysis seeks to answer. But before we discuss the questions and methods of the various forms of policy analysis, we look at the various purposes for conducting policy analysis.

WHO (2012) provides a list of possible purposes that forms a reasonable baseline. According to their guiding document, evaluation may focus on an "activity, project, programme, strategy, policy, topic, theme, sector, operational area or institutional performance." They should:

- Focus on expected and achieved accomplishments, examining the results chain, processes, contextual factors, and causality, in order to understand achievements or the lack thereof

- Determine the relevance, impact, effectiveness, efficiency, and sustainability of the interventions and contributions of the organization

- Provide evidence-based information that is credible, reliable, and useful, enabling the timely incorporation of findings, recommendations, and lessons learnt into the decision-making processes of the organization

- Be an integral part of each stage of the programming cycle and not only an end-of-programme activity (p. 1)

As a social worker, you are in a wonderful place to examine the implementation of policy. Now, it is understood that you might not have the time and resources to conduct major evaluations of major policies. But even small pieces can make for major contributions.

So what makes for a "good" evaluation? Well, again, that in part depends on the discipline and purpose of the evaluation. A slightly more "political" interpretation of what comprises a good evaluation comes from the CDC (CDC, 2011, p. 1), which suggest that a good evaluation must meet the standards of "utility, feasibility, propriety and accuracy." Similarly, the CDC offer a useful way of comparing program evaluation to policy evaluation. They suggest the major differences are:

- The level of analysis required (e.g., system or community level for policy evaluation; program level for program evaluation)

- The degree of control and clear "boundaries" may be more challenging with policy evaluation

- The ability to identify an equivalent comparison community may be more challenging with policy evaluation

- The scale and scope of data collection may be greater with policy evaluation

- Policy evaluation may require increased emphasis on the use of surveillance and administrative data

- The type and number of stakeholders involved may differ

Types of Policy Analysis

With the previous discussion in mind, there are several different types of policy analysis. Exhibit 12.1 demonstrates some of the various types, which, again, are based on the kinds of questions the analysis seeks to answer.

EXHIBIT 12.1

TYPES OF POLICY ANALYSIS

Descriptive analysis: Generally, this type attempts to understand the "what" of a policy, rather than "why." It includes the following questions:

- What is the target problem; how large is the problem; how is the problem defined?
- Who receives the benefit or sanction?
- What do beneficiaries receive? How do beneficiaries receive the benefit?
- How is it paid for?
- Does the policy reduce the size of the target problem? What remains to be done?

Historical analysis: This type attempts to understand how a policy "came to be." There are a number of questions that might be included, such as:

- When was the target problem first identified, and by whom? By whom and how was the problem defined?
- What policy alternatives existed?
- What groups or individuals supported and opposed the policy response?
- What was the evolution of the policy selected? What was the "legislative" chronology?
- What does the final policy include/not include?

Value analysis: This type attempts to understand the "why" of a policy. There are several different models, but generally they are all guided by some similar questions, that include:

- What social values does the policy hope to affect/support?
- What social values affected the definition and policy alternatives, and final selection?
- Has the policy actually achieved the desired value outcomes? Why or why not?

Power analysis: Closely related to the value analysis, this approach seeks to analyze the power relationships that affected the policy. There are two (of many) types as follows:

- Marxist analysis: This seeks to examine how the policy supports economic structures in society.
- Feminist analysis: This seeks to examine how a policy reinforces power relationships (such as patriarchy) in a society.

Economic analysis: These approaches attempt to analyze the economic characteristics of a policy. There are several types, but questions often include:

- What are the economic costs and benefits of the policy?
- Are there unanticipated consequences to the policy?
- Do the economic benefits exceed the economic or other types of costs?

Descriptive Analysis

The most ubiquitous type, and in fact one that often is a component of many types or may stand alone, is what may be called a descriptive analysis. The specific questions that comprise a descriptive analysis differ, but usually are guided by the kinds of questions presented by Terrell (2012). Specifically, these include:

- Social allocations: Who gets the benefit?
- Social provision: What is the benefit?
- Delivery: How are the benefits distributed?
- Finance: How is the benefit paid for?

Again, these questions apply to almost all kinds of policy analysis. It is critical to understand what a policy does before more substantive analyses that address more complicated questions.

Historical Analysis

In a similar vein, the second type of analysis, the historical analysis, which may also be a component of other analyses as well as a stand-alone approach, seeks to examine and describe the historical issues or legislative history associated with a given policy. Such an analysis may examine many different components of the history. For example, what interest groups or individuals supported and opposed the enactment of a piece of legislation. Or, if the policy was associated with a court decision or an Executive Order, what were the precipitating actions that led to the actions. (See Case 12.3 for an example of questions to ask about a state's policy on vaping.)

CASE 12.3   VAPING POLICY? THE SOCIAL WORKER'S ROLE IN EXAMINING NEW GOVERNMENT POLICY

So what questions should Jeff ask about the new state policy on vaping? Asked by his agency to develop a strategy to examine the policy effects on reduction of use, he knew there were more questions that could be assessed beyond whether use declined or not. In particular, he was interested in such things as why the policy was, well, rather weak. Why? What contributed to the law's limitations? Were politics involved? Or was the science underlying the law adequate? Or what about the role of tobacco lobbyists? Jeff knew his analysis would have to address these issues.

Values, Power, and Economic Analyses

There are several types of analysis that begin to look at deeper questions about the policy. The first of these are what might be called a value analysis. This type of analysis examines the values and beliefs that inform the policy. Values, as discussed in Chapter 11, Policy Practice: How Policy Is Made, serve several functions in policy. Such functions can include serving as goals for a policy, or as guides for processes of policy implementation. Analyses that examine values seek to "uncover" the informing values, or to assess how well the policy helps the society to achieve its values.

A good model of the application of this approach is found in Terrell's (2012) Dimensions of Social Welfare Policy. This model focuses on the dominant values of our political system: equality, equity, freedom, and then adequacy.

Closely related are evaluations that seek to examine what the relationship of the policy is to such things as power in a society. There are many permutations on this approach. For example, Marxist analyses attempt to determine how policies serve to maintain power relationships between various class groups. Feminist models, likewise, examine the relationship between dominant/subordinate groups. Such evaluations have been useful in the past in helping to clarify methods of oppression and how social structures are maintained to support such systems.

Finally, economic analyses are used as tools to examine the relative costs and benefits of both past and prospective policy choices. One of the most interesting aspects of these types of evaluations is how they have attempted to quantify noneconomic factors in policy assessments.

So which type should you do? It depends on your interests, your skills, and your resources. But even if you are unable to fully embark on a major evaluation, there are still many useful ways to contribute. For one thing, you may use the evaluation findings of others as you construct your policy briefs. Your goal may not be an altogether new policy. Indeed, you might be largely happy with what you see with the exception of some minor adjustments. How will policy makers know these adjustments are needed? Through the work you do. Bring needed changes to the attention of policy makers. That, in many situations, is the best and most useful thing you may do.

■ Summary

While this chapter does not address community organizing per se, there are a number of critical overlaps. Similarly, there are a number of wonderful models for community organizing that the social worker should be familiar with to be effective. Several wonderful consolidations of various models are available online (cUniversity of Kansas, 2015; StayWoke, n.d.), but a few themes stand out for special attention here. First and perhaps most important are the common purposes of both organizing and political mobilization and advocacy. Both domains are concerned with consolidating and/or creating power. In some cases, this is the process of empowerment, and in other cases this means using power to leverage.

In this chapter, we examined how social workers may participate in policy through what is called policy practice. Throughout the policy process, there are opportunities for social workers to engage policy. Among these are assisting to identify and characterize emerging problems when first encountering new problems. Then, the social worker can help to publicize and educate the policy making and general communities about the problems, and mobilize these groups to address the issue. At the stage of policy implementation, the social worker can participate in the regulatory process and help make the regulations through joining the commenting period. Further, engaging in organizational practice to provide the service as effectively as possible is necessary. And at the last stage of the policy process, the social worker can participate in policy analysis and evaluation. Information here can be used to feed back into the policy process and hopefully facilitate change as needed.

CASE SUMMARY   "UNDOCUMENTED AND HOMELESS"

Practice Setting Description

Jackie is a first-year master of social work student completing an internship at an inner-city family service agency in the Southwest. The agency is located in a section of the city that has a high crime rate, gang activity, and failing schools. The area has a diverse population with a large number of immigrants from Central and South America and a substantial African American population. The agency provides individual and family counseling services on a sliding fee scale. The agency also runs a number of educational and treatment groups as well as a temporary shelter for women and their children. Jackie has been assigned to work with the women and their children in the shelter. Her primary tasks are to provide concrete services and supportive counseling to the shelter residents.

Background Information

Elicia T and her daughter, Maria, are undocumented immigrants from Mexico. They have been in the United States for 5 years. Elicia and Maria fled to the area from another southwestern city to escape her abusive husband approximately 2 months ago. Elicia is 25 years old and Maria 8 years old. Elicia has a 2-year-old daughter, Sarah, who was placed in foster care because of suspected abuse in the home. Sarah is in a foster home in a small rural community in the state hundreds of miles from Elicia's current residence. Since moving to the area, Maria has not been attending school.

Elicia and Maria are currently residing in the agency's temporary shelter for families. They have been at the shelter for 2 weeks, and the agency has a 90-day limit. It is viewed as temporary housing, and the residents are only allowed to stay for 3 months. Prior to arriving at the shelter, Elicia and Maria were homeless and living on the streets.

Elicia is a high-school dropout and was a stay-at-home mother prior to leaving her husband and moving to a different part of the state. She chose to move there because she has two female cousins living in the area who are also undocumented immigrants. Elicia's native language is Spanish. She speaks some English but is not as comfortable speaking in English. Her English comprehension appears to be good. Maria speaks both English and Spanish well. When communicating with the staff, Maria acts as Elicia's interpreter since none of the staff at the shelter speak Spanish.

(continued)

CASE SUMMARY

Maria appears to be behind academically. She struggles reading simple children's books written in English. It is unknown if her ability to read in Spanish is better than her English reading skills.

Other than her two cousins, Elicia has no other sources of support in the community. Her cousins have young families and limited resources but are well established and connected to a Latino community in the city and the local Catholic church. Her cousins refused to let Elicia and Maria live with them while she was trying to find her own place and a job. They stated that they did not have enough room and are concerned they would get in trouble with their landlord if it was found out that they were letting people stay with them. They sent her to the local church for help, and she was given the address for the agency's shelter by the priest.

Elicia has been looking for housing in the Latino community. The housing market is tight with limited options, and she has been unable to find anything that she could possibly afford. The only affordable housing she found was a room in a rundown motel that rents by the hour or by the month. It is in an area of town known for drug dealing and sex work.

On arrival in the community, Elicia found occasional work for a house cleaning company. The company hires undocumented workers, pays them very low cash wages, and threatens to turn them in to Immigration and Customs Enforcement (ICE) if they complain. The job bosses also exploit their female workers sexually, threatening to turn them in if they do not comply. Elicia was fearful about applying for other jobs because of her illegal status. She considered turning to sex work to be able to take care of her children, but her Catholic upbringing and thoughts of how doing so would shame her family have kept her from doing so. She is in constant fear of being detained, separated from her children, and having them placed in foster care. She is also afraid that she will end up homeless again and forced to live on the streets or return to her abusive husband.

Elicia is extremely reluctant to sign up for any federally funded services, even those that she and her children are entitled to receiving. On the suggestion that she enroll for supplemental food through SNAP, Elicia became nervous and refused as she has heard that participation in SNAP services, and others like them, would draw the attention of ICE, and she had heard stories on the news of individuals being deported after signing up for such programs.

Presenting Problems

Elicia and her children are facing multiple obstacles. They need to find permanent, affordable housing and a job that pays enough to cover her housing and living expenses. In addition, Maria needs to be enrolled in school. Elicia also wants to regain custody of her youngest daughter in foster care.

Additionally, Elicia is experiencing an immense amount of stress, anxiety, and possibly post-traumatic stress disorder (PTSD). She described an instance where she could not calm down her breathing, and she felt lightheaded. She is very fearful of men and tries to avoid all contact with men in the community. She reports difficulty sleeping at night and feeling exhausted most of the time.

She is concerned about Maria. She has started acting out at the shelter, getting into fights with the other children, disobeying her mother, and being disrespectful and defiant to the staff and other adults. Elicia and Maria fight frequently, and when Elicia tries to discipline Maria, she throws a temper tantrum until Elicia gives up.

(continued)

CASE SUMMARY

Elicia has many strengths. She had the strength to leave her abusive husband and move to a different city. She loves her daughters. She wants desperately to keep Maria with her and hopes to have Sarah returned to her custody. She is resilient and has managed to survive and keep her daughter safe despite not having a place to stay, a job, and a limited support network. Additionally, Elicia is highly motivated to find her own accommodations and support her children.

■ Discussion Questions

1. What kinds of information about the client population would be useful to Jackie as she attempts to develop appropriate services for women like Elicia and girls like Maria?

2. What assumptions do you think affect the current social construction of the immigrant in America? How accurate do you think these assumptions are in the present case?

3. Looking at the policies that affect the services Elicia and Maria are eligible for in this case, what do you see that might be challenged and changed through legal action (the courts)? What policies do you think could only be changed by legislation?

4. How might Jackie publicize the situation of the clients in the community as a way of mobilizing support for some important policy changes?

■ References

Bainbridge, C. (2018). *Why social constructs are created*. Retrieved from https://www.verywellfamily .com/definition-of-social-construct-1448922

Barker, R. (2003). *Social work dictionary* (5th ed.). Baltimore, MD: NASW Press.

Birkenmaier, J., & Berg-Weger, M. (2007). *The practicum companion for social work: Integrating class and field work* (2nd ed.). Boston, MA: Pearson Education.

Borjas, G. J. (2003). The Labor Demand Curve Is Downward Sloping: Reexamining the Impact of Immigration on the Labor Market," *Quarterly Journal of Economics*, 1335–1374.

Bowman, B. (2014). *Report outlines constituent meeting do's and don'ts*. Retrieved from https://www .rollcall.com/news/report-outlines-constituent-meeting-dos-and-donts

Centers for Disease Control and Prevention. (2011). *Brief 1: Overview of policy evaluation*. Retrieved from https://www.cdc.gov/injury/pdfs/policy/brief%201-a.pdf

Centers for Disease Control and Prevention, National Vital Statistics System. (2018). *Mortality*. Atlanta: CDC. Retrieved from https://wonder.cdc.gov

Centers for Disease Control and Prevention. (2018). *Surveillance strategy report — A stepwise approach*. Retrieved from https://www.cdc.gov/surveillance/improving-surveillance/stepwise-approach.html

Center for Responsive Politics. (2018). *Cost of 2018 election to surpass $5 billion, CRP projects*. Retrieved from https://www.opensecrets.org/news/2018/10/cost-of-2018-election

Center for Responsive Politics. (2019a). *Election overview*. Retrieved from https://www.opensecrets.org/ overview/index.php?cycle=2018&type=A&display=A

Center for Responsive Politics. (2019b). *Top spenders.* Retrieved from https://www.opensecrets.org/lobby/top.php?indexType=s

Critchley, S. (2007). *Infinitely demanding: Ethics of commitment, politics of resistance.* Brooklyn, NY: Verso.

Domingo, A. (2015). *Introduction to technical writing: The policy brief.* Retrieved from https://www.slideshare.net/aedomingo/introduction-to-technical-writing-the-policy-brief

Edwards, D., & Lippucci, A. (1998). *Practicing American politics: An introduction to government.* New York, NY: Worth Publishers.

Faver, C. (2004). Relational spirituality and social caregiving. *Social Work, 49*(2), 241–249. doi:10.1093/sw/49.2.241.

Fiske, S., & Berdahl, J. (2007). Social power. In A. W. Kruglanski & E. T. Higgins (Eds.), *Social psychology, (2nd ed.). Handbook of basic principles* (pp. 678–744). New York, NY: Guilford Publications. Retrieved from https://www.guilford.com/excerpts/kruglanski.pdf

Florence, C. S., Zhou, C., Luo, F., & Xu, L. (2016). The economic burden of prescription opioid overdose, abuse, and dependence in the United States, 2013. *Medical Care, 54*(10), 901–906. doi:10.1097/MLR.0000000000000625

Florida Education Association. (n.d.a). Effective Lobbying Techniques. Retrieved from https://feaweb.org/effective-lobbying-techniques

French, J. R. P., Jr., & Raven, B. (1959). The bases of social power. In D. Cartwright (Ed.), *Studies in social power* (pp. 150–167). Oxford, England: University. Michigan.

Fussell, E. (2014). Warmth of the welcome: Attitudes toward immigrants and immigration policy in the United States. *Annual Review of Sociology, 40*(1), 479–498. doi:10.1146/annurev-soc-071913-043325

Heitshusen, V. (2017). *Senate committee hearings: Arranging witnesses, CRS report.* Congressional Research Service. Retrieved from https://www.senate.gov/CRSpubs/045a2fbf-0ad7-434b-9496-ab85db6dae6b.pdf

Heitshusen, V. (2018). *Types of committee hearings, CRS report congressional research service.* Retrieved from https://www.senate.gov/CRSpubs/cb39da50-6535-4824-9d2f-e5f1fcf0a3e4.pdf

Ingraham, C. (2017). Somebody just put a price tag on the 2016 election. It's a doozy. *Washington Post.* Retrieved from https://www.washingtonpost.com/news/wonk/wp/2017/04/14/somebody-just-put-a-price-tag-on-the-2016-election-its-a-doozy/?utm_term=.e5776b3fb8af

Kalla, J. L., & Broockman, D. E. (2016). Campaign contributions facilitate access to congressional officials: A randomized field experiment. *American Journal of Political Science, 60,* 545–558. doi:10.1111/ajps.12180

King, M. L. (1963). *Letter from a Birmingham jail.* Retrieved from https://www.africa.upenn.edu/Articles_Gen/Letter_Birmingham.html

Kollman, K. (1998). *Outside lobbying: Public opinion and interest group strategies.* Princeton, NJ: Princeton University Press.

Kornsweig, G., Osborne, D., Hovland, I., & Court, J. (2006). *CSOs, policy influence, and evidence use: A short survey.* London: ODI.

Mock, B. (2018). *Mapping where environmental justice is most threatened in the Carolinas.* Retrieved from https://www.citylab.com/equity/2018/09/mapping-where-environmental-justice-is-most-threatened-in-the-carolinas/570985

National Association of Social Workers. (2017). *Code of ethics.* Silver Spring, MD: Author. Retrieved from https://www.socialworkers.org/About/Ethics/Code-of-Ethics/Code-of-Ethics-English

National Education Association. (2019). *Writing effective letters to the editor.* Retrieved from http://www.nea.org/home/19683.htm

National Institutes of Health. (2019). *Opiates.* Retrieved from https://ghr.nlm.nih.gov/condition/opioid-addiction#statistics

O'Connor, K., Sabato, L., Haag, S., & Keith, G. (2004). *American government: Continuity and change.* Belmont, CA: Pearson Education.

Reisch, M. (2017). Why macro practice matters. *Human Service Organizations: Management, Leadership & Governance, 41*(1), 6–9. Retrieved from http://www.acosa.org/joomla/pdf/Reisch-2015-Why-macro-practice-matters.pdf

Schwartz, M., & Sanchez, E. (2016). *Social movements that have changed the world.* Global Citizen. Retrieved from https://www.globalcitizen.org/en/content/movements-social-change-apartheid-civil-rights-suf/

StayWoke. (n.d.). *Resistance manual.* Retrieved from https://www.resistancemanual.org/index.php?title=Tools_of_Resistance&oldid=13908

Tan, K. (2015). *Reconfiguring citizenship and national identity in the North American literary imagination.* Detroit, MI; Wayne Street University Press.

Terrell, P. (2012). *Dimensions of social welfare policy* (8th ed.). CA: Allyn & Bacon.

University of Kansas. (2015). *The community toolbox.* Retrieved from https://ctb.ku.edu/en

U.S. Census Bureau. (2017). *QuickFacts: United States.* Retrieved from https://www.census.gov/quickfacts/fact/table/US/PST045217

U.S. Department of Health and Human Services, Centers for Disease Prevention (2018). Mortality. Retrieved from https://wonder.cdc.gov.

U.S. Department of Homeland Security. (2019). *Yearbook of immigration statistics 2017.* Retrieved from https://www.dhs.gov/immigration-statistics/yearbook/2017

U.S. House of Representatives. (n.d.). *Congressional standards.* Retrieved from https://ethics.house.gov/casework/congressional-standards

U. S. Office of the Federal Register. (n.d.). *A guide to the rulemaking process.* Retrieved from https://www.federalregister.gov/uploads/2011/01/the_rulemaking_process.pdf

Vivolo-Kantor, A. M., Seth, P., Gladden, R M., Mattson, C. L., Baldwin, G. T., Kite-Powell, A., & Coletta, M. A. (March 9, 2018). *Vital signs: Trends in emergency department visits for suspected opioid overdoses--United States, July 2016-September 2017.* Retrieved from https://www.cdc.gov/mmwr/volumes/67/wr/mm6709e1.htm

Weber, M. (1978). *Economy and society* (G. Roth & C. Wittich, Trans.). Berkeley: University of California Press. (Original work published 1914.)

World Animal Net. (2017). Advocacy toolkit. Retrieved from http://worldanimal.net/advocacy-toolkit

World Health Organization. (2012). *Evaluation practice handbook.* Retrieved from https://apps.who.int/iris/bitstream/handle/10665/96311/9789241548687_eng.pdf;jsessionid=7EDFC70ED4E964FA133837A4C86E30F8?sequence=1

YouTube. (2019). *YouTube in numbers.* Retrieved from https://www.youtube.com/intl/en-GB/yt/about/press

PRACTICE-INFORMED RESEARCH

Carolyn is a school social worker at an elementary school complex. She meets with students individually and in groups. At times, teachers and other school personnel will seek out Carolyn's clinical expertise to determine how to address larger, school-wide concerns. Recently, the principal asked Carolyn to meet with her and several other employees to address recent concerns related to bullying that have arisen at school. During the meeting, all present were designated as the anti-bullying task force for the school and were charged with the duty of developing an anti-bullying policy and curriculum for the school to adopt and implement at the start of the next term.

During the initial task force meeting, each participant agreed to research anti-bullying programs and bring back their findings to the next meeting. At the second meeting, all of the participants shared what they had found. One member shared that she found out about an anti-bullying program that a neighboring school district is currently using. He reported that this program has been really successful in addressing bullying for that school based on conversations with teachers from that school. Carolyn asked how success was measured with this program, and the member was not able to answer that.

Another task force member shared an anti-bullying program that had been used in the past. She shared, "It has worked before, so it will work again." Again, Carolyn asked various follow-up questions, but the member was not able to answer her inquiries. A third member shared that if the team wanted to develop a successful anti-bullying program, they should adopt a "zero-tolerance" policy because that is what would make the most sense in order to reduce the problem of bullying. It did make logical sense, but Carolyn remembered her research courses and learning about ways of knowing. She recalled that, at times, logical does not mean that it is research supported.

After all of the other team members had shared their ideas, Carolyn provided her insights based on her research from professional publications. Carolyn shared that the professional organization that she is a member of routinely shares information on best practices related to school social work practice, and recently an issue was devoted to addressing bullying in the school setting. Carolyn shared this research with the group and presented her pitch to utilize an evidence-based practice to address the problem of concern.

LEARNING OBJECTIVES

This chapter addresses Competency 9: Evaluate Practice With Individuals, Families, Groups, Organizations, and Communities. It focuses on evaluating social work practice at the micro- and the mezzolevel. By the end of this chapter, you will be able to:

- Describe how positivism can influence social work research
- Understand how scientific inquiry informs social work practice

- Identify various ways of knowing, including the potential limitations of various ways
- Distinguish between qualitative and quantitative research methods
- Critically evaluate the value of research findings
- Identify social workers' ethical responsibilities related to evaluating program outcomes
- Plot single-system evaluation data on a line graph
- Interpret the clinical and visual significance of single-system evaluation data
- Use a logic model to organize a program evaluation
- Design a process evaluation of program implementation
- Design a program outcome evaluation
- Identify the characteristics of a culturally competent program evaluator and program evaluation

■ Competency 4: Engage in Practice-Informed Research and Research-Informed Practice

Social workers understand quantitative and qualitative research methods and their respective roles in advancing a science of social work and in evaluating their practice. Social workers know the principles of logic, scientific inquiry, and culturally informed and ethical approaches to building knowledge. Social workers understand that evidence that informs practice derives from multidisciplinary sources and multiple ways of knowing. They also understand the processes for translating research findings into effective practice. Social workers:

- Use practice experience and theory to inform scientific inquiry and research
- Apply critical thinking to engage in analysis of quantitative and qualitative research methods and research findings
- Use and translate research evidence to inform and improve practice, policy, and service delivery

■ Competency 9: Evaluate Practice With Individuals, Families, Groups, Organizations, and Communities

Social workers understand that evaluation is an ongoing component of the dynamic and interactive process of social work practice with, and on behalf of, diverse individuals, families, groups, organizations, and communities. Social workers recognize the importance of evaluating processes and outcomes to advance practice, policy, and service delivery effectiveness. Social workers understand theories of human behavior and the social environment, and critically evaluate and apply this knowledge in evaluating outcomes. Social workers understand qualitative and quantitative methods for evaluating outcomes and practice effectiveness. Social workers:

- Select and use appropriate methods for evaluation of outcomes

- Apply knowledge of human behavior and the social environment, person-in-environment, and other multidisciplinary theoretical frameworks in the evaluation of outcomes

- Critically analyze, monitor, and evaluate intervention and program processes and outcomes

- Apply evaluation findings to improve practice effectiveness at the micro-, mezzo-, and macrolevels

■ National Association of Social Workers (NASW) *Code of Ethics*

The NASW *Code of Ethics* (2017) value of competence is related to evaluating the practice effectiveness component of the Council on Social Work Education (CSWE) evaluating practice competency. To be a competent social work practitioner and to be committed to enhancing one's professional expertise requires an ongoing evaluation of one's practice effectiveness. Not knowing if your social work practice is doing what you hope to achieve in your work with clients is unethical. Social work ethics require that we evaluate our practice effectiveness to help ensure that our clients are receiving the help they need and the best services possible. Additionally, social work ethics require competence and the ongoing development of our professional expertise. Developing competence and expertise requires ongoing evaluation of our social work practice effectiveness.

The NASW *Code of Ethics* standard Evaluation and Research directly addresses the evaluating outcomes component of the Council on Social Work Education (CSWE) evaluating practice competency. This ethical standard has 17 subsections related to evaluating organizational and community interventions and outcomes. The subsections of the standard can be reviewed online (www.socialworkers.org/About/Ethics/Code-of-Ethics/Code-of-Ethics-English).

In sum, social workers have an ethical responsibility to evaluate program implementation and outcomes using appropriate research practices that protect human subjects. Social workers also have an ethical responsibility to avoid conflicts of interest in conducting evaluation of social work programs and interventions and to disseminate accurate evaluation findings.

▶ **Critical Thinking Question**

Based on the opening chapter case example:

1. What ethical principles and standards apply to Carolyn's evaluation plan? Why do they apply and what will Carolyn need to do to be compliant with the ethical principles?

■ Practice-Informed Research

Practice-informed research seeks to allow practice knowledge and experience to influence research conducted during the practice of social work. Research-informed practice requires social workers to integrate research into their practice. Practice-informed research occurs when social workers collect and analyze data during their practice with clients and use those findings to make practice decisions. The notion of conducting research or evaluation may seem daunting to some social workers. We encourage you to approach this task with an open mind. Many of the skills necessary to be an effective social worker are the same skills necessary to conduct effective practice-informed research. In practice, social workers identify problems and needs with clients. They then gather information during the assessment, select an intervention and monitor the intervention to determine effectiveness. Within the scope of research, the social worker also begins by looking at problems and needs. The social worker then gathers information and selects a means to collect data. The social worker then evaluates the data to determine the results. There are a variety of ways to describe research design. It is beyond the scope of this book to explore all types of research designs. However, we distinguish between quantitative and qualitative designs.

Quantitative Research

Quantitative research is a category of research where the data are statistically analyzed or quantified in some way. In its simplest form, quantitative research is often distinguished from qualitative research in that quantitative research emphasizes numeric data whereas qualitative research emphasizes data that are words and phrases. Both quantitative and qualitative designs are important components in social work research. The CSWE (2015) puts forth that social workers must be able to understand both quantitative and qualitative methods so that they can determine if their practice is effective and to monitor outcomes.

Quantitative research is a deductive approach to finding answers. A deductive approach means that you start with a premise or idea, and then, through a systematic process, lead to a conclusion. Quantitative research often begins with identifying a problem and then developing a research question. After a review of the current literature, a hypothesis is formed. Based on the research question, a design is selected and then data collection begins. After all of the data have been collected, the data are then analyzed using statistical means. The results are then interpreted and shared with others.

Qualitative Research

Qualitative research "seeks to explore and address concerns or topics that bridge knowledge, meaning, tangible experience, emotions and reflexive understanding to the applied practice of social work" (Carey, 2012, p. 8). Research that is qualitative in nature that is consistent with social work values can serve to

> ▶ **Critical Thinking Question**
> 1. In your own words, compare and contrast quantitative and qualitative research.

advance the profession's mission as it allows us to explore and gain a better understanding into the experiences of vulnerable populations (Reamer, 2012). While quantitative research looks at quantifiable data to analyze statistically, qualitative research looks at words in an attempt to identify codes or themes. Qualitative research designs are often much more flexible than quantitative designs by comparison (Maxwell, 2013).

Qualitative research is often critiqued in relation to positivism. At times, qualitative research has been viewed as "less scientific" than quantitative research. This is not the case. Both qualitative and quantitative methods, though different, are valuable and useful. When considering the strengths and limitations with each type of research, the researcher must consider the purpose of the research in order to determine which method would be the better fit. Ruch, Julkunen, and Epstein (2016) put forth that:

Qualitative research has always had to struggle to justify its existence and its distinctive characteristics, one of which is the focus on relationships in the research process. Consequently, discussions regarding how relationships are understood in qualitative research have largely been determined by the dominant discourse of objectivity associated with positivism, which configures the researcher and research subject as separate, rational individuals. From this positivist standpoint, subjectivity and any notion of relationship are problematic. The overriding endeavor is to minimize their significance – their interference in the research process – by rendering objective, as far as possible, any hint of subjectivity or relationality. In this context, reflexivity, another distinctive feature of qualitative research, is simply a means to an end, that is, the means by which subjectivity can be rendered objective, rather than being understood as important in its own right as a different source of knowing. (p. 29)

CASE 13.1   QUANTITATIVE OR QUALITATIVE RESEARCH DESIGNS

George works for an agency that provides supports for families with children who have disabilities. One of the agency's programs is respite care. Respite care provides families with a trained sitter so that they can leave the home to run errands or other tasks while the caregiver is home with the child. George feels like the respite program is a great benefit for families but noticed that it is not utilized often. George wants to determine why this is so. George has come up with two different ideas for gaining insights into this issue.

The first plan involves a quantitative design where George will review charts and determine the number of respite days used in the past 3 months. He will then begin sending families information about this program. After the intervention of sending information to families, George will begin tracking the number of respite days used. After 3 months, George will compare the number of days used before and after his intervention.

The second plan involves a qualitative design. George will send out flyers asking interested families to participate in a phone interview regarding how they feel about the respite program. If families call in, George has a list of three general questions to ask but is also open to letting clients lead the direction of the conversation around the topic of respite care.

George is unsure which design would be best for the agency and the respite care program. George met with his supervisor to share his ideas. Throughout the supervision process, both George and his supervisor agreed that they could learn beneficial information from both designs and discussed ways to integrate both to create a mixed-methods design.

Research to Improve Practice

Social workers should continually be seeking to improve their practice. As a profession, we value continued and ongoing education because we recognize that what we know is ever evolving. In addition to being concerned about improving our own practice, we should strive to improve the practice of our fellow social workers. One way that we can contribute to improving the practice of social workers is by sharing what we have found to be effective. This is often a common occurrence on an informal level in many social work organizations. We encourage social workers to be mindful about this process and go beyond informal sharing of "what works" and to formally share personal findings of ways to enhance, enrich, or improve professional practice. There are a variety of ways in which social workers can do this, which we explore now.

■ Evaluating Outcomes: Mezzopractice

Logic Model Revisited

A logic model is a graphic to visually represent the interrelations and connections among various parts of a program (Grinnel, Gabor, & Unrau, 2010). There are numerous advantages to a logic model including that it requires a focus on what is necessary in order for a program to meet its intended outcomes. If created in the right way, logic models can be useful for a variety of purposes. A well-constructed logic model can serve as a foundation for setting priorities within a program, evaluating and monitoring a program, as well as developing a strategic plan.

There are a variety of templates available for creating a logic model. For program evaluations, we prefer logic models that at a minimum have information on program inputs, goals, activities, outputs, and outcomes. Figure 13.1 describes each element of a logic model.

Logic models are very helpful in conducting process and outcome program evaluations, both of which are discussed later in this chapter. Table 13.1 presents a logic model developed for a substance abuse program for adolescents. The substance abuse program referenced in the logic model as ACRA is an evidence-based program called Adolescent Community

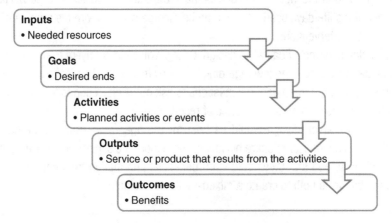

FIGURE 13.1 Elements of a logic model.

TABLE 13.1 Sample Logic Model: Adolescent Substance Abuse Program

INPUTS (RESOURCES)	SERVICE OR ACTIVITY	OUTPUT OBJECTIVES	OUTCOME OBJECTIVES
Program Resources	Goal 1: To decrease substance use among adolescents with histories of substance abuse.		
Program Director (1 FTE)	**Activity 1.1.** ACRA/ agency case management counseling services for substance using adolescents.	**Output Objective 1.1.** To provide 12-session ACRA/ agency case management services to 60 substance-using adolescents and their families during year 1.	**Outcome Objective 1.1.** At least 50% of the adolescent alcohol users decrease the number of days of drug use during the past 30 days by 33% between intake and discharge from the 12-week ACRA/agency program as measured by the Client Outcomes instrument.
Clinical Director (1 FTE)			
Case Managers (1.5 FTE)			
Program Evaluator (.25 FTE)		**Output Objective 1.2.** To provide 12-session ACRA/ agency case management services to 75 substance-using adolescents and their families during years 2 and 3.	**Outcome Objective 1.2.** At least 50% of the adolescent drug users decrease the number of days of drug use during the past 30 days by 33% between intake and discharge from the 12-week ACRA/ agency program as measured by the Client Outcomes instrument.
Research Assistant (.35 FTE)			
3 Interviewers (225 hrs. each)			
Statistical Consultant (25 hrs.)			**Outcome Objective 1.3.** At least 33% of the adolescent alcohol users decrease the number of days of alcohol use during the past 30 days by 25% between intake and 6 months post intake into the 12-week ACRA/agency program as measured by the Client Outcomes instrument.
Administrative Assistant (.5 FTE)			
Community Resources			
Youth Aid Panel			
Magisterial District Judges			**Outcome Objective 1.4.** At least 33% of the adolescent drug users decrease the number of days of drug use during the past 30 days by 25% between intake and 6 months post intake into the 12-week ACRA/agency program as measured by the Client Outcomes instrument.
School District			
Community Coalition			
Community Hospital			

(continued)

TABLE 13.1 Sample Logic Model: Adolescent Substance Abuse Program (continued)

INPUTS (RESOURCES)	SERVICE OR ACTIVITY	OUTPUT OBJECTIVES	OUTCOME OBJECTIVES
	Goal 2: To link adolescent substance users with appropriate community resources.		
	Activity 2.1. ACRA/agency case management referral/linkage services for substance-using adolescents.	**Output Objective 2.1.** To assess, each year, the service needs of 75 adolescent substance users and link those needing additional services with appropriate community resources. **Output Objective 2.2.** To provide follow-up case management referral/linkage services to all adolescent substance users referred to community resources.	**Outcome Objective 2.1.** 100% of the adolescent substance users with additional service needs will be linked with community resources as measured by the assessment instrument and client case records. **Outcome Objective 2.2.** At least 75% of the adolescent substance users referred to community resources will have followed up on the referral and contacted the community resource within 30 days of the referral as measured by the Client Outcomes instrument and client case records.
	Goal 3: To strengthen adolescent substance user's family support systems.		
	Activity 3.1. ACRA/agency case management family intervention services for substance using adolescents and their families.	**Output Objective 3.1.** To provide at least 2 adolescent/family sessions to 60 substance using adolescents during year 1. **Output Objective 3.2.** To provide at least 2 adolescent/family sessions to 75 substance using adolescents during years 2 and 3.	**Outcome Objective 3.1.** At least 50% of the adolescent substance user's scores on the Adolescent Happiness Scale will increase between initial assessment and discharge from the ACRA/agency case management program. **Outcome Objective 3.2.** At least 33% of the adolescent substance users' scores on the Adolescent Happiness Scale will increase between initial assessment and 6 months post intake in the ACRA/agency case management program.

ACRA, Adolescent Community Reinforcement Approach; FTE, full time equivalent.

Reinforcement Approach. The ACRA program consists of 10 individual sessions with the adolescent, two individual sessions with one or more caregivers, and two sessions with the adolescent and caregivers together. The intervention focuses on rearranging environmental contingencies so that abstaining from substances becomes more rewarding than using them. ACRA therapists teach adolescents how to find new reinforcers or enhance existing reinforcers for staying substance free, how to use existing community resources that were believed to support positive change, and how to develop a positive support system within the family. The logic model shown in Table 13.1 was used to develop the evaluation of the implementation of the program (process) and its outcome.

Process Evaluation

This type of program evaluation is sometimes called a formative evaluation. Grinnel et al. (2010) put forth that this type of evaluation serves to examine "how a program's services are delivered to clients and what administrative mechanisms exist within the program to support these services" (p. 129). Additionally, process evaluations look at routine aspects of daily operations. Within a process evaluation, activities and administration systems are explored regarding how they are organized and function. A process evaluation can be conducted at any time within an organization but often occurs early in program development. When used early in programs, process evaluations can be extremely helpful in identifying issues or glitches with the programs' functioning that can be addressed and rectified.

A process evaluation seeks to determine if there is program fidelity, which means that the program is operating as it had been intended. If outcomes are not being met, it may also be quite helpful to conduct a process evaluation in order to determine if there is an issue in program implementation that is causing the unmet outcomes. As you can see, process evaluations can be quite useful for a variety of reasons as they not only serve to improve a program's operation, but they can provide great insights into program practices and structure.

Once you decide to undertake a process evaluation, you should start by deciding what information you are hoping to gather. Once you know what information or data you would like to collect, you can then create your questions. As important as deciding what questions to ask is deciding whom you are going to ask. When conducting organizational evaluations, you need to be aware of the various stakeholders involved who may have vital information for you. Stakeholder is a term used to refer to those people who have an interest in your program. Stakeholders can be staff, administration, board of directors, funding sources, clients, community members, and other business or community partners.

▶ **Critical Thinking Questions**

1. Why is it important to conduct process evaluations?

2. In what ways are process evaluation similar to informal practice evaluations? In what ways are they different?

It is important to consider from whom you are going to collect information because your approach may need to be varied for each group. When collecting data for any purpose, it is important to be sure that your data collection methods are clear and straightforward. It is also a good idea to be considerate of the participants' time. Though you may want to collect as much data as possible, it would be impossible for most people to complete surveys or interviews that ask hundreds of questions. When conducting an organizational evaluation, such as a process evaluation, you are often collecting data from staff. Be mindful that staff already have a lot on their plates; so whenever possible, try to incorporate your data collection process into the existing flow of current program operations. It can be helpful to ask the staff what they think would be a good way to collect such data. User input can be a valuable insight when conducting a process evaluation.

You will then need to collect your information and create a system to manage the incoming data. Once you have gathered your data, you will need to analyze your findings. Upon analyzing your results, you should share your findings with others. After doing all of the work associated with a process evaluation, it is important to disseminate your results to others. As we have mentioned, you should tailor the delivery of your findings to meet the needs of the stakeholder groups again. For example, you may wish to present a written report or slide show to the board of directors of the program, but clients or community members may prefer something less formal, like a conversation and handouts.

Case 13.2 describes the process evaluation for the adolescent substance abuse program outlined in the logic model in Table 13.1. In this example, the process evaluation data were used to provide ongoing feedback to the program staff to ensure program fidelity in the delivery of the ACRA program to the participating adolescents and their families.

CASE 13.2   SAMPLE PROCESS EVALUATION PLAN

The process evaluation of the ACRA program will focus on two primary topics: (1) program implementation and (2) client feedback and perceptions.

Program Implementation. The evaluation team will closely monitor and document all aspects of program implementation. This component of the process evaluation will address the following questions:

- How closely did the implementation match the proposed plan?
- What types of deviations from the plan occurred?
- What led to the deviations?
- What were the effects of the deviations?
- What services were provided?
- Who provided the services?
- Who received the program services?
- What was the level of service provided?
- What were the costs of the services provided?

(continued)

CASE 13.2

All of the preceding questions are related to assessing program implementation. These data will be collected from program records, client records, staff interviews, and interviews with key informants from collaborating organizations. An emphasis of the implementation evaluation will be on fidelity to the ACRA model. The ACRA Global Procedure Checklist, the Therapist Skillfulness Scale, and the 15 individual ACRA Procedure Checklists will be used to access the fidelity of the implementation of the ACRA program.

Client Feedback and Perceptions. The second major topic of the process evaluation will focus on how clients perceive the program services and staff. This component will ascertain client feedback on all aspects of the program. The focus will be on documenting the clients' perceptions of what worked and what needs to be strengthened. These data will be collected each year from four focus groups, with approximately 10 former clients in each focus group. Two focus groups will be held at midyear with approximately 10 former adolescent clients, and two focus groups will be held with approximately 10 caregivers of former adolescent clients.

The focus group protocol that was used for meeting with the adolescent participants of the program is shown in Exhibit 13.1. A similar focus group protocol was used to interview the parent/caregivers.

EXHIBIT 13.1

SAMPLE FOCUS GROUP PROTOCOL

Directions

Please ask all of the adolescents to join you in a circle. Explain to them that you are going to ask them a few questions about the program, and that you want them to be as honest as possible. Tell them that your information will not be linked to any person.

Explain that the purpose of the focus group is to get feedback to improve the program.

Please ask the following questions of the group. Remember to try and get consensus about results—you do this by asking, "Does everyone agree?" and/or "Does anyone think differently."

You need not write down every word; just capture the consensus and/or the differences in what the group answers.

Questions

1.	Tell me about your case manager?

2.	Were your individual sessions with your case manager helpful?
3.	Were the sessions with your parents/caregiver helpful?
4.	In what ways did the program help you?
5.	How did the program help you in getting along with your parents?
6.	How did the program help you better understand yourself?
7.	How did the program help you in getting along with your peers?
8.	How did the program help you in making choices about substance use?
9.	What did you like best about the program?
10.	What did you like least about the program?
11.	What should the agency do to improve the program?

Outcome Evaluation

An outcome evaluation is a type of program evaluation that is sometimes called a summative evaluation. The primary purpose of an outcome evaluation is to determine to what extent the program is meeting its intended target by achieving its objectives. Through outcome evaluations, feedback related to program results can be given to program stakeholders, which increases the overall accountability of the program. It is beneficial to have a mechanism of providing feedback on a program in order to make program decisions, and an outcome evaluation can do just that.

The first step in conducting an outcome evaluation would be to examine the program objectives. Hopefully, the program has clearly outlined SMART objectives. SMART is an acronym used to describe objectives that are **s**pecific, **m**easurable, **a**ttainable, **r**elevant, and **t**ime-bound. It is important to understand where program objectives come from. Typically, a program begins with a mission statement. A mission statement is a written conceptual foundation that anchors the program based on what it is about and what it intends to do. From the mission statement, a vision statement can be derived. A vision statement is similar to a mission statement but focuses more on the future direction of the program. From these statements, goals are developed. Goals are broad statements that reflect the program's desired results. Then, from the goals, the objectives are created.

After exploring the program objectives, the next step in an outcome evaluation is to operationalize the variables you will be analyzing in your evaluation. You can then design your data collection and analysis processes and procedures. Then, similar to a process evaluation, you will want to be sure that you share your findings with program stakeholders. Case 13.3 is an outcome evaluation plan for the adolescent substance abuse program.

CASE 13.3   SAMPLE OUTCOME EVALUATION PLAN

Intervention Outcomes. The program logic model, found elsewhere in this proposal, lists the three program goals and their associated outcome objectives. The first program goal is to have the adolescent participants abstain from substance use. There are four outcomes associated with this goal. Two deal with substance use at discharge and at 6 months post intake and two deal with drug use at discharge and 6 months post intake. A Client Outcomes instrument will be used to measure the four outcomes associated with program goal 1. Program participants will be interviewed by evaluation team members using the instrument at intake, discharge, and 6 months post intake. To help meet the goal of completing follow-up interviews with at least 80% of the participants, a $20 mall certificate will be given to each adolescent who is interviewed. The participants' data will be entered into the program evaluation database that will be used to assess program outcomes.

The second program goal is to refer the adolescent participants to community resources. There are three outcomes associated with this goal. The assessment instrument and client case records will be used to measure the three outcomes related to assessment of resource needs and referral to community resources. The assessment instrument will be administered to program participants at intake and at 3, 6, and 12 months post intake by the program case managers. These data as well as

(continued)

CASE 13.3

information from the participants' case records will be entered into the program evaluation database that will be used to assess program outcomes.

The third program goal is to strengthen the adolescents' family support systems. There are two outcomes associated with this goal. The Perceived Social Support—Family Scale (PSS-Fa; Procidano & Heller, 1983) will be used to measure the family support outcomes listed in the logic model. The PSS-Fa will be administered by the program case managers along with the instrument. The PSS-Fa data will be entered into the program evaluation database that will be used to assess program outcomes.

Factors Associated With Outcomes. The second component of the outcome assessment consists of a multivariate analysis of individual, environment, and program factors that are associated with substance use, use of community resources, and family support. The data sources for these analyses will be the PSS-Fa, and client case records. As noted earlier, extensive time series data on a very larger number of scales and variables will be entered into an evaluation database for each adolescent participant. These data will be analyzed using SPSS for Windows. Regression analyses and analysis of variance will be used to identify the individual, environment, and program factors that are associated with the program outcomes at discharge and 6 months following intake.

Dissemination

It would be near pointless to gather and analyze data and to never share the findings with others. This fruitless endeavor should be avoided. Social workers who engage in research in their practice should share their findings. There are a variety of ways to share, or disseminate, r research findings. Three examples of dissemination that we explore include conference presentations, journal articles, and research reports.

Conference Presentations

Conferences are an excellent source to disseminate and to gain research information that can inform your practice. Conferences can vary in length, size, and scope. Some conferences are held with a very narrow focus on a particular topic or subject area, whereas other larger conferences have a plethora of options related to a variety of forms of practice and encourage general, theoretical presentations as well as empirical findings. Conferences can be an excellent way to stay connected with other professionals and networks.

Related to disseminating research, you can submit a proposal to present at a conference. You may present a poster session, a roundtable discussion, or a more traditional lecture-style presentation. In order to submit a proposal for a conference, the guidelines are often posted on the hosting organization's website. It is very important to read the directions closely and pay particular attention to deadlines for submission. Often when submitting a proposal, you will need to submit an abstract along with three learning objectives that participants will achieve by attending your session. The abstract is simply a short summary of what you intend to present. Learning objectives often begin with the phrase "participants will" followed by short statements of what they will accomplish by participating in the presentation. A sample abstract and learning objectives are available in Exhibit 13.2.

EXHIBIT 13.2

SAMPLE CONFERENCE ABSTRACT AND LEARNING OBJECTIVES

Abstract

Burnout is a state of exhaustion affecting the person mentally, physically, and spiritually as the result of ongoing exposure or involvement in the helping profession. Self-care is one way to buffer against burnout. To be competent professionals, we need to engage in regular self-care. Though there is research related to the prevalence of burnout among social work professionals, research on burnout among social work faculty and students is scant. This presentation sets forth to share new research collected from social work faculty and students related to rates of burnout and self-care. The presentation also explores current self-care strategies that are being implemented in social work education programs. Participants are provided with suggestions for decreasing rates of burnout and promoting appropriate self-care for social work faculty and students.

Learning Objectives

1. Participants will be able to describe burnout as it relates to social work education for faculty and students.

2. Participants will learn how to assess for levels of burnout and self-care in their social work programs among faculty and students.

3. Participants will be able to identify self-care strategies that can be incorporated into social work education to support both faculty and students.

Journal Articles

As college students, you are probably quite familiar with journal articles. Journal articles are one way that you can share your research findings with others. As you know, there are a wide variety of journals based on discipline, topic, or population. Many journal articles post a call for papers encouraging individuals to submit their own works to the journal for possible selection and publication. When considering submitting to a journal, it is important to attend to the guidelines for submission, which include such things as length and other requirements.

In the case of a peer-reviewed journal, your submission will be stripped of your identifiable information and shared with two reviewers. Each reviewer will read your paper and provide feedback and possible suggestions for revision. You will hear back from the journal regarding their decision. There are several common responses that you may hear back once you have submitted your article. The first response that you may hear back is that your paper has been accepted as is. This means that your paper will be published without any revisions necessary. The second response that you may hear back is that your paper is provisionally accepted with revisions. Based on the comments of the reviewers and editor, you may be asked to make changes to your paper; those are the revisions the journal is looking for. At this point, you may decide that you are willing to revise your work based on the reviewers' recommendations and resubmit. The final response that you may receive is that your paper has been rejected; even if it has been rejected, there will often be detailed notes as to why. Those notes can be extremely helpful in the future, the next time you submit a paper.

Research Reports

Research reports are formal papers that outline research in an organized fashion. Many social work education programs require their students to write at least one research report during their education. Table 13.2 outlines the main parts of a research report.

■ Social Justice Issue

A major social justice issue relevant to program evaluation is the cultural competence of the evaluator and cultural sensitivity of the evaluation design and process.

> When we conduct an evaluation, everything we do reflects our own cultural values and perspectives—from the evaluation purpose, the questions we develop, and the methodologies we select to our interpretation of the findings and the recommendations we make based on those findings. (Centers for Disease Control and Prevention [CDC], 2014, p. 3)

TABLE 13.2 Elements of a Research Report

Title	The title of your research report should represent what your report is all about succinctly. The APA sets forth that titles should be no more than 12 words.
Abstract	The abstract serves as a summary of the report. The APA (2010) asserts that a good abstract is accurate, nonevaluative, coherent and readable, and concise.
Introduction	The introduction serves to establish the foundation for your paper by demonstrating relevance.
Literature Review	A review of past and current scholarship on the topic you are addressing should be presented.
Research Question or Hypothesis	You should explicitly state your research question or hypothesis. This serves as the bridge into your research.
Methodology	Often referred to as the methods section, this portion of your paper outlines how you planned your research including sampling and intervention methods. You should clearly describe your research design.
Findings	The findings section is where you put forth your analyzed data results.
Discussion	The discussion allows for the findings to be explained. You should also address any limitations to your research. You can include any recommendations for future research and conclusions.
References	You should have a complete reference list that is formatted in APA style for all sources referenced in your report.

APA, American Psychological Association.

To conduct culturally competent program evaluations, the evaluator must appreciate the cultural context of the program and its stakeholders as well as acknowledge cultural differences in worldviews.

Culture is defined as the shared patterns of behaviors and interactions, cognitive constructs, and affective understanding that are learned through a process of socialization. These shared patterns identify the members of a culture group while also distinguishing those of another group. The NASW (2015) defines cultural competence as:

> the process by which individuals and systems respond respectfully and effectively to people of all cultures, languages, classes, races, ethnic backgrounds, religions, spiritual traditions, immigration status, and other diversity factors in a manner that recognizes, affirms, and values the worth of individuals, families, and communities and protects and preserves the dignity of each. (NASW, 2015, p. 13)

The Centers for Disease Control and Prevention guide (2014), shown in Table 13.3, lists action steps and questions to help ensure culturally competent program evaluations.

TABLE 13.3 Ensuring Cultural Competence in Evaluation

ACTION STEPS	QUESTIONS
Engage Stakeholders ▪ Assess cultural self-awareness. ▪ Request that stakeholders who reflect the diversity of the community be included throughout the evaluation. ▪ Lay clear ground rules for participation to establish equality. ▪ Build trust by talking openly with the community about the evaluation.	▪ Does the stakeholder group fully represent the diversity of the program's participants and others affected by the program? ▪ Are meaningful roles planned for stakeholders throughout the evaluation? ▪ Is there a distribution of power among stakeholders? To other distinctions related to status and social class? ▪ Are there multiple voices in planning, implementing, interpreting, and decision-making?
Describe the Program ▪ Conduct key informant interviews to clarify stakeholders' perspectives of the program. ▪ Hold an information-gathering session for stakeholders about the social and historical context of the program. ▪ Use models that resonate with the community.	▪ Are stakeholders' perspectives appropriately reflected? ▪ What is known about the strengths, assets, challenges, and barriers of the community, including the talents and expertise that individual community members or organizations bring? ▪ Are there "gatekeepers of knowledge" within the community that can help describe the social and political context of the program/community?
Focus the Evaluation Design ▪ Engage an experienced facilitator familiar with the community who can guide the development of evaluation questions that reflect stakeholders' values. ▪ Develop a visual chart that describes evaluation design options in such a way that all stakeholders understand the choices and the implications.	▪ What/whose values and perspectives are represented in the evaluation questions? ▪ Is the design appropriate to the evaluation questions as well as the cultural context and values of the community? ▪ Is the evidence considered credible by the community and stakeholders?

(continued)

TABLE 13.3 Ensuring Cultural Competence in Evaluation (*continued*)

ACTION STEPS	QUESTIONS
Gather Credible Evidence ■ Select culturally appropriate data collection instruments. ■ Develop data collection methods that factor in cultural and linguistic distinctions. ■ Adapt data collection processes to the stakeholder context.	■ Whose perspectives are accepted as credible evidence? Credible to whom? ■ Are the language, content, and design of the instruments culturally sensitive? Have the instruments been validated with their intended audiences? ■ Have verbal and nonverbal communication been addressed?
Justify Conclusions ■ Prior to developing final conclusions, discuss cultural implications during data analysis. ■ Involve diverse stakeholders in interpreting data. ■ Ensure that many stakeholders' voices are heard when making judgments.	■ How are different stakeholders' perspectives and values addressed in the analysis and interpretation of the evaluation findings? ■ Are conclusions validated by participants? ■ Are conclusions balanced with culturally appropriate recommendations and community capacity? ■ Are findings meaningful to the group or community of interest?
Ensure Use and Share Lessons Learned ■ Generate recommendations through an inclusive process by providing a role for various stakeholders to implement the evaluation findings. ■ Tailor dissemination of evaluation results to stakeholder needs. ■ Encourage the use of evaluation information by holding an inclusive meeting about developing an action plan for evaluation use.	■ Are communication mechanisms culturally appropriate? ■ Does the reporting method meet stakeholder needs (both the message and the messenger)? ■ Are the data presented in context, with efforts made to clarify issues and prevent misuse? ■ Has the community benefited as anticipated? How?

Source: From Centers for Disease Control and Prevention. (2014). *Practical Strategies for Culturally Competent Evaluation.* Atlanta, GA: U.S. Department of Health and Human Services. Retrieved from https://www.cdc.gov/dhdsp/docs/cultural_competence_guide.pdf

The action steps and questions in Table 13.3 are designed to help evaluators conduct culturally competent program evaluations. This is an important social justice issue. The potentially negative impact of program evaluations that are conducted from a worldview that is different from the community stakeholders is significant. Findings from such an evaluation may not reflect the perceptions of the community context and the cultural backgrounds of the participants, staff, and community stakeholders. These differences can result in loss of needed services and funding. This can also be stigmatizing and disempowering for those from nonmajority backgrounds and cultures. As social workers, we are called upon to "use a broad range of skills (micro, mezzo, and macro) and techniques that demonstrate an understanding of and respect for the importance of culture in practice, policy, and research" (NASW, 2015, p. 28). This applies to program evaluations as part of our mezzo–social work practice with organizations and communities.

Policy Issues

Related to research, social workers must be aware of policies at the organization, state, and federal levels. At the federal level, the National Research Act was passed by U.S. Congress in 1974. As a result of this Act, the National Commission for the Protection of Human Subjects of Biomedical and Behavioral Research was created. This commission was an interdisciplinary team. Social worker Dorothy Height was a member of this commission. The team members worked to share information related to researching vulnerable populations. Vulnerable populations that were addressed by the commission included children, prisoners, and those with mental illness. The Belmont Report that was discussed earlier in this textbook was one of the reports disseminated by this commission.

Social workers should use research to support all that they do. Social workers must not only utilize research to inform their practice; they must also use research to inform policy. As you know, social workers are called upon to be policy advocates. In order to be effective policy advocates, social workers must be aware of the current research and best practices to address conditions and situations that our clients face. It is the goal of social work to ameliorate circumstances that cause trouble, harm, or injustice to our clients. By following the evidence-based practice model process outlined earlier in this chapter, social workers can use similar skills to advocate for research-informed policies.

Social workers must be concerned with policy issues and must consider how research can assist and address those conditions. There are numerous policy issues that research can assist in better understanding and addressing. For the purpose of this chapter, we consider policy issues related to healthcare.

Research is clear that preventive healthcare and having adequate and appropriate access to medical resources including a primary care physician produce better medical outcomes and in the long run reduces cost and promotes better health. Social workers should be advocates for policies that increase insurance coverage and address the needs of individuals who may have insurance but cannot afford to use the insurance due to high deductibles.

Research and policy are closely interconnected. Furthermore, "the need for social work research to inform practices and policies, develop knowledge and promote issues of social justice is also increasing" (Berg, Hewson, & Fotheringham, 2012, p. 11).

■ Summary

This chapter focused on evaluating practice competency. The main components of this competency are evaluating practice effectiveness, which deals with the evaluation of micro–social work practice individuals, families, and groups. The second component is evaluating organization and community program outcomes.

The chapter began with a review of the NASW *Code of Ethics* (2017) values, ethical principles, and ethical standards related to practice evaluation. We then reviewed informal approaches to evaluation of practice effectiveness through supervision and self-reflection as well as different types of worker constructed measures that can be used in obtaining client feedback. More formal approaches to evaluating practice effectiveness were also reviewed in detail. This included identifying and evaluating reliability and validity of standardized measures, designing single-system evaluations, plotting single-system data, and interpreting results.

Evaluating program outcomes was also reviewed. The two major types of program evaluations were discussed. Process or normative evaluations are designed to collect data on the implementation of organizational and community programs. These types of evaluations are concerned with ensuring program fidelity and obtaining stakeholder feedback on what is working and not working in getting the program up and running. Program fidelity is critical if an evidence-based program is being implemented. It is important to make sure that the program is delivered in the way it was designed and empirically tested. We also reviewed developing outcome evaluations that measure the extent to which organization and community programs are achieving their stated goals and objectives. The chapter concluded with a discussion of the social justice issue of conducting culturally competent evaluations.

CASE SUMMARY   "UNDOCUMENTED AND HOMELESS"

Practice Setting Description

Jackie is a first-year master of social work student completing an internship at an inner-city family service agency in the Southwest. The agency is located in a section of the city that has a high crime rate, gang activity, and failing schools. The area has a diverse population with a large number of immigrants from Central and South America and a substantial African American population. The agency provides individual and family counseling services on a sliding fee scale. The agency also runs a number of educational and treatment groups as well as a temporary shelter for women and their children. Jackie has been assigned to work with the women and their children in the shelter. Her primary tasks are to provide concrete services and supportive counseling to the shelter residents.

Background Information

Elicia T and her daughter, Maria, are undocumented immigrants from Mexico. They have been in the United States for 5 years. Elicia and Maria fled to the area from another southwestern city to escape her abusive husband approximately 2 months ago. Elicia is 25 years old and Maria 8 years old. Elicia has a 2-year-old daughter, Sarah, who was placed in foster care because of suspected abuse in the home. Sarah is in a foster home in a small rural community in the state hundreds of miles from Elicia's current residence. Since moving to the area, Maria has not been attending school.

Elicia and Maria are currently residing in the agency's temporary shelter for families. They have been at the shelter for 2 weeks, and the agency has a 90-day limit. It is viewed as temporary housing, and the residents are only allowed to stay for 3 months. Prior to arriving at the shelter, Elicia and Maria were homeless and living on the streets.

Elicia is a high-school dropout and was a stay-at-home mother prior to leaving her husband and moving to a different part of the state. She chose to move there because she has two female

(continued)

CASE SUMMARY

cousins living in the area who are also undocumented immigrants. Elicia's native language is Spanish. She speaks some English but is not as comfortable speaking in English. Her English comprehension appears to be good. Maria speaks both English and Spanish well. When communicating with the staff, Maria acts as Elicia's interpreter since none of the staff at the shelter speak Spanish.

Maria appears to be behind academically. She struggles reading simple children's books written in English. It is unknown if her ability to read in Spanish is better than her English reading skills.

Other than her two cousins, Elicia has no other sources of support in the community. Her cousins have young families and limited resources but are well established and connected to a Latino community in the city and the local Catholic church. Her cousins refused to let Elicia and Maria live with them while she was trying to find her own place and a job. They stated that they did not have enough room and are concerned they would get in trouble with their landlord if it was found out that they were letting people stay with them. They sent her to the local church for help, and she was given the address for the agency's shelter by the priest.

Elicia has been looking for housing in the Latino community. The housing market is tight with limited options, and she has been unable to find anything that she could possibly afford. The only affordable housing she found was a room in a rundown motel that rents by the hour or by the month. It is in an area of town known for drug dealing and sex work.

On arrival in the community, Elicia found occasional work for a house cleaning company. The company hires undocumented workers, pays them very low cash wages, and threatens to turn them in to Immigration and Customs Enforcement (ICE) if they complain. The job bosses also exploit their female workers sexually, threatening to turn them in if they do not comply. Elicia was fearful about applying for other jobs because of her illegal status. She considered turning to sex work to be able to take care of her children, but her Catholic upbringing and thoughts of how doing so would shame her family have kept her from doing so. She is in constant fear of being detained, separated from her children, and having them placed in foster care. She is also afraid that she will end up homeless again and forced to live on the streets or return to her abusive husband.

Elicia is extremely reluctant to sign up for any federally funded services, even those that she and her children are entitled to receiving. On the suggestion that she enroll for supplemental food through SNAP, Elicia became nervous and refused as she has heard that participation in SNAP services, and others like them, would draw the attention of ICE, and she had heard stories on the news of individuals being deported after signing up for such programs.

Presenting Problems

Elicia and her children are facing multiple obstacles. They need to find permanent, affordable housing and a job that pays enough to cover her housing and living expenses. In addition, Maria needs to be enrolled in school. Elicia also wants to regain custody of her youngest daughter in foster care.

Additionally, Elicia is experiencing an immense amount of stress, anxiety, and possibly post-traumatic stress disorder (PTSD). She described an instance where she could not calm down her

(continued)

breathing, and she felt lightheaded. She is very fearful of men and tries to avoid all contact with men in the community. She reports difficulty sleeping at night and feeling exhausted most of the time.

She is concerned about Maria. She has started acting out at the shelter, getting into fights with the other children, disobeying her mother, and being disrespectful and defiant to the staff and other adults. Elicia and Maria fight frequently, and when Elicia tries to discipline Maria, she throws a temper tantrum until Elicia gives up.

Elicia has many strengths. She had the strength to leave her abusive husband and move to a different city. She loves her daughters. She wants desperately to keep Maria with her and hopes to have Sarah returned to her custody. She is resilient and has managed to survive and keep her daughter safe despite not having a place to stay, a job, and a limited support network. Additionally, Elicia is highly motivated to find her own accommodations and support her children.

■ Discussion Questions

1. Jackie has been asked by the director of the community service agency to design an evaluation of the shelter program. What should she do to ensure culturally competent program evaluation?

2. What is a possible goal for the shelter program?

3. What is a possible measurable outcome for the program goal?

4. How would you measure the outcome?

■ References

American Psychological Association. (2010). *Publication manual* (6th ed.). Washington, DC: Author.

Berg, B., Hewson, J., & Fotheringham, S. (2012). Collaborating to explore social work research ethics. *Canadian Social Work, 14*(1), 11–26. doi:10.1080/13691457.2010.516615

Carey, M. (2012). *Qualitative research skills for social work: Theory and practice*. Farnham, UK: Routledge.

Centers for Disease Control and Prevention. (2014). *Practical strategies for culturally competent evaluation*. Atlanta, GA: U.S. Department of Health and Human Services.

Council on Social Work Education. (2015). *Educational policy and accreditation standards*. Author.

Grinnel, R. M., Gabor, P., & Unrau, Y. A. (2010). *Program evaluation for social workers: Foundations of evidence based programs* (5th ed.). New York, NY: Oxford University Press.

Maxwell, J. A. (2013). *Qualitative research design: An interactive approach* (3rd ed.). Los Angeles, CA: Sage.

National Association of Social Workers. (2015). *Standards and indicators for cultural competence in social work practice*. Retrieved from https://www.socialworkers.org/LinkClick.aspx?fileticket=PonPTDEBrn4%3D&portalid=0

National Association of Social Workers. (2017). *Code of ethics*. Silver Spring, MD: Author. Retrieved from http://www.socialworkers.org

Procidano, M. E., & Heller, K. (1983). Measures of perceived social support from friends and from family: Three validation studies. *American Journal of Community Psychology, 11*, 1–24. doi:10.1007/BF00898416

Reamer, F. G. (2012). Ethics in qualitative research. In R. L. Miller, W. J. Reid, & A. E. Fortune (Eds.), *Qualitative research in social work* (2nd ed., pp. 35–60). New York, NY: Columbia University Press.

Ruch, G., Julkunen, I., & Epstein, I. (2016). *Relationship-based research in social work: understanding practice research*. London, UK: Jessica Kingsley Publishers.

INDEX